D1489373

MCKINNEY'S®
NEW YORK
RULES OF COURT

VOLUME IIA – FEDERAL
BANKRUPTCY COURTS

2018 EDITION

THOMSON REUTERS™

Mat#41846279

Francis U. and Mary F. Ritz Library
Dutchess Community College
Poughkeepsie, NY

© 2017 Thomson Reuters
All rights reserved

Copyright is not claimed as to any part of the original work prepared by a United States Government officer or employee as part of that person's official duties.

This publication was created to provide you with accurate and authoritative information concerning the subject matter covered; however, this publication was not necessarily prepared by persons licensed to practice law in a particular jurisdiction. The publisher is not engaged in rendering legal or other professional advice, and this publication is not a substitute for the advice of an attorney. If you require legal or other expert advice, you should seek the services of a competent attorney or other professional.

ISBN 978–0–314–68618–3

McKINNEY'S is registered in the U.S. Patent and Trademark Office.

West's and Westlaw are registered in the U.S. Patent and Trademark Office.
Thomson Reuters Westlaw is a trademark of Thomson Reuters and its affiliates.

PREFACE

Designed for use in the office or courtroom, this pamphlet contains New York federal bankruptcy rules.

WHAT'S NEW

McKinney's New York Rules of Court, Volume IIA – Federal Bankruptcy Court, 2018, includes rules and associated material governing practice before the New York federal courts. It is current with amendments received through September 1, 2017.

CONTACT US

For additional information or research assistance, call the reference attorneys at 1-800-REF-ATTY (1-800-733-2889). Contact our U.S. legal editorial department directly with your questions and suggestions by e-mail at editors.us-legal@tr.com.

Thank you for subscribing to this product. Should you have any questions regarding this product please contact Customer Service at 1-800-328-4880 or by fax at 1-800-340-9378. If you would like to inquire about related publications, or to place an order, please contact us at 1-888-728-7677 or visit us at legalsolutions.thomsonreuters.com.

THE PUBLISHER

October 2017

THOMSON REUTERS PROVIEW™

This title is one of many now available on your tablet as an eBook.

Take your research mobile. Powered by the Thomson Reuters ProView™ app, our eBooks deliver the same trusted content as your print resources, but in a compact, on-the-go format.

ProView eBooks are designed for the way you work. You can add your own notes and highlights to the text, and all of your annotations will transfer electronically to every new edition of your eBook.

You can also instantly verify primary authority with built-in links to WestlawNext® and KeyCite®, so you can be confident that you're accessing the most current and accurate information.

To find out more about ProView eBooks and available discounts, call 1-800-344-5009.

PUBLISHER'S FOREWORD

For the following contents, please refer to *McKinney's New York Rules of Court, Volume II — Federal District Courts, 2018 Edition:*

Federal Rules of Civil Procedure

Federal Rules of Evidence

Federal Rules of Appellate Procedure

Local Rules of the U.S. Court of Appeals, Second Circuit

Local Rules of the U.S. District Courts of New York

Rules Governing Multidistrict Litigation

Miscellaneous Fee Schedules

TABLE OF CONTENTS

TABLE OF CONTENTS

FEDERAL RULES OF BANKRUPTCY PROCEDURE

Including Amendments Effective December 1, 2017, absent contrary Congressional action

---

Rule 1001. Scope of Rules and Forms; Short Title

[Text of rule effective until December 1, 2017, absent contrary Congressional action.]

The Bankruptcy Rules and Forms govern procedure in cases under title 11 of the United States Code. The rules shall be cited as the Federal Rules of Bankruptcy Procedure and the forms as the Official Bankruptcy Forms. These rules shall be construed to secure the just, speedy, and inexpensive determination of every case and proceeding.

[Text of rule effective December 1, 2017, absent contrary Congressional action.]

The Bankruptcy Rules and Forms govern procedure in cases under title 11 of the United States Code. The rules shall be cited as the Federal Rules of Bankruptcy Procedure and the forms as the Official Bankruptcy Forms. These rules shall be construed, administered, and employed by the court and the parties to secure the just, speedy, and inexpensive determination of every case and proceeding.

(As amended Mar. 30, 1987, eff. Aug. 1, 1987; Apr. 30, 1991, eff. Aug. 1, 1991; Apr. 27, 2017, eff. Dec. 1, 2017, absent contrary Congressional action.)

PART I—COMMENCEMENT OF CASE: PROCEEDINGS RELATING TO PETITION AND ORDER FOR RELIEF

Rule 1002. Commencement of Case

(a) Petition

A petition commencing a case under the Code shall be filed with the clerk.

(b) Transmission to United States trustee

The clerk shall forthwith transmit to the United States trustee a copy of the petition filed pursuant to subdivision (a) of this rule.

(As amended Mar. 30, 1987, eff. Aug. 1, 1987; Apr. 30, 1991, eff. Aug. 1, 1991.)

Rule 1003. Involuntary Petition

(a) Transferor or transferee of claim

A transferor or transferee of a claim shall annex to the original and each copy of the petition a copy of all documents evidencing the transfer, whether transferred unconditionally, for security, or otherwise, and a signed statement that the claim was not transferred for the purpose of commencing the case and setting forth the consideration for and terms of the transfer. An entity that has transferred or acquired a claim for the purpose of commencing a case for liquidation under chapter 7 or for reorganization under chapter 11 shall not be a qualified petitioner.

(b) Joinder of petitioners after filing

If the answer to an involuntary petition filed by fewer than three creditors avers the existence of 12 or more creditors, the debtor shall file with the answer a list of all creditors with their addresses, a brief statement of the nature of their claims, and the amounts thereof. If it appears that there are 12 or more creditors as provided in § 303(b) of the Code, the court shall afford a reasonable opportunity for other creditors to join in the petition before a hearing is held thereon.

(As amended Mar. 30, 1987, eff. Aug. 1, 1987.)

Rule 1004. Involuntary Petition Against a Partnership

After filing of an involuntary petition under § 303(b)(3) of the Code, (1) the petitioning partners or other petitioners shall promptly send to or serve on each general partner who is not a petitioner a copy of the petition; and (2) the clerk shall promptly issue a summons for service on each general partner who is not a petitioner. Rule 1010 applies to the form and service of the summons.

(As amended Apr. 29, 2002, eff. Dec. 1, 2002.)

Rule 1004.1. Petition for an Infant or Incompetent Person

If an infant or incompetent person has a representative, including a general guardian, committee, conservator, or similar fiduciary, the representative may file a voluntary petition on behalf of the infant or incompetent person. An infant or incompetent person who does not have a duly appointed representative may file a voluntary petition by next friend or guardian ad litem. The court shall appoint a guardian ad litem for an infant or incompetent person who is a debtor and is not otherwise represented or shall make any other order to protect the infant or incompetent debtor.

(Added Apr. 29, 2002, eff. Dec. 1, 2002.)

Rule 1004.2. Petition in Chapter 15 Cases

(a) Designating center of main interests

A petition for recognition of a foreign proceeding under chapter 15 of the Code shall state the country where the debtor has its center of main interests. The petition shall also identify each country in which a foreign proceeding by, regarding, or against the debtor is pending.

(b) Challenging designation

The United States trustee or a party in interest may file a motion for a determination that the debtor's center of main interests is other than as stated in the petition for recognition commencing the chapter 15 case. Unless the court orders otherwise, the motion shall be filed no later than seven days before the date set for the hearing on the petition. The motion shall be transmitted to the United States trustee and served on the debtor, all persons or bodies authorized to administer foreign proceedings of the debtor, all entities against whom provisional relief is being sought under § 1519 of the Code, all parties to litigation pending in the United States in which the debtor was a party as of the time the petition was filed, and such other entities as the court may direct.

(Added Apr. 26, 2011, eff. Dec. 1, 2011.)

Rule 1005.   Caption of Petition

The caption of a petition commencing a case under the Code shall contain the name of the court, the title of the case, and the docket number. The title of the case shall include the following information about the debtor: name, employer identification number, last four digits of the social-security number or individual debtor's taxpayer-identification number, any other federal taxpayer-identification number, and all other names used within eight years before filing the petition. If the petition is not filed by the debtor, it shall include all names used by the debtor which are known to the petitioners.

(As amended Mar. 30, 1987, eff. Aug. 1, 1987; Mar. 27, 2003, eff. Dec. 1, 2003; Apr. 23, 2008, eff. Dec. 1, 2008.)

Rule 1006.   Filing Fee

(a) General requirement

Every petition shall be accompanied by the filing fee except as provided in subdivisions (b) and (c) of this rule. For the purpose of this rule, "filing fee" means the filing fee prescribed by 28 U.S.C. § 1930(a)(1)–(a)(5) and any other fee prescribed by the Judicial Conference of the United States under 28 U.S.C. § 1930(b) that is payable to the clerk upon the commencement of a case under the Code.

(b) Payment of filing fee in installments

[Text of subdivision (b)(1) effective until December 1, 2017, absent contrary Congressional action.]

(1) Application to pay filing fee in installments

A voluntary petition by an individual shall be accepted for filing if accompanied by the debtor's signed application, prepared as prescribed by the appropriate Official Form, stating that the debtor is unable to pay the filing fee except in installments.

[Text of subdivision (b)(1) effective December 1, 2017, absent contrary Congressional action.]

(1) Application to pay filing fee in installments

A voluntary petition by an individual shall be accepted for filing, regardless of whether any portion of the filing fee is paid, if accompanied by the debtor's signed application, prepared as prescribed by the appropriate Official Form, stating that the debtor is unable to pay the filing fee except in installments.

(2) Action on application

Prior to the meeting of creditors, the court may order the filing fee paid to the clerk or grant leave to pay in installments and fix the number, amount and dates of payment. The number of installments shall not exceed four, and the final installment shall be payable not later than 120 days after filing the petition. For cause shown, the court may extend the time of any installment, provided the last installment is paid not later than 180 days after filing the petition.

(3) Postponement of attorney's fees

All installments of the filing fee must be paid in full before the debtor or chapter 13 trustee may make further payments to an attorney or any other person who renders services to the debtor in connection with the case.

(c) Waiver of filing fee

A voluntary chapter 7 petition filed by an individual shall be accepted for filing if accompanied by the debtor's application requesting a waiver under 28 U.S.C. § 1930(f), prepared as prescribed by the appropriate Official Form.

(As amended Mar. 30, 1987, eff. Aug. 1, 1987; Apr. 23, 1996, eff. Dec. 1, 1996; Apr. 23, 2008, eff. Dec. 1, 2008; Apr. 27, 2017, eff. Dec. 1, 2017, absent contrary Congressional action.)

Rule 1007.   Lists, Schedules, Statements, and Other Documents; Time Limits

(a) Corporate ownership statement, list of creditors and equity security holders, and other lists

(1) Voluntary case

In a voluntary case, the debtor shall file with the petition a list containing the name and address of each entity included or to be included on Schedules D, E/F, G, and H as prescribed by the Official Forms. If the debtor is a corporation, other than a governmental unit, the debtor shall file with the petition a corporate ownership statement containing the information described in Rule 7007.1. The debtor shall file a supplemental statement promptly upon any change in circumstances that renders the corporate ownership statement inaccurate.

(2) Involuntary case

In an involuntary case, the debtor shall file, within seven days after entry of the order for relief, a list containing the name and address of each entity included or to be included on Schedules D, E/F, G, and H as prescribed by the Official Forms.

(3) Equity security holders

In a chapter 11 reorganization case, unless the court orders otherwise, the debtor shall file within 14 days after entry of the order for relief a list of the debtor's equity security holders of each class showing the number and kind of interests registered in the name of each holder, and the last known address or place of business of each holder.

(4) Chapter 15 case

In addition to the documents required under § 1515 of the Code, a foreign representative filing a petition for recognition under chapter 15 shall file with the petition: (A) a corporate ownership statement containing the information described in Rule 7007.1; and (B) unless the court orders otherwise, a list containing the names and addresses of all persons or bodies authorized to administer foreign proceedings of the debtor, all parties to litigation pending in the United States in which the debtor is a party at the time of the filing of the petition, and all entities against whom provisional relief is being sought under § 1519 of the Code.

(5) Extension of time

Any extension of time for the filing of the lists required by this subdivision may be granted only on motion for cause shown and on notice to the United States trustee and to any trustee, committee elected under § 705 or appointed under § 1102 of the Code, or other party as the court may direct.

(b) Schedules, statements, and other documents required

(1) Except in a chapter 9 municipality case, the debtor, unless the court orders otherwise, shall file the following schedules, statements, and other documents, prepared as prescribed by the appropriate Official Forms, if any:

    (A) schedules of assets and liabilities;

    (B) a schedule of current income and expenditures;

    (C) a schedule of executory contracts and unexpired leases;

    (D) a statement of financial affairs;

    (E) copies of all payment advices or other evidence of payment, if any, received by the debtor from an employer within 60 days before the filing of the petition, with redaction of all but the last four digits of the debtor's social-security number or individual taxpayer-identification number; and

    (F) a record of any interest that the debtor has in an account or program of the type specified in § 521(c) of the Code.

(2) An individual debtor in a chapter 7 case shall file a statement of intention as required by § 521(a) of the Code, prepared as prescribed by the appropriate Official Form. A copy of the statement of intention shall be served on the trustee and the creditors named in the statement on or before the filing of the statement.

(3) Unless the United States trustee has determined that the credit counseling requirement of § 109(h) does not apply in the district, an individual debtor must file a statement of compliance with the credit counseling requirement, prepared as prescribed by the appropriate Official Form which must include one of the following:

    (A) an attached certificate and debt repayment plan, if any, required by § 521(b);

    (B) a statement that the debtor has received the credit counseling briefing required by § 109(h)(1) but does not have the certificate required by § 521(b);

    (C) a certification under § 109(h)(3); or

    (D) a request for a determination by the court under § 109(h)(4).

(4) Unless § 707(b)(2)(D) applies, an individual debtor in a chapter 7 case shall file a statement of current monthly income prepared as prescribed by the appropriate Official Form, and, if the current monthly income exceeds the median family income for the applicable state and household size, the information, including calculations, required by § 707(b), prepared as prescribed by the appropriate Official Form.

(5) An individual debtor in a chapter 11 case shall file a statement of current monthly income, prepared as prescribed by the appropriate Official Form.

(6) A debtor in a chapter 13 case shall file a statement of current monthly income, prepared as prescribed by the appropriate Official Form, and, if the current monthly income exceeds the median family income for the applicable state and household size, a calculation of disposable income made in accordance with § 1325(b)(3), prepared as prescribed by the appropriate Official Form.

(7) Unless an approved provider of an instructional course concerning personal financial management has notified the court that a debtor has completed the course after filing the petition:

    (A) An individual debtor in a chapter 7 or chapter 13 case shall file a statement of completion of the course, prepared as prescribed by the appropriate Official Form; and

    (B) An individual debtor in a chapter 11 case shall file the statement if § 1141(d)(3) applies.

(8) If an individual debtor in a chapter 11, 12, or 13 case has claimed an exemption under § 522(b)(3)(A) in property of the kind described in § 522(p)(1) with a value in excess of the amount set out in § 522(q)(1), the debtor shall file a statement as to whether there is any proceeding pending in which the debtor may be found guilty of a felony of a kind described in § 522(q)(1)(A) or found liable for a debt of the kind described in § 522(q)(1)(B).

(c) Time limits

In a voluntary case, the schedules, statements, and other documents required by subdivision (b)(1), (4), (5), and (6) shall be filed with the petition or within 14 days thereafter, except as otherwise provided in subdivisions (d), (e), (f), and (h) of this rule. In an involuntary case, the schedules, statements, and other documents required by subdivision (b)(1) shall be filed by the debtor within 14 days after the entry of the order for relief. In a voluntary case, the documents required by paragraphs (A), (C), and (D) of subdivision (b)(3) shall be filed with the petition. Unless the court orders otherwise, a debtor who has filed a statement under subdivision (b)(3)(B), shall file the documents required by subdivision (b)(3)(A) within 14 days of the order for relief. In a chapter 7 case, the debtor shall file the statement required by subdivision (b)(7) within 60 days after the first date set for the meeting of creditors under § 341 of the Code, and in a chapter 11 or 13 case no later than the date when the last payment was made by the debtor as required by the plan or the filing of a motion for a discharge under § 1141(d)(5)(B) or § 1328(b) of the Code. The court may, at any time and in its discretion, enlarge the time to file the statement required by subdivision (b)(7). The debtor shall file the statement required by subdivision (b)(8) no earlier than the date of the last payment made under the plan or the date of the filing of a motion for a discharge under §§[1]

1141(d)(5)(B), 1228(b), or 1328(b) of the Code. Lists, schedules, statements, and other documents filed prior to the conversion of a case to another chapter shall be deemed filed in the converted case unless the court directs otherwise. Except as provided in § 1116(3), any extension of time to file schedules, statements, and other documents required under this rule may be granted only on motion for cause shown and on notice to the United States trustee, any committee elected under § 705 or appointed under § 1102 of the Code, trustee, examiner, or other party as the court may direct. Notice of an extension shall be given to the United States trustee and to any committee, trustee, or other party as the court may direct.

(d) List of 20 largest creditors in chapter 9 municipality case or chapter 11 reorganization case

In addition to the list required by subdivision (a) of this rule, a debtor in a chapter 9 municipality case or a debtor in a voluntary chapter 11 reorganization case shall file with the petition a list containing the name, address and claim of the creditors that hold the 20 largest unsecured claims, excluding insiders, as prescribed by the appropriate Official Form. In an involuntary chapter 11 reorganization case, such list shall be filed by the debtor within 2 days after entry of the order for relief under § 303(h) of the Code.

(e) List in chapter 9 municipality cases

The list required by subdivision (a) of this rule shall be filed by the debtor in a chapter 9 municipality case within such time as the court shall fix. If a proposed plan requires a revision of assessments so that the proportion of special assessments or special taxes to be assessed against some real property will be different from the proportion in effect at the date the petition is filed, the debtor shall also file a list showing the name and address of each known holder of title, legal or equitable, to real property adversely affected. On motion for cause shown, the court may modify the requirements of this subdivision and subdivision (a) of this rule.

(f) Statement of social security number

An individual debtor shall submit a verified statement that sets out the debtor's social security number, or states that the debtor does not have a social security number. In a voluntary case, the debtor shall submit the statement with the petition. In an involuntary case, the debtor shall submit the statement within 14 days after the entry of the order for relief.

(g) Partnership and partners

The general partners of a debtor partnership shall prepare and file the list required under subdivision (a), the schedules of the assets and liabilities, schedule of current income and expenditures, schedule of executory contracts and unexpired leases, and statement of financial affairs of the partnership. The court may order any general partner to file a statement of personal assets and liabilities within such time as the court may fix.

(h) Interests acquired or arising after petition

If, as provided by § 541(a)(5) of the Code, the debtor acquires or becomes entitled to acquire any interest in property, the debtor shall within 14 days after the information comes to the debtor's knowledge or within such further time the court may allow, file a supplemental schedule in the chapter 7 liquidation case, chapter 11 reorganization case, chapter 12 family farmer's debt adjustment case, or chapter 13 individual debt adjustment case. If any of the property required to be reported under this subdivision is claimed by the debtor as exempt, the debtor shall claim the exemptions in the supplemental schedule. The duty to file a supplemental schedule in accordance with this subdivision continues notwithstanding the closing of the case, except that the schedule need not be filed in a chapter 11, chapter 12, or chapter 13 case with respect to property acquired after entry of the order confirming a chapter 11 plan or discharging the debtor in a chapter 12 or chapter 13 case.

(i) Disclosure of list of security holders

After notice and hearing and for cause shown, the court may direct an entity other than the debtor or trustee to disclose any list of security holders of the debtor in its possession or under its control, indicating the name, address and security held by any of them. The entity possessing this list may be required either to produce the list or a true copy thereof, or permit inspection or copying, or otherwise disclose the information contained on the list.

(j) Impounding of lists

On motion of a party in interest and for cause shown the court may direct the impounding of the lists filed under this rule, and may refuse to permit inspection by any entity. The court may permit inspection or use of the lists, however, by any party in interest on terms prescribed by the court.

(k) Preparation of list, schedules, or statements on default of debtor

If a list, schedule, or statement, other than a statement of intention, is not prepared and filed as required by this rule, the court may order the trustee, a petitioning creditor, committee, or other party to prepare and file any of these papers within a time fixed by the court. The court may approve reimbursement of the cost incurred in complying with such an order as an administrative expense.

(*l*)[1] Transmission to United States trustee

The clerk shall forthwith transmit to the United States trustee a copy of every list, schedule, and statement filed pursuant to subdivision (a)(1), (a)(2), (b), (d), or (h) of this rule.

(m) Infants and incompetent persons

If the debtor knows that a person on the list of creditors or schedules is an infant or incompetent person, the debtor also shall include the name, address, and legal relationship of any person upon whom process would be served in an adversary proceeding against the infant or incompetent person in accordance with Rule 7004(b)(2).

(As amended Mar. 30, 1987, eff. Aug. 1, 1987; Apr. 30, 1991, eff. Aug. 1, 1991; Apr. 23, 1996, eff. Dec. 1, 1996; Apr. 23, 2001, eff. Dec. 1, 2001; Mar. 27, 2003, eff. Dec. 1, 2003; Apr. 25, 2005, eff. Dec. 1, 2005; Apr. 23, 2008, eff. Dec. 1, 2008; Mar. 26, 2009, eff. Dec. 1, 2009; Apr. 28, 2010, eff. Dec. 1, 2010; Apr. 23, 2012, eff. Dec. 1, 2012; Apr. 16, 2013, eff. Dec. 1, 2013; Apr. 29, 2015, eff. Dec. 1, 2015.)

1 So in original. Probably should be only one section symbol.

Rule 1008. Verification of Petitions and Accompanying Papers

All petitions, lists, schedules, statements and amendments thereto shall be verified or contain an unsworn declaration as provided in 28 U.S.C. § 1746.

(As amended Apr. 30, 1991, eff. Aug. 1, 1991.)

Rule 1009. Amendments of Voluntary Petitions, Lists, Schedules and Statements

(a) General right to amend

A voluntary petition, list, schedule, or statement may be amended by the debtor as a matter of course at any time before the case is closed. The debtor shall give notice of the amendment to the trustee and to any entity affected thereby. On motion of a party in interest, after notice and a hearing, the court may order any voluntary petition, list, schedule, or statement to be amended and the clerk shall give notice of the amendment to entities designated by the court.

(b) Statement of intention

The statement of intention may be amended by the debtor at any time before the expiration of the period provided in § 521(a) of the Code. The debtor shall give notice of the amendment to the trustee and to any entity affected thereby.

(c) Statement of social security number

If a debtor becomes aware that the statement of social security number submitted under Rule 1007(f) is incorrect, the debtor shall promptly submit an amended verified statement setting forth the correct social security number. The debtor shall give notice of the amendment to all of the entities required to be included on the list filed under Rule 1007(a)(1) or (a)(2).

(d) Transmission to United States trustee

The clerk shall promptly transmit to the United States trustee a copy of every amendment filed or submitted under subdivision (a), (b), or (c) of this rule.

(As amended Mar. 30, 1987, eff. Aug. 1, 1987; Apr. 30, 1991, eff. Aug. 1, 1991; Apr. 12, 2006, eff. Dec. 1, 2006; Apr. 23, 2008, eff. Dec. 1, 2008.)

Rule 1010. Service of Involuntary Petition and Summons

(a) Service of involuntary petition and summons

On the filing of an involuntary petition, the clerk shall forthwith issue a summons for service. When an involuntary petition is filed, service shall be made on the debtor. The summons shall be served with a copy of the petition in the manner provided for service of a summons and complaint by Rule 7004(a) or (b). If service cannot be so made, the court may order that the summons and petition be served by mailing copies to the party's last known address, and by at least one publication in a manner and form directed by the court. The summons and petition may be served on the party anywhere. Rule 7004(e) and Rule 4(*l*) F.R.Civ.P. apply when service is made or attempted under this rule.

(b) Corporate ownership statement

Each petitioner that is a corporation shall file with the involuntary petition a corporate ownership statement containing the information described in Rule 7007.1.

(As amended Mar. 30, 1987, eff. Aug. 1, 1987; Apr. 30, 1991, eff. Aug. 1, 1991; Apr. 22, 1993, eff. Aug. 1, 1993; Apr. 11, 1997, eff. Dec. 1, 1997; Apr. 23, 2008, eff. Dec. 1, 2008; Apr. 28, 2016, eff. Dec. 1, 2016.)

Rule 1011. Responsive Pleading or Motion in Involuntary Cases

(a) Who may contest petition

The debtor named in an involuntary petition may contest the petition. In the case of a petition against a partnership under Rule 1004, a nonpetitioning general partner, or a person who is alleged to be a general partner but denies the allegation, may contest the petition.

(b) Defenses and objections; when presented

Defenses and objections to the petition shall be presented in the manner prescribed by Rule 12 F.R.Civ.P. and shall be filed and served within 21 days after service of the summons, except that if service is made by publication on a party or partner not residing or found within the state in which the court sits, the court shall prescribe the time for filing and serving the response.

(c) Effect of motion

Service of a motion under Rule 12(b) F.R.Civ.P. shall extend the time for filing and serving a responsive pleading as permitted by Rule 12(a) F.R.Civ.P.

(d) Claims against petitioners

A claim against a petitioning creditor may not be asserted in the answer except for the purpose of defeating the petition.

(e) Other pleadings

No other pleadings shall be permitted, except that the court may order a reply to an answer and prescribe the time for filing and service.

(f) Corporate ownership statement

If the entity responding to the involuntary petition is a corporation, the entity shall file with its first appearance, pleading, motion, response, or other request addressed to the court a corporate ownership statement containing the information described in Rule 7007.1.

(As amended Mar. 30, 1987, eff. Aug. 1, 1987; Apr. 26, 2004, eff. Dec. 1, 2004; Apr. 23, 2008, eff. Dec. 1, 2008; Mar. 26, 2009, eff. Dec. 1, 2009; Apr. 28, 2016, eff. Dec. 1, 2016.)

Rule 1012. Responsive Pleading in Cross–Border Cases

(a) Who may contest petition

The debtor or any party in interest may contest a petition for recognition of a foreign proceeding.

(b) Objections and responses; when presented

Objections and other responses to the petition shall be presented no later than seven days before the date set for the hearing on the petition, unless the court prescribes some other time or manner for responses.

(c) Corporate ownership statement

If the entity responding to the petition is a corporation, then the entity shall file a corporate ownership statement containing the information described in Rule 7007.1 with its first appearance, pleading, motion, response, or other request addressed to the court.

(Added April 28, 2016, eff. Dec. 1, 2016.)

Rule 1013. Hearing and Disposition of a Petition in an Involuntary Case

(a) Contested petition

The court shall determine the issues of a contested petition at the earliest practicable time and forthwith enter an order for relief, dismiss the petition, or enter any other appropriate order.

(b) Default

If no pleading or other defense to a petition is filed within the time provided by Rule 1011, the court, on the next day, or as soon thereafter as practicable, shall enter an order for the relief requested in the petition.

(c) [Abrogated]

(As amended Apr. 30, 1991, eff. Aug. 1, 1991; Apr. 22, 1993, eff. Aug. 1, 1993.)

Rule 1014. Dismissal and Change of Venue

(a) Dismissal and transfer of cases

(1) Cases filed in proper district

If a petition is filed in the proper district, the court, on the timely motion of a party in interest or on its own motion, and after hearing on notice to the petitioners, the United States trustee, and other entities as directed by the court, may transfer the case to any other district if the court determines that the transfer is in the interest of justice or for the convenience of the parties.

(2) Cases filed in improper district

If a petition is filed in an improper district, the court, on the timely motion of a party in interest or on its own motion, and after hearing on notice to the petitioners, the United States trustee, and other entities as directed by the court, may dismiss the case or transfer it to any other district if the court determines that transfer is in the interest of justice or for the convenience of the parties.

(b) Procedure when petitions involving the same debtor or related debtors are filed in different courts

If petitions commencing cases under the Code or seeking recognition under chapter 15 are filed in different districts by, regarding, or against (1) the same debtor, (2) a partnership and one or more of its general partners, (3) two or more general partners, or (4) a debtor and an affiliate, the court in the district in which the first-filed petition is pending may determine, in the interest of justice or for the convenience of the parties, the district or districts in which any of the cases

should proceed. The court may so determine on motion and after a hearing, with notice to the following entities in the affected cases: the United States trustee, entities entitled to notice under Rule 2002(a), and other entities as the court directs. The court may order the parties to the later-filed cases not to proceed further until it makes the determination.

(As amended Mar. 30, 1987, eff. Aug. 1, 1987; Apr. 30, 1991, eff. Aug. 1, 1991; Apr. 30, 2007, eff. Dec. 1, 2007; Apr. 28, 2010, eff. Dec. 1, 2010; Apr. 25, 2014, eff. Dec. 1, 2014.)

Rule 1015. Consolidation or Joint Administration of Cases Pending in Same Court

(a) Cases involving same debtor

If two or more petitions by, regarding, or against the same debtor are pending in the same court, the court may order consolidation of the cases.

[Text of subdivision (b) effective until December 1, 2017, absent contrary Congressional action.]

(b) Cases involving two or more related debtors

If a joint petition or two or more petitions are pending in the same court by or against (1) a husband and wife, or (2) a partnership and one or more of its general partners, or (3) two or more general partners, or (4) a debtor and an affiliate, the court may order a joint administration of the estates. Prior to entering an order the court shall give consideration to protecting creditors of different estates against potential conflicts of interest. An order directing joint administration of individual cases of a husband and wife shall, if one spouse has elected the exemptions under § 522(b)(2) of the Code and the other has elected the exemptions under § 522(b)(3), fix a reasonable time within which either may amend the election so that both shall have elected the same exemptions. The order shall notify the debtors that unless they elect the same exemptions within the time fixed by the court, they will be deemed to have elected the exemptions provided by § 522(b)(2).

[Text of subdivision (b) effective December 1, 2017, absent contrary Congressional action.]

(b) Cases involving two or more related debtors

If a joint petition or two or more petitions are pending in the same court by or against (1) spouses, or (2) a partnership and one or more of its general partners, or (3) two or more general partners, or (4) a debtor and an affiliate, the court may order a joint administration of the estates. Prior to entering an order the court shall give consideration to protecting creditors of different estates against potential conflicts of interest. An order directing joint administration of individual cases of spouses shall, if one spouse has elected the exemptions under § 522(b)(2) of the Code and the other has elected the exemptions under § 522(b)(3), fix a reasonable time within which either may amend the election so that both shall have elected the same exemptions. The order shall notify the debtors that unless they elect the same exemptions within the time fixed by the court, they will be deemed to have elected the exemptions provided by § 522(b)(2).

(c) Expediting and protective orders

When an order for consolidation or joint administration of a joint case or two or more cases is entered pursuant to this rule, while protecting the rights of the parties under the Code, the court may enter orders as may tend to avoid unnecessary costs and delay.

(As amended Mar. 30, 1987, eff. Aug. 1, 1987; Apr. 23, 2008, eff. Dec. 1, 2008; Apr. 28, 2010, eff. Dec. 1, 2010; Apr. 27, 2017, eff. Dec. 1, 2017, absent contrary Congressional action.)

Rule 1016. Death or Incompetency of Debtor

Death or incompetency of the debtor shall not abate a liquidation case under chapter 7 of the Code. In such event the estate shall be administered and the case concluded in the same manner, so far as possible, as though the death or incompetency had not occurred. If a reorganization, family farmer's debt adjustment, or individual's debt adjustment case is pending under chapter 11, chapter 12, or chapter 13, the case may be dismissed; or if further administration is possible and in the best interest of the parties, the case may proceed and be concluded in the same manner, so far as possible, as though the death or incompetency had not occurred.

(As amended Apr. 30, 1991, eff. Aug. 1, 1991.)

Rule 1017. Dismissal or Conversion of Case; Suspension

(a) Voluntary dismissal; dismissal for want of prosecution or other cause

Except as provided in §§ 707(a)(3), 707(b), 1208(b), and 1307(b) of the Code, and in Rule 1017(b), (c), and (e), a case shall not be dismissed on motion of the petitioner, for want of prosecution or other cause, or by consent of the parties, before a hearing on notice as provided in Rule 2002. For the purpose of the notice, the debtor shall file a list of creditors with their addresses within the time fixed by the court unless the list was previously filed. If the debtor fails to file the list, the court may order the debtor or another entity to prepare and file it.

(b) Dismissal for failure to pay filing fee

(1) If any installment of the filing fee has not been paid, the court may, after a hearing on notice to the debtor and the trustee, dismiss the case.

(2) If the case is dismissed or closed without full payment of the filing fee, the installments collected shall be distributed in the same manner and proportions as if the filing fee had been paid in full.

(c) Dismissal of voluntary chapter 7 or chapter 13 case for failure to timely file list of creditors, schedules, and statement of financial affairs

The court may dismiss a voluntary chapter 7 or chapter 13 case under § 707(a)(3) or § 1307(c)(9) after a hearing on notice served by the United States trustee on the debtor, the trustee, and any other entities as the court directs.

(d) Suspension

The court shall not dismiss a case or suspend proceedings under § 305 before a hearing on notice as provided in Rule 2002(a).

(e) Dismissal of an individual debtor's chapter 7 case, or conversion to a case under chapter 11 or 13, for abuse

The court may dismiss or, with the debtor's consent, convert an individual debtor's case for abuse under § 707(b) only on motion and after a hearing on notice to the debtor, the trustee, the United States trustee, and any other entity as the court directs.

(1) Except as otherwise provided in § 704(b)(2), a motion to dismiss a case for abuse under § 707(b) or (c) may be filed only within 60 days after the first date set for the meeting of creditors under § 341(a), unless, on request filed before the time has expired, the court for cause extends the time for filing the motion to dismiss. The party filing the motion shall set forth in the motion all matters to be considered at the hearing. In addition, a motion to dismiss under § 707(b)(1) and (3) shall state with particularity the circumstances alleged to constitute abuse.

(2) If the hearing is set on the court's own motion, notice of the hearing shall be served on the debtor no later than 60 days after the first date set for the meeting of creditors under § 341(a). The notice shall set forth all matters to be considered by the court at the hearing.

(f) Procedure for dismissal, conversion, or suspension

(1) Rule 9014 governs a proceeding to dismiss or suspend a case, or to convert a case to another chapter, except under §§ 706(a), 1112(a), 1208(a) or (b), or 1307(a) or (b).

(2) Conversion or dismissal under §§ 706(a), 1112(a), 1208(b), or 1307(b) shall be on motion filed and served as required by Rule 9013.

(3) A chapter 12 or chapter 13 case shall be converted without court order when the debtor files a notice of conversion under §§ 1208(a) or 1307(a). The filing date of the notice becomes the date of the conversion order for the purposes of applying § 348(c) and Rule 1019. The clerk shall promptly transmit a copy of the notice to the United States trustee.

(As amended Mar. 30, 1987, eff. Aug. 1, 1987; Apr. 30, 1991, eff. Aug. 1, 1991; Apr. 22, 1993, eff. Aug. 1, 1993; Apr. 26, 1999, eff. Dec. 1, 1999; Apr. 17, 2000, eff. Dec. 1, 2000; Apr. 23, 2008, eff. Dec. 1, 2008.)

Rule 1018. Contested Involuntary Petitions; Contested Petitions Commencing Chapter 15 Cases; Proceedings to Vacate Order for Relief; Applicability of Rules in Part VII Governing Adversary Proceedings

Unless the court otherwise directs and except as otherwise prescribed in Part I of these rules, the following rules in Part VII apply to all proceedings contesting an involuntary petition or a chapter 15 petition for recognition, and to all proceedings to vacate an order for relief: Rules 7005, 7008–7010, 7015, 7016, 7024–7026, 7028–7037, 7052, 7054, 7056, and 7062. The court may direct that other rules in Part VII shall also apply. For the purposes of this rule a reference in the Part VII rules to adversary proceedings shall be read as a reference to proceedings contesting an involuntary petition or a chapter 15 petition for recognition, or proceedings to vacate an order for relief. Reference in the Federal Rules of Civil Procedure to the complaint shall be read as a reference to the petition.

(As amended Mar. 30, 1987, eff. Aug. 1, 1987; Apr. 28, 2010, eff. Dec. 1, 2010.)

Rule 1019. Conversion of a Chapter 11 Reorganization Case, Chapter 12 Family Farmer's Debt Adjustment Case, or Chapter 13 Individual's Debt Adjustment Case to a Chapter 7 Liquidation Case

When a chapter 11, chapter 12, or chapter 13 case has been converted or reconverted to a chapter 7 case:

(1) Filing of lists, inventories, schedules, statements

(A) Lists, inventories, schedules, and statements of financial affairs theretofore filed shall be deemed to be filed in the chapter 7 case, unless the court directs otherwise. If they have not been previously filed, the debtor shall comply with Rule 1007 as if an order for relief had been entered on an involuntary petition on the date of the entry of the order directing that the case continue under chapter 7.

(B) If a statement of intention is required, it shall be filed within 30 days after entry of the order of conversion or before the first date set for the meeting of creditors, whichever is earlier. The court may grant an extension of time for cause only on written motion filed, or oral request made during a hearing, before the time has expired. Notice of an extension shall be given to the United States trustee and to any committee, trustee, or other party as the court may direct.

(2) New filing periods

(A) A new time period for filing a motion under § 707(b) or (c), a claim, a complaint objecting to discharge, or a complaint to obtain a determination of dischargeability of any debt shall commence under Rules[1] 1017, 3002, 4004, or 4007, but a new time period shall not commence if a chapter 7 case had been converted to a chapter 11, 12, or 13 case and thereafter reconverted to a chapter 7 case and the time for filing a motion under § 707(b) or (c), a claim, a complaint objecting to discharge, or a complaint to obtain a determination of the dischargeability of any debt, or any extension thereof, expired in the original chapter 7 case.

(B) A new time period for filing an objection to a claim of exemptions shall commence under Rule 4003(b) after conversion of a case to chapter 7 unless:

(i) the case was converted to chapter 7 more than one year after the entry of the first order confirming a plan under chapter 11, 12, or 13; or

(ii) the case was previously pending in chapter 7 and the time to object to a claimed exemption had expired in the original chapter 7 case.

(3) Claims filed before conversion

All claims actually filed by a creditor before conversion of the case are deemed filed in the chapter 7 case.

(4) Turnover of records and property

After qualification of, or assumption of duties by the chapter 7 trustee, any debtor in possession or trustee previously acting in the chapter 11, 12, or 13 case shall, forthwith, unless otherwise ordered, turn over to the chapter 7 trustee all records and property of the estate in the possession or control of the debtor in possession or trustee.

(5) Filing final report and schedule of postpetition debts

(A) Conversion of chapter 11 or chapter 12 case

Unless the court directs otherwise, if a chapter 11 or chapter 12 case is converted to chapter 7, the debtor in possession or, if the debtor is not a debtor in possession, the trustee serving at the time of conversion, shall:

(i) not later than 14 days after conversion of the case, file a schedule of unpaid debts incurred after the filing of the petition and before conversion of the case, including the name and address of each holder of a claim; and

(ii) not later than 30 days after conversion of the case, file and transmit to the United States trustee a final report and account;

(B) Conversion of chapter 13 case

Unless the court directs otherwise, if a chapter 13 case is converted to chapter 7,

(i) the debtor, not later than 14 days after conversion of the case, shall file a schedule of unpaid debts incurred after the filing of the petition and before conversion of the case, including the name and address of each holder of a claim; and

(ii) the trustee, not later than 30 days after conversion of the case, shall file and transmit to the United States trustee a final report and account;

(C) Conversion after confirmation of a plan

Unless the court orders otherwise, if a chapter 11, chapter 12, or chapter 13 case is converted to chapter 7 after confirmation of a plan, the debtor shall file:

(i) a schedule of property not listed in the final report and account acquired after the filing of the petition but before conversion, except if the case is converted from chapter 13 to chapter 7 and § 348(f)(2) does not apply;

(ii) a schedule of unpaid debts not listed in the final report and account incurred after confirmation but before the conversion; and

(iii) a schedule of executory contracts and unexpired leases entered into or assumed after the filing of the petition but before conversion.

(D) Transmission to United States trustee

The clerk shall forthwith transmit to the United States trustee a copy of every schedule filed pursuant to Rule 1019(5).

(6) Postpetition claims; preconversion administrative expenses; notice

A request for payment of an administrative expense incurred before conversion of the case is timely filed under § 503(a) of the Code if it is filed before conversion or a time fixed by the court. If the request is filed by a governmental unit, it is timely if it is filed before conversion or within the later of a time fixed by the court or 180 days after the date of the conversion. A claim of a kind specified in § 348(d) may be filed in accordance with Rules 3001(a)–(d) and 3002. Upon the filing of the schedule of unpaid debts incurred after commencement of the case and before conversion, the clerk, or some other person as the court may direct, shall give notice to those entities listed on the schedule of the time for filing a request for payment of an administrative expense and, unless a notice of insufficient assets to pay a dividend is mailed in accordance with Rule 2002(e), the time for filing a claim of a kind specified in § 348(d).

(7) [Abrogated]

(As amended Mar. 30, 1987, eff. Aug. 1, 1987; Apr. 30, 1991, eff. Aug. 1, 1991; Apr. 23, 1996, eff. Dec. 1, 1996; Apr. 11, 1997, eff. Dec. 1, 1997; Apr. 26, 1999, eff. Dec. 1, 1999; Apr. 23, 2008, eff. Dec. 1, 2008; Mar. 26, 2009, eff. Dec. 1, 2009; Apr. 28, 2010, eff. Dec. 1, 2010.)

1 So in original. Probably should be "Rule".

Rule 1020. Small Business Chapter 11 Reorganization Case

(a) Small business debtor designation

In a voluntary chapter 11 case, the debtor shall state in the petition whether the debtor is a small business debtor. In an involuntary chapter 11 case, the debtor shall file within 14 days after entry of the order for relief a statement as to whether the debtor is a small business debtor. Except as provided in subdivision (c), the status of the case as a small business case shall be in accordance with the debtor's statement under this subdivision, unless and until the court enters an order finding that the debtor's statement is incorrect.

(b) Objecting to designation

Except as provided in subdivision (c), the United States trustee or a party in interest may file an objection to the debtor's statement under subdivision (a) no later than 30 days after the conclusion of the meeting of creditors held under § 341(a) of the Code, or within 30 days after any amendment to the statement, whichever is later.

(c) Appointment of committee of unsecured creditors

If a committee of unsecured creditors has been appointed under § 1102(a)(1), the case shall proceed as a small business

case only if, and from the time when, the court enters an order determining that the committee has not been sufficiently active and representative to provide effective oversight of the debtor and that the debtor satisfies all the other requirements for being a small business. A request for a determination under this subdivision may be filed by the United States trustee or a party in interest only within a reasonable time after the failure of the committee to be sufficiently active and representative. The debtor may file a request for a determination at any time as to whether the committee has been sufficiently active and representative.

(d) Procedure for objection or determination

Any objection or request for a determination under this rule shall be governed by Rule 9014 and served on: the debtor; the debtor's attorney; the United States trustee; the trustee; any committee appointed under § 1102 or its authorized agent, or, if no committee of unsecured creditors has been appointed under § 1102, the creditors included on the list filed under Rule 1007(d); and any other entity as the court directs.

(Added Apr. 11, 1997, eff. Dec. 1, 1997; amended Apr. 23, 2008, eff. Dec. 1, 2008; Mar. 26, 2009, eff. Dec. 1, 2009.)

Rule 1021. Health Care Business Case

(a) Health care business designation

Unless the court orders otherwise, if a petition in a case under chapter 7, chapter 9, or chapter 11 states that the debtor is a health care business, the case shall proceed as a case in which the debtor is a health care business.

(b) Motion

The United States trustee or a party in interest may file a motion to determine whether the debtor is a health care business. The motion shall be transmitted to the United States trustee and served on: the debtor; the trustee; any committee elected under § 705 or appointed under § 1102 of the Code or its authorized agent, or, if the case is a chapter 9 municipality case or a chapter 11 reorganization case and no committee of unsecured creditors has been appointed under § 1102, the creditors included on the list filed under Rule 1007(d); and any other entity as the court directs. The motion shall be governed by Rule 9014.

(Added Apr. 23, 2008, eff. Dec. 1, 2008.)

PART II—OFFICERS AND ADMINISTRATION; NOTICES; MEETINGS; EXAMINATIONS; ELECTIONS; ATTORNEYS AND ACCOUNTANTS

Rule 2001. Appointment of Interim Trustee Before Order for Relief in a Chapter 7 Liquidation Case

(a) Appointment

At any time following the commencement of an involuntary liquidation case and before an order for relief, the court on written motion of a party in interest may order the appointment of an interim trustee under § 303(g) of the Code. The

motion shall set forth the necessity for the appointment and may be granted only after hearing on notice to the debtor, the petitioning creditors, the United States trustee, and other parties in interest as the court may designate.

(b) Bond of movant

An interim trustee may not be appointed under this rule unless the movant furnishes a bond in an amount approved by the court, conditioned to indemnify the debtor for costs, attorney's fee, expenses, and damages allowable under § 303(i) of the Code.

(c) Order of Appointment

The order directing the appointment of an interim trustee shall state the reason the appointment is necessary and shall specify the trustee's duties.

(d) Turnover and report

Following qualification of the trustee selected under § 702 of the Code, the interim trustee, unless otherwise ordered, shall (1) forthwith deliver to the trustee all the records and property of the estate in possession or subject to control of the interim trustee and, (2) within 30 days thereafter file a final report and account.

(As amended Mar. 30, 1987, eff. Aug. 1, 1987; Apr. 30, 1991, eff. Aug. 1, 1991.)

Rule 2002. Notices to Creditors, Equity Security Holders, Administrators in Foreign Proceedings, Persons Against Whom Provisional Relief Is Sought in Ancillary and Other Cross–Border Cases, United States, and United States Trustee

(a) Twenty–one–day notices to parties in interest

Except as provided in subdivisions (h), (i), (*l*), (p), and (q) of this rule, the clerk, or some other person as the court may direct, shall give the debtor, the trustee, all creditors and indenture trustees at least 21 days' notice by mail of:

(1) the meeting of creditors under § 341 or § 1104(b) of the Code, which notice, unless the court orders otherwise, shall include the debtor's employer identification number, social security number, and any other federal taxpayer identification number;

(2) a proposed use, sale, or lease of property of the estate other than in the ordinary course of business, unless the court for cause shown shortens the time or directs another method of giving notice;

(3) the hearing on approval of a compromise or settlement of a controversy other than approval of an agreement pursuant to Rule 4001(d), unless the court for cause shown directs that notice not be sent;

(4) in a chapter 7 liquidation, a chapter 11 reorganization case, or a chapter 12 family farmer debt adjustment case, the hearing on the dismissal of the case or the conversion of the case to another chapter, unless the hearing is under § 707(a)(3) or § 707(b) or is on dismissal of the case for failure to pay the filing fee;

(5) the time fixed to accept or reject a proposed modification of a plan;

(6) a hearing on any entity's request for compensation or reimbursement of expenses if the request exceeds $1,000;

[Text of subdivisions (a)(7) and (8) effective until December 1, 2017, absent contrary Congressional action.]

(7) the time fixed for filing proofs of claims pursuant to Rule 3003(c); and

(8) the time fixed for filing objections and the hearing to consider confirmation of a chapter 12 plan.

[Text of subdivisions (a)(7), (8) and (9) effective December 1, 2017, absent contrary Congressional action.]

(7) the time fixed for filing proofs of claims pursuant to Rule 3003(c);

(8) the time fixed for filing objections and the hearing to consider confirmation of a chapter 12 plan; and

(9) the time fixed for filing objections to confirmation of a chapter 13 plan.

[Text of subdivision (b) effective until December 1, 2017, absent contrary Congressional action.]

(b) Twenty–eight–day notices to parties in interest

Except as provided in subdivision (*l*) of this rule, the clerk, or some other person as the court may direct, shall give the debtor, the trustee, all creditors and indenture trustees not less than 28 days' notice by mail of the time fixed (1) for filing objections and the hearing to consider approval of a disclosure statement or, under § 1125(f), to make a final determination whether the plan provides adequate information so that a separate disclosure statement is not necessary; and (2) for filing objections and the hearing to consider confirmation of a chapter 9, chapter 11, or chapter 13 plan.

[Text of subdivision (b) effective December 1, 2017, absent contrary Congressional action.]

(b) Twenty–eight–day notices to parties in interest

Except as provided in subdivision (*l*) of this rule, the clerk, or some other person as the court may direct, shall give the debtor, the trustee, all creditors and indenture trustees not less than 28 days' notice by mail of the time fixed (1) for filing objections and the hearing to consider approval of a disclosure statement or, under § 1125(f), to make a final determination whether the plan provides adequate information so that a separate disclosure statement is not necessary; (2) for filing objections and the hearing to consider confirmation of a chapter 9 or chapter 11 plan; and (3) for the hearing to consider confirmation of a chapter 13 plan.

(c) Content of notice

(1) Proposed use, sale, or lease of property

Subject to Rule 6004, the notice of a proposed use, sale, or lease of property required by subdivision (a)(2) of this rule shall include the time and place of any public sale, the terms and conditions of any private sale and the time fixed for filing objections. The notice of a proposed use, sale, or lease of property, including real estate, is sufficient if it generally describes the property. The notice of a proposed sale or lease of personally identifiable information under § 363(b)(1) of the Code shall state whether the sale is consistent with any policy prohibiting the transfer of the information.

(2) Notice of hearing on compensation

The notice of a hearing on an application for compensation or reimbursement of expenses required by subdivision (a)(6) of this rule shall identify the applicant and the amounts requested.

(3) Notice of hearing on confirmation when plan provides for an injunction

If a plan provides for an injunction against conduct not otherwise enjoined under the Code, the notice required under Rule 2002(b)(2) shall:

    (A) include in conspicuous language (bold, italic, or underlined text) a statement that the plan proposes an injunction;

    (B) describe briefly the nature of the injunction; and

    (C) identify the entities that would be subject to the injunction.

(d) Notice to equity security holders

In a chapter 11 reorganization case, unless otherwise ordered by the court, the clerk, or some other person as the court may direct, shall in the manner and form directed by the court give notice to all equity security holders of (1) the order for relief; (2) any meeting of equity security holders held pursuant to § 341 of the Code; (3) the hearing on the proposed sale of all or substantially all of the debtor's assets; (4) the hearing on the dismissal or conversion of a case to another chapter; (5) the time fixed for filing objections to and the hearing to consider approval of a disclosure statement; (6) the time fixed for filing objections to and the hearing to consider confirmation of a plan; and (7) the time fixed to accept or reject a proposed modification of a plan.

(e) Notice of no dividend

In a chapter 7 liquidation case, if it appears from the schedules that there are no assets from which a dividend can be paid, the notice of the meeting of creditors may include a statement to that effect; that it is unnecessary to file claims; and that if sufficient assets become available for the payment of a dividend, further notice will be given for the filing of claims.

(f) Other notices

Except as provided in subdivision (*l*) of this rule, the clerk, or some other person as the court may direct, shall give the debtor, all creditors, and indenture trustees notice by mail of:

    (1) the order for relief;

    (2) the dismissal or the conversion of the case to another chapter, or the suspension of proceedings under § 305;

    (3) the time allowed for filing claims pursuant to Rule 3002;

    (4) the time fixed for filing a complaint objecting to the debtor's discharge pursuant to § 727 of the Code as provided in Rule 4004;

    (5) the time fixed for filing a complaint to determine the dischargeability of a debt pursuant to § 523 of the Code as provided in Rule 4007;

    (6) the waiver, denial, or revocation of a discharge as provided in Rule 4006;

    (7) entry of an order confirming a chapter 9, 11, or 12 plan;

    (8) a summary of the trustee's final report in a chapter 7 case if the net proceeds realized exceed $1,500;

    (9) a notice under Rule 5008 regarding the presumption of abuse;

    (10) a statement under § 704(b)(1) as to whether the debtor's case would be presumed to be an abuse under § 707(b); and

    (11) the time to request a delay in the entry of the discharge under §§ 1141(d)(5)(C), 1228(f), and 1328(h). Notice of the time fixed for accepting or rejecting a plan pursuant to Rule 3017(c) shall be given in accordance with Rule 3017(d).

(g) Addressing notices

    (1) Notices required to be mailed under Rule 2002 to a creditor, indenture trustee, or equity security holder shall be addressed as such entity or an authorized agent has directed in its last request filed in the particular case. For the purposes of this subdivision—

    (A) a proof of claim filed by a creditor or indenture trustee that designates a mailing address constitutes a filed request to mail notices to that address, unless a notice of no dividend has been given under Rule 2002(e) and a later notice of possible dividend under Rule 3002(c)(5) has not been given; and

    (B) a proof of interest filed by an equity security holder that designates a mailing address constitutes a filed request to mail notices to that address.

    (2) Except as provided in § 342(f) of the Code, if a creditor or indenture trustee has not filed a request designating a mailing address under Rule 2002(g)(1) or Rule 5003(e), the notices shall be mailed to the address shown on the list of creditors or schedule of liabilities, whichever is filed later. If an equity security holder has not filed a request designating a mailing address under Rule 2002(g)(1) or Rule 5003(e), the notices shall be mailed to the address shown on the list of equity security holders.

    (3) If a list or schedule filed under Rule 1007 includes the name and address of a legal representative of an infant or incompetent person, and a person other than that representative files a request or proof of claim designating a name and mailing address that differs from the name and address of the representative included in the list or schedule, unless the court orders otherwise, notices under Rule 2002 shall be mailed to the representative included in the list or schedules and to the name and address designated in the request or proof of claim.

    (4) Notwithstanding Rule 2002(g)(1)–(3), an entity and a notice provider may agree that when the notice provider is directed by the court to give a notice, the notice provider shall give the notice to the entity in the manner agreed to and at the address or addresses the entity supplies to the notice provider. That address is conclusively presumed to be a proper address for the notice. The notice provider's failure to use the supplied address does not invalidate any notice that is otherwise effective under applicable law.

    (5) A creditor may treat a notice as not having been brought to the creditor's attention under § 342(g)(1) only if, prior to issuance of the notice, the creditor has filed a statement that designates the name and address of the person or organizational subdivision of the creditor responsible for receiving notices under the Code, and that describes the procedures established by the creditor to cause such notices to be delivered to the designated person or subdivision.

(h) Notices to creditors whose claims are filed

In a chapter 7 case, after 90 days following the first date set for the meeting of creditors under § 341 of the Code, the court may direct that all notices required by subdivision (a) of this rule be mailed only to the debtor, the trustee, all indenture trustees, creditors that hold claims for which proofs of claim have been filed, and creditors, if any, that are still permitted to file claims by reason of an extension granted pursuant to Rule 3002(c)(1) or (c)(2). In a case where notice of insufficient assets to pay a dividend has been given to creditors pursuant to subdivision (e) of this rule, after 90 days following the mailing of a notice of the time for filing claims pursuant to Rule 3002(c)(5), the court may direct that notices be mailed only to the entities specified in the preceding sentence.

(i) Notices to committees

Copies of all notices required to be mailed pursuant to this rule shall be mailed to the committees elected under § 705 or appointed under § 1102 of the Code or to their authorized agents. Notwithstanding the foregoing subdivisions, the court may order that notices required by subdivision (a)(2), (3) and (6) of this rule be transmitted to the United States trustee and be mailed only to the committees elected under § 705 or appointed under § 1102 of the Code or to their authorized agents and to the creditors and equity security holders who serve on the trustee or debtor in possession and file a request that all notices be mailed to them. A committee appointed under § 1114 shall receive copies of all notices required by subdivisions (a)(1), (a)(5), (b), (f)(2), and (f)(7), and such other notices as the court may direct.

(j) Notices to the United States

Copies of notices required to be mailed to all creditors under this rule shall be mailed (1) in a chapter 11 reorganization case, to the Securities and Exchange Commission at any place the Commission designates, if the Commission has filed either a notice of appearance in the case or a written request to receive notices; (2) in a commodity broker case, to the Commodity Futures Trading Commission at Washington, D.C.; (3) in a chapter 11 case, to the Internal Revenue Service at its address set out in the register maintained under Rule 5003(e) for the district in which the case is pending; (4) if the papers in the case disclose a debt to the United States other than for taxes, to the United States attorney for the district in which the case is pending and to the department, agency, or instrumentality of the United States through which the debtor became indebted; or (5) if the filed papers disclose a stock interest of the United States, to the Secretary of the Treasury at Washington, D.C.

(k) Notices to United States trustee

Unless the case is a chapter 9 municipality case or unless the United States trustee requests otherwise, the clerk, or some other person as the court may direct, shall transmit to the United States trustee notice of the matters described in subdivisions (a)(2), (a)(3), (a)(4), (a)(8), (b), (f)(1), (f)(2), (f)(4),

(f)(6), (f)(7), (f)(8), and (q) of this rule and notice of hearings on all applications for compensation or reimbursement of expenses. Notices to the United States trustee shall be transmitted within the time prescribed in subdivision (a) or (b) of this rule. The United States trustee shall also receive notice of any other matter if such notice is requested by the United States trustee or ordered by the court. Nothing in these rules requires the clerk or any other person to transmit to the United States trustee any notice, schedule, report, application or other document in a case under the Securities Investor Protection Act, 15 U.S.C. § 78aaa et.[1] seq.

(l) Notice by publication

The court may order notice by publication if it finds that notice by mail is impracticable or that it is desirable to supplement the notice.

(m) Orders designating matter of notices

The court may from time to time enter orders designating the matters in respect to which, the entity to whom, and the form and manner in which notices shall be sent except as otherwise provided by these rules.

(n) Caption

The caption of every notice given under this rule shall comply with Rule 1005. The caption of every notice required to be given by the debtor to a creditor shall include the information required to be in the notice by § 342(c) of the Code.

(o) Notice of order for relief in consumer case

In a voluntary case commenced by an individual debtor whose debts are primarily consumer debts, the clerk or some other person as the court may direct shall give the trustee and all creditors notice by mail of the order for relief within 21 days from the date thereof.

(p) Notice to a creditor with a foreign address

(1) If, at the request of the United States trustee or a party in interest, or on its own initiative, the court finds that a notice mailed within the time prescribed by these rules would not be sufficient to give a creditor with a foreign address to which notices under these rules are mailed reasonable notice under the circumstances, the court may order that the notice be supplemented with notice by other means or that the time prescribed for the notice by mail be enlarged.

(2) Unless the court for cause orders otherwise, a creditor with a foreign address to which notices under this rule are mailed shall be given at least 30 days' notice of the time fixed for filing a proof of claim under Rule 3002(c) or Rule 3003(c).

(3) Unless the court for cause orders otherwise, the mailing address of a creditor with a foreign address shall be determined under Rule 2002(g).

(q) Notice of petition for recognition of foreign proceeding and of court's intention to communicate with foreign courts and foreign representatives

(1) Notice of petition for recognition

After the filing of a petition for recognition of a foreign proceeding, the court shall promptly schedule and hold a hearing on the petition. The clerk, or some other person as the court may direct, shall forthwith give the debtor, all persons or bodies authorized to administer foreign proceedings of the debtor, all entities against whom provisional relief is being sought under § 1519 of the Code, all parties to litigation pending in the United States in which the debtor is a party at the time of the filing of the petition, and such other entities as the court may direct, at least 21 days' notice by mail of the hearing. The notice shall state whether the petition seeks recognition as a foreign main proceeding or foreign nonmain proceeding and shall include the petition and any other document the court may require. .If[1] the court consolidates the hearing on the petition with the hearing on a request for provisional relief, the court may set a shorter notice period, with notice to the entities listed in this subdivision.

(2) Notice of court's intention to communicate with foreign courts and foreign representatives

The clerk, or some other person as the court may direct, shall give the debtor, all persons or bodies authorized to administer foreign proceedings of the debtor, all entities against whom provisional relief is being sought under § 1519 of the Code, all parties to litigation pending in the United States in which the debtor is a party at the time of the filing of the petition, and such other entities as the court may direct, notice by mail of the court's intention to communicate with a foreign court or foreign representative.

(As amended Pub.L. 98–91, § 2(a), Aug. 30, 1983, 97 Stat. 607; Pub.L. 98–353, Title III, § 321, July 10, 1984, 98 Stat. 357; Mar. 30, 1987, eff. Aug. 1, 1987; Apr. 30, 1991, eff. Aug. 1, 1991; Apr. 22, 1993, eff. Aug. 1, 1993; Apr. 23, 1996, eff. Dec. 1, 1996; Apr. 11, 1997, eff. Dec. 1, 1997; Apr. 26, 1999, eff. Dec. 1, 1999; Apr. 17, 2000, eff. Dec. 1, 2000; Apr. 23, 2001, eff. Dec. 1, 2001; Mar. 27, 2003, eff. Dec. 1, 2003; Apr. 26, 2004, eff. Dec. 1, 2004; Apr. 25, 2005, eff. Dec. 1, 2005; Apr. 23, 2008, eff. Dec. 1, 2008; Mar. 26, 2009, eff. Dec. 1, 2009; Apr. 28, 2016, eff. Dec. 1, 2016; Apr. 27, 2017, eff. Dec. 1, 2017, absent contrary Congressional action.)

[1] So in original. Period probably should not appear.

Rule 2003. Meeting of Creditors or Equity Security Holders

(a) Date and place

Except as otherwise provided in § 341(e) of the Code, in a chapter 7 liquidation or a chapter 11 reorganization case, the United States trustee shall call a meeting of creditors to be held no fewer than 21 and no more than 40 days after the order for relief. In a chapter 12 family farmer debt adjustment case, the United States trustee shall call a meeting of creditors to be held no fewer than 21 and no more than 35 days after the order for relief. In a chapter 13 individual's debt adjustment case, the United States trustee shall call a meeting of creditors to be held no fewer than 21 and no more than 50 days after the order for relief. If there is an appeal from or a motion to vacate the order for relief, or if there is a motion to dismiss the case, the United States trustee may set a later date for the meeting. The meeting may be held at a regular place for holding court or at any other place designated by the United States trustee within the district convenient for the parties in interest. If the United States trustee designates a place for the meeting which is not regularly staffed by the United States trustee or an assistant who may preside at the meeting, the meeting may be held not more than 60 days after the order for relief.

(b) Order of meeting

(1) Meeting of creditors

The United States trustee shall preside at the meeting of creditors. The business of the meeting shall include the examination of the debtor under oath and, in a chapter 7 liquidation case, may include the election of a creditors' committee and, if the case is not under subchapter V of chapter 7, the election of a trustee. The presiding officer shall have the authority to administer oaths.

(2) Meeting of equity security holders

If the United States trustee convenes a meeting of equity security holders pursuant to § 341(b) of the Code, the United States trustee shall fix a date for the meeting and shall preside.

(3) Right to vote

In a chapter 7 liquidation case, a creditor is entitled to vote at a meeting if, at or before the meeting, the creditor has filed a proof of claim or a writing setting forth facts evidencing a right to vote pursuant to § 702(a) of the Code unless objection is made to the claim or the proof of claim is insufficient on its face. A creditor of a partnership may file a proof of claim or writing evidencing a right to vote for the trustee for the estate of a general partner notwithstanding that a trustee for the estate of the partnership has previously qualified. In the event of an objection to the amount or allowability of a claim for the purpose of voting, unless the court orders otherwise, the United States trustee shall tabulate the votes for each alternative presented by the dispute and, if resolution of such dispute is necessary to determine the result of the election, the tabulations for each alternative shall be reported to the court.

(c) Record of meeting

Any examination under oath at the meeting of creditors held pursuant to § 341(a) of the Code shall be recorded verbatim by the United States trustee using electronic sound recording equipment or other means of recording, and such record shall be preserved by the United States trustee and available for public access until two years after the conclusion of the meeting of creditors. Upon request of any entity, the United States trustee shall certify and provide a copy or transcript of such recording at the entity's expense.

(d) Report of election and resolution of disputes in a chapter 7 case

(1) Report of undisputed election

In a chapter 7 case, if the election of a trustee or a member of a creditors' committee is not disputed, the United States trustee shall promptly file a report of the election, including the name and address of the person or entity elected and a statement that the election is undisputed.

(2) Disputed election

If the election is disputed, the United States trustee shall promptly file a report stating that the election is disputed, informing the court of the nature of the dispute, and listing the name and address of any candidate elected under any alternative presented by the dispute. No later than the date on which the report is filed, the United States trustee shall mail a copy of the report to any party in interest that has made a request to receive a copy of the report. Pending disposition by the court of a disputed election for trustee, the interim trustee shall continue in office. Unless a motion for the resolution of the dispute is filed no later than 14 days after the United States trustee files a report of a disputed election for trustee, the interim trustee shall serve as trustee in the case.

(e) Adjournment

The meeting may be adjourned from time to time by announcement at the meeting of the adjourned date and time. The presiding official shall promptly file a statement specifying the date and time to which the meeting is adjourned.

(f) Special meetings

The United States trustee may call a special meeting of creditors on request of a party in interest or on the United States trustee's own initiative.

(g) Final meeting

If the United States trustee calls a final meeting of creditors in a case in which the net proceeds realized exceed $1,500, the clerk shall mail a summary of the trustee's final account to the creditors with a notice of the meeting, together with a statement of the amount of the claims allowed. The trustee shall attend the final meeting and shall, if requested, report on the administration of the estate.

(As amended Mar. 30, 1987, eff. Aug. 1, 1987; Apr. 30, 1991, eff. Aug. 1, 1991; Apr. 22, 1993, eff. Aug. 1, 1993; Apr. 26, 1999, eff. Dec. 1, 1999; Mar. 27, 2003, eff. Dec. 1, 2003; Apr. 23, 2008, eff. Dec. 1, 2008; Mar. 26, 2009, eff. Dec. 1, 2009; Apr. 26, 2011, eff. Dec. 1, 2011.)

Rule 2004. Examination

(a) Examination on motion

On motion of any party in interest, the court may order the examination of any entity.

(b) Scope of examination

The examination of an entity under this rule or of the debtor under § 343 of the Code may relate only to the acts, conduct, or property or to the liabilities and financial condition of the debtor, or to any matter which may affect the administration of the debtor's estate, or to the debtor's right to a discharge. In a family farmer's debt adjustment case under chapter 12, an individual's debt adjustment case under chapter 13, or a reorganization case under chapter 11 of the Code, other than for the reorganization of a railroad, the examination may also relate to the operation of any business and the desirability of its continuance, the source of any money or property acquired or to be acquired by the debtor for purposes of consummating a plan and the consideration given or offered therefor, and any other matter relevant to the case or to the formulation of a plan.

(c) Compelling attendance and production of documents

The attendance of an entity for examination and for the production of documents, whether the examination is to be conducted within or without the district in which the case is pending, may be compelled as provided in Rule 9016 for the attendance of a witness at a hearing or trial. As an officer of the court, an attorney may issue and sign a subpoena on behalf of the court for the district in which the examination is to be held if the attorney is admitted to practice in that court or in the court in which the case is pending.

(d) Time and place of examination of debtor

The court may for cause shown and on terms as it may impose order the debtor to be examined under this rule at any time or place it designates, whether within or without the district wherein the case is pending.

(e) Mileage

An entity other than a debtor shall not be required to attend as a witness unless lawful mileage and witness fee for one day's attendance shall be first tendered. If the debtor resides more than 100 miles from the place of examination when required to appear for an examination under this rule, the mileage allowed by law to a witness shall be tendered for any distance more than 100 miles from the debtor's residence at the date of the filing of the first petition commencing a case under the Code or the residence at the time the debtor is required to appear for the examination, whichever is the lesser.

(As amended Mar. 30, 1987, eff. Aug. 1, 1987; Apr. 30, 1991, eff. Aug. 1, 1991; Apr. 29, 2002, eff. Dec. 1, 2002.)

Rule 2005. Apprehension and Removal of Debtor to Compel Attendance for Examination

(a) Order to compel attendance for examination

On motion of any party in interest supported by an affidavit alleging (1) that the examination of the debtor is necessary for the proper administration of the estate and that there is reasonable cause to believe that the debtor is about to leave or has left the debtor's residence or principal place of business to avoid examination, or (2) that the debtor has evaded service of a subpoena or of an order to attend for examination, or (3) that the debtor has willfully disobeyed a subpoena or order to attend for examination, duly served, the court may issue to the marshal, or some other officer authorized by law, an order directing the officer to bring the debtor before the court without unnecessary delay. If, after hearing, the court finds the allegations to be true, the court shall thereupon cause the debtor to be examined forthwith. If necessary, the court shall fix conditions for further examination and for the debtor's obedience to all orders made in reference thereto.

(b) Removal

Whenever any order to bring the debtor before the court is issued under this rule and the debtor is found in a district other than that of the court issuing the order, the debtor may be taken into custody under the order and removed in accordance with the following rules:

(1) If the debtor is taken into custody under the order at a place less than 100 miles from the place of issue of the order, the debtor shall be brought forthwith before the court that issued the order.

(2) If the debtor is taken into custody under the order at a place 100 miles or more from the place of issue of the order, the debtor shall be brought without unnecessary delay before the nearest available United States magistrate judge, bankruptcy judge, or district judge. If, after hearing, the magistrate judge, bankruptcy judge, or district judge finds that an order has issued under this rule and that the person in custody is the debtor, or if the person in custody waives a hearing, the magistrate judge, bankruptcy judge, or district judge shall order removal, and the person in custody shall be released on conditions ensuring prompt appearance before the court that issued the order to compel the attendance.

(c) Conditions of release

In determining what conditions will reasonably assure attendance or obedience under subdivision (a) of this rule or appearance under subdivision (b) of this rule, the court shall be governed by the provisions and policies of title 18, U.S.C., § 3146(a) and (b).

(As amended Mar. 30, 1987, eff. Aug. 1, 1987; Apr. 22, 1993, eff. Aug. 1, 1993.)

Rule 2006. Solicitation and Voting of Proxies in Chapter 7 Liquidation Cases

(a) Applicability

This rule applies only in a liquidation case pending under chapter 7 of the Code.

(b) Definitions

(1) Proxy

A proxy is a written power of attorney authorizing any entity to vote the claim or otherwise act as the owner's attorney in fact in connection with the administration of the estate.

(2) Solicitation of proxy

The solicitation of a proxy is any communication, other than one from an attorney to a regular client who owns a claim or from an attorney to the owner of a claim who has requested the attorney to represent the owner, by which a creditor is asked, directly or indirectly, to give a proxy after or in contemplation of the filing of a petition by or against the debtor.

(c) Authorized solicitation

(1) A proxy may be solicited only by (A) a creditor owning an allowable unsecured claim against the estate on the date of the filing of the petition; (B) a committee elected pursuant to § 705 of the Code; (C) a committee of creditors selected by a majority in number and amount of claims of creditors (i) whose claims are not contingent or unliquidated, (ii) who are not disqualified from voting under § 702(a) of the Code and (iii) who were present or represented at a meeting of which all creditors having claims of over $500 or the 100 creditors having the largest claims had at least seven days' notice in

writing and of which meeting written minutes were kept and are available reporting the names of the creditors present or represented and voting and the amounts of their claims; or (D) a bona fide trade or credit association, but such association may solicit only creditors who were its members or subscribers in good standing and had allowable unsecured claims on the date of the filing of the petition.

(2) A proxy may be solicited only in writing.

(d) Solicitation not authorized

This rule does not permit solicitation (1) in any interest other than that of general creditors; (2) by or on behalf of any custodian; (3) by the interim trustee or by or on behalf of any entity not qualified to vote under § 702(a) of the Code; (4) by or on behalf of an attorney at law; or (5) by or on behalf of a transferee of a claim for collection only.

(e) Data required from holders of multiple proxies

At any time before the voting commences at any meeting of creditors pursuant to § 341(a) of the Code, or at any other time as the court may direct, a holder of two or more proxies shall file and transmit to the United States trustee a verified list of the proxies to be voted and a verified statement of the pertinent facts and circumstances in connection with the execution and delivery of each proxy, including:

(1) a copy of the solicitation;

(2) identification of the solicitor, the forwarder, if the forwarder is neither the solicitor nor the owner of the claim, and the proxyholder, including their connections with the debtor and with each other. If the solicitor, forwarder, or proxyholder is an association, there shall also be included a statement that the creditors whose claims have been solicited and the creditors whose claims are to be voted were members or subscribers in good standing and had allowable unsecured claims on the date of the filing of the petition. If the solicitor, forwarder, or proxyholder is a committee of creditors, the statement shall also set forth the date and place the committee was organized, that the committee was organized in accordance with clause (B) or (C) of paragraph (c)(1) of this rule, the members of the committee, the amounts of their claims, when the claims were acquired, the amounts paid therefor, and the extent to which the claims of the committee members are secured or entitled to priority;

(3) a statement that no consideration has been paid or promised by the proxyholder for the proxy;

(4) a statement as to whether there is any agreement and, if so, the particulars thereof, between the proxyholder and any other entity for the payment of any consideration in connection with voting the proxy, or for the sharing of compensation with any entity, other than a member or regular associate of the proxyholder's law firm, which may be allowed the trustee or any entity for services rendered in the case, or for the employment of any person as attorney, accountant, appraiser, auctioneer, or other employee for the estate;

(5) if the proxy was solicited by an entity other than the proxyholder, or forwarded to the holder by an entity who is neither a solicitor of the proxy nor the owner of the claim, a statement signed and verified by the solicitor or forwarder that no consideration has been paid or promised for the proxy, and whether there is any agreement, and, if so, the particulars thereof, between the solicitor or forwarder and any other entity for the payment of any consideration in connection with voting the proxy, or for sharing compensation with any entity, other than a member or regular associate of the solicitor's or forwarder's law firm which may be allowed the trustee or any entity for services rendered in the case, or for the employment of any person as attorney, accountant, appraiser, auctioneer, or other employee for the estate;

(6) if the solicitor, forwarder, or proxyholder is a committee, a statement signed and verified by each member as to the amount and source of any consideration paid or to be paid to such member in connection with the case other than by way of dividend on the member's claim.

(f) Enforcement of restrictions on solicitation

On motion of any party in interest or on its own initiative, the court may determine whether there has been a failure to comply with the provisions of this rule or any other impropriety in connection with the solicitation or voting of a proxy. After notice and a hearing the court may reject any proxy for cause, vacate any order entered in consequence of the voting of any proxy which should have been rejected, or take any other appropriate action.

(As amended Mar. 30, 1987, eff. Aug. 1, 1987; Apr. 30, 1991, eff. Aug. 1, 1991; Mar. 26, 2009, eff. Dec. 1, 2009.)

Rule 2007. Review of Appointment of Creditors' Committee Organized Before Commencement of the Case

(a) Motion to review appointment

If a committee appointed by the United States trustee pursuant to § 1102(a) of the Code consists of the members of a committee organized by creditors before the commencement of a chapter 9 or chapter 11 case, on motion of a party in interest and after a hearing on notice to the United States trustee and other entities as the court may direct, the court may determine whether the appointment of the committee satisfies the requirements of § 1102(b)(1) of the Code.

(b) Selection of members of committee

The court may find that a committee organized by unsecured creditors before the commencement of a chapter 9 or chapter 11 case was fairly chosen if:

(1) it was selected by a majority in number and amount of claims of unsecured creditors who may vote under § 702(a) of the Code and were present in person or represented at a meeting of which all creditors having unsecured claims of over $1,000 or the 100 unsecured creditors having the largest claims had at least seven days' notice in writing, and of which meeting written minutes reporting the names of the creditors present or represented and voting and the amounts of their claims were kept and are available for inspection;

(2) all proxies voted at the meeting for the elected committee were solicited pursuant to Rule 2006 and the lists and statements required by subdivision (e) thereof have been transmitted to the United States trustee; and

(3) the organization of the committee was in all other respects fair and proper.

(c) Failure to comply with requirements for appointment

After a hearing on notice pursuant to subdivision (a) of this rule, the court shall direct the United States trustee to vacate the appointment of the committee and may order other appropriate action if the court finds that such appointment failed to satisfy the requirements of § 1102(b)(1) of the Code.

(As amended Mar. 30, 1987, eff. Aug. 1, 1987; Apr. 30, 1991, eff. Aug. 1, 1991; Mar. 26, 2009, eff. Dec. 1, 2009.)

Rule 2007.1. Appointment of Trustee or Examiner in a Chapter 11 Reorganization Case

(a) Order to appoint trustee or examiner

In a chapter 11 reorganization case, a motion for an order to appoint a trustee or an examiner under § 1104(a) or § 1104(c) of the Code shall be made in accordance with Rule 9014.

(b) Election of trustee

(1) Request for an election

A request to convene a meeting of creditors for the purpose of electing a trustee in a chapter 11 reorganization case shall be filed and transmitted to the United States trustee in accordance with Rule 5005 within the time prescribed by § 1104(b) of the Code. Pending court approval of the person elected, any person appointed by the United States trustee under § 1104(d) and approved in accordance with subdivision (c) of this rule shall serve as trustee.

(2) Manner of election and notice

An election of a trustee under § 1104(b) of the Code shall be conducted in the manner provided in Rules 2003(b)(3) and 2006. Notice of the meeting of creditors convened under § 1104(b) shall be given as provided in Rule 2002. The United States trustee shall preside at the meeting. A proxy for the purpose of voting in the election may be solicited only by a committee of creditors appointed under § 1102 of the Code or by any other party entitled to solicit a proxy pursuant to Rule 2006.

(3) Report of election and resolution of disputes

(A) Report of undisputed election

If no dispute arises out of the election, the United States trustee shall promptly file a report certifying the election, including the name and address of the person elected and a statement that the election is undisputed. The report shall be accompanied by a verified statement of the person elected setting forth that person's connections with the debtor, creditors, any other party in interest, their respective attorneys and accountants, the United States trustee, or any person employed in the office of the United States trustee.

(B) Dispute arising out of an election

If a dispute arises out of an election, the United States trustee shall promptly file a report stating that the election is disputed, informing the court of the nature of the dispute, and listing the name and address of any candidate elected under any alternative presented by the dispute. The report shall be accompanied by a verified statement by each candidate elected under each alternative presented by the dispute, setting forth the person's connections with the debtor, creditors, any other party in interest, their respective attorneys and accountants, the United States trustee, or any person employed in the office of the United States trustee. Not later than the date on which the report of the disputed election is filed, the United States trustee shall mail a copy of the report and each verified statement to any party in interest that has made a request to convene a meeting under § 1104(b) or to receive a copy of the report, and to any committee appointed under § 1102 of the Code.

(c) Approval of appointment

An order approving the appointment of a trustee or an examiner under § 1104(d) of the Code shall be made on application of the United States trustee. The application shall state the name of the person appointed and, to the best of the applicant's knowledge, all the person's connections with the debtor, creditors, any other parties in interest, their respective attorneys and accountants, the United States trustee, or persons employed in the office of the United States trustee. The application shall state the names of the parties in interest with whom the United States trustee consulted regarding the appointment. The application shall be accompanied by a verified statement of the person appointed setting forth the person's connections with the debtor, creditors, any other party in interest, their respective attorneys and accountants, the United States trustee, or any person employed in the office of the United States trustee.

(Added Apr. 30, 1991, eff. Aug. 1, 1991; amended Apr. 11, 1997, eff. Dec. 1, 1997; Apr. 23, 2008, eff. Dec. 1, 2008.)

Rule 2007.2. Appointment of Patient Care Ombudsman in a Health Care Business Case

(a) Order to appoint patient care ombudsman

In a chapter 7, chapter 9, or chapter 11 case in which the debtor is a health care business, the court shall order the appointment of a patient care ombudsman under § 333 of the Code, unless the court, on motion of the United States trustee or a party in interest filed no later than 21 days after the commencement of the case or within another time fixed by the court, finds that the appointment of a patient care ombudsman is not necessary under the specific circumstances of the case for the protection of patients.

(b) Motion for order to appoint ombudsman

If the court has found that the appointment of an ombudsman is not necessary, or has terminated the appointment, the court, on motion of the United States trustee or a party in interest, may order the appointment at a later time if it finds that the appointment has become necessary to protect patients.

(c) Notice of appointment

If a patient care ombudsman is appointed under § 333, the United States trustee shall promptly file a notice of the appointment, including the name and address of the person appointed. Unless the person appointed is a State Long–Term Care Ombudsman, the notice shall be accompanied by a verified statement of the person appointed setting forth the person's connections with the debtor, creditors, patients, any other party in interest, their respective attorneys and accountants, the United States trustee, and any person employed in the office of the United States trustee.

(d) Termination of appointment

On motion of the United States trustee or a party in interest, the court may terminate the appointment of a patient care ombudsman if the court finds that the appointment is not necessary to protect patients.

(e) Motion

A motion under this rule shall be governed by Rule 9014. The motion shall be transmitted to the United States trustee and served on: the debtor; the trustee; any committee elected under § 705 or appointed under § 1102 of the Code or its authorized agent, or, if the case is a chapter 9 municipality case or a chapter 11 reorganization case and no committee of unsecured creditors has been appointed under § 1102, on the creditors included on the list filed under Rule 1007(d); and such other entities as the court may direct.

(Added Apr. 23, 2008, eff. Dec. 1, 2008. As amended Mar. 26, 2009, eff. Dec. 1, 2009.)

Rule 2008. Notice to Trustee of Selection

The United States trustee shall immediately notify the person selected as trustee how to qualify and, if applicable, the amount of the trustee's bond. A trustee that has filed a blanket bond pursuant to Rule 2010 and has been selected as trustee in a chapter 7, chapter 12, or chapter 13 case that does not notify the court and the United States trustee in writing of rejection of the office within seven days after receipt of notice of selection shall be deemed to have accepted the office. Any other person selected as trustee shall notify the court and the United States trustee in writing of acceptance of the office within seven days after receipt of notice of selection or shall be deemed to have rejected the office.

(As amended Mar. 30, 1987, eff. Aug. 1, 1987; Apr. 30, 1991, eff. Aug. 1, 1991; Mar. 26, 2009, eff. Dec. 1, 2009.)

Rule 2009. Trustees for Estates When Joint Administration Ordered

(a) Election of single trustee for estates being jointly administered

If the court orders a joint administration of two or more estates under Rule 1015(b), creditors may elect a single trustee for the estates being jointly administered, unless the case is under subchapter V of chapter 7 of the Code.

(b) Right of creditors to elect separate trustee

Notwithstanding entry of an order for joint administration under Rule 1015(b), the creditors of any debtor may elect a separate trustee for the estate of the debtor as provided in

§ 702 of the Code, unless the case is under subchapter V of chapter 7.

(c) Appointment of trustees for estates being jointly administered

(1) Chapter 7 liquidation cases

Except in a case governed by subchapter V of chapter 7, the United States trustee may appoint one or more interim trustees for estates being jointly administered in chapter 7 cases.

(2) Chapter 11 reorganization cases

If the appointment of a trustee is ordered, the United States trustee may appoint one or more trustees for estates being jointly administered in chapter 11 cases.

(3) Chapter 12 family farmer's debt adjustment cases

The United States trustee may appoint one or more trustees for estates being jointly administered in chapter 12 cases.

(4) Chapter 13 individual's debt adjustment cases

The United States trustee may appoint one or more trustees for estates being jointly administered in chapter 13 cases.

(d) Potential conflicts of interest

On a showing that creditors or equity security holders of the different estates will be prejudiced by conflicts of interest of a common trustee who has been elected or appointed, the court shall order the selection of separate trustees for estates being jointly administered.

(e) Separate accounts

The trustee or trustees of estates being jointly administered shall keep separate accounts of the property and distribution of each estate.

(As amended Mar. 30, 1987, eff. Aug. 1, 1987; Apr. 30, 1991, eff. Aug. 1, 1991; Mar. 27, 2003, eff. Dec. 1, 2003.)

Rule 2010. Qualification by Trustee; Proceeding on Bond

(a) Blanket bond

The United States trustee may authorize a blanket bond in favor of the United States conditioned on the faithful performance of official duties by the trustee or trustees to cover (1) a person who qualifies as trustee in a number of cases, and (2) a number of trustees each of whom qualifies in a different case.

(b) Proceeding on bond

A proceeding on the trustee's bond may be brought by any party in interest in the name of the United States for the use of the entity injured by the breach of the condition.

(As amended Mar. 30, 1987, eff. Aug. 1, 1987; Apr. 30, 1991, eff. Aug. 1, 1991.)

Rule 2011. Evidence of Debtor in Possession or Qualification of Trustee

(a) Whenever evidence is required that a debtor is a debtor in possession or that a trustee has qualified, the clerk may so certify and the certificate shall constitute conclusive evidence of that fact.

(b) If a person elected or appointed as trustee does not qualify within the time prescribed by § 322(a) of the Code, the clerk shall so notify the court and the United States trustee.

(As amended Apr. 30, 1991, eff. Aug. 1, 1991.)

Rule 2012. Substitution of Trustee or Successor Trustee; Accounting

(a) Trustee

If a trustee is appointed in a chapter 11 case or the debtor is removed as debtor in possession in a chapter 12 case, the trustee is substituted automatically for the debtor in possession as a party in any pending action, proceeding, or matter.

(b) Successor trustee

When a trustee dies, resigns, is removed, or otherwise ceases to hold office during the pendency of a case under the Code (1) the successor is automatically substituted as a party in any pending action, proceeding, or matter; and (2) the successor trustee shall prepare, file, and transmit to the United States trustee an accounting of the prior administration of the estate.

(As amended Mar. 30, 1987, eff. Aug. 1, 1987; Apr. 30, 1991, eff. Aug. 1, 1991.)

Rule 2013. Public Record of Compensation Awarded to Trustees, Examiners, and Professionals

(a) Record to be kept

The clerk shall maintain a public record listing fees awarded by the court (1) to trustees and attorneys, accountants, appraisers, auctioneers and other professionals employed by trustees, and (2) to examiners. The record shall include the name and docket number of the case, the name of the individual or firm receiving the fee and the amount of the fee awarded. The record shall be maintained chronologically and shall be kept current and open to examination by the public without charge. "Trustees," as used in this rule, does not include debtors in possession.

(b) Summary of record

At the close of each annual period, the clerk shall prepare a summary of the public record by individual or firm name, to reflect total fees awarded during the preceding year. The summary shall be open to examination by the public without charge. The clerk shall transmit a copy of the summary to the United States trustee.

(As amended Mar. 30, 1987, eff. Aug. 1, 1987; Apr. 30, 1991, eff. Aug. 1, 1991.)

Rule 2014. Employment of Professional Persons

(a) Application for an order of employment

An order approving the employment of attorneys, accountants, appraisers, auctioneers, agents, or other professionals pursuant to § 327, § 1103, or § 1114 of the Code shall be made only on application of the trustee or committee. The application shall be filed and, unless the case is a chapter 9 municipality case, a copy of the application shall be transmitted by the applicant to the United States trustee. The application shall state the specific facts showing the necessity for the employment, the name of the person to be employed, the reasons for the selection, the professional services to be rendered, any proposed arrangement for compensation, and, to the best of the applicant's knowledge, all of the person's connections with the debtor, creditors, any other party in interest, their respective attorneys and accountants, the United States trustee, or any person employed in the office of the United States trustee. The application shall be accompanied by a verified statement of the person to be employed setting forth the person's connections with the debtor, creditors, any other party in interest, their respective attorneys and accountants, the United States trustee, or any person employed in the office of the United States trustee.

(b) Services rendered by member or associate of firm of attorneys or accountants

If, under the Code and this rule, a law partnership or corporation is employed as an attorney, or an accounting partnership or corporation is employed as an accountant, or if a named attorney or accountant is employed, any partner, member, or regular associate of the partnership, corporation or individual may act as attorney or accountant so employed, without further order of the court.

(As amended Mar. 30, 1987, eff. Aug. 1, 1987; Apr. 30, 1991, eff. Aug. 1, 1991.)

Rule 2015. Duty to Keep Records, Make Reports, and Give Notice of Case or Change of Status

(a) Trustee or debtor in possession

A trustee or debtor in possession shall:

(1) in a chapter 7 liquidation case and, if the court directs, in a chapter 11 reorganization case file and transmit to the United States trustee a complete inventory of the property of the debtor within 30 days after qualifying as a trustee or debtor in possession, unless such an inventory has already been filed;

(2) keep a record of receipts and the disposition of money and property received;

(3) file the reports and summaries required by § 704(a)(8) of the Code, which shall include a statement, if payments are made to employees, of the amounts of deductions for all taxes required to be withheld or paid for and in behalf of employees and the place where these amounts are deposited;

(4) as soon as possible after the commencement of the case, give notice of the case to every entity known to be holding money or property subject to withdrawal or order of the debtor, including every bank, savings or building and loan association, public utility company, and landlord with whom the debtor has a deposit, and to every insurance company which has issued a policy having a cash surrender value payable to the debtor, except that notice need not be given to any entity who has knowledge or has previously been notified of the case;

(5) in a chapter 11 reorganization case, on or before the last day of the month after each calendar quarter during which there is a duty to pay fees under 28 U.S.C. § 1930(a)(6), file and transmit to the United States trustee a statement of any disbursements made during that quarter and of any fees payable under 28 U.S.C. § 1930(a)(6) for that quarter; and

(6) in a chapter 11 small business case, unless the court, for cause, sets another reporting interval, file and transmit to the United States trustee for each calendar month after the order for relief, on the appropriate Official Form, the report required by § 308. If the order for relief is within the first 15 days of a calendar month, a report shall be filed for the portion of the month that follows the order for relief. If the order for relief is after the 15th day of a calendar month, the period for the remainder of the month shall be included in the report for the next calendar month. Each report shall be filed no later than 21 days after the last day of the calendar month following the month covered by the report. The obligation to file reports under this subparagraph terminates on the effective date of the plan, or conversion or dismissal of the case.

(b) Chapter 12 trustee and debtor in possession

In a chapter 12 family farmer's debt adjustment case, the debtor in possession shall perform the duties prescribed in clauses (2)–(4) of subdivision (a) of this rule and, if the court directs, shall file and transmit to the United States trustee a complete inventory of the property of the debtor within the time fixed by the court. If the debtor is removed as debtor in possession, the trustee shall perform the duties of the debtor in possession prescribed in this paragraph.

(c) Chapter 13 trustee and debtor

(1) Business cases

In a chapter 13 individual's debt adjustment case, when the debtor is engaged in business, the debtor shall perform the duties prescribed by clauses (2)–(4) of subdivision (a) of this rule and, if the court directs, shall file and transmit to the United States trustee a complete inventory of the property of the debtor within the time fixed by the court.

(2) Nonbusiness cases

In a chapter 13 individual's debt adjustment case, when the debtor is not engaged in business, the trustee shall perform the duties prescribed by clause (2) of subdivision (a) of this rule.

(d) Foreign representative

In a case in which the court has granted recognition of a foreign proceeding under chapter 15, the foreign representative shall file any notice required under § 1518 of the Code within 14 days after the date when the representative becomes aware of the subsequent information.

(e) Transmission of reports

In a chapter 11 case the court may direct that copies or summaries of annual reports and copies or summaries of other reports shall be mailed to the creditors, equity security holders, and indenture trustees. The court may also direct the publication of summaries of any such reports. A copy of every report or summary mailed or published pursuant to this subdivision shall be transmitted to the United States trustee.

(As amended Mar. 30, 1987, eff. Aug. 1, 1987; Apr. 30, 1991, eff. Aug. 1, 1991; Apr. 23, 1996, eff. Dec. 1, 1996; Apr. 29, 2002, eff. Dec. 1, 2002; Apr. 23, 2008, eff. Dec. 1, 2008; Mar. 26, 2009, eff. Dec. 1, 2009; Apr. 23, 2012, eff. Dec. 1, 2012.)

Rule 2015.1.   Patient Care Ombudsman

(a) Reports

A patient care ombudsman, at least 14 days before making a report under § 333(b)(2) of the Code, shall give notice that the report will be made to the court, unless the court orders otherwise. The notice shall be transmitted to the United States trustee, posted conspicuously at the health care facility that is the subject of the report, and served on: the debtor; the trustee; all patients; and any committee elected under § 705 or appointed under § 1102 of the Code or its authorized agent, or, if the case is a chapter 9 municipality case or a chapter 11 reorganization case and no committee of unsecured creditors has been appointed under § 1102, on the creditors included on the list filed under Rule 1007(d); and such other entities as the court may direct. The notice shall state the date and time when the report will be made, the manner in which the report will be made, and, if the report is in writing, the name, address, telephone number, email address, and website, if any, of the person from whom a copy of the report may be obtained at the debtor's expense.

(b) Authorization to review confidential patient records

A motion by a patient care ombudsman under § 333(c) to review confidential patient records shall be governed by Rule 9014, served on the patient and any family member or other contact person whose name and address have been given to the trustee or the debtor for the purpose of providing information regarding the patient's health care, and transmitted to the United States trustee subject to applicable nonbankruptcy law relating to patient privacy. Unless the court orders otherwise, a hearing on the motion may not be commenced earlier than 14 days after service of the motion.

(Added Apr. 23, 2008, eff. Dec. 1, 2008; amended Mar. 26, 2009, eff. Dec. 1, 2009.)

Rule 2015.2.   Transfer of Patient in Health Care Business Case

Unless the court orders otherwise, if the debtor is a health care business, the trustee may not transfer a patient to another health care business under § 704(a)(12) of the Code unless the trustee gives at least 14 days' notice of the transfer to the patient care ombudsman, if any, the patient, and any family member or other contact person whose name and address has been given to the trustee or the debtor for the purpose of providing information regarding the patient's health care. The notice is subject to applicable nonbankruptcy law relating to patient privacy.

(Added Apr. 23, 2008, eff. Dec. 1, 2008; amended Mar. 26, 2009, eff. Dec. 1, 2009.)

Rule 2015.3.   Reports of Financial Information on Entities in Which a Chapter 11 Estate Holds a Controlling or Substantial Interest

(a) Reporting requirement

In a chapter 11 case, the trustee or debtor in possession shall file periodic financial reports of the value, operations, and profitability of each entity that is not a publicly traded corporation or a debtor in a case under title 11, and in which the estate holds a substantial or controlling interest. The reports shall be prepared as prescribed by the appropriate Official Form, and shall be based upon the most recent information reasonably available to the trustee or debtor in possession.

(b) Time for filing; service

The first report required by this rule shall be filed no later than seven days before the first date set for the meeting of creditors under § 341 of the Code. Subsequent reports shall be filed no less frequently than every six months thereafter, until the effective date of a plan or the case is dismissed or converted. Copies of the report shall be served on the United States trustee, any committee appointed under § 1102 of the Code, and any other party in interest that has filed a request therefor.

(c) Presumption of substantial or controlling interest; judicial determination

For purposes of this rule, an entity of which the estate controls or owns at least a 20 percent interest, shall be presumed to be an entity in which the estate has a substantial or controlling interest. An entity in which the estate controls or owns less than a 20 percent interest shall be presumed not to be an entity in which the estate has a substantial or controlling interest. Upon motion, the entity, any holder of an interest therein, the United States trustee, or any other party in interest may seek to rebut either presumption, and the court shall, after notice and a hearing, determine whether the estate's interest in the entity is substantial or controlling.

(d) Modification of reporting requirement

The court may, after notice and a hearing, vary the reporting requirement established by subdivision (a) of this rule for cause, including that the trustee or debtor in possession is not able, after a good faith effort, to comply with those reporting requirements, or that the information required by subdivision (a) is publicly available.

(e) Notice and protective orders

No later than 14 days before filing the first report required by this rule, the trustee or debtor in possession shall send notice to the entity in which the estate has a substantial or controlling interest, and to all holders—known to the trustee or debtor in possession—of an interest in that entity, that the trustee or debtor in possession expects to file and serve financial information relating to the entity in accordance with this rule. The entity in which the estate has a substantial or controlling interest, or a person holding an interest in that entity, may request protection of the information under § 107 of the Code.

(f) Effect of request

Unless the court orders otherwise, the pendency of a request under subdivisions (c), (d), or (e) of this rule shall not alter or stay the requirements of subdivision (a).

(Added Apr. 23, 2008, eff. Dec. 1, 2008; amended Mar. 26, 2009, eff. Dec. 1, 2009.)

Rule 2016. Compensation for Services Rendered and Reimbursement of Expenses

(a) Application for compensation or reimbursement

An entity seeking interim or final compensation for services, or reimbursement of necessary expenses, from the estate shall file an application setting forth a detailed statement of (1) the services rendered, time expended and expenses incurred, and (2) the amounts requested. An application for compensation shall include a statement as to what payments have theretofore been made or promised to the applicant for services rendered or to be rendered in any capacity whatsoever in connection with the case, the source of the compensation so paid or promised, whether any compensation previously received has been shared and whether an agreement or understanding exists between the applicant and any other entity for the sharing of compensation received or to be received for services rendered in or in connection with the case, and the particulars of any sharing of compensation or agreement or understanding therefor, except that details of any agreement by the applicant for the sharing of compensation as a member or regular associate of a firm of lawyers or accountants shall not be required. The requirements of this subdivision shall apply to an application for compensation for services rendered by an attorney or accountant even though the application is filed by a creditor or other entity. Unless the case is a chapter 9 municipality case, the applicant shall transmit to the United States trustee a copy of the application.

(b) Disclosure of compensation paid or promised to attorney for debtor

Every attorney for a debtor, whether or not the attorney applies for compensation, shall file and transmit to the United States trustee within 14 days after the order for relief, or at another time as the court may direct, the statement required by § 329 of the Code including whether the attorney has shared or agreed to share the compensation with any other entity. The statement shall include the particulars of any such sharing or agreement to share by the attorney, but the details of any agreement for the sharing of the compensation with a member or regular associate of the attorney's law firm shall not be required. A supplemental statement shall be filed and transmitted to the United States trustee within 14 days after any payment or agreement not previously disclosed.

(c) Disclosure of compensation paid or promised to bankruptcy petition preparer

Before a petition is filed, every bankruptcy petition preparer for a debtor shall deliver to the debtor, the declaration under penalty of perjury required by § 110(h)(2). The declaration shall disclose any fee, and the source of any fee, received from or on behalf of the debtor within 12 months of the filing of the case and all unpaid fees charged to the debtor. The declaration shall also describe the services performed and documents prepared or caused to be prepared by the bankruptcy petition preparer. The declaration shall be filed with the petition. The petition preparer shall file a supplemental statement within 14 days after any payment or agreement not previously disclosed.

(As amended Mar. 30, 1987, eff. Aug. 1, 1987; Apr. 30, 1991, eff. Aug. 1, 1991; Mar. 27, 2003, eff. Dec. 1, 2003; Mar. 26, 2009, eff. Dec. 1, 2009.)

Rule 2017. Examination of Debtor's Transactions With Debtor's Attorney

(a) Payment or transfer to attorney before order for relief

On motion by any party in interest or on the court's own initiative, the court after notice and a hearing may determine whether any payment of money or any transfer of property by the debtor, made directly or indirectly and in contemplation of the filing of a petition under the Code by or against the debtor or before entry of the order for relief in an involuntary case, to an attorney for services rendered or to be rendered is excessive.

(b) Payment or transfer to attorney after order for relief

On motion by the debtor, the United States trustee, or on the court's own initiative, the court after notice and a hearing may determine whether any payment of money or any transfer of property, or any agreement therefor, by the debtor to an attorney after entry of an order for relief in a case under the Code is excessive, whether the payment or transfer is made or is to be made directly or indirectly, if the payment, transfer, or agreement therefor is for services in any way related to the case.

(As amended Mar. 30, 1987, eff. Aug. 1, 1987; Apr. 30, 1991, eff. Aug. 1, 1991.)

Rule 2018. Intervention; Right to Be Heard

(a) Permissive intervention

In a case under the Code, after hearing on such notice as the court directs and for cause shown, the court may permit any interested entity to intervene generally or with respect to any specified matter.

(b) Intervention by Attorney General of a State

In a chapter 7, 11, 12, or 13 case, the Attorney General of a State may appear and be heard on behalf of consumer creditors if the court determines the appearance is in the public interest, but the Attorney General may not appeal from any judgment, order, or decree in the case.

(c) Chapter 9 municipality case

The Secretary of the Treasury of the United States may, or if requested by the court shall, intervene in a chapter 9 case. Representatives of the state in which the debtor is located may intervene in a chapter 9 case with respect to matters specified by the court.

(d) Labor unions

In a chapter 9, 11, or 12 case, a labor union or employees' association, representative of employees of the debtor, shall have the right to be heard on the economic soundness of a plan affecting the interests of the employees. A labor union or employees' association which exercises its right to be heard under this subdivision shall not be entitled to appeal any judgment, order, or decree relating to the plan, unless otherwise permitted by law.

(e) Service on entities covered by this rule

The court may enter orders governing the service of notice and papers on entities permitted to intervene or be heard pursuant to this rule.

(As amended Mar. 30, 1987, eff. Aug. 1, 1987; Apr. 30, 1991, eff. Aug. 1, 1991.)

Rule 2019. Disclosure Regarding Creditors and Equity Security Holders in Chapter 9 and Chapter 11 Cases

(a) Definitions

In this rule the following terms have the meanings indicated:

(1) "Disclosable economic interest" means any claim, interest, pledge, lien, option, participation, derivative instrument, or any other right or derivative right granting the holder an economic interest that is affected by the value, acquisition, or disposition of a claim or interest.

(2) "Represent" or "represents" means to take a position before the court or to solicit votes regarding the confirmation of a plan on behalf of another.

(b) Disclosure by groups, committees, and entities

(1) In a chapter 9 or 11 case, a verified statement setting forth the information specified in subdivision (c) of this rule shall be filed by every group or committee that consists of or represents, and every entity that represents, multiple creditors or equity security holders that are (A) acting in concert to advance their common interests, and (B) not composed entirely of affiliates or insiders of one another.

(2) Unless the court orders otherwise, an entity is not required to file the verified statement described in paragraph (1) of this subdivision solely because of its status as:

(A) an indenture trustee;

(B) an agent for one or more other entities under an agreement for the extension of credit;

(C) a class action representative; or

(D) a governmental unit that is not a person.

(c) Information required

The verified statement shall include:

(1) the pertinent facts and circumstances concerning:

(A) with respect to a group or committee, other than a committee appointed under § 1102 or § 1114 of the Code, the formation of the group or committee, including the name of each entity at whose instance the group or committee was formed or for whom the group or committee has agreed to act; or

(B) with respect to an entity, the employment of the entity, including the name of each creditor or equity security holder at whose instance the employment was arranged;

(2) if not disclosed under subdivision (c)(1), with respect to an entity, and with respect to each member of a group or committee:

(A) name and address;

(B) the nature and amount of each disclosable economic interest held in relation to the debtor as of the date the entity was employed or the group or committee was formed; and

(C) with respect to each member of a group or committee that claims to represent any entity in addition to the members of the group or committee, other than a committee appointed under § 1102 or § 1114 of the Code, the date of acquisition by quarter and year of each disclosable economic interest, unless acquired more than one year before the petition was filed;

(3) if not disclosed under subdivision (c)(1) or (c)(2), with respect to each creditor or equity security holder represented by an entity, group, or committee, other than a committee appointed under § 1102 or § 1114 of the Code:

(A) name and address; and

(B) the nature and amount of each disclosable economic interest held in relation to the debtor as of the date of the statement; and

(4) a copy of the instrument, if any, authorizing the entity, group, or committee to act on behalf of creditors or equity security holders.

(d) Supplemental statements

If any fact disclosed in its most recently filed statement has changed materially, an entity, group, or committee shall file a verified supplemental statement whenever it takes a position before the court or solicits votes on the confirmation of a plan. The supplemental statement shall set forth the material changes in the facts required by subdivision (c) to be disclosed.

(e) Determination of failure to comply; sanctions

(1) On motion of any party in interest, or on its own motion, the court may determine whether there has been a failure to comply with any provision of this rule.

(2) If the court finds such a failure to comply, it may:

(A) refuse to permit the entity, group, or committee to be heard or to intervene in the case;

(B) hold invalid any authority, acceptance, rejection, or objection given, procured, or received by the entity, group, or committee; or

(C) grant other appropriate relief.

(As amended Mar. 30, 1987, eff. Aug. 1, 1987; Apr. 30, 1991, eff. Aug. 1, 1991; Apr. 26, 2011, eff. Dec. 1, 2011.)

Rule 2020. Review of Acts by United States Trustee

A proceeding to contest any act or failure to act by the United States trustee is governed by Rule 9014.

(Added Apr. 30, 1991, eff. Aug. 1, 1991.)

(J) a motion to enlarge the time to file a reaffirmation agreement under Rule 4008(a) is pending;

(K) a presumption is in effect under § 524(m) that a reaffirmation agreement is an undue hardship and the court has not concluded a hearing on the presumption; or

(L) a motion is pending to delay discharge because the debtor has not filed with the court all tax documents required to be filed under § 521(f).

(2) Notwithstanding Rule 4004(c)(1), on motion of the debtor, the court may defer the entry of an order granting a discharge for 30 days and, on motion within that period, the court may defer entry of the order to a date certain.

(3) If the debtor is required to file a statement under Rule 1007(b)(8), the court shall not grant a discharge earlier than 30 days after the statement is filed.

(4) In a chapter 11 case in which the debtor is an individual, or a chapter 13 case, the court shall not grant a discharge if the debtor has not filed any statement required by Rule 1007(b)(7).

(d) Applicability of rules in Part VII and Rule 9014

An objection to discharge is governed by Part VII of these rules, except that an objection to discharge under §§[1] 727(a)(8), (a)(9), or 1328(f) is commenced by motion and governed by Rule 9014.

(e) Order of discharge

An order of discharge shall conform to the appropriate Official Form.

(f) Registration in other districts

An order of discharge that has become final may be registered in any other district by filing a certified copy of the order in the office of the clerk of that district. When so registered the order of discharge shall have the same effect as an order of the court of the district where registered.

(g) Notice of discharge

The clerk shall promptly mail a copy of the final order of discharge to those specified in subdivision (a) of this rule.

(As amended Mar. 30, 1987, eff. Aug. 1, 1987; Apr. 30, 1991, eff. Aug. 1, 1991; Apr. 23, 1996, eff. Dec. 1, 1996; Apr. 26, 1999, eff. Dec. 1, 1999; Apr. 17, 2000, eff. Dec. 1, 2000; Apr. 29, 2002, eff. Dec. 1, 2002; Apr. 23, 2008, eff. Dec. 1, 2008; Mar. 26, 2009, eff. Dec. 1, 2009; Apr. 28, 2010, eff. Dec. 1, 2010; Apr. 26, 2011, eff. Dec. 1, 2011; Apr. 16, 2013, eff. Dec. 1, 2013.)

[1] So in original. Probably should be only one section symbol.

Rule 4005. Burden of Proof in Objecting to Discharge

At the trial on a complaint objecting to a discharge, the plaintiff has the burden of proving the objection.

(As amended Mar. 30, 1987, eff. Aug. 1, 1987.)

Rule 4006. Notice of No Discharge

If an order is entered: denying a discharge; revoking a discharge; approving a waiver of discharge; or, in the case of an individual debtor, closing the case without the entry of a discharge, the clerk shall promptly notify all parties in interest in the manner provided by Rule 2002.

(As amended Mar. 30, 1987, eff. Aug. 1, 1987; Apr. 23, 2008, eff. Dec. 1, 2008.)

Rule 4007. Determination of Dischargeability of a Debt

(a) Persons entitled to file complaint

A debtor or any creditor may file a complaint to obtain a determination of the dischargeability of any debt.

(b) Time for commencing proceeding other than under § 523(c) of the Code

A complaint other than under § 523(c) may be filed at any time. A case may be reopened without payment of an additional filing fee for the purpose of filing a complaint to obtain a determination under this rule.

(c) Time for filing complaint under § 523(c) in a chapter 7 liquidation, chapter 11 reorganization, chapter 12 family farmer's debt adjustment case, or chapter 13 individual's debt adjustment case; notice of time fixed

Except as otherwise provided in subdivision (d), a complaint to determine the dischargeability of a debt under § 523(c) shall be filed no later than 60 days after the first date set for the meeting of creditors under § 341(a). The court shall give all creditors no less than 30 days' notice of the time so fixed in the manner provided in Rule 2002. On motion of a party in interest, after hearing on notice, the court may for cause extend the time fixed under this subdivision. The motion shall be filed before the time has expired.

(d) Time for filing complaint under § 523(a)(6) in a chapter 13 individual's debt adjustment case; notice of time fixed

On motion by a debtor for a discharge under § 1328(b), the court shall enter an order fixing the time to file a complaint to determine the dischargeability of any debt under § 523(a)(6) and shall give no less than 30 days' notice of the time fixed to all creditors in the manner provided in Rule 2002. On motion of any party in interest, after hearing on notice, the court may for cause extend the time fixed under this subdivision. The motion shall be filed before the time has expired.

(e) Applicability of Rules in Part VII

A proceeding commenced by a complaint filed under this rule is governed by Part VII of these rules.

(As amended Mar. 30, 1987, eff. Aug. 1, 1987; Apr. 30, 1991, eff. Aug. 1, 1991; Apr. 26, 1999, eff. Dec. 1, 1999; Apr. 23, 2008, eff. Dec. 1, 2008.)

Rule 4008. Filing of Reaffirmation Agreement; Statement in Support of Reaffirmation Agreement

(a) Filing of reaffirmation agreement

A reaffirmation agreement shall be filed no later than 60 days after the first date set for the meeting of creditors under § 341(a) of the Code. The reaffirmation agreement shall be accompanied by a cover sheet, prepared as prescribed by the appropriate Official Form. The court may, at any time and in its discretion, enlarge the time to file a reaffirmation agreement.

(b) Statement in support of reaffirmation agreement

The debtor's statement required under § 524(k)(6)(A) of the Code shall be accompanied by a statement of the total income and expenses stated on schedules I and J. If there is a difference between the total income and expenses stated on those schedules and the statement required under § 524(k)(6)(A), the statement required by this subdivision shall include an explanation of the difference.

(As amended Apr. 30, 1991, eff. Aug. 1, 1991; Apr. 23, 2008, eff. Dec. 1, 2008; Mar. 26, 2009, eff. Dec. 1, 2009.)

PART V—BANKRUPTCY COURTS AND CLERKS

Rule 5001. Courts and Clerks' Offices

(a) Courts always open

The courts shall be deemed always open for the purpose of filing any pleading or other proper paper, issuing and returning process, and filing, making, or entering motions, orders and rules.

(b) Trials and hearings; orders in chambers

All trials and hearings shall be conducted in open court and so far as convenient in a regular court room. Except as otherwise provided in 28 U.S.C. § 152(c), all other acts or proceedings may be done or conducted by a judge in chambers and at any place either within or without the district; but no hearing, other than one ex parte, shall be conducted outside the district without the consent of all parties affected thereby.

(c) Clerk's office

The clerk's office with the clerk or a deputy in attendance shall be open during business hours on all days except Saturdays, Sundays and the legal holidays listed in Rule 9006(a).

(As amended Mar. 30, 1987, eff. Aug. 1, 1987; Apr. 30, 1991, eff. Aug. 1, 1991; Apr. 23, 2008, eff. Dec. 1, 2008.)

Rule 5002. Restrictions on Approval of Appointments

(a) Approval of appointment of relatives prohibited

The appointment of an individual as a trustee or examiner pursuant to § 1104 of the Code shall not be approved by the court if the individual is a relative of the bankruptcy judge approving the appointment or the United States trustee in the region in which the case is pending. The employment of an individual as an attorney, accountant, appraiser, auctioneer, or other professional person pursuant to §§ 327, 1103, or 1114 shall not be approved by the court if the individual is a relative of the bankruptcy judge approving the employment. The employment of an individual as attorney, accountant, appraiser, auctioneer, or other professional person pursuant to §§ 327, 1103, or 1114 may be approved by the court if the individual is a relative of the United States trustee in the region in which the case is pending, unless the court finds that the relationship with the United States trustee renders the employment improper under the circumstances of the case. Whenever under this subdivision an individual may not be approved for appointment or employment, the individual's firm, partnership, corporation, or any other form of business association or relationship, and all members, associates and professional employees thereof also may not be approved for appointment or employment.

(b) Judicial determination that approval of appointment or employment is improper

A bankruptcy judge may not approve the appointment of a person as a trustee or examiner pursuant to § 1104 of the Code or approve the employment of a person as an attorney, accountant, appraiser, auctioneer, or other professional person pursuant to §§ 327, 1103, or 1114 of the Code if that person is or has been so connected with such judge or the United States trustee as to render the appointment or employment improper.

(As amended Apr. 29, 1985, eff. Aug. 1, 1985; Apr. 30, 1991, eff. Aug. 1, 1991.)

Rule 5003. Records Kept by the Clerk

(a) Bankruptcy dockets

The clerk shall keep a docket in each case under the Code and shall enter thereon each judgment, order, and activity in that case as prescribed by the Director of the Administrative Office of the United States Courts. The entry of a judgment or order in a docket shall show the date the entry is made.

(b) Claims register

The clerk shall keep in a claims register a list of claims filed in a case when it appears that there will be a distribution to unsecured creditors.

(c) Judgments and orders

The clerk shall keep, in the form and manner as the Director of the Administrative Office of the United States Courts may prescribe, a correct copy of every final judgment or order affecting title to or lien on real property or for the recovery of money or property, and any other order which the court may direct to be kept. On request of the prevailing party, a correct copy of every judgment or order affecting title to or lien upon real or personal property or for the recovery of money or property shall be kept and indexed with the civil judgments of the district court.

(d) Index of cases; certificate of search

The clerk shall keep indices of all cases and adversary proceedings as prescribed by the Director of the Administrative Office of the United States Courts. On request, the clerk shall make a search of any index and papers in the clerk's custody and certify whether a case or proceeding has been filed in or transferred to the court or if a discharge has been entered in its records.

(e) Register of mailing addresses of federal and state governmental units and certain taxing authorities

The United States or the state or territory in which the court is located may file a statement designating its mailing address. The United States, state, territory, or local governmental unit responsible for collecting taxes within the district in which the case is pending may also file a statement designating an address for service of requests under § 505(b) of the Code, and the designation shall describe where further information concerning additional requirements for filing such requests may be found. The clerk shall keep, in the form and manner as the Director of the Administrative Office of the United States Courts may prescribe, a register that includes the mailing addresses designated under the first sentence of this subdivision, and a separate register of the addresses designated for the service of requests under § 505(b) of the Code. The clerk is not required to include in any single register more than one mailing address for each department, agency, or instrumentality of the United States or the state or territory. If more than one address for a department, agency, or instrumentality is included in the register, the clerk shall also include information that would enable a user of the register to determine the circumstances when each address is applicable, and mailing notice to only one applicable address is sufficient to provide effective notice. The clerk shall update the register annually, effective January 2 of each year. The mailing address in the register is conclusively presumed to be a proper address for the governmental unit, but the failure to use that mailing address does not invalidate any notice that is otherwise effective under applicable law.

(f) Other books and records of the clerk

The clerk shall keep any other books and records required by the Director of the Administrative Office of the United States Courts.

(As amended Mar. 30, 1987, eff. Aug. 1, 1987; Apr. 17, 2000, eff. Dec. 1, 2000; Apr. 23, 2008, eff. Dec. 1, 2008.)

Rule 5004. Disqualification

(a) Disqualification of judge

A bankruptcy judge shall be governed by 28 U.S.C. § 455, and disqualified from presiding over the proceeding or contested matter in which the disqualifying circumstances[1] arises or, if appropriate, shall be disqualified from presiding over the case.

(b) Disqualification of judge from allowing compensation

A bankruptcy judge shall be disqualified from allowing compensation to a person who is a relative of the bankruptcy judge or with whom the judge is so connected as to render it improper for the judge to authorize such compensation.

(As amended Apr. 29, 1985, eff. Aug. 1, 1985; Mar. 30, 1987, eff. Aug. 1, 1987.)

[1] So in original. Probably should be "circumstance".

Rule 5005. Filing and Transmittal of Papers

(a) Filing

(1) Place of filing

The lists, schedules, statements, proofs of claim or interest, complaints, motions, applications, objections and other papers required to be filed by these rules, except as provided in 28 U.S.C. § 1409, shall be filed with the clerk in the district where the case under the Code is pending. The judge of that court may permit the papers to be filed with the judge, in which event the filing date shall be noted thereon, and they shall be forthwith transmitted to the clerk. The clerk shall not refuse to accept for filing any petition or other paper presented for the purpose of filing solely because it is not presented in proper form as required by these rules or any local rules or practices.

(2) Filing by electronic means

A court may by local rule permit or require documents to be filed, signed, or verified by electronic means that are consistent with technical standards, if any, that the Judicial Conference of the United States establishes. A local rule may require filing by electronic means only if reasonable exceptions are allowed. A document filed by electronic means in compliance with a local rule constitutes a written paper for the purpose of applying these rules, the Federal Rules of Civil Procedure made applicable by these rules, and § 107 of the Code.

(b) Transmittal to the United States trustee

(1) The complaints, motions, applications, objections and other papers required to be transmitted to the United States trustee by these rules shall be mailed or delivered to an office of the United States trustee, or to another place designated by the United States trustee, in the district where the case under the Code is pending.

(2) The entity, other than the clerk, transmitting a paper to the United States trustee shall promptly file as proof of such transmittal a verified statement identifying the paper and stating the date on which it was transmitted to the United States trustee.

(3) Nothing in these rules shall require the clerk to transmit any paper to the United States trustee if the United States trustee requests in writing that the paper not be transmitted.

(c) Error in filing or transmittal

A paper intended to be filed with the clerk but erroneously delivered to the United States trustee, the trustee, the attorney for the trustee, a bankruptcy judge, a district judge, the clerk of the bankruptcy appellate panel, or the clerk of the district court shall, after the date of its receipt has been noted thereon, be transmitted forthwith to the clerk of the bankruptcy court. A paper intended to be transmitted to the United States trustee but erroneously delivered to the clerk, the trustee, the attorney for the trustee, a bankruptcy judge, a district judge, the clerk of the bankruptcy appellate panel, or the clerk of the district court shall, after the date of its receipt has been noted thereon, be transmitted forthwith to the United States trustee. In the interest of justice, the court may order that a paper erroneously delivered shall be deemed filed with the clerk or transmitted to the United States trustee as of the date of its original delivery.

(As amended Mar. 30, 1987, eff. Aug. 1, 1987; Apr. 30, 1991, eff. Aug. 1, 1991; Apr. 22, 1993, eff. Aug. 1, 1993; Apr. 23, 1996, eff. Dec. 1, 1996; Apr. 12, 2006, eff. Dec. 1, 2006.)

Rule 5006. Certification of Copies of Papers

The clerk shall issue a certified copy of the record of any proceeding in a case under the Code or of any paper filed with the clerk on payment of any prescribed fee.

(As amended Apr. 30, 1991, eff. Aug. 1, 1991.)

Rule 5007. Record of Proceedings and Transcripts

(a) Filing of record or transcript

The reporter or operator of a recording device shall certify the original notes of testimony, tape recording, or other original record of the proceeding and promptly file them with the clerk. The person preparing any transcript shall promptly file a certified copy.

(b) Transcript fees

The fees for copies of transcripts shall be charged at rates prescribed by the Judicial Conference of the United States. No fee may be charged for the certified copy filed with the clerk.

(c) Admissibility of record in evidence

A certified sound recording or a transcript of a proceeding shall be admissible as prima facie evidence to establish the record.

(As amended Mar. 30, 1987, eff. Aug. 1, 1987; Apr. 30, 1991, eff. Aug. 1, 1991.)

Rule 5008. Notice Regarding Presumption of Abuse in Chapter 7 Cases of Individual Debtors

If a presumption of abuse has arisen under § 707(b) in a chapter 7 case of an individual with primarily consumer debts, the clerk shall within 10 days after the date of the filing of the petition notify creditors of the presumption of abuse in accordance with Rule 2002. If the debtor has not filed a statement indicating whether a presumption of abuse has arisen, the clerk shall within 10 days after the date of the filing of the petition notify creditors that the debtor has not filed the statement and that further notice will be given if a later filed statement indicates that a presumption of abuse has arisen. If a debtor later files a statement indicating that a presumption of abuse has arisen, the clerk shall notify creditors of the presumption of abuse as promptly as practicable.

(Added Apr. 23, 2008, eff. Dec. 1, 2008.)

[Rule 5009 nameline effective until December 1, 2017, absent contrary Congressional action]

Rule 5009. Closing Chapter 7 Liquidation, Chapter 12 Family Farmer's Debt Adjustment, Chapter 13 Individual's Debt Adjustment, and Chapter 15 Ancillary and Cross–Border Cases

[Rule 5009 nameline effective December 1, 2017, absent contrary Congressional action]

Rule 5009. Closing Chapter 7, Chapter 12, Chapter 13, and Chapter 15 Cases; Declaring Lien Satisfied

[Text of subdivision (a) effective until December 1, 2017, absent contrary Congressional action.]

(a) Cases under chapters 7, 12, and 13

If in a chapter 7, chapter 12, or chapter 13 case the trustee has filed a final report and final account and has certified that the estate has been fully administered, and if within 30 days no objection has been filed by the United States trustee or a party in interest, there shall be a presumption that the estate has been fully administered.

[Text of subdivision (a) effective December 1, 2017, absent contrary Congressional action.]

(a) Closing of cases under chapters 7, 12, and 13

If in a chapter 7, chapter 12, or chapter 13 case the trustee has filed a final report and final account and has certified that the estate has been fully administered, and if within 30 days no objection has been filed by the United States trustee or a party in interest, there shall be a presumption that the estate has been fully administered.

(b) Notice of failure to file Rule 1007(b)(7) statement

If an individual debtor in a chapter 7 or 13 case is required to file a statement under Rule 1007(b)(7) and fails to do so within 45 days after the first date set for the meeting of creditors under § 341(a) of the Code, the clerk shall promptly notify the debtor that the case will be closed without entry of a discharge unless the required statement is filed within the applicable time limit under Rule 1007(c).

(c) Cases under chapter 15

A foreign representative in a proceeding recognized under § 1517 of the Code shall file a final report when the purpose of the representative's appearance in the court is completed. The report shall describe the nature and results of the representative's activities in the court. The foreign representative shall transmit the report to the United States trustee, and give notice of its filing to the debtor, all persons or bodies authorized to administer foreign proceedings of the debtor, all parties to litigation pending in the United States in which the debtor was a party at the time of the filing of the petition, and such other entities as the court may direct. The foreign representative shall file a certificate with the court that notice has been given. If no objection has been filed by the United States trustee or a party in interest within 30 days after the certificate is filed, there shall be a presumption that the case has been fully administered.

[Text of subdivision (d) effective December 1, 2017, absent contrary Congressional action.]

(d) Order declaring lien satisfied

In a chapter 12 or chapter 13 case, if a claim that was secured by property of the estate is subject to a lien under applicable nonbankruptcy law, the debtor may request entry of an order declaring that the secured claim has been satisfied and the lien has been released under the terms of a confirmed plan. The request shall be made by motion and shall be served on the holder of the claim and any other entity the court designates in the manner provided by Rule 7004 for service of a summons and complaint.

(As amended Apr. 30, 1991, eff. Aug. 1, 1991; Apr. 28, 2010, eff. Dec. 1, 2010; Apr. 16, 2013, eff. Dec. 1, 2013; Apr. 27, 2017, eff. Dec. 1, 2017, absent contrary Congressional action.)

Rule 5010. Reopening Cases

A case may be reopened on motion of the debtor or other party in interest pursuant to § 350(b) of the Code. In a chapter 7, 12, or 13 case a trustee shall not be appointed by the United States trustee unless the court determines that a trustee is necessary to protect the interests of creditors and the debtor or to insure efficient administration of the case.

(As amended Mar. 30, 1987, eff. Aug. 1, 1987; Apr. 30, 1991, eff. Aug. 1, 1991.)

Rule 5011. Withdrawal and Abstention From Hearing a Proceeding

(a) Withdrawal

A motion for withdrawal of a case or proceeding shall be heard by a district judge.

(b) Abstention from hearing a proceeding

A motion for abstention pursuant to 28 U.S.C. § 1334(c) shall be governed by Rule 9014 and shall be served on the parties to the proceeding.

(c) Effect of filing of motion for withdrawal or abstention

The filing of a motion for withdrawal of a case or proceeding or for abstention pursuant to 28 U.S.C. § 1334(c) shall not stay the administration of the case or any proceeding therein before the bankruptcy judge except that the bankruptcy judge may stay, on such terms and conditions as are proper, proceedings pending disposition of the motion. A motion for a stay ordinarily shall be presented first to the bankruptcy judge. A motion for a stay or relief from a stay filed in the district court shall state why it has not been presented to or obtained from the bankruptcy judge. Relief granted by the district judge shall be on such terms and conditions as the judge deems proper.

(Added Mar. 30, 1987, eff. Aug. 1, 1987 and amended Apr. 30, 1991, eff. Aug. 1, 1991.)

Rule 5012. Agreements Concerning Coordination of Proceedings in Chapter 15 Cases

Approval of an agreement under § 1527(4) of the Code shall be sought by motion. The movant shall attach to the motion a copy of the proposed agreement or protocol and, unless the court directs otherwise, give at least 30 days' notice of any hearing on the motion by transmitting the motion to the United States trustee, and serving it on the debtor, all persons or bodies authorized to administer foreign proceedings of the debtor, all entities against whom provisional relief is being sought under § 1519, all parties to litigation pending in the United States in which the debtor was a party at the time of the filing of the petition, and such other entities as the court may direct.

(Added Apr. 28, 2010, eff. Dec. 1, 2010.)

PART VI—COLLECTION AND LIQUIDATION OF THE ESTATE

Rule 6001. Burden of Proof as to Validity of Postpetition Transfer

Any entity asserting the validity of a transfer under § 549 of the Code shall have the burden of proof.

Rule 6002. Accounting by Prior Custodian of Property of the Estate

(a) Accounting required

Any custodian required by the Code to deliver property in the custodian's possession or control to the trustee shall promptly file and transmit to the United States trustee a report and account with respect to the property of the estate and the administration thereof.

(b) Examination of administration

On the filing and transmittal of the report and account required by subdivision (a) of this rule and after an examination has been made into the superseded administration, after notice and a hearing, the court shall determine the propriety of the administration, including the reasonableness of all disbursements.

(As amended Mar. 30, 1987, eff. Aug. 1, 1987; Apr. 30, 1991, eff. Aug. 1, 1991; Apr. 22, 1993, eff. Aug. 1, 1993.)

Rule 6003. Interim and Final Relief Immediately Following the Commencement of the Case—Applications for Employment; Motions for Use, Sale, or Lease of Property; and Motions for Assumption or Assignment of Executory Contracts

Except to the extent that relief is necessary to avoid immediate and irreparable harm, the court shall not, within 21 days after the filing of the petition, issue an order granting the following:

(a) an application under Rule 2014;

(b) a motion to use, sell, lease, or otherwise incur an obligation regarding property of the estate, including a motion to pay all or part of a claim that arose before the filing of the petition, but not a motion under Rule 4001; or

(c) a motion to assume or assign an executory contract or unexpired lease in accordance with § 365.

(Added Apr. 30, 2007, eff. Dec. 1, 2007; amended Mar. 26, 2009, eff. Dec. 1, 2009; Apr. 26, 2011, eff. Dec. 1, 2011.)

Rule 6004. Use, Sale, or Lease of Property

(a) Notice of proposed use, sale, or lease of property

Notice of a proposed use, sale, or lease of property, other than cash collateral, not in the ordinary course of business shall be given pursuant to Rule 2002(a)(2), (c)(1), (i), and (k) and, if applicable, in accordance with § 363(b)(2) of the Code.

(b) Objection to proposal

Except as provided in subdivisions (c) and (d) of this rule, an objection to a proposed use, sale, or lease of property shall be filed and served not less than seven days before the date set for the proposed action or within the time fixed by the court. An objection to the proposed use, sale, or lease of property is governed by Rule 9014.

(c) Sale free and clear of liens and other interests

A motion for authority to sell property free and clear of liens or other interests shall be made in accordance with Rule 9014 and shall be served on the parties who have liens or other interests in the property to be sold. The notice required by subdivision (a) of this rule shall include the date of the hearing on the motion and the time within which objections may be filed and served on the debtor in possession or trustee.

(d) Sale of property under $2,500

Notwithstanding subdivision (a) of this rule, when all of the nonexempt property of the estate has an aggregate gross value less than $2,500, it shall be sufficient to give a general notice of intent to sell such property other than in the ordinary course of business to all creditors, indenture trustees, committees appointed or elected pursuant to the Code, the United States trustee and other persons as the court may direct. An objection to any such sale may be filed and served by a party in interest within 14 days of the mailing of the notice, or within the time fixed by the court. An objection is governed by Rule 9014.

(e) Hearing

If a timely objection is made pursuant to subdivision (b) or (d) of this rule, the date of the hearing thereon may be set in the notice given pursuant to subdivision (a) of this rule.

(f) Conduct of sale not in the ordinary course of business

(1) Public or private sale

All sales not in the ordinary course of business may be by private sale or by public auction. Unless it is impracticable, an itemized statement of the property sold, the name of each purchaser, and the price received for each item or lot or for the property as a whole if sold in bulk shall be filed on completion of a sale. If the property is sold by an auctioneer, the auctioneer shall file the statement, transmit a copy thereof to the United States trustee, and furnish a copy to the trustee, debtor in possession, or chapter 13 debtor. If the property is not sold by an auctioneer, the trustee, debtor in possession, or chapter 13 debtor shall file the statement and transmit a copy thereof to the United States trustee.

(2) Execution of instruments

After a sale in accordance with this rule the debtor, the trustee, or debtor in possession, as the case may be, shall execute any instrument necessary or ordered by the court to effectuate the transfer to the purchaser.

(g) Sale of personally identifiable information

(1) Motion

A motion for authority to sell or lease personally identifiable information under § 363(b)(1)(B) shall include a request for an order directing the United States trustee to appoint a consumer privacy ombudsman under § 332. Rule 9014 governs the motion which shall be served on: any committee elected under § 705 or appointed under § 1102 of the Code, or if the case is a chapter 11 reorganization case and no committee of unsecured creditors has been appointed under § 1102, on the creditors included on the list of creditors filed under Rule 1007(d); and on such other entities as the court may direct. The motion shall be transmitted to the United States trustee.

(2) Appointment

If a consumer privacy ombudsman is appointed under § 332, no later than seven days before the hearing on the motion under § 363(b)(1)(B), the United States trustee shall file a notice of the appointment, including the name and address of the person appointed. The United States trustee's notice shall be accompanied by a verified statement of the person appointed setting forth the person's connections with the debtor, creditors, any other party in interest, their respective attorneys and accountants, the United States trustee, or any person employed in the office of the United States trustee.

(h) Stay of order authorizing use, sale, or lease of property

An order authorizing the use, sale, or lease of property other than cash collateral is stayed until the expiration of 14 days after entry of the order, unless the court orders otherwise.

(As amended Mar. 30, 1987, eff. Aug. 1, 1987; Apr. 30, 1991, eff. Aug. 1, 1991; Apr. 26, 1999, eff. Dec. 1, 1999; Apr. 23, 2008, eff. Dec. 1, 2008; Mar. 26, 2009, eff. Dec. 1, 2009.)

Rule 6005. Appraisers and Auctioneers

The order of the court approving the employment of an appraiser or auctioneer shall fix the amount or rate of compensation. No officer or employee of the Judicial Branch of the United States or the United States Department of Justice shall be eligible to act as appraiser or auctioneer. No residence or licensing requirement shall disqualify an appraiser or auctioneer from employment.

(As amended Mar. 30, 1987, eff. Aug. 1, 1987; Apr. 30, 1991, eff. Aug. 1, 1991.)

Rule 6006. Assumption, Rejection or Assignment of an Executory Contract or Unexpired Lease

(a) Proceeding to assume, reject, or assign

A proceeding to assume, reject, or assign an executory contract or unexpired lease, other than as part of a plan, is governed by Rule 9014.

(b) Proceeding to require trustee to act

A proceeding by a party to an executory contract or unexpired lease in a chapter 9 municipality case, chapter 11 reorganization case, chapter 12 family farmer's debt adjustment case, or chapter 13 individual's debt adjustment case, to require the trustee, debtor in possession, or debtor to determine whether to assume or reject the contract or lease is governed by Rule 9014.

(c) Notice

Notice of a motion made pursuant to subdivision (a) or (b) of this rule shall be given to the other party to the contract or lease, to other parties in interest as the court may direct, and, except in a chapter 9 municipality case, to the United States trustee.

(d) Stay of order authorizing assignment

An order authorizing the trustee to assign an executory contract or unexpired lease under § 365(f) is stayed until the expiration of 14 days after the entry of the order, unless the court orders otherwise.

(e) Limitations

The trustee shall not seek authority to assume or assign multiple executory contracts or unexpired leases in one motion unless: (1) all executory contracts or unexpired leases to be assumed or assigned are between the same parties or are to be assigned to the same assignee; (2) the trustee seeks to assume, but not assign to more than one assignee, unexpired leases of real property; or (3) the court otherwise authorizes the motion to be filed. Subject to subdivision (f), the trustee may join requests for authority to reject multiple executory contracts or unexpired leases in one motion.

(f) Omnibus Motions

A motion to reject or, if permitted under subdivision (e), a motion to assume or assign multiple executory contracts or unexpired leases that are not between the same parties shall:

(1) state in a conspicuous place that parties receiving the omnibus motion should locate their names and their contracts or leases listed in the motion;

(2) list parties alphabetically and identify the corresponding contract or lease;

(3) specify the terms, including the curing of defaults, for each requested assumption or assignment;

(4) specify the terms, including the identity of each assignee and the adequate assurance of future performance by each assignee, for each requested assignment;

(5) be numbered consecutively with other omnibus motions to assume, assign, or reject executory contracts or unexpired leases; and

(6) be limited to no more than 100 executory contracts or unexpired leases.

(g) Finality of Determination

The finality of any order respecting an executory contract or unexpired lease included in an omnibus motion shall be determined as though such contract or lease had been the subject of a separate motion.

(As amended Mar. 30, 1987, eff. Aug. 1, 1987; Apr. 30, 1991, eff. Aug. 1, 1991; Apr. 22, 1993, eff. Aug. 1, 1993; Apr. 26, 1999, eff. Dec. 1, 1999; Apr. 30, 2007, eff. Dec. 1, 2007; Mar. 26, 2009, eff. Dec. 1, 2009.)

Rule 6007. Abandonment or Disposition of Property

(a) Notice of proposed abandonment or disposition; objections; hearing

Unless otherwise directed by the court, the trustee or debtor in possession shall give notice of a proposed abandonment or disposition of property to the United States trustee, all creditors, indenture trustees, and committees elected pursuant to § 705 or appointed pursuant to § 1102 of the Code. A party in interest may file and serve an objection within 14 days of the mailing of the notice, or within the time fixed by the court. If a timely objection is made, the court shall set a hearing on notice to the United States trustee and to other entities as the court may direct.

(b) Motion by party in interest

A party in interest may file and serve a motion requiring the trustee or debtor in possession to abandon property of the estate.

(c) [Abrogated]

(As amended Mar. 30, 1987, eff. Aug. 1, 1987; Apr. 30, 1991, eff. Aug. 1, 1991; Apr. 22, 1993, eff. Aug. 1, 1993; Mar. 26, 2009, eff. Dec. 1, 2009.)

Rule 6008. Redemption of Property From Lien or Sale

On motion by the debtor, trustee, or debtor in possession and after hearing on notice as the court may direct, the court may authorize the redemption of property from a lien or from a sale to enforce a lien in accordance with applicable law.

Rule 6009. Prosecution and Defense of Proceedings by Trustee or Debtor in Possession

With or without court approval, the trustee or debtor in possession may prosecute or may enter an appearance and defend any pending action or proceeding by or against the debtor, or commence and prosecute any action or proceeding in behalf of the estate before any tribunal.

Rule 6010. Proceeding to Avoid Indemnifying Lien or Transfer to Surety

If a lien voidable under § 547 of the Code has been dissolved by the furnishing of a bond or other obligation and the surety thereon has been indemnified by the transfer of, or the creation of a lien upon, nonexempt property of the debtor, the surety shall be joined as a defendant in any proceeding to avoid the indemnifying transfer or lien. Such proceeding is governed by the rules in Part VII.

(As amended Apr. 30, 1991, eff. Aug. 1, 1991.)

Rule 6011. Disposal of Patient Records in Health Care Business Case

(a) Notice by publication under § 351(1)(A)

A notice regarding the claiming or disposing of patient records under § 351(1)(A) shall not identify any patient by name or other identifying information, but shall:

(1) identify with particularity the health care facility whose patient records the trustee proposes to destroy;

(2) state the name, address, telephone number, email address, and website, if any, of a person from whom information about the patient records may be obtained;

(3) state how to claim the patient records; and

(4) state the date by which patient records must be claimed, and that if they are not so claimed the records will be destroyed.

(b) Notice by mail under § 351(1)(B)

Subject to applicable nonbankruptcy law relating to patient privacy, a notice regarding the claiming or disposing of patient records under § 351(1)(B) shall, in addition to including the information in subdivision (a), direct that a patient's family member or other representative who receives the notice inform the patient of the notice. Any notice under this subdivision shall be mailed to the patient and any family member or other contact person whose name and address have been given to the trustee or the debtor for the purpose of providing information regarding the patient's health care, to the Attorney General of the State where the health care facility is located, and to any insurance company known to have provided health care insurance to the patient.

(c) Proof of compliance with notice requirement

Unless the court orders the trustee to file proof of compliance with § 351(1)(B) under seal, the trustee shall not file, but shall maintain, the proof of compliance for a reasonable time.

(d) Report of destruction of records

The trustee shall file, no later than 30 days after the destruction of patient records under § 351(3), a report certifying that the unclaimed records have been destroyed and explaining the method used to effect the destruction. The report shall not identify any patient by name or other identifying information.

(Added Apr. 23, 2008, eff. Dec. 1, 2008.)

PART VII—ADVERSARY PROCEEDINGS

Rule 7001. Scope of Rules of Part VII

An adversary proceeding is governed by the rules of this Part VII. The following are adversary proceedings:

(1) a proceeding to recover money or property, other than a proceeding to compel the debtor to deliver property to the trustee, or a proceeding under § 554(b) or § 725 of the Code, Rule 2017, or Rule 6002;

[Text of subdivision (2) effective until December 1, 2017, absent contrary Congressional action.]

(2) a proceeding to determine the validity, priority, or extent of a lien or other interest in property, other than a proceeding under Rule 4003(d);

[Text of subdivision (2) effective December 1, 2017, absent contrary Congressional action.]

(2) a proceeding to determine the validity, priority, or extent of a lien or other interest in property, but not a proceeding under Rule 3012 or Rule 4003(d);

(3) a proceeding to obtain approval under § 363(h) for the sale of both the interest of the estate and of a co-owner in property;

(4) a proceeding to object to or revoke a discharge, other than an objection to discharge under §§[1] 727(a)(8), (a)(9), or 1328(f);

(5) a proceeding to revoke an order of confirmation of a chapter 11, chapter 12, or chapter 13 plan;

(6) a proceeding to determine the dischargeability of a debt;

(7) a proceeding to obtain an injunction or other equitable relief, except when a chapter 9, chapter 11, chapter 12, or chapter 13 plan provides for the relief;

(8) a proceeding to subordinate any allowed claim or interest, except when a chapter 9, chapter 11, chapter 12, or chapter 13 plan provides for subordination;

(9) a proceeding to obtain a declaratory judgment relating to any of the foregoing; or

(10) a proceeding to determine a claim or cause of action removed under 28 U.S.C. § 1452.

(As amended Mar. 30, 1987, eff. Aug. 1, 1987; Apr. 30, 1991, eff. Aug. 1, 1991; Apr. 26, 1999, eff. Dec. 1, 1999; Apr. 28, 2010, eff. Dec. 1, 2010; Apr. 27, 2017, eff. Dec. 1, 2017, absent contrary Congressional action.)

1 So in original. Probably should be only one section symbol.

Rule 7002. References to Federal Rules of Civil Procedure

Whenever a Federal Rule of Civil Procedure applicable to adversary proceedings makes reference to another Federal Rule of Civil Procedure, the reference shall be read as a reference to the Federal Rule of Civil Procedure as modified in this Part VII.

Rule 7003. Commencement of Adversary Proceeding

Rule 3 F.R.Civ.P. applies in adversary proceedings.

Rule 7004. Process; Service of Summons, Complaint

(a) Summons; service; proof of service

(1) Except as provided in Rule 7004(a)(2), Rule 4(a), (b), (c)(1), (d)(1), (e)–(j), (*l*), and (m) F.R.Civ.P. applies in adversary proceedings. Personal service under Rule 4(e)–(j) F.R.Civ.P. may be made by any person at least 18 years of age

who is not a party, and the summons may be delivered by the clerk to any such person.

(2) The clerk may sign, seal, and issue a summons electronically by putting an "s/" before the clerk's name and including the court's seal on the summons.

(b) Service by first class mail

Except as provided in subdivision (h), in addition to the methods of service authorized by Rule 4(e)–(j) F.R.Civ.P., service may be made within the United States by first class mail postage prepaid as follows:

(1) Upon an individual other than an infant or incompetent, by mailing a copy of the summons and complaint to the individual's dwelling house or usual place of abode or to the place where the individual regularly conducts a business or profession.

(2) Upon an infant or an incompetent person, by mailing a copy of the summons and complaint to the person upon whom process is prescribed to be served by the law of the state in which service is made when an action is brought against such a defendant in the courts of general jurisdiction of that state. The summons and complaint in that case shall be addressed to the person required to be served at that person's dwelling house or usual place of abode or at the place where the person regularly conducts a business or profession.

(3) Upon a domestic or foreign corporation or upon a partnership or other unincorporated association, by mailing a copy of the summons and complaint to the attention of an officer, a managing or general agent, or to any other agent authorized by appointment or by law to receive service of process and, if the agent is one authorized by statute to receive service and the statute so requires, by also mailing a copy to the defendant.

(4) Upon the United States, by mailing a copy of the summons and complaint addressed to the civil process clerk at the office of the United States attorney for the district in which the action is brought and by mailing a copy of the summons and complaint to the Attorney General of the United States at Washington, District of Columbia, and in any action attacking the validity of an order of an officer or an agency of the United States not made a party, by also mailing a copy of the summons and complaint to that officer or agency. The court shall allow a reasonable time for service pursuant to this subdivision for the purpose of curing the failure to mail a copy of the summons and complaint to multiple officers, agencies, or corporations of the United States if the plaintiff has mailed a copy of the summons and complaint either to the civil process clerk at the office of the United States attorney or to the Attorney General of the United States.

(5) Upon any officer or agency of the United States, by mailing a copy of the summons and complaint to the United States as prescribed in paragraph (4) of this subdivision and also to the officer or agency. If the agency is a corporation, the mailing shall be as prescribed in paragraph (3) of this subdivision of this rule. The court shall allow a reasonable time for service pursuant to this subdivision for the purpose of curing the failure to mail a copy of the summons and

complaint to multiple officers, agencies, or corporations of the United States if the plaintiff has mailed a copy of the summons and complaint either to the civil process clerk at the office of the United States attorney or to the Attorney General of the United States. If the United States trustee is the trustee in the case and service is made upon the United States trustee solely as trustee, service may be made as prescribed in paragraph (10) of this subdivision of this rule.

(6) Upon a state or municipal corporation or other governmental organization thereof subject to suit, by mailing a copy of the summons and complaint to the person or office upon whom process is prescribed to be served by the law of the state in which service is made when an action is brought against such a defendant in the courts of general jurisdiction of that state, or in the absence of the designation of any such person or office by state law, then to the chief executive officer thereof.

(7) Upon a defendant of any class referred to in paragraph (1) or (3) of this subdivision of this rule, it is also sufficient if a copy of the summons and complaint is mailed to the entity upon whom service is prescribed to be served by any statute of the United States or by the law of the state in which service is made when an action is brought against such a defendant in the court of general jurisdiction of that state.

(8) Upon any defendant, it is also sufficient if a copy of the summons and complaint is mailed to an agent of such defendant authorized by appointment or by law to receive service of process, at the agent's dwelling house or usual place of abode or at the place where the agent regularly carries on a business or profession and, if the authorization so requires, by mailing also a copy of the summons and complaint to the defendant as provided in this subdivision.

(9) Upon the debtor, after a petition has been filed by or served upon the debtor and until the case is dismissed or closed, by mailing a copy of the summons and complaint to the debtor at the address shown in the petition or to such other address as the debtor may designate in a filed writing.

(10) Upon the United States trustee, when the United States trustee is the trustee in the case and service is made upon the United States trustee solely as trustee, by mailing a copy of the summons and complaint to an office of the United States trustee or another place designated by the United States trustee in the district where the case under the Code is pending.

(c) Service by publication

If a party to an adversary proceeding to determine or protect rights in property in the custody of the court cannot be served as provided in Rule 4(e)-(j) F.R.Civ.P. or subdivision (b) of this rule, the court may order the summons and complaint to be served by mailing copies thereof by first class mail, postage prepaid, to the party's last known address, and by at least one publication in such manner and form as the court may direct.

(d) Nationwide service of process

The summons and complaint and all other process except a subpoena may be served anywhere in the United States.

(e) Summons: time limit for service within the United States

Service made under Rule 4(e), (g), (h)(1), (i), or (j)(2) F.R.Civ.P. shall be by delivery of the summons and complaint within 7 days after the summons is issued. If service is by any authorized form of mail, the summons and complaint shall be deposited in the mail within 7 days after the summons is issued. If a summons is not timely delivered or mailed, another summons will be issued for service. This subdivision does not apply to service in a foreign country.

(f) Personal jurisdiction

If the exercise of jurisdiction is consistent with the Constitution and laws of the United States, serving a summons or filing a waiver of service in accordance with this rule or the subdivisions of Rule 4 F.R.Civ.P. made applicable by these rules is effective to establish personal jurisdiction over the person of any defendant with respect to a case under the Code or a civil proceeding arising under the Code, or arising in or related to a case under the Code.

(g) Service on debtor's attorney

If the debtor is represented by an attorney, whenever service is made upon the debtor under this Rule, service shall also be made upon the debtor's attorney by any means authorized under Rule 5(b) F.R.Civ.P.

(h) Service of process on an insured depository institution

Service on an insured depository institution (as defined in section 3 of the Federal Deposit Insurance Act) in a contested matter or adversary proceeding shall be made by certified mail addressed to an officer of the institution unless—

(1) the institution has appeared by its attorney, in which case the attorney shall be served by first class mail;

(2) the court orders otherwise after service upon the institution by certified mail of notice of an application to permit service on the institution by first class mail sent to an officer of the institution designated by the institution; or

(3) the institution has waived in writing its entitlement to service by certified mail by designating an officer to receive service.

(As amended Mar. 30, 1987, eff. Aug. 1, 1987; Apr. 30, 1991, eff. Aug. 1, 1991; Oct. 22, 1994, Pub.L. 103–394, Title I, § 114, 108 Stat. 4118; Apr. 23, 1996, eff. Dec. 1, 1996; Apr. 26, 1999, eff. Dec. 1, 1999; Apr. 25, 2005, eff. Dec. 1, 2005; Apr. 12, 2006, eff. Dec. 1, 2006; Mar. 26, 2009, eff. Dec. 1, 2009; Apr. 25, 2014, eff. Dec. 1, 2014.)

Rule 7005. Service and Filing of Pleadings and Other Papers

Rule 5 F.R.Civ.P. applies in adversary proceedings.

Rule 7007. Pleadings Allowed

Rule 7 F.R.Civ.P. applies in adversary proceedings.

Rule 7007.1. Corporate Ownership Statement

(a) Required disclosure

Any corporation that is a party to an adversary proceeding, other than the debtor or a governmental unit, shall file two copies of a statement that identifies any corporation, other than a governmental unit, that directly or indirectly owns 10% or more of any class of the corporation's equity interests, or states that there are no entities to report under this subdivision.

(b) Time for Filing

A party shall file the statement required under Rule 7007.1(a) with its first appearance, pleading, motion, response, or other request addressed to the court. A party shall file a supplemental statement promptly upon any change in circumstances that this rule requires the party to identify or disclose.

(Added Mar. 27, 2003, eff. Dec. 1, 2003. As amended Apr. 30, 2007, eff. Dec. 1, 2007.)

Rule 7008. General Rules of Pleading

Rule 8 F.R.Civ.P. applies in adversary proceedings. The allegation of jurisdiction required by Rule 8(a) shall also contain a reference to the name, number, and chapter of the case under the Code to which the adversary proceeding relates and to the district and division where the case under the Code is pending. In an adversary proceeding before a bankruptcy court, the complaint, counterclaim, cross-claim, or third-party complaint shall contain a statement that the pleader does or does not consent to entry of final orders or judgment by the bankruptcy court.

(As amended Mar. 30, 1987, eff. Aug. 1, 1987; Apr. 25, 2014, eff. Dec. 1, 2014; Apr. 28, 2016, eff. Dec. 1, 2016.)

Rule 7009. Pleading Special Matters

Rule 9 F.R.Civ.P. applies in adversary proceedings.

Rule 7010. Form of Pleadings

Rule 10 F.R.Civ.P. applies in adversary proceedings, except that the caption of each pleading in such a proceeding shall conform substantially to the appropriate Official Form.

(As amended Apr. 30, 1991, eff. Aug. 1, 1991.)

Rule 7012. Defenses and Objections—When and How Presented—By Pleading or Motion— Motion for Judgment on the Pleadings

(a) When presented

If a complaint is duly served, the defendant shall serve an answer within 30 days after the issuance of the summons, except when a different time is prescribed by the court. The court shall prescribe the time for service of the answer when service of a complaint is made by publication or upon a party in a foreign country. A party served with a pleading stating a cross-claim shall serve an answer thereto within 21 days after service. The plaintiff shall serve a reply to a counterclaim in the answer within 21 days after service of the answer or, if a reply is ordered by the court, within 21 days after service of the order, unless the order otherwise directs. The United States or an officer or agency thereof shall serve an answer to a complaint within 35 days after the issuance of the summons, and shall serve an answer to a cross-claim, or a reply to a counterclaim, within 35 days after service upon the United States attorney of the pleading in which the claim is asserted. The service of a motion permitted under this rule alters these periods of time as follows, unless a different time is fixed by order of the court: (1) if the court denies the motion or postpones its disposition until the trial on the merits, the responsive pleading shall be served within 14 days after notice of the court's action; (2) if the court grants a motion for a more definite statement, the responsive pleading shall be served within 14 days after the service of a more definite statement.

(b) Applicability of Rule 12(b)–(i) F.R.Civ.P.

Rule 12(b)–(i) F.R.Civ.P. applies in adversary proceedings. A responsive pleading shall include a statement that the party does or does not consent to entry of final orders or judgment by the bankruptcy court.

(As amended Mar. 30, 1987, eff. Aug. 1, 1987; Apr. 23, 2008, eff. Dec. 1, 2008; Mar. 26, 2009, eff. Dec. 1, 2009; Apr. 28, 2016, eff. Dec. 1, 2016.)

Rule 7013. Counterclaim and Cross–Claim

Rule 13 F.R.Civ.P. applies in adversary proceedings, except that a party sued by a trustee or debtor in possession need not state as a counterclaim any claim that the party has against the debtor, the debtor's property, or the estate, unless the claim arose after the entry of an order for relief. A trustee or debtor in possession who fails to plead a counterclaim through oversight, inadvertence, or excusable neglect, or when justice so requires, may by leave of court amend the pleading, or commence a new adversary proceeding or separate action.

(As amended Mar. 30, 1987, eff. Aug. 1, 1987.)

Rule 7014. Third–Party Practice

Rule 14 F.R.Civ.P. applies in adversary proceedings.

Rule 7015. Amended and Supplemental Pleadings

Rule 15 F.R.Civ.P. applies in adversary proceedings.

Rule 7016. Pre–Trial Procedures

(a) Pretrial conferences; scheduling; management

Rule 16 F.R.Civ.P. applies in adversary proceedings.

(b) Determining procedure

The bankruptcy court shall decide, on its own motion or a party's timely motion, whether:

(1) to hear and determine the proceeding;

(2) to hear the proceeding and issue proposed findings of fact and conclusions of law; or

(3) to take some other action.

(As amended Apr. 28, 2016, eff. Dec. 1, 2016.)

Rule 7017. Parties Plaintiff and Defendant; Capacity

Rule 17 F.R.Civ.P. applies in adversary proceedings, except as provided in Rule 2010(b).

(As amended Apr. 30, 1991, eff. Aug. 1, 1991.)

Rule 7018. Joinder of Claims and Remedies

Rule 18 F.R.Civ.P. applies in adversary proceedings.

Rule 7019. Joinder of Persons Needed for Just Determination

Rule 19 F.R.Civ.P. applies in adversary proceedings, except that (1) if an entity joined as a party raises the defense that the court lacks jurisdiction over the subject matter and the defense is sustained, the court shall dismiss such entity from the adversary proceeding and (2) if an entity joined as a party properly and timely raises the defense of improper venue, the court shall determine, as provided in 28 U.S.C. § 1412, whether that part of the proceeding involving the joined party shall be transferred to another district, or whether the entire adversary proceeding shall be transferred to another district.

(As amended Mar. 30, 1987, eff. Aug. 1, 1987.)

Rule 7020. Permissive Joinder of Parties

Rule 20 F.R.Civ.P. applies in adversary proceedings.

Rule 7021. Misjoinder and Non–Joinder of Parties

Rule 21 F.R.Civ.P. applies in adversary proceedings.

Rule 7022. Interpleader

Rule 22(a) F.R.Civ.P. applies in adversary proceedings. This rule supplements—and does not limit—the joinder of parties allowed by Rule 7020.

(As amended Apr. 23, 2008, eff. Dec. 1, 2008.)

Rule 7023. Class Proceedings

Rule 23 F.R.Civ.P. applies in adversary proceedings.

Rule 7023.1. Derivative Actions

Rule 23.1 F.R.Civ.P. applies in adversary proceedings.

(As amended Apr. 23, 2008, eff. Dec. 1, 2008.)

Rule 7023.2. Adversary Proceedings Relating to Unincorporated Associations

Rule 23.2 F.R.Civ.P. applies in adversary proceedings.

Rule 7024. Intervention

Rule 24 F.R.Civ.P. applies in adversary proceedings.

Rule 7025. Substitution of Parties

Subject to the provisions of Rule 2012, Rule 25 F.R.Civ.P. applies in adversary proceedings.

Rule 7026. General Provisions Governing Discovery

Rule 26 F.R.Civ.P. applies in adversary proceedings.

Rule 7027. Depositions Before Adversary Proceedings or Pending Appeal

Rule 27 F.R.Civ.P. applies to adversary proceedings.

Rule 7028. Persons Before Whom Depositions May Be Taken

Rule 28 F.R.Civ.P. applies in adversary proceedings.

Rule 7029. Stipulations Regarding Discovery Procedure

Rule 29 F.R.Civ.P. applies in adversary proceedings.

Rule 7030. Depositions Upon Oral Examination

Rule 30 F.R.Civ.P. applies in adversary proceedings.

Rule 7031. Deposition Upon Written Questions

Rule 31 F.R.Civ.P. applies in adversary proceedings.

Rule 7032. Use of Depositions in Adversary Proceedings

Rule 32 F.R.Civ.P. applies in adversary proceedings.

Rule 7033. Interrogatories to Parties

Rule 33 F.R.Civ.P. applies in adversary proceedings.

Rule 7034. Production of Documents and Things and Entry Upon Land for Inspection and Other Purposes

Rule 34 F.R.Civ.P. applies in adversary proceedings.

Rule 7035. Physical and Mental Examination of Persons

Rule 35 F.R.Civ.P. applies in adversary proceedings.

Rule 7036. Requests for Admission

Rule 36 F.R.Civ.P. applies in adversary proceedings.

Rule 7037. Failure to Make Discovery: Sanctions

Rule 37 F.R.Civ.P. applies in adversary proceedings.

Rule 7040. Assignment of Cases for Trial

Rule 40 F.R.Civ.P. applies in adversary proceedings.

Rule 7041. Dismissal of Adversary Proceedings

Rule 41 F.R.Civ.P. applies in adversary proceedings, except that a complaint objecting to the debtor's discharge shall not be dismissed at the plaintiff's instance without notice to the trustee, the United States trustee, and such other persons as the court may direct, and only on order of the court containing terms and conditions which the court deems proper.

(As amended Apr. 30, 1991, eff. Aug. 1, 1991.)

Rule 7042. Consolidation of Adversary Proceedings; Separate Trials

Rule 42 F.R.Civ.P. applies in adversary proceedings.

Rule 7052. Findings by the Court

Rule 52 F.R.Civ.P. applies in adversary proceedings, except that any motion under subdivision (b) of that rule for amended or additional findings shall be filed no later than 14 days after entry of judgment. In these proceedings, the reference in Rule 52 F.R.Civ.P. to the entry of judgment under Rule 58 F.R.Civ.P. shall be read as a reference to the entry of a judgment or order under Rule 5003(a).

(As amended Mar. 26, 2009, eff. Dec. 1, 2009.)

Rule 7054. Judgments; Costs

(a) Judgments

Rule 54(a)–(c) F.R.Civ.P. applies in adversary proceedings.

(b) Costs; Attorney's Fees

(1) Costs Other Than Attorney's Fees. The court may allow costs to the prevailing party except when a statute of the United States or these rules otherwise provides. Costs against the United States, its officers and agencies shall be imposed only to the extent permitted by law. Costs may be taxed by the clerk on 14 days' notice; on motion served within seven days thereafter, the action of the clerk may be reviewed by the court.

(2) Attorney's Fees.

(A) Rule 54(d)(2)(A)–(C) and (E) F.R.Civ.P. applies in adversary proceedings except for the reference in Rule 54(d)(2)(C) to Rule 78.

(B) By local rule, the court may establish special procedures to resolve fee-related issues without extensive evidentiary hearings.

(As amended Apr. 23, 2012, eff. Dec. 1, 2012; Apr. 25, 2014, eff. Dec. 1, 2014.)

Rule 7055. Default

Rule 55 F.R.Civ.P. applies in adversary proceedings.

Rule 7056. Summary Judgment

Rule 56 F.R.Civ.P. applies in adversary proceedings, except that any motion for summary judgment must be made at least 30 days before the initial date set for an evidentiary hearing on any issue for which summary judgment is sought, unless a different time is set by local rule or the court orders otherwise.

(As amended Apr. 23, 2012, eff. Dec. 1, 2012.)

Rule 7058. Entering Judgment in Adversary Proceeding

Rule 58 F.R.Civ.P. applies in adversary proceedings. In these proceedings, the reference in Rule 58 F.R.Civ.P. to the civil docket shall be read as a reference to the docket maintained by the clerk under Rule 5003(a).

(Added Mar. 26, 2009, eff. Dec. 1, 2009.)

Rule 7062. Stay of Proceedings to Enforce a Judgment

Rule 62 F.R.Civ.P. applies in adversary proceedings.

(As amended Apr. 30, 1991, eff. Aug. 1, 1991; Apr. 26, 1999, eff. Dec. 1, 1999.)

Rule 7064. Seizure of Person or Property

Rule 64 F.R.Civ.P. applies in adversary proceedings.

Rule 7065. Injunctions

Rule 65 F.R.Civ.P. applies in adversary proceedings, except that a temporary restraining order or preliminary injunction may be issued on application of a debtor, trustee, or debtor in possession without compliance with Rule 65(c).

Rule 7067. Deposit in Court

Rule 67 F.R.Civ.P. applies in adversary proceedings.

Rule 7068. Offer of Judgment

Rule 68 F.R.Civ.P. applies in adversary proceedings.

Rule 7069. Execution

Rule 69 F.R.Civ.P. applies in adversary proceedings.

Rule 7070. Judgment for Specific Acts; Vesting Title

Rule 70 F.R.Civ.P. applies in adversary proceedings and the court may enter a judgment divesting the title of any party and vesting title in others whenever the real or personal property involved is within the jurisdiction of the court.

(As amended Mar. 30, 1987, eff. Aug. 1, 1987.)

Rule 7071. Process in Behalf of and Against Persons Not Parties

Rule 71 F.R.Civ.P. applies in adversary proceedings.

Rule 7087. Transfer of Adversary Proceeding

On motion and after a hearing, the court may transfer an adversary proceeding or any part thereof to another district pursuant to 28 U.S.C. § 1412, except as provided in Rule 7019(2).

(As amended Mar. 30, 1987, eff. Aug. 1, 1987.)

PART VIII—APPEALS TO DISTRICT COURT OR BANKRUPTCY APPELLATE PANEL

Rule 8001. Scope of Part VIII Rules; Definition of "BAP"; Method of Transmission

(a) General scope

These Part VIII rules govern the procedure in a United States district court and a bankruptcy appellate panel on appeal from a judgment, order, or decree of a bankruptcy court. They also govern certain procedures on appeal to a United States court of appeals under 28 U.S.C. § 158(d).

(b) Definition of "BAP"

"BAP" means a bankruptcy appellate panel established by a circuit's judicial council and authorized to hear appeals from a bankruptcy court under 28 U.S.C. § 158.

(c) Method of transmitting documents

A document must be sent electronically under these Part VIII rules, unless it is being sent by or to an individual who is not represented by counsel or the court's governing rules permit or require mailing or other means of delivery.

(As amended Mar. 30, 1987, eff. Aug. 1, 1987; Apr. 30, 1991, eff. Aug. 1, 1991; Apr. 11, 1997, eff. Dec. 1, 1997; Apr. 23, 2008, eff. Dec. 1, 2008; Mar. 26, 2009, eff. Dec. 1, 2009; Apr. 25, 2014, eff. Dec. 1, 2014.)

Rule 8002. Time for Filing Notice of Appeal

(a) In general

(1) Fourteen-day period

Except as provided in subdivisions (b) and (c), a notice of appeal must be filed with the bankruptcy clerk within 14 days after entry of the judgment, order, or decree being appealed.

(2) Filing before the entry of judgment

A notice of appeal filed after the bankruptcy court announces a decision or order—but before entry of the judgment, order, or decree—is treated as filed on the date of and after the entry.

(3) Multiple appeals

If one party files a timely notice of appeal, any other party may file a notice of appeal within 14 days after the date when the first notice was filed, or within the time otherwise allowed by this rule, whichever period ends later.

(4) Mistaken filing in another court

If a notice of appeal is mistakenly filed in a district court, BAP, or court of appeals, the clerk of that court must state on the notice the date on which it was received and transmit it to the bankruptcy clerk. The notice of appeal is then considered filed in the bankruptcy court on the date so stated.

(b) Effect of a motion on the time to appeal

(1) In general

If a party timely files in the bankruptcy court any of the following motions, the time to file an appeal runs for all parties from the entry of the order disposing of the last such remaining motion:

    (A) to amend or make additional findings under Rule 7052, whether or not granting the motion would alter the judgment;

    (B) to alter or amend the judgment under Rule 9023;

    (C) for a new trial under Rule 9023; or

    (D) for relief under Rule 9024 if the motion is filed within 14 days after the judgment is entered.

(2) Filing an appeal before the motion is decided

If a party files a notice of appeal after the court announces or enters a judgment, order, or decree—but before it disposes of any motion listed in subdivision (b)(1)—the notice becomes effective when the order disposing of the last such remaining motion is entered.

(3) Appealing the ruling on the motion

If a party intends to challenge an order disposing of any motion listed in subdivision (b)(1)—or the alteration or amendment of a judgment, order, or decree upon the motion—the party must file a notice of appeal or an amended notice of appeal. The notice or amended notice must comply with Rule 8003 or 8004 and be filed within the time prescribed by this rule, measured from the entry of the order disposing of the last such remaining motion.

(4) No additional fee

No additional fee is required to file an amended notice of appeal.

(c) Appeal by an inmate confined in an institution

(1) In general

If an inmate confined in an institution files a notice of appeal from a judgment, order, or decree of a bankruptcy court, the notice is timely if it is deposited in the institution's internal mail system on or before the last day for filing. If the institution has a system designed for legal mail, the inmate must use that system to receive the benefit of this rule. Timely filing may be shown by a declaration in compliance with 28 U.S.C. § 1746 or by a notarized state-

ment, either of which must set forth the date of deposit and state that first-class postage has been prepaid.

(2) Multiple appeals

If an inmate files under this subdivision the first notice of appeal, the 14–day period provided in subdivision (a)(3) for another party to file a notice of appeal runs from the date when the bankruptcy clerk dockets the first notice.

(d) Extending the time to appeal

(1) When the time may be extended

Except as provided in subdivision (d)(2), the bankruptcy court may extend the time to file a notice of appeal upon a party's motion that is filed:

    (A) within the time prescribed by this rule; or

    (B) within 21 days after that time, if the party shows excusable neglect.

(2) When the time may not be extended

The bankruptcy court may not extend the time to file a notice of appeal if the judgment, order, or decree appealed from:

    (A) grants relief from an automatic stay under § 362, 922, 1201, or 1301 of the Code;

    (B) authorizes the sale or lease of property or the use of cash collateral under § 363 of the Code;

    (C) authorizes the obtaining of credit under § 364 of the Code;

    (D) authorizes the assumption or assignment of an executory contract or unexpired lease under § 365 of the Code;

    (E) approves a disclosure statement under § 1125 of the Code; or

    (F) confirms a plan under § 943, 1129, 1225, or 1325 of the Code.

(3) Time limits on an extension

No extension of time may exceed 21 days after the time prescribed by this rule, or 14 days after the order granting the motion to extend time is entered, whichever is later.

(As amended Mar. 30, 1987, eff. Aug. 1, 1987; Apr. 30, 1991, eff. Aug. 1, 1991; Apr. 29, 1994, eff. Aug. 1, 1994; Apr. 11, 1997, eff. Dec. 1, 1997; Mar. 26, 2009, eff. Dec. 1, 2009; Apr. 25, 2014, eff. Dec. 1, 2014.)

Rule 8003. Appeal as of Right—How Taken; Docketing the Appeal

(a) Filing the notice of appeal

(1) In general

An appeal from a judgment, order, or decree of a bankruptcy court to a district court or BAP under 28 U.S.C. § 158(a)(1) or (a)(2) may be taken only by filing a notice of appeal with the bankruptcy clerk within the time allowed by Rule 8002.

(2) Effect of not taking other steps

An appellant's failure to take any step other than the timely filing of a notice of appeal does not affect the validity of the appeal, but is ground only for the district court or BAP to act as it considers appropriate, including dismissing the appeal.

(3) Contents

The notice of appeal must:

(A) conform substantially to the appropriate Official Form;

(B) be accompanied by the judgment, order, or decree, or the part of it, being appealed; and

(C) be accompanied by the prescribed fee.

(4) Additional copies

If requested to do so, the appellant must furnish the bankruptcy clerk with enough copies of the notice to enable the clerk to comply with subdivision (c).

(b) Joint or consolidated appeals

(1) Joint notice of appeal

When two or more parties are entitled to appeal from a judgment, order, or decree of a bankruptcy court and their interests make joinder practicable, they may file a joint notice of appeal. They may then proceed on appeal as a single appellant.

(2) Consolidating appeals

When parties have separately filed timely notices of appeal, the district court or BAP may join or consolidate the appeals.

(c) Serving the notice of appeal

(1) Serving parties and transmitting to the United States trustee

The bankruptcy clerk must serve the notice of appeal on counsel of record for each party to the appeal, excluding the appellant, and transmit it to the United States trustee. If a party is proceeding pro se, the clerk must send the notice of appeal to the party's last known address. The clerk must note, on each copy, the date when the notice of appeal was filed.

(2) Effect of failing to serve or transmit notice

The bankruptcy clerk's failure to serve notice on a party or transmit notice to the United States trustee does not affect the validity of the appeal.

(3) Noting service on the docket

The clerk must note on the docket the names of the parties served and the date and method of the service.

(d) Transmitting the notice of appeal to the district court or BAP; docketing the appeal

(1) Transmitting the notice

The bankruptcy clerk must promptly transmit the notice of appeal to the BAP clerk if a BAP has been established for appeals from that district and the appellant has not elected to have the district court hear the appeal. Otherwise, the bankruptcy clerk must promptly transmit the notice to the district clerk.

(2) Docketing in the district court or BAP

Upon receiving the notice of appeal, the district or BAP clerk must docket the appeal under the title of the bankruptcy case and the title of any adversary proceeding, and must identify the appellant, adding the appellant's name if necessary.

(As amended Mar. 30, 1987, eff. Aug. 1, 1987; Apr. 23, 2008, eff. Dec. 1, 2008; Mar. 26, 2009, eff. Dec. 1, 2009; Apr. 25, 2014, eff. Dec. 1, 2014.)

Rule 8004. Appeal by Leave—How Taken; Docketing the Appeal

(a) Notice of appeal and motion for leave to appeal

To appeal from an interlocutory order or decree of a bankruptcy court under 28 U.S.C. § 158(a)(3), a party must file with the bankruptcy clerk a notice of appeal as prescribed by Rule 8003(a). The notice must:

(1) be filed within the time allowed by Rule 8002;

(2) be accompanied by a motion for leave to appeal prepared in accordance with subdivision (b); and

(3) unless served electronically using the court's transmission equipment, include proof of service in accordance with Rule 8011(d).

(b) Contents of the motion; response

(1) Contents

A motion for leave to appeal under 28 U.S.C. § 158(a)(3) must include the following:

(A) the facts necessary to understand the question presented;

(B) the question itself;

(C) the relief sought;

(D) the reasons why leave to appeal should be granted; and

(E) a copy of the interlocutory order or decree and any related opinion or memorandum.

(2) Response

A party may file with the district or BAP clerk a response in opposition or a cross-motion within 14 days after the motion is served.

(c) Transmitting the notice of appeal and the motion; docketing the appeal; determining the motion

(1) Transmitting to the district court or BAP

The bankruptcy clerk must promptly transmit the notice of appeal and the motion for leave to the BAP clerk if a BAP has been established for appeals from that district and the appellant has not elected to have the district court hear the appeal. Otherwise, the bankruptcy clerk must promptly transmit the notice and motion to the district clerk.

(2) Docketing in the district court or BAP

Upon receiving the notice and motion, the district or BAP clerk must docket the appeal under the title of the bankruptcy case and the title of any adversary proceeding, and must identify the appellant, adding the appellant's name if necessary.

(3) Oral argument not required

The motion and any response or cross-motion are submitted without oral argument unless the district court or BAP orders otherwise.

(d) Failure to file a motion with a notice of appeal

If an appellant timely files a notice of appeal under this rule but does not include a motion for leave, the district court or BAP may order the appellant to file a motion for leave, or treat the notice of appeal as a motion for leave and either grant or deny it. If the court orders that a motion for leave be filed, the appellant must do so within 14 days after the order is entered, unless the order provides otherwise.

(e) Direct appeal to a court of appeals

If leave to appeal an interlocutory order or decree is required under 28 U.S.C. § 158(a)(3), an authorization of a direct appeal by the court of appeals under 28 U.S.C. § 158(d)(2) satisfies the requirement.

(As amended Mar. 30, 1987, eff. Aug. 1, 1987; Apr. 30, 1991, eff. Aug. 1, 1991; Apr. 25, 2014, eff. Dec. 1, 2014.)

Rule 8005. Election to Have an Appeal Heard by the District Court Instead of the BAP

(a) Filing of a statement of election

To elect to have an appeal heard by the district court, a party must:

(1) file a statement of election that conforms substantially to the appropriate Official Form; and

(2) do so within the time prescribed by 28 U.S.C. § 158(c)(1).

(b) Transmitting the documents related to the appeal

Upon receiving an appellant's timely statement of election, the bankruptcy clerk must transmit to the district clerk all documents related to the appeal. Upon receiving a timely statement of election by a party other than the appellant, the BAP clerk must transmit to the district clerk all documents related to the appeal and notify the bankruptcy clerk of the transmission.

(c) Determining the validity of an election

A party seeking a determination of the validity of an election must file a motion in the court where the appeal is then pending. The motion must be filed within 14 days after the statement of election is filed.

(d) Motion for leave without a notice of appeal—effect on the timing of an election

If an appellant moves for leave to appeal under Rule 8004 but fails to file a separate notice of appeal with the motion, the motion must be treated as a notice of appeal for purposes of determining the timeliness of a statement of election.

(As amended Mar. 30, 1987, eff. Aug. 1, 1987; Apr. 25, 2014, eff. Dec. 1, 2014.)

Rule 8006. Certifying a Direct Appeal to the Court of Appeals

(a) Effective date of a certification

A certification of a judgment, order, or decree of a bankruptcy court for direct review in a court of appeals under 28 U.S.C. § 158(d)(2) is effective when:

(1) the certification has been filed;

(2) a timely appeal has been taken under Rule 8003 or 8004; and

(3) the notice of appeal has become effective under Rule 8002.

(b) Filing the certification

The certification must be filed with the clerk of the court where the matter is pending. For purposes of this rule, a matter remains pending in the bankruptcy court for 30 days after the effective date under Rule 8002 of the first notice of appeal from the judgment, order, or decree for which direct review is sought. A matter is pending in the district court or BAP thereafter.

(c) Joint certification by all appellants and appellees

A joint certification by all the appellants and appellees under 28 U.S.C. § 158(d)(2)(A) must be made by using the appropriate Official Form. The parties may supplement the certification with a short statement of the basis for the certification, which may include the information listed in subdivision (f)(2).

(d) The court that may make the certification

Only the court where the matter is pending, as provided in subdivision (b), may certify a direct review on request of parties or on its own motion.

(e) Certification on the court's own motion

(1) How accomplished

A certification on the court's own motion must be set forth in a separate document. The clerk of the certifying court must serve it on the parties to the appeal in the manner required for service of a notice of appeal under Rule 8003(c)(1). The certification must be accompanied by an opinion or memorandum that contains the information required by subdivision (f)(2)(A)-(D).

(2) Supplemental statement by a party

Within 14 days after the court's certification, a party may file with the clerk of the certifying court a short supplemental statement regarding the merits of certification.

(f) Certification by the court on request

(1) How requested

A request by a party for certification that a circumstance specified in 28 U.S.C. §158(d)(2)(A)(i)-(iii) applies—or a request by a majority of the appellants and a majority of the appellees—must be filed with the clerk of the court where the matter is pending within 60 days after the entry of the judgment, order, or decree.

(2) Service and contents

The request must be served on all parties to the appeal in the manner required for service of a notice of appeal under Rule 8003(c)(1), and it must include the following:

    (A) the facts necessary to understand the question presented;

    (B) the question itself;

    (C) the relief sought;

    (D) the reasons why the direct appeal should be allowed, including which circumstance specified in 28 U.S.C. § 158(d)(2)(A)(i)-(iii) applies; and

    (E) a copy of the judgment, order, or decree and any related opinion or memorandum.

(3) Time to file a response or a cross-request

A party may file a response to the request within 14 days after the request is served, or such other time as the court where the matter is pending allows. A party may file a cross-request for certification within 14 days after the request is served, or within 60 days after the entry of the judgment, order, or decree, whichever occurs first.

(4) Oral argument not required

The request, cross-request, and any response are submitted without oral argument unless the court where the matter is pending orders otherwise.

(5) Form and service of the certification

If the court certifies a direct appeal in response to the request, it must do so in a separate document. The certification must be served on the parties to the appeal in the manner required for service of a notice of appeal under Rule 8003(c)(1).

(g) Proceeding in the court of appeals following a certification

Within 30 days after the date the certification becomes effective under subdivision (a), a request for permission to take a direct appeal to the court of appeals must be filed with the circuit clerk in accordance with F.R.App.P. 6(c).

(As amended Mar. 30, 1987, eff. Aug. 1, 1987; Apr. 30, 1991, eff. Aug. 1, 1991; Apr. 29, 1994, eff. Aug. 1, 1994; Mar. 26, 2009, eff. Dec. 1, 2009; Apr. 25, 2014, eff. Dec. 1, 2014.)

Rule 8007. Stay Pending Appeal; Bonds; Suspension of Proceedings

(a) Initial motion in the Bankruptcy Court

(1) In general

Ordinarily, a party must move first in the bankruptcy court for the following relief:

    (A) a stay of a judgment, order, or decree of the bankruptcy court pending appeal;

    (B) the approval of a supersedeas bond;

    (C) an order suspending, modifying, restoring, or granting an injunction while an appeal is pending; or

    (D) the suspension or continuation of proceedings in a case or other relief permitted by subdivision (e).

(2) Time to file

The motion may be made either before or after the notice of appeal is filed.

(b) Motion in the district court, the BAP, or the Court of Appeals on direct appeal

(1) Request for relief

A motion for the relief specified in subdivision (a)(1)—or to vacate or modify a bankruptcy court's order granting such relief—may be made in the court where the appeal is pending.

(2) Showing or statement required

The motion must:

    (A) show that moving first in the bankruptcy court would be impracticable; or

    (B) if a motion was made in the bankruptcy court, either state that the court has not yet ruled on the motion, or state that the court has ruled and set out any reasons given for the ruling.

(3) Additional content

The motion must also include:

    (A) the reasons for granting the relief requested and the facts relied upon;

    (B) affidavits or other sworn statements supporting facts subject to dispute; and

    (C) relevant parts of the record.

(4) Serving notice

The movant must give reasonable notice of the motion to all parties.

(c) Filing a bond or other security

The district court, BAP, or court of appeals may condition relief on filing a bond or other appropriate security with the bankruptcy court.

(d) Bond for a trustee or the United States

The court may require a trustee to file a bond or other appropriate security when the trustee appeals. A bond or other security is not required when an appeal is taken by the United States, its officer, or its agency or by direction of any department of the federal government.

(e) Continuation of proceedings in the Bankruptcy Court

Despite Rule 7062 and subject to the authority of the district court, BAP, or court of appeals, the bankruptcy court may:

    (1) suspend or order the continuation of other proceedings in the case; or

    (2) issue any other appropriate orders during the pendency of an appeal to protect the rights of all parties in interest.

(As amended Mar. 30, 1987, eff. Aug. 1, 1987; Apr. 30, 1991, eff. Aug. 1, 1991; Apr. 25, 2014, eff. Dec. 1, 2014.)

Rule 8008.　Indicative Rulings

(a)　Relief pending appeal

If a party files a timely motion in the bankruptcy court for relief that the court lacks authority to grant because of an appeal that has been docketed and is pending, the bankruptcy court may:

   (1)　defer considering the motion;

   (2)　deny the motion;　or

   (3)　state that the court would grant the motion if the court where the appeal is pending remands for that purpose, or state that the motion raises a substantial issue.

(b)　Notice to the court where the appeal is pending

The movant must promptly notify the clerk of the court where the appeal is pending if the bankruptcy court states that it would grant the motion or that the motion raises a substantial issue.

(c)　Remand after an indicative ruling

If the bankruptcy court states that it would grant the motion or that the motion raises a substantial issue, the district court or BAP may remand for further proceedings, but it retains jurisdiction unless it expressly dismisses the appeal. If the district court or BAP remands but retains jurisdiction, the parties must promptly notify the clerk of that court when the bankruptcy court has decided the motion on remand.

(As amended Mar. 30, 1987, eff. Aug. 1, 1987;　Apr. 23, 1996, eff. Dec. 1, 1996;　Apr. 25, 2014, eff. Dec. 1, 2014.)

Rule 8009.　Record on Appeal; Sealed Documents

(a)　Designating the record on appeal; statement of the issues

(1)　Appellant

(A)　The appellant must file with the bankruptcy clerk and serve on the appellee a designation of the items to be included in the record on appeal and a statement of the issues to be presented.

(B)　The appellant must file and serve the designation and statement within 14 days after:

   (i)　the appellant's notice of appeal as of right becomes effective under Rule 8002;　or

   (ii)　an order granting leave to appeal is entered.

A designation and statement served prematurely must be treated as served on the first day on which filing is timely.

(2)　Appellee and cross-appellant

Within 14 days after being served, the appellee may file with the bankruptcy clerk and serve on the appellant a designation of additional items to be included in the record. An appellee who files a cross-appeal must file and serve a designation of additional items to be included in the record and a statement of the issues to be presented on the cross-appeal.

(3)　Cross-appellee

Within 14 days after service of the cross-appellant's designation and statement, a cross-appellee may file with the bankruptcy clerk and serve on the cross-appellant a designation of additional items to be included in the record.

(4)　Record on appeal

The record on appeal must include the following:

● docket entries kept by the bankruptcy clerk;

● items designated by the parties;

● the notice of appeal;

● the judgment, order, or decree being appealed;

● any order granting leave to appeal;

● any certification required for a direct appeal to the court of appeals;

● any opinion, findings of fact, and conclusions of law relating to the issues on appeal, including transcripts of all oral rulings;

● any transcript ordered under subdivision (b);

● any statement required by subdivision (c);　and

● any additional items from the record that the court where the appeal is pending orders.

(5)　Copies for the Bankruptcy Clerk

If paper copies are needed, a party filing a designation of items must provide a copy of any of those items that the bankruptcy clerk requests.　If the party fails to do so, the bankruptcy clerk must prepare the copy at the party's expense.

(b)　Transcript of Proceedings

(1)　Appellant's duty to order

Within the time period prescribed by subdivision (a)(1), the appellant must:

(A)　order in writing from the reporter, as defined in Rule 8010(a)(1), a transcript of such parts of the proceedings not already on file as the appellant considers necessary for the appeal, and file a copy of the order with the bankruptcy clerk;　or

(B)　file with the bankruptcy clerk a certificate stating that the appellant is not ordering a transcript.

(2)　Cross-appellant's duty to order

Within 14 days after the appellant files a copy of the transcript order or a certificate of not ordering a transcript, the appellee as cross-appellant must:

(A)　order in writing from the reporter, as defined in Rule 8010(a)(1), a transcript of such additional parts of the proceedings as the cross-appellant considers necessary for the appeal, and file a copy of the order with the bankruptcy clerk;　or

(B)　file with the bankruptcy clerk a certificate stating that the cross-appellant is not ordering a transcript.

(3)　Appellee's or cross-appellee's right to order

Within 14 days after the appellant or cross-appellant files a copy of a transcript order or certificate of not ordering a transcript, the appellee or cross-appellee may order in writing from the reporter a transcript of such additional parts of the proceedings as the appellee or cross-appellee considers necessary for the appeal. A copy of the order must be filed with the bankruptcy clerk.

(4) Payment

At the time of ordering, a party must make satisfactory arrangements with the reporter for paying the cost of the transcript.

(5) Unsupported finding or conclusion

If the appellant intends to argue on appeal that a finding or conclusion is unsupported by the evidence or is contrary to the evidence, the appellant must include in the record a transcript of all relevant testimony and copies of all relevant exhibits.

(c) Statement of the evidence when a transcript is unavailable

If a transcript of a hearing or trial is unavailable, the appellant may prepare a statement of the evidence or proceedings from the best available means, including the appellant's recollection. The statement must be filed within the time prescribed by subdivision (a)(1) and served on the appellee, who may serve objections or proposed amendments within 14 days after being served. The statement and any objections or proposed amendments must then be submitted to the bankruptcy court for settlement and approval. As settled and approved, the statement must be included by the bankruptcy clerk in the record on appeal.

(d) Agreed statement as the record on appeal

Instead of the record on appeal as defined in subdivision (a), the parties may prepare, sign, and submit to the bankruptcy court a statement of the case showing how the issues presented by the appeal arose and were decided in the bankruptcy court. The statement must set forth only those facts alleged and proved or sought to be proved that are essential to the court's resolution of the issues. If the statement is accurate, it—together with any additions that the bankruptcy court may consider necessary to a full presentation of the issues on appeal—must be approved by the bankruptcy court and must then be certified to the court where the appeal is pending as the record on appeal. The bankruptcy clerk must then transmit it to the clerk of that court within the time provided by Rule 8010. A copy of the agreed statement may be filed in place of the appendix required by Rule 8018(b) or, in the case of a direct appeal to the court of appeals, by F.R.App.P. 30.

(e) Correcting or modifying the record

(1) Submitting to the Bankruptcy Court

If any difference arises about whether the record accurately discloses what occurred in the bankruptcy court, the difference must be submitted to and settled by the bankruptcy court and the record conformed accordingly. If an item has been improperly designated as part of the record on appeal, a party may move to strike that item.

(2) Correcting in other ways

If anything material to either party is omitted from or misstated in the record by error or accident, the omission or misstatement may be corrected, and a supplemental record may be certified and transmitted:

(A) on stipulation of the parties;

(B) by the bankruptcy court before or after the record has been forwarded; or

(C) by the court where the appeal is pending.

(3) Remaining questions

All other questions as to the form and content of the record must be presented to the court where the appeal is pending.

(f) Sealed documents

A document placed under seal by the bankruptcy court may be designated as part of the record on appeal. In doing so, a party must identify it without revealing confidential or secret information, but the bankruptcy clerk must not transmit it to the clerk of the court where the appeal is pending as part of the record. Instead, a party must file a motion with the court where the appeal is pending to accept the document under seal. If the motion is granted, the movant must notify the bankruptcy court of the ruling, and the bankruptcy clerk must promptly transmit the sealed document to the clerk of the court where the appeal is pending.

(g) Other necessary actions

All parties to an appeal must take any other action necessary to enable the bankruptcy clerk to assemble and transmit the record.

(As amended Mar. 30, 1987, eff. Aug. 1, 1987; Mar. 26, 2009, eff. Dec. 1, 2009; Apr. 25, 2014, eff. Dec. 1, 2014.)

Rule 8010. Completing and Transmitting the Record

(a) Reporter's duties

(1) Proceedings recorded without a reporter present

If proceedings were recorded without a reporter being present, the person or service selected under bankruptcy court procedures to transcribe the recording is the reporter for purposes of this rule.

(2) Preparing and filing the transcript

The reporter must prepare and file a transcript as follows:

(A) Upon receiving an order for a transcript in accordance with Rule 8009(b), the reporter must file in the bankruptcy court an acknowledgment of the request that shows when it was received, and when the reporter expects to have the transcript completed.

(B) After completing the transcript, the reporter must file it with the bankruptcy clerk, who will notify the district, BAP, or circuit clerk of its filing.

(C) If the transcript cannot be completed within 30 days after receiving the order, the reporter must request an extension of time from the bankruptcy clerk. The clerk must enter on the docket and notify the parties whether the extension is granted.

(D) If the reporter does not file the transcript on time, the bankruptcy clerk must notify the bankruptcy judge.

(b) Clerk's duties

(1) Transmitting the record—in general

Subject to Rule 8009(f) and subdivision (b)(5) of this rule, when the record is complete, the bankruptcy clerk must transmit to the clerk of the court where the appeal is pending either the record or a notice that the record is available electronically.

(2) Multiple appeals

If there are multiple appeals from a judgment, order, or decree, the bankruptcy clerk must transmit a single record.

(3) Receiving the record

Upon receiving the record or notice that it is available electronically, the district, BAP, or circuit clerk must enter that information on the docket and promptly notify all parties to the appeal.

(4) If paper copies are ordered

If the court where the appeal is pending directs that paper copies of the record be provided, the clerk of that court must so notify the appellant. If the appellant fails to provide them, the bankruptcy clerk must prepare them at the appellant's expense.

(5) When leave to appeal is requested

Subject to subdivision (c), if a motion for leave to appeal has been filed under Rule 8004, the bankruptcy clerk must prepare and transmit the record only after the district court, BAP, or court of appeals grants leave.

(c) Record for a preliminary motion in the District Court, BAP, or Court of Appeals

This subdivision (c) applies if, before the record is transmitted, a party moves in the district court, BAP, or court of appeals for any of the following relief:

- leave to appeal;
- dismissal;
- a stay pending appeal;
- approval of a supersedeas bond, or additional security on a bond or undertaking on appeal; or
- any other intermediate order.

The bankruptcy clerk must then transmit to the clerk of the court where the relief is sought any parts of the record designated by a party to the appeal or a notice that those parts are available electronically.

(As amended Apr. 25, 2014, eff. Dec. 1, 2014.)

Rule 8011. Filing and Service; Signature

(a) Filing

(1) With the clerk

A document required or permitted to be filed in a district court or BAP must be filed with the clerk of that court.

(2) Method and timeliness

(A) In general

Filing may be accomplished by transmission to the clerk of the district court or BAP. Except as provided in subdivision (a)(2)(B) and (C), filing is timely only if the clerk receives the document within the time fixed for filing.

(B) Brief or appendix

A brief or appendix is also timely filed if, on or before the last day for filing, it is:

(i) mailed to the clerk by first-class mail—or other class of mail that is at least as expeditious—postage prepaid, if the district court's or BAP's procedures permit or require a brief or appendix to be filed by mailing; or

(ii) dispatched to a third-party commercial carrier for delivery within 3 days to the clerk, if the court's procedures so permit or require.

(C) Inmate filing

A document filed by an inmate confined in an institution is timely if deposited in the institution's internal mailing system on or before the last day for filing. If the institution has a system designed for legal mail, the inmate must use that system to receive the benefit of this rule. Timely filing may be shown by a declaration in compliance with 28 U.S.C. § 1746 or by a notarized statement, either of which must set forth the date of deposit and state that first-class postage has been prepaid.

(D) Copies

If a document is filed electronically, no paper copy is required. If a document is filed by mail or delivery to the district court or BAP, no additional copies are required. But the district court or BAP may require by local rule or by order in a particular case the filing or furnishing of a specified number of paper copies.

(3) Clerk's refusal of documents

The court's clerk must not refuse to accept for filing any document transmitted for that purpose solely because it is not presented in proper form as required by these rules or by any local rule or practice.

(b) Service of all documents required

Unless a rule requires service by the clerk, a party must, at or before the time of the filing of a document, serve it on the other parties to the appeal. Service on a party represented by counsel must be made on the party's counsel.

(c) Manner of service

(1) Methods

Service must be made electronically, unless it is being made by or on an individual who is not represented by counsel or the court's governing rules permit or require service by mail or other means of delivery. Service may be made by or on an unrepresented party by any of the following methods:

(A) personal delivery;

(B) mail; or

(C) third-party commercial carrier for delivery within 3 days.

(2) When service is complete

Service by electronic means is complete on transmission, unless the party making service receives notice that the document was not transmitted successfully. Service by mail or by commercial carrier is complete on mailing or delivery to the carrier.

(d) Proof of service

(1) What is required

A document presented for filing must contain either:

(A) an acknowledgment of service by the person served; or

(B) proof of service consisting of a statement by the person who made service certifying:

(i) the date and manner of service;

(ii) the names of the persons served; and

(iii) the mail or electronic address, the fax number, or the address of the place of delivery, as appropriate for the manner of service, for each person served.

(2) Delayed proof

The district or BAP clerk may permit documents to be filed without acknowledgment or proof of service, but must require the acknowledgment or proof to be filed promptly thereafter.

(3) Brief or appendix

When a brief or appendix is filed, the proof of service must also state the date and manner by which it was filed.

(e) Signature

Every document filed electronically must include the electronic signature of the person filing it or, if the person is represented, the electronic signature of counsel. The electronic signature must be provided by electronic means that are consistent with any technical standards that the Judicial Conference of the United States establishes. Every document filed in paper form must be signed by the person filing the document or, if the person is represented, by counsel.

(As amended Apr. 25, 2014, eff. Dec. 1, 2014.)

Rule 8012. Corporate Disclosure Statement

(a) Who must file

Any nongovernmental corporate party appearing in the district court or BAP must file a statement that identifies any parent corporation and any publicly held corporation that owns 10% or more of its stock or states that there is no such corporation.

(b) Time to file; supplemental filing

A party must file the statement with its principal brief or upon filing a motion, response, petition, or answer in the district court or BAP, whichever occurs first, unless a local rule requires earlier filing. Even if the statement has already been filed, the party's principal brief must include a statement before the table of contents. A party must supplement its statement whenever the required information changes.

(As amended Apr. 25, 2014, eff. Dec. 1, 2014.)

Rule 8013. Motions; Intervention

(a) Contents of a motion; response; reply

(1) Request for relief

A request for an order or other relief is made by filing a motion with the district or BAP clerk, with proof of service on the other parties to the appeal.

(2) Contents of a motion

(A) Grounds and the relief sought

A motion must state with particularity the grounds for the motion, the relief sought, and the legal argument necessary to support it.

(B) Motion to expedite an appeal

A motion to expedite an appeal must explain what justifies considering the appeal ahead of other matters. If the district court or BAP grants the motion, it may accelerate the time to transmit the record, the deadline for filing briefs and other documents, oral argument, and the resolution of the appeal. A motion to expedite an appeal may be filed as an emergency motion under subdivision (d).

(C) Accompanying documents

(i) Any affidavit or other document necessary to support a motion must be served and filed with the motion.

(ii) An affidavit must contain only factual information, not legal argument.

(iii) A motion seeking substantive relief must include a copy of the bankruptcy court's judgment, order, or decree, and any accompanying opinion as a separate exhibit.

(D) Documents barred or not required

(i) A separate brief supporting or responding to a motion must not be filed.

(ii) Unless the court orders otherwise, a notice of motion or a proposed order is not required.

(3) Response and reply; time to file

Unless the district court or BAP orders otherwise,

(A) any party to the appeal may file a response to the motion within 7 days after service of the motion; and

(B) the movant may file a reply to a response within 7 days after service of the response, but may only address matters raised in the response.

(b) Disposition of a motion for a procedural order

The district court or BAP may rule on a motion for a procedural order—including a motion under Rule 9006(b) or (c)—at any time without awaiting a response. A party adversely affected by the ruling may move to reconsider, vacate, or modify it within 7 days after the procedural order is served.

(c) Oral argument

A motion will be decided without oral argument unless the district court or BAP orders otherwise.

(d) Emergency motion

(1) Noting the emergency

When a movant requests expedited action on a motion because irreparable harm would occur during the time needed to consider a response, the movant must insert the word "Emergency" before the title of the motion.

(2) Contents of the motion

The emergency motion must

(A) be accompanied by an affidavit setting out the nature of the emergency;

(B) state whether all grounds for it were submitted to the bankruptcy court and, if not, why the motion should not be remanded for the bankruptcy court to consider;

(C) include the e-mail addresses, office addresses, and telephone numbers of moving counsel and, when known, of opposing counsel and any unrepresented parties to the appeal; and

(D) be served as prescribed by Rule 8011.

(3) Notifying opposing parties

Before filing an emergency motion, the movant must make every practicable effort to notify opposing counsel and any unrepresented parties in time for them to respond. The affidavit accompanying the emergency motion must state when and how notice was given or state why giving it was impracticable.

(e) Power of a single BAP judge to entertain a motion

(1) Single judge's authority

A BAP judge may act alone on any motion, but may not dismiss or otherwise determine an appeal, deny a motion for leave to appeal, or deny a motion for a stay pending appeal if denial would make the appeal moot.

(2) Reviewing a single judge's action

The BAP may review a single judge's action, either on its own motion or on a party's motion.

(f) Form of documents; page limits; number of copies

(1) Format of a paper document

Rule 27(d)(1) F.R.App.P. applies in the district court or BAP to a paper version of a motion, response, or reply.

(2) Format of an electronically filed document

A motion, response, or reply filed electronically must comply with the requirements for a paper version regarding covers, line spacing, margins, typeface, and type style. It must also comply with the page limits under paragraph (3).

(3) Page limits

Unless the district court or BAP orders otherwise:

(A) a motion or a response to a motion must not exceed 20 pages, exclusive of the corporate disclosure statement and accompanying documents authorized by subdivision (a)(2)(C); and

(B) a reply to a response must not exceed 10 pages.

(4) Paper copies

Paper copies must be provided only if required by local rule or by an order in a particular case.

(g) Intervening in an appeal

Unless a statute provides otherwise, an entity that seeks to intervene in an appeal pending in the district court or BAP must move for leave to intervene and serve a copy of the motion on the parties to the appeal. The motion or other notice of intervention authorized by statute must be filed within 30 days after the appeal is docketed. It must concisely state the movant's interest, the grounds for intervention, whether intervention was sought in the bankruptcy court, why intervention is being sought at this stage of the proceeding, and why participating as an amicus curiae would not be adequate.

(As amended Mar. 30, 1987, eff. Aug. 1, 1987; Apr. 25, 2014, eff. Dec. 1, 2014.)

Rule 8014. Briefs

(a) Appellant's brief

The appellant's brief must contain the following under appropriate headings and in the order indicated:

(1) a corporate disclosure statement, if required by Rule 8012;

(2) a table of contents, with page references;

(3) a table of authorities—cases (alphabetically arranged), statutes, and other authorities—with references to the pages of the brief where they are cited;

(4) a jurisdictional statement, including:

(A) the basis for the bankruptcy court's subject-matter jurisdiction, with citations to applicable statutory provisions and stating relevant facts establishing jurisdiction;

(B) the basis for the district court's or BAP's jurisdiction, with citations to applicable statutory provisions and stating relevant facts establishing jurisdiction;

(C) the filing dates establishing the timeliness of the appeal; and

(D) an assertion that the appeal is from a final judgment, order, or decree, or information establishing the district court's or BAP's jurisdiction on another basis;

(5) a statement of the issues presented and, for each one, a concise statement of the applicable standard of appellate review;

(6) a concise statement of the case setting out the facts relevant to the issues submitted for review, describing the relevant procedural history, and identifying the rulings presented for review, with appropriate references to the record;

(7) a summary of the argument, which must contain a succinct, clear, and accurate statement of the arguments made in the body of the brief, and which must not merely repeat the argument headings;

(8) the argument, which must contain the appellant's contentions and the reasons for them, with citations to the authorities and parts of the record on which the appellant relies;

(9) a short conclusion stating the precise relief sought; and

(10) the certificate of compliance, if required by Rule 8015(a)(7) or (b).

(b) Appellee's brief

The appellee's brief must conform to the requirements of subdivision (a)(1)–(8) and (10), except that none of the following need appear unless the appellee is dissatisfied with the appellant's statement:

(1) the jurisdictional statement;

(2) the statement of the issues and the applicable standard of appellate review; and

(3) the statement of the case.

(c) Reply brief

The appellant may file a brief in reply to the appellee's brief. A reply brief must comply with the requirements of subdivision (a)(2)–(3).

(d) Statutes, rules, regulations, or similar authority

If the court's determination of the issues presented requires the study of the Code or other statutes, rules, regulations, or similar authority, the relevant parts must be set out in the brief or in an addendum.

(e) Briefs in a case involving multiple appellants or appellees

In a case involving more than one appellant or appellee, including consolidated cases, any number of appellants or appellees may join in a brief, and any party may adopt by reference a part of another's brief. Parties may also join in reply briefs.

(f) Citation of supplemental authorities

If pertinent and significant authorities come to a party's attention after the party's brief has been filed—or after oral argument but before a decision—a party may promptly advise the district or BAP clerk by a signed submission setting forth the citations. The submission, which must be served on the other parties to the appeal, must state the reasons for the supplemental citations, referring either to the pertinent page of a brief or to a point argued orally. The body of the submission must not exceed 350 words. Any response must be made within 7 days after the party is served, unless the court orders otherwise, and must be similarly limited.

(As amended Mar. 30, 1987, eff. Aug. 1, 1987; Apr. 25, 2014, eff. Dec. 1, 2014.)

Rule 8015. Form and Length of Briefs; Form of Appendices and Other Papers

(a) Paper copies of a brief

If a paper copy of a brief may or must be filed, the following provisions apply:

(1) Reproduction

(A) A brief may be reproduced by any process that yields a clear black image on light paper. The paper must be opaque and unglazed. Only one side of the paper may be used.

(B) Text must be reproduced with a clarity that equals or exceeds the output of a laser printer.

(C) Photographs, illustrations, and tables may be reproduced by any method that results in a good copy of the original. A glossy finish is acceptable if the original is glossy.

(2) Cover

The front cover of a brief must contain:

(A) the number of the case centered at the top;

(B) the name of the court;

(C) the title of the case as prescribed by Rule 8003(d)(2) or 8004(c)(2);

(D) the nature of the proceeding and the name of the court below;

(E) the title of the brief, identifying the party or parties for whom the brief is filed; and

(F) the name, office address, telephone number, and e-mail address of counsel representing the party for whom the brief is filed.

(3) Binding

The brief must be bound in any manner that is secure, does not obscure the text, and permits the brief to lie reasonably flat when open.

(4) Paper size, line spacing, and margins

The brief must be on 8 1/2-by-11 inch paper. The text must be double-spaced, but quotations more than two lines long may be indented and single-spaced. Headings and footnotes may be single-spaced. Margins must be at least one inch on all four sides. Page numbers may be placed in the margins, but no text may appear there.

(5) Typeface

Either a proportionally spaced or monospaced face may be used.

(A) A proportionally spaced face must include serifs, but sans-serif type may be used in headings and captions. A proportionally spaced face must be 14-point or larger.

(B) A monospaced face may not contain more than 10 1/2 characters per inch.

(6) Type Styles

A brief must be set in plain, roman style, although italics or boldface may be used for emphasis. Case names must be italicized or underlined.

(7) Length

(A) Page limitation

A principal brief must not exceed 30 pages, or a reply brief 15 pages, unless it complies with (B) and (C).

(B) Type-volume limitation

(i) A principal brief is acceptable if:

● it contains no more than 14,000 words; or

● it uses a monospaced face and contains no more than 1,300 lines of text.

(ii) A reply brief is acceptable if it contains no more than half of the type volume specified in item (i).

(iii) Headings, footnotes, and quotations count toward the word and line limitations. The corporate disclosure statement, table of contents, table of citations, statement with respect to oral argument, any addendum containing statutes, rules, or regulations, and any certificates of counsel do not count toward the limitation.

(C) Certificate of compliance

(i) A brief submitted under subdivision (a)(7)(B) must include a certificate signed by the attorney, or an unrepresented party, that the brief complies with the type-volume limitation. The person preparing the certificate may rely on the word or line count of the word-processing system used to prepare the brief.

The certificate must state either:

- the number of words in the brief; or

- the number of lines of monospaced type in the brief.

(ii) The certification requirement is satisfied by a certificate of compliance that conforms substantially to the appropriate Official Form.

(b) Electronically filed briefs

A brief filed electronically must comply with subdivision (a), except for (a)(1), (a)(3), and the paper requirement of (a)(4).

(c) Paper copies of appendices

A paper copy of an appendix must comply with subdivision (a)(1), (2), (3), and (4), with the following exceptions:

(1) An appendix may include a legible photocopy of any document found in the record or of a printed decision.

(2) When necessary to facilitate inclusion of odd-sized documents such as technical drawings, an appendix may be a size other than 8 1/2-by-11 inches, and need not lie reasonably flat when opened.

(d) Electronically filed appendices

An appendix filed electronically must comply with subdivision (a)(2) and (4), except for the paper requirement of (a)(4).

(e) Other documents

(1) Motion

Rule 8013(f) governs the form of a motion, response, or reply.

(2) Paper copies of other documents

A paper copy of any other document, other than a submission under Rule 8014(f), must comply with subdivision (a), with the following exceptions:

(A) A cover is not necessary if the caption and signature page together contain the information required by subdivision (a)(2).

(B) Subdivision (a)(7) does not apply.

(3) Other documents filed electronically

Any other document filed electronically, other than a submission under Rule 8014(f), must comply with the appearance requirements of paragraph (2).

(f) Local variation

A district court or BAP must accept documents that comply with the applicable requirements of this rule. By local rule, a district court or BAP may accept documents that do not meet all of the requirements of this rule.

(As amended Mar. 30, 1987, eff. Aug. 1, 1987; Mar. 26, 2009, eff. Dec. 1, 2009; Apr. 25, 2014, eff. Dec. 1, 2014.)

Rule 8016. Cross–Appeals

(a) Applicability

This rule applies to a case in which a cross-appeal is filed. Rules 8014(a)–(c), 8015(a)(7)(A)–(B), and 8018(a)(1)–(3) do not apply to such a case, except as otherwise provided in this rule.

(b) Designation of appellant

The party who files a notice of appeal first is the appellant for purposes of this rule and Rule 8018(a)(4) and (b) and Rule 8019. If notices are filed on the same day, the plaintiff, petitioner, applicant, or movant in the proceeding below is the appellant. These designations may be modified by the parties' agreement or by court order.

(c) Briefs

In a case involving a cross-appeal:

(1) Appellant's principal brief

The appellant must file a principal brief in the appeal. That brief must comply with Rule 8014(a).

(2) Appellee's principal and response brief

The appellee must file a principal brief in the cross-appeal and must, in the same brief, respond to the principal brief in the appeal. That brief must comply with Rule 8014(a), except that the brief need not include a statement of the case unless the appellee is dissatisfied with the appellant's statement.

(3) Appellant's response and reply brief

The appellant must file a brief that responds to the principal brief in the cross-appeal and may, in the same brief, reply to the response in the appeal. That brief must comply with Rule 8014(a)(2)–(8) and (10), except that none of the following need appear unless the appellant is dissatisfied with the appellee's statement in the cross-appeal:

(A) the jurisdictional statement;

(B) the statement of the issues and the applicable standard of appellate review; and

(C) the statement of the case.

(4) Appellee's reply brief

The appellee may file a brief in reply to the response in the cross-appeal. That brief must comply with Rule 8014(a)(2)–(3) and (10) and must be limited to the issues presented by the cross-appeal.

(d) Length

(1) Page limitation

Unless it complies with paragraphs (2) and (3), the appellant's principal brief must not exceed 30 pages; the appellee's principal and response brief, 35 pages; the appellant's response and reply brief, 30 pages; and the appellee's reply brief, 15 pages.

(2) Type-volume limitation

(A) The appellant's principal brief or the appellant's response and reply brief is acceptable if:

(i) it contains no more than 14,000 words; or

(ii) it uses a monospaced face and contains no more than 1,300 lines of text.

(B) The appellee's principal and response brief is acceptable if:

(i) it contains no more than 16,500 words; or

(ii) it uses a monospaced face and contains no more than 1,500 lines of text.

(C) The appellee's reply brief is acceptable if it contains no more than half of the type volume specified in subparagraph (A).

(D) Headings, footnotes, and quotations count toward the word and line limitations. The corporate disclosure statement, table of contents, table of citations, statement with respect to oral argument, any addendum containing statutes, rules, or regulations, and any certificates of counsel do not count toward the limitation.

(3) Certificate of compliance

A brief submitted either electronically or in paper form under paragraph (2) must comply with Rule 8015(a)(7)(C).

(e) Time to serve and file a brief

Briefs must be served and filed as follows, unless the district court or BAP by order in a particular case excuses the filing of briefs or specifies different time limits:

(1) the appellant's principal brief, within 30 days after the docketing of notice that the record has been transmitted or is available electronically;

(2) the appellee's principal and response brief, within 30 days after the appellant's principal brief is served;

(3) the appellant's response and reply brief, within 30 days after the appellee's principal and response brief is served; and

(4) the appellee's reply brief, within 14 days after the appellant's response and reply brief is served, but at least 7 days before scheduled argument unless the district court or BAP, for good cause, allows a later filing.

(As amended Mar. 30, 1987, eff. Aug. 1, 1987; Apr. 30, 1991, eff. Aug. 1, 1991; Apr. 25, 2014, eff. Dec. 1, 2014.)

Rule 8017. Brief of an Amicus Curiae

(a) When permitted

The United States or its officer or agency or a state may file an amicus-curiae brief without the consent of the parties or leave of court. Any other amicus curiae may file a brief only by leave of court or if the brief states that all parties have consented to its filing. On its own motion, and with notice to all parties to an appeal, the district court or BAP may request a brief by an amicus curiae.

(b) Motion for leave to file

The motion must be accompanied by the proposed brief and state:

(1) the movant's interest; and

(2) the reason why an amicus brief is desirable and why the matters asserted are relevant to the disposition of the appeal.

(c) Contents and form

An amicus brief must comply with Rule 8015. In addition to the requirements of Rule 8015, the cover must identify the party or parties supported and indicate whether the brief supports affirmance or reversal. If an amicus curiae is a corporation, the brief must include a disclosure statement like that required of parties by Rule 8012. An amicus brief need not comply with Rule 8014, but must include the following:

(1) a table of contents, with page references;

(2) a table of authorities—cases (alphabetically arranged), statutes, and other authorities—with references to the pages of the brief where they are cited;

(3) a concise statement of the identity of the amicus curiae, its interest in the case, and the source of its authority to file;

(4) unless the amicus curiae is one listed in the first sentence of subdivision (a), a statement that indicates whether:

(A) a party's counsel authored the brief in whole or in part;

(B) a party or a party's counsel contributed money that was intended to fund preparing or submitting the brief; and

(C) a person—other than the amicus curiae, its members, or its counsel—contributed money that was intended to fund preparing or submitting the brief and, if so, identifies each such person;

(5) an argument, which may be preceded by a summary and need not include a statement of the applicable standard of review; and

(6) a certificate of compliance, if required by Rule 8015(a)(7)(C) or 8015(b).

(d) Length

Except by the district court's or BAP's permission, an amicus brief must be no more than one-half the maximum length authorized by these rules for a party's principal brief. If the court grants a party permission to file a longer brief, that extension does not affect the length of an amicus brief.

(e) Time for filing

An amicus curiae must file its brief, accompanied by a motion for filing when necessary, no later than 7 days after the principal brief of the party being supported is filed. An amicus curiae that does not support either party must file its brief no later than 7 days after the appellant's principal brief is filed. The district court or BAP may grant leave for later filing, specifying the time within which an opposing party may answer.

(f) Reply brief

Except by the district court's or BAP's permission, an amicus curiae may not file a reply brief.

(g) Oral argument

An amicus curiae may participate in oral argument only with the district court's or BAP's permission.

(As amended Mar. 26, 2009, eff. Dec. 1, 2009; Apr. 25, 2014, eff. Dec. 1, 2014.)

Rule 8018. Serving and Filing Briefs; Appendices

(a) Time to serve and file a brief

The following rules apply unless the district court or BAP by order in a particular case excuses the filing of briefs or specifies different time limits:

(1) The appellant must serve and file a brief within 30 days after the docketing of notice that the record has been transmitted or is available electronically.

(2) The appellee must serve and file a brief within 30 days after service of the appellant's brief.

(3) The appellant may serve and file a reply brief within 14 days after service of the appellee's brief, but a reply brief must be filed at least 7 days before scheduled argument unless the district court or BAP, for good cause, allows a later filing.

(4) If an appellant fails to file a brief on time or within an extended time authorized by the district court or BAP, an appellee may move to dismiss the appeal—or the district court or BAP, after notice, may dismiss the appeal on its own motion. An appellee who fails to file a brief will not be heard at oral argument unless the district court or BAP grants permission.

(b) Duty to serve and file an appendix to the brief

(1) Appellant

Subject to subdivision (e) and Rule 8009(d), the appellant must serve and file with its principal brief excerpts of the record as an appendix. It must contain the following:

(A) the relevant entries in the bankruptcy docket;

(B) the complaint and answer, or other equivalent filings;

(C) the judgment, order, or decree from which the appeal is taken;

(D) any other orders, pleadings, jury instructions, findings, conclusions, or opinions relevant to the appeal;

(E) the notice of appeal; and

(F) any relevant transcript or portion of it.

(2) Appellee

The appellee may also serve and file with its brief an appendix that contains material required to be included by the appellant or relevant to the appeal or cross-appeal, but omitted by the appellant.

(3) Cross-appellee

The appellant as cross-appellee may also serve and file with its response an appendix that contains material relevant to matters raised initially by the principal brief in the cross-appeal, but omitted by the cross-appellant.

(c) Format of the appendix

The appendix must begin with a table of contents identifying the page at which each part begins. The relevant docket entries must follow the table of contents. Other parts of the record must follow chronologically. When pages from the transcript of proceedings are placed in the appendix, the transcript page numbers must be shown in brackets immediately before the included pages. Omissions in the text of documents or of the transcript must be indicated by asterisks. Immaterial formal matters (captions, subscriptions, acknowledgments, and the like) should be omitted.

(d) Exhibits

Exhibits designated for inclusion in the appendix may be reproduced in a separate volume or volumes, suitably indexed.

(e) Appeal on the original record without an appendix

The district court or BAP may, either by rule for all cases or classes of cases or by order in a particular case, dispense with the appendix and permit an appeal to proceed on the original record, with the submission of any relevant parts of the record that the district court or BAP orders the parties to file.

(As amended Mar. 30, 1987, eff. Aug. 1, 1987; Apr. 27, 1995, eff. Dec. 1, 1995; Apr. 25, 2014, eff. Dec. 1, 2014.)

Rule 8019. Oral Argument

(a) Party's statement

Any party may file, or a district court or BAP may require, a statement explaining why oral argument should, or need not, be permitted.

(b) Presumption of oral argument and exceptions

Oral argument must be allowed in every case unless the district judge—or all the BAP judges assigned to hear the appeal—examine the briefs and record and determine that oral argument is unnecessary because

(1) the appeal is frivolous;

(2) the dispositive issue or issues have been authoritatively decided; or

(3) the facts and legal arguments are adequately presented in the briefs and record, and the decisional process would not be significantly aided by oral argument.

(c) Notice of argument; postponement

The district court or BAP must advise all parties of the date, time, and place for oral argument, and the time allowed for each side. A motion to postpone the argument or to allow longer argument must be filed reasonably in advance of the hearing date.

(d) Order and contents of argument

The appellant opens and concludes the argument. Counsel must not read at length from briefs, the record, or authorities.

(e) Cross-appeals and separate appeals

If there is a cross-appeal, Rule 8016(b) determines which party is the appellant and which is the appellee for the purposes of oral argument. Unless the district court or BAP directs otherwise, a cross-appeal or separate appeal must be argued when the initial appeal is argued. Separate parties should avoid duplicative argument.

(f) Nonappearance of a party

If the appellee fails to appear for argument, the district court or BAP may hear the appellant's argument. If the appellant fails to appear for argument, the district court or BAP may hear the appellee's argument. If neither party appears, the case will be decided on the briefs unless the district court or BAP orders otherwise.

(g) Submission on briefs

The parties may agree to submit a case for decision on the briefs, but the district court or BAP may direct that the case be argued.

(h) Use of physical exhibits at argument; removal

Counsel intending to use physical exhibits other than documents at the argument must arrange to place them in the courtroom on the day of the argument before the court convenes. After the argument, counsel must remove the exhibits from the courtroom unless the district court or BAP directs otherwise. The clerk may destroy or dispose of the exhibits if counsel does not reclaim them within a reasonable time after the clerk gives notice to remove them.

(As amended Mar. 30, 1987, eff. Aug. 1, 1987; Apr. 25, 2014, eff. Dec. 1, 2014.)

Rule 8020. Frivolous Appeal and Other Misconduct

(a) Frivolous appeal—damages and costs

If the district court or BAP determines that an appeal is frivolous, it may, after a separately filed motion or notice from the court and reasonable opportunity to respond, award just damages and single or double costs to the appellee.

(b) Other misconduct

The district court or BAP may discipline or sanction an attorney or party appearing before it for other misconduct, including failure to comply with any court order. First, however, the court must afford the attorney or party reasonable notice, an opportunity to show cause to the contrary, and, if requested, a hearing.

(Added Apr. 11, 1997, eff. Dec. 1, 1997; Apr. 25, 2014, eff. Dec. 1, 2014.)

Rule 8021. Costs

(a) Against whom assessed

The following rules apply unless the law provides or the district court or BAP orders otherwise:

(1) if an appeal is dismissed, costs are taxed against the appellant, unless the parties agree otherwise;

(2) if a judgment, order, or decree is affirmed, costs are taxed against the appellant;

(3) if a judgment, order, or decree is reversed, costs are taxed against the appellee;

(4) if a judgment, order, or decree is affirmed or reversed in part, modified, or vacated, costs are taxed only as the district court or BAP orders.

(b) Costs for and against the United States

Costs for or against the United States, its agency, or its officer may be assessed under subdivision (a) only if authorized by law.

(c) Costs on appeal taxable in the bankruptcy court

The following costs on appeal are taxable in the bankruptcy court for the benefit of the party entitled to costs under this rule:

(1) the production of any required copies of a brief, appendix, exhibit, or the record;

(2) the preparation and transmission of the record;

(3) the reporter's transcript, if needed to determine the appeal;

(4) premiums paid for a supersedeas bond or other bonds to preserve rights pending appeal; and

(5) the fee for filing the notice of appeal.

(d) Bill of costs; objections

A party who wants costs taxed must, within 14 days after entry of judgment on appeal, file with the bankruptcy clerk, with proof of service, an itemized and verified bill of costs. Objections must be filed within 14 days after service of the bill of costs, unless the bankruptcy court extends the time.

(Added Apr. 25, 2014, eff. Dec. 1, 2014.)

Rule 8022. Motion for Rehearing

(a) Time to file; contents; response; action by the district court or BAP if granted

(1) Time

Unless the time is shortened or extended by order or local rule, any motion for rehearing by the district court or BAP must be filed within 14 days after entry of judgment on appeal.

(2) Contents

The motion must state with particularity each point of law or fact that the movant believes the district court or BAP has overlooked or misapprehended and must argue in support of the motion. Oral argument is not permitted.

(3) Response

Unless the district court or BAP requests, no response to a motion for rehearing is permitted. But ordinarily, rehearing will not be granted in the absence of such a request.

(4) Action by the district court or BAP

If a motion for rehearing is granted, the district court or BAP may do any of the following:

(A) make a final disposition of the appeal without reargument;

(B) restore the case to the calendar for reargument or resubmission; or

(C) issue any other appropriate order.

(b) Form of the motion; length

The motion must comply in form with Rule 8013(f)(1) and (2). Copies must be served and filed as provided by Rule 8011. Unless the district court or BAP orders otherwise, a motion for rehearing must not exceed 15 pages.

(Added Apr. 25, 2014, eff. Dec. 1, 2014.)

Rule 8023. Voluntary Dismissal

The clerk of the district court or BAP must dismiss an appeal if the parties file a signed dismissal agreement specifying how costs are to be paid and pay any fees that are due. An appeal may be dismissed on the appellant's motion on terms agreed to by the parties or fixed by the district court or BAP.

(Added Apr. 25, 2014, eff. Dec. 1, 2014.)

Rule 8024. Clerk's Duties on Disposition of the Appeal

(a) Judgment on appeal

The district or BAP clerk must prepare, sign, and enter the judgment after receiving the court's opinion or, if there is no opinion, as the court instructs. Noting the judgment on the docket constitutes entry of judgment.

(b) Notice of a judgment

Immediately upon the entry of a judgment, the district or BAP clerk must:

(1) transmit a notice of the entry to each party to the appeal, to the United States trustee, and to the bankruptcy clerk, together with a copy of any opinion; and

(2) note the date of the transmission on the docket.

(c) Returning physical items

If any physical items were transmitted as the record on appeal, they must be returned to the bankruptcy clerk on disposition of the appeal.

(Added Apr. 25, 2014, eff. Dec. 1, 2014.)

Rule 8025. Stay of a District Court or BAP Judgment

(a) Automatic stay of judgment on appeal

Unless the district court or BAP orders otherwise, its judgment is stayed for 14 days after entry.

(b) Stay pending appeal to the court of appeals

(1) In general

On a party's motion and notice to all other parties to the appeal, the district court or BAP may stay its judgment pending an appeal to the court of appeals.

(2) Time limit

The stay must not exceed 30 days after the judgment is entered, except for cause shown.

(3) Stay continued

If, before a stay expires, the party who obtained the stay appeals to the court of appeals, the stay continues until final disposition by the court of appeals.

(4) Bond or other security

A bond or other security may be required as a condition for granting or continuing a stay of the judgment. A bond or other security may be required if a trustee obtains a stay, but not if a stay is obtained by the United States or its officer or agency or at the direction of any department of the United States government.

(c) Automatic stay of an order, judgment, or decree of a bankruptcy court

If the district court or BAP enters a judgment affirming an order, judgment, or decree of the bankruptcy court, a stay of the district court's or BAP's judgment automatically stays the bankruptcy court's order, judgment, or decree for the duration of the appellate stay.

(d) Power of a court of appeals not limited

This rule does not limit the power of a court of appeals or any of its judges to do the following:

(1) stay a judgment pending appeal;

(2) stay proceedings while an appeal is pending;

(3) suspend, modify, restore, vacate, or grant a stay or an injunction while an appeal is pending; or

(4) issue any order appropriate to preserve the status quo or the effectiveness of any judgment to be entered.

(Added Apr. 25, 2014, eff. Dec. 1, 2014.)

Rule 8026. Rules by Circuit Councils and District Courts; Procedure When There Is No Controlling Law

(a) Local rules by circuit councils and district courts

(1) Adopting local rules

A circuit council that has authorized a BAP under 28 U.S.C. § 158(b) may make and amend rules governing the practice and procedure on appeal from a judgment, order, or decree of a bankruptcy court to the BAP. A district court may make and amend rules governing the practice and procedure on appeal from a judgment, order, or decree of a bankruptcy court to the district court. Local rules must be consistent with, but not duplicative of, Acts of Congress and these Part VIII rules. Rule 83 F.R.Civ.P. governs the procedure for making and amending rules to govern appeals.

(2) Numbering

Local rules must conform to any uniform numbering system prescribed by the Judicial Conference of the United States.

(3) Limitation on imposing requirements of form

A local rule imposing a requirement of form must not be enforced in a way that causes a party to lose any right because of a nonwillful failure to comply.

(b) Procedure when there is no controlling law

(1) In general

A district court or BAP may regulate practice in any manner consistent with federal law, applicable federal rules, the Official Forms, and local rules.

(2) Limitation on sanctions

No sanction or other disadvantage may be imposed for noncompliance with any requirement not in federal law, applicable federal rules, the Official Forms, or local rules unless the alleged violator has been furnished in the particular case with actual notice of the requirement.

(Added Apr. 25, 2014, eff. Dec. 1, 2014.)

Rule 8027. Notice of a Mediation Procedure

If the district court or BAP has a mediation procedure applicable to bankruptcy appeals, the clerk must notify the parties promptly after docketing the appeal of: (a) the requirements of the mediation procedure; and (b) any effect the mediation procedure has on the time to file briefs.

(Added Apr. 25, 2014, eff. Dec. 1, 2014.)

Rule 8028. Suspension of Rules in Part VIII

In the interest of expediting decision or for other cause in a particular case, the district court or BAP, or where appropriate the court of appeals, may suspend the requirements or provisions of the rules in Part VIII, except Rules 8001, 8002, 8003, 8004, 8005, 8006, 8007, 8012, 8020, 8024, 8025, 8026, and 8028.

(Added Apr. 25, 2014, eff. Dec. 1, 2014.)

PART IX—GENERAL PROVISIONS

Rule 9001. General Definitions

The definitions of words and phrases in §§ 101, 902, 1101, and 1502 of the Code, and the rules of construction in § 102, govern their use in these rules. In addition, the following words and phrases used in these rules have the meanings indicated:

(1) "Bankruptcy clerk" means a clerk appointed pursuant to 28 U.S.C. § 156(b).

(2) "Bankruptcy Code" or "Code" means title 11 of the United States Code.

(3) "Clerk" means bankruptcy clerk, if one has been appointed, otherwise clerk of the district court.

(4) "Court" or "judge" means the judicial officer before whom a case or proceeding is pending.

(5) "Debtor." When any act is required by these rules to be performed by a debtor or when it is necessary to compel attendance of a debtor for examination and the debtor is not a natural person: (A) if the debtor is a corporation, "debtor" includes, if designated by the court, any or all of its officers, members of its board of directors or trustees or of a similar controlling body, a controlling stockholder or member, or any other person in control; (B) if the debtor is a partnership, "debtor" includes any or all of its general partners or, if designated by the court, any other person in control.

(6) "Firm" includes a partnership or professional corporation of attorneys or accountants.

(7) "Judgment" means any appealable order.

(8) "Mail" means first class, postage prepaid.

(9) "Notice provider" means any entity approved by the Administrative Office of the United States Courts to give notice to creditors under Rule 2002(g)(4).

(10) "Regular associate" means any attorney regularly employed by, associated with, or counsel to an individual or firm.

(11) "Trustee" includes a debtor in possession in a chapter 11 case.

(12) "United States trustee" includes an assistant United States trustee and any designee of the United States trustee.

(As amended Mar. 30, 1987, eff. Aug. 1, 1987; Apr. 30, 1991, eff. Aug. 1, 1991; Apr. 25, 2005, eff. Dec. 1, 2005; Apr. 28, 2010, eff. Dec. 1, 2010.)

Rule 9002. Meanings of Words in the Federal Rules of Civil Procedure When Applicable to Cases Under the Code

The following words and phrases used in the Federal Rules of Civil Procedure made applicable to cases under the Code by these rules have the meanings indicated unless they are inconsistent with the context:

(1) "Action" or "civil action" means an adversary proceeding or, when appropriate, a contested petition, or proceedings to vacate an order for relief or to determine any other contested matter.

(2) "Appeal" means an appeal as provided by 28 U.S.C. § 158.

(3) "Clerk" or "clerk of the district court" means the court officer responsible for the bankruptcy records in the district.

(4) "District court," "trial court," "court," "district judge," or "judge" means bankruptcy judge if the case or proceeding is pending before a bankruptcy judge.

(5) "Judgment" includes any order appealable to an appellate court.

(As amended Mar. 30, 1987, eff. Aug. 1, 1987; Apr. 22, 1993, eff. Aug. 1, 1993.)

Rule 9003. Prohibition of Ex Parte Contacts

(a) General prohibition

Except as otherwise permitted by applicable law, any examiner, any party in interest, and any attorney, accountant, or employee of a party in interest shall refrain from ex parte meetings and communications with the court concerning matters affecting a particular case or proceeding.

(b) United States trustee

Except as otherwise permitted by applicable law, the United States trustee and assistants to and employees or agents of the United States trustee shall refrain from ex parte meetings and communications with the court concerning matters affecting a particular case or proceeding. This rule does not preclude communications with the court to discuss general problems of administration and improvement of bankruptcy administration, including the operation of the United States trustee system.

(As amended Mar. 30, 1987, eff. Aug. 1, 1987; Apr. 30, 1991, eff. Aug. 1, 1991.)

Rule 9004. General Requirements of Form

(a) Legibility; abbreviations

All petitions, pleadings, schedules and other papers shall be clearly legible. Abbreviations in common use in the English language may be used.

(b) Caption

Each paper filed shall contain a caption setting forth the name of the court, the title of the case, the bankruptcy docket number, and a brief designation of the character of the paper.

Rule 9005. Harmless Error

Rule 61 F.R.Civ.P. applies in cases under the Code. When appropriate, the court may order the correction of any error or defect or the cure of any omission which does not affect substantial rights.

Rule 9005.1. Constitutional Challenge to a Statute—Notice, Certification, and Intervention

Rule 5.1 F.R.Civ.P. applies in cases under the Code.

(Added Apr. 30, 2007, eff. Dec. 1, 2007.)

Rule 9006. Computing and Extending Time; Time for Motion Papers

(a) Computing time

The following rules apply in computing any time period specified in these rules, in the Federal Rules of Civil Procedure, in any local rule or court order, or in any statute that does not specify a method of computing time.

(1) Period stated in days or a longer unit

When the period is stated in days or a longer unit of time:

    (A) exclude the day of the event that triggers the period;

    (B) count every day, including intermediate Saturdays, Sundays, and legal holidays; and

    (C) include the last day of the period, but if the last day is a Saturday, Sunday, or legal holiday, the period

continues to run until the end of the next day that is not a Saturday, Sunday, or legal holiday.

(2) Period stated in hours

When the period is stated in hours:

    (A) begin counting immediately on the occurrence of the event that triggers the period;

    (B) count every hour, including hours during intermediate Saturdays, Sundays, and legal holidays; and

    (C) if the period would end on a Saturday, Sunday, or legal holiday, then continue the period until the same time on the next day that is not a Saturday, Sunday, or legal holiday.

(3) Inaccessibility of clerk's office

Unless the court orders otherwise, if the clerk's office is inaccessible:

    (A) on the last day for filing under Rule 9006(a)(1), then the time for filing is extended to the first accessible day that is not a Saturday, Sunday, or legal holiday; or

    (B) during the last hour for filing under Rule 9006(a)(2), then the time for filing is extended to the same time on the first accessible day that is not a Saturday, Sunday, or legal holiday.

(4) "Last day" defined

Unless a different time is set by a statute, local rule, or order in the case, the last day ends:

    (A) for electronic filing, at midnight in the court's time zone; and

    (B) for filing by other means, when the clerk's office is scheduled to close.

(5) "Next day" defined

The "next day" is determined by continuing to count forward when the period is measured after an event and backward when measured before an event.

(6) "Legal holiday" defined

"Legal holiday" means:

    (A) the day set aside by statute for observing New Year's Day, Martin Luther King Jr.'s Birthday, Washington's Birthday, Memorial Day, Independence Day, Labor Day, Columbus Day, Veterans' Day, Thanksgiving Day, or Christmas Day;

    (B) any day declared a holiday by the President or Congress; and

    (C) for periods that are measured after an event, any other day declared a holiday by the state where the district court is located. (In this rule, "state" includes the District of Columbia and any United States commonwealth or territory.)

(b) Enlargement

(1) In general

Except as provided in paragraphs (2) and (3) of this subdivision, when an act is required or allowed to be done at or within a specified period by these rules or by a notice given thereunder or by order of court, the court for cause shown may at any time in its discretion (1) with or without motion or notice order the period enlarged if the request therefor is made before the expiration of the period originally prescribed or as extended by a previous order or (2) on motion made after the expiration of the specified period permit the act to be done where the failure to act was the result of excusable neglect.

(2) Enlargement not permitted

The court may not enlarge the time for taking action under Rules 1007(d), 2003(a) and (d), 7052, 9023, and 9024.

(3) Enlargement governed by other rules

The court may enlarge the time for taking action under Rules 1006(b)(2), 1017(e), 3002(c), 4003(b), 4004(a), 4007(c), 4008(a), 8002, and 9033, only to the extent and under the conditions stated in those rules. In addition, the court may enlarge the time to file the statement required under Rule 1007(b)(7), and to file schedules and statements in a small business case under § 1116(3) of the Code, only to the extent and under the conditions stated in Rule 1007(c).

(c) Reduction

(1) In general

Except as provided in paragraph (2) of this subdivision, when an act is required or allowed to be done at or within a specified time by these rules or by a notice given thereunder or by order of court, the court for cause shown may in its discretion with or without motion or notice order the period reduced.

(2) Reduction not permitted

The court may not reduce the time for taking action under Rules 2002(a)(7), 2003(a), 3002(c), 3014, 3015, 4001(b)(2), (c)(2), 4003(a), 4004(a), 4007(c), 4008(a), 8002, and 9033(b). In addition, the court may not reduce the time under Rule 1007(c) to file the statement required by Rule 1007(b)(7).

(d) Motion papers

A written motion, other than one which may be heard ex parte, and notice of any hearing shall be served not later than seven days before the time specified for such hearing, unless a different period is fixed by these rules or by order of the court. Such an order may for cause shown be made on ex parte application. When a motion is supported by affidavit, the affidavit shall be served with the motion. Except as otherwise provided in Rule 9023, any written response shall be served not later than one day before the hearing, unless the court permits otherwise.

(e) Time of service

Service of process and service of any paper other than process or of notice by mail is complete on mailing.

(f) Additional time after service by mail or under Rule 5(b)(2)(D) or (F) F.R.Civ.P.

When there is a right or requirement to act or undertake some proceedings within a prescribed period after being served and that service is by mail or under Rule 5(b)(2)(D) (leaving with the clerk) or (F) (other means consented to) F.R.Civ.P., three days are added after the prescribed period would otherwise expire under Rule 9006(a).

(g) Grain storage facility cases

This rule shall not limit the court's authority under § 557 of the Code to enter orders governing procedures in cases in which the debtor is an owner or operator of a grain storage facility.

(As amended Mar. 30, 1987, eff. Aug. 1, 1987; Apr. 25, 1989, eff. Aug. 1, 1989; Apr. 30, 1991, eff. Aug. 1, 1991; Apr. 23, 1996, eff. Dec. 1, 1996; Apr. 26, 1999, eff. Dec. 1, 1999; Apr. 23, 2001, eff. Dec. 1, 2001; Apr. 25, 2005, eff. Dec. 1, 2005; Apr. 23, 2008, eff. Dec. 1, 2008; Mar. 26, 2009, eff. Dec. 1, 2009; Apr. 16, 2013, eff. Dec. 1, 2013; Apr. 28, 2016, eff. Dec. 1, 2016.)

Rule 9007.   General Authority to Regulate Notices

When notice is to be given under these rules, the court shall designate, if not otherwise specified herein, the time within which, the entities to whom, and the form and manner in which the notice shall be given. When feasible, the court may order any notices under these rules to be combined.

(As amended Mar. 30, 1987, eff. Aug. 1, 1987.)

Rule 9008.   Service or Notice by Publication

Whenever these rules require or authorize service or notice by publication, the court shall, to the extent not otherwise specified in these rules, determine the form and manner thereof, including the newspaper or other medium to be used and the number of publications.

Rule 9009.   Forms

[Text of rule effective until December 1, 2017, absent contrary Congressional action.]

Except as otherwise provided in Rule 3016(d), the Official Forms prescribed by the Judicial Conference of the United States shall be observed and used with alterations as may be appropriate. Forms may be combined and their contents rearranged to permit economies in their use. The Director of the Administrative Office of the United States Courts may issue additional forms for use under the Code. The forms shall be construed to be consistent with these rules and the Code.

[Text of rule effective December 1, 2017, absent contrary Congressional action.]

(a) Official forms

The Official Forms prescribed by the Judicial Conference of the United States shall be used without alteration, except as otherwise provided in these rules, in a particular Official Form, or in the national instructions for a particular Official Form. Official Forms may be modified to permit minor changes not affecting wording or the order of presenting information, including changes that:

(1) expand the prescribed areas for responses in order to permit complete responses;

(2) delete space not needed for responses; or

(3) delete items requiring detail in a question or category if the filer indicates—either by checking "no" or "none" or

by stating in words—that there is nothing to report on that question or category.

(b) Director's forms

The Director of the Administrative Office of the United States Courts may issue additional forms for use under the Code.

(c) Construction

The forms shall be construed to be consistent with these rules and the Code.

(As amended Apr. 30, 1991, eff. Aug. 1, 1991; Apr. 23, 2008, eff. Dec. 1, 2008; Apr. 27, 2017, eff. Dec. 1, 2017, absent contrary Congressional action.)

Rule 9010. Representation and Appearances; Powers of Attorney

(a) Authority to act personally or by attorney

A debtor, creditor, equity security holder, indenture trustee, committee or other party may (1) appear in a case under the Code and act either in the entity's own behalf or by an attorney authorized to practice in the court, and (2) perform any act not constituting the practice of law, by an authorized agent, attorney in fact, or proxy.

(b) Notice of appearance

An attorney appearing for a party in a case under the Code shall file a notice of appearance with the attorney's name, office address and telephone number, unless the attorney's appearance is otherwise noted in the record.

(c) Power of attorney

The authority of any agent, attorney in fact, or proxy to represent a creditor for any purpose other than the execution and filing of a proof of claim or the acceptance or rejection of a plan shall be evidenced by a power of attorney conforming substantially to the appropriate Official Form. The execution of any such power of attorney shall be acknowledged before one of the officers enumerated in 28 U.S.C. § 459, § 953, Rule 9012, or a person authorized to administer oaths under the laws of the state where the oath is administered.

(As amended Mar. 30, 1987, eff. Aug. 1, 1987; Apr. 30, 1991, eff. Aug. 1, 1991.)

Rule 9011. Signing of Papers; Representations to the Court; Sanctions; Verification and Copies of Papers

(a) Signature

Every petition, pleading, written motion, and other paper, except a list, schedule, or statement, or amendments thereto, shall be signed by at least one attorney of record in the attorney's individual name. A party who is not represented by an attorney shall sign all papers. Each paper shall state the signer's address and telephone number, if any. An unsigned paper shall be stricken unless omission of the signature is corrected promptly after being called to the attention of the attorney or party.

(b) Representations to the court

By presenting to the court (whether by signing, filing, submitting, or later advocating) a petition, pleading, written motion, or other paper, an attorney or unrepresented party is certifying that to the best of the person's knowledge, information, and belief, formed after an inquiry reasonable under the circumstances,[1]—

(1) it is not being presented for any improper purpose, such as to harass or to cause unnecessary delay or needless increase in the cost of litigation;

(2) the claims, defenses, and other legal contentions therein are warranted by existing law or by a nonfrivolous argument for the extension, modification, or reversal of existing law or the establishment of new law;

(3) the allegations and other factual contentions have evidentiary support or, if specifically so identified, are likely to have evidentiary support after a reasonable opportunity for further investigation or discovery; and

(4) the denials of factual contentions are warranted on the evidence or, if specifically so identified, are reasonably based on a lack of information or belief.

(c) Sanctions

If, after notice and a reasonable opportunity to respond, the court determines that subdivision (b) has been violated, the court may, subject to the conditions stated below, impose an appropriate sanction upon the attorneys, law firms, or parties that have violated subdivision (b) or are responsible for the violation.

(1) How initiated

(A) By motion

A motion for sanctions under this rule shall be made separately from other motions or requests and shall describe the specific conduct alleged to violate subdivision (b). It shall be served as provided in Rule 7004. The motion for sanctions may not be filed with or presented to the court unless, within 21 days after service of the motion (or such other period as the court may prescribe), the challenged paper, claim, defense, contention, allegation, or denial is not withdrawn or appropriately corrected, except that this limitation shall not apply if the conduct alleged is the filing of a petition in violation of subdivision (b). If warranted, the court may award to the party prevailing on the motion the reasonable expenses and attorney's fees incurred in presenting or opposing the motion. Absent exceptional circumstances, a law firm shall be held jointly responsible for violations committed by its partners, associates, and employees.

(B) On court's initiative

On its own initiative, the court may enter an order describing the specific conduct that appears to violate subdivision (b) and directing an attorney, law firm, or party to show cause why it has not violated subdivision (b) with respect thereto.

(2) Nature of sanction; limitations

A sanction imposed for violation of this rule shall be limited to what is sufficient to deter repetition of such conduct or comparable conduct by others similarly situated.

Subject to the limitations in subparagraphs (A) and (B), the sanction may consist of, or include, directives of a nonmonetary nature, an order to pay a penalty into court, or, if imposed on motion and warranted for effective deterrence, an order directing payment to the movant of some or all of the reasonable attorneys' fees and other expenses incurred as a direct result of the violation.

(A) Monetary sanctions may not be awarded against a represented party for a violation of subdivision (b)(2).

(B) Monetary sanctions may not be awarded on the court's initiative unless the court issues its order to show cause before a voluntary dismissal or settlement of the claims made by or against the party which is, or whose attorneys are, to be sanctioned.

(3) Order

When imposing sanctions, the court shall describe the conduct determined to constitute a violation of this rule and explain the basis for the sanction imposed.

(d) Inapplicability to discovery

Subdivisions (a) through (c) of this rule do not apply to disclosures and discovery requests, responses, objections, and motions that are subject to the provisions of Rules 7026 through 7037.

(e) Verification

Except as otherwise specifically provided by these rules, papers filed in a case under the Code need not be verified. Whenever verification is required by these rules, an unsworn declaration as provided in 28 U.S.C. § 1746 satisfies the requirement of verification.

(f) Copies of signed or verified papers

When these rules require copies of a signed or verified paper, it shall suffice if the original is signed or verified and the copies are conformed to the original.

(As amended Mar. 30, 1987, eff. Aug. 1, 1987; Apr. 30, 1991, eff. Aug. 1, 1991; Apr. 11, 1997, eff. Dec. 1, 1997.)

1 So in original. The comma probably should not appear.

Rule 9012.   Oaths and Affirmations

(a) Persons authorized to administer oaths

The following persons may administer oaths and affirmations and take acknowledgments: a bankruptcy judge, clerk, deputy clerk, United States trustee, officer authorized to administer oaths in proceedings before the courts of the United States or under the laws of the state where the oath is to be taken, or a diplomatic or consular officer of the United States in any foreign country.

(b) Affirmation in lieu of oath

When in a case under the Code an oath is required to be taken, a solemn affirmation may be accepted in lieu thereof.

(As amended Mar. 30, 1987, eff. Aug. 1, 1987; Apr. 30, 1991, eff. Aug. 1, 1991.)

Rule 9013.   Motions: Form and Service

A request for an order, except when an application is authorized by the rules, shall be by written motion, unless made during a hearing. The motion shall state with particularity the grounds therefor, and shall set forth the relief or order sought. Every written motion, other than one which may be considered ex parte, shall be served by the moving party within the time determined under Rule 9006(d). The moving party shall serve the motion on:

(a) the trustee or debtor in possession and on those entities specified by these rules; or

(b) the entities the court directs if these rules do not require service or specify the entities to be served.

(As amended Mar. 30, 1987, eff. Aug. 1, 1987; Apr. 16, 2013, eff. Dec. 1, 2013.)

Rule 9014.   Contested Matters

(a) Motion. In a contested matter not otherwise governed by these rules, relief shall be requested by motion, and reasonable notice and opportunity for hearing shall be afforded the party against whom relief is sought. No response is required under this rule unless the court directs otherwise.

(b) Service. The motion shall be served in the manner provided for service of a summons and complaint by Rule 7004 and within the time determined under Rule 9006(d). Any written response to the motion shall be served within the time determined under Rule 9006(d). Any paper served after the motion shall be served in the manner provided by Rule 5(b) F. R. Civ. P.

(c) Application of Part VII rules. Except as otherwise provided in this rule, and unless the court directs otherwise, the following rules shall apply: 7009, 7017, 7021, 7025, 7026, 7028–7037, 7041, 7042, 7052, 7054–7056, 7064, 7069, and 7071. The following subdivisions of Fed. R. Civ. P. 26, as incorporated by Rule 7026, shall not apply in a contested matter unless the court directs otherwise: 26(a)(1) (mandatory disclosure), 26(a)(2) (disclosures regarding expert testimony) and 26(a)(3) (additional pre-trial disclosure), and 26(f) (mandatory meeting before scheduling conference/discovery plan). An entity that desires to perpetuate testimony may proceed in the same manner as provided in Rule 7027 for the taking of a deposition before an adversary proceeding. The court may at any stage in a particular matter direct that one or more of the other rules in Part VII shall apply. The court shall give the parties notice of any order issued under this paragraph to afford them a reasonable opportunity to comply with the procedures prescribed by the order.

(d) Testimony of witnesses. Testimony of witnesses with respect to disputed material factual issues shall be taken in the same manner as testimony in an adversary proceeding.

(e) Attendance of witnesses. The court shall provide procedures that enable parties to ascertain at a reasonable time before any scheduled hearing whether the hearing will be an evidentiary hearing at which witnesses may testify.

(As amended Mar. 30, 1987, eff. Aug. 1, 1987; Apr. 26, 1999, eff. Dec. 1, 1999; Apr. 29, 2002, eff. Dec. 1, 2002; Apr. 26, 2004, eff. Dec. 1, 2004; Apr. 16, 2013, eff. Dec. 1, 2013.)

Rule 9015. Jury Trials

(a) Applicability of certain Federal Rules of Civil Procedure

Rules 38, 39, 47–49, and 51, F.R.Civ.P., and Rule 81(c) F.R.Civ.P. insofar as it applies to jury trials, apply in cases and proceedings, except that a demand made under Rule 38(b) F.R.Civ.P. shall be filed in accordance with Rule 5005.

(b) Consent to have trial conducted by bankruptcy judge

If the right to a jury trial applies, a timely demand has been filed pursuant to Rule 38(b) F.R.Civ.P., and the bankruptcy judge has been specially designated to conduct the jury trial, the parties may consent to have a jury trial conducted by a bankruptcy judge under 28 U.S.C. § 157(e) by jointly or separately filing a statement of consent within any applicable time limits specified by local rule.

(c) Applicability of Rule 50 F.R.Civ.P.

Rule 50 F.R.Civ.P. applies in cases and proceedings, except that any renewed motion for judgment or request for a new trial shall be filed no later than 14 days after the entry of judgment.

(Added Apr. 11, 1997, eff. Dec. 1, 1997; amended Mar. 26, 2009, eff. Dec. 1, 2009.)

Rule 9016. Subpoena

Rule 45 F.R.Civ.P. applies in cases under the Code.

(As amended Mar. 30, 1987, eff. Aug. 1, 1987.)

Rule 9017. Evidence

The Federal Rules of Evidence and Rules 43, 44 and 44.1 F.R.Civ.P. apply in cases under the Code.

Rule 9018. Secret, Confidential, Scandalous, or Defamatory Matter

On motion or on its own initiative, with or without notice, the court may make any order which justice requires (1) to protect the estate or any entity in respect of a trade secret or other confidential research, development, or commercial information, (2) to protect any entity against scandalous or defamatory matter contained in any paper filed in a case under the Code, or (3) to protect governmental matters that are made confidential by statute or regulation. If an order is entered under this rule without notice, any entity affected thereby may move to vacate or modify the order, and after a hearing on notice the court shall determine the motion.

(As amended Mar. 30, 1987, eff. Aug. 1, 1987.)

Rule 9019. Compromise and Arbitration

(a) Compromise

On motion by the trustee and after notice and a hearing, the court may approve a compromise or settlement. Notice shall be given to creditors, the United States trustee, the debtor, and indenture trustees as provided in Rule 2002 and to any other entity as the court may direct.

(b) Authority to compromise or settle controversies within classes

After a hearing on such notice as the court may direct, the court may fix a class or classes of controversies and authorize the trustee to compromise or settle controversies within such class or classes without further hearing or notice.

(c) Arbitration

On stipulation of the parties to any controversy affecting the estate the court may authorize the matter to be submitted to final and binding arbitration.

(As amended Mar. 30, 1987, eff. Aug. 1, 1987; Apr. 30, 1991, eff. Aug. 1, 1991; Apr. 22, 1993, eff. Aug. 1, 1993.)

Rule 9020. Contempt Proceedings

Rule 9014 governs a motion for an order of contempt made by the United States trustee or a party in interest.

(As amended Mar. 30, 1987, eff. Aug. 1, 1987; Apr. 30, 1991, eff. Aug. 1, 1991; Apr. 23, 2001, eff. Dec. 1, 2001.)

Rule 9021. Entry of Judgment

A judgment or order is effective when entered under Rule 5003.

(As amended Mar. 30, 1987, eff. Aug. 1, 1987; Mar. 26, 2009, eff. Dec. 1, 2009.)

Rule 9022. Notice of Judgment or Order

(a) Judgment or order of bankruptcy judge

Immediately on the entry of a judgment or order the clerk shall serve a notice of entry in the manner provided in Rule 5(b) F.R.Civ.P. on the contesting parties and on other entities as the court directs. Unless the case is a chapter 9 municipality case, the clerk shall forthwith transmit to the United States trustee a copy of the judgment or order. Service of the notice shall be noted in the docket. Lack of notice of the entry does not affect the time to appeal or relieve or authorize the court to relieve a party for failure to appeal within the time allowed, except as permitted in Rule 8002.

(b) Judgment or order of district judge

Notice of a judgment or order entered by a district judge is governed by Rule 77(d) F.R.Civ.P. Unless the case is a chapter 9 municipality case, the clerk shall forthwith transmit to the United States trustee a copy of a judgment or order entered by a district judge.

(As amended Mar. 30, 1987, eff. Aug. 1, 1987; Apr. 30, 1991, eff. Aug. 1, 1991; Apr. 23, 2001, eff. Dec. 1, 2001.)

Rule 9023. New Trials; Amendment of Judgments

Except as provided in this rule and Rule 3008, Rule 59 F.R.Civ.P. applies in cases under the Code. A motion for a new trial or to alter or amend a judgment shall be filed, and a court may on its own order a new trial, no later than 14 days after entry of judgment. In some circumstances, Rule 8008 governs post-judgment motion practice after an appeal has been docketed and is pending.

(As amended Mar. 26, 2009, eff. Dec. 1, 2009; Apr. 25, 2014, eff. Dec. 1, 2014.)

Rule 9024.   Relief From Judgment or Order

Rule 60 F.R.Civ.P. applies in cases under the Code except that (1) a motion to reopen a case under the Code or for the reconsideration of an order allowing or disallowing a claim against the estate entered without a contest is not subject to the one-year limitation prescribed in Rule 60(c), (2) a complaint to revoke a discharge in a chapter 7 liquidation case may be filed only within the time allowed by § 727(e) of the Code, and (3) a complaint to revoke an order confirming a plan may be filed only within the time allowed by § 1144, § 1230, or § 1330. In some circumstances, Rule 8008 governs post-judgment motion practice after an appeal has been docketed and is pending.

(As amended Apr. 30, 1991, eff. Aug. 1, 1991; Apr. 23, 2008, eff. Dec. 1, 2008; Apr. 25, 2014, eff. Dec. 1, 2014.)

Rule 9025.   Security: Proceedings Against Sureties

Whenever the Code or these rules require or permit the giving of security by a party, and security is given in the form of a bond or stipulation or other undertaking with one or more sureties, each surety submits to the jurisdiction of the court, and liability may be determined in an adversary proceeding governed by the rules in Part VII.

Rule 9026.   Exceptions Unnecessary

Rule 46 F.R.Civ.P. applies in cases under the Code.

Rule 9027.   Removal

(a) Notice of removal

(1) Where filed; form and content

A notice of removal shall be filed with the clerk for the district and division within which is located the state or federal court where the civil action is pending. The notice shall be signed pursuant to Rule 9011 and contain a short and plain statement of the facts which entitle the party filing the notice to remove, contain a statement that upon removal of the claim or cause of action, the party filing the notice does or does not consent to entry of final orders or judgment by the bankruptcy court, and be accompanied by a copy of all process and pleadings.

(2) Time for filing; civil action initiated before commencement of the case under the Code

If the claim or cause of action in a civil action is pending when a case under the Code is commenced, a notice of removal may be filed only within the longest of (A) 90 days after the order for relief in the case under the Code, (B) 30 days after entry of an order terminating a stay, if the claim or cause of action in a civil action has been stayed under § 362 of the Code, or (C) 30 days after a trustee qualifies in a chapter 11 reorganization case but not later than 180 days after the order for relief.

(3) Time for filing; civil action initiated after commencement of the case under the Code

If a claim or cause of action is asserted in another court after the commencement of a case under the Code, a notice of removal may be filed with the clerk only within the shorter of (A) 30 days after receipt, through service or otherwise, of a copy of the initial pleading setting forth the claim or cause of action sought to be removed, or (B) 30 days after receipt of the summons if the initial pleading has been filed with the court but not served with the summons.

(b) Notice

Promptly after filing the notice of removal, the party filing the notice shall serve a copy of it on all parties to the removed claim or cause of action.

(c) Filing in non-bankruptcy court

Promptly after filing the notice of removal, the party filing the notice shall file a copy of it with the clerk of the court from which the claim or cause of action is removed. Removal of the claim or cause of action is effected on such filing of a copy of the notice of removal. The parties shall proceed no further in that court unless and until the claim or cause of action is remanded.

(d) Remand

A motion for remand of the removed claim or cause of action shall be governed by Rule 9014 and served on the parties to the removed claim or cause of action.

(e) Procedure after removal

(1) After removal of a claim or cause of action to a district court the district court or, if the case under the Code has been referred to a bankruptcy judge of the district, the bankruptcy judge, may issue all necessary orders and process to bring before it all proper parties whether served by process issued by the court from which the claim or cause of action was removed or otherwise.

(2) The district court or, if the case under the Code has been referred to a bankruptcy judge of the district, the bankruptcy judge, may require the party filing the notice of removal to file with the clerk copies of all records and proceedings relating to the claim or cause of action in the court from which the claim or cause of action was removed.

(3) Any party who has filed a pleading in connection with the removed claim or cause of action, other than the party filing the notice of removal, shall file a statement that the party does or does not consent to entry of final orders or judgment by the bankruptcy court. A statement required by this paragraph shall be signed pursuant to Rule 9011 and shall be filed not later than 14 days after the filing of the notice of removal. Any party who files a statement pursuant to this paragraph shall mail a copy to every other party to the removed claim or cause of action.

(f) Process after removal

If one or more of the defendants has not been served with process, the service has not been perfected prior to removal, or the process served proves to be defective, such process or service may be completed or new process issued pursuant to Part VII of these rules. This subdivision shall not deprive any defendant on whom process is served after removal of the defendant's right to move to remand the case.

(g) Applicability of Part VII

The rules of Part VII apply to a claim or cause of action removed to a district court from a federal or state court and govern procedure after removal. Repleading is not necessary unless the court so orders. In a removed action in which the defendant has not answered, the defendant shall answer or present the other defenses or objections available under the rules of Part VII within 21 days following the receipt through service or otherwise of a copy of the initial pleading setting forth the claim for relief on which the action or proceeding is based, or within 21 days following the service of summons on such initial pleading, or within seven days following the filing of the notice of removal, whichever period is longest.

(h) Record supplied

When a party is entitled to copies of the records and proceedings in any civil action or proceeding in a federal or a state court, to be used in the removed civil action or proceeding, and the clerk of the federal or state court, on demand accompanied by payment or tender of the lawful fees, fails to deliver certified copies, the court may, on affidavit reciting the facts, direct such record to be supplied by affidavit or otherwise. Thereupon the proceedings, trial and judgment may be had in the court, and all process awarded, as if certified copies had been filed.

(i) Attachment or sequestration; securities

When a claim or cause of action is removed to a district court, any attachment or sequestration of property in the court from which the claim or cause of action was removed shall hold the property to answer the final judgment or decree in the same manner as the property would have been held to answer final judgment or decree had it been rendered by the court from which the claim or cause of action was removed. All bonds, undertakings, or security given by either party to the claim or cause of action prior to its removal shall remain valid and effectual notwithstanding such removal. All injunctions issued, orders entered and other proceedings had prior to removal shall remain in full force and effect until dissolved or modified by the court.

(As amended Mar. 30, 1987, eff. Aug. 1, 1987; Apr. 30, 1991, eff. Aug. 1, 1991; Apr. 29, 2002, eff. Dec. 1, 2002; Mar. 26, 2009, eff. Dec. 1, 2009; Apr. 28, 2016, eff. Dec. 1, 2016.)

Rule 9028. Disability of a Judge

Rule 63 F.R.Civ.P. applies in cases under the Code.

(As amended Mar. 30, 1987, eff. Aug. 1, 1987.)

Rule 9029. Local Bankruptcy Rules; Procedure When There Is No Controlling Law

(a) Local bankruptcy rules

(1) Each district court acting by a majority of its district judges may make and amend rules governing practice and procedure in all cases and proceedings within the district court's bankruptcy jurisdiction which are consistent with—but not duplicative of—Acts of Congress and these rules and

which do not prohibit or limit the use of the Official Forms. Rule 83 F.R.Civ.P. governs the procedure for making local rules. A district court may authorize the bankruptcy judges of the district, subject to any limitation or condition it may prescribe and the requirements of 83 F.R.Civ.P., to make and amend rules of practice and procedure which are consistent with—but not duplicative of—Acts of Congress and these rules and which do not prohibit or limit the use of the Official Forms. Local rules shall conform to any uniform numbering system prescribed by the Judicial Conference of the United States.

(2) A local rule imposing a requirement of form shall not be enforced in a manner that causes a party to lose rights because of a nonwillful failure to comply with the requirement.

(b) Procedure when there is no controlling law. A judge may regulate practice in any manner consistent with federal law, these rules, Official Forms, and local rules of the district. No sanction or other disadvantage may be imposed for noncompliance with any requirement not in federal law, federal rules, Official Forms, or the local rules of the district unless the alleged violator has been furnished in the particular case with actual notice of the requirement.

(As amended Mar. 30, 1987, eff. Aug. 1, 1987; Apr. 30, 1991, eff. Aug. 1, 1991; Apr. 27, 1995, eff. Dec. 1, 1995.)

Rule 9030. Jurisdiction and Venue Unaffected

These rules shall not be construed to extend or limit the jurisdiction of the courts or the venue of any matters therein.

(As amended Mar. 30, 1987, eff. Aug. 1, 1987.)

Rule 9031. Masters Not Authorized

Rule 53 F.R.Civ.P. does not apply in cases under the Code.

Rule 9032. Effect of Amendment of Federal Rules of Civil Procedure

The Federal Rules of Civil Procedure which are incorporated by reference and made applicable by these rules shall be the Federal Rules of Civil Procedure in effect on the effective date of these rules and as thereafter amended, unless otherwise provided by such amendment or by these rules.

(As amended Apr. 30, 1991, eff. Aug. 1, 1991.)

Rule 9033. Proposed Findings of Fact and Conclusions of Law

(a) Service

In a proceeding in which the bankruptcy court has issued proposed findings of fact and conclusions of law, the clerk shall serve forthwith copies on all parties by mail and note the date of mailing on the docket.

(b) Objections: time for filing

Within 14 days after being served with a copy of the proposed findings of fact and conclusions of law a party may serve and file with the clerk written objections which identify the specific proposed findings or conclusions objected to and state the grounds for such objection. A party may respond to another party's objections within 14 days after being served with a copy thereof. A party objecting to the bankruptcy judge's proposed findings or conclusions shall arrange promptly for the transcription of the record, or such portions of it as all parties may agree upon or the bankruptcy judge deems sufficient, unless the district judge otherwise directs.

(c) Extension of time

The bankruptcy judge may for cause extend the time for filing objections by any party for a period not to exceed 21 days from the expiration of the time otherwise prescribed by this rule. A request to extend the time for filing objections must be made before the time for filing objections has expired, except that a request made no more than 21 days after the expiration of the time for filing objections may be granted upon a showing of excusable neglect.

(d) Standard of review

The district judge shall make a de novo review upon the record or, after additional evidence, of any portion of the bankruptcy judge's findings of fact or conclusions of law to which specific written objection has been made in accordance with this rule. The district judge may accept, reject, or modify the proposed findings of fact or conclusions of law, receive further evidence, or recommit the matter to the bankruptcy judge with instructions.

(Added Mar. 30, 1987, eff. Aug. 1, 1987; amended Mar. 26, 2009, eff. Dec. 1, 2009; Apr. 28, 2016, eff. Dec. 1, 2016.)

Rule 9034. Transmittal of Pleadings, Motion Papers, Objections, and Other Papers to the United States Trustee

Unless the United States trustee requests otherwise or the case is a chapter 9 municipality case, any entity that files a pleading, motion, objection, or similar paper relating to any of the following matters shall transmit a copy thereof to the United States trustee within the time required by these rules for service of the paper:

(a) a proposed use, sale, or lease of property of the estate other than in the ordinary course of business;

(b) the approval of a compromise or settlement of a controversy;

(c) the dismissal or conversion of a case to another chapter;

(d) the employment of professional persons;

(e) an application for compensation or reimbursement of expenses;

(f) a motion for, or approval of an agreement relating to, the use of cash collateral or authority to obtain credit;

(g) the appointment of a trustee or examiner in a chapter 11 reorganization case;

(h) the approval of a disclosure statement;

(i) the confirmation of a plan;

(j) an objection to, or waiver or revocation of, the debtor's discharge;

(k) any other matter in which the United States trustee requests copies of filed papers or the court orders copies transmitted to the United States trustee.

(Added Apr. 30, 1991, eff. Aug. 1, 1991.)

Rule 9035. Applicability of Rules in Judicial Districts in Alabama and North Carolina

In any case under the Code that is filed in or transferred to a district in the State of Alabama or the State of North Carolina and in which a United States trustee is not authorized to act, these rules apply to the extent that they are not inconsistent with any federal statute effective in the case.

(Added Apr. 30, 1991, eff. Aug. 1, 1991; amended Apr. 11, 1997, eff. Dec. 1, 1997.)

Rule 9036. Notice by Electronic Transmission

Whenever the clerk or some other person as directed by the court is required to send notice by mail and the entity entitled to receive the notice requests in writing that, instead of notice by mail, all or part of the information required to be contained in the notice be sent by a specified type of electronic transmission, the court may direct the clerk or other person to send the information by such electronic transmission. Notice by electronic means is complete on transmission.

(Added Apr. 22, 1993, eff. Aug. 1, 1993; amended Apr. 25, 2005, eff. Dec. 1, 2005.)

Rule 9037. Privacy Protection for Filings Made With the Court

(a) Redacted filings

Unless the court orders otherwise, in an electronic or paper filing made with the court that contains an individual's social-security number, taxpayer-identification number, or birth date, the name of an individual, other than the debtor, known to be and identified as a minor, or a financial-account number, a party or nonparty making the filing may include only:

(1) the last four digits of the social-security number and taxpayer-identification number;

(2) the year of the individual's birth;

(3) the minor's initials; and

(4) the last four digits of the financial-account number.

(b) Exemptions from the redaction requirement

The redaction requirement does not apply to the following:

(1) a financial-account number that identifies the property allegedly subject to forfeiture in a forfeiture proceeding;

(2) the record of an administrative or agency proceeding unless filed with a proof of claim;

(3) the official record of a state-court proceeding;

(4) the record of a court or tribunal, if that record was not subject to the redaction requirement when originally filed;

(5) a filing covered by subdivision (c) of this rule; and

(6) a filing that is subject to § 110 of the Code.

(c) Filings made under seal

The court may order that a filing be made under seal without redaction. The court may later unseal the filing or order the entity that made the filing to file a redacted version for the public record.

(d) Protective orders

For cause, the court may by order in a case under the Code:

(1) require redaction of additional information; or

(2) limit or prohibit a nonparty's remote electronic access to a document filed with the court.

(e) Option for additional unredacted filing under seal

An entity making a redacted filing may also file an unredacted copy under seal. The court must retain the unredacted copy as part of the record.

(f) Option for filing a reference list

A filing that contains redacted information may be filed together with a reference list that identifies each item of redacted information and specifies an appropriate identifier that uniquely corresponds to each item listed. The list must be filed under seal and may be amended as of right. Any reference in the case to a listed identifier will be construed to refer to the corresponding item of information.

(g) Waiver of protection of identifiers

An entity waives the protection of subdivision (a) as to the entity's own information by filing it without redaction and not under seal.

(Added Apr. 30, 2007, eff. Dec. 1, 2007.)

PART X—UNITED STATES TRUSTEES [ABROGATED]

INDEX TO
FEDERAL RULES OF BANKRUPTCY PROCEDURE

UNITED STATES BANKRUPTCY APPELLATE PANEL FOR THE SECOND CIRCUIT [TERMINATED]

Terminated Effective June 30, 2000

ORDER. IN THE MATTER OF THE TERMINATION OF THE BANKRUPTCY APPELLATE PANEL SERVICE OF THE SECOND JUDICIAL CIRCUIT

Pursuant to 28 U.S.C. § 158(b)(1)(C) as amended by the Bankruptcy Reform Act of 1994, the Judicial Council of the Second Circuit has determined there are insufficient judicial resources available in the Second Circuit justifying the continuation of the Bankruptcy Appellate Panel Service in the Second Circuit; it is hereby

ORDERED that the Bankruptcy Appellate Panel Service of the Second Circuit is terminated and that appeals of final judgments, orders and decrees and of interlocutory orders and decrees of bankruptcy judges entered in cases and proceedings previously referred to the Bankruptcy Appellate Panel and its appointed judges shall henceforth be referred to and heard by the respective United States District Courts in the Second Circuit; and it is hereby

ORDERED that the Bankruptcy Appellate Panel Service of the Second Circuit and its authority to hear and determine appeals from judgments, orders and decrees entered by bankruptcy judges from districts within the Second Circuit shall be terminated effective Friday, June 30, 2000."

[Dated: June 30, 2000.]

UNITED STATES BANKRUPTCY COURT FOR THE SOUTHERN DISTRICT OF NEW YORK

Including Amendments Received Through
September 1, 2017

ELECTRONIC CASE FILING

Procedures for the Filing, Signing and Verification of Documents by Electronic Means.

SELECTED GENERAL ORDERS

PART I. COMMENCEMENT OF CASE; PROCEEDINGS RELATING TO PETITION AND ORDER FOR RELIEF

RULE 1001–1. SHORT TITLE; APPLICABILITY

(a) **Short Title.** These rules shall be known and cited as the "Local Bankruptcy Rules."

(b) **Applicability.**

(1) The Local Bankruptcy Rules shall apply to all cases in this district governed by the Bankruptcy Code.

(2) Rules 1 through 35 and 63 through 82 of the Former Local Bankruptcy Rules shall apply to all cases in this district governed by the Bankruptcy Act.

[Adopted effective April 15, 1997.]

Comment

This rule is derived from Former Local Bankruptcy Rule 1.

Pursuant to Bankruptcy Rule 9029, "[e]ach district court . . . may make and amend rules governing practice and procedure . . . which are not inconsistent with" the Bankruptcy Rules and "[i]n all cases not provided for by rule, the court may regulate its practice in any manner not inconsistent with" the Bankruptcy Rules. The Judges of this district have been authorized to make and amend rules of practice and procedure pursuant to an order of the District Court (Griesa, C.J.), dated December 1, 1994.

Pursuant to the Memorandum of the Administrative Office of the United States Courts, dated November 22, 1994, the appropriate citation form for a local bankruptcy rule, using the uniform numbers, is "LBR _____." For example, this rule would be cited as "LBR 1001–1." In a brief or other document in which the district prescribing the rule must be identified, this rule would be cited as "S.D.N.Y. LBR 1001–1."

Except with respect to cases under the Bankruptcy Act, these Local Bankruptcy Rules supersede the Former Local Bankruptcy Rules.

From time to time, the Court may issue standing orders to supplement these Local Bankruptcy Rules, copies of which may be obtained from the Clerk and are available on the Court's website at http://www.nysb.uscourts.gov.

Capitalized terms used in these Local Bankruptcy Rules are defined in Local Bankruptcy Rule 9001–1.

[Comment amended effective July 28, 1998; August 2, 2004.]

RULE 1002–1. FILING OF PETITION

(a) A petition commencing a case under the Bankruptcy Code may be filed in any office of the Clerk or by electronic means established by the Court.

(b) **Notice Regarding Filing of a Chapter 11 or Chapter 15 Petition.** To the extent practicable, when a prospective chapter 11 debtor or chapter 15 petitioner anticipates the need to seek orders for immediate relief, counsel for the debtor or petitioner shall contact the United States Trustee and the

Clerk prior to filing a voluntary petition for relief under chapter 11 or chapter 15 of the Bankruptcy Code, for the purpose of advising the United States Trustee and the Clerk of the anticipated filing of the petition (without disclosing the identity of the debtor or petitioner) and the matters on which the debtor or petitioner intends to seek immediate relief.

[Adopted effective April 15, 1997. Amended effective August 1, 2013; December 1, 2016.]

Comment

This rule is derived from Former Local Bankruptcy Rule 9(a).

Practitioners should refer to Local Bankruptcy Rule 5005–2, which governs filing by electronic means.

Subsection (b) of this rule was added in 2016. Subsection (b) is designed to alert the Court of impending motions seeking immediate first day relief and to give the United States Trustee time to review proposed, complex orders that may be entered at the conclusion of a "first day hearing," including debtor in possession orders, and the like.

[Comment amended effective July 28, 1998; August 2, 2004; August 1, 2013; December 1, 2016.]

RULE 1005–1. DEBTOR'S ADDRESS IN PETITION

If not included in the debtor's post office address, the petition also shall state the debtor's residence and place of business, including the street number, street, apartment or suite number, and zip code.

[Adopted effective April 15, 1997.]

Comment

This rule is derived from Former Local Bankruptcy Rule 50(a).

RULE 1007–1. DUTY TO FILE A LIST OF CREDITORS AND OTHER ENTITIES WITH THE PETITION UNDER BANKRUPTCY RULE 1007(a)(1)

(a) Duties Generally. The list of creditors and other entities required to be filed under Bankruptcy Rule 1007(a)(1), and the creditors' matrix, shall include the full name and complete mailing address, including street number or post office box, if any, and zip code. If a debt is owed to an agency or department of the United States, the list and matrix shall include the name and address of the particular agency or department to which such debt is owed.

(b) Attorneys Filing Electronically.

(1) Debtor's counsel, at the time of filing the petition, shall (i) file the list of creditors and other entities required under Bankruptcy Rule 1007(a)(1), and (ii) unless a claims and noticing agent has been retained by the debtor in accordance with Local Bankruptcy Rule 5075–1, upload the creditors' matrix into the CM/ECF creditors' database. Reference should be made to Procedures for Filing Creditors' List, which shall be available on the Court's website (http://www.nysb.uscourts.gov/content/procedures-filing-creditors-list).

(2) When amending a schedule to add a creditor or other entity required to be on the list filed under Bankruptcy Rule 1007(a)(1), debtor's counsel shall file the amended schedule on the docket and pay the applicable fee and, unless a claims and noticing agent has been retained by the debtor in accordance with Local Bankruptcy Rule 5075–1, upload the newly-added entity into the CM/ECF creditor database. Additionally, debtor's counsel shall serve any newly-added entity with notice of the case and file timely proof of service in accordance with Local Bankruptcy Rule 9078–1.

(3) When amending a schedule to modify an address, the filing of the amended schedule shall be accompanied by a letter indicating which entity is the subject of the modification and how the address has been modified.

(c) Debtors Not Represented by an Attorney.

(1) A debtor not represented by an attorney shall, at the time of filing the petition, file a paper document setting forth, for each creditor or other entity required to be on the list filed under Bankruptcy Rule 1007(a), the full name and complete mailing address, including street number or post office box, if any, and zip code. In addition to such paper document, the debtor shall provide the list required to be filed under Bankruptcy Rule 1007(a)(1) in an electronic format (such as a USB flash drive, or CD). Reference should be made to Procedures for Filing Creditors' List, which shall be available on the Court's website (http://www.nysb.uscourts.gov/content/procedures-filing-creditors-list).

(2) When amending a schedule to add a creditor or modify a creditor's address, the filing of the amended schedule shall be accompanied by (i) a letter indicating which creditor is being added or, if modification of a creditor's address is sought, which creditor is the subject of the modification and how the address has been modified, and (ii) payment of the applicable fee. Additionally, the debtor shall serve any newly-added creditor or other entity with notice of the case and file timely proof of service in accordance with Local Bankruptcy Rule 9078–1.

[Adopted effective April 15, 1997. Amended effective July 28, 1998; August 1, 2013; December 1, 2016.]

Comment

Filing requirements with respect to lists, statements, and schedules were governed by General Order M–192 until it was superseded by General Order M–408 in 2010.

This rule was amended in 2013 to include the requirements established by General Order M–408, relating to the debtor's duty to file the list of creditors. The Clerk's Office maintains a register of mailing addresses of federal and state governmental units and certain taxing authorities pursuant to Bankruptcy Rule 5003(e). The amendments in 2013 also make mandatory certain procedures which General Order M–408 indicated that the debtor or the debtor's attorney "should" follow. Other clarifying amendments were also made to this rule. General Order M–408 was abrogated and replaced by this local rule in 2013.

Subsection (c)(1) of this rule was amended in 2016 to remove the reference to "diskette" as an acceptable electronic format. This format is no longer supported.

[Comment amended effective August 2, 2004; August 1, 2013; December 1, 2016.]

RULE 1007–2. DEBTOR'S AFFIDAVIT AND PROPOSED CASE CONFERENCE ORDER TO BE FILED IN CHAPTER 11 CASES

(a) **Contents of Affidavit.** A debtor in a chapter 11 case shall file an affidavit setting forth:

(1) the nature of the debtor's business and a concise statement of the circumstances leading to the debtor's filing under chapter 11;

(2) if the case originally was commenced under chapter 7 or chapter 13, the name and address of any trustee appointed in the case and, in a case originally commenced under chapter 7, the names and addresses of the members of any creditors' committee;

(3) the names and addresses of the members of, and attorneys for, any committee organized prior to the order for relief in the chapter 11 case, and a brief description of the circumstances surrounding the formation of the committee and the date of its formation;

(4) the following information with respect to each of the holders of the twenty (20) largest unsecured claims, excluding insiders: the name, the address (including the number, street, apartment or suite number, and zip code, if not included in the post office address), the telephone number, the name(s) of person(s) familiar with the debtor's account, the amount of the claim, and an indication of whether the claim is contingent, unliquidated, disputed, or partially secured;

(5) the following information with respect to each of the holders of the five (5) largest secured claims: the name, the address (including the number, street, apartment or suite number, and zip code, if not included in the post office address), the amount of the claim, a brief description and an estimate of the value of the collateral securing the claim, and whether the claim or lien is disputed;

(6) summary of the debtor's assets and liabilities;

(7) the number and classes of shares of stock, debentures, or other securities of the debtor that are publicly held, and the number of holders thereof, listing separately those held by each of the debtor's officers and directors and the amounts so held;

(8) a list of all of the debtor's property in the possession or custody of any custodian, public officer, mortgagee, pledgee, assignee of rents, or secured creditor, or agent for any such entity, giving the name, address, and telephone number of each such entity and the court in which any proceeding relating thereto is pending;

(9) a list of the premises owned, leased, or held under other arrangement from which the debtor operates its business;

(10) the location of the debtor's substantial assets, the location of its books and records, and the nature, location, and value of any assets held by the debtor outside the territorial limits of the United States;

(11) the nature and present status of each action or proceeding, pending or threatened, against the debtor or its property where a judgment against the debtor or a seizure of its property may be imminent; and

(12) the names of the individuals who comprise the debtor's existing senior management, their tenure with the debtor, and a brief summary of their relevant responsibilities and experience.

(b) **Additional Information if Business is to Continue.** If the debtor intends to continue to operate its business, the affidavit shall so state and set forth:

(1) the estimated amount of the weekly payroll to employees (exclusive of officers, directors, stockholders, and partners) for the thirty (30) day period following the filing of the chapter 11 petition;

(2) the amount paid and proposed to be paid for services for the thirty (30) day period following the filing of the chapter 11 petition—

(A) if the debtor is a corporation, to officers, stockholders, and directors;

(B) if the debtor is an individual or a partnership, to the individual or the members of the partnership; and

(C) if a financial or business consultant has been retained by the debtor, to the consultant; and

(3) a schedule, for the thirty (30) day period following the filing of the chapter 11 petition, of estimated cash receipts and disbursements, net cash gain or loss, obligations and receivables expected to accrue but remain unpaid, other than professional fees, and any other information relevant to an understanding of the foregoing.

(c) **When to File.** In a voluntary chapter 11 case, the affidavit shall accompany the petition. In an involuntary chapter 11 case, the affidavit shall be filed within fourteen (14) days after the date on which (i) the order for relief is entered, or (ii) a consent to the petition is filed.

(d) **Waiver of Requirements.** Upon motion of the debtor on notice to the United States Trustee showing that it is impracticable or impossible to furnish any of the foregoing information, the Court may dispense with any of the foregoing provisions, with the exception of those contained in paragraphs (1), (2), (3), and (4) of subdivision (a) of this rule.

(e) **Proposed Case Conference Order.** There shall be submitted to the Court with the chapter 11 petition a proposed case conference order in the form available on the Court's website (http://www.nysb.uscourts.gov/sites/default/files/1007-2-e-procedures.docx). Any initial conference shall be conducted approximately thirty (30) days after the filing of the petition or at such other time as the Court may direct.

[Adopted effective April 15, 1997. Amended effective July 28, 1998; August 2, 2004; December 1, 2009.]

Comment

This rule is derived from Former Local Bankruptcy Rule 52, with the exception of subdivisions (a)(5) and (a)(11), which are derived from former Standing Order M–147.

Subdivision (e) of this rule, added in 1996, is intended to aid in the implementation of Local Bankruptcy Rule 9076–1.

Subdivision (c) of this rule was amended in 2009 to change the time period from fifteen (15) to fourteen (14) days. The purpose of the amendment was to conform the time period in this rule to the 2009 time-related amendments to the Federal Rules of Bankruptcy Procedure. Throughout the Bankruptcy Rules, as well as the Local Bankruptcy Rules, most time periods that are shorter than thirty (30) days were changed so that the number of days is in multiples of seven (7), thereby reducing the likelihood that time periods will end on a Saturday or Sunday.

[Comment amended effective July 28, 1998; December 1, 2009.]

RULE 1007-3. CORPORATE OWNERSHIP STATEMENT TO BE FILED BY DEBTOR THAT IS A PARTNERSHIP OR JOINT VENTURE

The Corporate Ownership Statement required to be filed by the debtor with the petition under Bankruptcy Rule 1007(a)(1) shall also be filed by any debtor that is a general or limited partnership or joint venture. In addition to the information required under Bankruptcy Rule 7007.1, the statement shall include the name and address of any corporation whose securities are publicly traded in which the debtor directly or indirectly owns 10% or more of any class of the corporation's equity interests, and any general or limited partnership or joint venture in which the debtor owns an interest.

[Adopted effective August 2, 2004. Amended effective December 1, 2009.]

Comment

Bankruptcy Rule 1007(a), as amended effective December 1, 2003, requires a Corporate Ownership Statement containing the information described in Bankruptcy Rule 7007.1 to be filed by the debtor with the petition. Bankruptcy Rule 1007(a), however, only refers to a debtor that is a corporation. "Corporation" is broadly defined under section 101(9) of the Bankruptcy Code (and includes, among other entities, limited liability companies and other unincorporated companies or associations), but it does not cover general or limited partnerships. The reasons for which this rule was enacted—to give the Judges of this Court information by which they can determine whether or not they need to recuse themselves in a particular case—apply equally with respect to debtors that are general and limited partnerships, and joint ventures. This local rule requires a similar disclosure with respect to business organizations of that character.

The heading of this rule was amended in 2009 to more accurately reflect the substance of the rule.

[Comment adopted effective August 2, 2004; amended effective December 1, 2009.]

RULE 1009-1. NOTICE OF AMENDMENT OF SCHEDULES IN CHAPTER 11 CASES

Whenever the debtor or trustee in a chapter 11 case amends the debtor's schedules to change the amount, nature, classification, or characterization of a debt owing to a creditor, the debtor or trustee promptly shall transmit notice of the amendment to the creditor.

[Adopted effective April 15, 1997.]

Comment

This rule is derived from Former Local Bankruptcy Rule 53.

The term "characterization," as used in this rule, includes a description of whether the debt is disputed or undisputed, fixed or contingent, and liquidated or unliquidated.

RULE 1010-1. CORPORATE OWNERSHIP STATEMENT TO BE FILED IN AN INVOLUNTARY CASE BY EACH PETITIONER THAT IS A PARTNERSHIP OR JOINT VENTURE

The Corporate Ownership Statement required to be filed under Bankruptcy Rule 1010(b) by each petitioner that is a corporation shall also be filed by each petitioner that is a general or limited partnership or joint venture.

[Effective December 1, 2009.]

Comment

Bankruptcy Rule 1010(b), which became effective on December 1, 2008, requires a Corporate Ownership Statement containing the information described in Bankruptcy Rule 7007.1 to be filed by each petitioner that is a corporation. Bankruptcy Rule 1010(b), however, only refers to a petitioner that is a corporation. "Corporation" is broadly defined under section 101(9) of the Bankruptcy Code (and includes, among other entities, limited liability companies and other unincorporated companies or associations), but it does not cover general or limited partnerships. The reasons for which this rule was enacted—to give the Judges of this Court information by which they can determine whether or not they need to recuse themselves in a particular case—apply equally with respect to petitioners that are general and limited partnerships, and joint ventures. This local rule requires a similar disclosure with respect to business organizations of that character.

[Comment effective December 1, 2009.]

RULE 1011-1. CORPORATE OWNERSHIP STATEMENT TO BE FILED BY A PARTNERSHIP OR JOINT VENTURE THAT IS A RESPONDENT TO AN INVOLUNTARY PETITION OR PETITION FOR RECOGNITION

The Corporate Ownership Statement required to be filed under Bankruptcy Rule 1011(f) by a corporation responding to an involuntary petition or a petition for recognition of a foreign proceeding shall also be filed by any entity responding to an involuntary petition or a petition for recognition of a foreign proceeding that is a general or limited partnership or joint venture. If the responding entity is the debtor, in addition to the information required under Bankruptcy Rule 7007.1, the statement shall include the information described in Bankruptcy Rule 1007-3.

[Effective December 1, 2009.]

Comment

Bankruptcy Rule 1011(f), which became effective on December 1, 2008, requires a Corporate Ownership Statement containing the information described in Bankruptcy Rule 7007.1 to be filed by any corporation responding to an involuntary petition or a petition for recognition of a foreign proceeding. "Corporation" is broadly defined under section 101(9) of the Bankruptcy Code (and includes, among other entities, limited liability companies and other unincorporated companies or associations), but it does not cover general or limited partnerships. The reasons for which this rule was enacted—to give the Judges of this Court information by which they can determine whether or not they need to recuse themselves in a particular case—apply equally with respect to responding entities that are general and limited partnerships, and joint ventures. This local rule requires a similar disclosure with respect to business organizations of that character. If the responding entity is the debtor, the additional information described in the second sentence of Local Bankruptcy Rule 1007–3 must be included.

[Comment effective December 1, 2009.]

RULE 1014–1. TRANSFER OF CASES

Unless the Court orders otherwise, whenever a case is ordered transferred from this district, the Clerk, promptly after entry of the order, shall effectuate the transfer of the case to the transferee court.

[Adopted effective April 15, 1997. Amended effective August 1, 2013.]

Comment

This rule is derived from Former Local Bankruptcy Rule 7 and is an adaptation of Civil Rule 83.1 of the Local District Rules. Although not expressly stated, this rule contemplates that whenever transfer of a case under the Bankruptcy Code is ordered by a District Judge, the District Clerk will transmit the order and related documents to the Clerk of the Bankruptcy Court.

This rule was amended in 2013 to eliminate the need for the Clerk to transmit certified copies or originals of documents in the age of electronic transmission. The District Court similarly amended Civil Rule 83.1 of the Local District Rules in recognition of the electronic filing of documents.

[Comment amended effective July 28, 1998; August 1, 2013.]

RULE 1020–1. SMALL BUSINESS ELECTION [REPEALED EFFECTIVE OCTOBER 17, 2015]

RULE 1073–1. ASSIGNMENT OF CASES AND PROCEEDINGS

(a) Cases. Where the street address of the debtor set forth on the petition is in (i) New York County or Bronx County, the Clerk shall assign the case to a Judge sitting in New York County; (ii) Rockland County or Westchester County, the Clerk shall assign the case to a Judge sitting in Westchester County; or (iii) Dutchess County, Orange County, Putnam County, Sullivan County or Ulster County, the Clerk shall assign the case to a Judge sitting in Dutchess County. No case assignment will be based upon a post office box address. Where more than one Judge is sitting in a county, cases, other than chapter 13 cases, shall be assigned by random selection so that each Judge shall be assigned approximately the same number of cases. The Judges may direct that chapter 13 cases be referred to the same Judge or Judges. The Clerk shall have no discretion in determining the Judge to whom any case is assigned; the action shall be solely ministerial.

(b) Cases Involving Affiliates. Cases involving debtors that are affiliates shall be assigned to the same Judge.

(c) Proceedings. Except as otherwise provided in the Bankruptcy Code or Bankruptcy Rules, the assignment of a case to a Judge includes the assignment of all proceedings arising under title 11 or arising in, or related to, a case under title 11.

(d) Removed Actions. A removed action that does not arise out of a case pending in this Court shall be deemed to have venue in the county in which the court from which it was removed is situated and be assigned to a Judge in the manner provided in subdivision (a) of this rule.

(e) Adversary Proceedings or Contested Matters in Cases Pending Outside of This Court. An adversary proceeding or contested matter that does not arise out of a case pending in this Court shall be designated by the Clerk to an office of the Clerk in New York County, Westchester County, or Dutchess County. In making the designation, the Clerk shall take into consideration the residence of the defendant, the convenience of litigants, counsel, and witnesses, and the place where the cause of action arose. Unless the Court orders otherwise, the county designated by the Clerk shall be the place of trial and all other proceedings. The designation shall be made at the time of commencement or transfer of the adversary proceeding or contested matter, and the Clerk shall give prompt notice thereof to the parties or their counsel. After the designation, the adversary proceeding or contested matter shall be assigned to a Judge in the manner provided in subdivision (a) of this rule. Objections, if any, to the designation shall be made, on notice to opposing counsel, before the Judge to whom the adversary proceeding or contested matter has been assigned.

(f) Assignments and Reassignments. The Chief Judge shall supervise and rule upon all assignments and reassignments of cases, adversary proceedings, contested matters, and actions.

[Adopted effective April 15, 1997. Amended effective July 28, 1998; August 2, 2004.]

Comment

This rule is derived from Former Local Bankruptcy Rule 5. This rule was amended in 2004 to eliminate the use of a post office box address as the basis for case assignment.

[Comment amended effective August 2, 2004.]

RULE 1074–1. CORPORATE RESOLUTION; PARTNERSHIP STATEMENT

(a) Corporate Resolution. A voluntary petition or consent to an involuntary petition filed by a corporation shall be accompanied by a copy of the duly attested corporate resolution authorizing, or other appropriate authorization for, the filing.

(b) Partnership Statement. A voluntary petition filed by, or consent to an involuntary petition filed on behalf of, a partnership shall be accompanied by a duly attested statement that all partners whose consent is required for the filing have consented.

[Adopted effective April 15, 1997.]

Comment

Subdivision (a) of this rule is derived from Former Local Bankruptcy Rule 51. Subdivision (b) of this rule was added in 1996.

[Comment amended effective July 28, 1998.]

PART II. OFFICERS AND ADMINISTRATION; NOTICES; MEETINGS; EXAMINATIONS; ELECTIONS; ATTORNEYS AND ACCOUNTANTS

RULE 2002–1. NOTICE TO UNITED STATES TRUSTEE

Unless the case is a chapter 9 case or the United States Trustee requests otherwise, any notice required to be given to creditors under Bankruptcy Rule 2002 also shall be given to the United States Trustee.

[Adopted effective April 15, 1997.]

Comment

This rule is derived from Former Local Bankruptcy Rule 36.

RULE 2002–2. NOTICE OF PROPOSED ACTION OR ORDER WHEN NOT PROCEEDING BY MOTION [REPEALED EFFECTIVE DECEMBER 1, 2016]

Comment

Local Rule 2002–2 was repealed in 2016. The content of Local Rule 2002–2 was combined with Local Rule 9074–1, and now appears under Local Rule 9074–1(c).

RULE 2002–4. NOTICE OF PETITION FOR RECOGNITION IN CHAPTER 15 CASE

A foreign representative commencing a chapter 15 case shall forthwith give the notice required by Bankruptcy Rule 2002(q)(1) and shall file proof of service in accordance with Local Bankruptcy Rule 9078–1. In addition to the information required under Bankruptcy Rule 2002(q), the notice shall include a statement that, at the hearing, the Court may order the scheduling of a case management conference to consider the efficient administration of the case.

[Adopted effective August 1, 2013.]

Comment

This rule was added in 2013 to include in the Local Bankruptcy Rules the notice requirements relating to chapter 15 cases promulgated by General Order M–323, with stylistic changes to conform to Bankruptcy Rule 2002(q)(1). The second sentence was added so that parties have notice that the Court may, at the hearing on the petition for recognition of a foreign proceeding, schedule a case management conference to consider the efficient administration of the case. General Order M–323 was abrogated and replaced by this local rule in 2013.

[Comment added effective August 1, 2013.]

RULE 2004–1. UNIFORM DEFINITIONS FOR EXAMINATIONS AND REQUESTS FOR PRODUCTION OF DOCUMENTS UNDER RULE 2004

Civil Rule 26.3 of the Local District Rules shall apply to requests for examinations and the production of documents under Bankruptcy Rule 2004.

[Adopted effective August 1, 2013.]

Comment

This rule was added in 2013 to clarify that the uniform definitions set forth in Civil Rule 26.3 of the Local District Rules are applicable to examinations and the production of documents under Bankruptcy Rule 2004. Pursuant to Local Bankruptcy Rule 7026–1, the uniform definitions are applicable to discovery requests in cases and proceedings.

[Comment added effective August 1, 2013.]

RULE 2007.1–1 ELECTION OF TRUSTEE IN CHAPTER 11 CASES

A meeting of creditors convened for the purpose of electing a chapter 11 trustee pursuant to section 1104(b) of the Bankruptcy Code shall be deemed a meeting of creditors under section 341 of the Bankruptcy Code.

[Adopted effective April 15, 1997.]

Comment

This rule clarifies that a meeting convened for the purpose of electing a chapter 11 trustee pursuant to section 1104(b) of the Bankruptcy Code satisfies the requirement of section 702(b) of the Bankruptcy Code that a trustee be elected at a meeting of creditors held under section 341 of the Bankruptcy Code.

RULE 2014–1. EMPLOYMENT OF PROFESSIONAL PERSONS

An application for the employment of a professional person pursuant to sections 327 and 328 of the Bankruptcy Code shall state the specific facts showing the reasonableness of the terms and conditions of the employment, including the terms of any retainer, hourly fee, or contingent fee arrangement.

[Adopted effective April 15, 1997.]

Comment

This rule is derived from Former Local Bankruptcy Rule 39.

The information required by Bankruptcy Rule 2014(a) and this rule may be contained in the same application.

RULE 2015–1. STORAGE OF BOOKS AND RECORDS

The trustee or debtor in possession may place in storage, at the expense of the estate, the debtor's books, records, and papers. If stored, electronic records shall be stored in their original electronic formats. Non-electronic records may be converted and stored in electronic format.

[Adopted effective April 15, 1997. Amended effective December 1, 2016.]

Comment

This rule is derived from Former Local Bankruptcy Rule 43.

This rule sets no time limit on the storage of books and records. On request, the Court may issue an appropriate order limiting storage of the debtor's books, records, and papers. Disposal of the debtor's books, records, and papers is governed by sections 363 and 554 of the Bankruptcy Code.

This rule was amended in 2016 to permit the electronic storage of documents. The estate may electronically store preexisting electronic records in their original formatting and may convert and store other documents in electronic format as well. The rule was intended to provide a more cost-effective alternative to store the debtor's books, records and papers.

RULE 2016–1. COMPENSATION OF PROFESSIONALS

(a) A person requesting an award of compensation or reimbursement of expenses for a professional shall comply with the *Amended Guidelines for Fees and Disbursements for Professionals in Southern District of New York Bankruptcy Cases* promulgated by the Court, which shall be available on the Court's website (http://www.nysb.uscourts.gov/sites/default/files/2016-1-a-Guidelines.pdf).

(b) A person requesting an award of compensation or reimbursement of expenses for a professional shall use in connection with the application a form order that conforms to the *Order Granting Application(s) for Allowance of Interim/Final Compensation and Reimbursement of Expenses* promulgated by the Court, including any applicable schedules, which shall be available on the Court's website (http://www.nysb.uscourts.gov/sites/default/files/2016-1-b-order.docx).

(c) A person requesting an order establishing procedures for monthly compensation and reimbursement of expenses for professionals shall comply with the *Procedures for Monthly Compensation and Reimbursement of Expenses of Professionals* promulgated by the Court, which shall be available on the Court's website (http://www.nysb.uscourts.gov/sites/default/files/2016-1-c-procedures.pdf).

[Adopted effective April 15, 1997. Amended effective July 28, 1998; August 1, 2013.]

Comment

This rule was amended in 2013 to better refer to the guidelines, procedures, and form orders promulgated by General Orders M–389, M–412, M–427, and M–447, and to state in the rule where practitioners may access them. These documents also may be obtained from the Clerk. The guidelines, procedures, and forms may be amended by the Court after giving notice and opportunity for comment as is appropriate.

[Comment added effective July 28, 1998. Amended effective August 2, 2004; December 1, 2009; August 1, 2013.]

RULE 2016–2. COMPENSATION OR REIMBURSEMENT OF EXPENSES IN CHAPTER 7 CASES

Unless the Court orders otherwise, a person seeking an award of compensation or reimbursement of expenses in a chapter 7 case shall file an application with the Clerk and serve a copy on the trustee and the United States Trustee not later than twenty-one (21) days prior to the date of the hearing on the trustee's final account. Failure to file and serve an application within the time prescribed by this rule may result in its disallowance. Unless the Court orders otherwise, the

United States Trustee shall file any objection to such application at least two (2) days prior to the date of the hearing.

[Adopted effective April 15, 1997. Amended effective December 1, 2009.]

Comment

This rule is derived from former Standing Order M–90.

This rule supplements Local Bankruptcy Rule 2016–1 and facilitates the expeditious closing of chapter 7 cases. Pursuant to Local Bankruptcy Rule 5009–1, the trustee is obligated to set forth the language contained in this rule, or words of similar import, on the notice of filing of a final account.

This rule was amended in 2009 to change the relevant time period from twenty (20) to twenty-one (21) days. The purpose of the amendment was to conform the time period in this rule to the 2009 time-related amendments to the Federal Rules of Bankruptcy Procedure. Throughout the Bankruptcy Rules, as well as the Local Bankruptcy Rules, most time periods that are shorter than thirty (30) days were changed so that the number of days is in multiples of seven (7), thereby reducing the likelihood that time periods will end on a Saturday or Sunday.

The two business day deadline in this rule was also amended in 2009 to delete the reference to "business" days so that the time period will be computed by calendar days, consistent with the 2009 amendments to Bankruptcy Rule 9006(a).

[Comment amended effective July 28, 1998; December 1, 2009.]

RULE 2090–1. ADMISSION TO PRACTICE; WITHDRAWAL AS ATTORNEY OF RECORD

(a) General. An attorney who may practice in the District Court pursuant to Civil Rule 1.3(a) and (b) of the Local District Rules may practice in this Court.

(b) Pro Hac Vice. Upon motion to the Court, a member in good standing of the bar of any state or of any United States District Court may be permitted to practice in this Court in a particular case, adversary proceeding, or contested matter.

(c) Repealed.

(d) Pro Se Designation of Address. An individual appearing pro se shall include the individual's residence address and telephone number in the individual's initial notice or pleading.

(e) Withdrawal as Attorney of Record. An attorney who has appeared as attorney of record may withdraw or be replaced only by order of the Court for cause shown.

(f) Exceptions. Rule 2090–1 shall not apply to (i) the filing of a proof of claim or interest, or (ii) an appearance by a child support creditor or such creditor's representative.

[Adopted effective April 15, 1997. Amended effective July 28, 1998; August 2, 2004.]

Comment

Subdivisions (a) and (b) of this rule are derived from Former Local Bankruptcy Rule 3. Subdivisions (d), (e), and (f)(i) of this rule are derived from Former Local Bankruptcy Rule 4 and are an adaptation of Civil Rules 1.3(c), (d), and 1.4 of the Local District Rules. Subdivision (f)(ii) of this rule, added in 1996, is derived from section 304(g) of the Bankruptcy Reform Act of 1994, which permits child support creditors or their representatives to appear and intervene without charge and without meeting any special local court rule requirements for attorney appearances.

Subdivision (c) of this rule, requiring a local address for service, was repealed in 2004 because it could have been construed to require retention of local counsel when the attorney for the debtor or for a petitioning creditor does not have an office located in the district. [Comment amended effective July 28, 1998; August 2, 2004.]

PART III. CLAIMS AND DISTRIBUTION TO CREDITORS AND EQUITY INTEREST HOLDERS; PLANS

RULE 3003–1. REQUESTS FOR ORDERS ESTABLISHING DEADLINES FOR FILING CLAIMS IN CHAPTER 11 CASES

A request for an order establishing a deadline for filing proofs of claim in a chapter 11 case shall conform to the *Procedural Guidelines for Filing Requests for Orders to Set the Last Date for Filing Proofs of Claim*, which shall available on the Court's website (http://www.nysb.uscourts.gov/sites/default/files/3003-1-guidelines.pdf).

[Adopted effective August 2, 2004. Amended effective August 1, 2013.]

Comment

Procedures for requesting deadlines for filing claims, traditionally known as "bar dates," were originally promulgated by General Order M–386.

This rule was amended in 2013 to better refer to the procedures promulgated by General Orders M–386, amended by General Order M–453 and to state in the rule the link to the Court's website where practitioners may access the governing procedures. These guidelines, which also may be obtained from the Clerk, may be further amended by the Court in the future after giving notice and opportunity for comment as is appropriate.

[Comment added effective August 2, 2004. Amended effective December 1, 2009; August 1, 2013.]

RULE 3008–1. RECONSIDERATION OF CLAIMS

No oral argument shall be heard on a motion to reconsider an order of allowance or disallowance of a claim unless the Court grants the motion and specifically orders that the matter be reconsidered upon oral argument. If a motion to reconsider is granted, notice and a hearing shall be afforded to parties in interest before the previous action taken with respect to the claim may be vacated or modified.

[Adopted effective April 15, 1997.]

Comment

This rule, added in 1996, is derived from the Advisory Committee Note to Bankruptcy Rule 3008 and Former Local Bankruptcy Rule 13(i).

[Comment amended effective July 28, 1998.]

RULE 3011–1. DISPOSITION OF UNCLAIMED FUNDS UNDER A CONFIRMED CHAPTER 11 PLAN

(a) A chapter 11 plan shall provide for the distribution of any unclaimed property that cannot be distributed pursuant to

section 347(b) of the Bankruptcy Code, including that any unclaimed property may be

(1) Reallocated pursuant to the absolute priority rule;

(2) Reallocated for distribution pursuant to the plan's distribution scheme; or

(3) Donated to a not-for-profit, non-religious organization designated to receive unclaimed property.

(b) If a confirmed chapter 11 plan does not provide for the disposition of unclaimed property that cannot be distributed pursuant to section 347(b) of the Bankruptcy Code, such unclaimed property shall be reallocated for distribution pursuant to the plan's distribution scheme.

(c) If a confirmed chapter 11 plan does not provide for the disposition of unclaimed property that cannot be distributed pursuant to section 347(b) of the Bankruptcy Code, and all claims have been paid in full, then the Court may, after notice and a hearing, approve a motion by the plan administrator, or similar appointee, to donate any unclaimed property to an appropriate not-for-profit, non-religious organization.

[Effective December 1, 2016.]

Comment

This rule was added in 2016. Section 347(b) governs the treatment of any property "remaining unclaimed" at the expiration of the time allowed for acts necessary for participation in a plan confirmed under chapter 9, 11 or 12. Section 1143 establishes a five year limit from the date the confirmation order is entered to take such acts. Under section 347(b), any "security, money, or other property" remaining unclaimed at this time reverts to the debtor or to the entity that acquired the assets of the debtor under the plan.

Section 347(b) may not provide a satisfactory result in the liquidating chapter 11 case of a debtor in which no entity acquires most of the debtor's assets and the debtor essentially ceases to exist. Although there may remain a shell entity to which assets can be returned, doing so may serve no useful purpose. The rule's proposed solution is to require the inclusion of preemptive provisions in the chapter 11 liquidating plan, to provide for the alternative distribution of any unclaimed property within five years of the date the confirmation order is entered. This would avoid the five year distribution deadline created by section 1143 and the resulting application of section 347(b).

RULE 3015–1. CHAPTER 13 PLANS: MODEL PLAN AND CONFIRMATION ORDER; TREATMENT OF DEBTOR'S ATTORNEY'S FEES AS ADMINISTRATIVE EXPENSES; SERVICE

(a) **Model Plan and Confirmation Order.** In a chapter 13 case, the plan shall conform to the model Chapter 13 Plan adopted by the Court, which shall be available in the Clerk's office and on the Court's website (http://www.nysb.uscourts. gov/sites/default/files/3015-1-plan.doc), and the confirmation order shall conform to the model Confirmation Order adopted by the Court, which shall be available in the Clerk's office and on the Court's website (http://www.nysb.uscourts.gov/sites/default/files/3015-1-order.doc).

(b) Notice and Hearing for Attorney's Fees to Be Treated as Administrative Expense. If the compensation, or any portion thereof, of the attorney for a chapter 13 debtor is to be treated as an administrative expense under the plan, the attorney shall provide adequate notice of that fact to the trustee, the United States Trustee, and all creditors. The notice shall be deemed adequate if the plan is transmitted timely to all parties in interest and states with particularity the timing and amount of any payments to be made to the attorney.

(c) Service of Plan. Unless the court orders otherwise, the debtor shall serve the plan and any amended plan that changes the treatment of any party on the chapter 13 trustee, the United States trustee, and all creditors at least twenty-eight (28) days, plus an additional three days if service is by mail, before the confirmation hearing. The debtor shall file timely proof of service in accordance with Local Bankruptcy Rule 9078-1.

[Adopted effective April 15, 1997. Amended effective July 28, 1998; December 1, 2009; August 1, 2013.]

Comment

Subdivision (a) of this rule was amended in 2013 to state in the rule the link to the Court's website where practitioners may access the referenced forms, which were originally promulgated by General Order M–384. General Order M–384 was abrogated and replaced by this Local Rule and General Order M–455.

Subdivision (c) of this rule was amended in 2013 to include the requirements established by General Order M–406, relating to service of chapter 13 plans. General Order M–406 was abrogated and replaced by this local rule.

[Comment added effective December 1, 2009. Amended effective August 1, 2013.]

RULE 3015–2. MODIFICATION OF CHAPTER 13 PLAN BEFORE CONFIRMATION

If the debtor seeks to modify a chapter 13 plan prior to confirmation, the debtor shall serve a copy of the modified plan on the chapter 13 trustee, the United States Trustee, and such creditors as the Court may direct.

[Adopted effective April 15, 1997.]

Comment

This rule is derived from Former Local Bankruptcy Rule 60 and supplements section 1323 of the Bankruptcy Code.

RULE 3015–3. HEARING ON CONFIRMATION OF CHAPTER 13 PLAN

The debtor shall attend the hearing on confirmation of the chapter 13 plan, unless the Court, upon application of the debtor on such notice as the Court directs, and for cause shown, orders otherwise.

[Adopted effective April 15, 1997.]

Comment

This rule is derived from Former Local Bankruptcy Rule 59.

RULE 3017–1. PROPOSED DISCLOSURE STATEMENTS IN CHAPTER 9 AND CHAPTER 11 CASES: TRANSMITTAL AND DISCLAIMER

(a) Transmittal. Unless the Court orders otherwise, the proponent of a plan shall transmit all notices and documents required to be transmitted by Bankruptcy Rule 3017(a). Upon request, the Clerk shall supply the proponent, at a reasonable cost, with any available matrix of creditors for the purpose of preparing address labels.

(b) Disclaimer Other Than in Small Business Cases. Except in a case where the debtor is a small business, before a proposed disclosure statement has been approved by the Court, the proposed disclosure statement shall have on its cover, in boldface type, the following language, or words of similar import:

This is not a solicitation of acceptance or rejection of the plan. Acceptances or rejections may not be solicited until a disclosure statement has been approved by the Bankruptcy Court. This disclosure statement is being submitted for approval but has not been approved by the Court.

(c) Disclaimer in Small Business Cases. In a case where the debtor is a small business, after conditional approval but before final approval of a proposed disclosure statement has been given, the proposed disclosure statement shall have on its cover, in boldface type, the following language, or words of similar import:

The debtor in this case is a small business. As a result, the debtor is permitted to distribute and has distributed this disclosure statement before its final approval by the court. If an objection to this disclosure statement is filed by a party in interest, final approval of this disclosure statement will be considered at or before the hearing on confirmation of the plan.

[Adopted effective April 15, 1997. Amended effective July 28, 1998; October 17, 2005.]

Comment

Subdivisions (a) and (b) of this rule are derived from Former Local Bankruptcy Rule 55. Subdivision (c) of this rule, added in 1996, is derived from section 217 of the Bankruptcy Reform Act of 1994.

Bankruptcy Rule 3017(a) provides that the plan and the disclosure statement shall be mailed with the notice of the hearing to the debtor, the trustee, each committee, the Securities and Exchange Commission, the United States Trustee, and any party in interest who requests in writing a copy of the disclosure statement or plan.

Bankruptcy Rule 2002(b) permits the Court to require a party other than the Clerk to bear the responsibility for transmitting the notices and documents specified in this rule.

The reasonable cost, if any, provided for in subdivision (a) of this rule is the fee prescribed by the Judicial Conference of the United States pursuant to 28 U.S.C. § 1930(b).

[Comment amended effective July 28, 1998.]

RULE 3018–1. CERTIFICATION OF ACCEPTANCE OR REJECTION OF PLANS IN CHAPTER 9 AND CHAPTER 11 CASES

(a) **Certification of Vote.** At least seven (7) days prior to the hearing on confirmation of a chapter 9 or chapter 11 plan, the proponent of a plan or the party authorized to receive the acceptances and rejections of the plan shall certify to the Court in writing the amount and number of allowed claims or allowed interests of each class accepting or rejecting the plan and any ballots not counted. A copy of the certification shall be served upon the debtor, the trustee, each committee, and the United States Trustee. The Court may find that the plan has been accepted or rejected on the basis of the certification.

(b) **Notice of Ineffective Election.** If a plan in a chapter 9 or chapter 11 case permits the holder of a claim or interest to make an election with respect to the treatment of the claim or interest, and for any reason the holder's election is deemed ineffective or otherwise is not counted by the person authorized to tabulate ballots, that person shall give notice of that fact to the holder at least seven (7) days prior to the hearing on confirmation.

[Adopted effective April 15, 1997. Amended effective July 28, 1998; December 1, 2009; December 1, 2016.]

Comment

Subdivision (a) of this rule is derived from Former Local Bankruptcy Rule 54 and is intended to permit the Court to rely on a certification in determining whether a plan has been accepted or rejected under section 1126 of the Bankruptcy Code. If an issue has been raised with respect to the acceptance or rejection of a plan, the Court may hold an evidentiary hearing. Where acceptances or rejections of a plan of reorganization have been solicited prior to the commencement of the case, the certification may be filed together with the petition.

Subdivision (b) of this rule, added in 1996, is intended to enable a creditor or interest holder who has the right to elect the treatment of its claim or interest on a ballot to be notified if its ballot was not counted or was rejected, and therefore that its election may not be effective.

Subdivisions (a) and (b) of this rule were amended in 2009 to change the time periods from five to seven days. The purpose of the amendment was to conform the time periods in this rule to the 2009 time- related amendments to the Federal Rules of Bankruptcy Procedure. Throughout the Bankruptcy Rules, as well as the Local Bankruptcy Rules, most time periods that are shorter than 30 days were changed so that the number of days is in multiples of seven, thereby reducing the likelihood that time periods will end on a Saturday or Sunday.

Subdivision (a) of the rule was amended in 2016 to require the proponent of the plan, or party authorized to receive votes on the plan, to include in the certification to the Court any ballots not counted. This was done to enhance transparency and increase access to voting results.

[Comment amended effective July 28, 1998; December 1, 2009; December 1, 2016.]

RULE 3018–2. ACCEPTANCES OR REJECTIONS OF PLAN SOLICITED BEFORE PETITION IN CHAPTER 11 CASES

A party seeking to obtain confirmation of any plan proposed and accepted before the commencement of a chapter 11 case shall comply with the *Procedural Guidelines for Prepackaged Chapter 11 Cases*, which shall be available on the Court's website   (http://www.nysb.uscourts.gov/sites/default/files/change_to3003-1-guidelines.pdf).

[Adopted effective July 28, 1998. Amended effective August 2, 2004; August 1, 2013.]

Comment

Procedures with respect to prepackaged chapter 11 plans were promulgated by General Order M–387. This rule was amended in 2013 to specify the title of the procedures promulgated by General Order M–387 and to state in the rule the link to the Court's website where practitioners may access the governing procedures. The procedures set forth in the *Procedural Guidelines for Prepackaged Chapter 11 Cases*, which also may be obtained from the Clerk, may be further amended by the Court after giving notice and opportunity for comment as is appropriate.

[Comment amended effective August 2, 2004; December 1, 2009; August 1, 2013.]

RULE 3019–1. MODIFICATION OF CHAPTER 11 PLAN BEFORE CLOSE OF VOTING

If the proponent of a chapter 11 plan files a modification of the plan after transmission of the approved disclosure statement and before the close of voting on the plan, the proponent shall serve a copy of the plan, as modified, upon the debtor, the trustee, each committee, the United States Trustee, all entities directly affected by the proposed modification, and such other entities as the Court may direct. On notice to such entities, the Court shall determine whether the modification adversely affects the treatment of the claim of any creditor or the interest of any equity security holder who has not accepted the modification in writing. If the Court determines that the modification is not adverse, the plan, as modified, shall be deemed accepted by all creditors and equity security holders who accepted the plan prior to modification. If the modification is adverse, the requirements of Bankruptcy Rule 3017 shall apply to the modified plan and any amendment of the disclosure statement necessitated by the modification.

[Adopted effective April 15, 1997.]

Comment

This rule is derived from Former Local Bankruptcy Rule 56.

Pursuant to section 1127(a) of the Bankruptcy Code, the proponent of a chapter 11 plan may modify the plan at any time before confirmation. While Bankruptcy Rule 3019 governs modification of a plan after acceptance and before confirmation, this rule governs modification subsequent to the transmission of an approved disclosure statement and before the close of voting.

RULE 3020–1. TIME FOR OBJECTING TO CONFIRMATION IN CHAPTER 9 AND CHAPTER 11 CASES

Unless the Court orders otherwise, objections to confirmation of a plan in a chapter 9 or chapter 11 case shall be filed not later than seven (7) days prior to the first date set for the hearing to consider confirmation of the plan.

[Adopted effective April 15, 1997. Amended effective December 1, 2009; August 1, 2013.]

Comment

This rule, which is derived from Former Local Bankruptcy Rule 57, designates a fixed time for objecting to confirmation as permitted by Bankruptcy Rule 3020(b)(1). The three (3) day deadline was amended to seven (7) days in 2009 to give the Court and the parties more time to consider objections before the confirmation hearing.

Former subdivision (b) of this rule required disclosure of the circumstances surrounding the withdrawal of, or failure to prosecute, any objections to confirmation. This subdivision was abrogated in 2013 so as to leave to the Court's discretion on a case-by-case basis whether to require disclosure, and the manner and extent of such disclosure, of the terms of any agreement between the plan proponent and the objecting party relating to the withdrawal of, or the failure to prosecute, an objection to confirmation of a plan.

[Comment amended effective December 1, 2009; August 1, 2013.]

RULE 3021–1. POST–CONFIRMATION REQUIREMENTS IN CHAPTER 11 CASES

(a) Unless the Court orders otherwise, within fourteen (14) days after the entry of an order confirming a chapter 11 plan, the plan proponent or other responsible person under the plan shall submit to the Court on presentment in accordance with Local Bankruptcy Rule 9074–1 a proposed order that shall contain a timetable with the steps proposed for achieving substantial consummation of the plan and entry of a final decree, including resolution of claims and resolution of avoidance and other bankruptcy court litigation outstanding or contemplated. The law firms or individuals responsible for safeguarding and accounting for the proceeds of all recoveries on behalf of the estate shall be identified.

(b) Unless the Court orders otherwise, the plan proponent or responsible person under the plan shall submit to the Court a report whenever necessary, but no less than every six months after the entry of the order issued in accordance with subdivision (a) of this rule, identifying the actions taken under the order, the location of and steps taken to protect any funds or other property recovered on behalf of the estate, and any necessary revisions to the timetable.

(c) Unless the Court orders otherwise, as a condition to serving as a liquidating trustee or a successor trustee to a post confirmation liquidating, or similar trust, the liquidating plan shall specify what steps the trustee shall take to monitor and ensure the safety of the trusts' assets.

[Adopted effective April 15, 1997. Amended effective July 28, 1998; August 2, 2004; December 1, 2009; August 1, 2013; December 1, 2016.]

Comment

This rule is derived from former Standing Order M–111. Where the circumstances warrant, the Court has the discretion to alter the time periods prescribed herein. This rule was amended in 2004 to repeal former subdivision (b) and delete paragraph (3) of the former Post–Confirmation Order and Notice form contained in subdivision (c), each of which related to the post-confirmation requirement to pay to the Clerk any special charges that may be assessed by the Court. The Court no longer assesses such charges.

Paragraph (3) of the former Post–Confirmation Order and Notice form contained in subdivision (c) of this rule was amended in 2009 to change the time period from fifteen (15) to fourteen (14) days. The purpose of the amendment was to conform the time period in this rule to the 2009 time-related amendments to the Federal Rules of Bankruptcy Procedure. Throughout the Bankruptcy Rules, as well as the Local Bankruptcy Rules, most time periods that are shorter than thirty (30) days were changed so that the number of days is in multiples of seven (7), thereby reducing the likelihood that time periods will end on a Saturday or Sunday.

This rule was amended in 2013 regarding post-confirmation requirements in chapter 11 cases. The "Post–Confirmation Order and Notice" form was abrogated.

Subsection (c) of this rule was added in 2016 to require the post-confirmation liquidating trustee to disclose the procedures that will be taken to secure the trusts' assets. Subsection (c) is not meant to expand or limit the scope of a trustee's fiduciary duties.

[Comment amended effective July 28, 1998; August 2, 2004; December 1, 2009; August 1, 2013; December 1, 2016.]

RULE 3022–1. CLOSING REPORTS IN CHAPTER 11 CASES

Unless the Court orders otherwise, within fourteen (14) days after the estate is fully administered and the Court has discharged any trustee serving in the case, the debtor, trustee, or estate representative, shall file and serve upon the United States Trustee a closing report substantially in the form available on the Court's website (http://www.nysb.uscourts.gov/sites/default/files/3022-1-report.docx).

[Adopted effective April 15, 1997. Amended effective July 28, 1998; December 1, 2009; August 1, 2013; December 1, 2016.]

Comment

This rule was amended in 2009 to change the time period from fifteen (15) to fourteen (14) days. The purpose of the amendment was to conform the time period in this rule to the 2009 time-related amendments to the Federal Rules of Bankruptcy Procedure. Throughout the Bankruptcy Rules, as well as the Local Bankruptcy Rules, most time periods that are shorter than thirty (30) days were changed so that the number of days is in multiples of seven (7), thereby reducing the likelihood that time periods will end on a Saturday or Sunday.

This rule was amended in 2013 to conform to section 350(a) of the Bankruptcy Code. Prior to its amendment, the rule required a closing report within fourteen (14) days following "substantial consummation," which required that distributions under the plan be commenced rather than completed. Despite substantial consummation, there may have remained unresolved claim allowance litigation, preference and fraudulent conveyance adversary proceedings, and other proceedings that should have been resolved before the case was closed. The amended language of this rule tracks section 350(a) on the closing of cases. This amended rule should give greater assistance to the Court, which is required by Bankruptcy Rule 3022 to enter a final decree closing the case after the estate is fully administered.

The amendment to this rule in 2013 also provides a link to the closing report form on the Court's website.

This rule was amended in 2016 to allow any estate representative to file and serve the closing report on the United States Trustee.

[Comment added effective December 1, 2009. Amended effective August 1, 2013; December 1, 2016.]

PART IV. THE DEBTOR: DUTIES AND BENEFITS
RULE 4001–1. RELIEF FROM AUTOMATIC STAY

(a) A party moving for relief from the automatic stay under section 362 of the Bankruptcy Code shall obtain a return date for the motion that is not more than thirty (30) days after the date on which the motion will be filed.

(b) If the debtor is an individual, the motion shall be supported by an affidavit, based on personal knowledge, attesting to the circumstances of any default with respect to an obligation related to the motion.

(c) If the debtor is an individual, a party moving for relief from the automatic stay under section 362 of the Bankruptcy Code relating to a mortgage on real property or a security interest in a cooperative apartment shall file, as an exhibit to the motion, a completed copy of the following form. Compliance with this subdivision shall constitute compliance with subdivision (b) of this rule.

[Adopted April 15, 1997. Amended effective August 2, 2004; August 4, 2008.]

Comment

This rule is derived from Former Local Bankruptcy Rule 44(a)

Bankruptcy Rule 4001(a) provides that a request for relief from the automatic stay shall be made by motion. Section 362(e) of the Bankruptcy Code contemplates that a hearing will commence within thirty (30) days from the date of the request for relief from the automatic stay. Local Bankruptcy Rule 9006–1 governs the time within which responsive papers may be served.

Subdivision (a) of this rule was amended in 2004 to put the burden of obtaining a timely return date on the movant. It does not attempt to deal with the ramifications of the movant's failure to comply with the rule.

Subdivision (b) of this rule was added in 2004 to assure the Court of the accuracy of allegations of default in cases concerning an individual debtor.

Subdivision (c) of this rule, which derives from General Order M–346 as amended by General Order M–347, was added in 2008 to assure the Court of the accuracy of allegations of default in proceedings relating to a mortgage on real property or a security interest in a cooperative apartment of an individual debtor. The Court may direct the submission of the form set forth in subdivision (c) of this rule in connection with other motions, including motions for adequate protection.

[Comment amended effective August 2, 2004; August 4, 2008.]

UNITED STATES BANKRUPTCY COURT SOUTHERN DISTRICT OF NEW YORK

--- X
<CASE CAPTION>   CASE NO. ___–____ (____)

--- X

RELIEF FROM STAY—REAL ESTATE AND
COOPERATIVE APARTMENTS

I, _____ <NAME AND TITLE> OF _____ <NAME OF ORGANIZATION/CORPORATION/MOVING PARTY> (HEREINAFTER, "MOVANT"), HEREBY DECLARE (OR CERTIFY, VERIFY, OR STATE):

BACKGROUND INFORMATION

1. REAL PROPERTY OR COOPERATIVE APARTMENT ADDRESS WHICH IS THE SUBJECT OF THIS MOTION: ___
_____

2. LENDER NAME: _____

3.   DATE OF MORTGAGE <MM/DD/YYYY>: _____

4.   POST-PETITION PAYMENT ADDRESS:

_____

_____

DEBT/VALUE REPRESENTATIONS

5.   TOTAL PRE-PETITION AND POST-PETITION INDEBTEDNESS OF DEBTOR(S) TO MOVANT AT THE TIME OF
FILING THE MOTION: $ _____

(Note: this amount may not be relied on as a "payoff" quotation.)

6.   MOVANT'S ESTIMATED MARKET VALUE OF THE REAL PROPERTY OR COOPERATIVE APARTMENT: $ _____

7.   SOURCE OF ESTIMATED VALUATION: _____

STATUS OF DEBT AS OF THE PETITION DATE

8.   TOTAL PRE-PETITION INDEBTEDNESS OF DEBTOR(S) TO MOVANT AS OF PETITION FILING DATE:
$ _____

   A.   AMOUNT OF PRINCIPAL: $ _____

   B.   AMOUNT OF INTEREST: $ _____

   C.   AMOUNT OF ESCROW (TAXES AND INSURANCE): $ _____

   D.   AMOUNT OF FORCED PLACE INSURANCE EXPENDED BY MOVANT: $ _____

   E.   AMOUNT OF ATTORNEYS' FEES BILLED TO DEBTOR(S) PRE-PETITION: $ _____

   F.   AMOUNT OF PRE-PETITION LATE FEES, IF ANY, BILLED TO DEBTOR(S): $ _____

9.   CONTRACTUAL INTEREST RATE: _____ (If interest rate is (or was) adjustable, please list the
rate(s) and date(s) the rate(s) was/were in effect on a separate sheet and attach the sheet as an
exhibit to this form; please list the exhibit number here: ___.)

10.   PLEASE EXPLAIN ANY ADDITIONAL PRE-PETITION FEES, CHARGES OR AMOUNTS CHARGED TO DEBT-
OR'S/DEBTORS' ACCOUNT AND NOT LISTED ABOVE:

_____

(If additional space is needed, please list the amounts on a separate sheet and attach the sheet as an
exhibit to this form; please list the exhibit number here: ___.)

AMOUNT OF ALLEGED POST–PETITION DEFAULT

(AS OF _____ <MM/DD/YYYY>)

11.   DATE LAST PAYMENT WAS RECEIVED: _____ <MM/DD/YYYY>

12.   ALLEGED TOTAL NUMBER OF PAYMENTS DUE POST-PETITION FROM FILING OF PETITION THROUGH PAY-
MENT DUE ON _____ <MM/DD/YYYY>: _____.

13.   PLEASE LIST ALL POST-PETITION PAYMENTS ALLEGED TO BE IN DEFAULT:

ALLEGED PAYMENT DUE DATE	ALLEGED AMOUNT DUE	AMOUNT RECEIVED	AMOUNT APPLIED TO PRINCIPAL	AMOUNT APPLIED TO INTEREST	AMOUNT APPLIED TO ESCROW	LATE FEE CHARGED (IF ANY)

Alleged Payment Due Date	Alleged Amount Due	Amount Received	Amount Applied to Principal	Amount Applied to Interest	Amount Applied to Escrow	Late Fee Charged (If Any)
TOTALS:	$	$	$	$	$	$

14. AMOUNT OF MOVANT'S ATTORNEYS' FEES BILLED TO DEBTOR FOR THE PREPARATION, FILING AND PROSECUTION OF THIS MOTION: $ _____

15. AMOUNT OF MOVANT'S FILING FEE FOR THIS MOTION: $ _____

16. OTHER ATTORNEYS' FEES BILLED TO DEBTOR POST-PETITION: $ _____

17. AMOUNT OF MOVANT'S POST-PETITION INSPECTION FEES: $ _____

18. AMOUNT OF MOVANT'S POST-PETITION APPRAISAL/BROKER'S PRICE OPINION: $ _____

19. AMOUNT OF FORCED PLACED INSURANCE OR INSURANCE PROVIDED BY THE MOVANT POST-PETITION: $ _____

20. SUM HELD IN SUSPENSE BY MOVANT IN CONNECTION WITH THIS CONTRACT, IF APPLICABLE: $ _____

21. AMOUNT OF OTHER POST-PETITION ADVANCES OR CHARGES, FOR EXAMPLE, TAXES, INSURANCE INCURRED BY DEBTOR, ETC.: $ _____

REQUIRED ATTACHMENTS TO MOTION

Please attach the following documents to this motion and indicate the exhibit number associated with the documents.

(1) Copies of documents that indicate Movant's interest in the subject property. For purposes of example only, a complete and legible copy of the promissory note or other debt instrument together with a complete and legible copy of the mortgage and any assignments in the chain from the original mortgagee to the current moving party. (Exhibit ___.)

(2) Copies of documents establishing proof of standing to bring this Motion. (Exhibit ___.)

(3) Copies of documents establishing that Movant's interest in the real property or cooperative apartment was perfected. For the purposes of example only, a complete and legible copy of the Financing Statement (UCC–1) filed with either the Clerk's Office or the Register of the county the property or cooperative apartment is located in. (Exhibit ___.)

CERTIFICATION FOR BUSINESS RECORDS

I CERTIFY THAT THE INFORMATION PROVIDED IN THIS FORM AND/OR ANY EXHIBITS ATTACHED TO THIS FORM (OTHER THAN THE TRANSACTIONAL DOCUMENTS ATTACHED AS REQUIRED BY PARAGRAPHS 1, 2 AND 3, IMMEDIATELY ABOVE) IS DERIVED FROM RECORDS THAT WERE MADE AT OR NEAR THE TIME OF THE OCCURRENCE OF THE MATTERS SET FORTH BY, OR FROM INFORMATION TRANSMITTED BY, A PERSON WITH KNOWLEDGE OF THOSE MATTERS, WERE KEPT IN THE COURSE OF THE REGULARLY CONDUCTED ACTIVITY; AND WERE MADE BY THE REGULARLY CONDUCTED ACTIVITY AS A REGULAR PRACTICE.

I FURTHER CERTIFY THAT COPIES OF ANY TRANSACTIONAL DOCUMENTS ATTACHED TO THIS FORM AS REQUIRED BY PARAGRAPHS 1, 2 AND 3, IMMEDIATELY ABOVE, ARE TRUE AND ACCURATE COPIES OF THE ORIGINAL DOCUMENTS. I FURTHER CERTIFY THAT THE ORIGINAL DOCUMENTS ARE IN MOVANT'S POSSESSION, EXCEPT AS FOLLOWS: _____.

DECLARATION

I, _____ <NAME AND TITLE> OF _____ <NAME OF MOVANT>, HEREBY DECLARE (OR CERTIFY, VERIFY, OR STATE) PURSUANT TO 28 U.S.C. § 1746 UNDER PENALTY OF PERJURY THAT THE FOREGOING IS TRUE AND CORRECT BASED ON PERSONAL KNOWLEDGE OF THE MOVANT'S BOOKS AND BUSINESS RECORDS.

EXECUTED AT _____ <CITY/TOWN>, ___ <STATE> ON THIS ___ DAY OF <MONTH>, 20 ___ <YEAR>.

<PRINT NAME>
<TITLE>
<MOVANT>
<STREET ADDRESS>
<CITY, STATE AND ZIP CODE>

RULE 4001–1.1 PAYMENT AND CURE OF PRE–PETITION JUDGMENT OF POSSESSION INVOLVING RESIDENTIAL PROPERTY

(a) A debtor is deemed to have complied with section 362(l)(1) of the Bankruptcy Code by:

(1) Making the required certification by completing Official Form 101A, Initial Statement About An Eviction Judgment Against You, including the landlord's name and address; and

(2) Delivering to the Clerk, together with the Voluntary Petition (or within one day of the filing, if the Voluntary Petition is filed electronically) a certified or cashier's check or money order, made payable to the lessor, in the amount of any rent that would become due during the thirty-day period after the filing of the petition.

(b) If the debtor complies with the requirements set forth in subdivision (a), the Clerk shall, within one day, send notice of compliance to the lessor who shall then have the option, exercisable no later than fourteen (14) days after the date of the notice, to consent to receive the check (in which event the lessor shall provide payment instructions), or file an objection to the debtor's certification, which objection shall constitute a request for hearing. A lessor is deemed to have consented to receive the check if the lessor does not respond within the fourteen (14) day deadline, in which event the Clerk shall send the check to the lessor at the address set forth in the debtor's certification.

[Adopted effective August 1, 2013. Amended effective December 1, 2015.]

Comment

This rule was added in 2013 to include in the Local Bankruptcy Rules the requirements established by General Order M–385, which relate to the requirements set forth in section 362(l)(1) of the Bankruptcy Code. General Order M–385 was abrogated and replaced by this local rule in 2013. This rule was amended in 2015 to conform to the new Official Form 101A, Initial Statement About An Eviction Judgment Against You, effective December 1, 2015.

RULE 4001–2. REQUESTS FOR USE OF CASH COLLATERAL OR TO OBTAIN CREDIT

(a) Contents of Motion. The following provisions, to the extent applicable, are added to the enumerated lists of material provisions set forth in Bankruptcy Rule 4001(b)(1)(B), (c)(1)(B), and (d)(1)(B):

(1) the amount of cash collateral the party seeks permission to use or the amount of credit the party seeks to obtain, including any committed amount or the existence of a borrowing base formula and the estimated availability under the formula;

(2) material conditions to closing and borrowing, including budget provisions;

(3) pricing and economic terms, including letter of credit fees, commitment fees, any other fees, and the treatment of costs and expenses of the lender, any agent for the lender, and their respective professionals;

(4) any effect on existing liens of the granting of collateral or adequate protection provided to the lender and any priority or super priority provisions;

(5) any carve-outs from liens or super priorities;

(6) any cross-collateralization provision that elevates pre-petition debt to administrative expense (or higher) status or that secures pre-petition debt with liens on post-petition assets (which liens the creditor would not otherwise have by virtue of the pre-petition security agreement or applicable law);

(7) any roll-up provision which applies the proceeds of post-petition financing to pay, in whole or in part, pre-petition debt or which otherwise has the effect of converting pre-petition debt to post-petition debt;

(8) any provision that would limit the Court's power or discretion in a material way, or would interfere with the exercise of the fiduciary duties, or restrict the rights and powers, of the trustee, debtor in possession, or a committee appointed under sections 1102 or 1114 of the Bankruptcy Code, or any other fiduciary of the estate, in connection with the operation, financing, use or sale of the business or property of the estate, but excluding any agreement to repay post-petition financing in connection with a plan or to waive any right to incur liens that prime or are pari passu with liens granted under section 364 of the Bankruptcy Code;

(9) any limitation on the lender's obligation to fund certain activities of the trustee, debtor in possession, or a committee appointed under sections 1102 or 1114 of the Bankruptcy Code;

(10) termination or default provisions, including events of default, any effect of termination or default on the automatic stay or the lender's ability to enforce remedies, any cross-default provision, and any terms that provide that the use of cash collateral or the availability of credit will cease on (i) the filing of a challenge to the lender's pre-petition lien or the lender's pre-petition claim based on the lender's pre-petition conduct; (ii) entry of an order granting relief from the automatic stay other than an order granting relief from the stay with respect to material assets; (iii) the grant of a change of venue with respect to the case or any adversary proceeding;

(iv) management changes or the departure, from the debtor, of any identified employees; (v) the expiration of a specified time for filing a plan; or (vi) the making of a motion by a party in interest seeking any relief (as distinct from an order granting such relief);

(11) any change-of-control provisions;

(12) any provision establishing a deadline for, or otherwise requiring, the sale of property of the estate;

(13) any provision that affects the debtor's right or ability to repay the financing in full during the course of the chapter 11 reorganization case;

(14) in jointly administered cases, terms that govern the joint liability of debtors including any provision described in subdivision (e) of this rule; and

(15) any provision for the funding of non-debtor affiliates with cash collateral or proceeds of the loan, as applicable, and the approximate amount of such funding.

(b) Disclosure of Efforts to Obtain Financing and Good Faith. A motion for authority to obtain credit shall describe in general terms the efforts of the trustee or debtor in possession to obtain financing, the basis on which the debtor determined that the proposed financing is on the best terms available, and material facts bearing on the issue of whether the extension of credit is being extended in good faith.

(c) Inadequacy of Notice After Event of Default.

(1) If the proposed order contains a provision that modifies or terminates the automatic stay or permits the lender to enforce remedies after an event of default, either the proposed order shall require at least seven (7) days' notice to the trustee or debtor in possession, the United States Trustee and each committee appointed under sections 1102 or 1114 of the Bankruptcy Code (or the largest creditors if no committee has been appointed under section 1102 of the Bankruptcy Code), before the modification or termination of the automatic stay or the enforcement of the lender's remedies, or the motion shall explain why such notice provision is not contained in the proposed order.

(2) If the proposed order contains a provision that terminates the use of cash collateral, either the proposed order shall require at least five (5) days' notice before the use of cash collateral ceases (provided that the use of cash collateral conforms to any budget in effect) or the motion shall explain why such notice provision is not contained in the proposed order.

(d) Carve-Outs. Any provision in a motion or proposed order relating to a carve-out from liens or super priorities shall disclose when a carve-out takes effect, whether it remains unaltered after payment of interim fees made before an event of default, and any effect of the carve-out on any borrowing base or borrowing availability under the post-petition loan. If a provision relating to a carve-out provides disparate treatment for the professionals retained by a committee appointed under sections 1102 or 1114 of the Bankruptcy Code, when compared with the treatment for professionals retained by the trustee or debtor in possession, or if the carve-out does not include fees payable to either the Bankruptcy Court or the United States Trustee, reasonable expenses of committee members (excluding fees and expenses of professionals employed by such committee members individually), and reasonable post-conversion fees and expenses of a chapter 7 trustee, or if a carve-out does not include the costs of investigating whether any claims or causes of action against the lender exist, there shall be disclosure thereof under subdivision (a) of this Local Rule and the motion shall contain a detailed explanation of the reasons therefor.

(e) Joint Obligations. In jointly-administered cases, if one or more debtors will be liable for the repayment of indebtedness for funds advanced to or for the benefit of another debtor, the motion and the proposed order shall describe, with specificity, any provisions of the agreement or proposed order that would affect the nature and priority, if any, of any interdebtor claims that would result if a debtor were to repay debt incurred by or for the benefit of another debtor.

(f) Investigation Period Relating to Waivers and Concessions as to Prepetition Debt. If a motion seeks entry of an order in which the debtor stipulates, acknowledges or otherwise admits to the validity, enforceability, priority, or amount of a claim that arose before the commencement of the case, or of any lien securing the claim, either the proposed order shall include a provision that permits a committee appointed under section 1102 of the Bankruptcy Code and other parties in interest to undertake an investigation of the facts relating thereto, and proceedings relating to such determination, or the motion shall explain why the proposed order does not contain such a provision. The minimum time period for such committee or other party in interest to commence, or to file a motion to obtain authority to commence, any related proceedings as representative of the estate shall ordinarily be sixty (60) days from the date of entry of the final order authorizing the use of cash collateral or the obtaining of credit, or such longer period as the Court orders for cause shown prior to the expiration of such period.

(g) Content of Interim Orders. A motion that seeks entry of an emergency or interim order before a final hearing under Bankruptcy Rule 4001(b)(2) or (c)(2) shall describe the amount and purpose of funds sought to be used or borrowed on an emergency or interim basis and shall set forth facts to support a finding that immediate or irreparable harm will be caused to the estate if immediate relief is not granted before the final hearing.

(h) Adequacy of Budget. If the debtor in possession or trustee will be subject to a budget under a proposed cash collateral or financing order or agreement, the motion filed under Bankruptcy Rule 4001(b), (c), or (d) shall include a statement by the trustee or debtor in possession as to whether it has reason to believe that the budget will be adequate, considering all available assets, to pay all administrative expenses due or accruing during the period covered by the financing or the budget.

(i) Notice. Notice of a preliminary or final hearing shall be given to the persons required by Bankruptcy Rules 4001(b)(3) and 4001(c)(3), as the case may be, the United States Trustee, and any other persons whose interests may be directly affected by the outcome of the motion or any provision of the proposed order.

(j) Presence at Hearing. Unless the court directs otherwise,

(1) counsel for each proposed lender, or for an agent representing such lender, shall be present at all preliminary and final hearings on the authority to obtain credit from such lender, and counsel for each entity, or for an agent of such entity, with an interest in cash collateral to be used with the entity's consent shall be present at all preliminary and final hearings on the authority to use such cash collateral; and

(2) a business representative of the trustee or debtor in possession, the proposed lender or an agent representing such lender, and any party objecting to the motion for authority to obtain credit, each with appropriate authority, must be present at, or reasonably available by telephone for, all preliminary and final hearings for the purpose of making necessary decisions with respect to the proposed financing.

(k) Provisions of the Proposed Order.

(1) *Findings of Fact.*

(A) A proposed order approving the use of cash collateral under section 363(c) of the Bankruptcy Code, or granting authority to obtain credit under section 364 of the Bankruptcy Code, shall limit the recitation of findings to essential facts, including the facts required under section 364 of the Bankruptcy Code regarding efforts to obtain financing on a less onerous basis and (where required) facts sufficient to support a finding of good faith under section 364(e) of the Bankruptcy Code, and shall not include any findings extraneous to the use of cash collateral or to the financing.

(B) A proposed emergency or interim order shall include a finding that immediate and irreparable loss or damage will be caused to the estate if immediate financing is not obtained and should state with respect to notice only that the hearing was held pursuant to Bankruptcy Rule 4001(b)(2) or (c)(2), that notice was given to certain parties in the manner described, and that the notice was, in the debtor's belief, the best available under the circumstances.

(C) A proposed final order may include factual findings as to notice and the adequacy thereof.

(D) To the extent that a proposed order incorporates by reference to, or refers to a specific section of, a pre-petition or post-petition loan agreement or other document, the proposed order shall also include a statement of such section's import.

(2) *Mandatory Provisions.* The proposed order shall contain all applicable provisions included in the enumerated lists of material provisions set forth in Bankruptcy Rule 4001(b)(1)(B), (c)(1)(B), and (d)(1)(B), as supplemented by subsection (a) of this Local Rule.

(3) *Cross–Collateralization and Rollups.* A proposed order approving cross-collateralization or a rollup shall include language that reserves the right of the Court to unwind, after notice and hearing, the post-petition protection provided to the pre-petition lender or the pay down of the pre-petition debt, whichever is applicable, in the event that there is a timely and successful challenge to the validity, enforceability, extent, perfection, or priority of the pre-petition lender's claims or liens, or a determination that the pre-petition debt was undersecured as of the petition date, and the cross-collateralization or rollup unduly advantaged the lender.

(4) *Waivers, Consents or Amendments With Respect to the Loan Agreement.* A proposed order may permit the parties to enter into waivers or consents with respect to the loan agreement or amendments thereof without the need for further court approval provided that (i) the agreement as so modified is not materially different from that approved, (ii) notice of all amendments is filed with the Court, and (iii) notice of all amendments (other than those that are ministerial or technical and do not adversely affect the debtor) are provided in advance to counsel for any committee appointed under sections 1102 or 1114 of the Bankruptcy Code, all parties requesting notice, and the United States Trustee.

(5) *Conclusions of Law.* A proposed interim order may provide that the debtor is authorized to enter into the loan or other agreement, but it shall not state that the Court has examined and approved the loan or other agreement.

(6) *Order to Control.* The proposed order shall state that to the extent that a loan or other agreement differs from the order, the order shall control.

(7) *Statutory Provisions Affected.* The proposed order shall specify those provisions of the Bankruptcy Code, Bankruptcy Rules and Local Rules relied upon as authority for granting relief, and shall identify those sections that are, to the extent permitted by law, being limited or abridged.

(8) *Conclusions of Law Regarding Notice.* A proposed final order may contain conclusions of law with respect to the adequacy of notice under section 364 of the Bankruptcy Code and Bankruptcy Rule 4001.

[Adopted effective April 15, 1997. Amended effective August 4, 2008; December 1, 2009.]

Comment

This rule was amended in its entirety in 2008 to conform to the 2007 amendments to Bankruptcy Rule 4001 and to replace the procedures for requests for the use of cash collateral or to obtain credit that were governed by former General Order M–274. Thus, this rule should be read in conjunction with Bankruptcy Rule 4001 as the requirements contained in this rule are meant to supplement, but not duplicate, Bankruptcy Rule 4001. This rule is not intended to fundamentally change practice under former General Order M–274, except as expressly provided.

As provided in former General Order M–274, a single motion may be filed seeking entry of an interim order and a final order, which orders would be normally entered at the conclusion of the preliminary hearing and the final hearing, respectively, as those terms are used in Bankruptcy Rules 4001(b)(2) and (c)(2). In addition, where circumstances warrant, the debtor may seek emergency relief for financing limited to the amount necessary to avoid immediate and irreparable harm to the estate pending the preliminary hearing, but in the usual case, only a preliminary and a final hearing will be required.

Notwithstanding the provisions of subsection (i), emergency and interim relief may be entered after the best notice available under the circumstances; however, emergency and interim relief will ordinarily not be considered unless the United States Trustee and the Court have had a reasonable opportunity to review the motion, the financing agreement, and the proposed interim order, and the Court normally will not approve provisions that directly affect the interests of landlords, taxing and environmental authorities and other third-parties without notice to them.

As suggested in former General Order M–274, prospective debtors may provide substantially complete drafts of the motion, interim order, and related financing documents to the United States Trustee in advance of a filing, on a confidential basis. Debtors are encouraged to provide drafts of financing requests, including proposed orders, to the United States Trustee as early as possible in advance of filing to provide that office with the opportunity to comment.

The hearing on a final order for use of cash collateral under section 363(c) of the Bankruptcy Code, or for authority to obtain credit under section 364 of the Bankruptcy Code will ordinarily not commence until there has been a reasonable opportunity for the formation of a creditors committee under section 1102 of the Bankruptcy Code and either the creditors committee's appointment of counsel or reasonable opportunity to do so.

Reasonable allocations in a carve-out provision may be proposed among (i) expenses of professionals retained by committees appointed in the case, (ii) expenses of professionals retained by the debtor, (iii) fees payable to either the Bankruptcy Court or the United States Trustee, (iv) the reasonable expenses of committee members, and (v) reasonable post-conversion fees and expenses of a chapter 7 trustee, and the lender may refuse to include in a carve-out the costs of litigation or other assertions of claims against it.

As provided in former General Order M–274, non-essential facts regarding pre-petition dealings and agreements may be included in an order approving the use of cash collateral or granting authority to obtain credit under a heading entitled "stipulations between the debtor and the lender" or "background."

As provided in former General Order M–274, an interim order will not ordinarily bind the Court with respect to the provisions of the final order provided that (i) the lender will be afforded all the benefits and protections of the interim order, including a lender's section 364(e) and 363(m) protection with respect to funds advanced during the interim period, and (ii) the interim order will not bind the lender to advance funds pursuant to a final order that contains provisions contrary to or inconsistent with the interim order.

Subdivision (c)(1) of this rule was amended in 2009 to change the time period from five (5) to seven (7) days. The purpose of the amendment was to conform the time period in this rule to the 2009 time-related amendments to the Federal Rules of Bankruptcy Procedure. Throughout the Bankruptcy Rules, as well as the Local Bankruptcy Rules, most time periods that are shorter than thirty (30) days were changed so that the number of days is in multiples of seven (7), thereby reducing the likelihood that time period will end on a Saturday or Sunday.

The deadlines in subdivisions (c)(1) and (c)(2) of this rule were also amended in 2009 to delete the references to "business" days so that the time periods will be computed by calendar days, consistent with the 2009 amendments to Bankruptcy Rule 9006(a). The three (3) day deadline in subdivision (c)(2) of this rule was amended in 2009 to change the time to five (5) days to compensate for the change in the computation of time under the 2009 amendments to Bankruptcy Rule 9006(a).

[Comment amended effective December 1, 2009.]

RULE 4001–3. REQUESTS FOR USE OF CASH COLLATERAL OR TO OBTAIN CREDIT [REPEALED EFFECTIVE AUGUST 4, 2008].

Comment

This rule was repealed in 2008 because of the amendments to Local Bankruptcy Rule 4001–2 made in 2008, which govern cash collateral and financing motions.

RULE 4002–1. DUTIES OF DEBTORS—PROCEDURES RELATING TO THE IMPLEMENTATION OF BANKRUPTCY CODE SECTION 521

(a) Payment Advices Required by Section 521(a)(1)(B)(iv). In a chapter 7, chapter 12, or chapter 13 case in which the debtor is an individual, copies of payment advices or other evidence of current income made available to the trustee under Bankruptcy Rule 4002(b)(2) shall not be filed with the Court.

(b) Request by Party in Interest for an Order of Dismissal Under Section 521(i)(2). If a party in interest requests an order of dismissal under section 521(i)(2) of the Bankruptcy Code, the following procedures shall apply:

(1) The party in interest shall serve a copy of the request on the debtor's attorney and the debtor at the same time that the party in interest sends the request to the Court.

(2) If the debtor objects to the request within seven (7) days of service, the debtor's objection will be treated as a request for a hearing, which the Court shall schedule promptly.

(3) No order of dismissal will be entered until the debtor's objection has been resolved, except that nothing herein shall affect the right of any party in interest to seek dismissal, or the authority of the Court to dismiss the case, pursuant to any other provision of applicable bankruptcy law.

[Adopted effective December 1, 2009. Amended effective August 1, 2013.]

Comment

This rule was amended in 2013 to include in the Local Bankruptcy Rules the provisions contained in General Order M–382, relating to section 521(a)(1)(B)(iv) and section 521(i)(2) of the Bankruptcy Code. Subdivision (a) of this rule expands the scope of General Order M–382 by making it applicable chapter 12 cases, as well as in chapter 7 and chapter 13 cases and is amended further to conform to, and not duplicate, Bankruptcy Rule 4002(b). General Order M–382 was abrogated and replaced by this local rule in 2013.

[Comment added effective December 1, 2009. Amended effective August 1, 2013.]

RULE 4003–1. EXEMPTIONS

(a) Amendment to Claim of Exemptions. An amendment to a claim of exemptions pursuant to Bankruptcy Rules 1009 and 4003 shall be filed and served by the debtor or dependent of the debtor on the trustee, the United States Trustee, and all creditors.

(b) Automatic Extension of Time to File Objections to Claim of Exemptions in Event of Amendment to Schedules to Add a Creditor. Unless the Court orders otherwise, if the schedules are amended to add a creditor, and the amendment is filed and served either (i) fewer than thirty (30) days prior to the expiration of the time set forth in Bankruptcy Rule 4003(b) for the filing of objections to the list of property claimed as exempt, or (ii) at any time after such filing deadline, the added creditor shall have thirty (30) days from the date of service of the amendment to file an objection to the list of property claimed as exempt.

[Adopted effective April 15, 1997. Amended effective July 28, 1998; August 2, 2004.]

Comment

Subdivision (a) of this rule is derived from Former Local Bankruptcy Rule 37. See Bankruptcy Rule 4003(b), which permits the trustee or any creditor to object to the list of property claimed as exempt within thirty (30) days following the conclusion of the meeting of creditors held pursuant to Bankruptcy Rule 2003(a), or the filing of any amendment to the list or supplemental schedules unless, within such period, the Court grants additional time.

[Comment amended effective July 28, 1998; August 2, 2004.]

RULE 4004–1. AUTOMATIC EXTENSION OF TIME TO FILE COMPLAINT OBJECTING TO DISCHARGE IN EVENT OF AMENDMENT [REPEALED EFFECTIVE AUGUST 1, 2013]

Comment

This rule was abrogated in 2013. The procedures for extending the time to object to the debtor's discharge are governed by Bankruptcy Rule 4004(b). The rights of a creditor that had not been scheduled in time to file a timely objection to discharge, or a timely motion to extend the time to file an objection to discharge, are matters governed by substantive law.

RULE 4004–2. DEBTOR'S CERTIFICATION CONCERNING DOMESTIC SUPPORT OBLIGATIONS IN A CASE UNDER CHAPTER 12 OR CHAPTER 13

(a) In a chapter 12 or chapter 13 case, within thirty (30) days before the date on which the last payment is due under the plan, or when the debtor files a motion to request a hardship discharge under section 1228(b) or section 1328(b) of the Bankruptcy Code, whichever is earlier, the Standing Trustee shall furnish the debtor with a Debtor's Certification Regarding Domestic Support Obligations, Director's Procedural Form B2830, which shall be available on the Court's website (http://www.nysb.uscourts.gov/official-bankruptcy-forms).

(b) The debtor shall complete, sign, and return to the Standing Trustee the Debtor's Certification Regarding Domestic Support Obligations when submitting the check for the last payment under the chapter 12 or chapter 13 plan or, if the debtor has filed a motion to request a hardship discharge, no later than the date of the hearing on the debtor's motion. In a joint case, each debtor must complete and sign a separate Debtor's Certification Regarding Domestic Support Obligations.

(c) The Standing Trustee shall attach the completed Debtor's Certification Regarding Domestic Support Obligations when electronically filing the Notice of Request for a Discharge or, in a case in which the debtor seeks a hardship discharge, shall otherwise make it available on the docket of that case.

[Adopted effective August 1, 2013. Amended effective December 1, 2015.]

Comment

This rule was added in 2013 to include in the Local Bankruptcy Rules the provisions established by General Order M–338, relating to the debtor's certifications regarding domestic support obligations. Though General Order M–338 provided that the Standing Trustee "should" furnish the debtor with the certification form, and "should" attach the completed form to the Notice of Request for a Discharge, this rule makes these provisions mandatory. General Order M–338 was abrogated and replaced by this local rule in 2013.

This rule was amended in 2015 to conform to the renumbering of the Director's Procedural Form B2830, effective December 1, 2015.

RULE 4007–1. AUTOMATIC EXTENSION OF TIME TO FILE COMPLAINT TO DETERMINE DISCHARGEABILITY OF A DEBT IN EVENT OF AMENDMENT [REPEALED EFFECTIVE AUGUST 1, 2013]

Comment

This rule was abrogated in 2013. The procedures for extending the time to file a complaint objecting to the dischargeability of a debt are governed by Bankruptcy Rule 4007. The rights of a creditor that had not been scheduled in time to file a timely complaint to determine the dischargeability of a debt are governed by substantive law, including section 523(a)(3) of the Bankruptcy Code.

[Comment added effective August 1, 2013.]

RULE 4007–2. WITHDRAWAL OR SETTLEMENT OF PROCEEDINGS TO DETERMINE DISCHARGE AND DISCHARGEABILITY

(a) **Withdrawal of Complaint.** In the event of the withdrawal of a complaint objecting to discharge or failure to prosecute an adversary proceeding objecting to discharge, no discharge shall be granted unless the debtor shall make and file an affidavit and the debtor's attorney shall make and file a certification that no consideration has been promised or given, directly or indirectly, for the withdrawal or failure to prosecute.

(b) **Settlement of Proceedings.** In all instances not governed by section 524(d) of the Bankruptcy Code, no adversary proceeding to determine the dischargeability of a debt shall be settled except pursuant to an order of the Court after due inquiry into the circumstances of any settlement, including the terms of any agreement entered into between the debtor and creditor relating to the payment of the debt, in whole or in part.

[Adopted effective April 15, 1997.]

Comment

This rule is derived from Former Local Bankruptcy Rule 48.

RULE 4008–1. REAFFIRMATION AGREEMENTS

A person filing a reaffirmation agreement shall adhere to the *Guidelines for Filing a Reaffirmation Agreement in the Southern District of New York*, which shall be available on the

Court's website (http://www.nysb.uscourts.gov/sites/default/files/4008-1-guidelines.pdf).

[Adopted effective August 1, 2013.]

Comment

This rule was added in 2013 to include in the Local Bankruptcy Rules the requirements established by General Order M–404, relating to reaffirmation agreements. The procedures set forth in the *Guidelines for Filing a Reaffirmation Agreement in the Southern District of New York* may be amended by the Court after giving notice and opportunity for comment as is appropriate. The *Guidelines*, which are available on the Court's website, also may be obtained from the Clerk.

[Comment added effective August 1, 2013.]

PART V. COURTS AND CLERKS

RULE 5001–1. CLERK'S OFFICE: HOURS; AFTER HOURS FILING

Unless otherwise posted on the Court's website, the offices of the Clerk shall be open Monday through Friday, from 8:30 a.m. to 5:00 p.m., except on legal and Court holidays, and shall be closed on Saturdays and Sundays. When the Clerk's Office is closed, papers not filed electronically may be filed with the Court by depositing them in the night depository maintained by the District Clerk and are deemed filed as of the date and time stamped thereon. Any required fees for such filings shall be delivered to the Clerk's Office no later than noon on the next day.

[Adopted effective April 15, 1997. Amended effective July 28, 1998; August 2, 2004; December 1, 2009; August 1, 2013.]

Comment

This rule is derived from Former Local Bankruptcy Rule 8 as modified to conform to Civil Rule 1.2 of the Local District Rules.

Bankruptcy Rule 5001(c) permits the adoption of a local rule setting forth the business hours of the Clerk.

The District Clerk maintains a night depository at the United States Courthouse located at 500 Pearl Street, New York, New York. The filing of papers in the District Court's night depository is intended to be used where exigent circumstances exist and is not intended as a regular alternative for filing papers with the Court during normal business hours or electronically at any time.

Under Former Local Bankruptcy Rule 8, papers filed in the District Court's night depository were deemed filed in the Court as of 8:30 a.m. the following business day. In accordance with Civil Rule 1.2 of the Local District Rules and *Greenwood v. New York*, 842 F.2d 636 (2d Cir. 1988), this rule deems papers deposited in the District Court's night depository to have been filed as of the date and time stamped thereon.

The next business day deadline in this rule was amended in 2009 to delete the reference to "business" so that the time period will be consistent with the 2009 amendments to Bankruptcy Rule 9006(a).

This rule was amended in 2013 to clarify that the times and days when the Clerk's Office is opened may be altered as posted on the Court's website.

[Comment amended effective July 28, 1998; August 2, 2004; December 1, 2009 August 1, 2013.]

RULE 5005–1. FILING PAPERS

Except as provided in Local Bankruptcy Rule 1002–1, unless submitted by electronic means, all papers may be submitted for filing in the Clerk's office located in any of the three divisions of the Court identified in Rule 1073–1(a). However, all chambers copies required by Rule 9070–1(b) shall be submitted in the Clerk's office located where the Judge assigned to the case or proceeding sits.

[Adopted effective April 15, 1997. Amended effective July 28, 1998; August 2, 2004.]

Comment

This rule is derived from Former Local Bankruptcy Rule 9(a).

[Comment amended effective July 28, 1998.]

RULE 5005–2. FILING BY ELECTRONIC MEANS

Unless the Court directs otherwise, all attorneys practicing in the Court, including attorneys admitted pro hac vice, are required to file all pleadings, motions, or other documents (except documents to be placed under seal) by electronic means, and all such documents required to be signed or verified shall be signed or verified by electronic means, in each case consistent with the *Procedures for the Filing, Signing, and Verification of Documents by Electronic Means* issued by the Court, which shall be available on the Court's website (http://www.nysb.uscourts.gov/sites/default/files/5005-2-procedures.pdf). If electronic filing, signing, or verification is not feasible in a particular situation, the Court may provide reasonable accommodation or excuse the requirement that documents be filed, signed, or verified by electronic means under the particular circumstances.

[Adopted effective July 28, 1998. Amended effective August 2, 2004; August 1, 2013.]

Comment

This rule, which implements the authority contained in Bankruptcy Rule 5005(a), was amended in 2013 to clarify that all attorneys practicing in the Court are required to file, sign, and verify pleadings, motions, and other documents by electronic means, unless the Court directs otherwise in a particular case or the document is filed under seal. If electronic filing is not feasible in a particular situation, the Clerk may provide a reasonable accommodation or excuse the requirements of this rule under the particular circumstances.

This rule was also amended in 2013 to specify the title of the procedures promulgated by General Order M–399 and to state in the rule the link to the Court's website where practitioners may access the governing procedures governing filing, signing, and verifying papers by electronic means. The procedures also may be obtained from the Clerk. It is anticipated that these guidelines will be amended from time to time to account for changes in technology or the law.

[Comment amended effective August 2, 2004; August 1, 2013.]

RULE 5005–3. PAYMENT OF COURT FEES

(a) Unless another form of payment is required by the Court, filers shall pay by credit card, through the CM/ECF system, all applicable filing fees at the time of filing or by the end of the day on which the filing occurred.

(b) If fees are not paid within four days of the date incurred, the filer shall be locked out of the CM/ECF system until full payment is made.

[Adopted effective August 1, 2013.]

Comment

This rule was added in 2013 to state the means and timing regarding payment of the filing fees, as well as the consequences of a failure to pay such fees.

[Comment added effective August 1, 2013.]

RULE 5009–1. FINAL REPORT AND ACCOUNT AND CLOSING REPORT IN A CHAPTER 7 CASE

(a) **Final Report and Account.** Unless the Court orders otherwise, the notice given by the trustee of the filing of a final report and account in the form prescribed by the United States Trustee in a chapter 7 case shall have on its face in bold type the following language, or words of similar import:

A person seeking an award of compensation or reimbursement of expenses shall file an application with the clerk and serve a copy on the trustee and the United States Trustee not later than twenty-one (21) days prior to the date of the hearing on the trustee's final account. Failure to file and serve such an application within that time may result in the disallowance of fees and expenses.

(b) **Closing Report in an Asset Case.** Unless the Court orders otherwise, in a chapter 7 asset case, the trustee shall file and serve upon the United States Trustee, together with the affidavit of final distribution, a closing report substantially in the form available on the Court's website (http://www.nysb.uscourts.gov/sites/default/files/5009-1-b-report.docx).

(c) **Closing Report in a No Asset Case.** In a chapter 7 no asset case, the trustee shall file a No Distribution Report as a virtual docket text entry in accordance with the guidelines promulgated by the Office of the United States Trustee.

[Adopted effective April 15, 1997. Amended effective July 28, 1998; December 1, 2009; August 1, 2013; December 1, 2016.]

Comment

Subdivision (a) of this rule is derived from former Standing Order M–90.

Subdivisions (b) and (c) of this rule, added in 1996, complement section 704(9) of the Bankruptcy Code. Although not specifying a particular time period, subdivision (b) of this rule contemplates that the trustee will file the closing report as soon as practicable after the filing of a final account and the final allowance of fees. Thereafter, the Clerk may close the case upon the entry of a final decree.

Subdivision (a) of this rule was amended in 2009 to change the time period from twenty (20) to twenty-one (21) days. The purpose of the amendment was to conform the time period in this rule to the 2009 time-related amendments to the Federal Rules of Bankruptcy Procedure. Throughout the Bankruptcy Rules, as well as the Local Bankruptcy Rules, most time periods that are shorter than thirty (30) days were changed so that the number of days is in multiples of seven, thereby reducing the likelihood that time periods will end on a Saturday or Sunday.

Subsection (c) of this rule was amended in 2013 to clarify that a separate form need not be attached to the "No Distribution" docket entry in a no asset chapter 7 case.

Subsection (a) was stylistically revised in 2016 to offset the warning language required. No substantive change was intended.

[Comment amended effective July 28, 1998; December 1, 2009; August 1, 2013; December 1, 2016.]

RULE 5009–2. CLOSING A CHAPTER 15 CASE

(a) **Closing the Case.** In a case under chapter 15 of the Bankruptcy Code, the Court shall close the case when there is a presumption under Bankruptcy Rule 5009(c) that the case has been fully administered or the Court, after notice and a hearing, determines that the purpose of the foreign representative's appearance in the chapter 15 case has been completed, whichever is earlier.

(b) **Reopening the Case.** A case under chapter 15 may be reopened to provide appropriate relief to the foreign representative or for other cause.

[Adopted effective August 1, 2013.]

Comment

This rule was added in 2013 to provide for the closing of a chapter 15 case, as well as reopening a case for cause.

The Bankruptcy Code and Bankruptcy Rules do not provide for the closing and reopening of a chapter 15 case, but impose certain reporting requirements on the foreign representative so that the Court is aware of the status of the case. In particular, section 1518 of the Bankruptcy Code imposes on the foreign representative the duty to promptly file a notice informing the Court of any substantial change in the status of the foreign proceeding or of the foreign representative's appointment, and of any other foreign proceeding regarding the debtor. Bankruptcy Rule 2015(d) requires the filing of such reports within 14 days after the foreign representative becomes aware of such information. Under Bankruptcy Rule 5009(c), the foreign representative is also required to file and transmit to the United States Trustee a final report describing the nature and results of the foreign representative's activities in the Court when the purpose of the foreign representative's appearance in the Court is completed, and to give notice of the report to certain parties. The foreign representative must file a certificate with the Court certifying that such notice has been given. Under Bankruptcy Rule 5009(c), if no objection has been filed within 30 days after the certificate is filed, there is a presumption that the case has been fully administered. At that time, the case should be closed. However, even in the absence of a certificate, the Court has the discretion, after notice and a hearing, to close the case if it finds that the purpose of the foreign representative's appearance in the case has been completed.

[Comment added effective August 1, 2013.]

RULE 5010–1. REOPENING CASES

(a) **Contents of Motion.** A motion to reopen a case pursuant to Bankruptcy Rule 5010 shall be in writing and state the name of the Judge to whom the case was assigned at the time it was closed.

(b) Reference. A motion to reopen a case shall be filed with the Clerk. The Clerk shall refer the motion to the Judge to whom the case was assigned at the time it was closed. If that Judge is no longer sitting, the motion shall be assigned in accordance with Local Bankruptcy Rule 1073–1.

[Adopted effective April 15, 1997. Amended effective July 28, 1998.]

Comment

This rule is derived from Former Local Bankruptcy Rule 11.

[Comment amended effective July 28, 1998.]

RULE 5011–1. WITHDRAWAL OF REFERENCE

A motion for withdrawal of the reference shall be filed with the Clerk of the Bankruptcy Court. The movant shall obtain from the Clerk of the Bankruptcy Court the District Court civil case number and name of the District Judge assigned to the motion, and shall thereafter file with the Clerk of the District Court a copy of the motion, the receipt for payment of the filing fee, three copies of the District Court Civil Cover Sheet, and a copy of any corporate ownership statement previously filed pursuant to Bankruptcy Rule 1007(a) or 7007.1, consistent with the *Instructions for Filing a Motion to Withdraw the Reference*, which shall be available on the Court's website (http://www.nysb.uscourts.gov/sites/default/files/5011-1-instructions.pdf). All subsequent papers relating to the motion shall be filed with the Clerk of the District Court.

[Adopted effective April 15, 1997. Amended effective August 1, 2013.]

Comment

This rule was amended in 2004 to specify the procedural requirements imposed on the party moving for withdrawal of the reference under 28 U.S.C. § 157(d).

This rule was amended in 2013 to clarify that the Bankruptcy Court Clerk now opens the motion to withdraw the reference on the District Court's electronic filing system. The movant must obtain the District Court civil case number and name of the District Judge assigned to the motion from the Clerk of the Bankruptcy Court, and thereafter file a copy of the motion and other specified papers with the Clerk of the District Court. The rule also has been amended to include a link to the *Instructions for Filing a Motion to Withdraw the Reference* on the Court's website.

[Comment added effective August 2, 2004. Amended effective August 1, 2013.]

RULE 5070–1. OBTAINING A RETURN DATE

Unless the Court orders otherwise, prior to serving a motion, cross-motion, or application, the moving party or applicant shall obtain a return date from the assigned Judge's chambers.

[Adopted effective April 15, 1997. Amended effective August 2, 2004; December 1, 2016.]

Comment

This rule is derived from former Standing Order M–99. Pursuant to Local Bankruptcy Rule 9004–2(b), the return date obtained under this rule shall be included in the upper right-hand corner of the caption of the motion or application.

The title of this rule was amended in 2016. No substantive change was intended.

RULE 5073–1. PHOTOGRAPHING, BROADCASTING, AND TELEVISING IN COURTROOMS AND ENVIRONS

The taking of photographs and the use of recording devices in a courtroom or its environs, except by officials of the Court in the conduct of the Court's business, and radio or television broadcasting from a courtroom or its environs, during the progress of, or in connection with, judicial proceedings or otherwise, whether or not the Court is actually in session, are prohibited.

[Adopted effective April 15, 1997.]

Comment

This rule is derived from Former Local Bankruptcy Rule 35 and is an adaptation of Civil Rule 1.8 of the Local District Rules.

This rule extends the District Court's restrictions to all bankruptcy courtrooms in this district, including those located in White Plains and Poughkeepsie.

[Comment amended effective July 28, 1998.]

RULE 5075–1. CLERK'S USE OF OUTSIDE SERVICES AND AGENTS; CLAIMS AND NOTICING AGENTS

(a) The Court may direct, subject to the supervision of the Clerk, the use of agents either on or off the Court's premises to file Court records, either by paper or electronic means, to issue notices, to maintain case dockets, to maintain Judges' calendars, and to maintain and disseminate other administrative information where the costs of such facilities or services are paid for by the estate.

(b)(1) In a case in which the number of creditors and equity security holders, in the aggregate, is 250 or more, the estate shall retain, subject to approval of the Court, a claims and noticing agent in accordance with the Protocol for the Employment of Claims And Noticing Agents under 28 U.S.C. § 156(c), which shall be available on the Court's website (http://www.nysb.uscourts.gov/sites/default/files/pdf/newClaimsAgents Protocol.pdf).

(2) With court approval, the estate may retain a claims and noticing agent in accordance with such protocol in a case in which the number of creditors and equity security holders, in the aggregate, is less than 250.

(3) The costs of services provided by such agent shall be paid by the estate. When the case is closed, the claims and noticing agent shall deliver to the Clerk a copy of the claims register.

(c) Upon request of the Clerk, the agent shall provide a copy of all electronic records maintained by the agent of the Clerk and shall provide public access to the Claims Registers, including complete proofs of claim with attachments, if any, without charge.

(d) The order providing for the retention of an agent under this rule shall provide for (i) the discharge of the agent at the conclusion of the case, or as otherwise provided by entry of an additional order by the Court, and (ii) the disposition of any records, documents and the like, that have been provided or delivered to such agent, whether in paper or electronic form in accordance with the *Protocol for the Employment of Claims Agents*.

[Adopted effective April 15, 1997. Amended effective August 1, 2013; December 1, 2016.]

Comment

This rule complements 28 U.S.C. § 156(c). Pursuant to the guidelines of the Judicial Conference of the United States, the Clerk is responsible for the security and integrity of all Court records.

This rule was amended in 2013 to add as new subdivision (b) the provisions of General Order M–409, relating to the use of claims and noticing agents, and to state in the rule the link to the Court's website where practitioners may access the governing protocols. The substance of former subdivision (b) has been deleted. The Clerk does not maintain duplicate electronic records of the claims register held by the claims and noticing agent. Such claims register is delivered to the Clerk upon the closing of the case. General Order M–409 was abrogated and replaced by this local rule in 2013.

Subsection (b) of this rule was stylistically revised in 2016. No substantive change was intended.

Subsection (c) of this rule was amended and subsection (d) was added in 2016 to require open access to claims registries in accordance with existing requirements and Clerk's Office procedures, as well as

section 107 of the Bankruptcy Code and Bankruptcy Rules 3002(b) and 5005(a).

[Comment amended effective August 1, 2013; December 1, 2016.]

RULE 5076–1. DEPOSIT FOR COURT RE-PORTING EXPENSES [REPEALED EFFECTIVE AUGUST 1, 2013]

Comment

This rule was abrogated in 2013 because court reporters are no longer used in Court proceedings.

[Comment added effective August 1, 2013.]

RULE 5078–1. PAYMENT OF FEES

Unless the Court orders otherwise, the Clerk shall not be required to render any service for which a fee is prescribed by statute or the Judicial Conference of the United States unless the fee is paid in advance.

[Adopted effective April 15, 1997.]

Comment

This rule is derived from Former Local Bankruptcy Rule 10 and is an adaptation of Civil Rule 1.7 of the Local District Rules.

An application for permission to make installment payments may be filed pursuant to Bankruptcy Rule 1006(b).

[Comment amended effective July 28, 1998.]

PART VI. COLLECTION AND LIQUIDATION OF THE ESTATE

RULE 6004–1. SALES OF PROPERTY, APPRAISALS, AND AUCTIONS

(a) Notice. The trustee may sell property of the estate that the trustee reasonably believes has an aggregate gross value of no more than $10,000 by public or private sale on seven (7) days' written notice to any party with an interest in such property, the landlord of the premises on which the property is located, and such other parties as the Court may direct. The notice of any proposed sale of property of the estate having an aggregate gross value of at least $2,500 shall include the time and place of the proposed sale, whether the sale will be public or private, and the terms and conditions of the proposed sale.

(b) Appraisals. Unless the Court orders otherwise, if an appraiser has been employed, the property to be appraised shall not be sold until after the appraisal has been filed.

(1) *Caption.* All appraisals filed with the Court shall have a cover sheet bearing the caption of the case in compliance with Local Bankruptcy Rule 9004–2 and the date, if any, of the proposed sale.

(2) *Filing and Access.* Unless the Court orders otherwise, any appraiser employed pursuant to section 327(a) of the Bankruptcy Code shall file with the Court and the United States Trustee each appraisal made of property of the estate not later than 12:00 noon on the day prior to the scheduled sale of the property. Each appraisal shall be kept under seal

upon filing and treated as confidential by the Court and the United States Trustee. Access to the appraisal may be had only by the Court, the United States Trustee, and such other parties as the Court may direct, and neither they nor the appraiser shall disclose any of the contents thereof until after the conclusion of the bidding at any sale of the appraised property, at which time the Court may order the appraisal to be unsealed. Unless the Court orders otherwise, the appraisal shall be unsealed six (6) months from the date on which the appraisal is filed.

(3) *Conformity With Auctioneer's Catalogue of Sale.* If property is to be appraised and sold at auction, upon request, the auctioneer promptly shall deliver the catalogue of sale to the appraiser. The appraisal shall conform to the catalogue to the greatest extent possible.

(c) Manner of Display and Conduct of Auction. Unless the Court orders otherwise, the auction shall be conducted in the following manner:

(1) the property shall be on public display for a reasonable period of time prior to the sale;

(2) prior to receiving bids, the auctioneer shall announce the terms of sale;

(3) where practicable, the property shall be offered for sale first in bulk and then in lots; and

(4) any property that is not to be included in the sale shall be set apart and conspicuously marked "not included in the

sale," and such fact shall be announced by the auctioneer before the sale.

(d) Joint Sales.

(1) If the trustee and a secured party, or other third party having an interest in the property, desire to conduct a joint auction sale, or if the joint sale of property in more than one (1) bankruptcy estate is anticipated to be more cost effective or beneficial for all the bankruptcy estates, the Court shall enter an order prior to the sale fixing the method of allocating the commissions and expenses of sale.

(2) The commissions and expenses incurred on behalf of one (1) bankruptcy estate in a joint auction sale shall not be charged to any other estate unless the motion requesting the joint auction reveals the identity and number of any other estate participants in the joint auction sale, and how such commissions and expenses shall be apportioned among them.

(3) Nothing in this rule shall prevent the trustee from participating in a joint sale with a non-debtor, provided it is in the best interest of the debtor's estate and its creditors.

(e) Proceeds of Sale. Upon receipt of the proceeds of sale, the auctioneer immediately shall deposit the proceeds in a separate account that the auctioneer maintains for each estate in accordance with the requirements of section 345(a) of the Bankruptcy Code. Unless the Court orders otherwise, payment of the gross proceeds of the sale, less the auctioneer's reimbursable expenses, shall be made promptly by the auctioneer to the trustee or debtor in possession, but in no event later than fourteen (14) days after the date on which the proceeds are received with respect to each item or lot sold.

(f) Report of Sale. Unless the Court orders otherwise, (i) within twenty-one (21) days after the last date of the auction, the auctioneer shall file a report with the Court and transmit a copy of the report to the United States Trustee, and (ii) if all proceeds of the auction have not been received by such date, the auctioneer shall file a supplemental report within fourteen (14) days after all proceeds have been received. The report shall set forth:

(1) the time, date, and place of the sale;

(2) the gross dollar amount of the sale;

(3) if property was sold in lots, a description of the items in each lot, the quantity in each lot, the dollar amount received for each lot, and any bulk bid(s) received;

(4) an itemized statement of expenditures, disbursements, and commissions allowable under Local Bankruptcy Rule 6005–1, including the name and address of the payee, together with the original receipts or canceled checks, or true copies thereof, for the expenditures or disbursements. Where labor charges are included, the report shall specify the days worked and the number of hours worked each day by each person and the last four digits of the person's social security number. If the canceled checks are not available at the time the report is filed, the report shall so state, and the canceled checks shall be filed as soon as they become available;

(5) where the auctioneer has a blanket insurance policy covering all sales conducted by the auctioneer, for which original receipts and canceled checks are not available, an explanation of how the insurance expense charged to the estate was computed;

(6) if any articles were withdrawn from the sale because of a third party claim of an interest therein, a separate itemized statement of the articles reflecting the names of such third parties;

(7) the names and addresses of all purchasers;

(8) the sign-in sheet, if any; otherwise, the approximate number of people attending the sale;

(9) the items for which there were no bids and the disposition of those items;

(10) the terms and conditions of sale that were read to the audience immediately prior to the commencement of the sale;

(11) a statement of the manner and extent of advertising of the sale;

(12) a statement of the manner and extent of the availability of the items for inspection; and

(13) any other information that the United States Trustee may request.

(g) Affidavit to Accompany Report of Sale. The auctioneer shall submit with the report of sale an affidavit stating: (i) that the auctioneer is a duly licensed auctioneer; (ii) the auctioneer's license number and place of business; (iii) the authority pursuant to which the auctioneer conducted the auction; (iv) the date and place of the auction; (v) that the labor and other expenses incurred on behalf of the estate as listed in the report of sale were reasonable and necessary; and (vi) that the gross proceeds of sale, exclusive of expenses, were remitted to the trustee or debtor in possession and the date of the remittance.

(h) Advertisement and Publication of Notice of Sale. An advertisement or publication of notice of a sale by auction or otherwise may be made without Court approval if it is sufficient to provide adequate notice of the sale and is advertised or published at least once in a newspaper of general circulation in the city or county in which the property is located. The advertisement or publication shall include: (i) the date, time, and place of the sale; (ii) a description of the property to be sold including, with respect to real property, the approximate acreage of any real estate outside the limits of any town or city, the street, lot, and block number of any real estate within any town or city, and a general statement of the character of any improvements upon the property; (iii) the terms and conditions of the sale; and (iv) the name, address, and telephone number of the trustee or debtor in possession. The Court may fix the manner and extent of advertising and publication at any time.

(i) No Order Needed to Confirm Sale. Unless a timely objection is made, no order of the Court shall be required to confirm a sale of property pursuant to this rule. The trustee, debtor, or debtor in possession may execute any documents and instruments that are necessary to complete the sale and shall file with the Court and transmit to the United States Trustee a report of the sale as required by Local Bankruptcy Rule 6004–1(f) when the sale is completed. On request, the Clerk shall issue a certificate stating that a notice of a proposed action, with proof of service, has been filed with the Court pursuant to Local Bankruptcy Rule 9074–1(c) and that no timely objection has been filed.

(j) Compliance With Guidelines of the Court. In addition to the foregoing requirements, parties conducting a sale of property of the estate, including trustees and auctioneers, shall comply with the Guidelines for the Conduct of Asset Sales by the Court, which shall be available on the Court's website (http://www.nysb.uscourts.gov/sites/default/files/6004-1-j-Guidelines.pdf).

[Adopted effective April 15, 1997. Amended effective July 28, 1998; August 2, 2004; December 1, 2009; August 1, 2013; December 1, 2016.]

Comment

Subdivision (a) of this rule was added in 1996. Subdivision (b) of this rule is derived from Former Local Bankruptcy Rule 40. Subdivisions (c), (d), (e), (f), and (g) of this rule are derived from Former Local Bankruptcy Rule 41. Subdivision (h) of this rule is derived from Former Local Bankruptcy Rule 42. Subdivision (i) of this rule is derived from Former Local Bankruptcy Rule 45(g).

Subdivision (d) of this rule was amended in 2004 to provide for joint sales of property from more than one estate. Subdivision (e) makes clear that the proceeds of an auction shall be turned over within the time specified, even if the auction has not yet concluded. Unlike subdivision (e), which requires the turnover of proceeds with respect to each lot or item of property, subdivision (f) contemplates the filing of a report within the time specified after the auction has been concluded and the supplementing of such report when the proceeds are received thereafter. Due to privacy concerns, subdivision (f) of this rule was amended in 2004 to delete the requirement that an auctioneer include in its report the social security numbers of people being paid labor charges.

The contents of a notice of a proposed sale are governed by Bankruptcy Rule 2002(c)(1).

In 2009, subdivision (a) of this rule was amended to change the time period from five (5) to seven (7) days, and subdivision (b) of this rule was amended to change the time period from ten (10) to fourteen (14) days. The purpose of these amendments was to conform the time periods in this rule to the 2009 time-related amendments to the Federal Rules of Bankruptcy Procedure. Throughout the Bankruptcy Rules, as well as the Local Bankruptcy Rules, most time periods that are shorter than thirty (30) days were changed so that the number of days is in multiples of seven (7), thereby reducing the likelihood that time periods will end on a Saturday or Sunday.

The business day deadline in subdivision (b)(2) of this rule was also amended in 2009 to delete the reference to "business" so that the time period will be consistent with the 2009 amendments to Bankruptcy Rule 9006(a).

Guidelines for the conduct of asset sales were promulgated by General Order M–383. This rule was amended in 2013 to specify the title of the procedures promulgated by General Order M–383 and to state in the rule the link to the Court's website where practitioners may access the governing procedures. The procedures also may be obtained from the Clerk. The procedures set forth in the Guidelines for the Conduct of Asset Sales may be amended by the Court after giving notice and opportunity for comment as is appropriate.

Subsection (i) was revised to conform to the 2016 amendments relocating Local Rule 2002–2, to Local Rule 9074–1(c). Subsection (i) now refers to Local Rule 9074–1(c), instead of Local Rule 2002–2.

[Comment amended effective July 28, 1998; August 2, 2004; December 1, 2009; August 1, 2013; December 1, 2016.]

RULE 6005–1. AUCTIONEERS

(a) No Official Auctioneer. There shall be no official auctioneer.

(b) Compensation. Unless the Court orders otherwise for cause, compensation and reimbursement of expenses shall be allowed to an auctioneer for sales of property as follows:

(1) commissions on each sale conducted by the auctioneer at the following rates:

(A) 10% of any gross proceeds of sale up to $50,000;

(B) 8% of any gross proceeds of sale in excess of $50,000 but not more than $75,000;

(C) 6% of any gross proceeds of sale in excess of $75,000 but not more than $100,000;

(D) 4% of any gross proceeds of sale in excess of $100,000 but not more than $150,000; and

(E) 2% of any gross proceeds of sale in excess of $150,000; and

(2) reimbursement for reasonable and necessary expenses directly related to the sale, including labor, printing, advertising, and insurance, but excluding workers' compensation, social security, unemployment insurance, and other payroll taxes. When directed by the trustee or debtor in possession to transport goods, the auctioneer shall be reimbursed for expenditures related thereto. No travel expenses shall be allowed, except as ordered by the Court.

(c) Purchase Prohibited. An auctioneer, or officer, director, stockholder, agent, or employee of an auctioneer, shall not purchase directly or indirectly, or have a financial interest in the purchase of, any property of the estate that the auctioneer has been employed to sell.

(d) Bond. An auctioneer employed pursuant to section 327 of the Bankruptcy Code shall not act until the auctioneer files with respect to each estate, at the auctioneer's expense, a surety bond in favor of the United States, to be approved, and in such sum as may be fixed, by the United States Trustee, which is conditioned upon:

(1) the faithful and prompt accounting for all monies and property that may come into the auctioneer's possession;

(2) compliance with all rules, orders, and decrees of the Court; and

(3) the faithful performance of the auctioneer's duties.

(e) Blanket Bond. In lieu of a bond in each case, an auctioneer may be permitted to file, at the auctioneer's own expense, a blanket bond covering all cases in which the auctioneer may act. The blanket bond shall be in favor of the United States in such sum as the United States Trustee shall fix and shall be conditioned for each estate on the same terms as bonds in separate estates.

(f) Application for Commissions. An auctioneer shall file an application with the Court for approval of commissions on not less than seven (7) days' notice to the debtor, the trustee, the United States Trustee, and each committee. No application shall be granted unless the report of sale referred to in Local Bankruptcy Rule 6004–1(f) has been filed.

(g) Repealed.

[Adopted effective April 15, 1997. Amended effective July 28, 1998; December 1, 2009; August 1, 2013.]

Comment

This rule is derived from Former Local Bankruptcy Rule 41.

Advertisements of auction sales are governed by Local Bankruptcy Rule 6004–1(h).

Subdivision (f) of this rule was amended in 2009 to change the time period from five (5) to seven (7) days. The purpose of the amendment was to conform the time period in this rule to the 2009 time-related amendments to the Federal Rules of Bankruptcy Procedure. Throughout the Bankruptcy Rules, as well as the Local Bankruptcy Rules, most time periods that are shorter than 30 days were changed so that the number of days is in multiples of seven, thereby reducing the likelihood that time periods will end on a Saturday or Sunday.

Subdivision (g) of this rule was repealed in 2013 so that the United States Trustee Guidelines governing auctioneers are not incorporated by reference into the Local Bankruptcy Rules.

[Comment amended effective July 28, 1998; December 1, 2009; August 1, 2013.]

RULE 6006–1. EXECUTORY CONTRACTS AND UNEXPIRED LEASES

(a) Motion to Assume, Reject, or Assign Executory Contract or Unexpired Lease. A motion to assume, reject, or assign an executory contract or unexpired lease shall be served in accordance with the time limits set forth in Local Bankruptcy Rule 9006–1(b), which may be waived or modified upon the written consent of all parties entitled to notice of the motion. In the event that a nonconsensual order is sought on less than fourteen (14) days' notice, Local Bankruptcy Rule 9077–1 shall govern and an actual hearing shall be held.

(b) Assumption of Executory Contract or Unexpired Lease in Chapter 7 Case.

(1) Unless the Court orders otherwise, in a chapter 7 case, a trustee moving to assume an executory contract or unexpired lease of residential real property or personal property of the debtor shall seek to obtain a return date for the hearing on the motion that is within sixty (60) days after the order for relief or, if the time to assume has been extended, before the expiration of such extended period. If the trustee files a motion to assume or to extend the time to assume or reject an executory contract or unexpired lease of residential real property or personal property, and the motion is filed not later than sixty (60) days after the order for relief (or, if the time to assume or reject the executory contract or unexpired lease has been extended previously by order of the Court, before the expiration of the extended time) with a return date no later than fourteen (14) days from the date of such filing, the time to assume or reject the executory contract or unexpired lease shall be extended automatically and without court order until the entry of the order resolving the motion.

(2) The assumption by an individual debtor of a lease of personal property that is no longer property of the estate pursuant to Section 365(p)(2)(A) of the Bankruptcy Code shall not require the approval of the Court. Any party in interest that request an order of the Court approving such an assumption shall in its request prominently state the reasons for seeking such an order notwithstanding its knowledge that an order of the Court is not required for such assumption.

(c) Motion to Assume Unexpired Lease of Nonresidential Real Property. Unless the Court orders otherwise, in a case under any chapter, a debtor, debtor in possession, or trustee moving to assume an unexpired lease of nonresidential real property under which the debtor is the lessee shall seek to obtain a return date for the hearing on the motion that is within one hundred twenty (120) days after the order for relief or, if the time to assume has been extended, before the expiration of such extended period. If the debtor, debtor in possession, or the trustee files a motion to assume or to extend the time to assume or reject an unexpired lease of nonresidential real property, and the motion is filed not later than one hundred-twenty (120) days after the order for relief (or, if the time to assume or reject the unexpired lease has been extended previously by order of the Court, before the expiration of the extended time) with a return date no later than fourteen (14) days from the date of such filing or, if the Court is unable, to schedule a return date within such fourteen (14) day period, or soon thereafter as the return date may be scheduled by the Court, the time to assume or reject the unexpired lease will be extended automatically and without court order until the entry of the order resolving the motion, except that the time for the debtor, debtor in possession, or trustee to assume or reject such unexpired lease shall not be extended beyond the date that is two hundred ten (210) days after the entry of the order for relief without the prior written consent of the landlord.

(d) Aircraft Equipment and Vessels. Unless the Court orders otherwise, a debtor in possession or trustee moving for approval of an agreement to perform all obligations of the debtor pursuant to section 1110(a)(1)(A) of the Bankruptcy Code shall seek to obtain a return date for the hearing on the motion that is within sixty (60) days after the order for relief or, if the time to assume has been extended by order of the Court, before the expiration of such extended period.

(e) Rolling Stock Equipment. Unless the Court orders otherwise, a trustee moving for approval of an agreement to perform all obligations of the debtor pursuant to section 1168(a)(1)(A) of the Bankruptcy Code shall seek to obtain a return date for the hearing on the motion that is within sixty (60) days after the date of commencement of the case or, if the time to assume has been extended by order of the Court, before the expiration of such extended period.

[Adopted effective April 15, 1997. Amended effective August 2, 2004; December 1, 2009; August 1, 2013.]

Comment

Subdivision (a) of this rule is derived from former Standing Order M–118. Subdivisions (b) and (c) of this rule are derived from Former Local Bankruptcy Rule 44(b) and (c). Subdivisions (d) and (e) of this rule, added in 1996, are derived from sections 1110 and 1168 of the Bankruptcy Code.

Section 365(d)(1) of the Bankruptcy Code contemplates that a hearing on a motion by a chapter 7 trustee to assume an executory contract or unexpired lease of residential real property or personal property of the debtor ordinarily will take place within sixty (60) days from the date of the order for relief. In addition, section 365(d)(4) of the Bankruptcy Code contemplates that a final hearing on a motion by a debtor, debtor in possession, or trustee to assume an unexpired lease of nonresidential real property of the debtor ordinarily will take place within one hundred twenty (120) days from the date of the order for relief.

Under section 365(d)(1) of the Bankruptcy Code, in a chapter 7 case, the Court may, for cause, extend the sixty (60)–day time period for assuming or rejecting an executory contract or unexpired lease of residential real property or personal property. Similarly, under section 365(d)(4), the Court may, for cause, extend the one hundred twenty (120)–day time period for assuming or rejecting an unexpired lease of nonresidential real property. In 2004, subdivisions (b) and (c) of this rule were amended to avoid the necessity of obtaining a "bridge order" extending these time periods in the event that a timely motion to assume or a timely motion to extend the time was filed but not resolved by the Court before the expiration of the time to assume or reject the contract or lease. Adequate cause for an extension of time to assume or reject the executory contract or unexpired lease until the Court rules on the motion exists by virtue of the fact that a motion to assume or to extend the time was filed in a timely manner. Any party in interest objecting to the extension of time may request a hearing on an expedited basis. To prevent abuse of the automatic extension, the return date of the motion must be no later than fourteen (14) days after the motion is filed.

Subdivision (a) of this rule was amended in 2009 to change the time period from ten (10) to fourteen (14) days. The purpose of the amendment was to conform the time period in this rule to the 2009 time-related amendments to the Federal Rules of Bankruptcy Procedure. Throughout the Bankruptcy Rules, as well as the Local Bankruptcy Rules, most time periods that are shorter than 30 days were changed so that the number of days is in multiples of seven (7), thereby reducing the likelihood that time periods will end on a Saturday or Sunday.

This rule was amended in 2013 to include in the new paragraph (2) of subdivision (b) the provisions of General Order M–415, which relates to an individual debtor's assumption of a lease of personal property under section 365(p) of the Bankruptcy Code. General Order M–415 was abrogated and replaced by this local rule in 2013.

Subdivision (c) was amended in 2013 so that the automatic extension of time would apply if the Court is unable to schedule a return date within fourteen (14) days after the motion is filed, provided that the return date is as soon thereafter as it may be scheduled by the Court. Subdivision (d) was amended in 2013 to update the Bankruptcy Code cross reference to reflect Bankruptcy Code amendments subsequent to this local rule's promulgation.

[Comment amended effective July 28, 1998; August 2, 2004; October 17, 2005; December 1, 2009; August 1, 2013.]

RULE 6007–1.   ABANDONMENT OR DISPOSITION OF PROPERTY

(a) Unless the Court orders otherwise, the notice of a proposed abandonment or disposition of property pursuant to Bankruptcy Rule 6007(a) shall describe the property to be abandoned or disposed of, state concisely the reason for the proposed abandonment or disposition, and, in the case of abandonment, identify the entity to whom the property is proposed to be abandoned.

(b) If the trustee files a notice of abandonment of a residential real property lease, other than a proprietary lease for a cooperative residence, the notice need only be served on the debtor and the landlord.

[Adopted effective April 15, 1997.]

Comment

This rule, added in 1996, simplifies the procedure for abandonment of an individual debtor's leased residence that is of no value to the estate so that the debtor may remain in such premises.

[Comment amended effective July 28, 1998.]

PART VII.   ADVERSARY PROCEEDINGS

RULE 7005–1.   FILING OF DISCOVERY– RELATED DOCUMENTS

(a) Except as provided in subdivision (b) of this rule, unless the Court orders otherwise, transcripts of depositions, exhibits to depositions, interrogatories, answers to interrogatories, document requests, responses to document requests, requests for admissions, and responses to requests for admissions shall not be filed with the Court.

(b) When discovery or disclosure material not on file with the Court is needed for an appeal, the necessary portion of that material may be filed with the Clerk.

[Adopted effective April 15, 1997.   Amended effective July 28, 1998.]

Comment

This rule is derived from Civil Rule 5.1 of the Local District Rules.

[Comment amended effective July 28, 1998.]

RULE 7007–1.   DISCOVERY–RELATED MOTION PRACTICE

(a) Attorney's Affidavit.   No discovery-related motion under Bankruptcy Rules 7026 through 7037 shall be heard unless counsel for the moving party files with the Court, at or prior to the hearing, an affidavit certifying that such counsel has conferred with counsel for the opposing party in a good faith effort to resolve by agreement the issues raised by the motion without the intervention of the Court and has been unable to reach an agreement. If any of the issues raised by motion have been resolved by agreement, the affidavit shall specify the issues so resolved and the issues remaining unresolved.

(b) Request for Informal Conference.   No discovery-related motion under Bankruptcy Rules 7026 through 7037 shall be heard unless counsel for the moving party first requests an informal conference with the Court and either the request has been denied or the discovery dispute has not been resolved as a consequence of the conference.

[Adopted effective April 15, 1997.]

Comment

This rule is derived from Former Local Bankruptcy Rule 13.

Subdivision (a) of this rule is an adaptation of Civil Rule 3(f) of the Former District Rules. Subdivision (b) of this rule is an adaptation of Civil Rule 37.2 of the Local District Rules.

[Comment amended effective July 28, 1998.]

RULE 7007.1–1. CORPORATE OWNERSHIP STATEMENT TO BE FILED BY A PARTNERSHIP OR JOINT VENTURE THAT IS A PARTY TO AN ADVERSARY PROCEEDING

The Corporate Ownership Statement required under Bankruptcy Rule 7007.1 shall also be filed by any party to an adversary proceeding, other than the debtor or a governmental entity, that is a general or limited partnership or joint venture.

[Adopted effective August 2, 2004. Amended effective December 1, 2009.]

Comment

Bankruptcy Rule 7007.1, effective December 1, 2003, requires a Corporate Ownership Statement to be filed for any corporation that is a party to an adversary proceeding other than the debtor or a governmental entity. "Corporation" is broadly defined under section 101(9) of the Bankruptcy Code (and includes, for instance, limited liability companies and other unincorporated companies or associations), but it does not cover general or limited partnerships. The reasons for which this rule was enacted—to give the Judges of this Court information by which they can determine whether or not they need to recuse themselves—apply equally to general and limited partnerships, and joint ventures. This local rule requires a similar disclosure with respect to business organizations of that character.

The heading of this rule was amended in 2009 to more accurately reflect the substance of the rule.

[Comment adopted effective August 2, 2004; amended effective December 1, 2009.]

RULE 7008–1. STATEMENT REGARDING CONSENT TO ENTRY OF ORDERS OR JUDGMENT IN CORE PROCEEDING [REPEALED EFFECTIVE DECEMBER 1, 2016]

Comment

This rule was repealed in 2016 in light of the new amendments to Bankruptcy Rule 7008.

RULE 7012–1. STATEMENT IN RESPONSIVE PLEADING REGARDING CONSENT TO ENTRY OF ORDERS OR JUDGMENT IN CORE PROCEEDING [REPEALED EFFECTIVE DECEMBER 1, 2016]

Comment

This rule was repealed in 2016 in light of the new amendments to Bankruptcy Rule 7012.

RULE 7016–1. SUBMISSION OF MARKED PLEADINGS

Unless the Court orders otherwise, marked pleadings are not required.

[Adopted effective April 15, 1997. Amended effective August 2, 2004.]

Comment

The Judges of the Court have determined that the benefits derived from the submission of marked pleadings normally do not justify the burdens on the plaintiff in submitting them, particularly in light of the information contained in pre-trial orders.

[Comment amended effective July 28, 1998; August 2, 2004.]

RULE 7016–2. INITIAL PRETRIAL CONFERENCE

The Court shall schedule an initial pretrial conference in all adversary proceedings. The date and time of the initial pretrial conference shall be set forth in the summons. Subsequent pretrial conferences may be scheduled in open court or by the Clerk as provided above. If a subsequent pretrial conference is scheduled in open court, the plaintiff shall file a notice of the date and time of such pretrial conference no later than forty-eight (48) hours after it was scheduled in open court.

Comment

This rule was added in 2013 to require a pretrial conference in every adversary proceeding and to specify the procedures for giving parties notice of the initial conference and any subsequent conferences.

RULE 7024–1. NOTICE OF CLAIM OF UNCONSTITUTIONALITY [REPEALED EFFECTIVE AUGUST 4, 2008]

Comment

This rule was repealed in 2008 as unnecessary because of the adoption in 2008 of Bankruptcy Rule 9005.1, which makes Rule 5.1 of the Federal Rules of Civil Procedure applicable to cases under the Bankruptcy Code. Rule 5.1 accomplishes the same objective as former Local Bankruptcy Rule 7024–1.

RULE 7026–1. UNIFORM DEFINITIONS IN DISCOVERY REQUESTS

Civil Rule 26.3 of the Local District Rules shall apply to discovery requests made in cases and proceedings commenced under the Bankruptcy Code.

[Adopted effective April 15, 1997. Amended effective July 28, 1998.]

Comment

This rule contains a technical change to reflect a renumbering of the applicable Local District Rule.

[Comment adopted effective July 28, 1998.]

RULE 7026–2. OPT–OUT FROM CERTAIN PROVISIONS OF RULE 26 OF THE FEDERAL RULES OF CIVIL PROCEDURE [REPEALED EFFECTIVE AUGUST 2, 2004]

RULE 7027–1. DEPOSITIONS PRIOR TO COMMENCEMENT OF ADVERSARY PROCEEDING OR PENDING APPEAL WHEN DEPOSITION IS MORE THAN 100 MILES FROM COURTHOUSE

If, prior to the commencement of an adversary proceeding or pending appeal, a proposed deposition pursuant to Bankruptcy Rule 7027 is sought to be taken at a location more than one hundred (100) miles from the courthouse, the Court may provide in the order therefor that, prior to the examination, the party seeking to take the deposition shall pay the expense of the attendance of one attorney for each adverse party, or expected adverse party, including reasonable attorney's fees. Unless the Court orders otherwise, any amounts paid pursuant to this subdivision shall be a taxable cost in the event the party taking the deposition is awarded costs of the adversary proceeding.

[Adopted effective April 15, 1997. Amended effective July 28, 1998.]

Comment

This rule is derived from Former Local Bankruptcy Rule 24 and is an adaptation of Civil Rule 30.1 of the Local District Rules.

[Comment amended effective July 28, 1998.]

RULE 7030–1. DEPOSITIONS UPON ORAL EXAMINATION MORE THAN 100 MILES FROM COURTHOUSE

If a proposed deposition upon oral examination is sought to be taken at a location more than one hundred (100) miles from the courthouse, the Court may provide in any order entered pursuant to Bankruptcy Rule 7030 that, prior to the examination, the party seeking to take the deposition shall pay the expense of the attendance of one attorney for each adverse party, or expected adverse party, including reasonable attorneys' fees. Unless the Court orders otherwise, any amounts paid pursuant to this subdivision shall be a taxable cost in the event that the party taking the deposition is awarded costs of the adversary proceeding.

[Adopted effective April 15, 1997. Amended effective December 1, 2016.]

Comment

This rule is derived from Former Local Bankruptcy Rule 24 and is an adaptation of Civil Rule 30.1 of the Local District Rules.

This title of this rule was stylistically amended in 2016 to conform to the language used in Local Rule 7027–1. No substantive change was intended.

[Comment amended effective July 28, 1998; December 1, 2016.]

RULE 7030–2. OPT–OUT FROM CERTAIN PROVISIONS OF RULE 30 OF THE FEDERAL RULES OF CIVIL PROCEDURE [REPEALED EFFECTIVE AUGUST 2, 2004]

RULE 7031–1. OPT–OUT FROM CERTAIN PROVISIONS OF RULE 31 OF THE FEDERAL RULES OF CIVIL PROCEDURE [REPEALED EFFECTIVE AUGUST 2, 2004]

RULE 7033–1. INTERROGATORIES

(a) **Restrictions.** At the commencement of discovery, interrogatories will be restricted to those questions seeking names of witnesses with knowledge or information relevant to the subject matter of the action, the computation of each category of damage alleged, and the existence, custodian, location, and general description of relevant documents, including pertinent insurance agreements, and other physical evidence, and information of a similar nature, to the extent such information has not already been provided under Rule 26(a)(1) of the Federal Rules of Civil Procedure.

(b) **Method of Obtaining Information.** During discovery, interrogatories, other than those seeking information described in subdivision (a) of this rule, may be served only if (i) they are a more practical method of obtaining the information sought than a request for production or a deposition or (ii) ordered by the Court.

(c) **What May Be Served.** Unless the Court orders otherwise, at the conclusion of each party's discovery, and prior to the discovery cut-off date, interrogatories seeking the claims and contentions of the opposing party may be served. Questions seeking the names of expert witnesses and the substance of their opinions also may be served if such information has not yet been supplied.

(d) **No Interrogatories to Be Unanswered.** No part of an interrogatory shall be left unanswered merely because an objection is interposed to another part of the interrogatory.

(e) **Objections or Requests for Relief.**

(1) In connection with any objection or request for relief with respect to interrogatories or answers to interrogatories, the party making the objection or request for relief shall (i) simultaneously file a copy of the interrogatories or answers to interrogatories and (ii) specify and quote verbatim each relevant interrogatory or answer and, immediately following each specification, set forth the basis of the objection or relief requested.

(2) If an objection or request for relief is made with respect to any interrogatory or portion thereof, the objection shall state all grounds with specificity. Any ground not stated in the objection or request for relief within the time provided by the Bankruptcy Rules, or any extensions thereof, shall be deemed waived.

(3) If a claim of privilege is asserted in an objection or request for relief with respect to any interrogatory or portion thereof, and an answer is not provided on the basis of the assertion, the objection or request for relief shall identify:

(A) the nature of the privilege being claimed and, if the privilege is being asserted in connection with a claim or defense governed by state law, the state's privilege rule being invoked; and

(B) unless divulgence of such information would cause disclosure of the allegedly privileged information:

1. for documents: (i) the type of document; (ii) the general subject matter of the document; (iii) the date of the document; and (iv) such other information as is sufficient to identify the document for a subpoena duces tecum, including, where appropriate, the author of the document, the addressee of the document, and, where not apparent, the relationship of the author to the addressee and the names of all entities that received a copy of the document.

2. for oral communications: (i) the name of the person making the communication, the names of any persons present while the communication was made, and, where not apparent, the relationship of the persons present to the person making the communication; (ii) the date and place of the communication; and (iii) the general subject matter of the communication.

(f) Reference to Records. If a party answers an interrogatory by reference to records from which the answer may be derived or ascertained, as permitted by Bankruptcy Rule 7033:

(1) the specification of documents to be produced shall be in sufficient detail to permit the interrogating party to locate and identify the records and ascertain the answer as readily as could the party from whom discovery is sought;

(2) the producing party shall also make available any computerized information or summaries thereof that it has, or can adduce by a relatively simple procedure, unless these materials are privileged or otherwise immune from discovery;

(3) the producing party shall also provide any relevant compilations, abstracts, or summaries in its custody or readily obtainable by it, unless these materials are privileged or otherwise immune from discovery; and

(4) unless the Court orders otherwise, the documents shall be made available for inspection and copying within fourteen (14) days after service of the answers to interrogatories or on a date agreed upon by the parties.

[Adopted effective April 15, 1997. Amended effective July 28, 1998; August 2, 2004; December 1, 2009; December 1, 2016.]

Comment

This rule is derived from Former Local Bankruptcy Rule 14 and is an adaptation of Civil Rules 5.1, 33.1, 33.3, and 37.1 of the Local District Rules, with the exception of subdivision (e)(1) of this rule, which is derived from Former Local Bankruptcy Rule 13.

The initial disclosures required under Fed. R. Civ. P. 26(a)(1) must be made in adversary proceedings. Because information previously sought by interrogatories will frequently have been obtained by those initial disclosures, this rule has been amended accordingly.

Subdivision (f)(4) of this rule was amended in 2009 to change the time period from ten (10) to fourteen (14) days. The purpose of the amendment was to conform the time period in this rule to the 2009 time-related amendments to the Bankruptcy Rules. Throughout the Bankruptcy Rules, as well as the Local Bankruptcy Rules, most time periods that are shorter than thirty (30) days were changed so that the number of days is in multiples of seven (7), thereby reducing the likelihood that time periods will end on a Saturday or Sunday.

Subsection (e)(2) was stylistically amended in 2016. No substantive change was intended.

[Comment amended effective July 28, 1998; August 2, 2004; December 1, 2009; December 1, 2016.]

RULE 7033–2. OPT–OUT FROM CERTAIN PROVISIONS OF RULE 33 OF THE FEDERAL RULES OF CIVIL PROCEDURE [REPEALED EFFECTIVE AUGUST 2, 2004]

RULE 7034–1. OBJECTIONS TO, AND REQUESTS FOR RELIEF WITH RESPECT TO, PRODUCTION OF DOCUMENTS

(a) In connection with any objection or request for relief with respect to document requests or answers thereto, the party making the objection or request for relief shall (i) simultaneously file a copy of the document request or answer and (ii) specify and quote verbatim each relevant document request or answer and, immediately following each specification, set forth the basis of the objection or relief requested.

(b) If an objection or request for relief is made with respect to any document request or portion thereof, the objection or request for relief shall state all grounds with specificity. Any ground not stated in the objection or request for relief within the time provided by the Bankruptcy Rules, or any extensions thereof, shall be deemed waived.

(c) If a claim of privilege is asserted in an objection or request for relief with respect to any document request or portion thereof, and an answer is not provided on the basis of the assertion, the objection or request for relief shall identify:

(1) the nature of the privilege being claimed and, if the privilege is being asserted in connection with a claim or defense governed by state law, the state's privilege rule being invoked; and

(2) unless divulgence of such information would cause disclosure of the allegedly privileged information: (i) the type of document; (ii) the general subject matter of the document; (iii) the date of the document; and (iv) such other information as is sufficient to identify the document for a subpoena duces tecum, including, where appropriate, the author of the document, the addressee of the document, and, where not apparent, the relationship of the author to the addressee, and the names of all entities that received a copy of the document.

[Adopted effective April 15, 1997. Amended effective July 28, 1998.]

Comment

This rule is derived from Former Local Bankruptcy Rule 14(e). Subdivision (a) of this rule is new and has been added to conform to subdivision (e)(1) of Local Bankruptcy Rule 7033–1.

Subdivision (c)(2) of this Rule has been modified to conform to subdivision (e)(3)(B)(1) of Local Bankruptcy Rule 7033–1.

[Comment amended effective July 28, 1998.]

RULE 7034–2. OPT–OUT FROM CERTAIN PROVISIONS OF RULE 34 OF THE FEDERAL RULES OF CIVIL PROCEDURE [REPEALED EFFECTIVE AUGUST 2, 2004]

RULE 7036–1. REQUESTS FOR ADMISSION

In connection with any objection to a request for admission, the objecting party shall (i) file a copy of the request for admission simultaneously with the filing of the objection, (ii) specify and quote verbatim in the objection each request to which the objection is made, and (iii) immediately following each specification, set forth the basis of the objection.

[Adopted effective April 15, 1997. Amended effective July 28, 1998.]

Comment

This rule is derived from Former Local Bankruptcy Rule 13(f) and is an adaptation of Civil Rule 37.1 of the Local District Rules.

[Comment amended effective July 28, 1998.]

RULE 7036–2. OPT–OUT FROM CERTAIN PROVISIONS OF RULE 36 OF THE FEDERAL RULES OF CIVIL PROCEDURE [REPEALED EFFECTIVE AUGUST 2, 2004]

RULE 7052–1. PROPOSED FINDINGS OF FACT AND CONCLUSIONS OF LAW

Before or after the announcement of its decision, the Court, on notice to all parties, may require one or more parties to submit proposed findings of fact and conclusions of law. Any party submitting proposed findings of fact and conclusions of law shall serve them on all other parties within the time fixed by the Court. The Court may also grant any party's request to submit counter-findings and conclusions, which shall be served on all other parties within the time fixed by the Court.

[Adopted effective April 15, 1997. Amended effective August 2, 2004; December 1, 2016.]

Comment

This rule is derived from Former Local Bankruptcy Rule 18 and is an adaptation of Civil Rule 23 of the Former District Rules.

This rule was amended in 2016 to give the Court the power to affirmatively authorize the submission of counter-findings and conclusions. The previous version of this rule allowed the parties to submit counter-findings and conclusion by right, unless the Court ordered simultaneous submissions. The content of the record on appeal is no longer limited by this rule.

[Comment amended effective July 28, 1998; December 1, 2016.]

RULE 7055–1. CERTIFICATE OF DEFAULT

A party applying for a certificate of default from the Clerk pursuant to Bankruptcy Rule 7055 shall submit an affidavit, together with proof of service, showing that (i) the party against whom a default is sought is not an infant, in the military, or an incompetent person, (ii) the party has failed to plead or otherwise defend the action, and (iii) the pleading to which no response has been made was properly served.

[Adopted effective July 28, 1998.]

Comment

This rule is derived from Civil Rule 55.1 of the Local District Rules.

RULE 7055–2. DEFAULT JUDGMENT

(a) By the Clerk. Upon issuance by the Clerk of a certificate of default, if the claim to which no response has been made only seeks payment of a sum certain and does not include a request for attorney's fees or other substantive relief, and if a default judgment is sought against all remaining parties to the action, the moving party may request that the Clerk enter a default judgment by submitting an affidavit, together with proof of service, showing the principal amount due and owing, not exceeding the amount sought in the claim to which no response has been made, plus interest, if any, computed by the party, with credit for all payments received to date clearly set forth, and costs, if any, pursuant to 28 U.S.C. § 1920.

(b) By the Court. In all other cases, the party seeking a judgment by default shall apply to the Court as described in Bankruptcy Rule 7055 and shall append to the application (i) the Clerk's certificate of default, (ii) a copy of the claim to which no response has been made, (iii) a proposed form of default judgment, and (iv) proof of service of the application.

[Adopted effective July 28, 1998.]

Comment

This rule is derived from Civil Rule 55.2 of the Local District Rules.

RULE 7056–1. SUMMARY JUDGMENT

(a) Unless the Court orders otherwise, no party shall file a motion for summary judgment without first seeking a pre-motion conference. The request for a pre-motion conference shall be made by letter, filed with the Court, on the docket of the case, and served on all other parties setting forth the issues to be presented in the motion and the grounds for relief. Unless the Court otherwise directs, the letter shall not exceed two pages in length.

(b) Upon any motion for summary judgment pursuant to Bankruptcy Rule 7056, there shall be annexed to the motion a separate, short, and concise statement, in numbered paragraphs, of the material facts as to which the moving party contends there is no genuine issue to be tried. Failure to submit the statement shall constitute grounds for denial of the motion.

(c) Papers opposing a motion for summary judgment shall include a correspondingly numbered paragraph responding to each numbered paragraph in the statement of the moving party, and if necessary, additional paragraphs containing a separate, short, and concise statement of additional material facts as to which it is contended that there is a genuine issue to be tried.

(d) Each numbered paragraph in the statement of material facts required to be served by the moving party shall be deemed admitted for purposes of the motion unless specifically controverted by a correspondingly numbered paragraph in the statement required to be served by the opposing party.

(e) Each statement by the movant or opponent pursuant to subdivisions (b) or (c) of this rule, including each statement controverting any statement of material fact by a movant or opponent, shall be followed by citation to evidence which would be admissible.

[Adopted effective April 15, 1997. Amended effective July 28, 1998; August 2, 2004; August 1, 2013.]

Comment

Subdivision (a) of this rule was added in 2004 because motions for summary judgment are frequently burdensome, in time and expense, for the Court and the parties. Parties frequently file motions for summary judgment when an objective examination would reveal triable issues of fact or when the Court might conclude that it would be more cost-effective to resolve all issues at trial, given that most trials in bankruptcy court are bench trials. Subdivision (a) provides the Court with an opportunity to notify the parties of its observations at a pre-motion conference. The rule does not limit a party's right to file a motion for summary judgment after the pre-motion conference.

Subdivisions (b) through (e) of this rule are derived from Former Local Bankruptcy Rule 13(h) and are an adaptation of Civil Rule 56.1 of the Local District Rules. The statement of material facts shall be sufficiently complete to permit the Court to render judgment on the claim or defense. These subdivisions were amended in 2004 to conform with the 2004 amendments to Local District Rule 56.1. Compare Local Bankruptcy Rule 7052–1 (Proposed Findings of Fact and Conclusions of Law).

This rule was amended in 2013 to impose a page limit on any letter requesting a pre-motion conference as a prerequisite for filing a motion for summary judgment. This limit will produce greater efficiency and will prevent parties from extensive briefing of issues in the letter requesting a pre-motion conference.

[Comment amended effective July 28, 1998; August 2, 2004; August 1, 2013.]

RULE 7087–1. TRANSFER OF ADVERSARY PROCEEDINGS [REPEALED EFFECTIVE AUGUST 2, 2004]

PART VIII. APPEALS

[Comment amended effective December 1, 2014.]

RULE 8003–1. COPIES OF NOTICE OF APPEAL FOR PRO SE PARTIES

Upon the filing of a notice of appeal, the appellant shall provide the Clerk with sufficient copies of the notice and address labels for all pro se parties to be served to permit the Clerk to comply with Bankruptcy Rule 8003(c).

[Former Rule 8004–1 adopted effective April 15, 1997. Amended and renumbered effective December 1, 2014.]

Comment

This rule is derived from Former Local Bankruptcy Rule 8004–1 and was renumbered to conform to the 2014 amendments to Part VIII of the Bankruptcy Rules and amended to require copies of the notice of appeal and address labels only for parties appearing pro se, which is consistent with the 2014 amendment to Bankruptcy Rule 8003(c). For all other parties, service of the notice of appeal is by electronic means pursuant to Bankruptcy Rule 8001(c). Although the appellant is required to provide address labels, envelopes should not be provided.

[Comment amended effective December 1, 2014.]

RULE 8007–1. SUPERSEDEAS BOND

(a) A supersedeas bond, where the judgment is for a sum of money only, shall be in the amount of the judgment plus 11% to cover interest and such damages for delay as may be awarded, plus $250 to cover costs.

(b) When the stay may be effected as of right solely by the giving of the supersedeas bond, but the judgment or order is not solely for a sum of money, the Court, on notice, shall fix the amount of the bond. In all other cases, the Court may, on notice, grant a stay on such terms as to security and otherwise as it may deem proper.

(c) On approval, a supersedeas bond shall be filed with the Clerk, and a copy thereof, with notice of filing, promptly served on all parties affected thereby. If the appellee raises objections to the form of the bond or to the sufficiency of the surety, the Court shall hold a hearing on notice to all parties.

[Former Rule 8005–1 adopted effective April 15, 1997. Amended effective July 28, 1998. Amended and renumbered effective December 1, 2014.]

Comment

This rule is derived from Former Local Bankruptcy Rule 8005–1 and was renumbered to conform to the 2014 amendments to Part VIII of the Bankruptcy Rules.

RULE 8009–1. RECORD ON APPEAL

(a) **Furnishing and Transmitting Record on Appeal.** Except as provided in subdivision (b) of this rule, a party filing a designation of items to be included in a record on appeal shall cause to be filed on the CM/ECF system, unless previously filed, a copy of each item designated and attached to the designation.

(b) **Documents of Unusual Bulk or Weight and Physical Exhibits.** Documents of unusual bulk or weight and physical exhibits shall remain in the custody of the attorney producing them, who shall permit their inspection by any party for the purpose of preparing the record on appeal and who shall be charged with the responsibility for their safekeeping and transportation to the appellate court.

[Former Rule 8007–1 adopted effective April 15, 1997. Amended effective July 28, 1998; August 2, 2004. Renumbered and amended effective December 1, 2014. Amended effective December 1, 2016.]

Comment

This rule is derived from Former Local Bankruptcy Rule 8007–1 and was renumbered to conform to the 2014 amendments to Part VIII of the Bankruptcy Rules.

In 2016, this comment was edited to clarify that any disputes relating to the content of the record on appeal shall be decided in accordance with Bankruptcy Rule 8009(e).

[Comment amended effective December 1, 2014; December 1, 2016.]

RULE 8010–1. NOTICE TO THE BANKRUPTCY COURT OF THE FILING OF A PRELIMINARY MOTION WITH AN APPELLATE COURT

Upon the filing of a preliminary motion, as defined in Federal Rule of Bankruptcy Procedure 8010(c), in the district court or court of appeals, that arises out of an order issued by this Court, the moving party shall also file the preliminary motion and notice thereof on this Court's CM/ECF system.

[Effective December 1, 2016.]

Comment

This rule was added in 2016. It is intended to provide notice to the bankruptcy court and all parties to the bankruptcy case of appellate motion practice relating to a decision or order entered in the bankruptcy case.

RULE 8024–1. ORDER, JUDGMENT, OR REMAND BY APPELLATE COURT

An order or judgment of an appellate court, when filed in the office of the Clerk, shall automatically become the order or judgment of the Court and be entered as such by the Clerk without further order. If the order or judgment of the appellate court remands for further proceedings, a motion for such further proceedings shall be referred to the Judge who heard the proceeding below unless the appellate court orders otherwise.

[Former Rule 8016–1 adopted effective April 15, 1997. Amended and renumbered effective December 1, 2014.]

Comment

This rule is derived from Former Local Bankruptcy Rule 8016–1 and was renumbered to conform to the 2014 amendments to Part VIII of the Bankruptcy Rules.

If a proceeding has been remanded by the appellate court, it is the responsibility of the parties to file a motion for further proceedings in the court to which it was remanded.

[Comment amended effective December 1, 2014.]

PART IX. GENERAL PROVISIONS

RULE 9001–1. DEFINITIONS

(a) **Definitions.** Unless inconsistent with the context, in these Local Bankruptcy Rules—

(1) *"Bankruptcy Act"* means the Bankruptcy Act of 1898, ch. 541, 30 Stat. 544 (repealed 1978);

(2) *"Bankruptcy Code"* means title 11 of the United States Code, as amended from time to time;

(3) *"Bankruptcy Rules"* means the Federal Rules of Bankruptcy Procedure and Official Bankruptcy Forms promulgated pursuant to 28 U.S.C. § 2075, as amended from time to time;

(4) *"Chief Judge"* means the Chief Judge of the Court;

(5) *"Clerk"* means the clerk or deputy clerk of the Court;

(6) *"CM/ECF"* means the Case Management/Electronic Case File System implemented in this Court, sometimes referred to herein as "ECF";

(7) *"Court"* means the United States Bankruptcy Court for the Southern District of New York;

(8) *"District Clerk"* means the clerk or deputy clerk of the District Court;

(9) *"District Court"* means the United States District Court for the Southern District of New York;

(10) *"District Judge"* means a United States District Judge appointed to, or sitting by designation in, the District Court;

(11) *"Former District Rules"* means the Rules for General, Civil, Criminal, Admiralty and Magistrate Judge Proceedings for the United States District Court for the Southern District of New York, effective from October 26, 1983 through April 15, 1997;

(12) *"Former Local Bankruptcy Rules"* means the United States Bankruptcy Court Southern District of New York Local Bankruptcy Rules, effective from April 21, 1986 through April 10, 1996;

(13) *"Judge"* means a bankruptcy judge appointed to or sitting by designation in the Court (or, with respect to a proceeding that has not been referred or which has been withdrawn, the District Judge);

(14) *"Local District Rules"* means the Local Rules for the United States District Court for the Southern and Eastern Districts of New York, as amended from time to time;

(15) *"Return Date"* means the date set for a hearing on a motion or application, and

(16) *"United States Trustee"* means the United States trustee or an assistant United States trustee for the Southern District of New York.

(b) **Rules of Construction.**

(1) Unless inconsistent with the context, the meanings of other words and phrases used in these Local Bankruptcy Rules shall be construed in accordance with the Bankruptcy Code and Bankruptcy Rules.

(2) Local Bankruptcy Rules containing references and URL links to guidelines, procedures, or forms on the Court's website shall be construed to mean such guidelines, procedures, and forms as amended from time to time.

(c) **Use of Terms "Documents" and "Papers."** The terms "documents" and "papers" as used in these Local Bankruptcy Rules include those filed or transmitted by electronic means.

[Adopted effective April 15, 1997. Amended effective July 28, 1998; August 2, 2004; August 1, 2013.]

Comment

Subdivisions (a) and (b) of this rule are derived from Former Local Bankruptcy Rule 2. Subdivision (c) of this rule was added in 1996.

Subdivision (a) of this rule was amended in 2013 to add the definition of "return date." This defined term was added to clarify that all references in the Local Bankruptcy Rules to return date mean the date set for a hearing on a motion or application, not the date on which objections or replies are due. Although an actual hearing may not be required in the absence of an objection or request for a hearing, the date set for a hearing in the event that a hearing is or becomes necessary is the "return date." The return date is often used in the Local Rules as a reference point for determining certain deadlines. See Local Bankruptcy Rule 9006–1.

Subdivision (b) of this rule was amended in 2013 to add paragraph (2), which provides that a reference to URL links and guidelines in these Local Bankruptcy Rules is to be construed as a reference to such guidelines, procedures, and forms as they may be amended by the Court from time to time.

[Comment amended effective July 28, 1998; August 1, 2013.]

RULE 9004–1. FORM OF PAPERS

(a) Papers Submitted for Filing. Papers submitted for filing shall

(1) be plainly typed or printed;

(2) not be bound or stapled;

(3) have no erasures or interlineations which materially deface them; and

(4) state on the face of the document:

(A) the name of the attorney for the filing party;

(B) the attorney's office and post office addresses; and

(C) the attorney's telephone number.

(b) Chambers copies and copies for the United States Trustee shall be bound or stapled and submitted in accordance with Local Bankruptcy Rule 9070–1.

[Adopted effective April 15, 1997. Amended effective July 28, 1998; August 2, 2004; August 4, 2008.]

Comment

This rule is derived from Former Local Bankruptcy Rule 9(b) and is an adaptation of Civil Rule 11.1 of the Local District Rules.

The general rules for form of papers are set forth in Bankruptcy Rule 9004 and Official Bankruptcy Forms 16A, 16B, 16C, and 16D.

This rule was amended in 2004 to conform to Civil Rule 11.1(b) of the Local District Rules to allow attorneys to use an identification number issued by the District Court instead of the last four digits of the attorney's social security number.

This rule was also amended in 2004 to clarify that pleadings no longer require litigation backs or covers.

This rule was amended in 2008 to conform to the repeal of Civil Rule 11.1(b) of the Local District Rules, which previously required that every pleading, written motion and other paper signed by an attorney include the attorney's initials and the last four digits of the attorney's social security number or any other four digit number registered by the attorney with the clerk of the court.

[Comment amended effective July 28, 1998; August 2, 2004; August 4, 2008.]

RULE 9004–2. CAPTION

(a) Papers submitted for filing shall bear the title of the case, the initials of the Judge to whom the case has been assigned, the docket number assigned to the case, and, if applicable, the adversary proceeding number.

(b) The return date and time of a motion, and time for serving any responsive papers, shall be included in the upper right-hand corner of the caption of the motion and all related pleadings. In addition, the CM/ECF docket number to which the filing relates shall be included in the upper right-hand corner of the caption of all responsive papers.

[Adopted effective April 15, 1997. Amended effective August 1, 2013.]

Comment

Subdivision (a) of this rule is derived from Former Local Bankruptcy Rule 9. Subdivision (b) of this rule is derived from former Standing Order M–99. The return date for a motion is obtained pursuant to Local Bankruptcy Rule 5070–1.

This rule was amended in 2013 to require that all motions and related pleadings include the deadline for filing objections or other responsive papers in the caption. In addition, for all objections or other responsive papers, the CM/ECF docket number for the proceeding must be included in the caption.

[Comment amended effective August 1, 2013.]

RULE 9006–1. TIME FOR SERVICE AND FILING OF MOTIONS AND ANSWERING PAPERS

(a) Discovery–Related Motions. Unless the Court orders otherwise, all motion papers under Bankruptcy Rules 7026 through 7037 shall be served at least seven (7) days before the return date. Where such service is made, any answering papers shall be served so as to ensure actual receipt not later than three (3) days before the return date.

(b) All Other Motions. Except as otherwise ordered by the Court, or required by the Bankruptcy Rules, all other motion papers shall be served at least fourteen (14) days before the return date. Where service is made at least fourteen (14) days before the return date, any answering papers shall be served so as to ensure actual receipt not later than seven (7) days before the return date, and reply papers shall be served so as to ensure actual receipt not later than 4:00 p.m. three (3) days before the return date, unless the Court orders otherwise.

(c) Time for Filing With Court. Unless the Court orders otherwise, all motions and answering papers shall be filed with the Clerk not later than one day following the date of service.

[Adopted effective April 15, 1997. Amended effective December 1, 2009; August 1, 2013; December 1, 2016.]

Comment

This rule is derived from Former Local Bankruptcy Rule 13(c) and is an adaptation of Civil Rule 6.1 of the Local District Rules. Subdivision (b) of this rule is an exercise of the Court's authority contained in Bankruptcy Rule 9006(d) to enlarge the time for service of motion papers.

In 2009, subdivision (a) of this rule was amended to change the time period from five (5) to seven (7) days, and subdivision (b) of this rule was amended to change the time period from ten (10) to fourteen (14) days. The purpose of these amendments was to conform the time periods in this rule to the 2009 time-related amendments to the Federal Rules of Bankruptcy Procedure. Throughout the Bankruptcy Rules, as well as the Local Bankruptcy Rules, most time periods that are shorter than thirty (30) days were changed so that the number of days is in multiples of seven (7), thereby reducing the likelihood that time periods will end on a Saturday or Sunday.

The one (1)–day deadline in subdivision (a) was changed to three (3) days, and the three (3) day deadline in subdivision (b) was changed to seven (7) days, to give the Court and the parties more time to consider the answering papers before the hearing.

The one business day deadline in subdivision (c) of this rule was also amended in 2009 to delete the reference to "business" so that the time period will be consistent with the 2009 amendments to Bankruptcy Rule 9006(a).

The Bankruptcy Rules require minimum notice periods longer than fourteen (14) days with respect to certain proposed actions. Although subdivision (b) is intended to enlarge the time for service of motions under Bankruptcy Rule 9006(d), it is not intended to shorten minimum time periods specified in the Bankruptcy Rules. For example, Bankruptcy Rule 2002(a)(3) requires at least twenty-one (21) days' notice of the hearing on approval of a compromise and settlement. Therefore, if a trustee moves for approval of a compromise and settlement under Rule 9019(a), the motion papers must be served at least 21 days before the hearing. Similarly, Rule 2002(a)(2) requires at least 21 days' notice of a proposed use, sale or lease of property, unless the Court shortens the time. The first sentence of subdivision (b) of this local rule was amended in 2013 to recognize such time periods required by the Bankruptcy Rules.

The second sentence of subdivision (b) was amended in 2013 to clarify that the seven-day requirement for service of answering papers applies when motion papers are served at least 14 days before the return date, even if the motion is served more than 14 days before the return date to comply with an applicable Bankruptcy Rule. For example, if a motion for approval of a compromise and settlement is served 21 days before return date to comply with Bankruptcy Rule 2002(a)(3), the answering papers must be served so as to ensure actual receipt at least seven days before the return date, unless the Court orders otherwise.

This rule was amended in 2016 to provide that replies, while permissible, must be received by the court no later than 4:00 p.m. three (3) days before the hearing date. Days should be counted in accordance with Bankruptcy Rule 9006(a).

[Comment amended effective July 28, 1998; December 1, 2009; August 1, 2013; December 1, 2016.]

RULE 9006–2. AUTOMATIC EXTENSION OF TIME WHEN TIMELY MOTION TO EXTEND TIME IS FILED

Unless otherwise provided in the Bankruptcy Code, the Bankruptcy Rules, the Local Bankruptcy Rules, or order of the Court, when a motion to extend the time to take any action is filed before the expiration of the period prescribed by the Bankruptcy Code, Bankruptcy Rules, Local Bankruptcy Rules, or order of the Court, with a return date that is no later than fourteen (14) days after the date of such filing or, if the Court is unable to schedule a return date within such period, as soon thereafter as the return date may be scheduled by the Court, the time shall automatically be extended until the Court resolves the motion to extend the time. An automatic extension under this rule shall not require the issuance or entry of an order extending the time.

[Adopted effective August 1, 2013.]

Comment

This rule was added in 2013 as an exercise of the Court's discretion to extend time under Bankruptcy Rule 9006(b) and to obviate the need for a "bridge order" in certain circumstances.

This local rule does not apply if an automatic bridge order would be inconsistent with a provision of the Bankruptcy Code, Bankruptcy Rules, Local Bankruptcy Rules, or order of the Court. For example, Local Bankruptcy Rule 9006–2 would not apply to motions to extend the time to file a plan or to confirm a plan in a small business case because, pursuant to section 1121(e)(3) of the Bankruptcy Code, such extensions require that the Court sign an extension order before the existing deadline expires. In addition, extensions of time for a lessee to assume or reject an unexpired lease of nonresidential real property are governed by Local Bankruptcy Rule 6006–1(c), which contains certain limitations, instead of Local Bankruptcy Rule 9006–2.

[Comment added effective August 1, 2013.]

RULE 9011–1. SIGNING OF PAPERS

(a) All pleadings, motions, and other papers that are submitted for filing, except a list, schedule, or statement, or amendments thereto, shall be signed by an attorney of record in the attorney's own name or, if there is no attorney, all papers submitted for filing shall be signed by the party. The name of the attorney or party shall be clearly printed or typed below the signature, together with the attorney's or party's address and telephone number.

(b) The signing of documents filed electronically shall be governed by the *Procedures for the Filing, Signing, and Verification of Documents by Electronic Means* issued by the Court, which shall be available on the Court's website (http://www.nysb.uscourts.gov/sites/default/files/5005-2-procedures.pdf). An original signed copy of the filing shall be maintained in the attorney's files.

(c) Any password required for electronic filing shall be used only by the attorney to whom the password is assigned and authorized members and employees of such attorney's firm.

[Adopted effective April 15, 1997. Amended effective August 2, 2004; August 4, 2008; August 1, 2013.]

Comment

This rule is an adaptation of Civil Rule 11.1 of the Local District Rules. This rule was amended in 2004 to conform to Civil Rule 11.1(b) of the Local District Rules to allow attorneys to use an identification number issued by the District Court instead of the last four digits of the attorney's social security number.

This rule was amended in 2008 to conform to the repeal of Civil Rule 11.1(b) of the Local District Rules, which previously required that every pleading, written motion and other paper signed by an attorney include the attorney's initials and the last four digits of the attorney's social security number or any other four digit number registered by the attorney with the clerk of the court.

Subdivision (a) was also amended in 2008 to conform to Rule 9011(a), which does not require an attorney's signature on lists, schedules, and statements.

Subdivision (b) was also amended in 2008 to provide that signing electronically filed documents is governed by the Court's standing order on electronically filed cases. This rule was amended in 2013 to specify the title to the procedures promulgated by General Order M–399 relating to electronic filing, signing and verification of documents, and to state the link to the Court's website where practitioners may access them. It is anticipated that these procedures, which also may be obtained from the Clerk, will be amended from time to time to account for changes in technology or the law.

[Comment amended effective July 28, 1998; August 2, 2004; August 4, 2008; August 1, 2013.]

RULE 9013–1. MOTION PRACTICE

(a) Rule or Statutory Basis. Each motion shall specify the rules and statutory provisions upon which it is predicated and the legal authorities that support the requested relief, either in the motion or in a separate memorandum of law. If such specification has not been made, the Court may strike the motion from the calendar.

(b) Entities to Receive Notice. In addition to all entities otherwise entitled to receive notice, notice of a motion shall be given to any entity believed to have or be claiming an interest in the subject matter of the proposed order or who, it is believed, otherwise would be affected by the proposed order.

[Adopted effective April 15, 1997. Amended effective July 28, 1998; August 4, 2008.]

Comment

This rule is derived from Former Local Bankruptcy Rule 13.

Local Bankruptcy Rule 7007–1 provides additional requirements for discovery-related motion practice.

This rule was amended in 2008 to delete the requirement that a separate memorandum of law be filed with every motion. A discussion of the law must be included in the motion or responsive pleading if a separate memorandum of law is not filed.

RULE 9014–1. CONTESTED MATTERS

Unless the Court orders otherwise, Rules 7(b) and 24 of the Federal Rules of Civil Procedure, as incorporated in Bankruptcy Rules 7007 and 7024, respectively, and Local Bankruptcy Rules 7005–1, 7007–1, 7016–1, 7024–1, 7026–1, 7027–1, 7030–1, 7033–1, 7034–1, 7036–1, 7052–1, 7055–1, 7055–2, and 7056–1, shall apply in contested matters.

[Adopted effective April 15, 1997. Amended effective July 28, 1998; August 2, 2004.]

Comment

This rule is an exercise of the Court's discretion under Bankruptcy Rule 9014 to make any rule in Part VII of the Bankruptcy Rules applicable to contested matters.

RULE 9014–2. FIRST SCHEDULED HEARING

The first scheduled hearing in a contested matter will not be an evidentiary hearing at which witnesses may testify, unless:

(a) the Court gives prior notice to the parties that such hearing will be an evidentiary hearing;

(b) the motion requests emergency relief and is made at the commencement of the case;

(c) the motion requests interim or final relief under sections 363(b), 363(c)(2)(B) or 364 of the Bankruptcy Code;

(d) the motion requests the Court's approval of rejection of an unexpired lease of real property under section 365(a) of the Bankruptcy Code, and a timely objection thereto is filed;

(e) the hearing is on confirmation of a plan in a case under chapter 9, chapter 11, chapter 12, or chapter 13 of the Bankruptcy Code; or

(f) Repealed.

[Adopted effective August 2, 2004.]

Comment

Bankruptcy Rule 9014(e), added in 2002, requires that the Court provide procedures that enable parties to ascertain at a reasonable time before any scheduled hearing whether the hearing will be an evidentiary hearing at which witnesses may testify. Local Rule 9014–2 was added in 2004 to provide such a procedure. Nothing in Local Rule 9014–2 precludes a party from requesting an evidentiary hearing at the first scheduled hearing and asking the Court to provide for notice thereof under paragraph (a).

Subdivision (f) of this rule was abrogated in 2013. Since this rule was adopted in 2004, there had been no general orders issued under subdivision (f), which could have made this paragraph misleading to practitioners. If the Court wants to specify another kind of contested matter in which an evidentiary hearing will be held at the first scheduled hearing, the Court may do so by amending this rule. Therefore, subdivision (f) is not necessary to give the Court flexibility to expand the list set forth in subdivisions (a) through (e).

[Comment adopted effective August 2, 2004.]

RULE 9015–1. JURY TRIALS

A statement of consent to have a jury trial conducted by a Bankruptcy Judge under 28 U.S.C. § 157(e) shall be filed not later than fourteen (14) days after the service of the last pleading directed to the issue for which the demand was made.

[Adopted effective July 28, 1998. Amended effective August 2, 2004; December 1, 2009.]

Comment

Section 157(e) of title 28 provides that a Bankruptcy Judge may conduct a jury trial on proper demand with the consent of the parties to the proceeding if the District Court has specifically designated the Bankruptcy Court to exercise such jurisdiction. The District Court, by order dated December 7, 1994, has specifically designated the Bankruptcy Court to conduct jury trials pursuant to section 157(e). Bankruptcy Rule 9015(b) provides that the time for filing a statement of consent to a jury trial shall be specified by local rule.

This rule provides a fourteen (14) day period for filing the statement of consent, which runs from the service of the last pleading, as specified in Bankruptcy Rule 7007.

This rule was amended in 2009 to change the time period from ten (10) to fourteen (14) days. The purpose of the amendment was to conform the time period in this rule to the 2009 time-related amendments to the Federal Rules of Bankruptcy Procedure. Throughout the Bankruptcy Rules, as well as the Local Bankruptcy Rules, most time periods that are shorter than 30 days were changed so that the number of days is in multiples of seven (7), thereby reducing the likelihood that time periods will end on a Saturday or Sunday.

[Comment amended effective August 2, 2004; December 1, 2009.]

RULE 9018–1. MOTIONS TO PUBLICLY FILE REDACTED DOCUMENTS AND TO FILE UNREDACTED DOCUMENTS UNDER SEAL

(a) Unless otherwise required by these Local Rules, the Bankruptcy Rules, the Bankruptcy Code, or order of this Court, requests to file under seal shall consist of two parts: (i) a motion to seal and (ii) the documents to be sealed.

(b) The motion to seal shall include:

(1) the grounds for sealing;

(2) the identity of any parties other than the moving party who will have access to the documents to be sealed;

(3) the duration of the seal;

(4) the time when the movant will either unseal the documents or retrieve the documents at the conclusion of the matter;

(5) a redacted copy of the documents sought to be sealed with only those redactions necessary to preserve confidentiality, made in good faith; and

(6) a proposed order that contains language indicating the order is without prejudice to the rights of any party in interest, or the United States Trustee, to seek to unseal the documents, or any part thereof.

(c) Upon filing the motion to seal, the moving party must hand deliver a copy of the motion to seal and the unredacted documents sought to be sealed to the Clerk's Office. The documents must be conspicuously marked "FILED UNDER PENDING MOTION TO SEAL."

[Effective December 1, 2016.]

Comment

This rule was added in 2016 to provide a uniform standard procedure for how to file motions under seal. The rule distinguishes between the motion, which should be filed publicly on the docket, and the documents to be sealed. The motion should include a redacted copy of the documents to be sealed. The time to file and serve the underlying motion for which purpose the motion to seal is being made should be in accordance with all applicable rules pertaining to service of the underlying motion.

RULE 9019-1. ALTERNATIVE DISPUTE RESOLUTION

Alternative dispute resolution shall be conducted in the manner required by the Procedures Governing Mediation of Matters and the Use of Early Neutral Evaluation and Mediation/Voluntary Arbitration in Bankruptcy Cases and Adversary Proceedings, which shall be available on the Court's web site (http://www.nysb.uscourts.gov/content/mediation-procedures).

[Adopted effective April 15, 1997. Amended effective January 26, 1999.]

Comment

Procedures governing mediation programs in bankruptcy cases and adversary proceedings were promulgated by General Order M–390. This rule was amended in 2013 to specify the title of the procedures promulgated by General Order M–390, amended by General Order M-452 and to state in the rule the link to the Court's website where practitioners may access the governing procedures. The Procedures Governing Mediation of Matters and the Use of Early Neutral Evaluation and Mediation/Voluntary Arbitration in Bankruptcy Cases and Adversary Proceedings, which also may be obtained from the Clerk, may be amended by the Court after giving notice and opportunity for comment as is appropriate.

RULE 9019-2. LOSS MITIGATION FOR INDIVIDUAL DEBTORS WITH RESIDENTIAL REAL PROPERTY AT RISK TO FORECLOSURE

Loss mitigation procedures for the facilitation of consensual resolutions for individual debtors whose residential real property is at risk of loss to foreclosure shall be governed by the Loss Mitigation Program Procedures promulgated by the Court, which shall be available on the Court's website (http://www.nysb.uscourts.gov/sites/default/files/LossMitigation Procedures.pdf).

Comment

This rule was promulgated in 2013 to include in the Local Bankruptcy Rules a reference to the Loss Mitigation Program Procedures established by General Order M-413 and modified by General Order M-451. These procedures, which also may be obtained from the Clerk, may be amended by the Court from time to time.

RULE 9020-1. DEFAULT SANCTIONS; IMPOSITION OF COSTS

(a) Default Sanctions. Failure of a party or counsel for a party to appear before the Court at a conference, complete the necessary preparations, or be prepared to proceed at the time set for trial or hearing may be considered an abandonment of the adversary proceeding or contested matter or a failure to prosecute or defend diligently, and an appropriate order of the Court may be entered against the defaulting party with respect to either a specific issue or the entire adversary proceeding or contested matter.

(b) Imposition of Costs. If the Judge finds that the sanctions in subdivision (a) of this rule are either inadequate or unjust to the parties, the Judge may assess reasonable costs directly against the party or counsel whose action has obstructed the effective administration of the Court's business.

[Adopted effective April 15, 1997.]

Comment

This rule is derived from Former Local Bankruptcy Rule 21 and is an adaptation of General Rule 5(b) and (c) of the Former District Rules.

[Comment amended effective July 28, 1998.]

RULE 9021-1. ENTRY OF ORDERS, JUDGMENTS, AND DECREES

The Clerk shall enter all orders, decrees, and judgments of the Court in the electronic filing system, which shall constitute docketing of the order, decree, or judgment for all purposes. The Clerk's notation on the appropriate docket of an order, judgment, or decree shall constitute the entry of the order, judgment, or decree.

[Adopted effective April 15, 1997. Amended effective July 28, 1998.]

Comment

This rule is derived from Former Local Bankruptcy Rule 19(a) and is an adaptation of Civil Rule 6.2 of the Local District Rules.

This rule supplements Bankruptcy Rule 9021, which provides that a judgment or order is effective when entered under Bankruptcy Rule 5003.

[Comment amended effective July 28, 1998; December 1, 2009.]

RULE 9023-1. MOTIONS FOR REARGUMENT

(a) A motion for reargument of a court order determining a motion shall be served within fourteen (14) days after the entry of the Court's order determining the original motion, or in the case of a court order resulting in a judgment, within fourteen (14) days after the entry of the judgment, and, unless the Court orders otherwise, shall be made returnable within the same amount of time as required for the original motion. The motion shall set forth concisely the matters or controlling decisions which counsel believes the Court has not considered. No oral argument shall be heard unless the Court grants the motion and specifically orders that the matter be re-argued orally.

(b) The expense of any party in obtaining all or any part of a transcript for purposes of a new trial or for amended findings may be a cost taxable against the losing party.

[Adopted effective April 15, 1997. Amended effective August 2, 2004; December 1, 2009.]

Comment

Subdivision (a) of this rule is derived from Former Local Bankruptcy Rule 13(j) and is an adaptation of Civil Rule 6.3 of the Local District Rules. Subdivision (b) of this rule is derived from Former Local Bankruptcy Rule 33 and is an adaptation of Civil Rule 12 of the Former District Rules.

This rule does not apply to motions made under Bankruptcy Rule 3008 or 9024.

Subdivision (a) of this rule was amended in 2004 to conform with the 2004 amendments to Local District Rule 6.3.

Subdivision (a) of this rule was amended in 2009 to change the time periods from ten (10) to fourteen (14) days. The purpose of the amendment was to conform the time periods in this rule to the 2009 time-related amendments to the Federal Rules of Bankruptcy Procedure. Throughout the Bankruptcy Rules, as well as the Local Bankruptcy Rules, most time periods that are shorter than thirty (30) days were changed so that the number of days is in multiples of seven (7), thereby reducing the likelihood that time periods will end on a Saturday or Sunday.

[Comment amended effective August 2, 2004; December 1, 2009.]

RULE 9025–1. SURETIES

(a) Execution by Surety Only. If a bond, undertaking, or stipulation is required, an instrument executed only by the surety shall be sufficient.

(b) Security for Bond. Except as otherwise provided by law, every bond, undertaking, or stipulation shall be secured by (i) the deposit of cash or government bonds in the amount of the bond, undertaking, or stipulation, (ii) the undertaking or guaranty of a corporate surety holding a certificate of authority from the Secretary of the Treasury, or (iii) the undertaking or guaranty of two individual residents of the Southern District or Eastern District of New York, each of whom owns real or personal property within such district with a value of twice the amount of the bond in excess of the surety's debts, liabilities, legal exemptions, and obligations on other bonds, guaranties, undertakings, or stipulations.

(c) Affidavit by Individual Surety. In the case of a bond, undertaking, or stipulation executed by individual sureties, each surety shall attach an affidavit of justification, giving the surety's full name, occupation, and residence and business addresses, and showing that the surety is not disqualified from acting as an individual surety under subdivision (d) of this rule.

(d) Persons Who May Not Act as Sureties. Members of the bar, administrative officers and employees of the Court, the marshal, and the marshal's deputies and assistants may not act as sureties in any pending case, adversary proceeding, or contested matter.

(e) Approval of Bonds of Corporate Sureties. Except as otherwise provided by sections 303 and 322(b) of the Bankruptcy Code, Bankruptcy Rule 2010, and Local Bankruptcy Rule 8005–1, all bonds, undertakings, and stipulations of corporate sureties holding certificates of authority from the Secretary of the Treasury, where the amount of such bonds or undertakings has been fixed by a Judge, an order of the Court, a statute, or Local Bankruptcy Rule 8007–1, may be approved by the Clerk

[Adopted effective April 15, 1997. Amended effective July 28, 1998; December 1, 2014.]

Comment

Subdivisions (a), (b), (c), and (d) of this rule are derived from Former Local Bankruptcy Rule 28 and are an adaptation of Civil Rule 65.1.1(a), (b), (d), and (e) of the Local District Rules. Subdivision (b) of this rule has been modified to conform to Civil Rule 65.1.1(b) of the Local District Rules. Subdivision (e) of this rule is derived from Former Local Bankruptcy Rule 29 and is an adaptation of Civil Rule 65.1.1(f) of the Local District Rules.

Subdivision (e) was amended in 2014 to change the reference to Local Bankruptcy Rule 8005–1 to Local Bankruptcy Rule 8007–1 to conform to the 2014 amendments to Part VIII of the Bankruptcy Rules.

[Comment amended effective July 28, 1998; December 1, 2014

RULE 9027–1. STATEMENT IN NOTICE OF REMOVAL REGARDING CONSENT TO ENTRY OF ORDERS OR JUDGMENT IN CORE PROCEEDING [REPEALED EFFECTIVE DECEMBER 1, 2016]

Comment

This rule was repealed in 2016 in light of Bankruptcy Rule 9027.

RULE 9027–2. STATEMENT REGARDING CONSENT TO ENTRY OF ORDERS OR JUDGMENT IN CORE PROCEEDING [REPEALED EFFECTIVE DECEMBER 1, 2016]

Comment

This rule was repealed in 2016 in light of Bankruptcy Rule 9027.

RULE 9028–1. ACTION IN ABSENCE OF ASSIGNED JUDGE

In the absence of an assigned Judge, any other Judge who is available may act temporarily in the absent Judge's place. To obtain the assistance of an available Judge, the parties shall communicate first with the chambers staff of the assigned Judge and, if chambers staff is unavailable, then with the Clerk.

[Adopted effective April 15, 1997. Amended effective July 28, 1998.]

Comment

This rule is derived from Former Local Bankruptcy Rule 6.

This rule is intended to assure that the business of the Court will not be impeded by the absence of an assigned Judge.

[Comment amended effective July 28, 1998.]

RULE 9033–1. PROPOSED FINDINGS AND CONCLUSIONS IN CERTAIN CORE PROCEEDINGS

If the Court determines that it cannot enter a final order or judgment consistent with Article III of the United States Constitution in a particular proceeding referred to the Court and designated as core under section 157(b) of title 28, and the Court hears the proceeding, Rule 9033(a), (b), and (c) of the Federal Rules of Bankruptcy Procedure shall apply as if it is a non-core proceeding.

[Adopted effective April 16, 2012.]

RULE 9037–1. REDACTION OF PERSONAL DATA IDENTIFIERS

(a) Compliance With Bankruptcy Rule 9037. All documents filed with the Court shall comply with Bankruptcy Rule 9037.

(b) Responsibility for Redaction. The responsibility for redacting personal data identifiers (as defined in Bankruptcy Rule 9037) rests solely with counsel, parties in interest and non-parties. The Clerk, or claims agent if one has been appointed, will not review each document for compliance with this Rule. In the event the Clerk, or claims agent if one has been appointed, discovers that personal identifier data or information concerning a minor individual has been included in a pleading, the Clerk, or claims agent if one has been appointed, is authorized, in its sole discretion, to restrict public access to the document in issue and inform the filer of the requirement to file a motion to redact.

(c) Motion to Redact Personal Identifiers. Notwithstanding the requirements of Bankruptcy Rule 9037, a party seeking to redact personal identifiers from a document or a proof of claim, already filed with the court, shall file a motion to redact the personal identifiers, in accordance with CM/ECF procedures, that identifies the proposed document for redaction by docket number or if applicable, by claim number. If a party seeks to redact documents filed in multiple cases, such as proofs of claim, the party must open a miscellaneous proceeding by filing a motion to redact with a list of all affected cases and/or documents, subject to fees in accordance with the Bankruptcy Court Miscellaneous Fee Schedule. Prior to filing the motion to redact, the party must contact the Clerk's Office to request that the Clerk's Office restrict the original image containing the personal data identifiers from public view on the docket.

(d) Notice. The filer shall include a certificate of service at the time the motion to redact is filed, showing service to the following recipients: the debtor, anyone whose personal information has been disclosed, the case trustee (if any) and the United States Trustee.

(e) Filing of Correctly Redacted Document or Claim. Unless otherwise ordered by the court, the party seeking redaction shall file a correctly redacted document or proof of claim within twenty-one days of the granting of the motion.

(f) Filing Motions to Reopen in Closed Cases. The granting of a motion to redact in a closed case is ministerial in nature and does not impact the administration of the case. For that reason, a party seeking redaction in a closed case does not need to file a motion to reopen the case, and no fee for reopening shall be collected by the clerk.

(g) Redaction Fee. In accordance with the provisions of the Bankruptcy Court Miscellaneous Fee Schedule, the party filing a motion to redact personal identifiers from a document or proof of claim must pay a fee for filing such motion to redact in each case.

[Effective December 1, 2016.]

Comment

This rule was added in 2016 to make clear that redactions are the responsibility of the filing party. The rule also addresses situations involving the need to redact the same information filed in multiple cases.

The fee for filing a motion to redact does not apply to transcripts. Pursuant to the Judicial Conference Policy, attorneys or any other entity requesting the redaction of personal identifiers on a transcript must file a *Notice of Intent to Request Redaction*. The procedures for redacting transcripts are available on the court's website. (http://www.nysb.uscourts.gov/sites/default/files/pdf/TranscriptRestrictionsRedactionGuidelines.pdf)

RULE 9070–1. COPIES OF FILED PAPERS

(a) Copy for United States Trustee. A hard copy of all papers filed with the Court, including those filed electronically, other than proofs of claim, shall be submitted to the Clerk for transmittal to the United States Trustee.

(b) Chambers Copy. Unless the Court directs otherwise, a copy of all complaints, answers, motions, applications, objections, and responses to any of the foregoing filed with the Court, other than proofs of claim, shall be marked "Chambers Copy" and delivered or mailed to the Clerk's office located in the division in which the assigned Judge sits on the same day as the papers are filed with the Clerk or, if filed electronically, not later than the next day.

[Adopted effective April 15, 1997. Amended effective July 28, 1998; August 2, 2004; December 1, 2009; August 1, 2013.]

Comment

The rule is derived from Former Local Bankruptcy Rule 9(d) and (e). The next business day deadline in subdivision (b) of this rule was amended in 2009 to delete the reference to "business" so that the time period will be consistent with the 2009 amendments to Bankruptcy Rule 9006(a).

Subdivision (b) was amended in 2013 to reduce the amount of paper submitted as chambers copies. Unless the Court directs otherwise, only certain papers specified in the rule, rather than all papers, must be delivered to chambers under this rule. Subdivision (b) of this rule was also amended to permit the mailing of chambers copies to the Court and to eliminate the requirement that papers must be delivered in unsealed envelopes.

[Comment amended effective December 1, 2009; August 1, 2013.]

RULE 9072–1. CUSTODY OF EXHIBITS

(a) Retention by Attorney. Unless the Court orders otherwise, exhibits shall not be filed with the Clerk, but shall be retained in the custody of the attorney who produced them in Court.

(b) Removal of Exhibits from Court. Exhibits that have been filed with the Clerk shall be removed by the party responsible for the exhibits (i) if no appeal has been taken, at the expiration of the time for taking an appeal, or (ii) if an appeal has been taken, within thirty (30) days after the record on appeal has been returned to the Clerk. Parties failing to comply with this rule shall be notified by the Clerk to remove their exhibits, and, upon their failure to do so within thirty (30) days of such notification, the Clerk may dispose of the exhibits.

[Adopted effective April 15, 1997. Amended effective July 28, 1998; December 1, 2014.]

Comment

This rule is derived from Former Local Bankruptcy Rule 27 and is an adaptation of Civil Rule 39.1 of the Local District Rules. Former subdivision (c) of this rule has been included, as modified, in Local Bankruptcy Rule 8009–1(b). As used in this rule, "exhibits" includes trial exhibits admitted in to evidence, in a case, adversary proceeding, or contested matter.

[Comment amended effective July 28, 1998; December 1, 2104.]

RULE 9074–1. SUBMISSION, SETTLEMENT OR PRESENTMENT OF ORDER, JUDGMENT, OR DECREE

(a) Submission or Settlement of an Order, Judgment, or Decree. Unless the Court orders otherwise, if, following a hearing or decision, the Court directs a party to submit or settle an order, judgment, or decree, the party, within fourteen (14) days of the issuance of the Court's ruling shall deliver the proposed order, judgment, or decree directly to the Judge's chambers upon not less than two days' notice to all parties to the adversary proceeding or contested matter, except that such notice period shall not apply if all parties to the adversary proceeding or contested matter have consented in writing to the proposed order, judgment, or decree. Failure to submit or settle an order, judgment, or decree within the fourteen (14) day period may result in the imposition of sanctions, including, without limitation, (i) dismissal for failure to prosecute or (ii) an award of attorney's fees. One (1) day notice is required of all counterproposals. Unless the Court orders otherwise, no proposed or counter-proposed order, judgment, or decree submitted or settled pursuant to this rule shall form a part of the record of the case, adversary proceeding, or contested matter.

(b) Notice of Motion Upon Presentment and Opportunity for Hearing With Respect to Certain Motions, Applications, and Objections.

(1) *Use.* Unless the Court orders otherwise, where it is anticipated that a motion, application, or objection of a type set forth below will be uncontested, the motion, application, or objection may be made upon notice of presentment conforming substantially to the appropriate form following this rule:

(A) Application to confirm a sale pursuant to Local Bankruptcy Rule 6004–1;

(B) Motion to extend the time to assume or reject a lease pursuant to section 365(d)(4) of the Bankruptcy Code;

(C) Motion for entry of a default judgment in an adversary proceeding pursuant to Bankruptcy Rule 7055 and Local Bankruptcy Rule 7055–2;

(D) Motion to extend the time to object to discharge or dischargeability pursuant to Bankruptcy Rule 4004 or 4007;

(E) Application to avoid a judicial lien that impairs an exemption pursuant to section 522(f) of the Bankruptcy Code;

(F) Application for an examination pursuant to Bankruptcy Rule 2004 to the extent that the application is not granted ex parte;

(G) Objection to a claim of exemption pursuant to Bankruptcy Rule 4003(b);

(H) Application to approve a loan modification under Local Bankruptcy Rule 9019–2;

(I) Request for a post-confirmation order pursuant to Local Bankruptcy Rule 3021–1;

(J) Application to employ a professional person pursuant to section 327(a) of the Bankruptcy Code; and

(K) Any other type of motion, application, or objection as ordered by the Court in the particular case.

(2) *Notice.* Unless the Court orders otherwise, notice of the presentment of an order pursuant to this subdivision shall be filed with the Clerk and a copy shall be delivered to the Judge's chambers and served upon the debtor, the trustee, each committee, the United States Trustee, all parties who have filed a notice of appearance and request for service of documents, and all other parties in interest. The notice shall comport with the notice requirements under the applicable provisions of the Bankruptcy Code, Bankruptcy Rules, and Local Bankruptcy Rules.

(3) *Objection; Opportunity for a Hearing.* A written objection, if any, to the proposed order, together with proof of service, shall be filed with the Clerk and a courtesy copy shall be delivered to the Judge's chambers at least three (3) days before the date of presentment. Unless the Court orders otherwise, no hearing will be held absent the timely filing of an objection. If an objection has been timely filed, the Court will notify the moving and objecting parties of the date and time of any hearing.

(c) Notice of Proposed Action or Order When "Notice and a Hearing" Are Required and a Motion Is Not Mandatory.

(1) *Contents of Notice.* Unless the Court orders otherwise, whenever "notice and a hearing" are specified in the Bankruptcy Code or Bankruptcy Rules but a motion is not mandatory, the entity proposing to act or obtain an order, in lieu of proceeding by motion, may give written notice, which, together with proof of service, shall be filed with the Clerk with a copy delivered to the Judge's chambers, setting forth:

(A) a statement of the action proposed to be taken or the order to be presented, including a concise statement of the terms and conditions of, and the reasons for, the proposed action or order;

(B) the date by which objections or responses to the proposed action or order shall be served and filed;

(C) the date and time when the action will be taken or the proposed order will be presented for signature if there is no objection, and a statement that the action will be taken or the order may be entered without a hearing unless a timely objection is made; and

(D) the date on which a hearing will be held if a timely objection is made, which date shall be obtained in the manner provided by Local Bankruptcy Rule 5070–1.

(2) *Time for Notice.* Unless the Court orders otherwise, if notice is to be given to all creditors under subdivision (1) of this rule, the notice shall be given at least twenty-one (21) days prior to the date on which the proposed action is to be taken or the proposed order is to be presented. If the Court issues an order requiring that notice be given to fewer than all creditors, the notice shall be given at least seven (7) days prior to such date.

(3) *Entities to Receive Notice.* Unless the Court orders otherwise, in addition to the requirements of Bankruptcy Rule 2002 and Local Bankruptcy Rule 2002–1, notice under subdivision (1) of this rule shall be given to any entity having or claiming an interest in the subject matter of the proposed action or order or who otherwise would be affected by the proposed action or order.

(4) *Objection.* Unless the Court orders otherwise, any objection to the proposed action or order shall be in writing, state with particularity the reasons for the objection, and be served on the party proposing the action or order so as to be received (i) at least seven (7) days prior to the date set for the hearing if at least twenty-one (21) days' notice has been given and (ii) at least one (1) day prior to the date set for the hearing if at least seven (7) [but less than twenty-one (21)] days' notice has been given. The objection, together with proof of service, shall be filed with the Clerk and a copy thereof shall be delivered to the Judge's chambers prior to the date set for the hearing.

(5) *Opportunity for a Hearing.* Unless the Court orders otherwise, no hearing will be held absent the timely filing of an objection. If an objection has been timely filed, the Court will notify the moving and objecting parties of the date and time of any hearing.

(d) Notice of Presentment of Order in Lieu of Hearing Where Notice and a Hearing Are Not Required.

(1) *Use.* If notice and a hearing are not required, and a motion is not mandatory, the form set forth in subdivision (d)(3) of this rule may be used for the submission of orders to the Court.

(2) *Notice.* Unless the Court orders otherwise, notice of the presentment of an order pursuant to this subdivision shall be filed with the Clerk, and a copy shall be delivered to the Judge's chambers and served upon the debtor, the trustee, each committee, the United States Trustee, all parties who have filed a notice of appearance and request for service of documents, and all other parties in interest on not less than three (3) days' notice.

(3) *Form.* A notice of presentment of a proposed order shall conform substantially to the appropriate form following this ruling.

(e) The Court shall consider a motion, application, objection, or proposed order made by notice of presentment under this Local Bankruptcy Rule on or after the date of presentment. Any motion, application, or proposed order made by notice of presentment under this Local Bankruptcy Rule shall include a copy of the proposed order. If there has been no objection or hearing date scheduled, and the presentment date has otherwise passed, the moving party shall promptly submit a copy of the proposed order to chambers.

[Adopted effective April 15, 1997. Amended effective July 28, 1998; August 4, 2008; December 1, 2009; August 1, 2013; December 1, 2016.]

Comment

Subdivision (a) of this rule, which is derived from Former Local Bankruptcy Rule 17 and is an adaptation of Civil Rule 77.1 of the Local District Rules, applies to the settlement of orders, judgments, and decrees following a hearing or decision. Subdivision (b) of this rule, which is derived from Former Local Bankruptcy Rule 46, applies in situations in which "notice and a hearing" are not required by the Bankruptcy Code. Subdivision (b) of this rule, formerly subdivision (c), is an adaptation of former Standing Order 186, applies only to the types of proceedings specified therein and where it is anticipated that the relief requested will be uncontested.

Subdivision (b)(1) of this rule, formerly subdivision (c)(1), was amended in 2008 to delete from the list of motions that may be made on presentment a motion to terminate the automatic stay pursuant to section 362 of the Bankruptcy Code in a chapter 13 case. The purpose of this amendment is to assure that the Court will properly hear, and consider the accuracy of, allegations of default in cases concerning an individual debtor. A motion is mandatory if required by the Bankruptcy Rules, the Local Bankruptcy Rules, or an order of the Court.

Times for the presentment of and objections to proposed orders are specified in this rule to promote uniformity in practice. If notice of presentment is given by mail, three (3) additional days must be added in accordance with Bankruptcy Rule 9006(f).

Subdivision (a) of this rule was amended in 2009 to change the time periods from fifteen (15) to fourteen (14) days. The purpose of the amendment was to conform the time periods in this rule to the 2009 time-related amendments to the Federal Rules of Bankruptcy Procedure. Throughout the Bankruptcy Rules, as well as the Local Bankruptcy Rules, most time periods that are shorter than thirty (30) days were changed so that the number of days is in multiples of seven (7), thereby reducing the likelihood that time periods will end on a Saturday or Sunday.

Subdivision (a) and the heading of this rule were amended in 2009 so that the rule also will apply when the Court directs a party to submit an order, judgment, or decree.

Subdivision (b)(1) of this rule, formerly subdivision (c)(1), was amended in 2013 to add items (H), (I) and (J), which permit the use of this procedure for applications to approve a loan modification and request for a post-confirmation order in a chapter 11 case and which clarify the Court's discretion to expand the uses of notices of presentment in a particular case.

Subdivision (e), formerly subdivision(d), was added in 2013 to clarify that the Court need not enter the order on the day of presentment. Other revisions were stylistic.

In 2016, Local Bankruptcy Rule 2002–2, governing notice of a proposed action or order when not proceeding by motion, was combined with Local Bankruptcy Rule 9074–1. What was Local Bankruptcy Rule 2002–2 is now Local Bankruptcy Rule 9074–1(c). Former subdivision (b) has been moved to the end of the rule, and is now subdivision (d). Former subdivision (c) has been moved up, and is now subdivision (b). What is now subdivision (c) used to be Local Bankruptcy Rule 2002–2. Former subdivision (d) has been moved down, and is now subdivision (e).

What is now Local Bankruptcy Rule 9074–1(c), previously Local Bankruptcy Rule 2002–2, is derived from Former Local Bankruptcy Rule 45. This rule provides a standard procedure that may be used whenever the Bankruptcy Code requires "notice and a hearing," including, without limitation, sections 363, 364, 554, and 725 of the Bankruptcy Code, where the entity proposing to act or obtain an order is not required, and does not intend, to proceed by motion.

The "notice and a hearing" requirements concerning the use, sale, or lease of property and the abandonment or other disposition of property are governed by Bankruptcy Rules 6004 and 6007, respectively. To the extent not inconsistent with those Bankruptcy Rules, this rule shall apply.

Local Bankruptcy Rule 9078–1 governs the filing of proofs of service of notices.

Subdivisions (c)(2) and (3), formerly subdivisions (b) and (d) of Local Rule 2002–2, were amended in 2009 to change the twenty (20) day time periods to twenty-one (21) days. The purpose of the amendment was to conform the time periods in this rule to the 2009 time-related amendments to the Federal Rules of Bankruptcy Procedure. Throughout the Bankruptcy Rules, as well as the Local Bankruptcy Rules, most time periods that are shorter than thirty (30) days were changed so that the number of days is in multiples of seven (7), thereby reducing the likelihood that time periods will end on a Saturday or Sunday.

The three (3) day deadline in subdivision (d) of this rule was amended to seven (7) days in 2009 to give parties more time to consider objections before the hearing.

In 2016, the title of Local Bankruptcy Rule 9074–1(a) was stylistically revised to refer to submission or settlement "of an" order. Substantively, subdivision (a) remains unchanged.

In 2016, pursuant to public comments received, Local Bankruptcy Rule 9074–1(b) was amended by adding a new subsection to the list of acceptable motions, applications or objections that may be done on presentment. The addition resulted in the relabeling of the catchall provision that was previously subsection (J), which now appears as subsection (K). New subsection (J) allows an application to employ a professional person under section 327(a) of the Bankruptcy Code to be done on presentment.

In 2016, the title of subsection (c) was revised to provide greater clarity. Instead of referring to *"Notice of Motion upon Presentment and Opportunity for Hearing with Respect to Certain Motions, Applications, and Objections,"* subsection (c) is now titled, *"Notice of Proposed Action or Order When "Notice and a Hearing" are Required and a Motion is Not Mandatory."* No substantive change was intended.

In 2016, what was Local Bankruptcy Rule 2002–2 and is now Local Bankruptcy Rule 9074–1(c), was stylistically renumbered and amended to conform to its new placement in the text of the Local Bankruptcy Rules. This rule was also amended by adding subsection (c)(5). The purpose of this addition was to clarify that anything heard on presentment will not be set for a hearing.

In 2016, the numeral in subsection (d) was added to the period of days listed therein to conform to the general style of the Local Bankruptcy Rules.

In 2016, subdivision (e) was stylistically revised to clearly refer to "this Local Bankruptcy Rule," instead of "this rule." No substantive change was intended.

[Comment amended effective July 28, 1998; August 4, 2008; December 1, 2009; August 1, 2013; December 1, 2016.]

NOTICE OF PRESENTMENT

UNITED STATES BANKRUPTCY COURT
SOUTHERN DISTRICT OF NEW YORK

Presentment Date and Time:
[Insert date and time]
<u>Objection Deadline</u>
[Insert date and time]

---x

[Caption of Case]   Chapter 11 Case No. _____

---x

NOTICE OF PRESENTMENT OF [INSERT TITLE OF ORDER]

PLEASE TAKE NOTICE that upon the annexed [application or motion] of [insert name of applicant or movant], the undersigned will present the attached proposed order to the Honorable [insert name], United States Bankruptcy Judge, for signature on [insert date] at 12:00 noon.

PLEASE TAKE FURTHER NOTICE that objections, if any, to the proposed order must be made in writing and received in the Bankruptcy Judge's chambers and by the undersigned not later than 11:30 a.m. [on that date.] The ECF docket number to which the filing relates shall be included in the upper right hand corner of the caption of all objections. Unless objections are received by that time, the order may be signed.

Dated: [place]
       [date]

[insert signature block]

To: [insert names and addresses
       of entities to receive notice]

NOTICE OF PRESENTMENT AND OPPORTUNITY FOR HEARING

UNITED STATES BANKRUPTCY COURT
SOUTHERN DISTRICT OF NEW YORK

Presentment Date and Time:
[Insert date and time]
Objection Deadline
[Insert date and time]

--x

[Caption of Case]   Chapter 11 Case No. _____

--x

NOTICE OF PRESENTMENT OF [INSERT TITLE OF ORDER]
AND
OPPORTUNITY FOR HEARING

PLEASE TAKE NOTICE that upon the annexed [application, motion, or objection] of [insert name of applicant, movant, or objectant], the undersigned will present the attached proposed order to the Honorable [insert name], United States Bankruptcy Judge, for signature on [insert a date conforming to the notice requirements under applicable rules for the particular type of application, motion, or objection] at 12:00 noon.

PLEASE TAKE FURTHER NOTICE that unless a written objection to the proposed order, with proof of service, is filed with the Clerk of the Court and a courtesy copy is delivered to the Bankruptcy Judge's chambers at least three days before the date of presentment, there will not be a hearing and the order may be signed.

PLEASE TAKE FURTHER NOTICE that if a written objection is timely filed, the Court will notify the moving and objecting parties of the date and time of the hearing and of the moving party's obligation to notify all other parties entitled to receive notice. The moving and objecting parties are required to attend the hearing, and failure to attend in person or by counsel may result in relief being granted or denied upon default.

PLEASE TAKE FURTHER NOTICE that the ECF docket number to which the filing relates shall be included in the upper right hand corner of the caption of all objections.

Dated: [place]
[date]
[insert signature block]

To: [insert names and addresses
of entities to receive notice]

RULE 9075–1. REQUEST FOR HEARING

An objection to a proposed action or order shall constitute a request for a hearing.

[Adopted effective April 15, 1997. Amended effective July 28, 1998.]

Comment

This rule is derived from Former Local Bankruptcy Rules 13(i) and 45.

RULE 9075–2. CERTIFICATE OF NO OBJECTION

(a) Filing a Certificate of No Objection. If a motion or application has been filed and appropriate notice thereof has been served, and no objection, responsive pleading, or request for a hearing with respect to the motion or application has been filed or served before forty-eight (48) hours after the expiration of the time to file an objection, counsel for the moving party may file a certificate of no objection ("CNO"), with a copy to chambers, stating that no objection, responsive pleading, or request for a hearing has been filed or served on the moving party. The CNO shall include the date of the filing and service of the motion or application, the deadline for filing an objection thereto, and a statement that counsel is filing the CNO not less than forty-eight (48) hours after the expiration of such deadline.

(b) Representations to the Court. By filing the CNO, counsel for the moving party represents to the Court that the moving party is unaware of any objection, responsive pleading, or request for a hearing with respect to the motion or application, that counsel has reviewed the Court's docket not less than forty-eight (48) hours after expiration of the time to file an objection, and that no objection, responsive pleading, or request for a hearing with respect to the motion or application appears thereon.

(c) Entry of Order and Cancellation of Scheduled Hearing. Unless an individual debtor not represented by an attorney is a party in the proceeding, or a hearing is required under the Bankruptcy Code or Bankruptcy Rules notwithstanding the absence of an objection, responsive pleading, or request for a hearing, upon receipt of the CNO, the Court may enter the order accompanying the motion or application without further pleading or hearing and, once the order is entered, the hearing scheduled on the motion or application shall be cancelled without further notice.

[Adopted effective August 1, 2013.]

Comment

This rule was added in 2013 to provide a procedure for counsel to inform the Court that no timely objection, responsive pleading, or request for a hearing has been filed or served and to request that the Court enter the proposed order without a hearing. It applies only in situations where appropriate notice of a motion has been given in accordance with the Bankruptcy Rules, Local Bankruptcy Rules, or order of the Court. This procedure is not available if the Court is required to hold a hearing notwithstanding the absence of an objection, responsive pleading, or request for a hearing, such as a hearing on confirmation of a plan in a chapter 11 or chapter 13 case or a hearing on reaffirmation of a debt requested by an individual debtor not represented by counsel.

[Comment added effective August 1, 2013.]

RULE 9076–1. STATUS CONFERENCES

(a) In General. Subject to the notice provisions of subdivision (c) of this rule, the Court, on its own motion or on request of a party in interest, may hold a conference, with or without a court reporter present, at any time during a case or proceeding, for any purpose consistent with the Bankruptcy Code, including:

(1) to address the posture and efficient administration of the case or proceeding; and

(2) to establish a case management or scheduling order.

(b) Request for Conference. A request for a conference may be made either in writing or orally at a hearing. Any request, whether written or oral, shall (i) specify the matters proposed to be addressed at the conference, (ii) identify the parties who have a direct interest in such matters, and (iii) include such further information as may assist the Court in evaluating whether a conference should be held and in conducting the conference. If a conference is requested for a date prior to the appointment of a creditors' committee and the retention of its counsel, the requesting party shall state why the conference should not be delayed until after the appointment and retention. If made in writing, the request shall be directed to the chambers of the Judge presiding over the case or proceeding and served, together with a copy of any papers submitted with the request, upon the following parties:

(1) in an adversary proceeding, to the parties to the adversary proceeding; or

(2) in a case or proceeding other than an adversary proceeding, to the debtor, the trustee, the United States Trustee, each official committee appointed to serve in the case (or, if no official committee has been appointed, the holders of the ten (10) largest unsecured claims), the holders of the five (5) largest secured claims, and each unofficial committee which previously has requested the opportunity to participate in conferences.

(c) Notice of Conference. If all necessary parties are present before the Court, the Judge may direct that a conference be held immediately without further notice. In the event that a conference is called under any other circumstances, unless the Court orders otherwise, as soon as practicable, the requesting party (or, if the conference is to be held on the Court's own motion, the debtor, the trustee, or such other party as the Court may direct) shall provide notice of the time, date, place, and purpose of the conference, to the parties required to be served under subdivision (b) of this rule.

(d) Submission of Proposed Case Management and Scheduling Orders. If one of the purposes of the conference is to establish a case management or scheduling order, unless the Court orders otherwise, the party requesting the conference (or, if the conference is to be held on the Court's own motion, the debtor, the trustee, or such other party as the Court may direct) shall submit to the Court prior to the conference, on notice to all necessary parties (as identified in subdivision (b) of this rule), a proposed case management or scheduling order. The submitting party in good faith shall attempt to obtain the consent of all necessary parties (as identified in subdivision (b) of this rule) with respect to the form of the order and indicate to the Court whether such consent has been obtained.

[Adopted effective April 15, 1997. Amended effective July 28, 1998.]

Comment

This rule is an exercise of the Court's authority under section 105(d) of the Bankruptcy Code.

RULE 9077–1. ORDERS TO SHOW CAUSE; EX PARTE ORDERS

(a) Orders to Show Cause. No order to show cause shall be granted except upon a clear and specific showing by affidavit of good and sufficient reasons why proceeding other than by notice of motion is necessary. The affidavit also shall state whether a previous application for similar relief has been made.

(b) Ex Parte Orders. No ex parte order in an adversary proceeding or contested matter shall be granted unless it is based upon an affidavit or motion showing cause for ex parte action as well as cause for the relief requested, and states whether a previous application for similar relief has been made.

[Adopted effective April 15, 1997. Amended effective July 28, 1998.]

Comment

Subdivision (a) of this rule is derived from Former Local Bankruptcy Rule 13(d) and is an adaptation of Civil Rule 6.1(d) of the Local District Rules. Subdivision (b) of this rule is derived from Former Local Bankruptcy Rule 19(b).

[Comment amended effective July 28, 1998.]

RULE 9078–1. CERTIFICATE OF SERVICE

Unless the Court orders otherwise, any party serving a pleading or other document shall file proof of service by the earlier of (i) three (3) days following the date of service, and (ii) the hearing date.

[Adopted effective April 15, 1997. Amended effective July 28, 1998; December 1, 2016.]

Comment

This rule is derived from Former Local Bankruptcy Rule 45(d).

Although Former Local Bankruptcy Rule 45(d) applied only to proofs of service of notices, this rule applies to proofs of service of all pleadings and documents. The general requirements for service of notices are contained in Local Bankruptcy Rule 2002–1.

ELECTRONIC CASE FILING
PROCEDURES FOR THE FILING, SIGNING AND VERIFICATION
OF DOCUMENTS BY ELECTRONIC MEANS

I. Registration for the Electronic Filing System.

A. *Accounts.*

1. Attorneys. Each attorney admitted to practice[1] in this Court shall be entitled to an account to the Court's Case Management/Electronic Case File (CM/ECF) System (referred to as "System" below) to permit the attorney to participate in the electronic retrieval and filing of documents on the System. Application guidelines are provided in paragraph B below.

2. Non–Attorneys. This Court has authorized the limited use of the System by non-attorneys who obtain a limited-access account. Application guidelines are provided in paragraph B below.

B. *Application for and Use of Account.*

1. Each applicant must submit a completed application form pursuant to the directions appearing on the Court's website [www.nysb.uscourts.gov]. Please note that separate application forms exist for attorneys and non-attorneys.

2. The Clerk's Office, upon completion of application processing, will use the email address provided by the applicant to send information pertaining to the new System account.

3. Each System Account Holder is responsible for the accuracy of the account information pertaining to his or her account. System Account Holders may change their Court-assigned passwords or other account information (*e.g.*, business address) by using the Account Maintenance option from the Utilities menu once they are logged into the System. **System Account Holders have a duty to update promptly their account information whenever there is a change in any of the listed information** (*e.g.*, a change in the System Account Holder's primary and/or secondary e-mail addresses or the relocation of the System Account Holder's law firm to a new address).

4. As a condition to receiving an account on the System, each applicant must agree to the terms stated in the application. Once an account is issued, each System Account Holder must agree to protect and maintain the accuracy and confidentiality of account information (*e.g.*, System account holder's password) and to stay current in terms of the hardware and software requirements established by the Court for System use. Furthermore, the System Account Holder, and any employees under the direction of the Account Holder, must undergo training on the System if requested by Staff of the Clerk's Office to do so.

5. The Clerk's Office is authorized to maintain a procedure for the issuance of a new password to a System Account Holder who has forgotten his or her password.

6. The Clerk of Court retains the discretion to cancel the password of a System Account Holder with respect to: a) any individual who misuses the System or does not comply with the provisions contained in these Procedures, b) an attorney who has been disbarred or has been suspended from practicing law, or c) an attorney who has been admitted pro hac vice and whose representation is completed.

II. Electronic Filing and Service of Documents.

A. *Filing.*

1. With limited exceptions due to privacy or other concerns, all motions, pleadings or other documents required to be filed with the Court in connection with a case shall be electronically filed on the System.

2. Except as provided in the next paragraph, all documents that form part of the motion or pleading and which are being filed at the same time and by the same party may be electronically filed together under one document number (*e.g.*, the motion and a supporting affidavit), with the exception of a memorandum of law. A memorandum of law must be filed separately and linked to the document (*e.g.*, motion) to which the memorandum pertains. All pleadings and memoranda of law must be filed in text-searchable portable document format (PDF), but exhibits may be scanned in accordance with the following paragraph.

3. Exhibits. All exhibits should be properly and <u>separately</u> identified when filed (*e.g.*, "Exhibit A—Mortgage Agreement"). Persons filing documents that reference *lengthy* exhibits not prepared in electronically produced text shall scan and electronically file only excerpts of the exhibits that are directly germane to the matter under consideration by the Court. Such exhibits must be clearly and prominently identified as excerpts, and the complete exhibit must be made available forthwith to counsel and the Court on request (and must be available in the Courtroom at any hearing pertaining to the matter). Persons filing excerpts of the exhibits pursuant to these Procedures do so without prejudice to their right to file additional excerpts or the complete exhibit with the Court at any time. Opposing parties may file additional excerpts if they believe that they are germane.

4. Title of Docket Entries. The System account holder electronically filing a document is responsible for designating a title for the document (*e.g.*, motion, application, etc.) and ensuring the proper use of System events[2] through the use of the System's search feature. The System account holder must review and become familiar with the System events in order to select the proper event for docketing.

5. Fees Payable to the Clerk. All filing fees incurred by the filing of documents shall be paid on-line. It is the System account holder's responsibility to have the means to pay on-line. With limited exceptions, ***filing fees are due at the time of filing.***

6. Proposed Orders. A person presenting a proposed order shall provide the presiding judge with the proposed order in word processing format—such as WordPerfect or Microsoft Word—and ***not*** portable document format (PDF). The presiding judge shall also be provided with a hard copy of the order and all related documents unless instructed by the judge's chambers to do otherwise.

7. Creditors' Matrix. A System account holder filing a case electronically must upload the creditors' matrix on the System and file the list of creditors (PDF) on the case docket. Both the matrix and the list shall include all parties listed—or to be listed—on Schedules D, E, F, G and H.[3]

B. *Service.*

1. Consent to Electronic Service. Whenever service is required to be made on a person who has requested, or is deemed to have requested, electronic notice in accordance with Federal Rule of Bankruptcy Procedure 9036 or the annexed order, the service may be made by serving the "Notice of Electronic Filing" generated by the System by e-mail, facsimile or hand delivery in the first instance, or by overnight mail if service by e-mail, facsimile or hand delivery is impracticable. The Court's issuance of an account to a System user constitutes a waiver of conventional service with respect to that user, who agrees to accept service in the manner described in the previous sentence. The automatic e-mailing of the "Notice of Filing" generated by the System does not constitute service.

2. Notwithstanding the preceding subparagraph, conventional service of documents in hard copy shall be required in the following circumstances:

a) Service of a complaint and summons in an adversary proceeding under Federal Rule of Bankruptcy Procedure 7004, service of a motion commencing a contested matter under Federal Rule of Bankruptcy Procedure 9014(b), or a subpoena issued under Federal Rule of Bankruptcy Procedure 9016;

b) Notice of the meeting of creditors required under Federal Rule of Bankruptcy Procedure 2002(a)(1);

c) Where delivery or service upon an agency of the United States—including the United States Attorney and the United States Trustee—or chambers is required by any federal or local rule or order of this Court; and

d) Where the debtor or debtor's attorney is required to serve—on the United States Trustee and the trustee assigned to the case—the petition, schedules, statement of financial affairs, other required documents and amendments to any of the afore-mentioned filings.

3. Means and Effect of Electronic Service and Notice. Whenever a document is filed, the System automatically sends notice of the filing via e-mail ("electronic notice") to the case trustee and all System account holders who have previously filed a document in the case or have otherwise elected to receive electronic notification in the case.[4] When mailed notice is to be sent by the Court through a service known as the Bankruptcy Noticing Center ("BNC"), the mailed notice is eliminated for any System account holder who has already received e-mail notification of that particular notice (except for the section 341(a) notice, which is sent by mail to *all* parties included

in the System database for that case, regardless of whether the addressee already received e-mail notification). However, case participants who do not have an account with the System or have only a limited-access account must be provided notice and service of any document filed electronically in accordance with the Federal Rules of Bankruptcy Procedure and the Local Bankruptcy Rules.

4. E–mail Addresses. All System account holders must maintain an active e-mail address to receive electronic notice and service from the System. Each System account holder has a duty to update promptly his or her account information on the System whenever there is a change in e-mail address. This applies to the System account holder's primary e-mail address as well as to any secondary e-mail addresses.

5. Withdrawal from a Particular Case. An account holder who is no longer involved in a particular case and wishes to stop receiving notification in that case may request to be removed from the electronic mailing list for that case by submitting to the Clerk's Office a signed letter so indicating.

C. *Signatures; Affidavits of Service.*

1. **Use of a System account to file a document on the System constitutes the signature of the System account holder.**

2. Every petition, pleading, motion and other paper served or filed in accordance with these Procedures shall contain signatures that conform to the following format: "/s/Jane Doe" or "s/ Jane Doe." Additionally, an attorney signing such pleading or other document shall conform to any standards established for the signatures of attorneys by the United States District Court for the Southern District of New York.

3. Petitions, lists, schedules, statements, amendments, pleadings, affidavits, stipulations and other documents which must contain original signatures, documents requiring verification under Federal Rule of Bankruptcy Procedure 1008, and unsworn declarations under 28 U.S.C. § 1746, shall be filed electronically and all signatures in any PDF document shall conform to the following format: "/s/ Jane Doe" or "s/ Jane Doe." The filer must maintain a hard copy of the originally executed document for the later of two years or the entry of a final order terminating the case or proceeding to which the document relates.

D. *Privacy Guidelines.* Anyone filing documents with the Court shall comply with all guidelines pertaining to the privacy of individuals, including the provisions of Federal Rule of Bankruptcy Procedure 9037 and any guidelines implementing the E–Government Act of 2002. Among the privacy guidelines is the mandate to redact the first five digits of individuals' Social Security Numbers in any document intended for filing with the Court.

III. Documents Filed Under Seal.

A. *Motion.* A motion to file documents under seal (but not the documents themselves) shall be filed electronically. If the motion itself contains confidential information, the movant shall serve and file electronically a redacted version clearly marked as such, and submit an unredacted version in camera. If requested by the Court, the movant shall deliver—to the presiding judge for in camera review—hard copies of those documents that the movant seeks to file under seal.

B. *Order.* The Court shall file electronically the order determining the motion.

C. *Copies. Documents to be filed under seal should NEVER be filed electronically on the System.* Instead, where the Court grants the motion, in whole or in part, the movant shall deliver the following to the Clerk's Office:

1. A hard copy of the documents to be filed under seal (the "sealed documents"), and

2. A CD or other electronic media containing the sealed documents in PDF along with a copy of the sealing order.

The CD or other electronic media shall be submitted in an envelope or CD mailer, clearly labeled with the case name and number, and if applicable, the document number assigned to the sealed document. Hard copies of the sealing order shall be attached to the hard copy of the sealed documents and to the CD (or other electronic media).

IV. Public Access to the System Docket.

A. *Internet Access.*

1. Access to View Docket and Documents Already Filed. Any person or organization may access the System at the Court's website: www.nysb.uscourts.gov. However, to gain access, an

account (providing login and password) must first be obtained from the *Public Access to Electronic Court Records Center* ("PACER"). With a PACER account, the account holder may view—on the Court's System—the docket in cases and proceedings and any documents filed in them. PACER account holders are charged for use of their accounts. [For additional information on PACER charges, *see* paragraph D. below and the PACER website: http://pacer.psc.uscourts.gov.]

   2.   Access to File Documents. An account to the Court's System is required to file a document electronically on the Court's System [see paragraph B. of Part I above].

B.   *Access at the Court.* Anyone may view a document free of charge that was filed on the System in the Office of the Clerk during specified hours, Monday through Friday.

C.   *Conventional Copies and Certified Copies.* Conventional copies and certified copies of electronically-filed documents may be purchased at any of the three divisional offices of the Clerk's Office [Manhattan, White Plains and Poughkeepsie] during specified hours, Monday through Friday. The fee for copying and certification shall be in accordance with the *Bankruptcy Court Miscellaneous Fee Schedule.*

D.   *Access Charges.* Charges required by the Judicial Conference of the United States, as authorized by 28 U.S.C. § 1930(b), for usage of the System to gain access to the Court's records, are assessed in accordance with the fees and procedures established by the Administrative Office of the United States Courts. Note that any such access charges are made by PACER and not by this Court.

E.   *Privacy Interests of Filers. Information posted on the System shall not be downloaded for uses inconsistent with the privacy concerns of debtors and third parties.*

[Dated: June 17, 2013.]

1 An attorney seeking admission to practice pro hac vice may obtain a System account for the purpose of filing electronically the motion for admission pro hac vice; however, the attorney should not make any other electronic filings until either the order is signed or the attorney has received permission from chambers. Once admission is granted by Court order, the attorney may continue using the System account but *only* in the case to which admission pro hac vice has been granted.

2 An "event" is a descriptive subject heading that, when properly selected by the System account holder, corresponds to the type of document being filed (*e.g.*, a System account holder would select the event, *"Certificate of Credit Counseling,"* for filing a credit counseling certificate and would select *"Motion, Relief from Stay"* for filing a motion for relief from the section 362 automatic stay).

3 Federal Rule of Bankruptcy Procedure 1007(a)(1).

4 The e-mail sent by the System contains a hyperlink to the filed document. PACER (Public Access to Electronic Court Records Center) permits certain e-mail recipients to have one view of the document via the hyperlink without incurring a charge; typically, PACER will not charge the attorney of record for this first view, and this applies to the attorney's primary e-mail account and any secondary e-mail accounts. Other recipients, such as those who have identified a case as being of interest, may be charged by PACER for accessing the document via the hyperlink.

SELECTED GENERAL ORDERS
GENERAL ORDER M–73.   IN THE MATTER OF LOCAL CHAPTER 12 BANKRUPTCY RULES

The Bankruptcy Judges having considered the report of the Advisory Committee on Bankruptcy Rules (the "Committee"), and it appearing that the Proposed Chapter 12 Bankruptcy Rules submitted by the Committee are acceptable to the Bankruptcy Judges of this District and that pursuant to Bankruptcy Rule 9029 they should be adopted as a supplement to the Local Bankruptcy Rules presently in effect in this District,

Now, it is

Ordered, that the annexed Chapter 12 Bankruptcy Rules be, and the same are hereby adopted as a supplement to the Local Bankruptcy Rules for the Southern District of New York, effective March 18, 1987.

[Dated: March 18, 1987.]

CHAPTER 12 BANKRUPTCY RULES SUPPLEMENT

Rule 12–1.   General Applicability of Bankruptcy Rules

The Bankruptcy Rules and Forms,[1] now in effect or as later amended, as supplemented by these rules govern procedure in cases under chapter 12 of title 11 of the United States Code.[2]

[1] Federal Bankruptcy Rules 1 et seq. and the Official Bankruptcy Forms are set out in 11 U.S.C.A.

[2] 11 U.S.C.A. § 1201 et seq.

Note: Section 305(b) of the Bankruptcy Judges, United States Trustees, and Family Farmer Bankruptcy Act of 1986, Pub.L. No. 99–554, 100 Stat. 3088, provides that the Bankruptcy Rules in effect on the day of enactment shall apply to chapter 12 family farmer's debt adjustment cases "to the extent practicable and not inconsistent" with chapter 12. Amendments to the Bankruptcy Rules are currently under consideration by the Supreme Court. This rule provides that if the proposed amendments become effective, the rules as amended will apply to chapter 12 cases.

Rule 12–2.   Adaptations of Certain Bankruptcy Rules

(1) The reference in Rule 1002(b)(1) to chapter 13 shall be read also as a reference to chapter 12.

(2) The reference in Rule 1007(a)(1) to a Chapter 13 Statement shall be read also as a reference to a Chapter 12 Statement, and the references in Rule 1007(c) and (h) to a chapter 13 case and a chapter 13 individual's debt adjustment case shall be read also as references to a chapter 12 case and a chapter 12 family farmer's debt adjustment case.

(3) The reference in Rule 1008 to Chapter 13 Statements shall be read also as a reference to Chapter 12 Statements.

(4) The references in Rule 1009 to a Chapter 13 Statement shall be read also as references to a Chapter 12 Statement.

(5) The references in Rule 1016 to an individual's debt adjustment case under chapter 13 shall be read also as references to a family farmer's debt adjustment case under chapter 12.

(6) The reference in Rule 1017(a) to § 1307(b) of the Code shall be read also as a reference to § 1208(b) of the Code.

(7) The references in Rule 1019 to a chapter 13 case shall be read also as references to a chapter 12 case.

(8) The reference in Rule 2004(b) to an individual's debt adjustment case under chapter 13 shall be read also as a reference to a family farmer's debt adjustment case under chapter 12.

(9) The references in Rule 2009(c)(3) to chapter 13 individual's debt adjustment cases and chapter 13 cases shall be read also as references to chapter 12 family farmer's debt adjustment cases and chapter 12 cases.

(10) The references in Rule 2015(b)(1) to chapter 13 trustee and debtor and chapter 13 individual's debt adjustment case shall be read also as references to chapter 12 trustee and debtor and chapter 12 individual's debt adjustment case.

(11) The reference in Rule 2018(b) to a chapter 13 case shall be read also as a reference to a chapter 12 case.

(12) The reference in Rule 3002(c) to a chapter 13 individual's debt adjustment case shall be read also as a reference to a chapter 12 family farmer's debt adjustment case.

(13) The references in the captions of Rule 3010 and Rule 3010(b) to chapter 13 individual's debt adjustment cases and chapter 13 cases shall be read also as references to chapter 12 family farmer's debt adjustment cases and chapter 12 cases.

(14) The reference in the caption to Rule 3011 to chapter 13 individual's debt adjustment cases shall be read also as a reference to chapter 12 family farmer's debt adjustment cases.

(15) The reference in Rule 3013 to § 1322(b)(1) of the Code shall be read also as a reference to § 1222(b)(1) of the Code.

(16) The reference in the caption of Rule 4007(c) to chapter 11 reorganization cases shall be read also as a reference to chapter 12 family farmer's debt adjustment cases.

(17) The reference in Rule 6006(b) to a chapter 13 individual's debt adjustment case shall be read also as a reference to a chapter 12 family farmer's debt adjustment case.

(18) The references in Rule 7001(5) and (8) to a chapter 13 plan shall be read also as references to a chapter 12 plan.

(19) The reference in Rule 7062 to § 1301 of the Code shall be read also as a reference to § 1201 of the Code.

(20) The reference in Rule 9011(a) to a Chapter 13 Statement shall be read also as a reference to a Chapter 12 Statement.

(21) The reference in Rule 9024 to § 1330 of the Code shall be read also as a reference to § 1230 of the Code.

(22) The reference in Rule X–1002(a)(1) to a Chapter 13 Statement shall be read also as a reference to a Chapter 12 Statement.

(23) The references in Rule X–1005(a)(3) to chapter 13 individual's debt adjustment cases and chapter 13 cases shall be read also as references to chapter 12 family farmer's debt adjustment cases and chapter 12 cases.

(24) The reference in Rule X–1007(b) to a chapter 13 individual's debt adjustment case shall be read also as a reference to a chapter 12 family farmer's debt adjustment case.

(25) Rule X–1008(a)(1) shall be read to include a reference to Rule 12–4.

Note: Many of the Bankruptcy Rules apply to cases under all chapters of the Code. Others apply only to specified chapters. Since the procedural aspects of chapters 12 and 13 are almost identical, the Bankruptcy Rules applicable to chapter 13 cases are appropriate for use in chapter 12 cases, and pursuant to § 305(b) of the 1986 Act, these rules are applicable to chapter 12 cases.

This rule provides that references in certain Bankruptcy Rules to chapter 13 or an aspect of a chapter 13 case shall be read to include a comparable reference to chapter 12 or an aspect of a chapter 12 case. Rule 1007(b) is omitted because Rule 12–3 covers the subject of filing schedules and statements.

Paragraph (16) makes Rule 4007(c), which fixes the time for filing a complaint under § 523(c) to determine the dischargeability of certain debts at 60 days from the first date set for the meeting of creditors, applicable in chapter 12 cases. Rule 4007(c) does not apply to chapter 13 cases because the § 523(c) debts are discharged pursuant to § 1328(a). Under § 1228(a) the chapter 12 discharge does not discharge the § 523(c) debts.

Rule 12–4 governs the filing and confirmation of a chapter 12 plan. Rule X–1008(a) requires that the United States trustee receive notice of and pleadings relating to important aspects of the case. Paragraph (25), in effect, expands Rule X–1008(a) to include the chapter 12 plan and confirmation matters.

Rule 12–3. Schedules and Statements Required

Unless the court orders otherwise, the debtor shall file with the court a Chapter 12 Statement conforming to Form No. 12–A or 12–B, whichever is appropriate, and a statement of financial affairs prepared as prescribed by Official Form No. 8. The budget included in the Chapter 12 Statement shall constitute the schedule of current income and expenditures.

Note: This rule is derived from Bankruptcy Rule 1007(b). Under § 109(f) of the Code, a chapter 12 debtor must have regular annual income. A plan may be confirmed over an objection only if the plan commits the debtor's projected disposable income for three years to payments under the plan. § 1225(b)(1)(B). The Chapter

12 Statement (Form No. 12–A or 12–B) required by this rule contains essential information for determining eligibility for commencing a chapter 12 case and the amount of the debtor's disposable income.

The time for the filing of the Chapter 12 Statement is prescribed by Bankruptcy Rule 1007(c).   Rule 12–2(2).

Rule 12–4. Filing and Confirmation of Plan

(a) **Time for Filing.** The debtor may file a chapter 12 plan with the petition. If a plan is not filed with the petition, it shall be filed within 90 days thereafter unless the court pursuant to § 1221 of the Code extends the time for filing the plan. If required by the court, the debtor shall furnish a sufficient number of copies of the plan, or any court approved summary of the plan, to enable the clerk to include a copy of the plan or summary with the notice of the hearing on confirmation of the plan.

(b) **Objections.** Objections to confirmation of the plan shall be filed with the court and served on the debtor, the trustee, and on any other entity designated by the court, within a time fixed by the court. An objection to confirmation is governed by Bankruptcy Rule 9014.

(c) **Hearing.** After notice as provided in subdivision (d) of this rule, the court shall conduct and conclude a hearing within the time prescribed by § 1224 of the Code and rule on confirmation of the plan. If no objection is timely filed, the court may determine that the plan has been proposed in good faith and not by any means forbidden by law without receiving evidence on those issues.

(d) **Notice.** The clerk, or some other person as the court may direct, shall give the debtor, the trustee, all creditors, and all equity security holders notice by mail of the time fixed for filing objections to and the hearing to consider confirmation of the plan. Unless the court fixes a shorter period, notice of the hearing shall be given not less than 15 days before the hearing. A copy of the plan or a court approved summary of the plan shall accompany the notice.

(e) **Order of Confirmation.** The order of confirmation shall conform to Official Form No. 31 and notice of entry thereof shall be mailed promptly by the clerk, or some other person as the court may direct, to the debtor, the trustee, all creditors, all equity security holders, and other parties in interest.

(f) **Retained Power.** Notwithstanding the entry of the order of confirmation, the court may enter all orders necessary to administer the estate.

Note: Section 1221 of the Code requires that the plan be filed within 90 days of the order for relief. The date of the order for relief is the date of the filing of the chapter 12 petition. See § 301 of the Code. Involuntary petitions are not permitted under chapter 12. Section 1224 requires that the confirmation hearing be held after "expedited notice." The confirmation hearing must be concluded within 45 days after the plan is filed unless the court extends the period for cause. This rule is derived from Bankruptcy Rules 3015 and 3020 and supplements the statutory requirements.

Subdivision (a) is derived from Bankruptcy Rule 3015. An extension of the time for the filing of a plan may be granted pursuant to § 1221 if the court finds "an extension is substantially justified." A summary of the plan may not be distributed unless approved by the court.

Subdivision (b) is derived from Bankruptcy Rule 3020(b)(1). Notice of the time for filing objections shall be included in the notice given pursuant to subdivision (d) of this rule.

Subdivision (c) is derived from Bankruptcy Rule 3020(b)(2). Section 1224 requires that the confirmation hearing be concluded within 45 days unless the court grants an extension for cause.

Subdivision (d). Section 1224 requires that there be "expedited notice" of the confirmation hearing. This rule establishes 15 days as the notice period. The court may shorten this time on its own motion or on motion of a party in interest. The coordination of the hearing date and the date for filing objections is determined by the court. The notice should include both dates and be accompanied by a copy of the plan or a court approved summary of the plan.

Subdivisions (e) and (f) are derived from Bankruptcy Rule 3020(c) and (d).

Form No. 12–A. Chapter 12 Statement of Individual Debtor

[Caption as in Official Form No. 1]

Chapter 12 Statement of Individual Debtor

[Each applicable question shall be answered or the failure to answer explained. If the answer is "none" or "not applicable," so state. If additional space is needed for the answer to any question, a separate sheet, properly identified and made a part hereof, should be used and attached.

The term "original petition," used in the following questions, shall mean the original petition filed under § 301 of the Code or, if the chapter 12 case was converted from another chapter of the Code, shall mean the petition by or against you which originated the first case.

Individual debtors must complete all questions. This form should be completed whether a married individual or a married individual and a spouse filed the petition. For convenience, the word "debtors" is used to refer to a married individual and spouse who have filed a chapter 12 petition. If such debtors' answers to any question are different, their respective answer shall be separately designated as the answer of the husband and the answer of the wife.]

1. <u>Filing Status.</u> (Check appropriate status.)
Unmarried individual   _____
Married individual and spouse are debtors   _____
Married individual is the sole debtor   _____

2. <u>Name and residence.</u>
   a. Full name
     Debtor or debtors.................................
     ....
     Spouse who is not a debtor ....
     ....
   b. Residence of the debtor or debtors
     (1) Mailing address of debtor or debtors ....
     ....
     City or town, state and zip code.
     (2) Mailing address of spouse who is not a debtor
     ....
     City or town, state and zip code.
     (3) Telephone number including area code
     Debtor or debtors ....
     ....
     Spouse who is not a debtor ....
     ....

3. <u>Summary of debt.</u>
Give amounts as of the date of the filing of the petition.
   a. <u>Noncontingent, liquidated debt.</u>
     (1) Amount of noncontingent, liquidated debt from farming operations. $.....
     (2) Amount of noncontingent, liquidated non-farm debt $.....
     (3) Total noncontingent, liquidated debt $.....
   b. <u>Contingent or unliquidated debt.</u>
     (1) Amount of contingent or unliquidated debt from farming operations $.....
     (2) Amount of contingent or unliquidated non-farm debt $.....
     (3) Total contingent or unliquidated debt $.....
   c. <u>Principal Residence.</u>
     Amount of non-farm debt that is secured by the principal residence of the debtor or debtors $.....

4. <u>Summary of income from last tax year.</u>
   a. Debtor or debtors' last tax year before the current tax year was calendar year 19___.
   b. Debtor or debtors' gross income for the last tax year before the current tax year $.....
   c. Amount of debtor or debtors' gross income for last tax year before the current tax year from farming operations $.....

5. <u>Nature of farming operations.</u> (Place an "X" on the appropriate line to identify each type of farming operation in which the debtor or debtors are engaged and supply the other information requested below.)
   a. Crops   _____
      Kind(s)...................................
      Acres owned.............leased ....
   b. Dairy operations   _____
      Acres owned.............leased ....
   c. Ranching   _____
      Kind(s)...................................
      Acres owned.............leased ....
   d. Poultry   _____
      Kind(s)...................................
      Acres owned.............leased ....
   e. Livestock   _____
      Kind(s)...................................
      Acres owned.............leased ....
   f. Production of poultry products   _____
      Kind(s)...................................
   g. Production of livestock products _____
      Kind(s)...................................

6. <u>Non-farming activities.</u>
   a. If a debtor or debtors are self employed in other than farming operations, state the nature thereof
      ....
      ....
   b. If a debtor or debtors are employed by others in either farming operations or non-farming activity, state the nature thereof
      ....
      ....
   c. If a spouse who is not a debtor is either self employed in other than farming operations or employed by others in either farming operations or non-farming activity, state the nature thereof.
      ....
      ....
   d. Give the name, address, and telephone number of each present employer of the debtor or debtors.
      ....
      ....
   e. Give the name, address, and telephone number of each present employer of a spouse who is not a debtor.
      ....
   f. State how long the debtor or debtors have been employed by each present employer.
      ....
   g. How long has the spouse who is not a debtor been employed by each present employer?
      ....

7. <u>Budget.</u>
   a. <u>Current income.</u>
      (1) Estimated gross income from farming operations for the next twelve months. (Include all government program payments.) $....
      (2) Income from non-farming activities:
          Give estimated average monthly income of debtor and spouse, consisting of:

                                         Debtor Spouse
          (A) Gross pay from employer (wages, salary, or commissions) $..... $.....

151

    (B) Take-home pay from employer (Gross pay less
          all deductions) $..... $.....

    (C) Regular income available from self employ-
          ment not included in item 7a(1) $..... $.....

    (D) Other income:

          Interest and dividends $..... $.....

          From real estate or personal property $..... $.....

          Social security $..... $.....

          Pension or other retirement income $..... $.....

          Other (specify)

          .... $..... $.....

    (E) Alimony, maintenance, or support payments:

          Payable to the debtor for the debtor's use $..... $.....

          Payable to the debtor for support of another
          (Attach additional sheet listing the name,
          age, and relationship to the debtor of per-
          sons for whose benefit payments are made) $..... $.....

    (F) Total estimated average monthly income from
          non-farming activities $..... $.....

If you anticipate receiving additional income on other than a monthly basis in the next year (such as an income tax refund) attach an additional sheet of paper and explain.

If you anticipate a substantial change in your income in the immediate future, attach an additional sheet of paper and explain.

    (4)[1] Total estimated income for next twelve months
          (twelve times total estimated average monthly
          income from non-farming activities (item
          7a(2)(F)) with any adjustment for a substantial
          change in such income plus income from farming
          operations (item 7a(1)). $.....

  b. Current expenses related to farming operations.

    (1) Real Property expenses. (Include expenses of the
          home of the debtor if the home is located on the
          debtor's property used in farming operations.)

          Give estimated current monthly expenditures con-
          sisting of:

          (A) Mortgage payment(s) $.....

          (B) Rental or lease payment(s) $.....

          (C) Real estate taxes $.....

          (D) Repairs & upkeep $.....

          Total real property expenses $.....

    (2) Other expenses.

          Give estimated current monthly expenditures for
          the debtor or debtors consisting of:

          (A) Installment or lease payments on equipment

          Specify .... $.....

                 .... $.....

                 .... $.....

                 .... $.....

          Total Monthly installment or lease payments
          on equipment $.....

          (B) Maintenance of equipment

          Service contracts $.....

          Other (specify)

          .... $.....

          .... $.....

          Total maintenance of equipment $.....

          (C) Utilities:

               Electricity $.....

               Fuel $.....

           Water $.....

           Telephone (business use) $.....

      Total utilities $.....

(D) Production expenses:

           Labor (gross) $.....

           Seed $.....

           Fertilizer $.....

           Feed $.....

           Pesticides $.....

           Veterinary, etc. $.....

           Other (specify)

           .... $.....

           .... $.....

           .... $.....

      Total production expenses $.....

(E) Miscellaneous expenses

      Give any expenses of farming operation not reflected above.

           (i) .... $.....

           (ii) .... $.....

           (iii) .... $.....

      Total miscellaneous expenses $.....

(3) Total estimated monthly expenses. $.....

(4) Total current yearly expenses related to farming operations (twelve times total estimated monthly expenses (item 7c(3))). $.....

  c.   Current expenses not related to farming operations.

Give estimated average current monthly expenditures for the individual debtor or debtors, consisting of:

      (1) Home expenses. (Complete this item c(1) only if the home is located on property not used in farming operations)

           (A) Rent or home loan payment (including any assessment or maintenance fee) $.....

           (B) Real estate taxes $.....

           (C) Utilities:

                Electricity $.....

                Gas $.....

                Water $.....

                Telephone (personal use) $.....

                Other (specify) $.....

                Total utilities $.....

           (D) Home maintenance (repairs and upkeep) $.....

           (E) Total of all home expenses $.....

      (2) Other expenses not related to farming activities.

           (A) Taxes (not deducted from wages or included in home loan payment or included in real estate taxes) $.....

           (B) Alimony, maintenance, or support payments (attach additional sheet listing name, age, and relationship of beneficiaries) $.....

           (C) Insurance (not deducted from wages)

                Life $.....

                Health $.....

                Auto $.....

                Homeowner's or Renter's $.....

                Other (specify)

                .... $.....

                Total insurance expenses $.....

           (D) Installment payments:

Auto $.....

Other (specify)

.... $.....

.... $.....

     Total installment payments $.....

(E) Transportation (not including auto payments) $.....

(F) Education (including tuition and school books) $.....

(G) Food $.....

(H) Clothing $.....

(I)   Medical, dental, and medicines $.....

(J) Telephone $.....

(K) Laundry and cleaning $.....

(L) Newspapers, periodicals and books $.....

(M) Recreation, clubs and entertainment $.....

(N) Charitable contributions $.....

(O) Other expenses (specify)

.... $.....

.... $.....

(P) Total of other expenses related to non-farming
      activities $.....

1 Pub. Note: There is no subdivision (3) in original.

If you anticipate a substantial change in your expenses in the immediate future, attach additional sheet of paper and explain.

           (3) Total expenses for next twelve months related to the debtor's non-farming activities (twelve times the total estimated current monthly expenses (item 7c(1)(E) plus item 7c(2)(P)) with an adjustment for any substantial change) $.....

    d.   Summary of budget information.

        (A) Total income for next twelve months (item 7a(4)) $.....

        (B) Total estimated expenses for next twelve months (item 7b(4) plus 7c(3)).   ($....)

               Available income ((A) minus (B)) $.....

8.   Dependents.

The debtor supports the following dependents (other than the debtor's spouse):

Name	Age	Relationship to Debtor
....	......	....
....	......	....
....	......	....
....	......	....

9.   Payment of Attorney.

    a.   How much have you agreed to pay or what property have you agreed to transfer to your attorney in connection with the case? $.....

    b.   How much have you paid or what have you transferred to the attorney? $.....

10.   Tax refunds and government program payments. (To be answered by debtor or debtors and, unless spouses are separated, by a spouse who is not a debtor.)

To what tax refunds (income or other) and government program payments, if any, is either of you, or may either of you be, entitled? (Give particulars, including information as to any refunds payable jointly to you and any other person. All such refunds should also be listed in Item 18(b).)

....

....

11.   Financial accounts, certificates of deposit and safe deposit boxes. (To be answered by debtor or debtors and, unless spouses are separated, by a spouse who is not a debtor.)

    a.   Does either of you currently have any accounts or certificates of deposit or shares in banks, savings and loan, thrift, building and loan and homestead associations, credit unions, brokerage houses, pension funds and the like? (If so, give name and address of each institution, number and nature of account, current balance, and name and address of every other person authorized to make withdrawals from the account. Such accounts should also be listed in Item 18(b).)

....
....

b. Does either of you currently keep any safe deposit boxes or other depositories? (If so, give name and address of bank or other depository, name and address of every other person who has a right of access thereto, and a brief description of the contents thereof, which should also be listed in Item 18(b).)

....
....

12. Prior Bankruptcy.
What cases under the Bankruptcy Act or Bankruptcy Code have previously been brought by or against you or either spouse filing a petition? (State the location of the bankruptcy court, the nature and number of each case, the date when it was filed, and whether a discharge was granted or denied, the case was dismissed, or a composition, arrangement, or plan was confirmed.)

....
....

13. Foreclosures, executions, and attachments. (To be answered by debtor or debtors and, unless spouses are separated, by a spouse who is not a debtor.)
a. Is any of the property of either of you, including real estate, involved in a foreclosure proceeding, in or out of court? (If so, identify the property and the person foreclosing.)

....
....

b. Has any property or income of either of you been attached, garnished, or seized under any legal or equitable process within the 90 days immediately preceding the filing of the original petition herein? (If so, describe the property seized, or person garnished, and who filed the law suit.)

....
....

14. Repossessions and returns. (To be answered by debtor or debtors and, unless spouses are separated, by a spouse who is not a debtor.)
Has any property of either of you been returned to, repossessed, or seized by the seller or by any other party, including a landlord, during the 90 days immediately preceding the filing of the original petition herein? (If so, give particulars, including the name and address of the party taking the property and its description and value.)

....
....

15. Transfers of Property. (To be answered by debtor or debtors and, unless spouses are separated, by a spouse who is not a debtor.)
a. Has either of you made any gifts, other than ordinary and usual presents to family members and charitable donations, during the year immediately preceding the filing of the original petition herein? (If so, give names and addresses of donees and dates, description and value of gifts.)

....
....

b. Has either of you made any other transfer, absolute or for the purpose of security, or any other disposition, of real or personal property during the year immediately preceding the filing of the original petition herein? (Give a description of the property, the date of the transfer or disposition, to whom transferred or how disposed of, and, if the transferee is a relative or insider, the relationship, the consideration, if any, received therefor, and the disposition of such consideration.)

....
....

16. <u>Debts.</u> (To be answered by debtor or debtors and by a spouse who is not a debtor.)
    a. <u>Debts Having Priority.</u>

(1) Nature of claim	(2) Name of creditor and complete mailing address including zip code	(3) Specify when claim was incurred and the consideration therefor: whether claim is subject to setoff, evidenced by a judgment, negotiable instrument, or other writing	(4) Indicate if claim is contingent, unliquidated, or disputed	(5) Amount of claim
. . . .	. . . .	. . . .	. . . .	. . . .
. . . .	. . . .	. . . .	. . . .	. . . .
. . . .	. . . .	. . . .	. . . .	. . . .
. . . .	. . . .	. . . .	. . . .	. . . .
. . . .	. . . .	. . . .	. . . .	. . . .
. . . .	. . . .	. . . .	. . . .	. . . .

1. Wages, salary, and commissions, including vacation, severance and sick leave pay owing to employees not exceeding $2,000 to each, earned within 90 days before filing of petition or cessation of business (if earlier specify date). $. . . . .

2. Contributions to employee benefit plans for services rendered within 180 days before filing of petition or cessation of business (if earlier specify date). $. . . . .

3. Deposits by individuals, not exceeding $900 for each purchase, lease, or rental of property or services for personal, family, or household use that were not delivered or provided. $. . . . .

4. Taxes owing [itemize by type of tax and taxing authority]
   (A) To the United States $. . . . .
   (B) To any state $. . . . .
   (C) To any other taxing authority $. . . . .
                                        Total $. . . . .

b. <u>Secured Debts.</u> List all debts which are or may be secured by real or personal property. (Indicate in the next to last column, if debt payable in installments, the amount of each installment, the installment period (monthly, weekly, or otherwise) and number of installments in arrears, if any. Indicate in last column whether husband or wife solely liable, or whether you are jointly liable.)

Creditor's name, account number and complete mailing address including zip code	Consideration or basis for debt	Amount claimed by creditor	If disputed, amount admitted by debtor	Description of collateral [include year and make of automobile]	Installment amount, period, and number of installments in arrears	Husband or wife solely liable, or jointly liable
. . . . . .	. . . . . .	. . . . . .	. . . . . .	. . . . . .	. . . . . .	. . . . . .
. . . . . .	. . . . . .	. . . . . .	. . . . . .	. . . . . .	. . . . . .	. . . . . .
. . . . . .	. . . . . .	. . . . . .	. . . . . .	. . . . . .	. . . . . .	. . . . . .
. . . . . .	. . . . . .	. . . . . .	. . . . . .	. . . . . .	. . . . . .	. . . . . .
. . . . . .	. . . . . .	. . . . . .	. . . . . .	. . . . . .	. . . . . .	. . . . . .

Total secured debts . . . .

c. <u>Unsecured Debts.</u> List all other debts, liquidated and unliquidated, including taxes, attorney fees, and tort claims.

Creditor's name, account number and complete mailing address including zip code	Consideration or basis for debt	Amount claimed by creditor	If disputed, amount admitted by debtor	Husband or wife solely liable, or jointly liable
. . . .	. . . .	. . . .	. . . .	. . . .
. . . .	. . . .	. . . .	. . . .	. . . .
. . . .	. . . .	. . . .	. . . .	. . . .
. . . .	. . . .	. . . .	. . . .	. . . .
. . . .	. . . .	. . . .	. . . .	. . . .

Total unsecured debts . . . .

17. Codebtors. (To be answered by debtor or debtors and by a spouse who is not a debtor.)

     a.   Are any other persons liable, as cosigners, guarantors, or in any other manner, on any of the debts of either of you or is either of you so liable on the debts of others? (If so, give particulars, indicating which spouse is liable and including names of creditors, nature of debt, names and addresses of codebtors, and their relationship, if any, to you.)

         ....

         ....

     b.   If so, have the codebtors made any payments on the debts? (Give name of each codebtor and amount paid by codebtor.)

         ....

         ....

     c.   Has either of you made any payments on the debts? (If so, specify total amount paid to each creditor, whether paid by husband or wife, and name of codebtor.)

         ....

         ....

         ....

18. Property and Exemptions. (To be answered by debtor or debtors and a spouse who is not a debtor.)

     a.   Real Property. List all real property owned at date of filing of original petition herein. (Indicate in next to last column whether an exemption is claimed and in last column whether owned solely by husband or wife, or jointly.)

Description and location of property	Name of any co-owner other than spouse	Present market value (without deduction for mortgage or other security interest)	Amount of mortgage or other security interest on this property	Name of mortgagee or other secured creditor	Value claimed exempt (specify federal or state statute creating the exemption)	Owned solely by husband or by wife, or jointly
....	....	....	....	....	....	....
....	....	....	....	....	....	....
....	....	....	....	....	....	....
....	....	....	....	....	....	....
....	....	....	....	....	....	....

     b.   Personal Property. List all other property owned by debtor or debtors and spouse who is not a debtor at date of filing of original petition herein. (Indicate in the next to last column whether an exemption is claimed and in last column whether owned solely by husband or wife, or jointly.)

Description	Location of property if not at debtor's residence	Name of any coowner other than spouse	Present market value (without deduction for mortgage or other security interest)	Amount of mortgage or other security interest on this property	Name of mortgagee or other secured creditor	Value claimed exempt (specify federal or state statute creating the exemption)	Owned solely by husband or wife or jointly
Autos [give year and make]	....	....	....	....	....	....	....
Farming equipment [give type & make]	....	....	....	....	....	....	....
Household goods	....	....	....	....	....	....	....
Personal effects	....	....	....	....	....	....	....

Cash or financial account

....

....

Other [specify]

....

....

Unsworn Declaration under Penalty of Perjury of Individual to Chapter 12 Statement

[To be signed by debtor or debtors]

I, ..., [an unmarried individual] [*or* a married individual] [*if both husband and wife are debtors* and I, ..., the spouse], declare under penalty of perjury that I have read the answers contained in the foregoing statement, consisting of ... sheets, and that they are true and complete to the best of my knowledge, information, and belief.

Executed on ....

....
Debtor

....
Debtor

Note: A Chapter 12 debtor must also prepare and file a statement of affairs as prescribed by Official Form No. 8. Rule 12.3.

Form No. 12–B.   Chapter 12 Statement of Partnership or Corporate Debtor

[Caption as in Official Form No. 1]

Chapter 12 Statement
of Partnership or Corporate Debtor

[Each applicable question shall be answered or the failure to answer explained. If the answer is "none" or "not applicable," so state. If additional space is needed for the answer to any question, a separate sheet, properly identified and made a part hereof, should be used and attached.

The term "original petition," used in the following questions, shall mean the original petition filed under § 301 of the Code or, if the chapter 12 case was converted from another chapter of the Code, shall mean the petition by or against you which originated the first case.

The questions are to be addressed to, and shall be answered on behalf of, the corporation or partnership, and the statement shall be certified by a duly authorized officer of the corporation or by a member of the partnership.]

  1.   Filing Status.   (Place an "X" on the appropriate line.)
      Corporation   _____
      Partnership   _____
      Limited Partnership   _____
  2.   Name, and other information.
     a.   Full name ....
     b.   Principal place of business of the debtor
        (1) Mailing address ....
        ....
        City or town, state and zip code.
        (2) Telephone number including area code
        ....

    (3) Date and the state of incorporation of the corporate debtor

....

    (4) Date and the state law under which the partnership debtor was formed

....

....

    (5) Name of the family or name of the family and relatives that conduct farming operations and own more than 50% of the stock or equity of the corporate or partnership debtor

....

....

3. Summary of debt.
   Give amounts as of the date of the filing of the petition.
   a. Noncontingent, liquidated debt.
       (1) Amount of noncontingent, liquidated debt from farming operations $.....
       (2) Amount of noncontingent, liquidated non-farm debt $.....
       (3) Total noncontingent, liquidated debt $.....
   b. Contingent or unliquidated debt.
       (1) Amount of contingent or unliquidated debt from farming operations $.....
       (2) Amount of contingent or unliquidated non-farm debt $.....
       (3) Total contingent or unliquidated debt $.....
   c. Principal Residence.
       Amount of non-farm debt that is secured by a dwelling owned by the corporate or partnership debtor and used as a principal residence by a shareholder or partner of the debtor $.....

4. Assets.
   a. Total value of assets $.....
   b. Value of assets related to farming operations $.....

5. Summary of income from last tax year.
   a. Debtor's last tax year before the current tax year was calendar year 19___ [or fiscal year _____ _____, 19___ to _____ _____, 19___]
   b. Debtor's gross income for the last tax year before the current tax year $.....
   c. Amount of debtor's gross income for last tax year before the current tax year from farming operations $.....

6. Nature of farming operations. (Place an "X" on the appropriate line to identify each type of farming operation in which the debtor is engaged and supply the other information requested below.)
   a. Crops   _____
       Kind(s)......................................
       Acres owned..............leased...............
   b. Dairy operations   _____
       Acres owned..............leased...............
   c. Ranching   _____
       Kind(s)......................................
       Acres owned..............leased...............
   d. Poultry   _____
       Kind(s)......................................
       Acres owned..............leased...............
   e. Livestock   _____
       Kind(s)......................................
       Acres owned..............leased...............
   f. Production of poultry products   _____

Kind(s) . . . .

g.　Production of livestock products
　　Kind(s) . . . .　　　　　———

7.　<u>Non-farming activities</u>.
　　If the debtor is engaged in business other than farming
　　operations, state the nature thereof
　　. . . . .
　　. . . . .

8.　<u>Budget</u>.
　　a.　<u>Current income</u>.
　　　　(1) Estimated gross income from farming operations
　　　　　　for the next twelve months. (Include all govern-
　　　　　　ment program payments.)　　　　　　　　　　　$ . . . . .
　　　　(2) Estimated gross income from non-farming activi-
　　　　　　ties for the next twelve months.　　　　　　　　$ . . . . .
　　　　(3) Total income　　　　　　　　　　　　　　　　　$ . . . . .
　　b.　<u>Current expenses related to farming operations</u>.
　　　　(1) <u>Real Property expenses</u>. (<u>Include expenses of a
　　　　　　home of a shareholder or partner of the debtor if
　　　　　　the home is located on the debtor's property
　　　　　　used in farming operations</u>.)
　　　　　　Give estimated current monthly expenditures con-
　　　　　　sisting of:
　　　　　　(A) Mortgage payment(s)　　　　　　　　　　$ . . . . .
　　　　　　(B) Rental or lease payment(s)　　　　　　　$ . . . . .
　　　　　　(C) Real estate taxes　　　　　　　　　　　$ . . . . .
　　　　　　(D) Repairs & upkeep　　　　　　　　　　　$ . . . . .
　　　　　　　　Total real property expenses　　　　　　　　　　$ . . . . .
　　　　(2) <u>Other expenses</u>.
　　　　　　Give estimated current average monthly expendi-
　　　　　　tures consisting of:
　　　　　　(A) Installment or lease payments on equipment
　　　　　　　　Specify . . . .　$ . . . . .
　　　　　　　　　　　. . . . .　$ . . . . .
　　　　　　　　　　　. . . . .　$ . . . . .
　　　　　　　　　　　. . . . .　$ . . . . .
　　　　　　　　Total Monthly installment or lease payments
　　　　　　　　　　on equipment　　　　　　　　　　　　　　　$ . . . . .
　　　　　　(B) Maintenance of equipment
　　　　　　　　Service contracts　　　　　　　　　　　　$ . . . . .
　　　　　　　　Other (<u>specify</u>)
　　　　　　　　. . . . .　$ . . . . .
　　　　　　　　. . . . .　$ . . . . .
　　　　　　　　Total maintenance of equipment　　　　　　　　$ . . . . .
　　　　　　(C) Utilities
　　　　　　　　Electricity　　　　　　　　　　　　　　$ . . . . .
　　　　　　　　Fuel　　　　　　　　　　　　　　　　　$ . . . . .
　　　　　　　　Water　　　　　　　　　　　　　　　　$ . . . . .
　　　　　　　　Telephone (business use)　　　　　　　　$ . . . . .
　　　　　　　　Total utilities　　　　　　　　　　　　　　　　$ . . . . .
　　　　　　(D) Production expenses:
　　　　　　　　Labor (gross)　　　　　　　　　　　　　$ . . . . .
　　　　　　　　Seed　　　　　　　　　　　　　　　　　$ . . . . .
　　　　　　　　Fertilizer　　　　　　　　　　　　　　$ . . . . .
　　　　　　　　Feed　　　　　　　　　　　　　　　　　$ . . . . .
　　　　　　　　Pesticides　　　　　　　　　　　　　　$ . . . . .
　　　　　　　　Veterinary, etc.　　　　　　　　　　　$ . . . . .
　　　　　　　　Other (<u>specify</u>)
　　　　　　　　. . . . .　$ . . . . .
　　　　　　　　. . . . .　$ . . . . .
　　　　　　　　. . . . .　$ . . . . .

Total production expenses $.....

(E) Miscellaneous expenses

Give any expenses of farming operation not reflected above

(i) .... $.....

(ii) .... $.....

(iii) .... $.....

Total miscellaneous expenses $.....

(3) Total estimated monthly expenses $.....

(4) Total current expenses related to farming operations

(twelve times total estimated monthly expenses (item 8c(3)) $.....

c. Current expenses related to non-farming activities.

Estimated expenses of the debtor's non-farming activities for the next twelve months $.....

d. Summary of budget information.

(A) Debtor's total estimated income for next twelve months (item 8a(3)). $.....

(B) Debtor's total estimated expenses for next twelve months (item 8b(4) plus item 8c). ($....)

Available Income ((A) minus (B)) $.....

9. Payment of Attorney.

a. How much has the debtor agreed to pay or what property has the debtor agreed to transfer to its attorney in connection with the case? $.....

b. How much has the debtor paid or what has the debtor transferred to its attorney? $.....

10. Tax refunds and government program payments.

To what tax refunds (income or other) and government program payments, if any, is the debtor entitled? (Give particulars, including information as to any refunds payable jointly to the debtor and any other person. All such refunds should also be listed in Item 18(b)).

....

....

11. Financial accounts, certificates of deposit and safe deposit boxes.

a. Does the debtor currently have any accounts or certificates of deposit or shares in banks, savings and loan, thrift, building and loan and homestead associations, credit unions, brokerage houses, pension funds and the like? (If so, give name and address of each institution, number and nature of account, current balance, and name and address of every person authorized to make withdrawals from the account. Such accounts should also be listed in Item 18(b).)

....

....

b. Does the debtor currently have any safe deposit boxes or other depositories? (If so, give name and address of bank or other depository, name and address of every person who has a right of access thereto, and a brief description of the contents thereof, which should also be listed in Item 18(b).)

....

....

12. Prior Bankruptcy.

What cases under the Bankruptcy Act or Bankruptcy Code have previously been brought by or against the debtor? (State the location of the bankruptcy court, the nature and number of each case, the date when it was filed, and whether a discharge was granted or denied, whether the case was dismissed, or whether an arrangement or plan was confirmed.)

. . . .

. . . .

13.   <u>Foreclosures, executions, and attachments</u>.

     a.   Is any of the property of debtor, including real estate, involved in a foreclosure proceeding, in or out of court? (If so, identify the property and the person foreclosing.)

. . . .

     b.   Has any property or income of debtor been attached, garnished, or seized under any legal or equitable process within the 90 days immediately preceding the filing of the original petition herein? (If so, describe the property seized, or person garnished, and who filed the law suit.)

. . . .

. . . .

14.   <u>Repossessions and returns</u>.

Has any property of debtor been returned to or been repossessed or seized by the seller or by any other party, including a landlord, during the 90 days immediately preceding the filing of the original petition herein? (If so, give particulars, including the name and address of the party obtaining the property and its description and value.)

. . . .

. . . .

15.   <u>Transfers of Property</u>.

     a.   Has the debtor made any gifts, during the year immediately preceding the filing of the original petition herein? (If so, give names and addresses of donees and dates, description and value of gifts.)

. . . .

     b.   Has the debtor made any other transfer, absolute or for the purpose of security, or any other disposition, of real or personal property during the year immediately preceding the filing of the original petition herein? (Give a description of the property, the date of the transfer or disposition, to whom transferred or how disposed of, and, if the transferee is an insider, the relationship, the consideration, if any, received therefor, and the disposition of such consideration.)

. . . .

. . . .

16.   Debts.

     a.   <u>Debts Having Priority</u>.

(1)	(2)	(3)	(4)	(5)
Nature of claim	Name of creditor and complete mailing address including zip code	Specify when claim was incurred and the consideration therefor; whether claim is subject to setoff, evidenced by a judgment, negotiable instrument, or other writing	Indicate if claim is contingent, unliquidated, or disputed	Amount of claim
. . . .	. . . .	. . . .	. . . .	. . . .
. . . .	. . . .	. . . .	. . . .	. . . .
. . . .	. . . .	. . . .	. . . .	. . . .
. . . .	. . . .	. . . .	. . . .	. . . .
. . . .	. . . .	. . . .	. . . .	. . . .

1. Wages, salary, and commissions, including vacation, severance and sick leave pay owing to employees not exceeding $2,000 to each earned within 90 days before filing of petition or cessation of business (if earlier specify date). $.....
2. Contributions to employee benefit plans for services rendered within 180 days before filing of petition or cessation of business (if earlier specify date). $.....
3. Deposits by individuals, not exceeding $900 for each purchase, lease, or rental of property or services for personal, family, or household use that were not delivered or provided. $.....
4. Taxes owing [itemize by type of tax and taxing authority]
   (A) To the United States $.....
   (B) To any state $.....
   (C) To any other taxing authority $.....
   Total $.....

    b.   Secured Debts. List all debts which are or may be secured by real or personal property. (Indicate in the last column, if debt payable in installments, the amount of each installment, the installment period (monthly, weekly, or otherwise) and number of installments in arrears, if any.)

Creditor's name, account number and complete mailing address including zip code	Consideration or basis for debt	Amount claimed by creditor	If disputed, amount admitted by debtor	Description of collateral [include year and make of vehicles]	Installment amount, period, and number of installments in arrears
....	....	....	....	....	....
....	....	....	....	....	....
....	....	....	....	....	....
....	....	....	....	....	....
....	....	....	....	....	....
....	....	....	....	....	....

Total secured debts ....

    c.   Unsecured Debts. List all other debts, liquidated and unliquidated, including taxes, attorney fees, and tort claims.

Creditor's name, account number and complete mailing address including zip code	Consideration or basis for debt	Amount claimed by creditor	If disputed, amount admitted by debtor
....	....	....	....
....	....	....	....
....	....	....	....
....	....	....	....
....	....	....	....
....	....	....	....

Total unsecured debts ....

17. Codebtors.
    a. Are any other persons liable, as cosigners, guarantors, or in any other manner, on any of the debts of the debtor or is the debtor so liable on the debts of others? (If so, give particulars including names of creditors, nature of debt, names and addresses of codebtors, and their relationship, if any, to the debtor.)

       ....
       ....
       ....

    b. If so, have the codebtors made any payments on the debts? (Give name of each codebtor and amount paid by codebtor.)

       ....
       ....
       ....

163

    c.   Has the debtor made any payments on the debts?   (If so, specify total amount paid to each creditor and name of codebtor.)

. . . .

. . . .

. . . .

18.   Property.

    a.   Real Property.   List all real property owned at date of filing of original petition herein.

Description and location of property	Name of any co-owner	Present market value (without deduction for mortgage or other security interest)	Amount of mortgage or other security interest on this property	Name of mortgagee or other secured creditor
. . . .	. . . .	. . . .	. . . .	. . . .
. . . .	. . . .	. . . .	. . . .	. . . .
. . . .	. . . .	. . . .	. . . .	. . . .
. . . .	. . . .	. . . .	. . . .	. . . .
. . . .	. . . .	. . . .	. . . .	. . . .

    b.   Personal Property.   List all other property owned by debtor at date of filing of original petition herein.

Description	Location of property if not at debtor's farm	Name of any co-owner	Present market value (without deduction for mortgage or other security interest)	Amount of mortgage or other security interest on this property	Name of mortgagee or other secured creditor
Autos [give year and make]					
. . . .	. . . . . .	. . . . . .	. . . .	. . . .	. . . .
Farming equipment [give type and make]	. . . . . .	. . . . . .	. . . .	. . . .	
. . . .	. . . . . .	. . . . . .	. . . .	. . . .	. . . .
Other equipment and office furnishings	. . . . . .	. . . . . .	. . . .	. . . .	
. . . .	. . . . . .	. . . . . .	. . . .	. . . .	. . . .
Cash or financial account	. . . . . .	. . . . . .	. . . .	. . . .	
. . . .	. . . . . .	. . . . . .	. . . .	. . . .	. . . .
Other [specify]	. . . . . .	. . . . . .	. . . .	. . . .	
. . . .	. . . . . .	. . . . . .	. . . .	. . . .	. . . .
. . . .	. . . . . .	. . . . . .	. . . .	. . . .	. . . .

Unsworn Declaration under Penalty of Perjury on Behalf of Corporation or Partnership to Chapter 12 Statement

I, ..., [the president or other officer or an authorized agent of the corporation] [or a member or an authorized agent of the partnership] named as debtor in this case, declare under penalty of perjury that I have read the answers contained in the foregoing statement, consisting of . . . sheets, and that they are true and correct to the best of my knowledge, information, and belief.

Executed on . . . .

Signature: . . . .

Note: A chapter 12 debtor must also prepare and file a statement of affairs as prescribed by Official Form No. 8. Rule 12.3.

GENERAL ORDER M–138.   FILING A LIST OF CREDITORS IN A BANKRUPTCY CASE

If a Debtor files a Petition with more than **ten (10)** but less than **one thousand (1000)** creditors and equity security holders, the Petition **shall** be accompanied by a separate, additional creditor list on floppy disk, in addition to the list or schedules included within the petition. The disk shall be filed in a sealed 8 1/2″ x 11″ envelope and shall contain names and post office addresses, including zip codes, of the debtor's creditors, the debtor, the debtor's attorney, the United States Trustee and if a debt is owing to the United States then to the particular agency or department, if known, to which such debt is owing. The floppy disk shall be filed in accordance with the format and specifications annexed as Exhibit "A" and shall include a certification by the debtor that the information entered on the floppy disk is true, complete and correct.

An attorney who is filing several petitions simultaneously, including one or more petitions with more than **ten (10)** but less than **one thousand (1000)** creditors and equity security holders, in lieu of providing an additional, individual disk list of creditors and equity security holders for each petition with more than **ten (10)** creditors and equity security holders, may submit a single floppy disk if the total number of creditors listed does not exceed **one thousand (1000) creditors.**

The disk shall be submitted in a sealed 8½″ x 11″ envelope and shall contain the lists of creditors and equity security holders for each of the petitions filed, including names and post office addresses, with zip codes, of the debtor's creditors, the debtor, the debtor's attorney, the United States Trustee and if a debt is owing to the United States, then to the particular agency or department, if known, to which such debt is owing. The floppy disk shall be filed in accordance with the format and specifications annexed as Exhibit "B" and shall include a certification by the debtor that information contained on the floppy disk is true, complete, and correct.

The foregoing requirement may be waived only upon submission of a written affidavit by an attorney or a pro se debtor, attesting to a lack of capacity to comply with the requirement. The waiver shall be accompanied by a matrix filed in accordance with the format and specifications annexed as Exhibit "C."

If a Debtor files a Petition with **one thousand (1000)** or more creditors and equity security holders, the Debtor **shall** immediately contact the clerk of court to determine if the claims process should be undertaken pursuant to 28 U.S.C. § 156(c).

[Dated: December 8, 1994.]

EXHIBIT "A"

Floppy Disk—Single Case (More than 10 but less than 1000 Creditors)

The additional list of creditors on floppy disk shall be filed in a sealed 8½″ x 11″ envelope. The debtor's name and address, social security/taxpayer identification number, chapter filed under and attorney name, address and telephone number shall appear on the envelope. The disk should be in the following format:

1. Must be 3.5″ or 5.25″;

2. Must be formatted for use on an IBM or compatible PC;

3. Contain one ASCII file;

4. One case per file;

5. One file per disk;

6. File must be named "creditor.scn";

7. The first line of the file must be the name of the debtor. If the disk is not filed with the petition, then the case number must be substituted for the debtor name (***9412345***); use three asterisks before and after the case number.

8. The second line must be blank;

9. Start the list of creditors on the third line;

10. The address must be 4 lines or less;

11. Each line of the address must contain no more than 30 characters;

12. Each address must be separated by two blank lines;

13. The state name can be either two characters or written out fully, however the state name **cannot** contain periods (i.e. "N.Y." is invalid but "NY" and "New York" are valid);

14. There should be no trailing blanks after the zip code; and

15. No more than 1000 creditors should be listed on one disk.

EXHIBIT "B"

Floppy disk: Multiple Cases (lists of creditors with more than 10 creditors per case but no more than 1000 creditors for all cases entered on the disk)

The disk must be tiled in a sealed 8½″ x 11″ envelope. The debtors' names and addresses, social security/taxpayer identification numbers, chapter filed under and the attorney name, address and telephone number shall appear on the envelope. The floppy disk shall be segmented by individual debtor and shall conform to the following format and specifications:

1. Must be 3.5″ or 5.25″;

2. Must be formatted for use on an IBM or compatible PC;

3. Contain one ASCII file;

4. One file per disk;

5. File must be named "creditor.scn";

6. The first line for each case on the tile must be the name of the debtor. If the disk is not tiled with the petitions, then the case numbers must be substituted for the debtors' names (***9412345***); use three asterisks before and after each case number.

7. The second line must be blank;

8. Start the list of creditors on the third line;

9. The address must be 4 lines or less;

10. Each line of the address must not contain more than 30 characters;

11. Each address must be separated by two blank lines;

12. State name can be either two characters or written out fully, however the state name cannot contain periods (i.e. "N.Y." is invalid but "NY" and "New York" are valid);

13. There should be no trailing blanks after the zip code;

14. No more than 1000 creditors should be listed;

15. After the last creditor for each case, there should be five blank lines before listing the name (or case number) of the next debtor., and

16. Follow instructions B.6–12.

FOR FURTHER INFORMATION ON FORMATTING OR DISK PREPARATION, CONTACT PATRICK DELL'ARENA AT (212) 668–2870 EXT.3522 OR VITO GENNA AT (212) 668–2870 EXT. 3521.

EXHIBIT "C"

MATRIX (Must be filed with Attorney Affidavit of Lack of Capacity to Prepare a Disk)

The matrix shall be filed in a **sealed** envelope, **unfolded** and **unstapled**, with the debtor's name and address, social security/taxpayer identification number and attorney name, address, telephone number and chapter of filing affixed to the envelope. The matrix should be in the following format:

1. Printed on clean white 8½″ x 11″ paper;

2. Contain no more than 10 addresses to a page;

3. Contain absolutely **no** headers, footers, page numbers, or other extraneous marks that are not directly material to a creditor name or address;

4. Be in all capital letters;

5. Each address must be no more than 4 lines;

6. Each line of the address must be 30 characters or less;

7. Each address must be separated by one blank line; and

8. Be an original document and not a copy.

Example: JOHN Q. PUBLIC, DEBTOR

EDWARD NEWBERRY, D.D.S.
3038 MEADE
SAN DIEGO, CA 92116

GROSSMONT ORTHOPEDIC MEDICAL GROUP
5565 GROSSMONT CENTER DRIVE
LA MESA, CA 92326

GROSSMONT DISTRICT HOSPITAL
P.O. BOX 158
LA MESA, CA 92041

AFFILIATED PHYSICAL THERAPY
SPRING VALLEY, CA 92078

UNION TRIBUNE
P.O. BOX 15337
SAN DIEGO, CA 92115

GENERAL ORDER M-139. IN THE MATTER OF DESIGNATION OF BANKRUPTCY JUDGES TO CONDUCT JURY TRIALS

And now, this 7th day of December 1994, the United States District Court for the Southern District of New York hereby specially designates the bankruptcy judges of this district to conduct jury trials pursuant to 28 U.S.C. § 157(e).

[Dated: December 7, 1994.]

GENERAL ORDER M-289. ORDER LIMITING FED.R.CIV.P. 26 IN CONTESTED MATTERS

By resolution of the Board of Judges for the Southern District of New York, it is resolved that the following subdivisions of Fed. R. Civ. P. 26, as incorporated by Fed. R. Bankr. P. 7026, shall not apply in a contested matter unless the court directs otherwise: 26(a)(1)(mandatory disclosure), 26(a)(2)(disclosures regarding expert testimony) and 26(a)(3)(additional pre-trial disclosure), and 26(f)(mandatory meeting before scheduling conference/discovery plan).

[Dated: November 19, 2003.]

GENERAL ORDER M-293. ORDER IMPOSING SANCTIONS ON ATTORNEYS DISCIPLINED BY THE COMMITTEE ON GRIEVANCES

WHEREAS, Southern District of New York Local Civil Rule 1.5(a) states that the Committee on Grievances appointed by the board of judges of the District Court, and under the direction of the chief judge, shall have charge of all matters relating to the discipline of attorneys and pursuant to Local Civil Rule 1.5(d)(4), the Committee on Grievances may impose discipline or take other actions as justice may require, including disbarment and suspension.

WHEREAS, Southern District of New York Local Rule of Bankruptcy Procedure 2090-1(a), states that an attorney who may practice in the District Court pursuant to Civil Rule 1.3(a) and (b) of the

Local District Rules may practice in this Court, and Local Rule of Bankruptcy Procedure 2090–1(b), further states that an attorney in good standing of the bar of any state or of any United States District Court may be admitted pro hac vice to practice in this Court in a particular case, adversary proceeding or contested matter; and

WHEREAS, the rules governing the Court's Electronic Case Filing System restrict the issuance of general System passwords that authorize the filing of documents on the Court's Electronic Filing System to attorneys admitted to practice in this Court; it is hereby

ORDERED that the Clerk of the Court is directed to revoke the general System password issued to any attorney who has been disbarred or suspended by the District Court pursuant to Local Civil Rule 1.5, or whose right to practice pro hac vice in this Court has been revoked, without prejudice, however, to that person's right to apply for a limited-access password that the Court makes available to non-attorneys.

[Dated: December 19, 2003.]

GENERAL ORDER M–293. CLAIMS BAR DATE PURSUANT TO RULE 3002(c)(5), FEDERAL RULES OF BANKRUPTCY PROCEDURE

Rule 3002(c)(5) of the Federal Rules of Bankruptcy Procedure provides:

If notice of insufficient assets to pay a dividend was given to creditors pursuant to Rule 2002(e), and subsequently the trustee notifies the court that payment of a dividend appears possible, the clerk shall notify the creditors of that fact and that they may file proofs of claim within 90 days after the mailing of the notice.

In this District notices sent pursuant to Rule 3002(c)(5) are mailed by a notice provider and the Bankruptcy Clerk, who prepares the notice that includes the date certain by which the proofs of claim are to be filed, and who is unable to know when the notice will be mailed. Consequently, for purposes of Rule 3002(c)(5) the date of mailing shall be deemed to be four days after transmission by the Bankruptcy Clerk to the notice provider, and the Bankruptcy Clerk shall use 94 days after transmission to the notice provider to calculate the bar date for filing claims under Rule 3002(c)(5).

The Bankruptcy Judges of this District having considered this clarification to Rule 3002(c)(5) and agreeing this practice should be adopted.

NOW, it is

ORDERED, that, effective immediately, any notices transmitted to a notice provider by the Bankruptcy Clerk shall use 94 days after transmission to calculate the bar date for filing claims under Rule 3002(c)(5).

[Dated: February 17, 2005.]

GENERAL ORDER M–306. ORDER REGARDING THE REASSIGNMENT OF CERTAIN CHAPTER 7 CASES

WHEREAS, a feature of the Court's CM/ECF System automatically assigns a judge to a chapter 7 case soon after filing on CM/ECF, but does not automatically assign affiliated cases to the same judge in accordance with Local Bankruptcy Rule 1073–1(b); and

WHEREAS, the incorrect automatic assignment, which is most likely to occur in the Manhattan divisional office, presently requires approval of the Chief Judge each time the Clerk must reassign a chapter 7 case to the judge already presiding over the affiliated debtor's case, it is hereby

ORDERED that the Clerk is directed to reassign any chapter 7 case filed in the Manhattan divisional office where, after the automatic assignment of a judge, it becomes necessary to reassign the chapter 7 case to the judge who is assigned to a pending case of the same debtor or an affiliate of the debtor.

[Dated: August 4, 2005.]

AMENDED GENERAL ORDER M–311.   IN RE: PROCEDURES FOR PAYMENT AND CURE OF PRE–PETITION JUDGMENT OF POSSESSION INVOLVING RESIDENTIAL PROPERTY [M–352]

WHEREAS, the Bankruptcy Abuse Prevention and Consumer Protection Act of 2005, as codified in 11 U.S.C. §§ 362(b)(22) and 362(l), creates certain rights and obligations with respect to the cure of a monetary default giving rise to a pre-petition judgment of possession regarding residential property in which the debtor resides as a tenant under a lease or rental agreement, it is hereby

ORDERED, that the debtor shall be deemed to have complied with 11 U.S.C. § 362(l)(1) by:

1.   Making the required certification by completing the four check boxes, **including the landlord's name and address**, listed in the voluntary petition under the section entitled "Statement by a Debtor who Resides as a Tenant of Residential Property"; and

2.   Delivering to the Clerk, together with the petition (or within one business day of the filing, if the petition is filed electronically) (a) a certified or cashier's check or money order, made payable to the lessor, in the amount of any rent that would become due during the 30 day period after the filing of the petition, and (b) a copy of the judgment of possession; and it is further

ORDERED, that if the debtor complies with the preceding paragraph, the Clerk of the Court shall, within one business day, send notice of compliance to the lessor who shall then have the option, exercisable within ten days of the date of the notice, (1) to consent to receive the check in which event the lessor shall provide payment instructions, or (2) object to the debtor's certification, which objection shall constitute a request for a hearing; and it is further

ORDERED, that if the lessor does not respond within the 10 day deadline, the lessor shall be deemed to have consented to receive the check, and the Clerk shall send the check to the lessor at the address set forth in the debtor's certification.

[Dated: April 28, 2008.]

GENERAL ORDER M–313.   CRIMINAL REFERRALS OF CERTAIN BANKRUPTCY CRIMES

WHEREAS, the Bankruptcy Abuse and Prevention and Consumer Protection Act of 2005 enacted section 158 of title 28 regarding, inter alia, the designation of certain individuals within the Department of Justice with primary responsibility for carrying out enforcement activities in addressing violations of 18 U.S.C. §§ 152 and 157 relating to abusive reaffirmations of debt or materially fraudulent statements in bankruptcy schedules that are intentionally false or intentionally misleading; and

WHEREAS, 18 U.S.C. § 158(d) directs the bankruptcy courts to establish procedures for referring any case that may contain a materially fraudulent statement in a bankruptcy schedule to the individuals designated under 18 U.S.C. § 158; it is hereby

ORDERED, that in addition to the obligations imposed under 18 U.S.C. § 3057, any person having reasonable grounds to believe that a bankruptcy schedule contains a materially fraudulent statement in violation of 18 U.S.C. §§ 152 or 157 shall report such violation to one or more of the individuals designated under 18 U.S.C. § 158 by completing the attached referral form or otherwise providing the same information in writing.

[Dated: November 30, 2005.]

**United States Bankruptcy Court for the
Southern District of New York**

**NOTIFICATION STATEMENT
REGARDING POTENTIAL
VIOLATION OF 18 U.S.C. § 152 OR 157**

TO: _____ POSITION:_____
FROM: _____ TITLE (if any): _____

DATE: _____ SIGNATURE _____

1. Background Information

a. Name of Debtor _____

   i. Case number _____

   ii. Debtor's Address _____

   iii. Debtor's Telephone no. _____

b. Debtor's Attorney _____

   i. Address _____

   ii. Telephone no. _____

c. Name of Trustee (if any) _____

   i. Address _____

   ii. Telephone no. _____

2. Case Chapter

a. Under what chapter was the case originally filed: 7 ( ); 11( ); 12 ( ); 13 ( )

b. Under what chapter is the case now pending: 7 ( ); 11( ); 12 ( ); 13 ( )

c. Type of Case: Voluntary ( ); Involuntary ( )

3. Report all facts and circumstances of the offense or offenses believed to have been committed (provide as complete a description as possible), including the following:

a. Identify the schedule that contains the materially fraudulent statement.

b. Explain why the statement is materially fraudulent.

c. Provide the names, addresses, and telephone numbers of persons with knowledge of an information relating to the suspected offense.

d. Disclose any other pertinent information regarding the suspected offense.

GENERAL ORDER M–320. RULES GOVERNING PROCEDURES FOR APPOINTMENT OF PRO BONO COUNSEL IN BANKRUPTCY PROCEEDINGS FROM A BANKRUPTCY PRO BONO PANEL

The Court having issued General Order M–68, dated May 8, 1985, adopting the "Rules Governing Appointment of Pro Bono Counsel" (the "Old Rules"); and the Bankruptcy Judges of this District having subsequently adopted the annexed "Rules Governing Procedures for Appointment of Pro Bono Counsel in Bankruptcy Proceedings From a Bankruptcy Pro Bono Panel" (the "New Rules") to replace the Old Rules; it is hereby

ORDERED, that General Order M–68 is vacated; and it is further

ORDERED, that the New Rules are adopted.

[Dated: February 15, 2006.]

UNITED STATES BANKRUPTCY COURTS
FOR THE
SOUTHERN AND EASTERN DISTRICTS
OF NEW YORK

RULES GOVERNING PROCEDURES FOR APPOINTMENT OF PRO BONO COUNSEL IN BANKRUPTCY PROCEEDINGS FROM A BANKRUPTCY PRO BONO PANEL

The following procedures shall govern the appointment of pro bono counsel from a bankruptcy pro bono panel to represent pro se parties in bankruptcy proceedings when such parties lack the resources to retain counsel by any other means.

1. Bankruptcy Pro Bono Panel. There shall be a bankruptcy pro bono panel (the "Panel") of attorneys and law firms who are willing to accept appointment to represent pro se parties in bankruptcy proceedings when such parties lack the resources to retain counsel. Registration forms to participate in the Panel shall be available at the Clerk's office in the Southern and Eastern District Bankruptcy Courts, on each court's respective website (Southern District: www.nysb.uscourts.gov; Eastern District: www.nyeb.uscourts.gov) and through the Panel Administrator (as defined in Rule 3).

2. **Composition of Bankruptcy Pro Bono Panel.** The Panel will consist of the following:

(a) *Law Firms.* Law firms, including public interest law firms, may register to participate on the Panel as firms by completing a registration form setting forth, among other things: (i) the firm's mailing and website addresses; (ii) the name of the attorney or pro bono coordinator with the firm designated as Panel liaison, along with such individual's electronic mail address, phone number and facsimile number; (iii) the number of attorneys employed by the firm; (iv) the ability of participating attorneys to represent non-English speaking clients, and the languages that can be accommodated; and (v) preference, if any, for appointment between courthouses. Where a firm is appointed to an action, the appointment will be directed to the Panel liaison and appearance in the action may be entered by the firm or the assigned attorney, at the firm's option.

(b) *Individual Attorneys.* Attorneys who are willing to accept appointment to represent pro se parties may register to participate on the Panel by completing a registration form setting forth, among other things: (i) the name, mailing address and website address, if any, of the attorney, along with the attorney's electronic mail address, phone number and facsimile number; (ii) the firm or organization, if any, with which the attorney is affiliated; (iii) the number of years the attorney has been admitted to practice; (iv) the attorney's principal practice areas; (v) the attorney's experience in bankruptcy and/or litigation matters; (vi) the ability of the attorney to represent non-English speaking clients; (vii) the courts in which the attorney is admitted to practice; and

(viii) the attorney's preference, if any, for appointment between the courthouses.

(c) *Attorney Instructors in Law School Clinical Programs.* The Southern and Eastern District Bankruptcy Courts may authorize a clinical program, under the auspices of one or more law schools accredited by the American Bar Association and located in the Southern or Eastern District, through which students, appropriately supervised by an attorney instructor, may appear in matters referred to the Panel. An attorney instructor may apply to participate on the Panel by completing a registration form setting forth, among other things: (i) the name, mailing address and website address of the law school administering the clinical program; (ii) the number of students involved in the clinical program; (iii) the practices of the clinical program in supervising participating students; (iv) the name, mailing address and website address, if any, of the attorney instructor, along with the attorney instructor's electronic mail address, phone number and facsimile number; (v) the firm or organization, if any, with which the attorney instructor is affiliated; (vi) the name and mailing address of the supervisor of the clinical program, along with the supervisor's electronic mail address, phone number and facsimile number; (vii) the number of years the attorney instructor has been admitted to practice; (viii) the attorney instructor's principal practice areas; (ix) the attorney instructor's experience in bankruptcy and/or litigation matters; (x) the ability of the attorney instructor and the clinical program to represent non-English speaking clients; (xi) the courts in which the attorney instructor is admitted to practice; and (xii) preference, if any, for appointment between the courthouses.

(d) Information on a registration form may be amended at any time by letter. An attorney or firm may by letter withdraw from the Panel at any time subject to Rule 6 (Relief From Appointment).

(e) Nothing in these rules shall restrict the authority of a bankruptcy judge to appoint pro bono counsel by other means, including direct appointment or appointment through organizations other than the pro bono panel established by these rules, whether or not the counsel appointed is a member of such panel.

3. **Panel Administrator.** A list of law firms, individual attorneys and attorney instructors who have registered to participate on the Panel shall be maintained by a representative of the City Bar Justice Center (hereinafter, the "Panel Administrator"). The Panel Administrator may receive assistance in administering the Panel from members of the Association of the Bar of the City of New York's Committee on Bankruptcy and Corporate Reorganization, from the New York City Bankruptcy Assistance Project and from other qualified organizations. The Panel Administrator may remove an attorney or firm from the Panel at any time. It is not intended that the Panel Administrator shall be responsible for supervising attorneys appointed to represent clients. The Southern and Eastern District Bankruptcy Courts may appoint additional Panel Administrators. Attorneys and law firms participating in the Panel are not required to be members of any bar association.

4. Appointment Procedure.

(a) Whenever a bankruptcy judge concludes that appointment of counsel from the Panel may be warranted and the client consents, the judge may request, on the record or in writing, that the Panel Administrator select counsel from the Panel. The judge's chambers shall inform the Panel Administrator of the appointment and any scheduled court dates and provide the Panel Administrator with a copy of the docket sheet and any necessary pleadings. The Panel Administrator may, in its discretion, if deemed desirable in specific cases, select counsel not on the Panel or select a specific attorney on the Panel who is especially qualified to undertake the representation. The Panel Administrator may direct the applicant to a bar association referral service in any case where it appears that adequate counsel fees may be awarded as provided by statute. The provisions of the Bankruptcy Code relating to the appointment of counsel by the court shall be complied with.

(b) Pro bono counsel will be appointed only for individuals who have appeared pro se and are unable to afford counsel, or who had counsel but were unable to pay for litigated matters. Such persons may be requested to file with the court an in forma pauperis affidavit affirming they lack the resources to retain counsel. In determining whether to request that the Panel Administrator select counsel from the Panel for appointment, the judge may take the following factors into account: (i) the nature and complexity of the matter in which the pro bono counsel is to represent the client; (ii) the apparent potential merit of the claim or issue involved; (iii) the inability of the client to retain counsel by other means; (iv) the degree to which the interests of justice will be served by the appointment of counsel, including the benefit the court may derive from the assistance of the appointed counsel; and (v) any other factors deemed appropriate. It is not intended that counsel will be appointed for any party prior to the filing of a petition under Title 11 of the U.S. Code. These rules are not intended to provide any party with a right to have counsel appointed.

(c) It is intended that counsel will be appointed to represent debtors only on a specific contested matter or adversary proceeding rather than generally with respect to the bankruptcy case, and counsel's responsibilities shall be limited only to such matter or proceeding. Counsel also may be appointed to represent non-debtors in connection with specific contested matters, adversary proceedings or other litigated matters arising in or relating to a bankruptcy case.

(d) Upon receiving a request, as set forth in Rule 4(a), to select counsel from the Panel, it is expected that the Panel Administrator shall forward a request for pro bono counsel to members of the Panel via electronic mail or otherwise. Panel members may contact the Panel Administrator to indicate their interest in accepting a case. Appointments of counsel generally shall be on a first-come first-served basis; provided, however, that the Panel Administrator may select counsel on other bases where appropriate. If several Panel members are interested in the same case, a wait list may be established. The Panel Administrator shall forward a notice of appointment, along with the client's name and contact information, to the selected Panel member. In the event no Panel member accepts the assignment, the Panel Administrator shall so inform the client and the judge's chambers and no further attempts at assignment shall be required.

5. Responsibilities of the Appointed Attorney.

(a) Upon receiving a notice of appointment, counsel shall obtain, either through the applicable Case Management/Electronic Case Files System or otherwise, and review the case file and, if deemed appropriate, communicate with the client, but must advise the client that s/he has not yet decided whether to accept the appointment. Counsel shall determine as soon as practicable, and within such time prior to the matter's next scheduled hearing date so as to permit another appointment to be made, whether to accept the representation. Upon accepting the representation, and upon the client's consent, counsel shall file a notice of appearance and inform other counsel as appropriate. The notice of appearance shall, if appropriate, specify the discrete matter or matters upon which pro bono counsel is to represent the client and further state that all pleadings and other papers shall continue to be served upon the client as well as upon pro bono counsel. Pro bono counsel shall send a copy of the notice of appearance to the client, the judge's chambers and the Panel Administrator. The Panel Administrator shall maintain a record of all assigned matters.

(b) Upon accepting an appointment and filing a notice of appearance, counsel shall fully discuss the merits of the matter with the client. Counsel may, if appropriate, explore with the client the possibility of resolving the dispute by other means, including but not limited to seeking a negotiated settlement or proceeding to mediation. If, after consultation with counsel, the client decides to prosecute or defend the action, counsel shall represent the party until the attorney-client relationship is terminated in the ordinary course in connection with the matter as to which counsel was appointed or until terminated as provided for herein.

(c) If the appointed attorney after reviewing the file reasonably anticipates a need to request relief from appointment, the attorney shall, before discussing the merits of the case with the client, advise the client that a procedure for such relief exists. Where the attorney did not reasonably anticipate the need for such relief prior to discussing the merits of the case with the client, the attorney may request the waiver at any time the need for such relief becomes apparent. The attorney should then request the client to execute a limited waiver of the attorney client privilege permitting the attorney to disclose under seal to the Court the attorney's reasons for seeking to be relieved of the appointment. The waiver should indicate that the application for relief will be a privileged court document and may not be used in the litigation. The client's refusal to execute a waiver shall not preclude the attorney from applying for relief.

6. Relief From Appointment.

(a) Prior to filing a notice of appearance and within the time period set forth in Rule 5(a), if counsel does not wish to accept an appointment due to lack of time, personal preference or any other ground set forth below, or upon the client's request, counsel shall promptly inform the Panel Administrator, who will attempt to reassign the case to another Panel member. In the event no Panel member accepts the assignment, the Panel Administrator shall so inform the client and the judge's chambers and no further attempts at assignment shall be required.

(b) Subsequent to filing a notice of appearance, pro bono counsel may apply pursuant to the Court's Local Rules to be relieved of an appointment on any grounds available to an attorney-of record except for the non-payment of fees or expenses.

(c) An application by counsel for relief from an appointment on any of the grounds set forth above must be made promptly upon counsel acquiring knowledge of the facts leading to the application.

(d) If counsel wishes to be relieved from an appointment on any of the grounds set forth in Rule 6(b) or similar grounds, counsel shall send a request to that effect to the client, stating the grounds for relief. If the client does not object to the request for relief, counsel shall so advise the Panel Administrator and submit a proposed order, endorsed by the Panel Administrator, to the court. If the client objects to the request for relief, counsel shall submit the request and the grounds therefor to the judge's chambers for consideration, along with a proposed order, in a document to be kept under seal and not to be available in discovery or otherwise used in connection with the matter or any other litigation. Counsel shall provide a copy of the request and proposed order to the client and the Panel Administrator.

(e) If an order for relief from appointment is entered, the judge may request, on the record or in writing, that the Panel Administrator attempt to reassign the case to another Panel member. In the event no Panel member accepts the assignment, the Panel Administrator shall so inform the client and the judge's chambers and no further attempts at reassignment shall be required.

7. Discharge. A party for whom counsel has been appointed may request the judge, on the record or in writing, to discharge such counsel from the representation. The client shall provide a copy of any written request to the appointed counsel. When such a request is supported by good cause (e.g., substantial disagreement between the party and counsel on strategy), the order of discharge shall be granted and the appointed counsel shall duly inform the Panel Administrator and the client. The judge may request, on the record or in writing, that the Panel Administrator attempt to reassign the case to another Panel member. In the event no Panel member accepts the assignment, the Panel Administrator shall so inform the client and the judge's chambers and no further attempts at reassignment shall be required.

8. Expenses. There being no public funds available for the purpose, appointed counsel or the firm may advance the expenses of the matter.

9. Compensation for Services.

(a) No payment of money or other valuable consideration shall be demanded or accepted in connection with the services rendered by pro bono counsel.

(b) Notwithstanding paragraph (a), the matter may be one for which compensation for legal services may become available to the appointed counsel under the Bankruptcy Code or other authority. Upon appropriate application by appointed counsel, and taking into consideration counsel's initial agreement to take the matter without compensation, the judge may award fees to the appointed counsel or law firm for services rendered, as permitted by applicable law.

(c) If, after appointment, the appointed counsel discovers that the party is able to pay for legal services, counsel shall bring this information to the attention of the Panel Administrator. Upon appropriate motion, the court may relieve counsel from the representation and permit the party to retain other counsel or proceed pro se.

10. Duration of Representation.

(a) Subject to the provisions of Rules 10(b) and (c), appointed counsel shall represent the party in connection with the matter on which counsel was appointed from the date counsel enters an appearance until a final order or judgment is entered in the matter and reasonable efforts have been made to enforce the order or judgment, or until counsel has been relieved from appointment by the court. If the bankruptcy case is continuing after the matter is concluded, counsel shall inform the client in writing with a copy to the Panel Administrator that counsel's responsibilities have concluded and that the party is again proceeding pro se.

(b) If an appealable order or judgment is entered in connection with the matter, counsel shall inform the client of the possibility of appeal and, if the client requests, file a notice of appeal, a designation of the items to be included in the record on appeal and a statement of the issues to be presented, or assist the party in filing such papers.

(c) In the event the party desires to take an appeal from an appealable order or judgment, or if such order or judgment is appealed by another party, counsel is encouraged but not required to represent the party on the appeal and in any proceeding that may ensue upon an order of remand. If counsel elects not to represent the client on the appeal or remand, counsel shall give prompt notice of such election to the Panel Administrator who may attempt to reassign the matter to another Panel member or refer the client to the pro se panel of the court to which the appeal is taken.

(d) Nothing in these rules shall be read to affect: (i) an attorney's responsibilities under the Code of Professional Responsibility or applicable law; or (ii) the manner in which and to whom a notice of appearance or notice of withdrawal must be given under the Federal Rules of Bankruptcy Procedure, the Local Bankruptcy Rules, or any order of the court in the particular bankruptcy case.

GENERAL ORDER M–383. AMENDING GENERAL ORDER M–331, RE GUIDELINES FOR THE CONDUCT OF ASSET SALES

By resolution of the Board of Judges of the Southern District of New York, it is resolved that in order to expedite the review and determination of applications to conduct asset sales, it is hereby

ORDERED that the Amended Guidelines for the Conduct of Asset Sales (the "Amended Guidelines"), annexed hereto, are adopted and shall be effective December 1, 2009; and it is further

ORDERED that all sales applications filed in the United States Bankruptcy Court for the Southern District of New York, and all proceedings and orders relating to such applications, shall conform substantially to these Amended Guidelines.

[Dated: November 18, 2009.]

AMENDED GUIDELINES FOR THE CONDUCT OF ASSET SALES

The United States Bankruptcy Court for the Southern District of New York (the "Court") has established the following guidelines (the "Guidelines") for the conduct of asset sales under section 363(b) of 11 U.S.C. §§ 101 et seq. (the "Bankruptcy Code"). The Guidelines are designed to help practitioners identify issues that typically are of concern to parties and the Court, so that, among other things, determinations can be made, if necessary, on an expedited basis.

By offering the Guidelines, this Court does not address the circumstances under which an asset sale or asset sale process is appropriate or express a preference for asset sales under section 363(b) of the Bankruptcy Code as opposed to those conducted in the context of confirming a chapter 11 plan, address other substantive legal issues, or establish any substantive rules. However, the Guidelines do require disclosure of the "Extraordinary Provisions," discussed below, pertaining to the conduct of asset sales, which ordinarily will not be approved without good cause shown for such Extraordinary Provisions, or compelling circumstances, and reasonable notice.

The Guidelines are intended to supplement the requirements of section 363(b) and 365 of the Bankruptcy Code, Rules 2002 and 6004 of the Federal Rules of Bankruptcy Procedure (the "Bankruptcy Rules"), and Rules 6004–1 and 6005–1 of the Court's Local Rules.

I. MOTIONS

A. Motion Content. When an auction is contemplated, the debtor[1] should file a single motion seeking the entry of two orders to be considered at two separate hearings. The first order (the "Sale Procedures Order") will approve procedures for the sale process, including any protections for an initial bidder, or stalking horse buyer, and the second order (the "Sale Order") will approve the sale to the successful bidder at the auction. If no auction procedures or stalking horse buyer protection provisions are contemplated, only one order (the Sale Order) and one hearing is required. If no auction is contemplated or the debtor has not actively solicited or will not actively solicit higher and better offers, the motion seeking approval of the sale should explain why the debtor proposes to structure the sale in such manner.[2]

1. The proposed purchase agreement, or a form of proposed agreement acceptable to the debtor if the debtor has not yet entered into an agreement with a proposed buyer, should be attached to the motion.

2. The motion also should include a copy of the proposed order(s), particularly if the order(s) include any Extraordinary Provisions.

3. The motion must comply in form with the Local Rules.

4. If a hearing is required under section 363(b) of the Bankruptcy Code in connection with the sale of personally identifiable information subject to a privacy policy of the debtor, the motion should request appointment of a consumer privacy ombudsman under section 332 of the Bankruptcy Code.

B. Bidding Procedures. Generally, the Court will entertain a motion for approval, in a Sale Procedures Order, of proposed bidding procedures if such procedures are, as a matter of reasonable business judgment, likely to maximize the sale price. Such procedures must not chill the receipt of higher and better offers and must be consistent with the seller's fiduciary duties. It is recommended that such procedures include the following:[3]

1. *Qualification of Bidders.* An entity that is seeking to become a qualified bidder will deliver financial information by a stated deadline to the debtor and other key parties (ordinarily excluding other bidders)[4] reasonably demonstrating such bidder's ability to consummate a sale on the terms proposed. Such financial information, which may be provided confidentially, if appropriate, may include current audited or verified financial statements of, or verified financial commitments obtained by, the potential bidder (or, if the potential bidder is an entity formed for the purpose of acquiring the property to be sold, the party that will bear liability for a breach). To be qualified, a prospective bidder also may be required by a stated deadline to make a non-binding expression of interest and execute a reasonable form of non-disclosure agreement before being provided due diligence access to non-public information.

2. *Qualification of Bids Prior to Auction.*

(a) The bidding procedures should state the criteria for a qualifying bid and any deadlines for (i) submitting such a bid and (ii) notification whether the bid constitutes a qualifying bid.

(b) The bidding procedures may require each qualified bid to be marked against the form of a stalking horse agreement or a template of the debtor's preferred sale terms, showing amendments and other modifications (including price and other terms) proposed by the qualified bidder. The proposed bidding procedures may, but are not required to, limit bidding to the terms of a stalking horse agreement or preferred form of agreement; for example, bidding on less than all of the assets proposed to be acquired by an initial, or stalking horse, bidder normally should be permitted, unless such bidding is inconsistent with the purpose of the sale.

(c) A qualified bid should clearly identify all conditions to the qualified bidder's obligation to consummate the purchase.

(d) A qualified bid should include a good faith deposit, which will be non-refundable if the bidder is selected as the successful bidder and fails to consummate the purchase (other than as a result of a breach by the seller) and refundable if it is not selected as the successful bidder (other than as a result of its own breach). The amount of, and precise rules governing, the good faith deposit will be determined on a case-by-case basis, but generally each qualified bidder, including any initial, or stalking horse, bidder, should be required to make the same form of deposit.

3. *Backup Buyer.* The Sale Procedures Order may provide that the debtor in the reasonable exercise of its judgment may accept and close on the second highest qualified bid received if the winning bidder fails to close the transaction within a specified period. In such case, the debtor would

retain the second highest bidder's good faith deposit until such bidder was relieved of its obligation to be a back-up buyer.

4. *Stalking Horse or Initial Bidder Protections/Bidding Increments.*

(a) No–Shop or No–Solicitation Provisions. Limited no-shop or no-solicitation provisions may be permissible, in unusual circumstances, if they are necessary to obtain a sale, they are consistent with the debtor's fiduciary duties and they do not chill the receipt of higher or better offers. Such provisions must be prominently disclosed in the motion, with particularity. If the relevant documents do not include a "fiduciary out" provision, the debtor must disclose the fact of and the reason for the exclusion of the provision.

(b) Break–Up/Topping Fees and Expense Reimbursement. The propriety of any break-up or topping fees and other bidding protections (such as the estate's proposed payment of out-of-pocket expenses incurred by a bidder in connection with the proposed transaction or the compensation of a bidder for lost opportunity costs) will be determined on a case-by-case basis. Generally such obligations should be payable only from the proceeds of a higher or better transaction entered into with a third party within a reasonable time of the closing of the sale. Such provisions must be set forth with particularity, and conspicuously disclosed in the motion.

(c) Bidding Increments. If a proposed sale contemplates the granting of a break-up or topping fee or expense reimbursement, the initial bidding increment must be more than sufficient to pay the maximum amount payable thereunder. Additional bidding increments should not be so high that they chill further bids, or so low that they provide insubstantial consideration to the estate.

(d) Rebidding. If a break-up or topping fee is requested, the Sale Procedures Order should state whether the stalking horse will be deemed to waive the break-up or topping fee by rebidding. In the absence of a waiver, the Sales Procedure Order should state whether the stalking horse will receive a "credit" equal to the break-up or topping fee when bidding at the auction.

5. *Auction Procedures.*

(a) If an auction is proposed, the Sale Procedures Order generally should provide that the auction will be conducted openly, and that each bidder will be informed of the terms of the previous bid. The motion should explain the rationale for proposing a different auction format in the Sale Procedures Order.

(b) If a professional auctioneer will conduct the auction, the parties should refer to the statutory provisions and rules governing the conduct of professional auctioneers. *See* Bankruptcy Rule 6004 and Rules 6004–1 and 6005–1 of the Local Bankruptcy Rules for the Southern District of New York (the "Local Rules").

(c) If the auction is sufficiently complex or disputes can reasonably be expected to arise, it is advisable at the sale procedures hearing to ask the Court whether it will consider conducting the auction in open court, or otherwise be available to resolve disputes. If the debtor proposes to conduct the auction outside the presence of the judge, the actual bidding should be transcribed or videotaped to ensure a record, or the motion should explain why this is not advisable.

(d) Each bidder is expected to confirm at the auction that it has not engaged in any collusion with respect to the bidding or the sale.

(e) The Sale Procedures Order should provide that, absent irregularities in the conduct of the auction, or reasonable and material confusion during the bidding, the Court will not consider bids made after the auction has been closed, or the motion should explain why this is not advisable.

C. Sale Motion. With regard to the proposed sale, the motion and the evidence presented or proffered at any sale hearing should be sufficient to enable the Court to make the following findings: (1) a sound business reason exists for the transaction; (2) the property has been adequately marketed, the purchase price constitutes the highest or otherwise best offer and provides fair and reasonable consideration; (3) the proposed transaction is in the best interests of the debtor's estate, its creditors, and where relevant, its interest holders; (4) the transaction has been proposed and negotiated in good faith; (5) adequate and reasonable notice has been provided; (6) the "free and clear" requirements of section 363(f) of the Bankruptcy Code, if applicable, have been met; (7) if applicable, the sale is consistent with the debtor's privacy policy concerning personally identifiable information, or, after appointment of a consumer ombudsman in accordance with section 332 of the Bankruptcy Code and notice and a hearing, no showing was made that such sale would violate applicable nonbankruptcy law; (8) the requirements of section 365 of the Bankruptcy Code have been met in respect of the proposed assumption and assignment or rejection of any executory contracts and unexpired leases; (9) where necessary, the debtor's board of directors or other governing body has authorized the proposed transaction; and (10) the debtor and the purchaser have entered into the transaction without collusion, in good faith, and from arm's-length bargaining positions, and neither party has engaged in any conduct that would cause or permit the agreement to be avoided under section 363(n) of the Bankruptcy Code.

1. *Sound Business Purpose.* A debtor must demonstrate the facts that support a finding that a sound business reason exists for the sale.

2. *Marketing Efforts.* A debtor must demonstrate facts that support a finding that the property to be sold has been marketed adequately.

3. *Purchase Price.* A debtor must demonstrate that fair and reasonable value will be received and that the proffered purchase price is the highest or best under the circumstances. If a bid includes deferred payments or any equity component, a debtor should discuss its assessment of the creditworthiness of competing bidders, if any, and the proposed buyer's ability to realize the projected earnings upon which future payments or other forms of consideration to the estate are based. Any material purchase price adjustment provisions should be identified.

4. *Assumption and Assignment of Contracts and Leases.* A debtor must demonstrate at a minimum: (a) that it or the assignee/acquiror has cured or will promptly cure all existing defaults under the agreement(s), and (b) that the assignee/acquiror can provide adequate assurance that it will perform under the terms of the agreement(s) to be assumed and assigned under section 365 of the Bankruptcy Code. Additional notice and opportunity for a hearing may be required, if the offer sought to be approved at the sale hearing is submitted by a different entity than the initial, stalking horse bidder or the winning bid identifies different contracts or leases for assumption and assignment, or rejection, than the initial bid that was noticed for approval. If this possibility exists, the sale motion should acknowledge the debtor will provide such additional notice and opportunity to object under such circumstances.

D. Extraordinary Provisions. The following provisions must be disclosed conspicuously <u>in a separate section</u> of the sale motion and, where applicable, in the related proposed Sale Procedures Order or Sale Order, and the motion must provide substantial justification therefor:[5]

1. *Sale to Insider.* If the motion proposes a sale to an insider, as defined in the Bankruptcy Code, the motion must disclose what measures have been taken to ensure the fairness of the sale process and the proposed transaction.

2. *Agreements with Management.* The sale motion must disclose whether the proposed buyer has discussed or entered into any agreements with management or key employees regarding compensation or future employment, the material terms of any such agreements, and what measures have been taken to ensure the fairness of the sale and the proposed transaction in the light of any such agreements.

3. *Private Sale/No Competitive Bidding.* If no auction is contemplated, the debtor has agreed to a limited no-shop or no-solicitation provision, or the debtor has otherwise not sought or is not actively seeking higher or better offers, the sale motion must so state and explain why such sale is likely to maximize the sale price.

4. *Deadlines that Effectively Limit Notice.* If the proposed transaction includes deadlines for the closing or Court approval of the Sale Procedures Order or the Sale Order that have the effect of limiting notice to less than that discussed in II, below, the sale motion must provide an explanation.

5. *No Good Faith Deposit.* If any qualified bidder, including a stalking horse, is excused from submitting a good faith deposit, the sale motion must provide an explanation.

6. *Interim Arrangements with Proposed Buyer.* If a debtor is entering into any interim agreements or arrangements with the proposed purchaser, such as interim management arrangements (which, if out of the ordinary course, also must be subject to notice and a hearing under section 363(b) of the Bankruptcy Code), the sale motion must disclose the terms of such agreements.

7. *Use of Proceeds.* If a debtor proposes to release sale proceeds on or after the closing without further Court order, or to provide for a definitive allocation of sale proceeds between or among various sellers or collateral, the sale motion must describe the intended disposition of such amounts and the rationale therefor.

8. *Tax Exemption.* If the debtor is seeking to have the sale declared exempt from taxes under section 1146(a) of the Bankruptcy Code, the sale motion must prominently disclose the type of tax (e.g., recording tax, stamp tax, use tax, capital gains tax) for which the exemption is sought. It is not

sufficient to refer simply to "transfer" taxes. In addition, the debtor must identify the state or states in which the affected property is located.

9. *Record Retention.* If the debtor proposes to sell substantially all of its assets, the sale motion must confirm that the debtor will retain, or have reasonable access to, its books and records to enable it to administer its bankruptcy case.

11.* *Sale of Avoidance Actions.* If the debtor seeks to sell its rights to pursue avoidance claims under chapter 5 of the Bankruptcy Code, the sale motion must so state and provide an explanation of the basis therefor.

* [**Publisher's Note:** So in original.]

12. *Requested Findings as to Successor Liability.* If the debtor seeks findings limiting the purchaser's successor liability, the sale motion must disclose the adequacy of the debtor's proposed notice of such requested relief and the basis for such relief. Generally, the proposed Sale Order should not contain voluminous findings with respect to successor liability, or injunctive provisions except as provided in III, below.

13. *Future Conduct.* If the debtor seeks a determination regarding the effect of conduct or actions that may or will be taken after the date of the Sale Order, the sale motion must set forth the legal authority for such a determination.

14. *Requested Findings as to Fraudulent Conveyance.* If debtor seeks a finding to the effect that the sale does not constitute a fraudulent conveyance, it must explain why a finding that the purchase price is fair and reasonable is not sufficient.

15. *Sale Free and Clear of Unexpired Leases.* If the debtor seeks to sell property free and clear of a possessory leasehold interest, license or other right, the debtor must identify the non-debtor parties whose interests will be affected, and explain what adequate protection will be provided for those interests.

16. *Relief from Bankruptcy Rule 6004(h).* If the debtor seeks relief from the fourteen-day stay imposed by Bankruptcy Rule 6004(h), the sale motion must disclose the business or other basis for such request.

II. NOTICE

A. **General.** Notice is always required under section 363(b); however, a hearing is required only if there are timely objections or the Court otherwise schedules a hearing.

B. **Notice of Proposed Sale Procedures.**

1. *Notice Parties.* Notice should be limited to those parties-in-interest best situated to articulate an objection to the limited relief sought at this stage, including:

(a) counsel for official and informal committees of creditors, equity holders, retirees, etc.;

(b) office of the United States Trustee;

(c) postpetition lenders;

(d) indenture trustees;

(e) agent for prepetition lenders;

(f) entities who have requested notice under Bankruptcy Rule 2002;

(g) all entities known or reasonably believed to have asserted a lien, encumbrance, claim or other interest in any of the assets offered for sale; and

(h) parties to executory contracts and unexpired leases proposed to be assumed and assigned, or rejected as part of the proposed transaction.

To provide additional marketing of the assets, the debtor also should send a copy of the motion to entities known or reasonably believed to have expressed an interest in acquiring any of the assets offered for sale. Nothing herein is meant to imply that prospective bidders have standing to be heard with respect to the Sales Procedures.

2. *Notice Period.* As a general matter, the minimum 21–day notice period set forth in Bankruptcy Rule 2002(a) can be shortened with respect to the request for approval of a proposed Sale Procedures Order, that does not involve Extraordinary Provisions and complies with these

Guidelines, without compromising the finality of the proposed transaction. The 14–day notice period provided for in Local Rule 9006–1(b) should provide sufficient time, under most circumstances, to enable any parties-in-interest to file an objection to proposed sale procedures.

3. *Contents of Notice.* Notice should comport with Bankruptcy Rules 2002 and 6004.

C. Notice of Sale.

1. *Notice Parties.* Generally the proposed sale requires more expansive notice than proposed sale procedures. (But see footnote 2, above, regarding omnibus procedures for de minimis sales.) Notice should ordinarily be given to:[6]

(a) counsel for official and informal committees of creditors, equity holders, retirees, etc.;

(b) office of the United States Trustee;

(c) entities who have requested notice under Bankruptcy Rule 2002[7] (and, if the proposed sale is of substantially all of the debtor's assets, all known creditors of the debtor);

(d) postpetition lenders;

(e) indenture trustees;

(f) agent for prepetition lenders;

(g) all entities known or reasonably believed to have asserted a lien, encumbrance, claim or other interest in any of the assets offered for sale;

(h) all parties to executory contracts or unexpired leases to be assumed and assigned, or rejected as part of the transaction;

(i) all affected federal, state and local regulatory (including, for example, environmental agencies) and taxing authorities,[8] including the Internal Revenue Service;

(j) if applicable, a consumer privacy ombudsman appointed under section 332 of the Bankruptcy Code; and

(k) the Securities and Exchange Commission (if appropriate).

If the contemplated sale implicates the anti-trust laws of the United States, or a debt (other than for taxes) is owed by the debtor to the United States government, notice also should be given to:

(*l*) the Federal Trade Commission;

(m) the Assistant Attorney General in charge of the Antitrust Division of the Department of Justice; and

(n) the United States Attorney's Office.

To provide additional marketing of the assets, notice also should be sent to any entities known or reasonably believed to have expressed an interest in acquiring any of the assets.

See I.C.4, above for circumstances in which it may be required, based on changes in the proposed transaction that had originally been noticed, to give additional notice to parties to executory contracts and unexpired leases proposed to be assumed and assigned or rejected under section 365 of the Bankruptcy Code.

2. *Notice Period.* The statutory 20–day notice period should not be shortened for notice of the actual sale without a showing of good cause. The service of a prior notice or order, that discloses an intention to conduct a sale but does not state a specific sale date, does not affect the 20–day notice period.

3. *Contents of Notice.* Proper notice should comport with Bankruptcy Rules 2002 and 6004 and should include:

(a) the Sale Procedures Order (including the date, time and place of any auction, the bidding procedures related thereto, the objection deadline for the sale motion and the date and time of the sale hearing);

(b) reasonably specific identification of the assets to be sold;

(c) the proposed form of asset purchase agreement, or instructions for promptly obtaining a copy;

(d) if appropriate, representations describing the sale as being free and clear of liens, claims, interests and other encumbrances (other than any claims and defenses of a consumer under any consumer credit transaction that is subject to the Truth in Lending Act or a consumer credit contract (as defined in 16 C.F.R. § 433.1, as amended), with all such liens, claims, interests and other encumbrances attaching with the same validity and priority to the sale proceeds;

(e) any commitment by the buyer to assume liabilities of the debtor; and

(f) notice of proposed cure amounts and the right and deadline to object thereto and otherwise to object to the proposed assumption and assignment, or rejection of executory contracts and unexpired leases (see I.C.4, above for additional notice that debtor may need to acknowledge may be required).[9]

III. SALE ORDER

The Court discourages unduly long sale orders that contain unnecessary and redundant provisions. In the typical case, the findings should be limited to those set out in I.C, supra, tailored to the particular case. The decretal paragraphs should also be limited, and if more than one decretal paragraph deals with the same subject matter or form of relief, the proponent of the Sale Order should explain the reason in a separate pleading. Finally, if the order contains a decretal paragraph that approves the purchase agreement or authorizes the debtor to execute the purchase agreement, it should not also contain separate decretal paragraphs that approve specific provisions of the purchase agreement or declare their legal effect.

With these admonitions, the Court may enter a Sale Order containing the following, if substantiated through evidence presented or proffered in the motion or at the sale hearing:

A. Approval of Sale and Purchase Agreement. The order should authorize the debtor to (1) execute the purchase agreement, along with any additional instruments or documents that may be necessary to implement the purchase agreement, provided that such additional documents do not materially change its terms; (2) consummate the sale in accordance with the terms and conditions of the purchase agreement and the instruments and agreements contemplated thereby; and (3) take all further actions as may reasonably be requested by the purchaser for the purpose of transferring the assets.[10]

B. Transfer of Assets. The assets will be transferred free and clear of all liens, claims, encumbrances and interests in such property, other than any claims and defenses of a consumer under any consumer credit transaction subject to the Truth in Lending Act or a consumer credit contract, as defined in 16 C.F.R. § 433.1 (and as may be amended), with all such interests attaching to the sale proceeds with the same validity and priority, and the same defenses, as existed immediately prior to the sale,[11] and persons and entities holding any such interests will be enjoined from asserting such interests against the purchaser, its successors or assigns, or the purchased assets, unless the purchaser has otherwise agreed.

C. Assumption and Assignment of Executory Contracts and Leases to Purchaser. The debtor will be authorized and directed to assume and assign to the purchaser executory contracts and leases free and clear of all liens, claims, encumbrances and interests, with all such interests attaching to the sale proceeds with the same validity and priority as they had in the assets being sold (provided, however, that in certain circumstances additional notice may be required before assumption and assignment or rejection of executory contracts and leases can be granted. See I.C.4, above.)

D. Statutory Provisions. The proposed order should specify those sections of the Bankruptcy Code and Bankruptcy Rules that are being relied on, and identify those sections, such as Bankruptcy Rule 6004(h), that are, to the extent permitted by law, proposed to be limited or abridged.

E. Good Faith/No Collusion. The transaction has been proposed and entered into by the debtors and the purchaser without collusion, in good faith, and from arm's-length bargaining positions. The proposed Sale Order should also specify that neither the debtor nor the purchaser have engaged in any conduct that would cause or permit the transaction to be avoided under Bankruptcy Code section 363(n).

[Dated: December 1, 2009.]

[1] The term "debtor" includes "debtor in possession" and "trustee," as appropriate under the particular circumstances.

[2] With the exception of providing for such disclosure, these Guidelines do not express a preference for public over private sales as a means to maximize the sale price.

[3] When multiple asset sales over time are expected, a debtor should consider seeking Court approval of global bidding procedures to avoid the need to obtain Court approval of procedures for each such sale. Similarly, the debtor should consider

seeking Court approval of global notice and other appropriate procedures to facilitate sales of assets of limited value or *de minimis* sales that do not warrant an auction or a separate motion for each sale. What constitutes a de minimis sale will depend on the facts of each case. *See* Local Rule 6004–1.

4 It is expected that the debtor will also share its evaluation of bids with key parties-in-interest, such as representatives of official committees, and that it will in its reasonable judgment identify the winning bidder only after consultation with such parties.

5 The fact that a similar provision was included in an order entered in a different case does not constitute a justification.

6 In larger cases, a sale of significant assets may also require notice of the proposed sale in publications of national circulation or other appropriate publications.

7 In the case of publicly traded debt securities, notice to indenture trustees and record holders may be sufficient to the extent that the identity of beneficial holders is not known.

8 Notice must be given to applicable taxing authorities, including the state attorney general or other appropriate legal officer, affected by the relief requested under section 1146(a) of the Bankruptcy Code.

9 This notice may be provided in a separate schedule sent only to the parties to such agreements.

10 Each and every federal, state and local government agency or department may be directed to accept any and all documents and instruments necessary and appropriate to consummate the transactions contemplated by the purchase agreement.

11 If any person or entity that has filed financing statements, mortgages, mechanic's liens, lis pendens, or other documents evidencing interests in the assets has not delivered to the debtor prior to the closing date termination statements, instruments of satisfaction, and/or releases of all such interests, the debtor may be authorized and directed to execute and file such statements, instruments, releases and other documents on behalf of such person or entity.

The debtor should try to anticipate whether there are any complex allocation issues presented by the proposed "free and clear" relief.

GENERAL ORDER M–396. IN THE MATTER OF PERSONAL ELECTRONIC DEVICES

At its meeting of March 2010, the Board of Judges of the Bankruptcy Court, Southern District of New York, approved adoption of the following general order of the Court, *effective April 1, 2010:*

(a) No one other than court officials engaged in the conduct of court business shall bring any Personal Electronic Device into the Courthouse[1] *except as permitted by this order*. Any violation of this order may result in sanctions including, but not limited to, fines and forfeiture of the privileges granted herein.

(b) An *attorney,*[2] *and only an attorney,* may bring a Personal Electronic Device[3] into the Courthouse. In order to comply with this order, identification will be required by the U.S. Marshals upon entry into the Courthouse. A photo ID will be necessary to evidence one's status as an attorney. A photo ID may be used in conjunction with another form of ID to establish attorney status.

(c) All sound emitting capabilities including, without limitation, any ring tone or vibrating sound, *must* be turned off whenever a Personal Electronic Device is in the Courthouse. Any capability of a Personal Electronic Device to make or record images or sounds shall be turned off during all times the device is in the Courthouse. Nothing herein modifies the policy or rules of the Judicial Conference of the United States (JCUS) or this Court regarding prohibiting the taking of photographs, the use of recording devices and broadcasting in or from the Courthouse.[4]

(d) Telephone calls may be made from Personal Electronic Devices *only* in *designated* areas in the Courthouse. All use of a Personal Electronic Device *must* comply with posted signage. Attorneys speaking on their phones are expected to do so with common courtesies being mindful of their surroundings. Failure to adhere to these restrictions *will* be grounds to suspend the privilege granted herein.

(e) The Chief Judge may suspend the privilege of bringing a Personal Electronic Device into the Courthouse under this order. Any attorney whose privilege is suspended may seek review or reinstatement by petitioning the Board of Judges in writing.

[Dated: March 23, 2010.]

1 This order applies only to the Manhattan and Poughkeepsie Courthouses. The White Plains and Middletown Courthouses are governed by the District Court's Standing Order M10–468 dated February 17, 2010, Southern District of New York.

2 Any other person may request permission from the presiding judge to bring a Personal Electronic Device into the Courthouse by contacting that judge's chambers.

3 "Personal Electronic Device" includes any cellular telephone, smartphone, Palm Pilot, iPhone, BlackBerry, and other comparable personal digital assistant device. An attorney with both a cellular telephone and a Blackberry or similar device, may take both into the Courthouse provided, however, that the devices belong, or are assigned, to that attorney.

4 *See* Local Bankruptcy Rule 5073–1.

GENERAL ORDER M-400. IN THE MATTER OF PERSONAL ELECTRONIC DEVICES (MEMBERS OF THE MEDIA)

WHEREAS, General Order M-396, signed on March 23, 2010, established guidelines pertaining to attorneys' use of Personal Electronic Devices[1] while in the Courthouse;[2]

WHEREAS, the established guidelines do not address the use of Personal Electronic Devices by members of the media in the Courthouse;

WHEREAS, the Board of Judges has determined that the use of Personal Electronic Devices by members of the media in the Courthouse should be authorized; it is hereby

ORDERED, that members of the media possessing press credentials[3] may bring a Personal Electronic Device into the Courthouse subject to the restrictions and obligations set forth in General Order M-396.

[Dated: May 19, 2010.]

[1] "Personal Electronic Device" includes any cellular telephone, smartphone, Palm Pilot, iPhone, BlackBerry, and other comparable personal digital assistant device.

[2] This order applies only to the Manhattan and Poughkeepsie Courthouses. The White Plains and Middletown Courthouses are governed by the District Court's Standing Order M10-468, dated February 17, 2010, Southern District of New York.

[3] Press credentials are defined herein as any credentials issued by a governmental unit or a recognized general media company establishing that the person identified therein as a member of the media.

GENERAL ORDER M-411. IN RE: ADOPTION OF AMENDED VERSION OF INTERIM RULE 1007-1

WHEREAS, this Court, by means of **General Order M-363**, signed December 9, 2008, adopted Interim Rule 1007-I, which implements the 2008 amendments to 11 U.S.C. § 707(b) providing a temporary exclusion from the application of the means test for certain members of the National Guard and Reserves; and

WHEREAS, this Court, by means of **General Order M-391,** signed December 28, 2009, adopted an amended version of Interim Rule 1007-I conforming the rule to the 2009 amendments to the Federal Rules of Bankruptcy Procedure; and

WHEREAS, in 2010, the Judicial Conference of the United States approved amendments to Interim Rule 1007-I to conform the rule to the 2010 amendments to Federal Rule of Bankruptcy Procedure 1007;

NOW THEREFORE, the United States Bankruptcy Court for the Southern District of New York adopts the amended version of Interim Rule 1007-I,* which shall apply only to chapter 7 cases commenced during the three-year period beginning December 19, 2008.

[Dated: November 10, 2010.]

*[**Publisher's Note:** For the text of Interim Rule 1007-I currently in effect in matters before this Court, see General Order M-440, dated October 22, 2012, post.]

GENERAL ORDER M-412. IN THE MATTER OF: ORDER ESTABLISHING PROCEDURES FOR MONTHLY COMPENSATION AND REIMBURSEMENT OF EXPENSES OF PROFESSIONALS [AMENDING GENERAL ORDER M-388]

By resolution of the Board of Judges for the United States Bankruptcy Court for the Southern District of New York, it is resolved that in order to further provide professionals with clear and concise procedures for monthly compensation and reimbursement of expenses in chapter 11 cases (the "Monthly Fee Order"), all Monthly Fee Orders filed in the Bankruptcy Court for the Southern District of New York shall conform substantially to the official Monthly Fee Order form annexed hereto.

NOW, THEREFORE, IT IS ORDERED that the annexed official Monthly Fee Order, amending General Order M-388, is adopted, effective December 21, 2010 and shall apply to all Monthly Fee Orders signed on or after that date.

[Dated: December 21, 2010.]

UNITED STATES BANKRUPTCY COURT
SOUTHERN DISTRICT OF NEW YORK

In re:)
)   Chapter 11
)   Case Nos.: ___ –B– ___ (___)
         Debtors.   )   through ___ –B– ___ (___)
)   (Jointly Administered)
)

ORDER PURSUANT TO 11 U.S.C. §§ 105(a) AND 331
ESTABLISHING PROCEDURES FOR MONTHLY COMPENSATION
AND REIMBURSEMENT OF EXPENSES OF PROFESSIONALS

[NAMES OF DEBTORS], debtors and debtors-in-possession (collectively, the "Debtors"), move, by a motion dated _____ ___, 20 ___ (the "Motion"), for an order, pursuant to §§ 105(a) and 331 of the United States Bankruptcy Code (the "Code"), establishing procedures for monthly compensation and reimbursement of expenses of professionals retained by order of this Court, and this Court having determined that the relief requested in the Motion is in the best interests of the Debtors, their estates, and creditors; and it appearing that proper and adequate notice has been given by service of the Motion on the Office of the United States Trustee, counsel to each official committee (if no committee is appointed, the 20 largest unsecured creditors), counsel to all post-petition lenders (or counsel to their agent(s)), and all parties who filed a notice of appearance; and that no other or further notice is necessary; and upon the record of the hearing herein; and upon the representation of the Debtors that this estate is administratively solvent; and after due deliberation thereon; and good and sufficient cause appearing therefor, it is hereby

ORDERED, that except as may otherwise be provided in Court orders authorizing the retention of specific professionals, all professionals in these cases may seek monthly compensation in accordance with the following procedure:

(a) On or before the twentieth (20th) day of each month following the month for which compensation is sought, each professional seeking compensation under this Order shall serve a monthly statement ("Monthly Fee Statement"), by hand or overnight delivery on (i) _____, the officer designated by the Debtors to be responsible for such matters; (ii) counsel to the Debtors; (iii) counsel to all official committees; (iv) counsel for the Office of the United States Trustee, 33 Whitehall Street, 21st Floor, New York, New York 10004 (Attn: _____, Esq.); (vi) counsel to all post-petition lenders or their agent(s); and (v) _____ (anyone else the Court may designate);

(b) On or before the twentieth (20th) day of each month following the month for which compensation is sought, each professional seeking compensation under this Order shall file a Monthly Fee Statement with the Court; however, a courtesy copy need not be delivered to the Judge's chambers. The Monthly Fee Order does not alter the fee application requirements outlined in §§ 330 and 331 of the Code. Professionals are still required to serve and file interim and final applications for approval of fees and expenses in accordance with the relevant provisions of the Code, the Federal Rules of Bankruptcy Procedure and the Local Rules for the United States Bankruptcy Court, Southern District of New York;

(c) Each Monthly Fee Statement must contain a list of the individuals—and their respective titles (e.g., attorney, accountant, or paralegal)—who provided services during the statement period, their respective billing rates, the aggregate hours spent by each individual, a reasonably detailed breakdown of the disbursements incurred (no professional should seek reimbursement of an expense which would otherwise not be allowed pursuant to the Court's Administrative Orders dated June 24, 1991 and April 21, 1995 or the United States Trustee Guidelines for Reviewing Applications for Compensation and Reimbursement of Expenses Filed under 11 U.S.C. § 330 dated January 30, 1996), and contemporaneously maintained time entries for each individual in increments of tenths (1/10) of an hour;

(d) If any party in interest has an objection to the compensation or reimbursement sought in a particular Monthly Fee Statement, such party shall, by no later than the thirty-fifth (35th) day following the month for which compensation is sought, file with the Court and serve upon the professional whose Monthly Fee Statement is objected to, and the other persons designated to receive statements in paragraph (a), a written "Notice of Objection To Fee Statement," setting forth the nature of the objection and the amount of fees or expenses at issue;

(e) At the expiration of the thirty-five (35) day period, the Debtors shall promptly pay eighty percent (80%) of the fees and one hundred percent (100%) of the expenses identified in each Monthly Fee Statement to which no objection has been served in accordance with paragraph (d);

(f) If a Notice of Objection to Fee Statement is filed, the Debtors shall withhold payment of that portion of the Monthly Fee Statement to which the objection is directed and promptly pay the remainder of the fees and disbursements in the percentages set forth in paragraph (e) unless the professional whose statement is objected to seeks an order from the Court, upon notice and a hearing, directing payment to be made;

(g) If the parties to an objection are able to resolve their dispute following the filing of a Notice of Objection to Fee Statement and if the party whose Monthly Fee Statement was objected to files (a) a statement indicating that the objection is withdrawn and describing in detail the terms of the resolution, then the Debtors shall promptly pay, in accordance with paragraph (e), that portion of the Monthly Fee Statement which is no longer subject to an objection;

(h) All objections that are not resolved by the parties or Court order, shall be preserved and presented to the Court at the next interim or final fee application hearing to be heard by the Court (see paragraph (j), below);

(i) The service of an objection in accordance with paragraph (d) shall not prejudice the objecting party's right to object to any fee application made to the Court in accordance with the Code on any ground whether raised in the objection or not. Furthermore, the decision by any party not to object to a Monthly Fee Statement shall not be a waiver of any kind or prejudice that party's right to object to any fee application subsequently made to the Court in accordance with the Code;

(j) Approximately every 120 days, but no more than every 150 days, each of the professionals shall serve and file with the Court an application for interim or final Court approval and allowance, pursuant to sections 330 and 331 of the Bankruptcy Code (as the case may be), of the compensation and reimbursement of expenses requested;

(k) Any professional who fails to file an application seeking approval of compensation and expenses previously paid under this Order when due shall (1) be ineligible to receive further monthly payments of fees or expenses as provided herein until further order of the Court, and (2) may be required to disgorge any fees paid since retention or the last fee application, whichever is later;

(*l*) The pendency of an application or a Court order that payment of compensation or reimbursement of expenses was improper as to a particular statement shall not disqualify a professional from the future payment of compensation or reimbursement of expenses as set forth above, unless otherwise ordered by the Court;

(m) Neither the payment of, nor the failure to pay, in whole or in part, monthly compensation and reimbursement as provided herein shall have any effect on this Court's interim or final allowance of compensation and reimbursement of expenses of any professionals;

(n) Counsel for each official committee may, in accordance with the foregoing procedure for monthly compensation and reimbursement of professionals, collect and submit statements of expenses, with supporting vouchers, from members of the committee he or she represents; provided, however, that such committee counsel ensures that these reimbursement requests comply with this Court's Administrative Orders dated June 24, 1991 and April 21, 1995;

and it is further

ORDERED, that each professional may seek, in its first request for compensation and reimbursement of expenses pursuant to this Order, compensation for work performed and reimbursement for expenses incurred during the period beginning on the date of the professional's retention and ending on _____, 20 ___; and it is further

ORDERED, that the amount of fees and disbursements sought be set out in U.S. dollars (if the fees and disbursements are to be paid in foreign currency, the amount shall be set out in U.S. dollars and the conversion amount in the foreign currency, calculated at the time of the submission of the application); and it is further

ORDERED, that the Debtors shall include all payments to professionals on their monthly operating reports, detailed so as to state the amount paid to each of the professionals; and it is further

ORDERED, that any party may object to requests for payments made pursuant to this Order on the grounds that the Debtors have not timely filed monthly operating reports, remained current with their administrative expenses and 28 U.S.C. § 1930 fees, or a manifest exigency exists by seeking a further order of this Court, otherwise, this Order shall continue and shall remain in effect during the pendency of this case; and it is further

ORDERED, that all time periods set forth in this Order shall be calculated in accordance with Federal Rule of Bankruptcy Procedure 9006(a); and it is further

ORDERED, that any and all other and further notice of the relief requested in the Motion shall be, and hereby is, dispensed with and waived; provided, however, that the Debtors must serve a copy of this Order on all entities specified in paragraph (a) hereof.

Dated: New York, New York

———— ——, 20——

[Dated: December 21, 2010.]

GENERAL ORDER M–418. IN THE MATTER OF DEPOSIT AND INVESTMENT OF REGISTRY FUNDS [SUPERCEDED BY GENERAL ORDER M–502 EFFECTIVE OCTOBER 5, 2016]

GENERAL ORDER M–427. IN RE: ADOPTION OF NEW FEE APPLICATION SCHEDULES

Amended General Orders M–284, M–291, and M–425

WHEREAS, by Amended General Order # M–129, the Board of Judges adopted a form order with annexed exhibits (the "Schedules") for granting applications for allowance of interim/final compensation and reimbursement of expenses;

WHEREAS, the Board of Judges revised the Schedules pursuant to General Orders 284, 291 and 425, and has determined to add Schedule C to be used by applicants seeking payment of professional fees and reimbursements of expenses in cases filed under chapter 13; it is hereby

ORDERED, that Schedule A (Current Interim Fee Period) and Schedule B (Final Fee Application Totals) shall be used by applicants seeking payment of professional fees and reimbursement of expenses in all cases other than cases filed under chapter 13; and it is further

ORDERED, that Schedule C shall be used by applicants seeking payment of professional fees and reimbursement of expenses in all cases filed under chapter 13; and it is further

ORDERED, that the form order, originally adopted by General Order 284 and adopted again by this General Order, shall continue to be used by applicants seeking payment of professional fees and reimbursement of expenses; and it is further

ORDERED, that newly adopted Schedule C, referred to above, shall be used in conjunction with chapter 13 fee applications filed with the Court after fourteen (14) days of the signing of this General Order.

UNITED STATES BANKRUPTCY COURT
SOUTHERN DISTRICT OF NEW YORK

————————————————— x

In re: Chapter
                                     Case No.

————————————————— x

ORDER GRANTING APPLICATION(S) FOR ALLOWANCE OF INTERIM/FINAL COMPENSATION AND REIMBURSEMENT OF EXPENSES

Upon consideration of Application(s) for Allowance of Interim/Final Compensation and Reimbursement of Expenses (the "Application(s)") for professional services rendered and expenses incurred during the period commencing _____, 20 ___ through _____, 20 ___; and a hearing having been held before this court to consider the Application(s) on _____ 20 ___; and notice having been given pursuant to Federal Rules of Bankruptcy Procedure 2002(a)(7) and (c)(2); and due consideration having been given to any responses thereto; and sufficient cause having been shown therefor, it is hereby;

ORDERED that the Application(s) is/are granted to the extent set forth in Schedule "A".

Dated: New York, New York
_____, 20 ___

_____
United States Bankruptcy Judge

Case No.:   **CURRENT INTERIM FEE PERIOD**   Schedule A
Case Name: **[Insert Date Range]**

(1) Applicant	(2) Date/Document Number of Application	(3) Interim Fees Requested on Application	(4) Fees Allowed	(5) Fees to be Paid for Current Fee Period	(6) Fees to be Paid for Prior Fee Period(s) (if any) (i.e., Holdback Release)	(7) Total Fees to be Paid	(8) Interim Expenses Requested	(9) Expenses to be Paid for Current Fee Period

Revised September 2011   DATE ON WHICH ORDER WAS SIGNED: _____   INITIALS: _____ USBJ

Case No.:   **FINAL FEE APPLICATION TOTALS**   Schedule B
Case Name: **[Insert Date Range]**

(1) Applicant	(2) Total Fees Requested	(3) Total Fees Paid	(4) Total Expenses Requested	(5) Total Expenses Paid

Revised September 2011   DATE ON WHICH ORDER WAS SIGNED: _____   INITIALS: _____ USBJ

Case No.:   **Chapter 13 Fee Application**   **Schedule C**
Case Name: **[Insert Date Range]**

(1) Applicant	(2) Initial Fee Charged	(3) Amount of Initial Fee Paid	(4) Amount of Initial Fee Filed as Administrative Claim	(5) Amount of Initial Expenses Collected	(6) Additional Fees Requested	(7) Additional Expenses Requested	(8) Amount of Additional Fee Awarded	(9) Amount of Additional Expenses Awarded

Revised September 2011   DATE ON WHICH ORDER WAS SIGNED: _____   INITIALS: _____ USBJ

[Dated: December 21, 2011.]

GENERAL ORDER M–429.   IN RE: EXTENSION OF APPLICABILITY OF INTERIM RULE 1007–I

WHEREAS, this Court, by means of **General Order M–363** (signed December 9, 2008), adopted Interim Rule 1007–I, which implements the 2008 amendments to 11 U.S.C. § 707(b) providing a temporary exclusion from the application of the means test for certain members of the National Guard and Reserves;

WHEREAS, this Court, by means of **General Order M–391** (signed December 28, 2009), adopted the amended version of Interim Rule 1007–I,* as amended by the Judicial Conference of the United States; and

WHEREAS, the President of the United States, on December 13, 2011, signed into law the National Guard and Debt Relief Extension Act of 2011, which extended—for four additional years (until December 18, 2015)—the temporary exclusion from the application of the means test for certain members of the National Guard and Reserves; it is, therefore,

ORDERED that the applicability of Interim Rule 1007–I to cases filed in this district is extended for so long as such exclusion from the means test remains operative under federal law.

[Dated: December 21, 2011.]

* [**Publisher's Note:** For the text of Interim Rule currently in effect in matters before this Court, *see* General Order M–440, dated October 22, 2012, *post.*]

GENERAL ORDER M–431.   AMENDED STANDING ORDER OF REFERENCE [AMENDED STANDING ORDER OF REFERENCE 12–MISC–32][DISTRICT COURT ORDER]

In the Matter of: Standing Order of Reference re: Title 11

M10–468

Pursuant to 28 U.S.C. Section 157(a) any or all cases under title 11 and any or all proceedings arising under title 11 or arising in or related to a case under title 11 are referred to the bankruptcy judges for this district.

If a bankruptcy judge or district judge determines that entry of a final order or judgment by a bankruptcy judge would not be consistent with Article III of the United States Constitution in a particular proceeding referred under this order and determined to be a core matter, the bankruptcy judge shall, unless otherwise ordered by the district court, hear the proceeding and submit proposed findings of fact and conclusions of law to the district court. The district court may treat any order of the bankruptcy court as proposed findings of fact and conclusions of law in the event the district court concludes that the bankruptcy judge could not have entered a final order or judgment consistent with Article III of the United States Constitution.

[Dated: January 31, 2012.]

GENERAL ORDER M-440. IN RE: ADOPTION OF AMENDED VERSION OF INTERIM RULE 1007-I

WHEREAS, this Court, by means of **General Order M-363**, signed December 9, 2008, adopted Interim Rule 1007-I, which implements the 2008 amendments to 11 U.S.C. § 707(b) providing a temporary exclusion from the application of the means test for certain members of the National Guard and Reserves; and

WHEREAS, this Court, by means of **General Order M-391**, signed December 28, 2009, and **General Order M-411**, signed November 10, 2010, adopted amended versions of Interim Rule 1007-I conforming the rule to amendments to the Federal Rules of Bankruptcy Procedure; and

WHEREAS, this Court, by means of **General Order M-429**, signed December 21, 2011, extended the applicability of Interim Rule 1007-I for so long as the exclusion from the means test remains operative under federal law; and

WHEREAS, the Judicial Conference of the United States approved amendments to Interim Rule 1007-I to conform the rule to the 2012 amendment to Federal Rule of Bankruptcy Procedure 1007 taking effect on December 1, 2012;

NOW THEREFORE, the United States Bankruptcy Court for the Southern District of New York adopts the amended version of Interim Rule 1007-I, and such amended rule shall become effective on December 1, 2012 and shall remain operative pursuant to the provisions set forth in **General Order M-429**.

Interim Rule 1007-I.[1] Lists, Schedules, Statements, and Other Documents; Time Limits; Expiration of Temporary Means Testing Exclusion[2]

* * * * *

(b) Schedules, Statements, and Other Documents Required.

* * * * *

(4) *Unless either*: (A) § 707(b)(2)(D)(I) applies, or (B) § 707(b)(2)(D)(ii) applies and the exclusion from means testing granted therein extends beyond the period specified by Rule 1017(e), an individual debtor in a chapter 7 case shall file a statement of current monthly income prepared as prescribed by the appropriate Official Form, and, if the current monthly income exceeds the median family income for the applicable state and household size, the information, including calculations, required by § 707(b), prepared as prescribed by the appropriate Official Form.

* * * * *

(c) Time Limits. In a voluntary case, the schedules, statements, and other documents required by subdivision (b)(1), (4), (5), and (6) shall be filed with the petition or within 14 days thereafter, except as otherwise provided in subdivisions (d), (e), (f), (h), and (n) of this rule. In an involuntary case, the list in subdivision (a)(2), and the schedules, statements, and other documents required by subdivision (b)(1) shall be filed by the debtor within 14 days of the entry of the order for relief. In a voluntary case, the documents required by paragraphs (A), (C), and (D) of subdivision (b)(3) shall be filed with the petition. Unless the court orders otherwise, a debtor who has filed a statement under subdivision (b)(3)(B), shall file the documents required by subdivision (b)(3)(A) within 14 days of the order for relief. In a chapter 7 case, the debtor shall file the statement required by subdivision (b)(7) within 60 days after the first date set for the meeting of creditors under § 341 of the Code, and in a chapter 11 or 13 case no later than the date when the last payment was made by the debtor as required by the plan or the filing of a motion for a discharge under § 1141(d)(5)(B) or § 1328(b) of the Code. The court may, at any time and in its discretion, enlarge the time to file the statement required by subdivision (b)(7). The debtor shall file the statement required by subdivision (b)(8) no earlier than the date of the last payment made under the plan or the date of the filing of a motion for a discharge under §§ 1141(d)(5)(B), 1228(b), or 1328(b) of the Code. Lists, schedules, statements, and other documents filed prior to the conversion of a case to another chapter shall be deemed filed in the converted case unless the court directs otherwise. Except as provided in § 1116(3), any extension of time to file schedules, statements, and other documents required under this rule may be granted only on motion for cause shown and on notice to the United States trustee, any committee elected under § 705 or appointed under § 1102 of the Code, trustee, examiner, or other party as the court may direct. Notice of an extension shall be given to the United States trustee and to any committee, trustee, or other party as the court may direct.

* * * * *

(n) Time Limits for, and Notice to, Debtors Temporarily Excluded from Means Testing.

(1) An individual debtor who is temporarily excluded from means testing pursuant to § 707(b)(2)(D)(ii) of the Code shall file any statement and calculations required by subdivision (b)(4) no later than 14 days after the expiration of the temporary exclusion if the expiration occurs within the time specified by Rule 1017(e) for filing a motion pursuant to § 707(b)(2).

(2) If the temporary exclusion from means testing under § 707(b)(2)(D)(ii) terminates due to the circumstances specified in subdivision (n)(1), and if the debtor has not previously filed a statement and calculations required by subdivision (b)(4), the clerk shall promptly notify the debtor that the required statement and calculations must be filed within the time specified in subdivision (n)(1).

[Dated: December 1, 2012.]

1 Interim Rule 1007–I has been adopted by the bankruptcy courts to implement the National Guard and Reservists Debt Relief Act of 2008, Public Law No: 110–438, as amended by Public Law No. 112–64. The amended Act, which provides a temporary exclusion from the application of the means test for certain members of the National Guard and reserve components of the Armed Forces, applies to bankruptcy cases commenced in the seven-year period beginning December 19, 2008.

2 Incorporates (1) time amendments to Rule 1007 which took effect on December 1, 2009, and (2) an amendment, effective December 1, 2010, which extended the time to file the statement of completion of a course in personal financial management in a chapter 7 case filed by an individual debtor.

GENERAL ORDER M–447. RE: AMENDED GUIDELINES FOR FEES AND DISBURSEMENTS FOR PROFESSIONALS IN SOUTHERN DISTRICT OF NEW YORK BANKRUPTCY CASES

Superseding General Orders M–104, M–151 M–291, M–389, M–446

By resolution of the Board of Judges for the United States Bankruptcy Court for the Southern District of New York, it is resolved that in order to further provide professionals with clear and concise procedures for compensation and reimbursement of expenses and to combine into one order the requirements heretofore promulgated by this Court and the United States Trustee, applications for compensation and reimbursement of expenses filed in the Bankruptcy Court for the Southern District of New York shall conform substantially to the following.

A. Contents of Applications for Compensation and Reimbursement of Expenses. All applications should include sufficient detail to demonstrate compliance with the standards set forth in 11 U.S.C. § 330. The fee application should also contain sufficient information about the case and the applicant to facilitate a review without searching for relevant information in other documents. The following will facilitate review of the application.

(1) *Information about the Applicant and the Application.* The following information should be provided in every fee application:

(i) Date the bankruptcy petition was filed, date of the order approving employment, identity of the party represented, date services commenced, and whether the applicant is seeking compensation under a provision of the Bankruptcy Code other than section 330.

(ii) Terms and conditions of employment and compensation, source of compensation, existence and terms controlling use of a retainer, and any budgetary or other limitations on fees.

(iii) Names and hourly rates of all applicant's professionals and paraprofessionals who billed time, explanation of any changes in hourly rates from those previously charged, and statement of whether the compensation is based on the customary compensation charged by comparably skilled practitioners in cases other than cases under title 11.

(iv) Whether the application is interim or final, and the dates of previous orders on interim compensation or reimbursement of expenses along with the amounts requested and the amounts allowed or disallowed, amounts of all previous payments, and amount of any allowed fees and expenses remaining unpaid.

(v) Whether the person on whose behalf the applicant is employed has been given the opportunity to review the application and whether that person has approved the requested amount.

(vi) When an application is filed more than once every 120 days after the order for relief or after a prior application to the Court, the date and terms of the order allowing leave to file at shortened intervals.

(vii) Time period of the services or expenses covered by the application.

(2) *Case Status.* The following information should be provided to the extent that it is known to or can be reasonably ascertained by the applicant:

(i) In a chapter 7 case, a summary of the administration of the case including all moneys received and disbursed in the case, when the case is expected to close, and, if applicant is seeking an interim award, whether it is feasible to make an interim distribution to creditors without prejudicing the rights of any creditor holding a claim of equal or higher priority.

(ii) In a chapter 11 case, whether a plan and disclosure statement have been filed and, if not yet filed, when the plan and disclosure statement are expected to be filed; whether all quarterly fees have been paid to the United States Trustee; and whether all monthly operating reports have been filed.

(iii) In a chapter 12 or 13 case, where the debtor's attorney is the applicant, whether the application complies with section 330(a)(4)(B); whether the application is in accordance with the 2016(b) statement that was filed at the beginning of the case; and whether approval of the application would have an effect on the debtor's plan.

(iv) In every case, the amount of cash on hand or on deposit, the amount and nature of accrued unpaid administrative expenses, and the amount of unencumbered funds in the estate.

(v) In every case, any material changes in the status of the case that occur after the filing of the fee application should be raised, orally or in writing, at the hearing on the application or, if a hearing is not required, prior to the expiration of the time period for objection.

(3) *Summary Sheet.* All applications should contain a summary or cover sheet that provides a synopsis of the following information:

(i) Total compensation and expenses requested and any amount(s) previously requested;

(ii) Total compensation and expenses previously awarded by the court;

(iii) Name and applicable billing rate for each person who billed time during the period, and date of bar admission for each attorney;

(iv) Total hours billed and total amount of billing for each person who billed time during billing period; and

(v) Computation of blended hourly rate for persons who billed time during period, excluding paralegal or other paraprofessional time.

(4) *Project Billing Format.*

(i) To facilitate effective review of the application, all time and service entries should be arranged by project categories. The project categories set forth in Exhibit A should be used to the extent applicable. A separate project category should be used for administrative matters and, if payment is requested, for fee application preparation.

(ii) The Court has discretion to determine that the project billing format is not necessary in a particular case or in a particular class of cases.

(iii) Each project category should contain a narrative summary of the following information:

    a. a description of the project, its necessity and benefit to the estate, and the status of the project including all pending litigation for which compensation and reimbursement are requested;

    b. identification of each person providing services on the project; and

    c. a statement of the number of hours spent and the amount of compensation requested for each professional and paraprofessional on the project.

(vi)* Time and service entries are to be reported in chronological order under the appropriate project category.

(vii) Time entries should be kept contemporaneously with the services rendered in time periods of tenths of an hour. Services should be noted in detail, with each service showing a separate time entry and not combined or "lumped" together; however, tasks performed on a project which total a de minimis amount of time can be combined or lumped together if they do not exceed 0.5 hours on a daily aggregate. Time entries for telephone calls, letters, and other communications should give sufficient detail to identify the parties to and the nature of the communication. Time entries for court hearings and conferences should identify the subject of the hearing or conference. If more than one professional from the applicant firm attends a hearing or conference, the applicant should explain the need for multiple attendees.

(5) *Reimbursement for Actual, Necessary Expenses.* Except to the extent that paragraph F, infra, is to the contrary, the following factors are relevant to a determination that an expense is proper:

(i) Whether the expense is reasonable and economical.

(ii) Whether the requested expenses are customarily charged to non-bankruptcy clients of the applicant.

(iii) Whether applicant has provided a detailed itemization of all expenses including the date incurred, description of expense (e.g., type of travel, type of fare, rate, destination), method of computation, and, where relevant, name of the person incurring the expense and purpose of the expense. Itemized expenses should be identified by their nature (e.g., long distance telephone, copy costs, messengers, computer research, airline travel, etc.) and by the month incurred. Unusual items require more detailed explanations and should be allocated, where practicable, to specific projects.

(iv) Whether applicant has prorated expenses where appropriate between the estate and other cases (e.g., travel expenses applicable to more than one case) and has adequately explained the basis for any such proration.

(v) Whether expenses incurred by the applicant to third parties are limited to the actual amounts billed to, or paid by, the applicant on behalf of the estate.

(vi) Whether applicant can demonstrate that the amount requested for expenses incurred in-house reflect the actual cost of such expenses to the applicant, or the actual cost cannot easily be determined.

(vii) Whether the expenses appear to be in the nature nonreimbursable overhead. Overhead consists of all continuous administrative or general costs incident to the operation of the applicant's office and not particularly attributable to an individual client or case. Overhead includes, but is not limited to: word processing, proofreading, administrative and other clerical services; rent, utilities, office equipment and furnishings; insurance, taxes, local telephones and monthly car phone charges;, lighting, heating and cooling; and library and publication charges.

(viii) Whether applicant has adhered to allowable rates for expenses as fixed by local rule or order of the Court.

B. Certification.

(1) Each application for fees and disbursements must contain a certification by the professional designated by the applicant with the responsibility in the particular case for compliance with these Amended Guidelines (the "Certifying Professional"), that (a) the Certifying Professional has read the application; (b) to the best of the Certifying Professional's knowledge, information and belief formed after reasonable inquiry, the fees and disbursements sought fall within these Amended Guidelines, except as specifically noted in the certification and described in the fee application; (c) except to the

extent that fees or disbursements are prohibited by these Amended Guidelines, the fees and disbursements sought are billed at rates and in accordance with practices customarily employed by the applicant and generally accepted by the applicant's clients; and (d) in providing a reimbursable service, the applicant does not make a profit on the service, whether the service is performed by the applicant in-house or through a third party.

(2) Each application for fees and disbursements must contain a certification by the Certifying Professional that the trustee, debtor, and, where applicable, the chair of each official committee, have been provided, not later than 21 days after the end of each month, with a statement of the fees and disbursements accrued during such month. The statement must contain a list of professionals and paraprofessionals providing services, their respective billing rates, the aggregate hours spent by each professional and paraprofessional, a general description of services rendered, a reasonably detailed breakdown of the disbursements incurred and an explanation of billing practices.

(3) Each application for fees and disbursements must contain a certification by the Certifying Professional that the trustee and, in a chapter 11 case, the chair of each official committee and the debtor have all been provided with a copy of the relevant fee application at least 14 days before the date set by the court or any applicable rules for filing fee applications.

C. Confidentiality Requests. If an applicant believes that there is a need to omit any information or description of services as privileged or confidential, the applicant must first get the approval of the court; provided, however, that if such a request is granted, the court may require that any application also contain a set of unredacted time records for in camera inspection.

D. Fee Enhancement.

(1) Any request for an enhancement of fees over the fee which would be derived from the applicable hourly rates multiplied by the hours expended or from the court order authorizing retention must be specifically identified in the application, including the amount being requested, and the justification for the requested enhancement must be set forth in detail.

(2) Any request for such an enhancement of fees must be set forth in the summary sheet required by these Amended Guidelines.

E. Voluntary Reduction of Fees or Disbursements. If an applicant is not requesting all of the fees or disbursements to which it might be entitled based on the applicable hourly rates multiplied by the hours expended or based on the court order authorizing retention, the voluntary reduction must be identified in the application, including the amount of the reduction taken. If the voluntary reduction pertains to services which that continue to appear in the detailed description of services rendered or to disbursements that continue to be listed, the entries for which no compensation or reimbursement is sought must be identified.

F. Provisions Regarding Disbursements.

(1) *No Enhanced Charges for Disbursements.* Except to the extent that disbursements are prohibited by these Amended Guidelines, the disbursements sought must be billed at rates, and in accordance with, practices customarily employed by the applicant and generally accepted by the applicant's clients.

(2) *Photocopies.* Photocopies shall be reimbursable at the lesser of $ 0.10 per page or cost.

(3) *Overtime Expense.* No overtime expense for non-professional and paraprofessional staff shall be reimbursable unless fully explained and justified. Any such justification must indicate, at a minimum, that:

(i) Services after normal closing hours are absolutely necessary for the case; and

(ii) That charges are for overtime expenses paid. The reasonable expenses of a professional required to work on the case after 8:00 p.m. are reimbursable provided that, if the professional dines before 8:00 p.m., the expense is reimbursable only if the professional returns to the office to work for at least one and one half hours. In any event, the expense for an individual's meal may not exceed $20.00.

G. Form of Order. To ensure that the accuracy of the Public Record of Compensation Awarded to Trustees, Examiners, and Professionals is maintained pursuant to Federal Rule of Bankruptcy Procedure 2013, the form of order and schedules promulgated by the Board of Judges and found on the Court's website shall be used.

The foregoing Guidelines have been approved by the Board of Judges and shall be subject to annual review as to adjustments to disbursement/ reimbursement amounts set forth hereinabove in Provision F.

This order shall become effective on February 5, 2013, and apply to all fee applications filed on or after that date.

EXHIBIT A

PROJECT CATEGORIES

Here is a list of suggested project categories for use in most bankruptcy cases. Only one category should be used for a given activity. Professionals should make their best effort to be consistent in their use of categories, whether within a particular firm or by different firms working on the same case. It would be appropriate for all professionals to discuss the categories In advance and agree generally on how activities will be categorized. This list is not exclusive. The application may contain additional categories as the case requires. They are generally more applicable to attorneys in chapter 7 and chapter 11, but may be used by all professionals as appropriate.

ASSET ANALYSIS AND RECOVERY: Identification and review of potential assets including causes of action and non-litigation recoveries.

ASSET DISPOSITION: Sales, leases (§ 365 matters), abandonment and related transaction work.

BUSINESS OPERATIONS: Issues related to debtor-in-possession operating in chapter 11 such as employee, vendor, tenant issues and other similar problems.

CASE ADMINISTRATION: Coordination and compliance activities, including preparation of statement of financial affairs; schedules; list of contracts; United States Trustee interim statements and operating reports; contacts with the United States Trustee; general creditor inquiries.

CLAIMS ADMINISTRATION AND OBJECTIONS: Specific claim inquiries; bar date motions; analyses, objections and allowances of claims.

EMPLOYEE BENEFITS/PENSIONS: Review issues such as severance, retention, 401K coverage and continuance of pension plan.

FEE/EMPLOYMENT APPLICATIONS: Preparations of employment and fee applications for self or others; motions to establish interim procedures.

FEE/EMPLOYMENT OBJECTIONS: Review of and objections to the employment and fee applications of others.

FINANCING: Matters under §§ 361, 363 and 364 including cash collateral and secured claims; loan document analysis.

LITIGATION: There should be a separate category established for each matter (e.g. XYZ Litigation).

MEETINGS OF CREDITORS: Preparing for and attending the conference of creditors, the § 341(a) meeting and other creditors' committee meetings.

PLAN AND DISCLOSURE STATEMENT: Formulation, presentation and confirmation; compliance with the plan confirmation order, related orders and rules; disbursement and case closing activities, except those related to the allowance and objections to allowance of claims.

RELIEF FROM STAY PROCEEDINGS: Matters relating to termination or continuation of automatic stay under § 362.

The following categories are generally more applicable to accountants and financial advisors, but may be used by all professionals as appropriate.

ACCOUNTING/AUDITING: Activities related to maintaining and auditing books of account, preparation of financial statements and account analysis.

BUSINESS ANALYSIS: Preparation and review of company business plan; development and review of strategies; preparation and review of cash flow forecasts and feasibility studies.

CORPORATE FINANCE: Review financial aspects of potential mergers, acquisitions and disposition of company or subsidiaries.

DATA ANALYSIS: Management information systems review, installation and analysis, construction, maintenance and reporting of significant case financial data, lease rejection, claims, etc.

LITIGATION CONSULTING: Providing consulting and expert witness services relating to various bankruptcy matters such as insolvency, feasibility, avoiding actions; forensic accounting, etc.

RECONSTRUCTION ACCOUNTING: Reconstructing books and records from past transactions and bringing accounting current.

TAX ISSUES: Analysis of tax issues and preparation of state and federal tax returns.

VALUATION: Appraise or review appraisals of assets.

[Dated: January 29, 2013.]

* [Publisher's Note: So in original.]

GENERAL ORDER M–451. IN RE: ADOPTION OF MODIFIED LOSS MITIGATION PROGRAMS
I. PURPOSE

The Loss Mitigation Program is designed to function as a forum for debtors and lenders to reach consensual resolution whenever a debtor's residential property is at risk of foreclosure. The Loss Mitigation Program aims to facilitate resolution by opening the lines of communication between the debtors' and lenders' decision-makers. While the Loss Mitigation Program stays certain bankruptcy deadlines that might interfere with the negotiations or increase costs to the Loss Mitigation Parties, the Loss Mitigation Program also encourages the parties to finalize any agreement under Bankruptcy Court protection, instead of seeking dismissal of the bankruptcy case.

II. LOSS MITIGATION DEFINED

The term "Loss Mitigation" is intended to describe the full range of solutions that may avert either the loss of a debtor's property to foreclosure, increased costs to the lender, or both. Loss mitigation commonly consists of the following general types of agreements, or a combination of them: loan modification, loan refinance, forbearance, short sale, or surrender of the property in full satisfaction. The terms of a Loss Mitigation solution will vary in each case according to the particular needs and goals of the parties.

III. ELIGIBILITY

The following definitions are used to describe the types of parties, properties and loans that are eligible for participation in the Loss Mitigation Program:

A. Debtor. The term "Debtor" means any individual debtor in a case filed under chapter 7, 11, 12, or 13 of the Bankruptcy Code, including joint debtors.

B. Property. The term "Property" means any real property or cooperative apartment used as a principal residence in which an eligible Debtor holds an interest.

C. Loan. The term "Loan" means any mortgage, lien or extension of money or credit secured by eligible Property or stock shares in a residential cooperative, regardless of whether or not the Loan (1) is considered to be "subprime" or "non-traditional," (2) was in foreclosure prior to the bankruptcy filing, (3) is the first or junior mortgage or lien on the Property, or (4) has been "pooled," "securitized," or assigned to a servicer or to a trustee.

D. Creditor. The term "Creditor" refers to any secured creditor whether it be the holder, mortgage servicer or trustee of an eligible Loan. If the Creditor participating in Loss Mitigation is not the direct holder of the loan, the Creditor is deemed to have full consent to act on behalf of the holder. If such consent has not been given, the Creditor must object to the Loss Mitigation Request and provide the name of the holder, trustee, or other entity that has the ability to participate in Loss Mitigation.

E. Loss Mitigation Parties. The term "Loss Mitigation Parties" refers to the Debtor and the Creditor bound by a Loss Mitigation Order to participate in Loss Mitigation.

IV. ADDITIONAL PARTIES

A. Other Creditors. Where it may be necessary or desirable to obtain a global resolution, any party may request, or the Bankruptcy Court may direct, that multiple Creditors participate in Loss Mitigation.

B. Co–Debtors and Third Parties. Where the participation of a co-debtor or other third party may be necessary or desirable, any party may request, or the Bankruptcy Court may direct, that such party participate in Loss Mitigation, to the extent that the Bankruptcy Court has jurisdiction over the party, or if the party consents to participation in Loss Mitigation.

C. Chapter 13 Trustee. The Chapter 13 Trustee has the duty in section 1302(b)(4) of the Bankruptcy Code to "advise, other than on legal matters, and assist the debtor in performance under the plan." Any party may request, or the Bankruptcy Court may direct, the Chapter 13 Trustee to participate in Loss Mitigation to the extent that such participation would be consistent with the Chapter 13 Trustee's duty under the Bankruptcy Code.

D. Mediator. At any time, a Debtor or Creditor participating in the Loss Mitigation Program may request, or the Bankruptcy Court may order, the appointment of an independent mediator from the United States Bankruptcy Court for the Southern District of New York's Register of Mediators, which may be viewed at http://www.nysb.uscourts.gov/mediators.html. A mediator will assist in Loss Mitigation in accordance with these Procedures and Local Rule 9019–1.

V. COMMENCEMENT OF LOSS MITIGATION

Parties are encouraged to request Loss Mitigation as early in a case as possible, but Loss Mitigation may be initiated at any time prior to the entry of a discharge order, by any of the following methods:

A. By the Debtor.

1. In section C of the Model Chapter 13 Plan, a Chapter 13 Debtor may indicate an interest in discussing Loss Mitigation with a particular Creditor. Upon requesting same in the Chapter 13 Plan, the Debtor must serve said plan on the Creditor and file proof of same on the Electronic Case Filing System ("ECF"). If the Creditor fails to object within fourteen (14) days of service of the plan the Debtor shall submit an order approving the Loss Mitigation Request (the *"Loss Mitigation Order"*[1]) and the Bankruptcy Court may enter the order. A copy of the Southern District of New York's *"Model Chapter 13 Plan"* can be found on the Bankruptcy Court's website under "Chapter 13 Forms." The Debtor may request Loss Mitigation in the plan for one Loan without regard for whether the Loan is a first or second mortgage loan. In order to request Loss Mitigation on a second Loan, the Debtor must file a separate Loss Mitigation Request.

2. A Debtor may file a request for Loss Mitigation ("Loss Mitigation Request") with a particular Creditor. The Creditor shall have fourteen (14) days to object. If no objection is filed, the Debtor shall submit a *"Loss Mitigation Order"* and the Bankruptcy Court may enter the *"Loss Mitigation Order."* A copy of the *"Loss Mitigation Request by the Debtor"* and the *"Loss Mitigation Order"* can be found on the Bankruptcy Court's website under the "Loss Mitigation" tab.

3. Upon entry of the *"Loss Mitigation Order"*, the Debtor must serve same upon the appropriate Creditor and file proof of service on ECF. If the Creditor is a domestic or foreign corporation, partnership, or other unincorporated association, service must be made by mailing a copy of the plan to a physical address and to the attention of an officer. A copy of the *"Loss Mitigation Order"*, can be found on the Bankruptcy Court's website.

4. If a Creditor has filed a motion requesting relief from the automatic stay pursuant to section 362 of the Bankruptcy Code (a "Lift-Stay Motion"), at any time prior to the conclusion of the hearing on the Lift-Stay Motion, the Debtor may file a Loss Mitigation Request. The Debtor and Creditor shall appear at the scheduled hearing on the Lift-Stay Motion, and the Bankruptcy Court will consider the Loss Mitigation Request and any opposition by the Creditor.

B. By a Creditor. A Creditor may file a Loss Mitigation Request. The Creditor must serve said request on the Debtor and Debtor's counsel and file proof of service on ECF. The Debtor shall have seven (7) days after service of the request to object. If no objection is filed, the Creditor shall submit a Loss Mitigation Order and the Bankruptcy Court may enter the Loss Mitigation Order. Upon entry of the Loss Mitigation Order, the Creditor is to serve same upon Debtor and Debtor's counsel and file proof of same on ECF. The form *"Loss Mitigation Request-By the Creditor"* can be found on the Bankruptcy Court's website.

C. By the Bankruptcy Court. The Bankruptcy Court may enter a *"Loss Mitigation Order"* at any time, provided that the Loss Mitigation Parties that will be bound by the *"Loss Mitigation Order"* have had notice and an opportunity to object.

D. Opportunity to Object. Where any party files an objection, a "Loss Mitigation Order" shall not be entered until the Bankruptcy Court has held a hearing to consider the objection. At the hearing, a party objecting to Loss Mitigation must present specific reasons why it believes that Loss Mitigation would not be successful. If a party objects on the grounds that Loss Mitigation has been requested in bad faith, the assertion must be supported by evidence.

VI. LOSS MITIGATION ORDER

A. Order. A separate *"Loss Mitigation Order"* shall be submitted for each Loss Mitigation Request, regardless of the method used for making the request.

B. Deadlines. A *"Loss Mitigation Order"* shall contain set time frames for all of the following:

1. The date by which the Loss Mitigation Parties shall designate contact persons and disclose contact information.

2. The date by which each Creditor must transmit any information request to the Debtor.

3. The date by which the Debtor must transmit any information request to each Creditor.

4. The date by which a written status report must be filed and the date and time set for a status conference at which a verbal report must be provided. Where a written report is required, it should generally be filed not later than seven (7) days before the initial Loss Mitigation status conference ("Initial Status Conference").

C. Effect. Whenever a *"Loss Mitigation Order"* is entered, the following shall apply to the Loss Mitigation Parties:

1. Unless otherwise ordered by the Bankruptcy Court, all communications between the Loss Mitigation Parties shall be made through the designated contacts' attorneys.

2. Except where necessary to prevent irreparable injury, loss or damage, a Creditor shall not file a Lift-Stay Motion while Loss Mitigation is pending.

3. Any Lift-Stay Motion filed by the Creditor prior to the entry of the *"Loss Mitigation Order"* shall be adjourned to a date after the *"Order Terminating Loss Mitigation and Final Report,"* and the stay shall be extended pursuant to section 362(e) of the Bankruptcy Code.

4. In a Chapter 13 case, the deadline by which a Creditor must object to confirmation of the Chapter 13 plan shall be extended to permit the Creditor an additional fourteen (14) days after the filing of the *"Order Terminating Loss Mitigation and Final Report."*

5. All communications and information exchanged by the Loss Mitigation Parties during Loss Mitigation will be inadmissible in any subsequent proceeding pursuant to Federal Rule of Evidence 408.

6. Unless otherwise ordered by the Bankruptcy Court, in a Chapter 7 case, the entry of the "Loss Mitigation Order" defers the entry of an order granting the Debtor's discharge until one day after an "Order Terminating Loss Mitigation and Final Report" is filed, pursuant to Federal Rule of Bankruptcy Procedure 4004(c)(2). The time to object to the Debtor's discharge or the dischargeability of a debt is NOT extended by this Order.

VII. DUTIES UPON COMMENCEMENT OF LOSS MITIGATION

Upon entry of a Loss Mitigation Order, the Loss Mitigation Parties shall have the following duties:

A.   Good Faith. The Loss Mitigation Parties shall negotiate in good faith. A party that fails to participate in Loss Mitigation in good faith may be subject to sanctions.

B.   Contact Information.

1. *The Debtor.* Unless the Debtor has already done so in the Chapter 13 plan or Loss Mitigation Request, the Debtor shall file and serve a written notice on each Creditor, indicating the manner in which the Creditor should contact the Debtor.

2. *The Creditor.* Unless a Creditor has already done so as part of a Loss Mitigation Request, each Creditor shall provide written notice to the Debtor by filing and serving its Creditor Affidavit on the Debtor in which it identifies: 1) the name, address and direct telephone number of the contact person who has full settlement authority; and 2) the attorney representing it in the Loss Mitigation.

C.   Document Exchange.

1.   The Creditor shall serve upon the Debtor and Debtor's attorney a request for information using the *"Creditor Loss Mitigation Affidavit"* form within seven (7) days of service of the *"Loss Mitigation Order."* The Creditor shall file same on ECF. The *"Creditor Loss Mitigation Affidavit"* can be found on the Bankruptcy Court's website.

2.   The Debtor shall serve upon the Creditor a response to Creditor's request for information using the *"Debtor Loss Mitigation Affidavit"* form within fourteen (14) days of service of the Creditor Loss Mitigation Affidavit. The Debtor shall file only the *Debtor Loss Mitigation Affidavit* on ECF. A copy of the *"Debtor Loss Mitigation Affidavit"* can be found on the Bankruptcy Court's website.

D.   Status Report. The Loss Mitigation Parties shall provide a written report to the Bankruptcy Court regarding the status of Loss Mitigation within the timeframe set by the Bankruptcy Court in the *"Loss Mitigation Order."* The status report shall state whether one or more Loss Mitigation sessions have been conducted, whether a resolution was reached, and whether one or more of the Loss Mitigation Parties believe that additional Loss Mitigation sessions would be likely to result in either a partial or complete resolution.

E.   Bankruptcy Court Approval. The Loss Mitigation Parties shall seek Bankruptcy Court approval of any resolution or Settlement reached during Loss Mitigation.

VIII.   LOSS MITIGATION PROCESS

A.   Initial Contact. Following entry of a *"Loss Mitigation Order,"* the contact person designated by each Creditor shall contact the Debtor's designated contact person and any other Loss Mitigation Party within the timeframe provided in the *"Loss Mitigation Order."* The Debtor through its designated contact person may contact any other Loss Mitigation Party at any time. The purpose of the initial contact is to create a framework for discussion at the Loss Mitigation sessions and to ensure that each of the Loss Mitigation Parties will be prepared to participate in the Loss Mitigation session-it is not intended to limit additional issues or proposals that may arise during the session. During the initial contact phase, the Loss Mitigation Parties should hold a telephone conference to discuss the following:

1.   The types of Loss Mitigation solutions under consideration by each party.

2.   A plan for the exchange of required information prior to the Loss Mitigation session, including the due date for the Debtor to complete and return any information request or other Loss Mitigation paperwork that each Creditor may require.

B.   Loss Mitigation Sessions Between the Parties. Loss Mitigation sessions between the parties may be conducted in person, telephonically or via video conference. At the conclusion of each Loss Mitigation session, the Loss Mitigation Parties should discuss whether additional sessions are necessary and set the time and method for conducting any additional sessions, including a schedule for the exchange of any further information or documentation that may be required.

C.   Status Conferences With the Bankruptcy Court. The Initial Status Conference shall be set by the Bankruptcy Court in the "Loss Mitigation Order" and may be adjourned at the discretion of the Bankruptcy Court. At any time during the pendency of Loss Mitigation, a loss Mitigation Party may request a settlement conference or status conference with the Bankruptcy Court.

D.   Settlement Authority. Each Loss Mitigation Party must have a person with full settlement authority present at every Loss Mitigation status conference. During a status conference or settlement conference with the Bankruptcy Court, the person with full settlement authority must either attend the conference in person or be available by telephone or video conference beginning thirty (30) minutes prior to the start of the conference.

IX. DURATION AND TERMINATION

A. Duration. Once a *"Loss Mitigation Order"* has been entered by the Bankruptcy Court, it shall remain in effect until an *"Order Terminating Loss Mitigation and Final Report"* is filed.

B. Early Termination.

1. Upon Request of a Loss Mitigation Party: A Loss Mitigation Party may request that Loss Mitigation be terminated by filing the form *"Request for Termination of Loss Mitigation"* which can be found on our website stating the reasons for the request. Except where immediate termination is necessary to prevent irreparable injury, loss or damage, the request shall be made on notice to all other Loss Mitigation Parties, and the Bankruptcy Court may schedule a hearing to consider the termination request.

2. Sua Sponte Termination of Loss Mitigation: The Bankruptcy Court may terminate Loss Mitigation sua sponte at any time for failure to comply with the Loss Mitigation Program Procedures.

3. Dismissal of the Bankruptcy Case:

a. Other than at the request of a Chapter 13 Debtor, or the motion of the United States Trustee or Trustee for failure to comply with requirements under the Bankruptcy Code: Except where a Chapter 13 Debtor requests voluntary dismissal, or upon motion, a case shall not be dismissed during Loss Mitigation unless the Loss Mitigation Parties have provided the Bankruptcy Court with a status report that is satisfactory to the Bankruptcy Court. The Bankruptcy Court may schedule a further status conference with the Loss Mitigation Parties prior to dismissal of the case.

b. Upon the request of a Chapter 13 Debtor: **A Debtor is not required to request dismissal of the bankruptcy case as part of any resolution or settlement that is offered or agreed to during Loss Mitigation.** Where a Chapter 13 Debtor requests voluntary dismissal of the bankruptcy case during a pending Loss Mitigation, the Debtor's dismissal request shall indicate whether the Debtor agreed to any settlement or resolution from a Loss Mitigation Party during Loss Mitigation or intends to accept an offer of settlement made by a Loss Mitigation Party during Loss Mitigation.

X. SETTLEMENT

The Bankruptcy Court will consider any agreement or resolution reached during Loss Mitigation (a "Settlement") and may approve the Settlement, subject to the following provisions:

1. *Implementation.* A Settlement may be noticed and implemented in any manner permitted by the Bankruptcy Code and Federal Rules of Bankruptcy Procedure ("Bankruptcy Rules"), including, but not limited to, a stipulation, sale, plan of reorganization or amended plan of reorganization; and a Motion to Approve Loan Modification.

2. *Fees, Costs, or Charges.* If a Settlement provides for a Creditor to receive payment or reimbursement of any fee, cost or charge that arose from Loss Mitigation, such fees, costs or charges shall be disclosed to the Debtor and to the Bankruptcy Court prior to approval of the Settlement.

3. *Signatures.* Consent to the Settlement shall be acknowledged in writing by (1) the Creditor representative who participated in Loss Mitigation, (2) the Creditor's attorney, (3) the Debtor, and (4) the Debtor's attorney, if applicable.

4. *Hearing.* Where a Debtor is represented by counsel, a Settlement may be approved by the Bankruptcy Court without further notice, or upon such notice as the Bankruptcy Court directs, unless additional notice or a hearing is required by the Bankruptcy Code or Bankruptcy Rules. Where a Debtor is not represented by counsel, a Settlement shall not be approved until after the Bankruptcy Court has conducted a hearing at which the Debtor shall appear in person.

5. *Dismissal Not Required.* A Debtor is not required to request dismissal of the bankruptcy case in order to effectuate a Settlement. In order to ensure that the Settlement is enforceable, the Loss Mitigation Parties should seek Bankruptcy Court approval of the Settlement.

6. Any Settlement provided to the Bankruptcy Court for its approval shall have the Agreement attached as an exhibit.

XI. ORDER TERMINATING LOSS MITIGATION AND FINAL REPORT

The Loss Mitigation Parties shall file with the Bankruptcy Court an *"Order Terminating Loss Mitigation and Final Report"*

1. when the Bankruptcy Court enters an order-after a motion is made by one of the parties to Loss Mitigation (for example, a motion asking the Court to approve a Settlement)-where such order brings to a close the Loss Mitigation;

2. when the Bankruptcy Court approves a Settlement that has been presented to the Court, which provides resolution of the Loss Mitigation; or

3. when a Loss Mitigation's request for termination has been granted upon the record of a Loss Mitigation hearing.

Loss Mitigation is not "terminated" unless an *"Order Terminating Loss Mitigation and Final Report"* is entered by the Bankruptcy Court. Where a case has two or more requests for Loss Mitigation, a separate *"Order Terminating Loss Mitigation and Final Report"* must be filed for each request.

XII. FORMS

All of the Loss Mitigation forms may be found on the Bankruptcy Court's website under the ""Loss Mitigation" tab. These forms must be used. The Bankruptcy Court may revise the forms from time to time without the need to update the Loss Mitigation Program Procedures.

XIII. COORDINATION WITH OTHER PROGRAMS

[Provisions may be added in the future to provide for coordination with other Loss Mitigation programs, including programs in the New York State Unified Court System.]

[Dated: June 12, 2013.]

1 Italicized words in quotations indicate that there is a form by the same name on the Bankruptcy Court's website. These forms should be used whenever applicable.

GENERAL ORDER M–452. IN RE: PROCEDURES GOVERNING MEDIATION OF MATTERS AND THE USE OF EARLY NEUTRAL EVALUATION AND MEDIATION/VOLUNTARY ARBITRATION IN BANKRUPTCY CASES AND ADVERSARY PROCEEDINGS

Amending and restating M–143, M–211 and M–390

Whereas, on November 12, 1993, this court entered General Order M–117 adopting procedures governing the mediation of matters in bankruptcy cases and adversary proceedings before this court (the "Court Annexed Mediation Program"); and

Whereas, on January 18, 1995, this court entered General Order M–143 amending and superseding General Order M–117 and setting forth the Court Annexed Mediation Program in Rules 1.0 through 8.0 of General Order M–143; and

Whereas, in order to expand the Court Annexed Mediation Program to include the use of Early Neutral Evaluation and Mediation/Voluntary Arbitration, as referred to in 28 U.S.C. § 651 through § 658, on October 20, 1999, this court entered General Order M–211, supplementing General Order M–143 by (i) providing that the provisions of General Order M–143, set forth in Rules 1.0 through 8.0, be entitled "Court Annexed Alternative Dispute Resolution Program" and apply to Early Neutral Evaluation and (ii) adding procedures governing Mediation/Voluntary Arbitration set forth in Rules 9.0 through 13.0; and

Whereas, in order to conform certain time periods set forth in its procedures to the 2009 time-related amendments to the Federal Rules of Bankruptcy Procedure (the "Bankruptcy Rules") and amend, restate and supersede General Orders M–143 and M–211 to combine them into one General Order, and to continue to include Early Neutral Evaluation within the Court Annexed Alternative Dispute Resolution Program, this Court entered General Order M–390; and

Whereas the procedures set forth in General Order M–390 may now be found on the Court's website as the "Procedures Governing the Mediation of Matters and the Use of Early Neutral Evaluation and Mediation and Voluntary Arbitration in Bankruptcy Cases and Adversary Proceedings,"

NOW, THEREFORE, IT IS

ORDERED, that the revised Procedures Governing the Mediation of Matters and the Use of Early Neutral Evaluation and Mediation and Voluntary Arbitration in Bankruptcy Cases and Adversary Proceedings, annexed hereto, are adopted, effective August 1, 2013, and shall be available in the Clerk's Office and on the Court's web site; and it is further

ORDERED, that the Court may modify the Procedures Governing the Mediation of Matters and the Use of Early Neutral Evaluation and Mediation and Voluntary Arbitration in Bankruptcy Cases and Adversary Proceedings from time to time by duly adopted General Order, making the revised Procedures available in the Clerk's Office and on the Court's website no less than fourteen (14) days before the effective date.

[Dated: June 28, 2013.]

UNITED STATES BANKRUPTCY COURT
SOUTHERN DISTRICT OF NEW YORK

PROCEDURES GOVERNING MEDIATION OF MATTERS AND THE USE OF EARLY NEUTRAL EVALUATION AND MEDIATION/ VOLUNTARY ARBITRATION IN BANKRUPTCY CASES AND ADVERSARY PROCEEDINGS

The procedures governing the mediation of matters and the use of early neutral evaluation and mediation and voluntary arbitration in bankruptcy cases and adversary proceedings in the United States Bankruptcy Court, Southern District of New York (the "Mediation Procedures") are set forth in the following Rules:

1.0 Assignment of Matters to Mediation.

1.1 *By Court Order.* The Court may order assignment of a matter to mediation upon its own motion, or upon a motion by any party in interest or the U.S. Trustee. The motion by a party in interest must be filed promptly after filing the initial document in the matter. Notwithstanding assignment of a matter or proceeding to mediation, it shall be set for the next appropriate hearing on the Court docket in the normal course of setting required for such a matter.

1.2 *Stipulation of Counsel.* Any matter may be referred to mediation upon stipulated order submitted by counsel of record or by a party appearing pro se.

1.3 *Types of Matters Subject to Mediation.* Unless otherwise ordered by the presiding judge, any adversary proceeding, contested matter or other dispute may be referred by the Court to mediation.

1.4 *Mediation Procedures.* Upon assignment of a matter to mediation, these Procedures shall become binding on all parties subject to such mediation.

2.0 The Mediator.

2.1 *Mediation Register.* The Clerk of the United States Bankruptcy Court for the Southern District of New York shall establish and maintain a Register of Persons Qualifying under Rule 2.1.A.

A. Application and Qualification Procedures for Mediation Register. To qualify for the Mediation Register of this Court, a person must apply and meet the following minimum qualifications:

(1) For General Services as a Mediator. A person must have been a member of the bar in any state or the District of Columbia for at least five (5) years; currently a member of the bar in

good standing of any state or the District of Columbia; be admitted to practice in the Southern District of New York; and be certified by the Chief Judge to be competent to perform the duties of a mediator. Each person certified as a mediator should take the oath or affirmation prescribed by 28 U.S.C. § 453 before serving as a mediator.

(2) For Services as a Mediator where the Court Has Determined the Need for Special Skills.

(a) A person must have been authorized to practice for at least four (4) years under the laws of the State of New York as a professional, including but not limited to, an accountant, real estate broker, appraiser, engineer or other professional. Notwithstanding the requirement for authorization to practice under the laws of the State of New York, an investment banker professional who has been practicing for a period of at least four (4) years shall be eligible to serve as a mediator; and

(b) Be an active member in good standing, or if retired, have been a member in good standing, of any applicable professional organization;

(c) Not have:

(i) Been suspended, or have had a professional license revoked, or have pending any proceeding to suspend or revoke such license; or

(ii) Resigned from applicable professional organization while an investigation into allegations of misconduct which would warrant suspension, disbarment or professional license revocation was pending; or

(iii) Have been convicted of a felony.

B. Removal from Mediation Register. A person shall be removed from the Mediation Register either at the person's request or by Court order. If removed from the Register by Court order, the person shall not be returned to the Register absent a Court order obtained upon motion to the Chief Judge and affidavit sufficiently explaining the circumstances of such removal and reasons justifying the return of the person to the Register.

2.2 *Appointment of the Mediator.*

A. The parties will ordinarily choose a mediator from the Register for appointment by the Court. If the parties cannot agree upon a mediator within seven (7) days of assignment to mediation, the Court shall appoint a mediator and alternate mediator.

B. In the event of a determination by the Court that there are special issues presented which suggest reference to an appropriately experienced mediator other than the mediator chosen by the parties, then the Court shall appoint a mediator and an alternate mediator.

C. If the mediator is unable to serve, the mediator shall file within seven (7) days after receipt of the notice of appointment, a notice of inability to accept appointment and immediately serve a copy upon the appointed alternate mediator. The alternate mediator shall become the mediator for the matter if such person fails to file a notice of inability to accept appointment within seven (7) days after filing of the original mediator's notice of inability. If neither can serve, the Court will appoint another mediator and alternate mediator.

2.3 *Disqualification of a Mediator.* Any person selected as a mediator may be disqualified for bias or prejudice as provided in 28 U.S.C. § 144 or if not, disinterested under 11 U.S.C. § 101. Any party selected as a mediator shall be disqualified in any matter where 28 U.S.C. § 455 would require disqualification if that person were a justice, judge or magistrate.

3.0 The Mediation.

3.1 *Time and Place of Mediation.* Upon consultation with all attorneys and pro se parties subject to the mediation, the mediator shall fix a reasonable time and place for the initial mediation conference of the parties with the mediator and promptly shall give the attorneys and pro se parties advance written notice of the conference. The conference shall be set as soon after the entry of the mediation order and as long in advance of the Court's final evidentiary hearing as practicable. To ensure prompt dispute resolution, the mediator shall have the duty and authority to establish the time for all mediation activities, including private meetings between the mediator and parties and the submission of relevant documents. The mediator shall have the authority to establish a deadline for the parties to act upon a proposed settlement or upon a settlement recommendation from the mediator.

3.2 *Mediation Conference.* A representative of each party shall attend the mediation conference, and must have complete authority to negotiate all disputed amounts and issues. The mediator shall control all procedural aspects of the mediation. The mediator shall also have the discretion to require that the party representative or a non-attorney principal of the party with settlement authority be present at any conference. The mediator shall also determine when the parties are to be present in the conference room. The mediator shall report any willful failure to attend or participate in good faith in the mediation process or conference. Such failure may result in the imposition of sanctions by the Court.

3.3 *Recommendations of the Mediator.* The mediator shall have no obligation to make written comments or recommendations; provided, however, that the mediator may furnish the attorneys for the parties and any pro se party with a written settlement recommendation. Any such recommendation shall not be filed with the Court.

3.4 *Post–Mediation Procedures.* Promptly upon conclusion of the mediation conference, and in any event no later than 3:00 P.M. two (2) days prior to the date fixed for hearing referred to in Rule 1.1, the mediator shall file a final report showing compliance or noncompliance with the requirements of this General Order by the parties and the mediation results. If in the mediation the parties reach an agreement regarding the disposition of the matter, they shall determine who shall prepare and submit to the Court a stipulated order or judgment, or joint motion for approval of compromise of controversy (as appropriate), within twenty-one (21) days of the conference. Failure to timely file such a stipulated order or judgment or motion when agreement is reached shall be a basis for the Court to impose appropriate sanctions. Absent such a stipulated order or judgment or motion, no party shall be bound by any statement made or action taken during the mediation process. If the mediation ends in an impasse, the matter will be heard or tried as scheduled.

3.5 *Termination of Mediation.* Upon receipt of the mediator's final report, the mediation will be deemed terminated, and the mediator excused and relieved from further responsibilities in the matter without further Court order.

3.6 *Withdrawal from Mediation.* Any matter referred pursuant to mediation may be withdrawn from mediation by the judge assigned to the matter at any time upon determination for any reason the matter is not suitable for mediation. Nothing in these Mediation Procedures shall prohibit or prevent any party in interest, the U.S. Trustee or the mediator from filing a motion to withdraw a matter from mediation for cause.

4.0 Compensation of Mediators. The mediator's compensation shall be on such terms as are satisfactory to the mediator and the parties, and subject to Court approval if the estate is to be charged with such expense. In the event that the mediator and the parties cannot agree on terms of compensation, then the Court shall fix such terms as are reasonable and just.

5.0 Confidentiality.

5.1 *Confidentiality as to the Court and Third Parties.* Any statements made by the mediator, by the parties or by others during the mediation process shall not be divulged by any of the participants in the mediation (or their agents) or by the mediator to the Court or to any third party. All records, reports, or other documents received or made by a mediator while serving in such capacity shall be confidential and shall not be provided to the Court, unless they would be otherwise admissible. The mediator shall not be compelled to divulge such records or to testify in regard to the mediation in connection with any arbitral, judicial or other proceeding, including any hearing held by the Court in connection with the referred matter. Nothing in this section, however, precludes the mediator from reporting the status (though not content) of the mediation effort to the Court orally or in writing, or from complying with the obligation set forth in 3.2 to report failures to attend or to participate in good faith.

5.2 *Confidentiality of Mediation Effort.* Rule 408 of the Federal Rules of Evidence shall apply to mediation proceedings. Except as permitted by Rule 408, no person may rely on or introduce as evidence in connection with any arbitral, judicial or other proceeding, including any hearing held by this Court in connection with the referred matter, any aspect of the mediation effort, including, but not limited to:

   A. Views expressed or suggestions made by any party with respect to a possible settlement of the dispute;

   B. Admissions made by the other party in the course of the mediation proceedings;

   C. Proposals made or views expressed by the mediator.

6.0 Immunity. The Mediators shall be immune from claims arising out of acts or omissions incident to their service as Court appointees in this Mediation Program. See *Wagshal v. Foster*, 28 F.3d 1249 (D.C. Cir. 1994).

7.0 Consensual Modification of Mediation Procedures. Additional rules and procedures for the mediation may be negotiated and agreed upon by the mediator and the parties at any time during the mediation process.

8.0 Compliance With the U.S. Code, Bankruptcy Rules, and Court Rules and Orders. Nothing in these Procedures shall relieve any debtor, party in interest, or the U.S. Trustee from complying with this Court's orders or Local Rules, U.S. Code, or the Bankruptcy Rules, including times fixed for discovery or preparation for any Court hearing pending on the matter.

9.0 Assignment of Disputes to Mediation/Voluntary Arbitration.

9.1 *Stipulation of Parties.* The Court may refer a dispute pending before it to mediation, and, upon consent of the parties, to arbitration if and to the extent that the mediation is unsuccessful. At the conclusion of mediation, after the parties have failed to reach agreement and upon voluntary stipulation of the parties, the mediator, if qualified as an arbitrator, may hear and arbitrate the dispute.

A. Referral to Arbitration pursuant to Bankruptcy Rule 9019(c). Except as provided in subdivision (B) the Court may authorize the referral of a matter to final and binding arbitration under Bankruptcy Rule 9019(c) if:

(1) The issue does not arise in an adversary proceeding; or

(2) The issue arises in an adversary proceeding in which the amount in controversy has a dollar value greater than $150,000, the issue is procedural or non-dispositive (such as a discovery dispute), and the Court retains jurisdiction to decide, after presentation of evidence, the adversary proceeding.

B. Referral of Adversary Proceeding to Arbitration pursuant to 28 U.S.C. § 654. With the consent of the parties, under 28 U.S.C. § 654, the Court may authorize the referral to arbitration of an adversary proceeding in which the matter in controversy has a dollar value that does not exceed $150,000, subject to the following provisions:

(1) Determination De Novo of Arbitration Awards under 28 U.S.C. § 654.

(a) Time for Filing Demand. Within 30 days after the filing of an arbitration award with the Clerk of Court in an adversary proceeding governed by Rule 9.1(B), any party may file a written demand for a determination *de novo* with the Court.

(b) Action Restored to Court Docket. Upon a demand for a determination *de novo*, the action shall be restored to the docket of the Court and treated for all purposes as if had not been referred to arbitration.

(c) Exclusion of Evidence of Arbitration. The Court shall not admit at the determination *de novo* any evidence that there has been an arbitration proceeding, the nature or amount of any award, or any other matter concerning the conduct of the arbitration proceeding, unless—

(i) The evidence would otherwise be admissible in the Court under the Federal Rules of Evidence; or

(ii) The parties have otherwise stipulated.

(2) Arbitration awards in a proceeding governed by Rule 9.1(B) shall be entered as the judgment of the Court after the time has expired for requesting a determination *de novo*. The judgment so entered shall be subject to the same provisions of law and shall have the same force and effect as a judgment of the Court, except that the judgment shall not be subject to review in any other Court by appeal or otherwise.

(a) Filing and Effect of Arbitration Award. The Clerk of the Court shall place under seal the contents of any arbitration award made under Rule 9.1(B) of this Court Annexed Alternative Dispute Resolution Program and the contents shall not be known to any judge who might be assigned to the matter until the Court has entered a final judgment in the action or the action has otherwise terminated.

C. Safeguards in Consent to Voluntary Arbitration. Matters referred to mediation where the parties do not reach agreement are allowed to proceed to voluntary arbitration under Rule 9.1(A) or Rule 9.1(B) by consent expressly reflected and filed with the Court where—

(1) Consent to arbitration is freely and knowingly obtained; and

(2) No party or attorney is prejudiced for refusing to participate in arbitration.

10.0 The Arbitrator.

10.1 *Powers of Mediator/Arbitrator.* A mediator/arbitrator to whom an action is referred shall have the power, after a good faith attempt to mediate, and upon consent of the parties, to—

A. Conduct arbitration hearings consistent with Rule 9.1 above;

B. Administer oaths and affirmations; and

C. Make awards.

10.2 *Standards for Certification as an Arbitrator.* In addition to fulfilling the requirements found in Rule 2.0 The Mediator, a person qualifying as a Mediator/Arbitrator shall be certified as an arbitrator through a qualifying mediation/arbitration program which includes an ethics component on how to retain neutrality when changing the process.

10.3 *Immunity.* All individuals serving as Mediator/Arbitrator in the Court Annexed Alternative Dispute Resolution Program are performing quasi-judicial functions and are entitled to the immunities and protections that the law accords to persons serving in such capacity.

10.4 *Subpoenas.* The Federal Rules of Civil Procedure and Bankruptcy Procedure apply to subpoenas for the attendance of witnesses and the production of documents at a Voluntary Arbitration hearing.

11.0 Arbitration Award and Judgment.

11.1 An arbitration award made by a Mediator/Arbitrator, along with proof of service of such award on the other party by the prevailing party, shall be filed promptly after the arbitration hearing is concluded with the Clerk of the Court.

12.0 Compensation of Mediator/Arbitrator. The Mediator/Arbitrator's compensation shall be consistent with Rule 4.0 Compensation of Mediator as described above.

12.1 *Transportation Allowances.* Subject to Court approval, if the estate is to be charged with such expense, the Mediator/Arbitrator may be reimbursed for actual transportation expenses necessarily incurred in the performance of duties.

13.0 Notice of Court Annexed Alternate Dispute Resolution Program. The Court, at the first scheduled pre-trial conference, shall give notice of dispute resolution alternatives substantially in compliance with Form I.

[Dated: August 1, 2013.]

GENERAL ORDER M–454. IN RE: AMENDED PROCEDURAL GUIDELINES FOR PREPACKAGED CHAPTER 11 CASES

Amending M–387

By resolution of the Board of Judges of the United States Bankruptcy Court for the Southern District of New York, in an attempt to provide bankruptcy practitioners with guidelines in dealing with practical matters when filing a prepackaged chapter 11 case, including filing all documents on the Court's Electronic Case Filing System, this Court entered General Order M–387 adopting Prepackaged Chapter 11 Case Guidelines, as amended, effective December 1, 2009, and providing that the Guidelines may be revised from time to time,

NOW, THEREFORE, IT IS

ORDERED that the revised Procedural Guidelines for Prepackaged Chapter 11 Cases in the United States Bankruptcy Court for the Southern District of New York (the "Guidelines"), annexed hereto, are adopted, effective August 1, 2013, and shall be available in the Clerk's Office and on the Court's web site; and it is further

ORDERED, that the Court may modify the Guidelines from time to time by duly adopted General Order, making the revised Guidelines available in the Clerk's Office and on the Court's website no less than fourteen (14) days before the effective date.

[Dated: June 28, 2013.]

UNITED STATES BANKRUPTCY COURT
SOUTHERN DISTRICT OF NEW YORK

PROCEDURAL GUIDELINES FOR PREPACKAGED CHAPTER 11 CASES IN THE UNITED STATES BANKRUPTCY COURT FOR THE SOUTHERN DISTRICT OF NEW YORK

I. Goals. The purpose of this document is to establish uniform guidelines for commencing and administering "Prepackaged Chapter 11 cases" in the United States Bankruptcy Court for the Southern District of New York (the "Court"). Specifically, this document defines "Prepackaged Chapter 11 case" and attempts to provide bankruptcy practitioners with help in dealing with practical matters which either is not addressed at all by statute or rules or are addressed indirectly in a piecemeal fashion by statutes, general rules, and/or local rules that were not enacted specifically with Prepackaged Chapter 11 cases in mind. Although each case is different, many issues are common to all prepackaged cases. Judicial economy, as well as procedural predictability for debtors and creditors, will be enhanced by promulgation of uniform guidelines to deal with these common issues. The guidelines are advisory only; the Court retains the power to depart from them.

In order to ease the burden on practitioners and the Court, Chief Judge Tina L. Brozman convened a Committee of Judges, Attorneys, Clerk's Office Staff and the United States Trustee to assist in developing a uniform set of procedures applicable to Prepackaged Chapter 11 cases filed in the Southern District of New York. Those meetings resulted in a General Order adopted by the Court on February 2, 1999, after a vote of the Board of Judges, which established the following procedural guidelines for Prepackaged Chapter 11 cases.

II. Definition of Prepackaged Chapter 11 Case. For purposes of these guidelines, a "Prepackaged Chapter 11 case" is one in which the Debtor, substantially contemporaneously with the filing of its chapter 11 petition, files a Confirmation Hearing Scheduling Motion For Prepackaged Plan in substantially the form annexed hereto as Exhibit A and satisfying the criteria set forth in Part III(A) below ("Prepack Scheduling Motion"), plan, disclosure statement (or other solicitation document), and voting certification.

III. Criteria for Prepackaged Chapter 11 Case; Contents of Prepack Scheduling Motion.

A. *Content of Prepack Scheduling Motion.* The Prepack Scheduling Motion shall:

(i) Represent that (x) the solicitation of all votes to accept or reject the Debtor's plan required for confirmation of that plan was completed prior to commencement of the Debtor's chapter 11 case or in accordance with section 1125(g), and that no additional solicitation of votes on that plan is contemplated by the Debtor, or (y) the solicitation of all votes to accept or reject the Debtor's plan required for confirmation of that plan has been deemed adequate by the Court pursuant to Part III(C)(ii) below such that no additional solicitation will be required;

(ii) Represent that the requisite acceptances of such plan have been obtained from each class of claims or interests as to which solicitation is required except as provided in Part III(A)(iii) below; and

(iii) With respect to any class of interests that has not accepted the plan whether or not it is deemed not to have accepted the plan under section 1126(g), represent that the Debtor is requesting confirmation under section 1129(b); and

(iv) Request entry of an order scheduling the hearing (x) on confirmation of the plan and (y) to determine whether the Debtor has satisfied the requirements of either 11 U.S.C. § 1126(b)(1) or 11 U.S.C. § 1126(b)(2), for a date that is not more than ninety (90) days following the petition date.

B. *Confirmation Pursuant to 11 U.S.C. § 1129(b)(2)(C).* A chapter 11 case may constitute a "Prepackaged Chapter 11 case" for purposes of these guidelines notwithstanding the fact that the Debtor proposes to confirm the Plan pursuant to 11 U.S.C. § 1129(b)(2)(C) as to a class of interests.

C. *Filing of Petition after Solicitation Has Commenced But Before Expiration of Voting Deadline.* Unless the Court orders otherwise, if a chapter 11 case is commenced by or against the Debtor, or if a chapter 7 case is commenced against the Debtor and converted to a chapter 11 case by the Debtor pursuant to 11 U.S.C. § 706(a), after the Debtor has transmitted all solicitation materials to holders of claims and interests whose vote is sought but before the deadline for casting acceptances or rejections of the Debtor's plan (the "Voting Deadline"),

(i) The Debtor and other parties in interest shall be permitted to accept but not solicit ballots until the Voting Deadline; and

(ii) After notice and a hearing, the Court shall determine the effect of any and all such votes.

D. *Applicability of Guidelines to Cases Involving Cramdown of Classes of Claims and "Partial Prepackaged Chapter 11 Cases."* The Court may, upon request of the Debtor or other party in interest in an appropriate case, apply some or all of these guidelines to

(i) Cases in which the Debtor has satisfied the requirements of Part III(A)(i) above but intends to seek confirmation of the plan pursuant to 11 U.S.C. § 1129(b) as to a class of claims (a) which is deemed not to have accepted the plan under 11 U.S.C. § 1126(g); (b) which is receiving or retaining property under or pursuant to the plan but whose members' votes were not solicited prepetition and whose rejection of the plan has been assumed by the Debtor for purposes of confirming the plan; or (c) which is receiving or retaining property under or pursuant to the plan and which voted prepetition to reject the plan, as long as no class junior to such rejecting class is receiving or retaining any property under or pursuant to the plan; and

(ii) "Partial Prepackaged Chapter 11 Cases"—i.e., cases in which acceptances of the Debtor's plan were solicited prior to the commencement of the case from some, but not all, classes of claims or interests whose solicitation is required to confirm the Debtor's plan.

IV. Prefiling Notification to United States Trustee and Clerk of the Court.

A. *Notice of Proposed Filing to United States Trustee.* At least three (3) days prior to the anticipated filing date of the Prepackaged Chapter 11 case, the Debtor should (i) notify the United States Trustee of the Debtor's intention to file a prepackaged Chapter 11 case and (ii) supply the United States Trustee with two (2) copies of the Debtor's plan and disclosure statement (or other solicitation document).

B. *Notice of Proposed "First Day Orders" to United States Trustee.* If possible, drafts of all First Day Motions (as defined in Part VI.A. below), with the proposed orders attached as exhibits, should be furnished to the United States Trustee at least three (3) days in advance of the filing of the petition or as soon as practicable after the filing of an involuntary petition.

C. *Notice of Proposed Filing to Clerk of Court.* At least three (3) days prior to the anticipated filing date of the Prepackaged Chapter 11 case, counsel for the Debtor, without disclosing the name of the Debtor, should contact the Clerk of the Court to discuss the anticipated filing, the amount of the Debtor's assets, number and type of creditors, procedures for handling public inquiries (i.e., the names, addresses and telephone numbers of the persons to whom such inquiries should be directed), procedures for handling claims and proofs of claim or interest, whether the Debtor will request the Court to set a last date to file proofs of claim or interest, and related matters. On request, the Clerk of the Court will reserve a last date to file proofs of claim or interest for the Debtor. The Clerk of the Court will not assign the case to or discuss the case with a judge until the petition is filed.

V. Filing of Prepackaged Chapter 11 Case.

A. *Electronic Case Filing Via the Internet.* The Court has established and requires electronic filing of all chapter 11 cases on the Internet. Information on electronic filing procedures is available on the Court's website at: http://www.nysb.uscourts.gov. In electronically filing a Prepackaged Chapter 11 case, the Debtor should file the petition(s) first, followed by the affidavit pursuant to Local Rule 1007–2 and the motions and proposed orders, and should file lengthy documents, such as the disclosure statement (or other solicitation materials) and plan, last. Electronically filing lengthy documents last will expedite the filing process.

B. *Proposed Orders as Exhibits to Electronically Filed Motions.* All "First Day Motions" (as defined in Part VI(A) below) shall have attached as an exhibit, a copy of the proposed order sought to be signed.

C. *Paper Copies Furnished to Assigned Judge.* As soon as practicable, following filing of a Prepackaged Chapter 11 case, the Debtor shall furnish to the judge assigned to the case, a paper copy of the Plan, the Disclosure Statement (or other solicitation document), "First Day Motions" (with Proposed Orders attached as exhibits), any other filed Motion and any Order To Show Cause on which the Court's signature is requested. Proposed Orders should be presented in electronic format in Word or WordPerfect or other Windows-based format. (See Electronic Filing Procedures). To the extent that documents filed by the Debtor at or following the commencement of the Debtor's chapter 11 case differ in substance from the versions supplied to the United States Trustee under

Parts VI(A) and IV(B) above, the Debtor shall furnish to the United States Trustee two (2) paper copies of any such documents that have been modified, preferably blacklined to show changes.

D. *Abeyance of Local Rule 1007–2(e)*. Notwithstanding Local Rule 1007–2(e), a proposed case conference order need not be submitted to the Court unless the confirmation hearing is delayed until a date that is more than ninety (90) days following the petition date.

VI. First Day Orders.

A. *Motions for Request for Entry of Immediate Orders*. "First Day Orders" are orders which the Debtor seeks to have entered by the Court on or shortly after the filing of the petition. The request for a First Day Order should be made by motion (a "First Day Motion") in accordance with Local Rule 9013–1, and a copy of the proposed First Day Order should be filed with and attached as an exhibit to the First Day Motion.

B. *Purpose of First Day Orders*. Generally, the purpose of First Day Orders is to deal with administrative matters ("Administrative Orders") and to ensure that the Debtor's business and operations are stabilized and conducted in a manner consistent with past practice and the proposed plan, pending consideration of confirmation of that plan ("Operational Orders"). While the Court recognizes the necessity and desirability of entertaining appropriate First Day Motions, the terms and conditions of First Day Orders (particularly Operational Orders) necessarily will depend upon the facts and circumstances of the case, the terms of the plan, the notice given, and related factors, and will take into account the needs of the Debtor and the rights of other parties in interest.

C. *Typical First Day Motions and Orders*. First Day Orders typically entertained by the Court on or within one (1) day of the later of the petition date or the date of filing of the First Day Motions include (but are not limited to) the following:

1. Prepack Scheduling Motion, setting forth the information required in Part III above.[1]

2. Motion for Order Directing Joint Administration of Debtors' Cases if more than one case is commenced.

3. Motion for Order Authorizing Debtor to Mail Initial Notices, including the Notice of Meeting of Creditors under 11 U.S.C. § 341(a).

4. Motion for Order (i) Dispensing with the Requirement of Filing any or all Schedules and Statement of Financial Affairs in the Event the Debtor is not seeking to bar and subsequently discharge all or certain categories of debt (ii) extending Debtor's time for filing schedules and statement of financial affairs to a specified date.

5. Motion for an Order Setting the Last Date for Filing Proofs of Claim or interest if the Debtor has determined that a deadline should be set.

6. Applications to Employ Appropriate Professionals, which may include:

- attorneys
- accountants
- financial advisors.

If accountants, investment advisors, vote tabulators, solicitation agents or similar non-legal professionals were retained pre-petition and are not seeking any payment in connection with the plan or the case in addition to payments that they received prior to the filing of the petition ("Additional Post–Petition Payments"), such professionals need not be retained pursuant to 11 U.S.C. § 327 and may continue to provide services to the Debtor with respect to the plan and the case (e.g., testifying at the confirmation/disclosure adequacy hearing); provided, however, that the post-petition services provided by accountants and financial advisors who have not been retained pursuant to 11 U.S.C. § 327 shall not include any work of a substantive nature, such as, for example, the preparation of new financial data, even if such accountants and financial advisors are not seeking any Additional Post–Petition Payments.

7. Motion for Order Authorizing Employment and Payment without Fee Applications of Professionals used in ordinary course of business, not to exceed a specified individual and aggregate amount.

8. Motion for Order Establishing Procedures for Compensation and Reimbursement of Expenses of Professionals.

9. Motion for Order Authorizing Debtor to Maintain Existing Bank Accounts and Cash Management System, and to continue using existing business forms (including checks) without

"debtor-in-possession" designation. Any motion should describe the proposed cash management system and, in cases where money will be transferred between Debtors or from a Debtor to a non-debtor affiliate, represent why such transfers are desirable from the Debtor's perspective that the Debtor(s) will maintain records of all post-petition intercompany transfers of funds and describe what repayment terms exist.

10.   Motion Under 11 U.S.C. § 363 for Interim Order Authorizing Debtor's Use of Cash Collateral on an Emergency Basis, pending a hearing, and providing adequate protection.

11.   Motion Under 11 U.S.C. § 364 for Interim Order Authorizing Debtor to Obtain Post–Petition Financing on an Emergency Basis, pending a hearing.

12.   Motion Under 11 U.S.C. § 345(b) for Order Authorizing Debtor to Deviate from Enumerated Permitted Investments set forth in 11 U.S.C. § 345. Motion should disclose the amount of funds which the Debtor proposes to invest outside the statute's enumerated permitted investments and the proposed types of investments to be made. If the Debtor proposes to invest or deposit money in or with an entity that has not satisfied the requirement of 11 U.S.C. § 345(b) (a "Non–Qualified Entity") the First Day Motion should demonstrate and explain why such an investment or deposit is necessary and, to the extent known, why the Non–Qualified Entity cannot or has not satisfied the requirements of 11 U.S.C. § 345(b).

13.   Motion for an Order Authorizing Debtor to Pay (i) Pre–Petition Wages, Salaries and Commissions (including vacation, severance and sick leave pay) Earned by an Individual in an amount not to exceed specified per employee and aggregate amounts, which amounts shall be set forth in the Motion. If the Motion requests authority to pay amounts in excess of the amount set forth in 11 U.S.C. § 104(b) per employee, then a list of the names and position/job titles of all employees as to whom those payments will be made shall be attached. However, the propriety of those requests shall be considered on a case by case basis. The Motion also shall state whether, and the extent to which, the claims proposed to be paid constitute priority claims under 11 U.S.C. § 507 ("Priority Claims") and, if such claims are not Priority Claims, the Motion should explain why those claims should be afforded the treatment requested in the Motion. The Motion may also ask the Court to direct banks to honor prepetition checks for such amounts and authorize the Debtor to replace prepetition checks that have been dishonored.

14.   Motion for an Order Authorizing Debtor to Pay Claims for Contribution to Employee Benefit Plans in an amount not to exceed a specified amount, which amount shall be set forth in the Motion. If the Motion requests authority to pay amounts in excess of the amounts set forth in 11 U.S.C. § 507(a)(5) (as modified by 11 U.S.C. § 104(b)), then a list of the names and position/job titles of all employees as to whom those payments will be made shall be attached. However, the propriety of those requests shall be considered on a case by case basis. The Motion also shall state whether, and the extent to which, the claims proposed to be paid constitute Priority Claims and, if such claims are not Priority Claims, the Motion should explain why those claims should be afforded the treatment requested in the Motion.

15.   Motion for an Order Authorizing Debtor to Reimburse Employee Business Expenses in an amount not to exceed a specified amount per employee and not to exceed a specified aggregate amount, which amounts shall be set forth in the Motion. The Motion also shall state whether, and the extent to which, the claims proposed to be paid constitute Priority Claims and, if such claims are not Priority Claims, the Motion should explain why those claims should be afforded the treatment requested in the Motion.

16.   Motion for an Order Authorizing Debtor to Pay Creditors whose prepetition claims will be paid in full in cash on consummation under the Debtor's plan, not to exceed a specified aggregate amount, which amount shall be set forth in the Motion. The Motion should disclose the types of claims that the Debtor proposes to pay (e.g., trade creditors supplying goods; trade creditors supplying services; professionals involved in the routine, day-to-day operations and business of the Debtor). The Motion also shall state whether, and the extent to which, the claims proposed to be paid constitute Priority Claims and, if such claims are not Priority Claims; the Motion should explain why those should be afforded the treatment requested in the Motion.

17.   Motion for an Order Authorizing Debtor to Honor Pre–Petition Customer Claims (e.g., refund of deposits, lay-a-way plans) and Warranties, not to exceed specified aggregate and per claimant amounts, which amounts shall be set forth in the Motion. The Motion also shall state whether, and the extent to which, the claims proposed to be paid constitute Priority Claims and, if such claims are not Priority Claims, the Motion should explain why those claims should be afforded the treatment requested in the Motion.

18. Motion for an Order Authorizing Continued Performance without Assumption under Key Executory Contracts, including payment of prepetition amounts due and owing thereunder in an amount not to exceed specified aggregate and per claimant amounts. The Motion shall list and state all contracts subject to the motion and whether, and the extent to which, the claims proposed to be paid are believed to be Priority Claims and, if such claims are not Priority Claims, the Motion should explain why those claims should be afforded the treatment requested in the Motion.

19. Motion for Interim Order Prohibiting Utilities from Altering, Refusing or Discontinuing Service on Account of Pre–Petition Claims and Establishing Procedures for Determining Requests for Additional Adequate Assurance.

20. In a case involving a sale of any or all of the Debtor's assets, Motion for Order Authorizing and Scheduling Auction at which the Debtor may sell its assets free and clear of claims and interests and approving auction procedures and related matters

D. *Request for Related Relief Need Not be Filed in Separate Motions.* Motions for related relief under First Day Orders referred to above need not be filed as separate motions. For example, in a given case it may be appropriate to combine cash collateral and financing motions, or deal with all employee-related matters in a single motion.

VII. Voting Period; Ballot; Multiple Votes; Notice Presumptions.

A. *Voting Period Guidelines.* Fed.R.Bankr.P. 3018(b) requires the Court to consider whether "an unreasonably short" time was prescribed for creditors and equity security holders to accept or reject the plan. Under ordinary circumstances, in determining whether the time allowed for casting acceptances and rejections on the Debtor's plan satisfied Fed.R. Bankr. P. 3018(b), the Court will approve as reasonable:

1. For securities listed or admitted to trading on the New York Stock Exchange or American Stock Exchange or any international exchanges quoted on NASDAQ, and for securities publicly traded on any other national securities exchange ("Publicly Traded Securities"), a twenty-one (21) day voting period, measured from the date of commencement of mailing.

2. For securities which are not Publicly Traded Securities and for debt for borrowed money which is not evidenced by a Publicly Traded Security, a fourteen (14) day voting period, measured from the date of commencement of mailing.

3. For all other claims and interests, a twenty-one (21) day voting period, measured from the date of commencement of mailing.

B. *Shorter or Longer Voting Period.* Nothing herein is intended to preclude (i) a shorter voting period if it is justified in a particular case, or (ii) any party in interest from demonstrating that the presumptions set forth above were not reasonable in a particular case.

C. *Ballot.*

1. The Debtor may, but shall not be required to, use a ballot substantially in the form of the Official Form of Ballot For Accepting or Rejecting A Plan (the "Prepackaged Chapter 11 Case Ballot Form attached as Exhibit 'B'") in connection with a prepackaged plan solicitation.

2. Prepackaged Chapter 11 Master Ballot Form attached as Exhibit 'C'" may be used to report voting by beneficial owners of claims and interests.

3. The ballot may include information in addition to that set forth on the Official Ballot Form, and may request and provide space for the holder of a claim or interest to vote on matters in addition to the plan. By way of example, the ballot may seek and record (i) votes relating to an exchange offer, (ii) consents to or votes with respect to benefits plans, and (iii) elections provided for in the plan (or exchange offer).

D. *Multiple Votes.* If the holder of a claim or interest changes its vote during the pre-petition voting period, only the last timely ballot cast by such holder shall be counted in determining whether the Plan has been accepted or rejected unless the Disclosure Statement (or other solicitation document) clearly provides for some other procedure for determining votes on the prepackaged plan. If a holder of a claim or interest wants to change a vote post-petition, Rule 3018(a) requires a showing of cause and Court approval.

E. *Notice Guidelines.* Fed.R.Bankr. P. 3018(b) requires the Court to consider whether the plan was transmitted to substantially all creditors and equity security holders of the same class. In making that determination, the Court will take into account (i) whether the Debtor transmitted the plan and disclosure statement (or other solicitation document) in substantial compliance with applicable non-bankruptcy law, rules, or regulations and, (ii) the fact that creditors and equity security holders who are not record holders of the securities upon which their claims or interests are based generally assume the risk associated with their decision to hold their securities in "street name."

VIII. Organizational Meeting; Creditors' Committee.

A.   Unless the Court finds that a meeting of creditors need not be convened pursuant to section 341(e), after the filing of the chapter 11 petition, the Debtor shall notify creditors of the date, time and place of the meeting of creditors pursuant to 11 U.S.C. § 341(a), as well as the other information set forth in Part X.B.2 below.   The date set for the section 341(a) meeting should be no more than forty (40) days after the filing of the petition.

B.   If a meeting of creditors pursuant to 11 U.S.C. § 341(a) has not yet been convened prior to the date upon which the plan is confirmed, no such meeting will be convened if the Order Confirming the Plan or Order entered substantially contemporaneously therewith contains a provision waiving the convening of such a meeting.

C.   Typically, no creditors' committee will be appointed in a Prepackaged Chapter 11 case where the unsecured creditors are unimpaired.   However, where members of a pre-petition committee seek to serve as a member of an official creditor's committee, they shall demonstrate to the United States Trustee their compliance with Fed.R.Bankr.P. 2007(b).

IX. Last Date for Filing Proofs of Claim or Interest.

A.   A last date to file proofs of claim or interest will not be set unless the Debtor seeks an order fixing such a deadline for filing proofs of claim or proofs of interest.

B.   As provided in Part IV(C) above, the Debtor should consult with the Clerk of the Court in advance of the filing of the case to discuss whether a last date to file proofs of claim or interest will be sought, the need for appointment of a Claims' Agent for the Court (at the Debtor's expense), and related matters.

C.   If a Claims' Agent is appointed, such agent shall docket all proofs of claim and proofs of interest and deliver to the Debtor complete copies of the proofs of claim and interest, along with a complete claims and interest docket, not later than five (5) days after the last date to file proofs of claim or interest.

D.   Fed.R.Bankr.P. 2002(a)(7) requires at least twenty-one (21) days' notice by mail of the last day to file proofs of claim or interest.   Unless the Court orders otherwise, creditors whose mailing addresses are outside the United States shall be given at least thirty (30) days notice of the last day to file proofs of claim or interest as required by Fed.R.Bankr.P. 2002(p)(2).

E.   Paper copies of the notice of the last date to file proofs of claim or interest must be mailed as required under Fed.R.Bankr.P. 2002(a)(7).

X. Notice.

A.   *In General.*   Notice of the filing of the Plan and Disclosure Statement (or other solicitation document) and of the hearing to consider compliance with disclosure requirements and confirmation of the Plan must be given to all parties-in-interest.   Paper copy of a notice must be mailed;   service of a notice of electronic filing will not suffice.   No further distribution of the Plan and Disclosure Statement (or other solicitation document) beyond that which occurred pre-petition is required unless requested by a party-in-interest.

B.   *Hearing Notice.*

1.   Where the Disclosure Statement has not been approved by the Court prior to confirmation, the Debtor shall prepare and mail paper copies to all parties-in-interest of a Notice of Confirmation Hearing and Approval of Disclosure Statement (or other solicitation documents) in substantially the form annexed hereto as Exhibit "D" (the "Hearing Notice").   The Hearing Notice must set forth:

• (i) the date, time and place of the hearing to consider compliance with disclosure requirements and confirmation of the Plan, and (ii) the date and time by which objections to the foregoing must be filed and served;

• include a chart summarizing plan distributions;

- set forth the name, address and telephone number of the person from whom copies of the Plan and Disclosure Statement (or other solicitation document) can be obtained (at the Debtor's expense); and

- state that the Plan and Disclosure Statement (or other solicitation document) can be viewed electronically and explain briefly how electronic access to these documents may be obtained.

2.   Either the Hearing Notice or a separate notice must:

- set forth the date, time and place of the section 341(a) meeting and state that such meeting will not be convened if (i) the Plan is confirmed prior to the date set for the section 341(a) meeting and (ii) the order confirming the Plan (or order entered substantially contemporaneously therewith) contains a provision waiving the convening of such a meeting.

C. *Service.*

1.   The Hearing Notice shall be served upon (i) record (registered) holders of debt and equity securities (determined as of the record date established in the disclosure statement or other solicitation document) that were entitled to vote on the Plan, (ii) record (registered) holders of all other claims and interests of any class (determined as of a record date that is not more than fourteen (14) days prior to the date of the filing of the petition), (iii) all other creditors listed in the Debtor's schedules, unless Debtor is not seeking to bar and subsequently discharge claims, in which case schedules may not be required to be filed, (iv) the United States Trustee, (v) all indenture trustees, (vi) any committee(s) that may have been appointed in the case, and (vii) the United States in accordance with Fed.R.Bankr.P. 2002(j).

2.   The Debtor shall inform the Court of the proposed procedures for transmitting the Hearing Notice to beneficial holders of stock, bonds, debentures, notes, and other securities, and the Court shall determine the adequacy of those procedures and enter such orders as it deems appropriate.

D. *Time Period.* The Official Notice shall be mailed at least twenty-eight (28) days prior to the scheduled hearing date on confirmation of the plan and adequacy of disclosure unless the Court shortens such notice period.

XI. Combined Hearings. The hearings on the Debtor's compliance with either 11 U.S.C. § 1126(b)(1) or 11 U.S.C. § 1126(b)(2), as applicable, and on confirmation of the plan in a Prepackaged Chapter 11 case shall be combined whenever practicable.

EXHIBIT "A"

UNITED STATES BANKRUPTCY COURT
SOUTHERN DISTRICT OF NEW YORK

In re:	Chapter 11 Case No.
[NAME],	_____(__)
Debtor.	Tax ID No. _____

SCHEDULING MOTION FOR
PREPACKAGED CHAPTER 11 CASE

TO THE HONORABLE UNITED STATES BANKRUPTCY JUDGE:

The **[NAME OF DEBTOR]**, as debtor and debtor in possession (the

"Debtor"), respectfully represents:

<u>Background</u>

1.   **[Brief background of the Debtor].**

<u>Jurisdiction and Venue</u>

2.   This Court has jurisdiction to consider this application pursuant to 28 U.S.C.

§§ 157 and 1334. Consideration of this application is a core proceeding pursuant to 28 U.S.C.

§ 157(b). Venue of this proceeding is proper in this district pursuant to 28 U.S.C. §§ 1408 and

1409.

<u>The Debtor's Business</u>

3.   **[Brief Description of the Debtor's business].**

<u>The Proposed Plan of Reorganization</u>

4.   **[Brief description of the proposed plan of reorganization].**

PREPACK SCHEDULING MOTION   Case No.

A:\#133728 V2 - PREPACK SCHEDULING MOTION.DOC

<u>This Court Should Schedule a Hearing</u>
<u>To Consider Confirmation of the Proposed Plan</u>

5.   Pursuant to section 1128(a) of the Bankruptcy Code, the Debtor requests that the

Court set a hearing to consider confirmation of the Plan. Section 1128(a) of the Bankruptcy

Code provides that "[after notice, the Court shall hold a hearing on confirmation of a plan]."

6.   **[Summarize results of pre-petition solicitation].**

7.   **[Indicate whether Debtor requests that confirmation hearing and**

disclosure hearing be combined]. [Indicate proposed date and time for

confirmation/disclosure hearings].

8.   The Debtor proposes to publish notice of the Confirmation and Disclosure

Compliance Hearing (the "Hearing Notice") **[insert where notice will be published]. [Indicate**

whether the proposed notice schedule complies with the minimum twenty-eight (28) days

notice required under Rules 2002(b) and 3017(a) of the Federal Rules of Bankruptcy

Procedure (the "Bankruptcy Rules".][1]

9.   In addition to the Hearing Notice, the Debtor will transmit, in accordance with

Bankruptcy Rule 3017(d), via first class mail, postage prepaid, a copy of the Disclosure

Statement and the Plan to all holders of claims against, or equity interests in, the Debtor other

than **[insert parties who received such materials pursuant to the prepetition solicitation],**

which are the parties to whom the Disclosure Statement and Plan have already been

transmitted pursuant to the prepetition solicitation.

<u>Notice</u>

10.   Notice of this application has been given to **[insert names of persons to**

whom notice has been given] which shall include the U.S. Trustee, **[others?].**

---

[1] A form of Hearing Notice, which includes a summary of the Plan, also is appended to the Guidelines.

11.   No previous application for the relief sought herein has been made to this or any other court.

WHEREFORE the Debtor respectfully requests entry of an order granting the relief requested herein and granting the Debtor such other and further relief as is just.

Dated: _____, _____

By: _____

[signing attorney]
Attorneys for Debtor

EXHIBIT "B"

NO PERSON HAS BEEN AUTHORIZED TO GIVE ANY INFORMATION OR ADVICE, OR TO MAKE ANY REPRESENTATION, OTHER THAN WHAT IS INCLUDED IN THE MATERIALS MAILED WITH THIS BALLOT.

_____

[NAME OF DEBTOR],

    Debtor.

[DEBTOR'S ADDRESS]

Tax ID No. _____

_____

BALLOT FOR ACCEPTING OR REJECTING PREPACKAGED
PLAN OF REORGANIZATION OF [NAME OF DEBTOR]
UNDER CHAPTER 11 OF THE BANKRUPTCY CODE BALLOT
FOR VOTING __% NOTES
(Class __: __% NOTE CLAIMS)
[Insert Exact Name of Notes/Bonds, If Applicable]*
[Insert CUSIP #, If Applicable]

If you are a beneficial owner of **[NAME OF SECURITIES]** (the __% Notes") issued by **[NAME OF DEBTOR]**, please use this Ballot to cast your vote to accept or reject the chapter 11 plan of reorganization (the "Plan") which is being proposed by **[DEBTOR]**. The Plan is Exhibit **[ ]** to the Disclosure Statement, dated _____, ____, (the "Disclosure Statement"), which accompanies this Ballot. The Plan can be confirmed by the Bankruptcy Court and thereby made binding upon you if it is accepted by the holders of two-thirds in amount and more than one-half in number of claims in each class that vote on the Plan, and by the holders of two-thirds in amount of equity security interests in each class that vote on the Plan, and if it otherwise satisfies the requirements of section 1129(a) of the Bankruptcy Code. [If the requisite acceptances are not obtained, the Bankruptcy Court may nonetheless confirm the Plan if it finds that the Plan provides fair and equitable treatment to, and does not discriminate unfairly against, the class or classes rejecting it, and otherwise satisfies the requirements of section 1129(b) of the Bankruptcy Code.]

IMPORTANT

VOTING DEADLINE: __:____.M., EASTERN TIME ON _____, ____.
REVIEW THE ACCOMPANYING DISCLOSURE STATEMENT FOR THE PLAN.
[BALLOTS WILL NOT BE ACCEPTED BY FACSIMILE TRANSMISSION.]
DO NOT RETURN ANY SECURITIES WITH THIS BALLOT. This Ballot is *not* a letter of transmittal and may *not* be used for any purpose other than to cast votes to accept or reject the Plan.

_____

* This form ballot does not contemplate multiple securities within the same class.

[Ballot Code]

A:\#75698 V2 - BAL6038T.03A.DOC

HOW TO VOTE

1. COMPLETE ITEM 1 (if not already filled out by your nominee) AND ITEM 2 AND COMPLETE ITEM 3 (if applicable).

2. REVIEW THE CERTIFICATIONS CONTAINED IN ITEM 4.

3. **SIGN THE BALLOT** (unless your Ballot has already been signed or "prevalidated" by your nominee).

4. RETURN THE BALLOT IN THE PRE-ADDRESSED POSTAGE-PAID ENVELOPE (if the enclosed envelope is addressed to your nominee, make sure your nominee receives your Ballot in time to submit it before the Voting Deadline).

5. YOU WILL RECEIVE A SEPARATE BALLOT FOR EACH ISSUE OF SECURITIES YOU OWN WHICH IS ENTITLED TO BE VOTED UNDER THE PLAN.

6. YOU MUST VOTE *ALL YOUR* __% NOTES *EITHER* TO ACCEPT *OR* TO REJECT THE PLAN AND MAY NOT SPLIT YOUR VOTE.

Item 1.   **Principal Amount of __% Notes Voted.** The undersigned certifies that as of [the record date] the undersigned was either the beneficial owner, or the nominee of a beneficial owner, of __% Notes in the following aggregate unpaid principal amount (insert amount in the box below). If your __% Notes are held by a nominee on your behalf and you do not know the amount, please contact your nominee immediately.

> $

Item 2.   **Vote.** The beneficial owner of the __% Notes identified in Item 1 votes as follows (check one box only   —if you do not check a box your vote will not be counted):

         O to **Accept** the Plan.   O to **Reject** the Plan.

Item 3.   **Identify All Other __% Notes Voted.** By returning this Ballot, the beneficial owner of the __% Notes identified in Item 1 certifies that (a) this Ballot is the only Ballot submitted for the __% Notes owned by such beneficial owner, except for the __% Notes identified in the following table, and (b) *all* Ballots for __% Notes submitted by the beneficial owner indicate the same vote to accept or reject the Plan that the beneficial owner has indicated in Item 2 of this Ballot (please use additional sheets of paper if necessary):

ONLY COMPLETE ITEM 3 IF YOU HAVE SUBMITTED OTHER BALLOTS

Account Number	Name of Holder*	Principal Amount of Other __% Notes Voted
		$
		$

       * Insert your name if the notes are held by you in record name or, if held in street name, insert the name of your broker or bank.

Item 4.   **Authorization.** By returning this Ballot, the beneficial owner of the __% Notes identified in Item 1 certifies that it (a) has full power and authority to vote to accept or reject the Plan with respect to the __% Notes listed in Item 1, (b) was the beneficial owner of the __% Notes described in Item 1 on _____, and (c) has received a copy of the Disclosure Statement (including the exhibits thereto) and understands that the solicitation of votes for the Plan is subject to all the terms and conditions set forth in the Disclosure Statement.

Name:_____
        (Print or Type)

Social Security or Federal Tax I.D. No.:_____
                          (Optional)

Signature:_____

By:_____
        (If Appropriate)

Title:_____
        (If Appropriate)

Street   Address:

City,   State,   Zip   Code:

Telephone Number: (___)_____

Date Completed:_____

No fees, commissions, or other remuneration will be payable to any broker, dealer, or other person for soliciting votes on the Plan. This Ballot shall not constitute or be deemed a proof of claim or equity interest or an assertion of a claim or equity interest.

> **YOUR VOTE MUST BE FORWARDED IN AMPLE TIME FOR YOUR VOTE TO BE RECEIVED BY [DEBTOR or DEBTOR'S AGENT], BY ___:___ .M., EASTERN TIME, ON _____, _____, OR YOUR VOTE WILL NOT BE COUNTED. IF THE ENCLOSED ENVELOPE IS ADDRESSED TO YOUR NOMINEE, MAKE SURE YOUR NOMINEE RECEIVES YOUR BALLOT IN TIME TO SUBMIT IT BEFORE THE VOTING DEADLINE.**

A:\#75698 V2 - BAL603#T.03A.DOC   3

IF YOU HAVE ANY QUESTIONS REGARDING THIS BALLOT OR THE VOTING PROCEDURES, OR IF YOU NEED A BALLOT OR ADDITIONAL COPIES OF THE DISCLOSURE STATEMENT OR OTHER ENCLOSED MATERIALS, PLEASE CALL [DEBTOR or DEBTOR'S AGENT], AT _____.

EXHIBIT "C"

NO PERSON HAS BEEN AUTHORIZED TO GIVE ANY INFORMATION OR
ADVICE, OR TO MAKE ANY REPRESENTATION, OTHER THAN WHAT IS
INCLUDED IN THE MATERIALS MAILED WITH THIS BALLOT.

——————————————————

[NAME OF DEBTOR],
            Debtor.
[DEBTOR'S ADDRESS]

Tax ID No. _____

——————————————————

**MASTER BALLOT FOR ACCEPTING OR REJECTING
PREPACKAGED PLAN OF REORGANIZATION OF
[NAME OF DEBTOR]
TO BE FILED UNDER CHAPTER 11 OF THE BANKRUPTCY CODE
MASTER BALLOT FOR VOTING __% NOTES
(Class __ : __% NOTE CLAIMS)
[Insert exact name of Notes/Bonds]*
[Insert CUSIP # If Applicable]**

> THE **VOTING DEADLINE** BY WHICH YOUR MASTER BALLOT MUST BE *RECEIVED* BY [DEBTOR or
> DEBTOR'S AGENT] IS __ : ____ .M., EASTERN TIME ON _____, ____. IF YOUR MASTER BALLOT
> IS NOT RECEIVED ON OR BEFORE THE VOTING DEADLINE, THE VOTES REPRESENTED BY YOUR
> MASTER BALLOT WILL <u>NOT</u> BE COUNTED.

This Master Ballot is to be used by you, as a broker, bank, or other nominee (or as their proxy holder or
agent) (each of the foregoing, a "Nominee"), for beneficial owners of **[NAME OF SECURITIES]** (the
"__% Notes") issued by **[NAME OF DEBTOR]**, to transmit the votes of such holders in respect of their
__% Notes to accept or reject the chapter 11 plan of reorganization (the "Plan") described in, and attached
as Exhibit "__" to the Disclosure Statement, dated _____, ____ (the "Disclosure Statement") provided
to you. Before you transmit such votes, please review the Disclosure Statement carefully, including the
voting procedures explained in Section __.

The Plan can be confirmed by the Bankruptcy Court and thereby made binding upon you and the beneficial
owners of __% Notes for which you are the Nominee if it is accepted by the holders of two-thirds in
amount and more than one-half in number of claims in each class that vote on the Plan, and by the holders
of two-thirds in amount of equity security interests in each class that vote on the Plan, and if it otherwise
satisfies the requirements of section 1129(a) of the Bankruptcy Code. [If the requisite acceptances are not
obtained, the Bankruptcy Court may nonetheless confirm the Plan if it finds that the Plan provides fair and
equitable treatment to, and does not discriminate unfairly against, the class or classes rejecting it, and
otherwise satisfies the requirements of section 1129(b) of the Bankruptcy Code.]

PLEASE READ AND FOLLOW THE ATTACHED INSTRUCTIONS CAREFULLY. COMPLETE, SIGN, AND DATE
THIS MASTER BALLOT, AND RETURN IT SO THAT IT IS RECEIVED BY [DEBTOR or DEBTOR'S AGENT] ON OR
BEFORE THE VOTING DEADLINE OF __ : ____ .M., EASTERN TIME, ON _____, ____. IF THIS MASTER
BALLOT IS NOT COMPLETED, SIGNED, AND TIMELY RECEIVED, THE VOTES TRANSMITTED BY THIS
MASTER BALLOT WILL NOT BE COUNTED.

——————————————————

         * This form ballot does not contemplate multiple securities within the same class.

[Master Ballot Code]

A:\#75697 V2 - BAL6035T.05A.DOC

Item 1. Certification of Authority to Vote. The undersigned certifies that as of the _____, ____ record date, the undersigned (please check the applicable box):

☐ Is a broker, bank, or other nominee for the beneficial owners of the aggregate principal amount of __% Notes listed in Item 2 below, and is the registered holder of such securities, or

☐ Is acting under a power of attorney and/or agency (a copy of which will be provided upon request) granted by a broker, bank, or other nominee that is the registered holder of the aggregate principal amount of __% Notes listed in Item 2 below, or

☐ Has been granted a proxy (an original of which is attached hereto) from a broker, bank, or other nominee, or a beneficial owner, that is the registered holder of the aggregate principal amount of __% Notes listed in Item 2 below,

and, accordingly, has full power and authority to vote to accept or reject the Plan on behalf of the beneficial owners of the __% Notes described in Item 2 below.

Item 2. Class __ (__% Note Claims) Vote. The undersigned transmits the following votes of beneficial owners in respect of their __% Notes, and certifies that the following beneficial owners of __% Notes, as identified by their respective customer account numbers set forth below, are beneficial owners of such securities as of the _____, ____ record date and have delivered to the undersigned, as Nominee, Ballots casting such votes (Indicate in the appropriate column the aggregate principal amount voted for each account, or attach such information to this Master Ballot in the form of the following table. Please note: Each beneficial owner must vote *all* his, her, or its Class __ claims (__% Notes) *either* to accept or reject the Plan, and may *not* split such vote.):

Your Customer Account Number for Each Beneficial Owner of __% Notes	Principal Amount of __% Notes Voted to ACCEPT the Plan		Principal Amount of __% Notes Voted to REJECT the Plan
1.	$	OR	$
2.	$	OR	$
3.	$	OR	$
4.	$	OR	$
5.	$	OR	$
6.	$	OR	$
7.	$	OR	$
8.	$	OR	$
9.	$	OR	$
10.	$	OR	$
TOTALS	$		$

Item 3.　Certification As to Transcription of Information From Item 3 As to Other ___% Notes Voted by Beneficial Owners. The undersigned certifies that the undersigned has transcribed in the following table the information, if any, provided by beneficial owners in Item 3 of the ___% Note Ballots, identifying any other ___% Notes for which such beneficial owners have submitted other Ballots:

TRANSCRIBE FROM ITEM 3 OF [ ]% NOTES BALLOT:

YOUR customer account number for each beneficial owner who completed Item 3 of the ___% Note Ballot	Account Number (Transcribe from Item 3 of ___% Note Ballot)	Name Holder (Transcribe from Item 3 of ___% Note Ballot)	Principal Amount of Other ___% Notes Voted (Transcribe from Item 3 of ___% Note Ballot)
1.			$
2.			$
3.			$
4.			$
5.			$
6.			$
7.			$
8.			$
9.			$
10.			$

3

Item 4. Certification. By signing this Master Ballot, the undersigned certifies that each beneficial owner of ___% Notes listed in Item 2, above, has been provided with a copy of the Disclosure Statement, including the exhibits thereto, and acknowledges that the solicitation of votes is subject to all the terms and conditions set forth in the Disclosure Statement.

Name of Broker, Bank, or Other Nominee:

_____

(Print or Type)

Name of Proxy Holder or Agent for Broker,
Bank, or Other Nominee (if applicable):

_____
                              (Print or Type)

Social Security or Federal Tax I.D. No.: _____
                                                    (If Applicable)

Signature: _____

By: _____
                                        (If Appropriate)

Title: _____
                                        (If Appropriate)

Street Address: _____

City, State, Zip Code: _____

Telephone Number: ( ) _____

Date Completed: _____

THIS MASTER BALLOT MUST BE RECEIVED BY [DEBTOR or DEBTOR'S AGENT], BEFORE ___:____.M., EASTERN TIME, ON _____, ____OR THE VOTES TRANSMITTED HEREBY WILL NOT BE COUNTED.

[PLEASE NOTE: BALLOTS AND MASTER BALLOTS WILL *NOT* BE ACCEPTED BY FACSIMILE TRANSMISSION.]

IF YOU HAVE ANY QUESTIONS REGARDING THIS MASTER BALLOT OR THE VOTING PROCEDURES, OR IF YOU NEED ADDITIONAL COPIES OF THE MASTER BALLOT, BALLOTS, DISCLOSURE STATEMENT, OR OTHER RELATED MATERIALS, PLEASE CALL [DEBTOR or DEBTOR'S AGENT], AT _____.

A:\#75697 V2 - BAL6038T.05A.DOC   4

INSTRUCTIONS FOR COMPLETING THE MASTER BALLOT

VOTING DEADLINE:

The Voting Deadline is ___:___ __m., Eastern Time, on _____, _____, unless extended by the Debtor. To have the vote of your customers count, you must complete, sign, and return this Master Ballot so that it is received by **[DEBTOR or DEBTOR'S AGENT]**, **[ADDRESS]**, *on or before* the Voting Deadline.

HOW TO VOTE:

If you are both the registered owner *and* beneficial owner of any principal amount of __% Notes and you wish to vote such __% Notes, you may complete, execute, and return to [DEBTOR or DEBTOR'S AGENT] *either* a __% Note Ballot or a __% Note Master Ballot.

If you are transmitting the votes of any beneficial owners of __% Notes other than yourself,

you may *either*:

1. Complete and execute the __% Note Ballot (other than Items 2 and 3) and deliver to the beneficial owner such "prevalidated" __% Note Ballot, along with the Disclosure Statement and other materials requested to be forwarded. The beneficial owner should complete Items 2 and 3 of that Ballot and return the completed Ballot to [DEBTOR or DEBTOR'S AGENT] so as to be received before the Voting Deadline;

OR

2. For any __% Note Ballots you do not "prevalidate":

Deliver the __% Note Ballot to the beneficial owner, along with the Disclosure Statement and other materials requested to be forwarded, and take the necessary actions to enable such beneficial owner to (i) complete and execute such Ballot voting to accept or reject the Plan, and (ii) return the complete, executed Ballot to you in sufficient time to enable you to complete the Master Ballot and deliver it to **[DEBTOR or DEBTOR'S AGENT]** before the Voting Deadline; and

With respect to all __% Note Ballots returned to you, you must properly complete the Master Ballot, as follows:

a. Check the appropriate box in Item 1 on the Master Ballot;

b. Indicate the votes to accept or reject the Plan in Item 2 of this Master Ballot, as transmitted to you by the beneficial owners of __% Notes. To identify such beneficial owners without disclosing their names, please use the customer account number assigned by you to each such beneficial owner, or if no such customer account number exists, please assign a number to each account (making sure to retain a separate list of each beneficial owner and the assigned number). **IMPORTANT: BENEFICIAL OWNERS MAY** *NOT* **SPLIT THEIR VOTES. EACH BENEFICIAL OWNER MUST VOTE** *ALL* **HIS, HER, OR ITS __% NOTES** *EITHER* **TO ACCEPT OR REJECT THE PLAN. IF ANY BENEFICIAL OWNER HAS ATTEMPTED TO SPLIT SUCH VOTE, PLEASE CONTACT [DEBTOR or DEBTOR'S AGENT] IMMEDIATELY.** Any Ballot or Master Ballot which is validly executed but which does not indicate acceptance or rejection of the Plan by the indicated beneficial owner or which impermissibly attempts to split a vote will not be counted;

c. Please note that Item 3 of this Master Ballot requests that you transcribe the information provided by each beneficial owner from Item 3 of each completed __% Note Ballot relating to other __% Notes voted;

d. Review the certification in Item 4 of the Master Ballot;

e. Sign and date the Master Ballot, and provide the remaining information requested;

A:\#75697 V2 - BAL6038T.05A.DOC   5

f.   If additional space is required to respond to any item on the Master Ballot, please use additional sheets of paper clearly marked to indicate the applicable Item of the Master Ballot to which you are responding;

g.   Contact **[DEBTOR or DEBTOR'S AGENT]** to arrange for delivery of the completed Master Ballot to its offices; and

h.   Deliver the completed, executed Master Ballot so that it is actually   *received* by **[DEBTOR or DEBTOR'S AGENT]** on or before the Voting Deadline. For each completed, executed ___% Note Ballot returned to you by a beneficial owner, either forward such Ballot (along with your Master Ballot) to **[DEBTOR or DEBTOR'S AGENT]** or retain ___% Note Ballot in your files for one such year from the Voting Deadline.

PLEASE NOTE:

This Master Ballot is *not* a letter of transmittal and may *not* be used for any purpose other than to cast votes to accept or reject the Plan. Holders should not surrender, at this time, certificates representing their securities. **[DEBTOR or DEBTOR'S AGENT]** will not accept delivery of any such certificates surrendered together with this Master Ballot. Surrender of securities for exchange may only be made by you, and will only be accepted pursuant to a letter of transmittal which will be furnished to you by the Debtor following confirmation of the Plan by the United States Bankruptcy Court.

No Ballot or Master Ballot shall constitute or be deemed a proof of claim or equity interest or an assertion of a claim or equity interest.

No fees or commissions or other remuneration will be payable to any broker, dealer, or other person for soliciting votes on the Plan. [We will, however, upon request, reimburse you for customary mailing and handling expenses incurred by you in forwarding the Ballots and other enclosed materials to the beneficial owners of ___% Notes held by you as a nominee or in a fiduciary capacity. We will also pay all transfer taxes, if any, applicable to the transfer and exchange of your securities pursuant to and following confirmation of the Plan.]

> **NOTHING CONTAINED HEREIN OR IN THE ENCLOSED DOCUMENTS SHALL RENDER YOU OR ANY OTHER PERSON THE AGENT OF THE DEBTOR [OR THE DEBTOR'S AGENT], OR AUTHORIZE YOU OR ANY OTHER PERSON TO USE ANY DOCUMENT OR MAKE ANY STATEMENTS ON BEHALF OF ANY OF THEM WITH RESPECT TO THE PLAN, EXCEPT FOR THE STATEMENTS CONTAINED IN THE ENCLOSED DOCUMENTS.**

A:\#75697 V2 - BAL6038T.05A.DOC   6

IF YOU HAVE ANY QUESTIONS REGARDING THIS MASTER BALLOT OR THE VOTING PROCEDURES, OR IF YOU NEED ADDITIONAL COPIES OF THE MASTER BALLOT, BALLOTS, DISCLOSURE STATEMENT, OR OTHER RELATED MATERIALS, PLEASE CALL [DEBTOR or DEBTOR'S AGENT], AT _____.

A:\#75697 V2 - BAL6038T.05A.DOC   7

EXHIBIT "D"

**UNITED STATES BANKRUPTCY COURT
SOUTHERN DISTRICT OF NEW YORK**

--x

In re   :

                                 Chapter 11 Case No.

[NAME],   :   ___—___ (___)

             Debtor.   :

[DEBTOR'S ADDRESS]   :   Tax ID No.

                                    _____

--x

**SUMMARY OF PLAN OF REORGANIZATION AND NOTICE OF HEARING TO
CONSIDER (I) DEBTOR'S COMPLIANCE WITH DISCLOSURE
REQUIREMENTS AND (II) CONFIRMATION OF PLAN OF REORGANIZATION**

NOTICE IS HEREBY GIVEN as follows:

1. On _____ ___, ___ (the "Petition Date"), **[NAME OF DEBTOR]**, the above-captioned debtor (the "Debtor"), filed with the United States Bankruptcy Court for the Southern District of New York (the "Bankruptcy Court") a proposed plan of reorganization (the "Plan") and a proposed disclosure statement (the "Disclosure Statement") pursuant to §§ 1125 and 1126(b) of title 11 of the United States Code (the "Bankruptcy Code"). Copies of the Plan and the Disclosure Statement may be obtained upon request of Debtor's counsel at the address specified below and are on file with the Clerk of the Bankruptcy Court, **[ADDRESS]**, where they are available for review between the hours of 9:00 a.m.–4:30 p.m. The Plan and Disclosure Statement also are available for inspection on the Bankruptcy Court's internet site at www.nysb.uscourts.gov.

Summary of Plan of Reorganization

2. [Provide one paragraph general description of salient Plan provisions, including whether proponent requests confirmation pursuant to 11 U.S.C. § 1129(b).] Votes on the Plan were solicited prior to the Petition Date. The following chart summarizes the treatment provided by the Plan to each class of claims and interests and indicates the acceptance or rejection of the Plan by each class entitled to vote.

CLASS	CLASS DESCRIPTION	IMPAIRMENT/TREATMENT	ACCEPT/ REJECT

Hearing to Consider Compliance with Disclosure Requirements

3. A hearing to consider compliance with the disclosure requirements, any objections to the Disclosure Statement, and any other matter that may properly come before the Bankruptcy Court will be held before the Honorable _____, United States Bankruptcy Judge, in Room ___ of the United States Bankruptcy Court, **[ADDRESS]**, on _____ at _: ___ a_.m. or as soon thereafter as counsel may be heard (the "Disclosure Compliance Hearing"). The Disclosure Compliance Hearing may be adjourned from time to time without further notice other than an announcement of the adjourned date or dates at the Disclosure Compliance Hearing or at an adjourned Disclosure Compliance Hearing and will be available on the electronic case filing docket.

4. Any objections to the Disclosure Statement shall be in writing, shall conform to the Federal Rules of Bankruptcy Procedure and the Local Rules of the Bankruptcy Court, shall set forth the name of the objector, the nature and amount of any claims or interests held or asserted by the objector against the estate or property of the Debtor, the basis for the objection, and the specific grounds therefor, and shall be filed with the Bankruptcy Court at the address specified in the previous paragraph, with a copy delivered directly to Chambers, together with proof of service thereof, and served upon the following persons so as to be received on or before _____ ___, ___, at 5:00 p.m. (Eastern Time):

(i) **[NAME AND ADDRESS OF DEBTOR'S COUNSEL]**

(ii) **[NAME AND ADDRESS OF COMMITTEE COUNSEL]**

(iii) **[NAME AND ADDRESS OF BANK COUNSEL]**

(iv) **[NAME AND ADDRESS OF INDENTURE TRUSTEE]**

(v) OFFICE OF THE UNITED STATES TRUSTEE
33 Whitehall Street, 21st Floor
New York, NY 10004
Attn: Carolyn S. Schwartz, Esq.

[AND IF APPLICABLE:]

(vi) OFFICE OF THE UNITED STATES ATTORNEY FOR THE SOUTHERN DISTRICT OF NEW YORK
One St. Andrew's Plaza
New York, NY 10007
Attn: Mary Jo White, Esq.

(vii) SECURITIES AND EXCHANGE COMMISSION
7 World Trade Center
New York, NY 10048
Attn: Nathan M. Fuchs, Esq.

UNLESS AN OBJECTION IS TIMELY SERVED AND FILED IN ACCORDANCE WITH THIS NOTICE, IT MAY NOT BE CONSIDERED BY THE BANKRUPTCY COURT.

Hearing on Confirmation of the Plan

5. A hearing to consider confirmation of the Plan, any objections thereto, and any other matter that may properly come before the Bankruptcy Court shall be held before the Honorable _____, United States Bankruptcy Judge, in Room ___ of the United States Bankruptcy Court, **[ADDRESS]**, immediately following the Disclosure Compliance Hearing referred to above or at such later time as determined by the Bankruptcy Court at the conclusion of the Disclosure Compliance Hearing (the "Confirmation Hearing"). The Confirmation Hearing may be adjourned from time to time without further notice other than an announcement of the adjourned date or dates at the Confirmation Hearing or at an adjourned Confirmation Hearing.

6. Objections to the Plan, if any, shall be in writing, shall conform to the Federal Rules of Bankruptcy Procedure and the Local Rules of the Bankruptcy Court, shall set forth the name of the objector, the nature and amount of any claims or interests held or asserted by the objector against the estate or property of the Debtor, the basis for the objection, and the specific grounds therefor, and shall be filed with the Bankruptcy Court at the address specified in the previous paragraph, with a copy delivered directly to Chambers, together with proof of service thereof, and served upon the persons set forth in paragraph 4 above so as to be received on or before _____ ___, ___, at 5:00 p.m. (Eastern Time). **UNLESS AN OBJECTION IS TIMELY SERVED AND FILED IN ACCORDANCE WITH THIS NOTICE, IT MAY NOT BE CONSIDERED BY THE BANKRUPTCY COURT.**

7. The times fixed for the Confirmation Hearing and objections to confirmation of the Plan may be rescheduled by the Bankruptcy Court in the event that the Bankruptcy Court does not find compliance with the disclosure requirements on _____, ___. Notice of the rescheduled date or dates, if any, will be provided by an announcement at the Disclosure Compliance Hearing or at an adjourned Disclosure Compliance Hearing and will be available on the electronic case filing docket.

Section 341(a) Meeting

8. A meeting pursuant to section 341(a) of the Bankruptcy Code (the "Section 341(a) Meeting") shall be held at the United States Bankruptcy Court, in room ___, [**ADDRESS**], on _____ ___, ___ at ___: ___.m. Such meeting will not be convened if (i) the Plan is confirmed prior to the date set forth above for the Section 341(a) Meeting and (ii) the order confirming the Plan (or order entered substantially contemporaneously therewith) contains a provision waiving the convening of a Section 341(a) Meeting.

Dated: New York, New York

_____, _____

BY ORDER OF THE COURT

_____

United States Bankruptcy Judge

[NAME, ADDRESS, AND
TELEPHONE NUMBER
OF DEBTOR'S COUNSEL]

[Dated: June 28, 2013.]

1 In the event solicitation has not been completed prior to the petition date, an alternative first day motion should be submitted consistent with sections III(A)(i) and III(C).

GENERAL ORDER M-455. IN RE: ADOPTION OF MODEL CHAPTER 13 PLAN AND CONFIRMATION ORDER

Amending M-384

By resolution of the Board of Judges for the United States Bankruptcy Court for the Southern District of New York, it is decided that General Order M-384 shall be amended and in all cases filed under Chapter 13 of the Bankruptcy Code, the debtor's plan shall conform to the model Plan and the debtor's confirmation order shall conform to the model Confirmation Order adopted by the judges of this court, copies of which are attached to this order. The relevant provisions of Federal Rule of Bankruptcy Procedure 3015 and Local Rules of Bankruptcy Procedure 3015–1 and 3015–2 shall govern as to when a plan shall be filed, served, and modified in a Chapter 13 case.

The model Plan and Confirmation Order shall be available in the Clerk's Office and on the Court's web site. The court may modify the model Plan and Confirmation Order from time to time by duly adopted General Order, making the revised model Plan and Confirmation Order available in the clerk's office and on the court's web site no less than 30 days before its effective date.

NOW, THEREFORE, IT IS ORDERED that the model Chapter 13 Plan and Confirmation Order, annexed hereto, shall apply to all Chapter 13 plans filed and all Chapter 13 confirmation orders signed on or after August 1, 2013.

[Dated: June 28, 2013.]

Attorney name

Firm name (if applicable)

Attorney address

Attorney city, state zip

Attorney phone number, Attorney fax number

Attorney email

UNITED STATES BANKRUPTCY COURT
SOUTHERN DISTRICT OF NEW YORK

---x

In re   Case No.   –   (   )

                          ,   **CHAPTER 13 PLAN**

                          Debtor(s).

SSN xxx–xx– _____   SSN xxx–xx– _____

---x

Plan Definitions: If this is a joint case, use of the term "Debtor" shall also mean Debtors. The term "Trustee" shall always refer to Jeffrey L. Sapir, the Chapter 13 Standing Trustee for this court, or his substitute. The term "Bankruptcy Rule" shall refer to the Federal Rules of Bankruptcy Procedure. The term "Local Rule" shall refer to the Local Rules of Bankruptcy Procedure of the United States Bankruptcy Court for the Southern District of New York. The term "Petition" refers to Debtor's bankruptcy petition filed with the court on _____, 20 ___. The term "Real Property Used as a Principal Residence" includes cooperative apartments.

☐ This is an Amended or Modified Plan. The reasons for filing this Amended or Modified Plan are: _____.

In all respects, this Plan shall comply with the provisions of the Bankruptcy Code, Bankruptcy Rules and Local Rules.

Section A Plan Payments and Payment Duration	The future earnings of Debtor are submitted to the supervision and control of the Trustee. Debtor will make the first Plan payment no later than thirty (30) days after the date this Petition was filed. The Debtor shall make ___ [number] monthly payments to the Trustee as follows:

$ ___ each month, from [month] _____, 20 ___
through [month] _____, 20 ___.
$ ___ each month, from [month] _____, 20 ___
through [month] _____, 20 ___.
$ ___ each month, from [month] _____, 20 ___
through [month] _____, 20 ___.

☐ Lump-sum payment(s) in the following amount(s):

☐ All tax refunds in excess of $1500 (less any cash exemptions in the first year, if applicable).

☐ Pursuant to 11 U.S.C. § 1325(b)(4), the applicable commitment period is 60 months, **or**

☐ Pursuant to 11 U.S.C. § 1325(b)(4), the applicable commitment period is 36 months.

☐ Debtor's annual commitment period is 36 months and Debtor moves to extend to 60 months for the following reasons: (*check all that apply*)

☐ Debtor is not able to propose a feasible plan in a period of less than 60 months. Debtor's proposed monthly payment will constitute an affordable budget that the Debtor will be able to maintain.

☐ Payments greater than that proposed by this plan for 60 months would create an economic hardship for the Debtor.

☐ Creditors will not be prejudiced by this application for extension of Debtor's plan payments from 36 to 60 months.

Payment Terms

The Debtor will pay the amounts listed above to the Trustee by bank check, certified check, teller's check, or money order sent to the following address:

> Jeffrey L. Sapir, Esq., Chapter 13 Trustee
> 399 Knollwood Road, Suite 102
> White Plains, New York 10603

OPTIONAL: Debtor may pay his or her Plan payments to the Trustee by way of an employer pay order, pursuant to 11 U.S.C. § 1325(c). If Debtor selects this option, please check here: ☐

Upon selecting this option, Debtor hereby consents to the **immediate** entry of an order directing Debtor's employer to deduct from Debtor's wages the amount specified in this section and transmit that amount directly to the Trustee on Debtor's behalf. Debtor also agrees to notify the Trustee immediately upon change or termination of employment. A proposed order outlining Debtor's intention shall be submitted to the court for consideration upon the filing of this Plan.

☐ Non–Debtor Contributions. Identify the source and monthly amount to be contributed to the Plan from any person or entity other than the Debtor (a "Non–Debtor Contributor"): _____.

Prior to confirmation of this Plan, each Non–Debtor Contributor must either (1) file an affidavit with the court confirming the amounts that will be contributed to the Plan or (2) consent to entry of an employer pay order for the amount to be contributed to the Plan.

Section B
Trustee's Fee

Pursuant to 28 U.S.C. § 586(e), the Trustee may collect the percentage fee from all payments and property received, not to exceed 10%.

Section C
Loss Mitigation
(Optional)
This section applies only to the Debtor's Real Property Used as a Principal Residence.

☐ By checking this box and completing this section, the Debtor requests loss mitigation pursuant to General Order M–413, which establishes a court-ordered loss mitigation program, pursuant to which parties may deal with issues such as a loan modification, loan refinance, short sale, or surrender in full satisfaction, concerning the Debtor's Real Property Used as a Principal Residence. *[Identify the property, loan and creditor for which you are requesting loss mitigation]*:

_____

The Debtor hereby permits the Secured Creditor(s) listed above to contact (check all that apply):

> ☐ The Debtor directly.
> ☐ Debtor's bankruptcy counsel.
> ☐ Other: _____.

(Debtor is not required to dismiss this bankruptcy Petition during the loss mitigation discussions. Any agreement reached during the loss mitigation discussions may be approved pursuant to an amended plan, and the terms may be set forth in Section H, below.)

Section D
Treatment of Claims

☐ See Section H, Varying Provisions.

Except as otherwise ordered by the court, the Trustee will make disbursements to creditors after the court enters an order confirming this Plan. Unless otherwise provided in Section H (below), disbursements by the Trustee shall be pro rata as outlined below.

Category 1
Attorney's Fees pursuant to 11 U.S.C. § 507(a)(2).

Attorney's fees. Counsel for the Debtor has received a prepetition retainer of $ _____, to be applied against fees and costs incurred. Fees and costs exceeding the retainer shall be paid from funds held by the Chapter 13 Trustee as an administrative expense after application to and approval by the court pursuant to Bankruptcy Rule 2016.

☐ Not Applicable.

Category 2
Claims Secured by a
Mortgage on the
Debtor's Real Proper-
ty Used as a Principal
Residence

☐ Not Applicable.

☐ See Section H,
Varying Provisions.

Category 2 applies only to claims secured by a mortgage on the Debtor's Real Property Used as a Principal Residence.

Category 2 Definitions: For the purposes of this Category 2, any reference to the term "Secured Creditor" means mortgagees, a creditor whose interest is secured by a mortgage on Debtor's real property, a holder and/or servicer of a claim secured by a lien, mortgage and/or deed of trust and/or any other similarly situated creditor, servicing agent and/or their assigns. The term "Mortgage" shall include references to mortgages, liens, deeds of trust and any other similarly situated interest in the Debtor's Real Property Used as a Principal Residence. The term "Contract" shall refer to any contract or similar agreement pertaining to the Mortgage. The term "Prepetition Arrearages" shall refer to an amount owed by the Debtor to the Secured Creditor prior to the filing of Debtor's petition. The term "Post–Petition Payment" means any payment that first becomes due and payable by the Debtor to the Secured Creditor after the filing of the petition pursuant to the Mortgage or Contract.

Confirmation of this Plan shall impose an affirmative duty on the Secured Creditor and Debtor to do all of the following, as ordered:

(a) Prepetition Arrearages.

(i) For purposes of this Plan, Prepetition Arrearages shall include all sums included in the allowed claim and shall have a "0" balance upon entry of the Discharge Order in this case. In the event that a Secured Creditor listed in this section fails to timely file a proof of claim in this case, by this Plan the Debtor shall be deemed to have timely filed a proof of claim on behalf of each such Secured Creditor pursuant to 11 U.S.C. § 501(c), in the amount set forth below in Section D, Category 2(a)(iv).

(ii) No interest will be paid on Prepetition Arrearages unless otherwise stated.

(iii) Payments made by the Trustee on Debtor's Prepetition Arrearages shall be applied **only** to those Prepetition Arrearages and not to any other amount owed by Debtor to the Secured Creditor.

(iv) Information Regarding the Arrearages.

Secured Creditor & Property Description	Value of Collateral and Valuation Method	Arrearage Amount	Arrearage Owed As Of
[Name or state "none"]	$[Value] [Valuation method]	$[Amount]	[Date]
[Address and Brief property description]			
[Add rows as needed]			

(v) If Debtor pays the amount(s) specified in section (iv) (above), while making all required Post–Petition Payments (see below), Debtor's mortgage will be reinstated according to its original terms, extinguishing any right of the Secured Creditor to recover any amount alleged to have arisen prior to the filing of Debtor's petition.

(b) Post–Petition Payments.

Debtor shall pay the following Post–Petition Payments directly to the Secured Creditor listed below during the pendency of the Plan:

Secured Creditor & Property Description	Payment Amount	Payment Timing

[Name or state "none"]	$[Amount]	[How Often Payment is Due]

[Address Where Post–Petition Payments will be sent]

[Add rows as needed]

A Secured Creditor receiving Post–Petition Payments directly from the Debtor pursuant to this section must comply with Section E, below, with regard to any Notice of Contract Change (as defined in Section E) or other applicable notice as required by Section E or Bankruptcy Rule 3002.1. The Debtor shall make the Post–Petition Payments in the amount set forth on the most recent Notice of Contract Change or other applicable notice as required by Section E or Bankruptcy Rule 3002.1.

(c) Return and/or Reallocation of Distribution Payment Made to Secured Creditor.

If a Secured Creditor withdraws its claim, the sum allocated towards the payment of the Secured Creditor's claim shall be distributed by the Trustee to Debtor's remaining creditors. If the Secured Creditor has received monies from the Trustee (Distribution Payment) and returns those monies to the Trustee, the monies returned shall be distributed to the Debtor's remaining creditors. If Debtor has proposed a plan that repays his or her creditors in full, then these monies will be returned to the Debtor.

(d) Important Additional Provisions

Secured Creditors in Category 2 must comply with the "Additional Terms Applicable to Creditors and Secured Creditors" in Section E, below, regarding the following: (1) any claim for additional amounts during the pendency of the Debtor's case due to a change in the terms of the Mortgage; (2) any claim for Outstanding Obligations (defined below) that may arise during the pendency of the Debtor's case; or (3) any claim for compensation of services rendered or expenses incurred by the Secured Creditor during the pendency of the Debtor's case. Failure to comply with Section E may result in disallowance of such claims.

Category 3
Executory Contracts
& Unexpired Leases

☐ Not Applicable.

☐ See Section H, Varying Provisions.

Pursuant to 11 U.S.C. § 1322(b), Debtor assumes or rejects the following unexpired lease(s) or executory contract(s). For an executory contract or unexpired lease with an arrearage to cure, the arrearage will be cured in the Plan with regular monthly payments to be paid directly to the creditor or landlord ("Creditor") by the Debtor. The arrearage amount will be adjusted to the amount set forth in the Creditor's proof of claim, unless an objection to such amount is filed, in which event it shall be adjusted to the amount allowed by the court.

(a) Assumed.

Creditor & Property Description	Estimated Arrearage Amount	Arrearage Through Date
[Creditor name or state "none"]	$[Amount]	[Date]
[Address and brief property description]		

[Add rows as needed]

(b) Rejected.

Creditor & Property Description	Estimated Arrearage Amount	Arrearage Through Date

[Creditor name or state $[Amount]   [Date]
"none"]

[Address and brief
property description]

[Add rows as needed]

(c) Post–Petition Payments for Assumed Executory Contracts and Unexpired Leases.

Debtor shall make the following Post–Petition Payments directly to the Creditor:

Creditor & Property Description	Payment Amount	Payment Timing
[Creditor name or state "none"]	*$[Amount to be paid]*	*[How Often Payment is Due]*
[Address Post–Petition Payments will be sent]		

[Add rows as needed]

A Creditor receiving Post–Petition Payments directly from the Debtor pursuant to this section must comply with Section E, below, with regard to any Notice of Contract Change (as defined in Section E) or other applicable notice as required by Section E or Bankruptcy Rule 3002.1. The Debtor shall make the Post–Petition Payments in the amount set forth on the most recent Notice of Contract Change or other applicable notice as required by Section E or Bankruptcy Rule 3002.1.

(d) Important Additional Provisions.

Creditors in Category 3 must comply with the "Additional Terms Applicable to Creditors and Secured Creditors" in Section E, below, regarding any of the following: (1) any claim for additional amounts during the pendency of the Debtor's case due to a change in the terms of the executory contract or unexpired lease; (2) any claim for Outstanding Obligations (defined below) that may arise during the pendency of the Debtor's case; or (3) any claim for compensation of services rendered or expenses incurred by the Creditor during the pendency of the Debtor's case. Failure to comply with Section E may result in disallowance of such claims.

Category 4
Claims Secured by Personal Property, a Combination of Personal and Real Property, and Real Property Not Used as Debtor's Principal Residence

Category 4 applies to claims secured by personal property, a combination of personal and real property, and real property not used as the Debtor's principal residence.

Category 4 Definitions: The term "Secured Claim" shall refer to claims secured by personal property, a combination of personal and real property, and real property not used as the Debtor's principal residence. For purposes of this Category 4, any reference to the term "Secured Creditor" shall include, in addition to the definition of Secured Creditor in Category 2, any creditor whose interest is secured by an interest in any of the Debtor's property.

☐ Not Applicable.

☐ See Section H, Varying Provisions.

(a) List of Category 4 Claims.

Pursuant to 11 U.S.C. § 1325(a), the Secured Creditor listed below shall be paid the amount shown as their Secured Claim under this Plan. However, if the amount listed in the Secured Creditor's proof of claim is less than the amount of the Secured Claim listed below, the lesser of the two amounts will be paid. In the event that a Secured Creditor listed below fails to timely file a proof of claim in this case, by this Plan the Debtor shall be deemed to have timely filed a proof of claim on behalf of each such Secured Creditor, in the amount set forth below.

Creditor and Property Description	Debt Amount	Value of Collateral and Valuation Method	Amount To Be Paid on Claim	Interest Rate
[name, property address and description or state "none"]	*$[Amount]*	*$[value] [valuation method]*	*$[Amount to be paid or amount to pay debt in full]*	*[Interest rate, even if zero]*

[Add rows as needed]

(b) Adequate Protection.

If applicable, adequate protection shall be provided as follows: _____

[describe and provide the basis for calculation, or state not applicable]

(c) Post–Petition Payments.

Debtor shall pay the following Post–Petition Payments directly to the Secured Creditor listed below during the pendency of the Plan:

Secured Creditor & Property Description	Payment Amount	Payment Timing
[Name or state "none"] *[Address Where Post–Petition Payments will be sent]*	*$[Amount]*	*[How Often Payment is Due]*

[Add rows as needed]

A Secured Creditor receiving Post–Petition Payments directly from the Debtor pursuant to this section must comply with Section E, below, with regard to any Notice of Contract Change (as defined in Section E) or other applicable notice as required by Section E or Bankruptcy Rule 3002.1. The Debtor shall make the Post–Petition Payments in the amount set forth on the most recent Notice of Contract Change or other applicable notice as required by Section E or Bankruptcy Rule 3002.1.

(d) Return and/or Reallocation of Distribution Payment Made to Secured Creditor.

If a Secured Creditor withdraws its claim, the sum allocated towards the payment of the Secured Creditor's claim shall be distributed by the Trustee to Debtor's remaining creditors. If the Secured Creditor has received monies from the Trustee (Distribution Payment) and returns those monies to the Trustee, the monies returned shall be distributed to the Debtor's remaining creditors. If Debtor has proposed a plan that repays his or her creditors in full, then these monies will be returned to the Debtor.

(e) Important Additional Provisions.

In addition to any requirements set forth in any applicable Bankruptcy Rules, Secured Creditors in Category 4 must comply with the "Additional Terms Applicable to Creditors and Secured Creditors" in Section E, below, regarding the following: (1) any claim for additional amounts during the pendency of the Debtor's case due to a change in the terms of the Contract; (2) any claim for Outstanding Obligations (defined below) that may arise during the pendency of the Debtor's case; or (3) any claim for compensation of services rendered or expenses incurred by the Secured Creditor during the pendency of the Debtor's case. Failure to comply with Section E may result in disallowance of such claims.

Category 5
Priority, Unsecured
Claims

☐ Not Applicable.

☐ See Section H,
Varying Provisions.

All allowed claims entitled to pro rata priority treatment under 11
U.S.C. § 507 shall be paid in full in the following order:

(a) Unsecured Domestic Support Obligations.

Debtor shall remain current on all such obligations that come due
after filing the Debtor's Petition.
Unpaid obligations incurred before the Petition date are to be cured
by the Plan payments.

Creditor Status	Estimated Arrearages
[Status, e.g., child, spouse, former spouse or domestic partner]	$ *[Amount Owed through Date]*

[Add rows as needed]

(b) Other Unsecured Priority Claims.

Creditor	Type of Priority Debt	Amount Owed
[Creditor name or state "none"]	*[description]*	$*[Amount]*

[Add rows as needed]

Category 6
Codebtor Claims

☐ Not Applicable.

☐ See Section H,
Varying Provisions.

Category 6 Definition: The term " Codebtor" refers to _____.

The following Codebtor claims are to be paid pro rata until the
allowed amounts of such claims are paid in full.

Creditor	Codebtor Name	Estimated Debt Amount
[Creditor name or state "none"]	*[Codebtor Name]*	$*[Amount]*

[Add rows as needed]

Category 7
Nonpriority,
Unsecured Claims.

☐ Not Applicable.

☐ See Section H,
Varying Provisions.

Allowed unsecured, nonpriority claims shall be paid pro rata from the
balance of payments made under the Plan.

Section E
Additional Terms Ap-
plicable to Creditors
and Secured Creditors

Section E Definitions: The definitions in Section D also apply to this
Section. The term "Agreement" includes any executory contract,
unexpired lease, Mortgage (as defined in Section D) or Contract (as
defined in Section D).

*I. SECURED CREDITOR WITH SECURITY INTEREST IN
DEBTOR'S PRINCIPAL RESIDENCE.* A Secured Creditor with a
security interest in the Debtor's principal residence shall comply with
the provisions of Bankruptcy Rule 3002. 1, including the timely filing
of the notices required by subdivisions (b) and (c) of Bankruptcy Rule
3002.1 and the statement required by subdivision (g) of that rule. A
Secured Creditor's compliance with the provisions of Bankruptcy Rule
3002.1 satisfies any duty to provide notice under this Section E.

*II. CREDITOR OR SECURED CREDITOR WITH SECURITY
INTEREST IN PROPERTY OTHER THAN THE DEBTOR'S
PRINCIPAL RESIDENCE.*

(1) Notice of Contract Change.

(a) At any time during the pendency of Debtor's case, a Creditor or Secured Creditor must file on the Claims Register and serve upon the Trustee, Debtor, and Debtor's counsel (if applicable), at least thirty (30) days before the change is to take place, or a payment at a new amount is due, a notice (the "Notice of Contract Change") outlining any change(s) in the amount owed by Debtor under any Agreement, including any change(s) in the interest rate, escrow payment requirement, insurance premiums, change in payment address or other similar matters impacting the amount owed by Debtor under such Agreement (each a "Contract Change"). Additional amounts owed by the Debtor due to a Contract Change **may be disallowed by the Court** to the extent the amounts (i) were not reflected in a Notice of Contract Change filed as required by this subsection, and (ii) exceed the amount set forth in the proof of claim filed by the Creditor or Secured Creditor or deemed filed under this Plan.

(b) Within thirty (30) days of receipt of the Notice of Contract Change (defined above), Debtor shall either adjust the Post–Petition Payment to the amount set forth in the Notice of Contract Change, or file a motion with the court, objecting to the payment amount listed in the Notice of Contract Change and the stating reasons for the objection.

(c) The provisions set forth in this article are in addition to any requirements set forth in any applicable Bankruptcy Rules.

(2) Notice of Outstanding Obligations.

(a) At any time during the pendency of the Debtor's case, a Creditor or Secured Creditor shall file on the Claims Register and serve upon the Trustee, Debtor, and Debtor's counsel (if applicable) a notice containing an itemization of any obligations arising after the filing of this case that the Creditor or Secured Creditor believes are recoverable against the Debtor or against the Debtor's property (the "Outstanding Obligations"). Outstanding Obligations include, but are not limited to, all fees, expenses, or charges incurred in connection with any Agreement, such as any amounts that are due or past due related to unpaid escrow or escrow arrearages; insurance premiums; appraisal costs and fees; taxes; costs associated with the maintenance and/or upkeep of the property; and other similar items. Within thirty (30) days after the date such Outstanding Obligations were incurred, a Notice of Outstanding Obligations shall be filed on the Claims Register, sworn to by the Creditor or Secured Creditor pursuant to 28 U.S.C. § 1746, referencing the paragraph(s) (or specific section(s) and page number(s)) in the Agreement that allows for the reimbursement of the services and/or expenses.

(b) The Debtor reserves the right to file a motion with the court, objecting to the amounts listed in the Notice of Outstanding Obligations and stating the reasons for the objection. The bankruptcy court shall retain jurisdiction to resolve disputes relating to any Notice of Outstanding Obligations.

(c) The provisions set forth in this article are in addition to any requirements set forth in any applicable Bankruptcy Rules.

III. APPLICATION FOR REIMBURSEMENT OF COSTS AND FEES OF PROFESSIONALS. Pursuant to Bankruptcy Rule 2016 and Local Rule 2016–1, and in addition to any required notice or statement to be filed under Bankruptcy Rule 3002.1 (if applicable) or this Section E, a Creditor or Secured Creditor must file an application with the court if it wishes to be compensated from the Debtor or the estate for services rendered or expenses incurred by its professionals after Debtor's filing of this Petition and before the issuance of the Notice of Discharge. The application shall include a detailed statement setting forth (1) the services rendered, time expended and expenses incurred, and (2) the amounts requested. The application shall include a statement sworn to by the Creditor or Secured Creditor pursuant to 28 U.S.C. § 1746 that references the paragraph number(s) (or specific section(s) and page number(s)) in the Agreement that allows for the reimbursement of the services and/or expenses. A Creditor or Secured Creditor may request approval of multiple fees and expenses in a single application, and any application under this subsection must be filed not later than thirty (30) days after the issuance of the Notice of Discharge in this case. **Failure to comply with the provisions in this subsection may result in disallowance by the Court of such fees and expenses.** The Debtor reserves the right to object to any application filed under this subsection. This subsection will not apply to the extent that the court has previously approved a Creditor or Secured Creditor's fees or expenses pursuant to an order or conditional order.

Section F
Lien Retention

Except those expunged by order after appropriate notice pursuant to a motion or adversary proceeding, a Secured Creditor shall retain its liens as provided in 11 U.S.C. § 1325(a).

Section G
Surrendered
Property

Debtor surrenders the following property and upon confirmation of this Plan or as otherwise ordered by the court, bankruptcy stays are lifted as to the collateral to be surrendered.

☐ Not Applicable.

Claimant	Property To Be Surrendered
[Name or state "none"]	*[Brief description of property]*

[Add rows as needed]

Section H
Varying
Provisions

The Debtor submits the following provisions that vary from the Local Plan Form, Sections (A) through (G):

[Please state "none," or state the provision with reference to relevant paragraphs.]

Section I
Tax Returns,
Operating Reports
and Tax Refunds

(1) Tax Returns. While the case is pending, the Debtor shall timely file tax returns and pay taxes or obtain appropriate extensions and send a copy of either the tax return or the extension to the Trustee pursuant to 11 U.S.C. § 521(f) within thirty (30) days of filing with the taxing authority.

(2) Operating Reports. If Debtor is self-employed or operates a business either individually or in a corporate capacity, Debtor shall provide the Trustee with monthly operating reports throughout the entirety of the case.

(3) Tax Refunds. The Debtor may voluntarily elect to contribute tax refunds as lump-sum payments in Section A of this Plan. Unless the Debtor has proposed a plan that repays his or her creditors in full, the court may order the Debtor to contribute a portion of the tax refunds to the Plan. The amount to be contributed shall be determined by the court on a case-by-case basis.

Section J
Funding Shortfall

Debtor will cure any funding shortfall before the Plan is deemed completed.

Section K
Debtor's Duties

(1) *Insurance.* Debtor shall maintain insurance as required by law, contract, security agreement or Order of this court.

(2) *Payment Records to Trustee.* Debtor shall keep and maintain records of payments made to Trustee.

(3) *Payment Records to Secured Creditor(s)*. Debtor shall keep and maintain records of post-petition payments made to Secured Creditor(s).

(4) *Donation Receipts*. Where applicable, Debtor shall keep a record of all charitable donations made during the pendency of this case and maintain receipts received.

(5) *Domestic Support Obligation(s)*. Debtor shall maintain a record of all domestic support obligation payments paid directly to the recipient pursuant to a separation agreement, divorce decree, applicable child support collection unit order or other court's order. The Debtor must also complete and sign the "Certification Regarding Domestic Support Obligations" required by General Order M–338. The Certification should be returned to the Trustee when submitting the last payment under this Plan.

(6) *Change in Address*. Debtor must notify the court and the Trustee if the address or contact information changes during the pendency of the case. Notification must be made in writing within fifteen (15) days of when the change takes place.

(7) *Disposal of Property*. Debtor shall not sell, encumber, transfer or otherwise dispose of any Real Property or personal property with a value of more than $1,000 without first obtaining court approval.

(8) **This plan or amended plan has been served on all creditors more than 28 days, plus 3 additional days if service is by mail, before confirmation hearing. A certificate of service as required by Bankruptcy Rule 2002(b) and Local Bankruptcy Rules 3015–1(c) and 9078–1 has been filed.**

Debtor's Signature

Dated: _____, New York
_____, 20 ___.

_____   _____
Debtor   Debtor

_____   _____
Address   Address

Attorney's Signature   _____   _____
Attorney for Debtor   Date

Attorney Certification

I, the undersigned attorney for the Debtor, hereby certify that the foregoing chapter 13 Plan conforms to the pre-approved chapter 13 plan promulgated pursuant to [Local Bankruptcy Rule ___] of the United States Bankruptcy Court for the Southern District of New York.

_____   _____
Attorney for Debtor   Date

**UNITED STATES BANKRUPTCY COURT
SOUTHERN DISTRICT OF NEW YORK**

--x

In re   Case No.   –   (   )

                                CHAPTER 13

              ,

Debtor(s).

SSN xxx–xx– _____   SSN xxx–xx– _____
--x

ORDER CONFIRMING CHAPTER 13 PLAN

<u>Definitions</u>: If this is a joint case, use of the term "Debtor" shall also means Debtors. The term "Trustee" shall always refer to Jeffrey L. Sapir, the Chapter 13 Standing Trustee for this court, or his substitute. The term "Bankruptcy Rule" shall refer to the Federal Rules of Bankruptcy Procedure. The term "Local Rule" shall refer to the Local Rules of Bankruptcy Procedure of the United States Bankruptcy Court for the Southern District of New York. The term "Petition" refers to Debtor's bankruptcy petition filed with the court on _____, 20____. **Other definitions used in the Debtor's Plan apply to this Order.**

The Debtor's plan was filed on _____, and (if applicable) was modified on _____ (the "Plan"). The Plan or a summary of the Plan was transmitted to creditors pursuant to Bankruptcy Rule 3015 and Local Rule 3015–1(c) and 3015–2. The Court finds that the Plan meets the requirements of 11 U.S.C. § 1325.

IT IS ORDERED THAT:

The Plan is hereby CONFIRMED, and the following provisions shall apply:

PAYMENTS

The Debtor shall make ____ [number] monthly payments to the Trustee as follows:

$ ____ each month, from [month] _____, 20 ____ through [month] _____, 20____.

$ ____ each month, from [month] _____, 20 ____ through [month] _____, 20____.

$ ____ each month, from [month] _____, 20 ____ through [month] _____, 20____.

☐ Lump-sum payment(s) in the following amount(s): $ ___ on _____, 20 ___; and/or

☐ All tax refunds in excess of $1500 (less any cash exemptions in the first year, if applicable).

Unless the Debtor consented in the Plan to entry of a pay order, the Debtor will pay the amounts listed above to the Trustee by bank check, certified check, teller's check, or money order sent to the following address:

Jeffrey L. Sapir, Esq., Chapter 13 Trustee
399 Knollwood Road, Suite 102
White Plains, New York 10603

DISBURSEMENTS

Disbursements by the Trustee shall be pro rata as outlined below, and as set forth more fully in the Plan.

Category 1 (Attorney's Fees). The following fees—in excess of the portion of the pre-petition flat fee actually received prior to filing—have been approved by the court as follows:

Remainder of unpaid flat fee initially charged	$
Amount of fees approved by separate application	$ _____
Total fees	$

Category 2 (Claims Secured by a Mortgage on the Debtor's Real Property Used as a Principal Residence). By this Order, an affirmative duty is imposed on the Secured Creditor and Debtor to do all of the following:

(a) Prepetition Arrearages.

(i) For purposes of this Plan, Prepetition Arrearages shall include all sums included in the allowed claim and shall have a "0" balance upon entry of the Discharge Order in this case.

(ii) No interest will be paid on Prepetition Arrearages unless otherwise stated.

(iii) Payments made by the Trustee on Debtor's Prepetition Arrearages shall be applied **only** to those Prepetition Arrearages and not to any other amount owed by Debtor to the Secured Creditor.

(iv) Information Regarding the Arrearages.

[Insert Table in Section D, Category 2(a)(iv) of the Plan, if applicable.]

☐ Not Applicable.

(v) If Debtor pays the amount(s) specified in section (iv) (above), while making all required Post–Petition Payments (see below), Debtor's mortgage will be reinstated according to its original terms, extinguishing any right of the Secured Creditor to recover any amount alleged to have arisen prior to the filing of Debtor's petition.

(b) Post–Petition Payments.

Debtor shall pay the following Post–Petition Payments directly to the Secured Creditor listed below during the pendency of the Plan:

[Insert Table in Section D, Category 2(b) of the Plan, if applicable.]

☐ Not Applicable.

A Secured Creditor receiving Post–Petition Payments directly from the Debtor pursuant to this section must comply with Section E of the Plan, with regard to any Notice of Contract Change (as defined in Section E). The Debtor shall make the Post–Petition Payments in the amount set forth on the most recent Notice of Contract Change.

(c) Return and/or Reallocation of Distribution Payment Made to Secured Creditor.

If a Secured Creditor withdraws its claim, the sum allocated towards the payment of the Secured Creditor's claim shall be distributed by the Trustee to Debtor's remaining creditors. If the Secured Creditor has received monies from the Trustee (Distribution Payment) and returns those monies to the Trustee, the monies returned shall be distributed to the Debtor's remaining creditors. If Debtor has proposed a plan that repays his or her creditors in full, then these monies will be returned to the Debtor.

Category 3 (Executory Contracts and Unexpired Leases). Pursuant to 11 U.S.C. § 1322(b), Debtor assumes or rejects the following unexpired lease(s) or executory contract(s). For an executory contract or unexpired lease with an arrearage to cure, the arrearage will be cured as provided below, with regular monthly payments to be paid directly to the creditor or landlord ("Creditor") by the Debtor.

(a) Assumed.

[Insert Table in Section D, Category 3(a) of the Plan, if applicable.]

☐ Not Applicable.

(b) Rejected.

[Insert Table in Section D, Category 3(b) of the Plan, if applicable.]

☐ Not Applicable.

(c) Post–Petition Payments for Assumed Executory Contracts and Unexpired Leases.

[Insert Table in Section D, Category 3(c) of the Plan, if applicable.]

☐ Not Applicable.

A Creditor receiving Post–Petition Payments directly from the Debtor pursuant to this section must comply with Section E of the Plan, with regard to any Notice of Contract Change (as defined in Section E). The Debtor shall make the Post–Petition Payments in the amount set forth on the most recent Notice of Contract Change.

Category 4 (Claims Secured by Personal Property, a Combination of Personal and Real Property, and Real Property Not Used as Debtor's Principal Residence).

(a) List of Category 4 Claims.

[Insert Table in Section D, Category 4(a) of the Plan, if applicable.]

☐ Not Applicable.

(b) Adequate Protection.

The Secured Creditor received the following amounts as adequate protection post-petition and prior to confirmation: _____.

☐ Not Applicable.

(c) Post–Petition Payments.

Debtor shall pay the following Post–Petition Payments directly to the Secured Creditor listed below during the pendency of the Plan:

[Insert Table in Section D, Category 4(c) of the Plan, if applicable.]

☐ Not Applicable.

A Secured Creditor receiving Post–Petition Payments directly from the Debtor pursuant to this section must comply with Section E in the Plan, with regard to any Notice of Contract Change (as defined in Section E). The Debtor shall make the Post–Petition Payments in the amount set forth on the most recent Notice of Contract Change.

(d) Return and/or Reallocation of Distribution Payment Made to Secured Creditor.

If a Secured Creditor withdraws its claim, the sum allocated towards the payment of the Secured Creditor's claim shall be distributed by the Trustee to Debtor's remaining creditors. If the Secured Creditor has received monies from the Trustee (Distribution Payment) and returns those monies to the Trustee, the monies returned shall be distributed to the Debtor's remaining creditors. If Debtor has proposed a plan that repays his or her creditors in full, then these monies will be returned to the Debtor.

Category 5 (Priority, Unsecured Claims). All allowed claims entitled to pro rata priority treatment under 11 U.S.C. § 507 shall be paid in full in the following order:

(a) Unsecured Domestic Support Obligations.

Debtor shall remain current on all such obligations that come due after filing the Debtor's Petition. Unpaid obligations incurred before the Petition date are to be cured as follows:

[Insert Table in Section D, Category 5(a) of the Plan, if applicable.]

☐ Not Applicable.

(b) Other Unsecured Priority Claims.

[Insert Table in Section D, Category 5(b) of the Plan, if applicable.]

☐ Not Applicable.

Category 6 (Codebtor Claims). The following Codebtor (as defined in the Plan) claims are to be paid pro rata until the allowed amounts of such claims are paid in full.

[Insert Table in Section D, Category 6 of the Plan, if applicable.]

☐ Not Applicable.

Category 7 (Nonpriority, Unsecured Claims). Allowed unsecured, nonpriority claims shall be paid pro rata from the balance of payments made under the Plan.

☐ Not Applicable.

WARNING TO CREDITORS

Section E of the Plan requires Secured Creditors and Creditors (as defined in the Plan) receiving distributions above and/or listed in Category 2, 3 and 4 of the Plan to file (1) a **Notice of Contract Change** (defined in Section E of the Plan), (2) a claim for Outstanding Obligations (a **Notice of Outstanding Obligations**, defined in Section E of the Plan), (3) any notice or statement required by Bankruptcy Rule 3002.1 if such rule is applicable, and (4) pursuant to Bankruptcy Rule 2016 and Local Rule 2016–1, an **application for reimbursement of costs and fees** incurred by their professionals post-petition and prior to the issuance of a Notice of Discharge in this case. *Failure to comply with Section E of the Plan may result in disallowance of such claims.*

DEBTOR'S DUTIES

Tax Returns. While the case is pending, the Debtor shall timely file tax returns and pay taxes or obtain appropriate extensions and send a copy of either the tax return or the extension to the Trustee pursuant to 11 U.S.C. § 521(f) within thirty (30) days of filing with the taxing authority.

Operating Reports. If Debtor is self-employed or operates a business either individually or in a corporate capacity, Debtor shall provide the Trustee with monthly operating reports throughout the entirety of the case.

Insurance. Debtor shall maintain insurance as required by law, contract, security agreement or Order of this court.

Payment Records to Trustee. Debtor shall keep and maintain records of payments made to Trustee.

Payment Records to Secured Creditor(s). Debtor shall keep and maintain records of post-petition payments made to Secured Creditor(s).

Donation Receipts. Where applicable, Debtor shall keep a record of all charitable donations made during the pendency of this case and maintain receipts received.

Domestic Support Obligation(s). Debtor shall maintain a record of all domestic support obligation payments paid directly to the recipient pursuant to a separation agreement, divorce decree, applicable child support collection unit order or other court's order. The Debtor must also complete and sign the "Certification Regarding Domestic Support Obligations" required by General Order M–338. The Certification should be returned to the Trustee when submitting the last payment under this Plan.

Change in Address. Debtor must notify the court and the Trustee if the address or contact information changes during the pendency of the case. Notification must be made in writing within fifteen (15) days of when the change takes place.

Disposal of Property. Debtor shall not sell, encumber, transfer or otherwise dispose of any real property or personal property with a value of more than $1,000 without first obtaining court approval.

ADDITIONAL AND VARYING PROVISIONS

The following, additional provisions are hereby incorporated as part of the Plan:

_____.

☐ Not Applicable.

Debtor will cure any funding shortfall before the Plan is deemed completed.

Property of the estate is hereby vested in the Debtor except where the Plan specifically provides otherwise.

CONFIRMATION ORDER CONTROLS

Additional provisions set forth in the Plan shall apply unless they are inconsistent with a specific provision of this Order. If any provision of the Plan is inconsistent with this Order, the provisions of this Order shall control.

Dated: _____

_____
United States Bankruptcy Judge

GENERAL ORDER M–502. IN RE: IN THE MATTER OF DEPOSIT AND INVESTMENT OF REGISTRY FUNDS

The Court, having determined that it is necessary to adopt local procedures to ensure uniformity in the deposit, investment, and tax administration of funds in the Court's Registry,

IT IS ORDERED that the following shall govern the receipt, deposit, and investment of registry funds:

1.0. Receipt of Funds.

1.1. No money shall be sent to the Court or its officers for deposit in the Court's registry without a court order signed by the presiding judge in the case or proceeding.

1.2. The party making the deposit or transferring funds to the Court's registry shall serve the order permitting the deposit or transfer on the Clerk of Court.

1.3. Unless provided for elsewhere in this Order, all monies ordered to be paid to the Court or received by its officers in any case pending or adjudicated shall be deposited with the Treasurer of the United States in the name and to the credit of this Court pursuant to 28 U.S.C. § 2041 through depositories designated by the treasury to accept such deposit on its behalf.

2.0. Investment of Registry Funds.

2.1. Where, by order of the Court, funds on deposit with the Court are to be placed in some form of interest-bearing account or invested in a court-approved, interest-bearing instrument in accordance with Rule 67 of the Federal Rules of Civil Procedure, the Court Registry Investment System

(CRIS), administered by the Administrative Office of the United States Courts under 28 U.S.C. § 2045, shall be the only investment mechanism authorized.

2.2.   Interpleader funds deposited under 28 U.S.C. § 1335 meet the IRS definition of a Disputed Ownership Fund (DOF), a taxable entity that requires tax administration. Unless otherwise ordered by the court, interpleader funds shall be deposited in the DOF established within the CRIS and administered by the Administrative Office of the United States Courts, which shall be responsible for meeting all DOF tax administration requirements.

2.3.   The Director of Administrative Office of the United States Courts is designated as custodian for all CRIS funds. The Director or the Director's designee shall perform the duties of custodian. Funds held in the CRIS remain subject to the control and jurisdiction of the Court

2.4.   Money from each case deposited in the CRIS shall be "pooled" together with those on deposit with Treasury to the credit of other courts in the CRIS and used to purchase Government Account Series securities through the Bureau of Public Debt, which will be held at Treasury, in an account in the name and to the credit of the Director of Administrative Office of the United States Courts. The pooled funds will be invested in accordance with the principles of the CRIS Investment Policy as approved by the Registry Monitoring Group.

2.5.   An account will be established in the CRIS Liquidity Fund titled in the name of the case giving rise to the deposit invested in the fund. Income generated from fund investments will be distributed to each case based on the ratio each account's principal and earnings has to the aggregate principal and income total in the fund after the CRIS fee has been applied. Reports showing the interest earned and the principal amounts contributed in each case will be prepared and distributed to each court participating in the CRIS and made available to litigants and/or their counsel.

2.6.   For each interpleader case, an account shall be established in the CRIS Disputed Ownership Fund, titled in the name of the case giving rise to the deposit invested in the fund. Income generated from fund investments will be distributed to each case after the DOF fee has been applied and tax withholdings have been deducted from the fund. Reports showing the interest earned and the principal amounts contributed in each case will be available through the FedInvest/CMS application for each court participating in the CRIS and made available to litigants and/or their counsel. On appointment of an administrator authorized to incur expenses on behalf of the DOF in a case, the case DOF funds should be transferred to another investment account as directed by court order.

3.0.   Fees and Taxes.

3.1.   The custodian is authorized and directed by this Order to deduct the CRIS fee of an annualized 10 basis points on assets on deposit for all CRIS funds, excluding the case funds held in the DOF, for the management of investments in the CRIS. According to the Court's Miscellaneous Fee Schedule, the CRIS fee is assessed from interest earnings to the pool before a pro rata distribution of earnings is made to court cases.

3.2.   The custodian is authorized and directed by this Order to deduct the DOF fee of an annualized 20 basis points on assets on deposit in the DOF for management of investments and tax administration. According to the Court's Miscellaneous Fee Schedule, the DOF fee is assessed from interest earnings to the pool before a pro rata distribution of earnings is made to court cases. The custodian is further authorized and directed by this Order to withhold and pay federal taxes due on behalf of the DOF.

4.0.   Transition From Former Investment Procedure.

4.1.   The Clerk of Court is further directed to develop a systematic method of redemption of all existing investments and their transfer to the CRIS.

4.2.   Deposits to the CRIS DOF will not be transferred from any existing CRIS Funds. Only new deposits pursuant to 28 U.S.C. 1335 from the effective date of this order will be placed in the CRIS DOF.

4.3.   Parties not wishing to transfer certain existing registry deposits into the CRIS may seek leave to transfer them to the litigants or their designees on proper motion and approval of the judge assigned to the specific case.

4.4.   This Order supersedes and abrogates all prior orders of this Court regarding the deposit and investment of registry funds.

[Dated: October 5, 2016.]

INDEX TO UNITED STATES BANKRUPTCY COURT
FOR THE SOUTHERN DISTRICT OF NEW YORK

UNITED STATES BANKRUPTCY COURT FOR THE EASTERN DISTRICT OF NEW YORK

Including Amendments Received Through
September 1, 2017

———————

RULE 1001–1. SHORT TITLE; APPLICABILITY

(a) **Short Title.** These rules shall be known as the "E.D.N.Y. Local Bankruptcy Rules."

(b) **Applicability.**

(i) The E.D.N.Y. Local Bankruptcy Rules, as amended as of December 5, 2012, shall apply to all cases and proceedings in this Court.

(ii) The appropriate citation form for an E.D.N.Y. Local Bankruptcy Rule is "E.D.N.Y. LBR _____." For example, this rule shall be cited as "E.D.N.Y. LBR 1001–1."

(c) Modification or Suspension. In the interest of justice or for cause, the Court may modify or suspend the requirements set forth in these rules.

[Effective July 1, 1997. Amended effective July 1, 1999; May 28, 2008; December 1, 2009; December 5, 2012.]

Reference: Individual chambers rules of Judges, when applicable.

PART I. COMMENCEMENT OF CASE; PROCEEDINGS RELATING TO PETITION AND ORDER FOR RELIEF

RULE 1002–1. FILING OF PETITION

(a) Petition.

(i) A petition commencing a case under any chapter of the Bankruptcy Code in which the debtor's address is located in Kings, Richmond, or Queens County shall be filed in the office of the Clerk in the Brooklyn courthouse or designated as a Brooklyn case if filed electronically.

(ii) A petition commencing a case under any chapter of the Bankruptcy Code in which the debtor's address is located in Nassau or Suffolk County shall be filed in the office of the Clerk in the Central Islip courthouse or designated as a Central Islip case if filed electronically.

(b) Electronic Filing. Notwithstanding subdivision (a) of this rule, a petition commencing a case under any chapter of the Bankruptcy Code shall be filed by electronic means in the manner specified by the General Order on Electronic Filing Procedures and these rules.

(c) Incomplete Filing. In the event that a petition is submitted without full compliance with all requirements, the Clerk shall accept the same for filing and shall provide the debtor, debtor's counsel and the trustee, if any, with a notice of the deficiencies.

[Effective July 1, 1997. Amended effective July 1, 1998; July 1, 1999; May 28, 2008.]

Cross Reference: E.D.N.Y. LBR 1073–1, 9011–1.

References: Bankruptcy Code § 521; Court's Website; General Order on Electronic Filing Procedures.

RULE 1005–1. DEBTOR'S ADDRESS IN PETITION

If the debtor's post office address is not the debtor's residence or place of business, the petition shall also state the debtor's residence or place of business, including the street number, street, apartment or suite number and zip code.

[Effective July 1, 1997.]

RULE 1005–2. AMENDING CAPTION TO CORRECT DEBTOR'S NAME

If the debtor's name is incorrect in the caption of the petition, the debtor shall file an application and proposed order amending the caption to correct the debtor's name.

[Effective May 28, 2008.]

Reference: Court's Website.

Committee Note: A form of order is located at the intake counter of the Clerk's Office and at the Court's Website.

RULE 1007–1. LIST OF CREDITORS

(a) Creditor List. In addition to the schedules, a list shall be filed which sets forth the names of all creditors in alphabetical order (the "Creditor List"). The Creditor List shall also set forth the post office address, zip code, and the specific amount of debt, if known, owed to each listed creditor. The provider of the Creditor List shall certify that it is accurate.

(b) Schedules and Lists Filed After Filing of Petition. Schedules D, E, and F, which were not submitted at the time of filing of the petition but are filed thereafter, shall be accompanied by (i) Local Form No. USBC–64 entitled "Affidavit Pursuant to Local Rule 1007–1(b)" and (ii) the applicable filing fee.

[Effective July 1, 1997. Amended effective July 1, 1999; May 28, 2008; December 1, 2015.]

Cross–Reference: E.D.N.Y. LBR 1009–1

References: Court's Website

Committee Note: Local Form No. USBC–64 is available at the intake counter of the Clerk's office and at the Court's Website

RULE 1007–2. EXEMPTIONS AND WAIVERS REGARDING CREDIT COUNSELING REQUIREMENT; WAIVER OF PERSONAL FINANCIAL MANAGEMENT COURSE

(a) A motion pursuant to Bankruptcy Code § 109(h)(3)(B) for a further exemption from the credit counseling requirement imposed by Bankruptcy Code § 109(h)(1) shall be made on notice to the trustee and the United States trustee, and shall explain the circumstances which warrant the relief requested.

(b) A motion pursuant to Bankruptcy Code § 109(h)(4) for a waiver of the credit counseling requirement imposed by Bankruptcy Code § 109(h)(1) or a waiver of the requirement to file a statement regarding completion of an instructional course concerning personal financial management imposed by Bankruptcy Code § 727(a)(11) shall be on notice to the trustee and the United States trustee and should be supported by documentary evidence of the debtor's entitlement to the relief requested.

[Effective July 1, 1997. Amended effective May 28, 2008.]

References: Bankruptcy Code §§ 109(h)(1), (3) and (4), 727(a)(11).

RULE 1007–3. MAILING MATRIX

(a) General Requirements.

(i) The debtor shall file a mailing matrix which shall include, in alphabetical order, the name and last known mailing address (including zip codes) for every scheduled creditor. The mailing matrix shall also include those agencies and officers of the United States entitled to receive notice under Bankruptcy Rule 2002(j). The mailing matrix shall be filed at the time the list of creditors required by Bankruptcy Rule 1007(a) is filed.

(ii) If the debtor is a partnership, the mailing matrix shall contain the names and current mailing addresses of each general and limited partner.

(iii) If the debtor is a corporation, the mailing matrix shall contain: (1) the names and current mailing addresses of the present officers and directors and the position held by each, or if none, the immediate past officers and past directors; and (2) the name and address of any person who may be served pursuant to Bankruptcy Rule 7004(b)(3). In addition, the debtor shall file with its list of equity security holders a separate mailing matrix containing the name and last known address or place of business of each equity security holder.

(b) Accuracy of Information Provided and Amendment of Mailing Matrix.
The debtor and debtor's attorney are responsible for the preparation of the mailing matrix and any amendments thereto. Upon the need for any amendment to a mailing matrix, the debtor shall file an amended creditor mailing matrix together with a list of all creditors who were added or deleted. The debtor shall file Local Form No. USBC–44 entitled "Verification of Mailing Matrix/List of Creditors."

[Effective July 1, 1997. Amended effective May 28, 2008; December 1, 2009.]

References: Court's Website; General Order on Electronic Filing Procedures.

Committee Note: Specifications for preparation of the mailing matrix are available at the intake counter of the Clerk's office and at the Court's Website. Local Form No. USBC–44 is available at the intake counter of the Clerk's office and at the Court's Website.

RULE 1007–4. DEBTOR'S AFFIDAVIT TO BE FILED IN CHAPTER 11 CASES

(a) Contents of Affidavit.
In addition to the requirements set forth in Bankruptcy Rule 1007, a debtor in a chapter 11 case shall file an affidavit setting forth:

(i) whether the debtor is a small business debtor within the meaning of Bankruptcy Code § 101(51D);

(ii) the nature of the debtor's business and a statement of the circumstances leading to the debtor's filing under chapter 11;

(iii) in a case originally commenced under chapter 7, 12 or 13, the name and address of any trustee appointed in the case and, in a case originally commenced under chapter 7, the names and addresses of the members of any creditors' committee elected under Bankruptcy Code § 705;

(iv) the names and addresses of the members of, and professionals employed by, any committee organized prior to the order for relief in the chapter 11 case, and a description of the circumstances surrounding the formation of the committee and the date of its formation;

(v) with respect to each of the holders of the 20 largest general unsecured claims, excluding insiders: name, address (including the number, street, apartment or suite number, and zip code, if not included in the post office address), telephone number, name(s) of person(s) familiar with the debtor's account, amount of the claim, and whether the claim is contingent, unliquidated, disputed, or partially secured;

(vi) with respect to each of the holders of the 5 largest secured claims: name, address (including the number, street, apartment or suite number, and zip code, if not included in the post office address), amount of the claim, a description and an estimate of the value of the collateral securing the claim, and whether the claim or lien is disputed;

(vii) a summary of the debtor's assets and liabilities;

(viii) the number and classes of shares of stock, debentures, or other securities of the debtor that are publicly held, and the number of record holders thereof, listing separately those held by each of the debtor's officers and directors and the amounts so held;

(ix) a list of all of the debtor's property in the possession or custody of any custodian, public officer, mortgagee, pledgee, assignee of rents, or secured creditor, or agent for any such entity, giving the name, address, and telephone number of each such entity, the title of any proceeding relating thereto, and the court in which it is pending;

(x) a list of the premises owned, leased, or held under any other arrangement from which the debtor operates its business;

(xi) the location of the debtor's significant assets, the location of its books and records, and the nature, location, and value of any assets held by the debtor outside the territorial limits of the United States;

(xii) the nature and present status of each action or proceeding, pending or threatened, against the debtor or its property where a judgment against the debtor or a seizure of its property may be imminent;

(xiii) the names of the debtor's existing senior management, their tenure with the debtor, and a summary of their relevant responsibilities and experience;

(xiv) the estimated amount of the weekly payroll to employees (exclusive of officers, directors, stockholders, partners and members) for the 30–day period following the filing of the chapter 11 petition;

(xv) the amount paid and proposed to be paid for services for the 30–day period following the filing of the chapter 11 petition—

(A) if the debtor is a corporation, to officers and directors;

(B) if the debtor is an individual or a partnership, to the individual or the members of the partnership; and

(C) if a financial or business consultant has been retained by the debtor, to the consultant;

(xvi) a schedule, for the 30–day period following the filing of the chapter 11 petition, of estimated cash receipts and disbursements, net cash gain or loss, obligations and receivables expected to accrue but remaining unpaid, other than professional fees, and any other information relevant to an understanding of the foregoing; and

(xvii) such additional information as may be necessary to fully inform the Court of the debtor's rehabilitation prospects.

(b) When to File. In a chapter 11 case, upon the entry of an order for relief, the affidavit shall be filed forthwith, but no later than 14 days after the date on which the order for relief is entered.

(c) Waiver of Requirements. Upon motion of the debtor on notice to the United States trustee showing that it is impracticable or impossible to furnish any of the foregoing information, the Court may waive any of the foregoing provisions, with the exception of those contained in paragraphs (i) through (vii) of subdivision (a) of this rule.

[Effective May 28, 2008. Amended effective December 1, 2009.]

References: Bankruptcy Code §§ 101(51D), 705.

RULE 1009–1. AMENDMENTS OF VOLUNTARY PETITIONS, LISTS, SCHEDULES AND STATEMENTS

(a) Effectuation of Amendment. An order is not required to file an amended voluntary petition, list, schedule, or statement by the debtor. Amendments to Schedules D, E, or F shall be accompanied by (i) Local Form No. USBC–63 entitled "Affidavit Pursuant to Local Rule 1009–1(a)" and (ii) the applicable filing fee. An amendment shall not be effective until proof of service in accordance with subdivision (b) of this rule has been filed. If a creditor is added or deleted, an amended mailing matrix shall also be filed.

(b) Notice of Amendment. A complete copy of the voluntary petition, list, schedule, or statement, as amended, together with Local Form No. USBC–63, shall be served by the amending party upon:

(i) the United States trustee;

(ii) the trustee;

(iii) all creditors who were added or deleted; and

(iv) any other party affected thereby.

If the amendment affects claimed exemptions, the amending party must also serve all creditors. If the amendment adds a creditor, the papers to be served on such creditor shall consist of the amendment, together with copies of all notices previously sent to creditors that appear in the Court's docket, including without limitation the notice informing creditors of the date by which all proofs of claim must be filed. If the amendment modifies an existing creditor's claim, service on such creditor shall include any notices informing creditors of the date by which proofs of claim must be filed.

[Effective July 1, 1997. Amended effective July 1, 1999; May 28, 2008; December 1, 2009; December 1, 2015.]

Cross–Reference: E.D.N.Y. LBR 3007–2, 4003–1, 9004–1

References: Court's Website; General Order on Electronic Filing Procedures

Committee Note: Local Form No. USBC–63 is available at the intake counter of the Clerk's office and at the Court's Website

RULE 1013–1. INVOLUNTARY PETITIONS

(a) Entry of Order for Relief Upon Default of Alleged Debtor. An order for relief shall be entered if proof of service of the summons and involuntary petition has been filed and the alleged debtor has not timely responded.

(b) Notice of Entry. Upon entry of an order for relief in an involuntary case, the Clerk shall forthwith serve a copy of the order with notice of entry upon the petitioners, the debtor, the debtor's attorney of record, if any, and the United States trustee.

(c) Dismissal. The Court may dismiss the case if proof of service of the summons and involuntary petition pursuant to Bankruptcy Rule 7004 is not timely filed.

[Effective July 1, 1997. Amended effective May 28, 2008.]

Reference: Bankruptcy Rule 7004.

RULE 1017–1. DISMISSAL OF CASE AFTER CONVERSION

If a case has been converted from chapter 11 to chapter 7, and the trustee is seeking to dismiss the case for failure of the debtor to attend the meeting of creditors under Bankruptcy Code § 341, the trustee must file an affidavit setting forth what efforts, if any, have been made to locate and serve the debtor.

[Effective July 1, 1997. Amended effective May 28, 2008.]

RULE 1073–1. ASSIGNMENT OF CASES AND PROCEEDINGS

(a) Assignment of Cases. The Clerk shall randomly assign cases to the Judges. Notwithstanding the foregoing, the Court may adopt internal procedures whereby cases are assigned to Judges sitting in Brooklyn or Central Islip depending upon the location of the debtor's address.

(b) Petitions of Affiliates or Related Cases. Notwithstanding subdivision (a) of this rule, cases involving affiliated or related debtors shall be assigned to the Judge to whom the first such case was assigned, and any case subsequently filed by a debtor who has previously filed a petition shall be assigned to the Judge to whom the last such case was assigned.

(c) Assignments and Reassignments. Notwithstanding the provisions of this rule, the Chief Judge may, in the interests of justice or the proper administration of the Court, assign or re-assign cases or proceedings.

[Effective July 1, 1997. Amended effective March 1, 1998; July 1, 1999; May 28, 2008.]

Cross–Reference: E.D.N.Y. LBR 1002–1.

RULE 1073–2. DISCLOSURE OF RELATED CASES

(a) Definition of Related Cases. Cases shall be deemed "Related Cases" for purposes of this rule and E.D.N.Y. LBR 1073–1 if the earlier case was pending at any time within 8 years before the filing of the current petition, and the debtors in such cases:

(i) are the same;

(ii) are spouses or ex-spouses;

(iii) are affiliates, as defined in Bankruptcy Code § 101(2);

(iv) are general partners in the same partnership;

(v) are a partnership and one or more of its general partners;

(vi) are partnerships which share one or more common general partners; or

(vii) have, or within 180 days of the commencement of either of the Related Cases had, an interest in property that was or is included in the property of the other debtor's estate under Bankruptcy Code § 541(a).

(b) Disclosure of Related Cases.

(i) A petition commencing a case shall be accompanied by Local Form No. USBC–2 entitled "E.D.N.Y. LBR 1073–2 Statement."

(ii) The E.D.N.Y. LBR 1073–2 Statement shall be executed by the debtor or any other petitioner under penalty of perjury and shall disclose, to the petitioner's best knowledge, information, and belief:

(A) whether any Related Case is pending or has been pending at any time;

(B) the name of the debtor in such Related Case;

(C) the case number of such Related Case;

(D) the district and division in which such Related Case is or was pending;

(E) the Judge to whom such Related Case was assigned;

(F) the current status of such Related Case;

(G) the manner in which the cases are related; and

(H) any real property listed in a debtor's Schedule A, which was also listed in a Schedule A filed in a Related Case.

(c) Sanctions. The failure to fully and truthfully provide all information required by the E.D.N.Y. LBR 1073–2 Statement may subject the debtor or any other petitioner and their attorney to appropriate sanctions, including without limitation, conversion, the appointment of a trustee, or the dismissal of the case with prejudice.

[Effective July 1, 1999. Amended effective May 28, 2008; December 1, 2015.]

Cross–Reference: E.D.N.Y. LBR 1073–1

References: Bankruptcy Code §§ 101(2), 541(a); Court's Website

Committee Note: Local Form No. USBC–2 is available at the Court's Website and at the intake counter of the Clerk's office

RULE 1073–3. CORPORATE DISCLOSURE

(a) Who Must File. Any corporation that is a debtor shall file a statement that identifies any corporation that directly or indirectly owns 10% or more of any class of the debtor's equity interests, or states that there are no entities to report under this subdivision (the "E.D.N.Y. LBR 1073–3 Statement").

(b) Time for Filing.

(i) In a voluntary case, the debtor shall file the E.D.N.Y. LBR 1073–3 Statement with the petition.

(ii) In an involuntary case, the debtor shall file the E.D.N.Y. LBR 1073–3 Statement within 14 days after the entry of the order for relief.

(iii) Upon any change in the information required under this rule, the debtor shall promptly file an amended E.D.N.Y. LBR 1073–3 Statement.

[Effective May 28, 2008. Amended effective December 1, 2009.]

Reference: Bankruptcy Rule 7007.1; Federal Rule of Civil Procedure 7.1.

RULE 1074–1. CORPORATE RESOLUTION; PARTNERSHIP STATEMENT

(a) Corporate Resolution. A voluntary petition or consent to an involuntary petition filed by a corporation shall be accompanied by a duly attested copy of the corporate resolution authorizing, or other appropriate authorization for, the filing.

(b) Partnership or Limited Liability Partnership Statements. A voluntary petition filed by, or consent to an involuntary petition filed on behalf of, a partnership or limited liability partnership shall be accompanied by a duly attested statement that all partners whose consent is required for the filing have consented.

(c) Limited Liability Company Statements. A voluntary petition filed by, or consent to an involuntary petition filed on behalf of a limited liability company shall be accompanied by a duly attested statement by the managing member, or by at least one member if there is no managing member, that the filing is duly authorized.

[Effective July 1, 1997. Amended effective May 28, 2008.]

PART II. OFFICERS AND ADMINISTRATION; NOTICES; MEETINGS; EXAMINATIONS; ELECTIONS; ATTORNEYS AND ACCOUNTANTS

RULE 2002–1. NOTICES OF PRESENTMENT

(a) Contents of Notice of Presentment. Whenever "notice and a hearing" (as defined in Bankruptcy Code § 102(1)) are specified in the Bankruptcy Code or Bankruptcy Rules but a hearing is not mandatory, the entity proposing to act or obtain an order, in lieu of proceeding by notice of hearing, may proceed by filing a motion or application with the Clerk, together with proof of service and a notice of presentment. The notice of presentment shall set forth:

(i) the date by which objections or responses to the proposed action or order shall be served and filed;

(ii) the date and time when the action will be taken or the proposed order will be presented for signature if there is no objection, and a statement that the action will be taken or the order may be entered without a hearing unless a timely objection is made; and

(iii) the date on which a hearing will be held if a timely objection is made.

(b) Proposed Order. A copy of the proposed order shall be filed and served along with the notice of presentment.

(c) Time for Notice. A notice of presentment under subdivision (a) of this rule shall provide at least 21 days' notice of the date set for the proposed action or the presentment of the proposed order. If papers are served by first-class mail, an additional 3 days shall be added to the minimum service requirement. If papers are served by overnight mail or courier, an additional day shall be added to the minimum service requirement.

(d) Entities to Receive Notice. In addition to the requirements of Bankruptcy Rule 2002 and E.D.N.Y. LBR 2002–2, a notice of presentment under subdivision (a) of this rule shall be served upon any entity having or claiming an interest in the subject matter of the proposed action or order or who otherwise would be affected by the proposed action or order.

(e) Objection. Any objection to the proposed action or order shall be in writing, set forth the nature of the objector's interest in the estate, state the reasons and legal basis for the objection, and be served on the proponent and filed at least 7 days prior to the date set for the proposed action or the presentment of the proposed order. The objection and proof of service shall be filed and a courtesy copy shall be provided to chambers.

[Effective July 1, 1997. Amended effective July 1, 1999; May 28, 2008; December 1, 2009.]

Cross–References: E.D.N.Y. LBR 2002–2, 3015–2, 4001–1, 5070–1.

Committee Note: Each Judge's chambers should also be consulted regarding the relief that may be sought by notice of presentment.

RULE 2002–2. NOTICE TO GOVERNMENTAL AGENCIES

(a) United States Trustee. Unless the case is a chapter 9 case or the United States trustee requests otherwise, any notice required to be given to creditors also shall be given to the United States trustee. Notices to the United States trustee shall be sent to the address specified at the Court's Website.

(b) Internal Revenue Service. Except as otherwise requested by it, any notices required to be given to the Internal Revenue Service shall also be given to the United States Attorney for the Eastern District of New York and the Tax Division of the U.S. Department of Justice. Notices to these entities shall be sent to the addresses specified at the Court's Website.

(c) New York State Department of Taxation and Finance. Except as otherwise requested by it, any notices required to be given to the New York State Department of Taxation and Finance shall also be given to the New York State Attorney General. Notices to these entities shall be sent to the addresses specified at the Court's Website.

[Effective July 1, 1997. Amended effective July 1, 1999; May 28, 2008.]

Reference: Court's Website.

Committee Note: The addresses referred to in this local rule are available at the intake counter of the Clerk's office and at the Court's Website.

RULE 2003–1. MANDATORY DISCLOSURES IN CHAPTER 13 CASES

(a) In all chapter 13 cases, the debtor shall provide the following documents to the trustee no later than 7 days before the first date set for the meeting of creditors pursuant to Bankruptcy Code § 341(a):

(i) copies of all payment advices or other evidence of payment received within 60 days before the date of the filing of the petition, by the debtor from any employer of the debtor, or a written statement that such proof of income does not exist;

(ii) copies of affidavits of contribution and copies of all payment advices or other evidence of payment received within 60 days before the date of the filing of the petition, by each person contributing to the proposed plan or to payment of expenses of the debtor's household;

(iii) except in cases where the debtor proposes to pay 100% to unsecured creditors, documentation (other than tax assessments) of the current value of all real property, condominiums, cooperative apartments, vacant land, cemetery plots and/or timeshares in which the debtor has an ownership interest. If a valuation is prepared by a real estate broker, then the broker shall (A) have personally inspected the premises, (B) maintain an office in the vicinity of the premises, and (C) provide information on 4 recent comparable sales. All valuations must be less than 90 days old prior to filing;

(iv) copies of leases for all real property for which the debtor is lessor;

(v) in a case where the debtor had a prior chapter 13 case pending within a year of the filing date, a copy of a detailed affidavit of changed circumstances, describing the disposition of each prior case and explaining how the debtor's circumstances have changed; and

(vi) copies of canceled checks, receipts, money orders, or other documentation of payment of all mortgage installments, real property lease payments, auto loan payments, and co-op or condo maintenance and management fees that have come due since the petition was filed.

(b) A debtor shall provide the following documents to the trustee no later than 7 days before the first date set for confirmation of the chapter 13 plan:

(i) copies of canceled checks, receipts, money orders or other documentation of payment of all mortgage installments and real property lease payments that have come due since the disclosure was made under subdivision (a)(vi) of this rule;

(ii) a copy of an affidavit by the debtor stating:

(A) whether the debtor has paid all amounts that are required to be paid under a domestic support obligation and that first became payable after the date of the filing of the petition if the debtor is required by a judicial or administrative order or by statute to pay such domestic support obligation; or

(B) that the debtor has no domestic support obligations; and

(iii) a copy of an affidavit by the debtor stating whether the debtor has filed all applicable federal, state, and local tax returns as required by Bankruptcy Code § 1308.

(c) A debtor shall file the original affidavits required under subdivisions (a)(ii) and (v), and (b)(ii) and (iii) of this rule.

(d) A debtor shall promptly provide to the trustee any other documents within the scope of Bankruptcy Rule 2004(b) that the trustee may request from time to time.

[Effective July 1, 1999. Amended effective May 28, 2008; December 1, 2009.]

Cross–Reference: E.D.N.Y. LBR 4002–1.

References: Bankruptcy Code §§ 1308, 1325(a)(8), (9); Bankruptcy Rule 2004(b).

RULE 2004–1. ASSERTION OF CLAIM OF PRIVILEGE, UNIFORM DEFINITIONS IN DISCOVERY REQUESTS, AND COUNSEL FEES ON TAKING DEPOSITIONS MORE THAN 100 MILES FROM THE COURTHOUSE, IN RULE 2004 EXAMINATIONS

District Rules 26.2, 26.3 and 30.1 shall apply to requests for the production of documents under Bankruptcy Rule 2004.

[Effective December 5, 2012.]

References: District Rules 26.2, 26.3 and 30.1.

RULE 2014–1. EMPLOYMENT OF PROFESSIONAL PERSONS

(a) In addition to the requirements set forth in Bankruptcy Rule 2014(a), an application for the employment of a professional person pursuant to Bankruptcy Code §§ 327, 1103 or 1114 shall state:

(i) the terms and conditions of the employment, including the terms of any retainer, hourly fee, or contingent fee arrangement;

(ii) all compensation already paid or promised to the professional person in contemplation of or in connection with the services to be performed, and the specific source of such compensation; and

(iii) whether the professional person has previously rendered any professional services to the trustee, debtor, debtor in possession, the extent thereof and the status of the compensation therefor.

(b) In addition to the requirements set forth in Bankruptcy Rule 2014(a), the application referred to in subdivision (a) shall be accompanied by a verified statement of the person to be employed stating that such person does not hold or represent an interest adverse to the estate except as specifically disclosed therein, and where employment is sought pursuant to Bankruptcy Code § 327(a), that the professional is disinterested.

(c) In a chapter 11 case, in addition to the requirements set forth in Bankruptcy Rule 2014(a), the verified statement required to accompany an application for approval of the employment of an attorney under § 327(a) of the Bankruptcy Code shall include a statement setting forth the attorney's qualifications and experience in handling chapter 11 cases to enable the Court to evaluate the attorney's competence to represent the trustee or debtor in possession in conducting the case.

(d) In addition to the requirements set forth in subdivisions (a) and (b), and Bankruptcy Rule 2014(a), an application seeking authorization to employ an accountant shall include a verified statement by an authorized representative of the accounting firm that sets forth:

(i) whether or not the accountant is a certified public accountant; and

(ii) the estimated cost of the accountant's proposed services, the basis of such estimate and the extent to which the accountant is familiar with the books or accounts of the debtor.

(e) All ex parte proposed orders and supporting documentation for employment of any professional must be submitted to the United States trustee for review prior to filing.

[Effective July 1, 1997. Amended effective May 28, 2008; August 19, 2011.]

Cross–Reference: E.D.N.Y. LBR 6005–1.

References: Bankruptcy Code §§ 327, 1103.

RULE 2015–1. MONTHLY REPORTS IN ALL CHAPTER 11, 12 AND BUSINESS CHAPTER 13 CASES

The debtor in possession or trustee in all chapter 11 and 12 cases, or a chapter 13 debtor engaged in business within the meaning of Bankruptcy Code § 1304(a), shall file and serve upon the United States trustee and counsel for the creditors' committee (if any) in a chapter 11 or 12 case, or the trustee in a chapter 13 case, and provide to chambers, a verified monthly report no later than the 20th day of each month, which shall be completed in the manner prescribed by the United States trustee Guidelines, and in the case of a small business chapter 11 debtor, in accordance with Bankruptcy Code § 308 when such provisions shall become effective. Failure to file required reports may constitute cause for dismissal or conversion of the case.

[Effective July 1, 1997. Amended effective May 28, 2008.]

References: Bankruptcy Code §§ 308, 1304(a).

RULE 2015–2. STORAGE OF BOOKS AND RECORDS

The trustee or debtor in possession may place in storage, at the expense of the estate, the debtor's books, records, and papers.

[Effective December 5, 2012.]

Comment

This rule sets no time limit on the storage of books and records. On request, the Court may issue an appropriate order limiting storage of the debtor's books, records, and papers. Disposal of the debtor's books, records, and papers is governed by §§ 363 and 554 of the Bankruptcy Code.

RULE 2016–1. COMPENSATION OF PROFESSIONALS

A person seeking an award of compensation or reimbursement of expenses shall comply with the requirements contained in any fee guidelines promulgated by the United States trustee.* A copy of the order authorizing the retention of the professional shall accompany all such applications.

[Effective July 1, 1997. Amended effective July 1, 1999; May 28, 2008.]

   * [**Publisher's Note:** *See also* General Order 613, *post.*]

RULE 2016–2. FINAL COMPENSATION OR REIMBURSEMENT OF EXPENSES IN CHAPTER 7 CASES

A person seeking a final award of compensation or reimbursement of expenses in a chapter 7 case shall file and serve an application on the trustee and the United States trustee no later than 21 days prior to the date of the hearing on the trustee's final account. Failure to file and serve an application within the time prescribed by this rule may result in its disallowance. Objections, if any, to such application shall be filed at least 7 days prior to the date of the hearing.

[Effective July 1, 1997. Amended effective May 28, 2008; December 1, 2009.]

RULE 2017–1. DESCRIPTION OF PRE–PETITION SERVICES OF DEBTOR'S COUNSEL IN CHAPTER 7 OR 13 CASES

Upon the filing of a chapter 7 or 13 case, the attorney for the debtor shall submit a statement, together with and in addition to the statement required by Bankruptcy Rule 2016(b), containing:

(i) a description of pre-petition services performed for and on behalf of the debtor in contemplation of the petition;

(ii) an itemization of the services performed by each member, associate, or paraprofessional of the firm;

(iii) the time spent in the performance thereof, including the dates upon which the services were rendered and the time spent on each date;

(iv) an itemization of expenses incurred by the debtor's attorney; and

(v) the firm's billing rates for comparable services for each member, associate or paraprofessional.

[Effective July 1, 1997. Amended effective May 28, 2008.]

Reference: Bankruptcy Rule 2016(b).

RULE 2090–1. PRACTICE BEFORE THE COURT; WITHDRAWAL AS ATTORNEY OF RECORD; SUSPENSION

(a) **General.** An attorney who may practice in the District Court pursuant to District Rule 1.3 may practice in this Court.

(b) **Pro Hac Vice.** Upon motion made in accordance with District Rule 1.3(c), a member in good standing of the bar of any state or of any United States District Court may be permitted to practice in this Court in a particular case, adversary proceeding, or contested matter.

A member in good standing of the bar of any state or of any United States District Court whose involvement in the case is limited to filing a notice of appearance under Bankruptcy Rule 2002, filing a proof of claim or interest, or representing a child support creditor, may appear for those purposes without obtaining authorization to appear pro hac vice.

(c) **Pro Se.** An individual may appear pro se. Such an individual shall include his or her residence or place of business address and telephone number on every paper filed with the court.

(d) **Withdrawal or Substitution of Attorneys of Record.** An attorney who has been authorized to be retained or has appeared as the attorney of record for any party in any case or adversary proceeding may not withdraw or be relieved or displaced except by order after notice to the party represented, any adversaries (if applicable), the United States trustee and the trustee. An application for such an order shall include a showing by affidavit of satisfactory reasons for withdrawal or displacement and the posture of the case, including the status of any pending matters.

(e) Suspension.

(i) Any attorney admitted to practice before this Court may, for good cause shown, after notice and a hearing, be suspended from practice before the Court for an indefinite period, pending the outcome of disciplinary proceedings in the District Court.

(ii) Grounds for suspension include conviction in another court of a serious crime; disbarment, suspension or reprimand by another court, with or without the attorney's consent; or resignation from the bar of another court while an investigation into allegations of misconduct is pending.

(iii) In all pending cases in which a suspended attorney has made an appearance, the Clerk shall issue notice of the suspension to any party affected thereby.

(iv) The Court may order a suspended attorney to return any fees received in cases currently before the Court, pending the outcome of disciplinary proceedings in the District Court.

[Effective July 1, 1997. Amended effective May 28, 2008.]

References: District Rules 1.3, 1.4 and 1.5; Bankruptcy Rule 9014; Court's Website.

Committee Note: Forms to request authorization to appear pro hac vice, and a proposed order are available at the intake counter of the Clerk's office and at the Court's Website.

RULE 2090–2. APPEARANCE BY DEBTOR'S COUNSEL IN ADVERSARY PROCEEDINGS, CONTESTED MATTERS, ETC.

(a) In General. The attorney of record for a debtor, or an attorney acting of counsel to such attorney and who is knowledgeable in all aspects of the case, shall appear on behalf of the debtor in every aspect of the case, including but not limited to appearing at the Bankruptcy Code § 341 meeting and any adjournments thereof, and defending an adversary proceeding, contested matter, motion, or application filed against the debtor during the pendency of the bankruptcy case. Except as provided in subdivisions (b) and (c) of this rule, an attorney of record for a debtor shall not exclude from the attorney's representation of the debtor any aspect of the case, including but not limited to, appearing at the Bankruptcy Code § 341 meeting and any adjournment thereof, and defending an adversary proceeding, contested matter, motion, or application filed against the debtor during the pendency of the bankruptcy case.

(b) Exclusion of Adversary Proceeding Defense from Scope of Representation. If the debtor's pre-petition written retainer agreement with the attorney of record excludes the defense of an adversary proceeding from the agreed scope of representation, and if the attorney will not for that reason appear on the debtor's behalf in the adversary proceeding, and unless the debtor has obtained new counsel for the defense of such adversary proceeding and that counsel has appeared in the adversary proceeding, the attorney shall, within 14 days of service of the summons and complaint, file and serve on the debtor and counsel for the plaintiff a signed copy of the relevant portions of the retainer agreement (which may be redacted, subject to further disclosure upon direction by the Court, to the extent required to protect privileged or proprietary information, but which must include the signature page) and an affirmation setting forth:

(i) that such attorney has not been retained to represent the debtor in the adversary proceeding and for that reason will not undertake the representation;

(ii) the applicable provisions of the attorney's written retainer agreement with the debtor;

(iii) that such attorney, following the commencement of the adversary proceeding, has advised the debtor of:

(A) the nature of the adversary proceeding and the claims asserted therein;

(B) the debtor's obligation to file and serve an appropriate response to the initial pleading and the consequences of failing timely to answer or move with respect to the pleading;

(C) the requirements of form and time limits applicable to the preparation, filing and service of a responsive pleading; and

(D) how to serve and file a responsive pleading; and

(iv) if the attorney is, despite best efforts, unable to contact the debtor to communicate the information described in subdivision (b)(iii) of this rule, the affirmation shall also set forth the nature of the attorney's efforts to contact the debtor.

(c) Relief from Representation of Chapter 11 or Chapter 13 Debtor Upon Conversion to Chapter 7. Notwithstanding the requirements of subdivision (a) of this rule, upon conversion of a chapter 11 or chapter 13 case to a case under chapter 7, counsel for the debtor or chapter 11 trustee, if one was appointed, is relieved from any further obligation to represent the debtor or the chapter 11 trustee in the bankruptcy case, except that such counsel shall assist the debtor or chapter 11 trustee in the performance of their duties upon conversion under any applicable statute or rule.

(d) Relief from Representation of the Debtor Under Other Circumstances. Applications for relief from representation of a debtor under circumstances other than those described in subdivision (b) of this rule shall be made pursuant to E.D.N.Y. LBR 2090–1. The filing of a withdrawal application pursuant to E.D.N.Y. LBR 2090–1 does not suspend the requirements of subdivision (a) of this rule or toll the running of the time limitations applicable to the interposition of responses to papers initiating adversary proceedings, contested matters, motions, or any other application against the debtor.

(e) Sanctions. An attorney of record for a debtor who fails or refuses without reasonable excuse to represent the debtor in any aspect of the case, including but not limited to appearing at the Bankruptcy Code § 341 meeting and any adjournments thereof, and defending an adversary proceeding, contested matter, motion, or application filed against the debtor during the pendency of the bankruptcy case (other than any attorney who excludes the defense of adversary proceedings from the attorney's representation of the debtor in accordance with subdivision (b) of this rule and who complies with all of the requirements of subdivision (b) of this rule) may, after notice and a hearing, be sanctioned pursuant to this rule and may be ordered to disgorge fees paid in connection with the case pursuant to Bankruptcy Rule 2017.

[Adopted effective July 1, 1999. Amended effective May 28, 2008; December 1, 2009.]

Cross–Reference: E.D.N.Y. LBR 2090–1.

Reference: Bankruptcy Rule 2017.

PART III. CLAIMS AND DISTRIBUTION TO CREDITORS AND EQUITY INTEREST HOLDERS; PLANS

RULE 3007–1. OBJECTIONS TO CLAIMS

A motion to reduce, expunge, or reclassify a claim shall have attached thereto a copy of the proof of claim as filed (without exhibits) which identifies the claimant by name and the claim number. Each reference to a filed claim in the moving papers and any proposed order to be entered thereon shall refer to the claim both by name of the claimant and claim number. The title of the motion shall refer to the claim by claim number.

[Effective July 1, 1997. Amended effective July 1, 1999.]

Committee Note: Each Judge's chambers should be consulted regarding procedures for filing omnibus objections to claims.

RULE 3007–2. MODIFICATION OF SCHEDULES OF CLAIMS

If a claim is scheduled by the debtor and is not listed as disputed, contingent, or unliquidated, and a proof of claim has not been filed under Bankruptcy Rules 3003, 3004 and/or 3005, the debtor may not object to the claim. The debtor may amend the debtor's schedules under Bankruptcy Rule 1009 and provide notice as required by E.D.N.Y. LBR 1009–1(b). If the amendment modifies a creditor's scheduled claim or adds a creditor to the schedules of claims and if the deadline by which proofs of claim must be filed has expired or will expire in less than 30 days, the creditor shall have 30 days from the effective date of amendment to file a proof of claim.

[Effective May 28, 2008.]

Cross–Reference: E.D.N.Y. LBR 1009–1.

References: Bankruptcy Rules 1009, 3003, 3004, 3005.

RULE 3015–1. CHAPTER 13 PLAN

(a) Service of Plan. A chapter 13 debtor shall

serve the plan on the trustee and all creditors within 7 days of filing the plan and file proof of service thereof.

(b) Notice and Hearing for Attorney's Fees to Be Treated as Administrative Expense. If the compensation, or any portion thereof, of the attorney for a chapter 13 debtor is to be treated as an administrative expense under the plan, the attorney shall provide notice of that fact to the debtor, the trustee, the United States trustee, and all creditors. Separate notices shall not be required if the plan, or a summary of the plan, states the date(s) and amount of any payments to be made to the attorney, and is served upon all parties in interest at least 14 days prior to the confirmation hearing.

[Effective July 1, 1997. Amended effective May 28, 2008; December 1, 2009.]

RULE 3015–2. CHAPTER 13 PLAN MODIFICATION

(a) Modification of Chapter 13 Plan Before Confirmation. If a debtor in a chapter 13 case proposes to modify his or her chapter 13 plan before confirmation, and the modification of the chapter 13 plan adversely affects the treatment of the claim of any creditor, the debtor shall serve a copy of the modified plan on the trustee and on all creditors not later than 14 days prior to the hearing on confirmation or any adjournment thereof.

(b) Modification of Chapter 13 Plan After Confirmation. If a debtor in a chapter 13 case proposes to modify his or her chapter 13 plan after confirmation, the debtor shall proceed by motion or on presentment in accordance with E.D.N.Y. LBR 2002–1, if there is compliance with Bankruptcy Rule 3015(g). A copy of the proposed modified plan shall be attached to the motion or notice of presentment.

[Effective July 1, 1997. Amended effective May 28, 2008; December 1, 2009.]

Cross–Reference: E.D.N.Y. LBR 2002–1.

RULE 3015–3. HEARING ON CONFIRMATION OF CHAPTER 13 PLAN

Unless excused, the debtor and debtor's attorney shall attend the hearing on confirmation of the chapter 13 plan.

[Effective July 1, 1997.]

RULE 3016–1. OMISSION OF SEPARATE DISCLOSURE STATEMENT IN CHAPTER 11 SMALL BUSINESS CASES: DISCLAIMER

When a chapter 11 case is a small business case as defined in Bankruptcy Code § 101(51C), and the Court finds that the plan provides adequate information under Bankruptcy Code § 1125(f)(1) and a separate disclosure statement is unnecessary, such plan shall have on its cover, in boldface type, the following language or words of similar import:

THE DEBTOR IN THIS CASE IS A SMALL BUSINESS. THE COURT HAS CONDITIONALLY FOUND THAT THIS PLAN PROVIDES ADEQUATE INFORMATION AS REQUIRED UNDER 11 U.S.C. § 1125(a)(1). AS A RESULT, THE DEBTOR MAY DISTRIBUTE THIS PLAN WITHOUT FILING A DISCLOSURE STATEMENT. IF A PARTY IN INTEREST FILES AN OBJECTION TO THIS PLAN BASED ON LACK OF ADEQUATE INFORMATION, THE COURT SHALL MAKE A FINDING REGARDING COMPLIANCE WITH 11

U.S.C. § 1125(a)(1) AT OR BEFORE THE HEARING ON CONFIRMATION OF THE PLAN.

[Effective May 28, 2008.]

References: Bankruptcy Code §§ 101(51C), 1125(f)(1); Bankruptcy Rule 3017.1.

RULE 3017–1. PROPOSED DISCLOSURE STATEMENTS IN CHAPTER 9 AND 11 CASES: TRANSMITTAL AND DISCLAIMER

(a) Transmittal. The proponent of a plan shall transmit all notices and documents required to be transmitted by Bankruptcy Rule 3017(a).

(b) Disclaimer. Before a proposed disclosure statement has been approved, it shall have on its cover, in boldface type, the following language or words of similar import:

THIS IS NOT A SOLICITATION OF ACCEPTANCE OR REJECTION OF THE PLAN. ACCEPTANCES OR REJECTIONS MAY NOT BE SOLICITED UNTIL A DISCLOSURE STATEMENT HAS BEEN APPROVED BY THE BANKRUPTCY COURT. THIS DISCLOSURE STATEMENT IS BEING SUBMITTED FOR APPROVAL BUT HAS NOT BEEN APPROVED BY THE COURT.

(c) Disclosure Statement Disclaimer in Small Business Cases. When a chapter 11 case is a small business case as defined in Bankruptcy Code § 101(51C), after conditional approval, but before final approval of a proposed disclosure statement has been given, such statement shall have on its cover, in boldface type, the following language or words of similar import:

THE DEBTOR IN THIS CASE IS A SMALL BUSINESS. AS A RESULT, THE DEBTOR MAY DISTRIBUTE THIS DISCLOSURE STATEMENT BEFORE ITS FINAL APPROVAL BY THE COURT. IF AN OBJECTION TO THIS DISCLOSURE STATEMENT IS FILED BY A PARTY IN INTEREST, FINAL APPROVAL OF THIS DISCLOSURE STATEMENT WILL BE CONSIDERED AT OR BEFORE THE HEARING ON CONFIRMATION OF THE PLAN.

[Effective July 1, 1997. Amended effective May 28, 2008.]

Reference: Bankruptcy Code § 101(51C).

RULE 3018–1. SUMMARY AND CERTIFICATION OF ACCEPTANCE OR REJECTION OF PLANS IN CHAPTER 9 AND 11 CASES

(a) Summary of Ballots and Notice of Cramdown. At least 7 days prior to the hearing on confirmation of a chapter 9 or 11 plan, the proponent of the plan shall file, and serve upon the United States trustee and counsel to any committee appointed in the case, a one-page statement setting forth the following information:

(i) a summary of the ballots received;

(ii) whether the proponent proposes to confirm the plan over the objection of one or more impaired classes; and

(iii) whether any witnesses other than the proponent's witness in favor of the plan are expected to testify as to any facts relevant to confirmation (testimony by the proponent on behalf of the plan is required).

(b) Certification of Vote. Prior to the hearing on confirmation of a chapter 9 or 11 plan, the proponent of a plan or the party authorized to receive the acceptances and rejections of the plan shall file a certification setting forth the amount and number of allowed claims or allowed interests of each class accepting or rejecting the plan. A copy of the certification shall be served upon the debtor, the trustee, each committee, and the United States trustee. The Court may find that the plan has been accepted or rejected on the basis of the certification.

(c) Notice of Ineffective Election. If a plan in a chapter 9 or 11 case permits the holder of a claim or interest to make an election with respect to the treatment of the claim or interest, and if the holder's election is deemed ineffective or otherwise is not counted by the person authorized to tabulate ballots, that person shall give notice of that fact to the holder at least 7 days prior to the hearing on confirmation.

[Effective July 1, 1997. Amended effective July 1, 1999; May 28, 2008; December 1, 2009.]

RULE 3019–1. MODIFICATION OF CHAPTER 11 PLAN BEFORE CLOSE OF VOTING

If the proponent of a chapter 11 plan files a modification of the plan after transmission of the approved disclosure statement and before the close of voting on the plan, the proponent shall serve a copy of the plan, as modified, upon the debtor, the trustee, each committee, the United States trustee, all entities directly affected by the proposed modification, and such other entities as the Court may direct. On notice to such entities, the Court shall determine whether the modification adversely affects the treatment of the claim of any creditor or the interest of any equity security holder who has not accepted the modification in writing. If the Court determines that the modification is not adverse, the plan, as modified, shall be deemed accepted by all creditors and equity security holders who accepted the plan prior to modification. If the modification is adverse, the requirements of Bankruptcy Rule 3017 shall apply to the modified plan and any amendment of the disclosure statement necessitated by the modification.

[Effective December 5, 2012.]

Reference: Bankruptcy Rule 3017

Comment

Pursuant to § 1127(a) of the Bankruptcy Code, the proponent of a chapter 11 plan may modify the plan at any time before confirmation. While Bankruptcy Rule 3019 governs modification of a plan after acceptance and before confirmation, this rule governs modification subsequent to the transmission of an approved disclosure statement and before the close of voting.

RULE 3020–1. TIME FOR OBJECTING TO CONFIRMATION IN CHAPTER 9 AND 11 CASES; WITHDRAWAL OF OBJECTIONS

(a) Objections to Confirmation. Objections to confirmation of a plan shall be filed at least 7 days prior to the hearing to consider confirmation of the plan.

(b) Withdrawal of Objections. If an objection to confirmation of a plan is withdrawn, the proponent shall disclose to the Court the reasons for the withdrawal, including the terms of any agreement precipitating the withdrawal of the objection.

[Effective July 1, 1997. Amended effective May 28, 2008; December 1, 2009.]

RULE 3020–2. CONFIRMATION ORDERS IN CHAPTER 9 AND 11 CASES

A proposed order confirming a chapter 9 or 11 plan shall have annexed a copy of the plan to be confirmed.

[Effective May 28, 2008. Amended effective December 1, 2009.]

RULE 3022–1. FINAL DECREE

In a chapter 11 case, within 14 days following the full administration of the estate, the plan proponent shall file, on notice to the United States trustee, an application and a proposed order for a final decree pursuant to Bankruptcy Rule 3022. Upon request, the Court may reduce or extend the time to file such application.

[Effective May 28, 2008. Amended effective December 5, 2012.]

PART IV. THE DEBTOR: DUTIES AND BENEFITS

RULE 4001–1. RELIEF FROM AUTOMATIC STAY

(a) By Motion. If a motion for relief from the automatic stay under Bankruptcy Code § 362 is made returnable more than 30 days after the date filed, the movant shall be deemed to have consented to the continuation of the automatic stay through the hearing date.

(b) By Presentment. If a motion for relief from the automatic stay under Bankruptcy Code § 362 is made by presentment as set forth in E.D.N.Y. LBR 2002–1, and a hearing is scheduled, the time limitation set forth in Bankruptcy Code § 362(e) is deemed waived.

[Effective July 1, 1997. Amended effective May 28, 2008; December 5, 2012.]

Cross–References: E.D.N.Y. LBR 2002–1, 5070–1.

Reference: Bankruptcy Code § 362

RULE 4001–2. ORDERS CONFIRMING THE INAPPLICABILITY OF THE AUTOMATIC STAY

A request for an order pursuant to Bankruptcy Code §§ 362(c)(4)(A)(ii) or (j) shall be on notice to the debtor, the debtor's attorney, if any, and the trustee and shall include evidence of entitlement to the order.

[Effective May 28, 2008.]

References: Bankruptcy Code § 362(c)(4)(A)(ii), (j).

RULE 4001–3. ORDERS CONTINUING OR IMPOSING THE AUTOMATIC STAY

A motion for an order pursuant to Bankruptcy Code § 362(c)(3)(B) continuing the automatic stay or an order pursuant to Bankruptcy Code § 362(c)(4)(B) imposing the automatic stay shall be on notice to all parties in interest, including but not limited to, all creditors and the trustee.

[Effective July 1, 1997. Amended effective May 28, 2008.]

References: Bankruptcy Code § 362(c)(3)(B), (c)(4)(B).

RULE 4001–4. PAYMENT AND CURE OF PRE–PETITION JUDGMENT OF POSSESSION INVOLVING RESIDENTIAL PROPERTY

(a) A debtor seeking to obtain a 30–day stay of eviction pursuant to Bankruptcy Code § 362(b)(22) and (*l*) shall:

(i) provide the landlord's name and address in the certification required under Bankruptcy Code § 362(*l*)(1);

(ii) deliver to the Clerk, together with the petition (or, if the petition is filed electronically, no later than the day after the filing), a certified or cashier's check or money order, made payable to the lessor, in the amount of any rent that would become due during the 30–day period after the filing of the petition;

(iii) serve the landlord with a copy of the debtor's petition;

(iv) file a copy of the judgment for possession, if available; and

(v) if the landlord objects to the debtor's certification, attend the hearing on such objection.

(b) A debtor who obtained a 30–day stay pursuant to Bankruptcy Code § 362(b)(22) and (*l*) and who wishes to extend the stay beyond the 30–day period shall comply with subdivision (a) of this rule and, within the 30–day period after the filing of the petition, shall:

(i) cure the entire monetary default that gave rise to the judgment of possession; and

(ii) if the landlord objects to the debtor's certification under Bankruptcy Code § 362(*l*)(2) that the entire monetary default that gave rise to the judgment of possession has been cured, attend the hearing on such objection.

[Effective May 28, 2008. Amended effective December 1, 2009.]

Reference: Bankruptcy Code § 362(b)(22), (*l*).

RULE 4001–5. CASH COLLATERAL AND OBTAINING CREDIT

(a) Motions. In addition to the requirements set forth in Bankruptcy Rule 4001, all motions to use cash collateral and to obtain credit pursuant to Bankruptcy Code §§ 363 and 364 ("Financing Motions") shall recite whether the proposed form of order and/or underlying cash collateral stipulation or loan agreement contains any provision of the type indicated below, identify the location of any such provision in the proposed form of order, cash collateral stipulation and/or loan agreement, and state the justification for the inclusion of such provision:

(i) the absence of any carve-out for professional fees, or provisions that provide treatment for the professionals retained by the debtor that is different than that provided for the professionals retained by a creditors' committee with respect to a professional fee carve-out;

(ii) provisions that require the debtor to pay the secured creditor's expenses and attorneys' fees in connection with the proposed financing or use of cash collateral, without any notice or review by the Office of the United States trustee, creditors' committee (if formed), or the Court; or

(iii) provisions that exclude from a carve-out any request for professional fees related to the investigation of whether the secured creditor's lien is valid and/or properly perfected.

(b) Interim Relief. When Financing Motions are filed with the Court on or shortly after the date of entry of the order for relief, the Court may grant interim relief on shortened notice. Such interim relief is intended to avoid immediate and irreparable harm to the estate pending a final hearing. In the absence of extraordinary circumstances, the Court will not approve ex parte interim financing orders that include any of the provisions listed in Bankruptcy Rule 4001 and in subdivision (a)(i)–(iii), inclusive, of this rule.

[Effective May 28, 2008. Amended effective December 1, 2009.]

References: Bankruptcy Code §§ 363 and 364.

Committee Note: This rule is not intended to supersede or duplicate Bankruptcy Rule 4001, but imposes additional requirements on proponents of cash collateral and financing motions.

RULE 4002–1. PERSONAL IDENTIFIERS AND TAX INFORMATION OF THE DEBTOR

(a) Debtor's Duty to Redact Personal Identifiers. An individual debtor providing information to the trustee or a creditor pursuant to Bankruptcy Code § 521(e) shall redact personal identifiers as follows:

(i) if an individual's social security number, alien registration number, or tax identification number is included, only the last four digits of that number shall appear;

(ii) if minor children are identified by name, only the children's initials shall appear;

(iii) if an individual's date of birth is included, only the year shall appear; and

(iv) if financial account numbers are provided, only the last four digits of these numbers shall appear.

(b) Electronic Filing of Debtor's Tax Information. All tax information electronically filed shall be entered under the event titled "Tax Documents" (Category–Other) in the CM/ECF event list.

(c) Procedure for Requesting Tax Information Filed With the Court Pursuant to Bankruptcy Code § 521(f). Any party in interest seeking access to a debtor's tax information that is filed with the Court pursuant to Bankruptcy Code

§ 521(f) shall file a motion with the Court on notice to the debtor and the debtor's attorney, if any. A motion requesting access to such information shall include:

(i) a description of the movant's status in the case;

(ii) a description of the specific tax information sought;

(iii) a statement indicating that the information cannot be obtained by the movant from any other sources; and

(iv) an explanation of the movant's need for the tax information.

(d) Procedure for Obtaining Access to Tax Information Filed With the Court Pursuant to Bankruptcy Code § 521(f) After Access to the Tax Information Is Granted. Any party in interest whose motion seeking to obtain access to a debtor's tax information filed pursuant to Bankruptcy Code § 521(f) was granted by the Court shall present to the Clerk a copy of the Court's order granting such movant access to the tax information and a valid, government issued picture identification card in order to obtain such tax information.

(e) Confidentiality of Personal Identifiers. Any party in interest who obtains the personal identifiers listed in subdivision (a) of this rule shall keep such information confidential and shall disclose it only to an employee or financial or legal advisor with a need to know such information in connection with the bankruptcy case. Any person or entity who uses, discloses, or disseminates personal identifiers in a manner inconsistent with this rule may be found in contempt of court and may be subject to penalties therefor.

(f) Confidentiality of Tax Information. Any party in interest who obtains tax information of the debtor shall keep such information confidential and shall disclose only to the extent necessary in connection with the case or related adversary proceeding. Any party in interest who seeks to disclose tax information of the debtor for any other purpose shall seek authority to do so by motion on notice to the debtor and the debtor's attorney, if any. Any person or entity who discloses a debtor's tax information in a manner inconsistent with this rule may be found in contempt of court and may be subject to penalties therefor.

(g) Waiver of Protection of Personal Identifiers. An individual debtor waives the protection of subdivisions (e) of this rule as to personal identifiers provided to the trustee or a creditor pursuant to Bankruptcy Code § 521(e) to the extent such personal identifiers are not redacted in accordance with subdivision (a) of this rule.

[Effective May 28, 2008.]

References: Bankruptcy Code § 521(e); Bankruptcy Rule 9037; Director of the Administrative Office of the United States Courts' Interim Guidance Regarding Tax Information under 11 U.S.C. § 521 dated Sept. 20, 2005.

RULE 4003–1. AMENDMENT TO CLAIM OF EXEMPTIONS

An amendment to a claim of exemptions pursuant to Bankruptcy Rules 1009 and 4003 and these rules shall be filed and served on the trustee, the United States trustee, all creditors, and other parties in interest. An amendment shall not be effective until proof of service is filed, which shall be done within 7 days of service.

[Effective July 1, 1997. Amended effective May 28, 2008; December 1, 2009.]

Cross–Reference: E.D.N.Y. LBR 1009–1.

Reference: Bankruptcy Rule 1009.

RULE 4003–2. OBJECTION TO A CLAIM OF EXEMPTION [ABROGATED EFFECTIVE DECEMBER 1, 2009]

RULE 4004–1. SETTLEMENT OR DISMISSAL OF PROCEEDINGS OBJECTING TO DISCHARGE

A complaint objecting to discharge may be settled or dismissed only if the debtor or representative of the objecting party files an affidavit or affirmation setting forth what consideration, if any, has been paid or promised to the objecting party. The affidavit or affirmation must be served upon the trustee, all creditors, and other parties in interest.

[Formerly Rule 4004–2, redesignated effective May 28, 2008.]

RULE 4007–1. SETTLEMENT OR DISMISSAL OF PROCEEDINGS OBJECTING TO DISCHARGEABILITY

In all instances not governed by Bankruptcy Code § 524(d), an adversary proceeding objecting to dischargeability of a debt may be settled or dismissed only if a proponent of the settlement or dismissal files an affidavit or affirmation setting forth the terms of any agreement entered into between the debtor and creditor relating to the payment of the debt in whole or in part.

[Effective July 1, 1997. Formerly Rule 4007–2, redesignated effective May 28, 2008.]

Reference: Bankruptcy Code § 524(d).

PART V. COURTS AND CLERKS

RULE 5001–1. CLERK'S OFFICE: CONTACT INFORMATION

(a) Mailing Addresses.

Brooklyn Cases:
United States Bankruptcy Court
Eastern District of New York
271–C Cadman Plaza East
Suite 1595
Brooklyn, New York 11201–1800

Central Islip Cases:
United States Bankruptcy Court
Eastern District of New York
290 Federal Plaza
Central Islip, New York 11722

(b) Physical Addresses and Phone Numbers.

Brooklyn Office:
United States Bankruptcy Court
Conrad B. Duberstein Courthouse
271–C Cadman Plaza East
Brooklyn, New York 11201–1800
Phone No. (347) 394–1700

Central Islip Office:
United States Bankruptcy Court
Alphonse M. D'Amato
U.S. Courthouse
290 Federal Plaza
Central Islip, New York 11722
Phone No. (631) 712–6200

(c) Website Address. The Court's Website is located at www.nyeb.uscourts.gov.

[Effective July 1, 1997. Amended effective July 1, 1999; May 28, 2008; December 1, 2009.]

RULE 5001–2. CLERK'S OFFICE: HOURS; AFTER HOURS FILING

The offices of the Clerk shall be open Monday through Friday between the hours of 9:00 a.m. and 4:30 p.m., except on legal or court holidays, and shall be closed on Saturdays and Sundays. When the Clerk's office is closed, papers relating to cases pending in Brooklyn may be submitted in a night depository located in the courthouse lobby of the United States District Court, 225 Cadman Plaza East, Brooklyn, New York 11201. When the Clerk's office is closed, papers relating to cases pending in Central Islip may be submitted in a night depository located in the courthouse lobby of the Alfonse M. D'Amato U.S. Courthouse, 290 Federal Plaza, Central Islip, New York 11722. If the Alfonse M. D'Amato U.S. Courthouse is closed, papers may be submitted in a night depository located in the courthouse lobby of the United States District Court, 225 Cadman Plaza East, Brooklyn, New York 11201. If the papers are deposited in a night depository, they will be deemed filed as of the exact time and date stamped on the papers.

Persons may review records, request files for review, review dockets, request dockets for review, or make a public inquiry at the Clerk's office between the hours of 9:00 a.m. and 4:00 p.m. Telephone inquiries to the Clerk's office may be made between the hours of 9:00 a.m. and 4:00 p.m.

[Amended effective December 1, 2009.]

Committee Note: Parties shall consult the Court's Website for the hours of accessibility to the night depositories in each Court location.

RULE 5005–1. FILING BY ELECTRONIC MEANS

(a) Password and Registration.

(i) *Attorneys.* An attorney admitted to practice before the Court may obtain a password to permit the attorney to file documents electronically. An attorney may register to use the electronic filing system by filing a password application.

(ii) *Limited Creditors.* Creditors may register for limited use of the electronic filing system by filing a password application.

(b) Filing Requirements.

(i) All motions, pleadings, memoranda of law, exhibits, and other documents required to be filed with the Court in connection with a case and documents filed under seal in accordance with E.D.N.Y. LBR 9018, shall be electronically filed over the Internet. No later than the day after the electronic filing, a chambers copy shall be filed with the Clerk to the attention of the appropriate Judge's chambers, which copy is to be marked "Chambers Copy." The date and time of the electronic filing shall be the official date and time of the filing of the document.

(ii) Proofs of claim may be filed electronically. A "Chambers Copy" shall not be filed with the Clerk.

(iii) All documents that form part of a motion or pleading, and which are being filed at the same time and by the same party, except for a memorandum of law, may be electronically filed together under one docket number. A memorandum of law shall be filed separately and shall indicate the motion or pleading to which it relates.

(iv) Relevant excerpts of exhibits that are not in electronic form shall be scanned and electronically filed. Such document excerpts shall be identified as excerpts, shall not exceed 20 pages, and shall state that the entire document is in the possession of the filing party and is available upon request. The complete exhibit shall be made available forthwith to counsel on request, and shall be available in the courtroom at any hearing on the matter. Persons filing excerpts of exhibits pursuant to these procedures do so without prejudice to their right to file additional excerpts or the entire exhibit with the Court at any time. Opposing parties may file any additional excerpts that they believe to be germane. Chambers copies of complete exhibits shall be provided to the Court on request.

[Effective July 1, 1997. Amended effective May 28, 2008. Superseded effective January 1, 2009, see General Order 536 *post*. Amended effective December 1, 2009.]

Cross–Reference: E.D.N.Y. LBR 9018–1.

Reference: General Order on Electronic Filing Procedures.

Committee Note: Attorney and Limited Creditor ECF password applications are available at the intake counter of the Clerk's office and at the Court's Website.

Former E.D.N.Y. LBR 5005–1 was stricken, and Former E.D.N.Y. LBR 5005–2 was redesignated E.D.N.Y. 5005–1.

RULE 5010–1. REOPENING CASES

(a) Contents of Motion. A motion to reopen a case pursuant to Bankruptcy Code § 350(b) and Bankruptcy Rule 5010 shall state the name of the Judge to whom the case had been assigned and the date on which the case was closed.

(b) Assignment of Matter. The Clerk shall assign the motion to the Judge to whom the case had been assigned at the time it was closed. If that Judge is no longer sitting, the motion shall be assigned in accordance with E.D.N.Y. LBR 1073–1.

(c) Filing Fee. A filing fee shall be due at the time of making a motion to reopen a case (including a motion to reopen for the purpose of filing a personal financial management certificate) in the same amount as the filing fee prescribed by 28 U.S.C. § 1930(a) for commencing a new case on the date of reopening, except that no filing fee shall be due if the reopening is requested to correct an administrative error, or for actions related to the debtor's discharge. The Court may defer or waive the filing fee under appropriate circumstances.

[Effective July 1, 1997. Amended effective July 1, 1999; May 28, 2008.]

Cross–Reference: E.D.N.Y. LBR 1073–1.

References: Bankruptcy Code §§ 111, 350(b), 727; Bankruptcy Rule 4006; 28 U.S.C. § 1930(a).

RULE 5011–1. WITHDRAWAL OF REFERENCE

A motion for withdrawal of the reference shall be filed with the Court, and the Clerk shall transmit the motion to the District Clerk promptly and so notify the movant. The movant shall be responsible for notifying all other parties. Following the transmittal of the motion, all further papers with respect to the motion shall be filed in the District Court.

[Effective July 1, 1997. Amended effective May 28, 2008.]

RULE 5070–1. CALENDARS AND SCHEDULING

(a) Obtaining Return Date. Prior to serving a motion or application, the moving party or applicant shall obtain a return date from the Court's Website, if appropriate, or from the Judge's courtroom deputy or chambers.

(b) Adjournments Without Date. Any matter adjourned without date and not restored to the calendar within 60 days may be deemed withdrawn without prejudice.

[Effective July 1, 1997. Amended effective May 28, 2008.]

Cross–References: E.D.N.Y. LBR 2002–1, 4001–1.

Committee Note: Parties shall consult the Court's Website for each Judge's procedures with respect to the designation of return and adjournment dates.

RULE 5073–1. CAMERAS, RADIO, RECORDERS AND OTHER ELECTRONIC DEVICES [ABROGATED EFFECTIVE MAY 28, 2008]

Committee Note: Parties are directed to the Court's Website for the Court's policy on cameras, radio, recorders, and other electronic devices.

RULE 5075–1. USE OF SERVICES AND AGENTS

The Court may permit, subject to the supervision of the Clerk, the use of services and agents to maintain Court records, issue notices, file certain documents, and maintain and disseminate other administrative information when the costs of such services and agents are paid for by the estate.

[Effective July 1, 1997. Amended effective May 28, 2008.]

Cross–References: E.D.N.Y. LBR 3007–1, 3007–2.

RULE 5080–1. FEES—GENERAL

Except as otherwise authorized by statute, rule, or order, the Clerk shall not render any service for which a fee is prescribed by statute or by the Judicial Conference of the United States unless the fee has been paid or waived, or an application for waiver of the filing fee under applicable law is pending.

[Effective July 1, 1997. Amended effective July 1, 1999; May 28, 2008.]

References: 28 U.S.C. § 1930, Bankruptcy Rule 1006.

PART VI. COLLECTION AND LIQUIDATION OF THE ESTATE

RULE 6004–1. SALE OF PROPERTY, APPRAISALS AND AUCTIONS

(a) **Conflict of Interest.** An appraiser, auctioneer, or officer, director, stockholder, agent, employee, or insider of an appraiser or auctioneer, or any relative of any of the foregoing, shall not purchase, directly or indirectly, or have a financial interest in the purchase of, any property of the estate that the appraiser or auctioneer has been employed to appraise or sell.

(b) **Notice of Sale of Estate Property by Private Sale.** A party seeking to sell property of the estate outside the ordinary course of business shall give the notice required by Bankruptcy Rule 2002(a)(2) and, if applicable, Bankruptcy Rule 6004(g). Such notice shall contain:

(i) a general description of the property;

(ii) a statement explaining where a complete description or inventory of the property may be obtained or examined;

(iii) the terms of sale, including the upset price, if any, the procedures for bidding on the property to be sold, and the terms of any pending offer proposed to be accepted;

(iv) the place, date, and time of the sale;

(v) the place, date, and time the property may be examined prior to the sale;

(vi) the date by which objections to the sale must be filed with the Court;

(vii) the date of the hearing to consider any objections to the sale; and

(viii) the name and address of the trustee, if any.

(c) **Manner of Display and Conduct of Auction.** The auction shall be conducted in the following manner:

(i) the property shall be on public display for a reasonable period of time prior to the auction;

(ii) prior to receiving bids, the auctioneer shall announce the terms of sale;

(iii) when practicable, the property shall be offered for sale first in bulk and then in lots; and

(iv) any property that is not to be included in the auction shall be set apart and conspicuously marked "not included in the sale," and such fact shall be announced by the auctioneer before the auction.

(d) **Joint Auctions.** Whenever the trustee and a secured party, or other third party having an interest in the property, desire to conduct a joint auction, the Court may enter an order fixing the method of allocating the commissions and expenses of sale.

(e) **Proceeds of Auction.** Upon receipt of the proceeds of sale, the auctioneer shall immediately deposit the proceeds in a separate account that the auctioneer maintains for the estate in accordance with Bankruptcy Code § 345(a). Payment of the gross proceeds of the sale shall be made promptly by the auctioneer to the trustee or debtor in possession, but in no event later than 7 days after the proceeds are received.

(f) **Report of Auction.** Within 21 days after the last date of the auction, the auctioneer shall file a verified report and provide the report to the trustee and the United States trustee. If all proceeds of the auction have not been received by such date, the auctioneer shall file a supplemental report within 14 days after all proceeds have been received. The report shall set forth:

(i) the time, date, and place of the auction;

(ii) the gross dollar amount received at the auction;

(iii) if property was sold in lots, a description of the items in each lot, the quantity in each lot, the dollar amount received for each lot, and any bulk bid(s) received;

(iv) an itemized statement of expenditures, disbursements, and commissions allowable under E.D.N.Y. LBR 6005–1, including the name and address of the payee and receipts or canceled checks for the expenditures or disbursements. When labor charges are included, the report shall specify the days worked and the number of hours worked each day by each person supported, by an affidavit from every person receiving compensation which also sets forth all amounts received. If the canceled checks are not available at the time the report is filed, the report shall so state, and the canceled checks shall be filed as soon as they become available;

(v) when the auctioneer has a blanket insurance policy covering all sales conducted by the auctioneer, a statement of how any insurance expense charged to the estate was computed;

(vi) if any articles were withdrawn from the auction because of a third party claim of an interest therein, a statement of the articles and the names of the third parties;

(vii) the names and addresses of all purchasers;

(viii) the sign-in sheet, or, if none, the approximate number of people attending the auction;

(ix) the items for which there were no bids and the disposition of those items;

(x) the terms of sale that were announced prior to receiving bids;

(xi) a statement of the manner and extent of advertising of the auction, including a copy of the published advertisement and a certificate of publication;

(xii) a statement of the manner and extent of the availability of the items for inspection;

(xiii) a copy of the order retaining the auctioneer; and

(xiv) any other information that the trustee, the United States trustee, or the Court may request.

(g) Affidavit to Accompany Report of Auction. The auctioneer shall submit with the report of auction an affidavit stating:

(i) whether the auctioneer is duly licensed;

(ii) the auctioneer's license number and place of business;

(iii) the authority pursuant to which the auctioneer conducted the auction;

(iv) the date and place of the auction;

(v) that the labor and other expenses incurred on behalf of the estate as listed in the report of auction were reasonable and necessary; and

(vi) that the gross proceeds were remitted to the trustee or debtor in possession and the date of the remittance.

(h) Notice of Sale by Auction; Advertisement and Publication. An advertisement or publication of notice of a sale by auction or otherwise may be made without Court approval if it is sufficient to provide adequate notice of the sale and is advertised or published at least once in a newspaper of general circulation in the city or county in which the property is located. The advertisement or publication shall include:

(i) the date, time, and place of the sale;

(ii) a description of the property to be sold;

(iii) the terms and conditions of the sale; and

(iv) the name, address, and telephone number of the auctioneer.

The Judge may fix the manner and extent of advertising and publication at any time.

(i) No Order Needed to Confirm Sale. Unless a timely objection is made, an order of the Court shall not be required to confirm a sale of property otherwise authorized by the Bankruptcy Code, the Bankruptcy Rules, or Court order. The trustee, debtor, or debtor in possession may execute any documents and instruments that are necessary to complete the sale, and shall file with the Clerk and transmit to the United States trustee a report of the sale as required by Bankruptcy Rule 6004(f) when the sale is completed. On request, the Clerk shall issue a certificate stating that a notice of a proposed auction, with proof of service, has been filed pursuant to E.D.N.Y. LBR 2002–1 and that no timely objection has been filed.

[Effective July 1, 1997. Amended effective July 1, 1999; May 28, 2008; December 1, 2009.]

Cross–References: E.D.N.Y. LBR 2002–1, 2014–1, 6005–1, 9018–1.

References: Bankruptcy Code § 245(a); Bankruptcy Rules 2002, 6004, General Order on Electronic Filing Procedures.

RULE 6005–1. AUCTIONEERS

(a) Retention of Auctioneer. A debtor in possession or trustee may retain the services of an auctioneer, subject to prior Court approval.

(b) Compensation. An auctioneer may be allowed to receive commissions and reimbursement of expenses for sales of property, subject to Court approval, in an amount not to exceed:

(i) commissions on each sale conducted by the auctioneer at the following rates:

(A) 10% of any gross proceeds of sale up to $50,000;

(B) 8% of any gross proceeds of sale in excess of $50,000 but not more than $75,000;

(C) 6% of any gross proceeds of sale in excess of $75,000 but not more than $100,000;

(D) 4% of any gross proceeds of sale in excess of $100,000 but not more than $150,000; and

(E) 2% of any gross proceeds of sale in excess of $150,000; and

(ii) reimbursement for reasonable and necessary expenses directly related to the sale, including labor, printing, advertising, and insurance, but excluding workers' compensation, social security, unemployment insurance, and other payroll taxes. When directed by the trustee or debtor in possession to transport goods, the auctioneer may be reimbursed for expenditures related thereto. No travel expenses shall be allowed, except as ordered by the Court.

(c) Bond. An auctioneer employed pursuant to Bankruptcy Code § 327 shall not act until the auctioneer files and provides to the United States trustee, with respect to each estate, at the auctioneer's expense, a surety bond in favor of the United States, to be approved, and in such sum as may be fixed, by the United States trustee, conditioned upon:

(i) the faithful and prompt accounting for all monies and property that may come into the auctioneer's possession;

(ii) compliance with all rules, orders, and decrees of the Court; and

(iii) the faithful performance of the auctioneer's duties.

(d) Blanket Bond. In lieu of a bond in each case, an auctioneer may file, at the auctioneer's own expense, a blanket bond covering all cases in which the auctioneer may act. The blanket bond shall be in favor of the United States in such sum as the United States trustee shall fix and shall be conditioned for each estate on the same terms as bonds in separate estates.

(e) Application for Commissions and Reimbursement of Expenses. An auctioneer shall file an application with the Clerk for approval of commissions and reimbursement of expenses and give notice in accordance with Bankruptcy Rule 2002(a). An application may not be granted if the report of sale and accompanying affidavit described in E.D.N.Y. LBR 6004–1(f) and (g) have not been filed. The application shall state whether the debtor or the trustee has any objection to such application.

[Effective July 1, 1997. Amended effective May 28, 2008.]

Cross–References: E.D.N.Y. LBR 2014–1, 6004–1, 9025–1.

Reference: Bankruptcy Code § 327; Bankruptcy Rule 2002.

RULE 6006–1. EXECUTORY CONTRACTS AND UNEXPIRED LEASES

(a) Motion to Assume Executory Contract or Unexpired Lease in Chapter 7 Case. Unless the Court orders otherwise, in a chapter 7 case, a trustee moving to assume an executory contract or unexpired lease of residential real property or personal property of the debtor shall seek to obtain a return date for the hearing on the motion that is within 60 days after the order for relief or, if the time to assume has been extended, before the expiration of such extended period. If the trustee files a motion to assume or to extend the time to assume or reject an executory contract or unexpired lease of residential real property or personal property, and the motion is filed prior to the expiration of the time to assume or reject such executory contract or unexpired lease with a return date no later than 14 days from the date of the expiration of the time to assume or reject such executory contract or unexpired lease, the trustee shall file with its motion a proposed order seeking an extension for cause under § 365(d)(1) of the time to assume or reject the executory contract or unexpired lease to the date of the hearing on the motion, which order may be entered without further notice or a hearing.

(b) Motion to Assume Unexpired Lease of Nonresidential Real Property. Unless the Court orders otherwise, in a case under any chapter, a debtor, debtor in possession, or trustee moving to assume an unexpired lease of nonresidential real property under which the debtor is the lessee shall seek to obtain a return date for the hearing on the motion that is within 120 days after the order for relief or, if the time to assume has been extended, before the expiration of such extended period. If the debtor, debtor in possession, or trustee files a motion to assume or to extend the time to assume or reject an unexpired lease of nonresidential real property, and the motion is filed prior to the expiration of the time to assume or reject the unexpired lease with a return date no later than 14 days from the date of the expiration of the time to assume or reject such lease, the debtor, debtor in possession, or trustee shall file with its motion a proposed order seeking an extension for cause under § 365(d)(4)(B)(i) of the time to assume or reject the unexpired lease to the date of the hearing on the motion, which order may be entered without further notice or a hearing, except that the time for the debtor, debtor in possession, or trustee to assume or reject such unexpired lease shall not be extended beyond the date that is 210 days after the entry of the order for relief without the prior written consent of the landlord.

[Effective December 5, 2012.]

References: Bankruptcy Code §§ 365(d)(1), 365(d)(4)(B)(i)

Comment

§ 365(d)(1) of the Bankruptcy Code contemplates that a hearing on a motion by a chapter 7 trustee to assume an executory contract or unexpired lease of residential real property or personal property of the debtor ordinarily will take place within 60 days from the date of the order for relief. Likewise, § 365(d)(4) of the Bankruptcy Code contemplates that a final hearing on a motion by a debtor, debtor in possession, or trustee to assume an unexpired lease of nonresidential real property of the debtor ordinarily will take place within 60 days from the date of the order for relief.

Under § 365(d)(1) of the Bankruptcy Code, in a chapter 7 case, the Court may, for cause, extend the 60–day time period for assuming or rejecting an executory contract or unexpired lease of residential real property or personal property. Similarly, under § 365(d)(4), the Court may, for cause, extend the 120–day time period for assuming or rejecting an unexpired lease of nonresidential real property. Adequate cause for an extension of time to assume or reject the executory contract or unexpired lease until the Court rules on the motion exists by virtue of the fact that a motion to assume or to extend the time was filed in a timely manner. Any party in interest objecting to the extension of time may request a hearing on an expedited basis. To prevent abuse of the automatic extension, the return date of the motion must be no later than 14 days after the expiration of the period.

RULE 6007–1. ABANDONMENT OR DISPOSITION OF PROPERTY

Notice of a proposed abandonment or disposition of property pursuant to Bankruptcy Rule 6007(a) shall describe the property to be abandoned or disposed of and state the reason for the proposed abandonment or disposition.

[Effective July 1, 1997. Amended effective May 28, 2008.]

PART VII. ADVERSARY PROCEEDINGS

RULE 7005–1. FILING OF DISCOVERY–RELATED DOCUMENTS

Transcripts of depositions, exhibits to depositions, interrogatories, responses to interrogatories, document requests, responses to document requests, requests for admissions, and responses to requests for admissions are not required to be filed, but may be filed when necessary for the consideration of a matter by the Court.

[Effective July 1, 1997. Amended effective July 1, 1999; May 28, 2008; December 1, 2009.]

Cross–Reference: E.D.N.Y. LBR 8007–1.

RULE 7007–1. DISCOVERY RELATED MOTIONS

A discovery motion under Bankruptcy Rules 7026 through 7037 shall be supported by an affidavit or affirmation certifying that the moving party has made a good faith effort to confer with the opposing party to resolve the issues raised by the motion by agreement and without judicial intervention, but has been unable to reach an agreement. The affidavit or affirmation shall describe the efforts to resolve the discovery dispute without judicial intervention. The affidavit or affirmation shall specify any issues so resolved and the issues remaining unresolved. The affidavit or affirmation shall be filed and served together with the motion.

[Effective July 1, 1997. Amended effective May 28, 2008.]

Cross–References: E.D.N.Y. LBR 9006–1, 9013–1.

References: Bankruptcy Rules 7026, 7037.

RULE 7007.1-1. CORPORATE OWNERSHIP STATEMENT TO BE FILED BY A PARTNERSHIP OR JOINT VENTURE THAT IS A PARTY TO AN ADVERSARY PROCEEDING

The Corporate Ownership Statement required under Bankruptcy Rule 7007.1 shall also be filed by any party to an adversary proceeding, other than the debtor or a governmental entity, that is a general or limited partnership or joint venture.

[Effective December 5, 2012.]

Comment

Bankruptcy Rule 7007.1, effective December 1, 2003, requires a Corporate Ownership Statement to be filed for any corporation that is a party to an adversary proceeding other than the debtor or a governmental entity. "Corporation" is broadly defined under § 101(9) of the Bankruptcy Code (and includes, for instance, limited liability companies and other unincorporated companies or associations), but it does not cover general or limited partnerships. The reasons for which this rule was enacted—to give the Judges of this Court information by which they can determine whether or not they need to recuse themselves—apply equally to general and limited partnerships, and joint ventures. This local rule requires a similar disclosure with respect to business organizations of that character.

RULE 7016-1. SUBMISSION OF MARKED PLEADINGS

Unless the Court orders otherwise, marked pleadings are not required.

[Effective December 5, 2012.]

Comment

The Judges of the Court have determined that the benefits derived from the submission of marked pleadings normally do not justify the burdens on the plaintiff in submitting them, particularly in light of the information contained in pre-trial orders.

RULE 7026-1. ASSERTION OF CLAIM OF PRIVILEGE AND UNIFORM DEFINITIONS IN DISCOVERY REQUESTS

District Rules 26.2 and 26.3 shall apply to discovery requests made in cases and proceedings commenced under the Bankruptcy Code.

[Effective December 5, 2012.]

References: District Rules 26.2 and 26.3

RULE 7026-2. COOPERATION AMONG COUNSEL IN DISCOVERY

(a) Counsel are expected to cooperate with each other, consistent with the interests of their clients, in all phases of the discovery process and to be courteous in their dealings with each other, including in matters relating to scheduling and timing of various discovery procedures.

(b) Discovery requests shall be read reasonably in the recognition that the attorney serving them generally does not have the information being sought and the attorney receiving them generally does have such information or can obtain it from the client.

[Effective December 5, 2012.]

Comment

This rule is an adaptation of District Rule 26.4.

RULE 7030-1. COUNSEL FEES ON TAKING DEPOSITIONS MORE THAN 100 MILES FROM THE COURTHOUSE

District Rule 30.1 shall apply when a deposition upon oral examination is to be taken at a place more than one hundred (100) miles from the courthouse.

[Effective December 5, 2012.]

Comment

This rule is an adaptation of District Rule 30.1.

RULE 7033-1. INTERROGATORIES

(a) **Restrictions.** During discovery, interrogatories will be restricted to those questions seeking names of witnesses with knowledge or information relevant to the subject matter of the action, the computation of each category of damage alleged, and the existence, custodian, location, and general description of relevant documents, including pertinent insurance agreements, and other physical evidence, and information of a similar nature, to the extent such information has not already been provided under Federal Rule of Civil Procedure 26(a)(1).

(b) **Method of Obtaining Information.** During discovery, interrogatories, other than those seeking information described in subdivision (a) of this rule, may be served only if (i) they are a more practical method of obtaining the information sought than a request for production or a deposition or (ii) ordered by the Court.

(c) **What May Be Served.** At the conclusion of each party's discovery, and prior to the discovery cut-off date, interrogatories seeking the claims and contentions of the opposing party may be served. Questions seeking the names of expert witnesses and the substance of their opinions also may be served if such information has not yet been supplied.

(d) **No Interrogatories to Be Unanswered.** No part of an interrogatory shall be left unanswered merely because an objection is interposed to another part of the interrogatory.

(e) **Objections.**

(1) In connection with any objection to interrogatories or answers to interrogatories, the party making the objection shall specify and quote verbatim each relevant interrogatory or answer and, immediately following each specification, set forth the basis of the objection.

(2) If an objection is made to any interrogatory or portion thereof, the objection shall state all grounds with specificity. Any ground not stated in the objection within the time provided by the Bankruptcy Rules, or any extensions thereof, shall be deemed waived.

(f) Reference to Records. If a party answers an interrogatory by reference to records from which the answer may be derived or ascertained, as permitted by Bankruptcy Rule 7033:

(1) the specification of documents to be produced shall be in sufficient detail to permit the interrogating party to locate and identify the records and ascertain the answer as readily as could the party from whom discovery is sought;

(2) the producing party shall also make available any computerized information or summaries thereof that it has, or can adduce by a relatively simple procedure, unless these materials are privileged or otherwise immune from discovery;

(3) the producing party shall also provide any relevant compilations, abstracts, or summaries in its custody or readily obtainable by it, unless these materials are privileged or otherwise immune from discovery; and

(4) the documents shall be made available for inspection and copying within 14 days after service of the answers to interrogatories or on a date agreed upon by the parties.

[Effective December 5, 2012.]

References: Federal Rule of Civil Procedure 26(a)(1)

Comment

This rule is an adaptation of District Rules 33.3 and 37.1, with the exception of subdivision (e)(1) of this rule.

The initial disclosures required under Federal Rule of Civil Procedure 26(a)(1) must be made in adversary proceedings. Because information previously sought by interrogatories will frequently have been obtained by those initial disclosures, subdivision (a) of this rule has been amended accordingly.

RULE 7034–1. OBJECTIONS TO PRODUCTION OF DOCUMENTS

(a) In connection with any objection to document requests or answers thereto, the party making the objection shall specify and quote verbatim each relevant document request or answer and, immediately following each specification, set forth the basis of the objection.

(b) If an objection is made to any document request or portion thereof, the objection shall state all grounds with specificity. Any ground not stated in the objection within the time provided by the Bankruptcy Rules, or any extensions thereof, shall be deemed waived.

[Effective December 5, 2012.]

RULE 7036–1. REQUESTS FOR ADMISSIONS

In connection with any objection to a request for admission, the objecting party shall (i) specify and quote verbatim in the objection each request to which the objection is made and (ii) immediately following each specification, set forth the basis of the objection.

[Effective December 5, 2012.]

Comment

This rule is an adaptation of District Rule 37.1.

RULE 7054–1. TAXABLE COSTS

District Rule 54.1 applies in cases and adversary proceedings.

[Effective July 1, 1997. Amended effective May 28, 2008.]

Reference: District Rule 54.1

RULE 7055–1. DEFAULT JUDGMENT

A default judgment may be sought only by motion, which shall be served on the defaulting party, the defaulting party's attorney, if any, and, except in an adversary proceeding to determine dischargeability, the trustee.

[Effective July 1, 1997. Amended effective May 28, 2008; December 1, 2009.]

RULE 7056–1. SUMMARY JUDGMENT

A motion for summary judgment pursuant to Bankruptcy Rule 7056 shall include a separate statement of the material facts as to which the moving party contends there is no genuine issue to be tried. Failure to submit such a statement may be grounds for denial of the motion. The opposition to a motion for summary judgment shall include a separate statement of the material facts as to which it is contended that there exists a genuine issue to be tried. All material facts set forth in the statement required to be served by the moving party will be deemed to be admitted by the opposing party unless controverted by the statement required to be served by the opposing party. Each statement of material fact by a movant or opponent must be followed by citation to evidence which would be admissible, set forth as required by Federal Rule of Civil Procedure 56(e).

[Effective July 1, 1997. Amended effective May 28, 2008.]

Reference: Federal Rule of Civil Procedure 56(e).

PART VIII. APPEALS

RULE 8004–1. COPIES OF NOTICE OF APPEAL AND CERTIFICATION FOR DIRECT APPEAL TO CIRCUIT COURT

No later than the day after the filing of a notice of appeal, the appellant shall provide the Clerk with sufficient copies of the notice of appeal or certification for direct appeal and address labels for all parties to be served to permit the Clerk to comply with Bankruptcy Rule 8004.

[Effective July 1, 1997. Amended effective May 28, 2008; December 1, 2009.]

RULE 8006–1. RECORD ON APPEAL

(a) Designation of Items. When a party files a designation of items to be included in a record on appeal pursuant to

Bankruptcy Rule 8006 and an item is not docketed in electronic format, or only an excerpted version of an item is on the docket, that party shall provide the Clerk with a full copy of such designated item. The Clerk shall transmit to the District Clerk, as the record on appeal, the full copies of such items. A party shall electronically file in the bankruptcy case any item that party has designated that does not already appear on the docket.

(b) Exhibits Not Designated. Exhibits not designated to be included in a record on appeal shall remain in the custody of the attorney who has possession of such exhibits, who shall have the responsibility of promptly forwarding them to the clerk of the appellate court upon that clerk's request.

(c) Filing Papers Relating to the Appeal. Upon the docketing of the notice of appeal in the District Court, all papers relating to the appeal shall be filed electronically with the District Clerk, except for a request for a stay pending appeal, which must be filed in accordance with Bankruptcy Rule 8005.

[Redesignated and amended effective May 28, 2008. Amended effective December 1, 2009.]

Reference: Bankruptcy Rules 8005 and 8007.

RULE 8016–1. ORDER, JUDGMENT OR REMAND BY APPELLATE COURT

An order or judgment of an appellate court, when filed in the office of the Clerk, shall become the order or judgment of the Court and be entered as such by the Clerk without further order. If the order or judgment of the appellate court remands for further proceedings, a motion for such further proceedings shall be made by the appropriate party within 21 days of the remand and referred to the Judge who heard the proceeding below, unless the appellate court orders otherwise.

[Effective July 1, 1997. Amended effective May 28, 2008; December 1, 2009.]

PART IX.   GENERAL PROVISIONS

RULE 9001–1.   DEFINITIONS

(a) Definitions. Unless inconsistent with the context, in these rules—

(i) *"Bankruptcy Code"* or *"Code"* means title 11 of the United States Code, as amended from time to time;

(ii) *"Bankruptcy Rules"* means the Federal Rules of Bankruptcy Procedure and Official Bankruptcy Forms promulgated pursuant to 28 U.S.C. § 2075, as amended from time to time;

(iii) *"Chief Judge"* means the Chief Judge of the Court;

(iv) *"Clerk"* means the clerk or a deputy clerk of the Court;

(v) *"Court"* means the United States Bankruptcy Court for the Eastern District of New York and any Judge;

(vi) *"Court's Website"* means www.nyeb.uscourts.gov;

(vii) *"District Clerk"* means the clerk or a deputy clerk of the District Court;

(viii) *"District Court"* means the United States District Court for the Eastern District of New York;

(ix) *"District Judge"* means a United States District Judge or a judge appointed to, or sitting by designation in, the District Court;

(x) *"District Rules"* means the Local Rules of the United States District Courts for the Southern and Eastern Districts of New York;

(xi) *"Electronic Case Filing"* or *"ECF"* means the Electronic Case File System implemented in this Court;

(xii) *"Former E.D.N.Y. Local Bankruptcy Rules"* means the United States Bankruptcy Court Eastern District of New York Local Bankruptcy Rules, effective May 28, 2008, as revised;

(xiii) *"General Order on Electronic Filing Procedures"* means the Revised General Order on Electronic Filing Procedures, dated December 26, 2002, as amended from time to time;

(xiv) *"Judge"* means a bankruptcy judge appointed to or sitting by designation in the United States Bankruptcy Court for the Eastern District of New York (or, with respect to a proceeding that has not been referred or which has been withdrawn, the District Judge); and

(xv) *"United States trustee"* means the Office of the United States trustee for Region 2 or its authorized representative for the Eastern District of New York.

(b) Construction.

(i) Unless inconsistent with the context or stated otherwise above, words and phrases used in these rules shall be construed in accordance with the definitions and rules of construction set forth in the Bankruptcy Code and Bankruptcy Rules.

(ii) Unless inconsistent with the context or stated otherwise, the singular shall be construed to include the plural, and the plural shall be construed to include the singular.

(c) Use of Terms "Documents" and "Papers." The terms "documents" and "papers" as used in these rules include those filed or transmitted by electronic means.

[Effective July 1, 1997. Amended effective May 28, 2008; December 1, 2009.]

RULE 9004–1.   PAPERS—REQUIREMENTS OF FORM

(a) Papers Submitted for Filing.

(i) Papers filed shall:

(A) be plainly typed, printed, or copied;

(B) have no erasures or interlineations which materially deface them; and

(C) be signed in accordance with Bankruptcy Rule 9011.

(ii) Papers filed shall be on 8 ½″ × 11″ paper and shall not be stapled or otherwise bound on the side.

(b) Amendments. An amendment filed as a matter of right or allowed by order shall be filed in a form that is complete, including exhibits, and shall not incorporate by reference any prior paper.

(c) Chambers Copy. A paper copy of each document filed, other than petitions, schedules, and proofs of claim, shall be marked "Chambers Copy" and delivered to the Clerk no later than the day after filing.

[Effective July 1, 1997. Amended effective May 28, 2008; December 1, 2009.]

Cross–References: E.D.N.Y. LBR 5005–1, 5005–2.

RULE 9004–2. CAPTION—PAPERS, GENERAL

(a) All papers submitted for filing shall have a caption stating "United States Bankruptcy Court, Eastern District of New York" and shall include the title and chapter of the case. Subsequent to the filing of the petition for relief, all papers shall also include the case number and the Judge code. All papers filed in an adversary proceeding shall also contain the full title of the lawsuit and the adversary proceeding case number. Except for involuntary petitions, all petitions for relief shall also set forth the last four digits of the debtor's social security number and/or any other federal tax identification number of the debtor.

(b) In consolidated cases, the docket number for the lead case shall be listed first and shall be followed by the docket numbers of all cases contained in the consolidation in ascending order.

(c) The return date and time of a motion shall be included in the upper right hand corner of the caption of the motion and all related papers.

[Effective July 1, 1997. Amended effective May 28, 2008.]

Cross–Reference: E.D.N.Y. LBR 5070–1.

RULE 9005.1–1. NOTICE OF CLAIM OF UNCONSTITUTIONALITY

If a party raises a question concerning the constitutionality of an act of Congress or a state legislative body, that party shall notify the Court of the existence of the question, the title of the case and proceeding, the statute in question, and the grounds upon which it is claimed to be unconstitutional.

[Effective May 28, 2008. Amended effective December 1, 2009.]

Cross–Reference: E.D.N.Y. LBR 9014–1.

Reference: 28 U.S.C. § 2403.

RULE 9006–1. TIME FOR SERVICE AND FILING OF MOTIONS AND ANSWERING PAPERS

(a) Motions. Unless otherwise provided by these rules, the Bankruptcy Rules, or by Court order:

(i) all motion papers shall be served at least 14 days before the hearing date;

(ii) any answering papers shall be served so as to be received not later than 7 days before the hearing date;

(iii) any reply papers shall be served and filed, and a paper copy shall be delivered to the Clerk's office, at least 3 days prior to the hearing date.

Any party filing papers with the Court within 3 days prior to a hearing date shall contact chambers to advise that such papers have been filed.

(b) Time for Filing with Clerk. All motions and answering papers (except reply papers as provided in subdivision (a) of this rule) shall be filed no later than the day after the date of service.

(c) Extra Time for Service. If papers are served by first-class mail, an additional 3 days shall be added to the minimum service requirement. If papers are served by overnight mail or courier, an additional day shall be added to the minimum service requirement.

[Effective July 1, 1997. Amended effective July 1, 1999; May 28, 2008; December 1, 2009.]

Cross–References: E.D.N.Y. LBR 5005–1, 7007–1, 9013–1.

Reference: Bankruptcy Rule 2002.

RULE 9011–1. SIGNING OF PAPERS

(a) Whenever Bankruptcy Rule 9011(a) requires a paper to be signed by an attorney or by a party acting pro se, the name of the attorney or party pro se shall be printed or typed below the signature.

(b) Electronic Signatures. Whenever any applicable statute, rule, or order requires a document to be signed and the document is electronically filed, the document shall contain an electronic signature or a scanned copy of the original signature. An electronic signature shall consist of "s/" followed by the first and last name of the person signing. The original executed document and any original exhibits, shall be maintained by the filer for two years after the entry of a final order closing the case or proceeding. On request of the Court, the filer shall provide an original document for review.

(c) An electronic filing password shall be used only by the attorney to whom the password is assigned and authorized members and employees of such attorney's firm.

[Effective July 1, 1997. Amended effective May 28, 2008; December 1, 2009.]

Cross–References: E.D.N.Y. LBR 1002–1(c) and (d), 5005–2.

Reference: 28 U.S.C. § 1746; Bankruptcy Rule 1008.

RULE 9013–1. MOTION PRACTICE

(a) Rule or Statutory Basis. A motion shall be in writing, unless made during a hearing, and shall specify the rules and statutory provisions upon which it is based and the legal authorities that support the requested relief, either in the motion or in a separate memorandum of law, and the factual grounds for relief. Failure to provide this information may be grounds to strike the motion from the calendar or deny the motion.

(b) Responsive Papers. A response to a written motion shall be in writing and shall state the factual grounds upon which relief is opposed, and the legal authorities that support the respondent's position, either in the response or in a separate memorandum of law. Failure to provide this information may be grounds to strike the response or to grant the motion by default.

(c) Proposed Order. Whenever possible, a motion shall be accompanied by a proposed order.

(d) Entities to Receive Notice. In addition to the notice required by any applicable Bankruptcy Rule or local rule, notice of a motion shall be given to any entity having or claiming an interest in the subject matter of the proposed action or order or who otherwise would be affected by the proposed action or order.

(e) Proof of Service. Unless the movant is proceeding by order to show cause or has otherwise requested that the Court issue an order scheduling a hearing under E.D.N.Y. LBR 9077–1, all motions, documents, or proposed orders shall be filed with proof of service on all relevant parties.

(f) Hearing and Oral Argument Required. Except as provided in E.D.N.Y. LBR 2002–1, a hearing and oral argument is required on all calendar matters unless the Court directs that no hearing is required.

(g) Motions to Avoid Liens. Motions seeking relief pursuant to Bankruptcy Code § 522(f) shall be supported by an affidavit or affirmation stating:

(i) the date of filing of the bankruptcy petition;

(ii) a description of the judgments to be avoided (*e.g.*, name of judgment holder, date and place of docketing of the judgment, amount of judgment);

(iii) the amount of each lien on the property (including all mortgages); and

(iv) the amount of the exemption claimed by the debtor.

Such motion shall also be supported by evidence showing the fair market value of the property as of the date of the filing of the bankruptcy petition; copies of tax assessments or a statement by a debtor or counsel regarding the value of the property are not sufficient. Copies of relevant documents must also be annexed as exhibits, including, *e.g.*, the lien search from the County Clerk's office and pay-off statements from the mortgage holders.

[Effective July 1, 1997. Amended effective July 1, 1999; May 28, 2008.]

Cross–References: E.D.N.Y. LBR 1002–1, 2002–2, 5005–1, 7007–1, 9006–1, 9023–1, 9077–1.

References: Bankruptcy Code § 522(f); Bankruptcy Rule 2002.

RULE 9014–1. CONTESTED MATTERS

Bankruptcy Rule 7016(f) and E.D.N.Y. LBR 7005–1, 7007–1, 7007.1–1, 7016–1, 7026–1, 7026–2, 7030–1, 7033–1, 7034–1, 7036–1, 7054–1, and 7056–1 shall apply in contested matters.

Any reference to adversary proceedings in such rules shall be deemed for this purpose a reference to contested matters.

[Effective July 1, 1997. Amended effective May 28, 2008; December 5, 2012.]

Cross–References: E.D.N.Y. LBR 7005–1, 7007–1, 7007.1–1, 7016–1, 7026–1, 7026–2, 7030–1, 7033–1, 7034–1, 7036–1, 7054–1, 7056–1

References: Bankruptcy Rule 7016(f)

RULE 9014–2. FIRST SCHEDULED HEARING

At the first scheduled hearing in a contested matter, the parties should be prepared to conduct an evidentiary hearing, at which witnesses may testify, if:

(a) the motion requests emergency relief;

(b) the motion requests interim or final relief under § 363(c)(2)(B) or § 364 of the Bankruptcy Code;

(c) the motion requests a continuation of the automatic stay under § 362(c)(3)(B) or imposition of the automatic stay under § 362(c)(4)(B); or

(d) the hearing is on confirmation of a plan in a case under chapter 9, chapter 11 or chapter 12 of the Bankruptcy Code.

The first scheduled hearing in all other types of contested matters will not be an evidentiary hearing at which witnesses may testify unless the Court gives prior notice to the parties that such hearing will be an evidentiary hearing.

[Effective December 5, 2012.]

References: Bankruptcy Code §§ 363(c)(2)(B), 362(c)(3)(B), 364

Comment

Bankruptcy Rule 9014(e), added in 2002, requires that the Court provide procedures that enable parties to ascertain at a reasonable time before any scheduled hearing whether the hearing will be an evidentiary hearing at which witnesses may testify. Nothing in E.D.N.Y. LBR 9014–2 precludes a party from requesting an evidentiary hearing at the first scheduled hearing and asking the Court to provide for notice thereof in accordance with the final paragraph of the rule.

RULE 9018–1. DOCUMENTS FILED UNDER SEAL

(a) Motion. A motion to file a document under seal (but not the document itself) shall be filed electronically. If the motion itself contains confidential information, the movant shall serve and file electronically a redacted version clearly marked as such, and submit an unredacted version for *in camera* review.

(b) Delivery of Sealed Documents. If the Court grants a motion to file a document under seal, in whole or in part, the movant shall deliver to the Clerk:

(i) the documents to be filed under seal (the "sealed documents") and the proposed sealing order in an envelope clearly marked "Under Seal"; and

(ii) an electronically stored document submitted in physical form containing the sealed documents in "pdf" format and the proposed sealing order in a word processing format.

(c) Destruction of Documents Filed Under Seal. Sealed documents shall be destroyed when the bankruptcy case is closed.

[Effective May 28, 2008. Amended effective December 1, 2009.]

Reference: General Order on Electronic Case Filing.

RULE 9019–1. ALTERNATIVE DISPUTE RESOLUTION—MEDIATION

(a) Assignment of a Matter to Mediation. The Court may direct any dispute arising in any case or proceeding (collectively, "Matter") to mediation sua sponte or upon the request of one or more party in interest. The Court may determine which parties in interest shall participate in the mediation. If a Matter is assigned to mediation, the parties shall comply with all applicable pleading, discovery, and other deadlines and scheduling requirements.

(b) Appointment of a Mediator. The mediation participants shall select a mediator and at least one alternate from the Mediation Register of approved mediators kept by the Clerk within 7 days of the entry of the order assigning the matter to mediation. If the mediation participants cannot agree within that time, or if the Court determines that selection of a mediator by the Court is appropriate, then the Court shall appoint a mediator. Within 7 days of the selection of a mediator, the mediation participants and the mediator shall submit a proposed consent order appointing the mediator and describing the mediation procedures, including the terms of the mediator's compensation and expense reimbursement (the "Mediation Order"). Procedures that are not set forth in the Mediation Order shall be governed by agreement of the parties, by this rule, or by the mediator.

The proposed Mediation Order shall be accompanied by a verified statement by the mediator stating that such person does not hold or represent an interest adverse to the estate, except as specifically disclosed therein, and that such person is disinterested.

(c) Mediation Procedures.

(i) Unless the Court orders otherwise, the mediator and the mediation participants shall agree on the time and location for the initial mediation conference, which shall take place as soon as practicable after the entry of the Mediation Order, but no later than 30 days after the entry of the Mediation Order. The mediator may require the mediation participants to submit or exchange documents or information, including a mediation statement, before the initial mediation conference.

(ii) Each mediation participant that is an individual shall attend the mediation conference in person. Each mediation participant that is a government entity shall attend in person by a representative who has, to the extent practicable, authority to settle the matter. All other mediation participants shall attend the mediation conference in person through a representative with authority to settle the matter. The mediator may permit telephonic or video participation in the mediation conference in appropriate circumstances.

(iii) The mediator shall determine the time and place for the mediation, including mediation conferences and caucuses between the mediator and a mediation participant, and the submission or exchange of documents or information. The mediator may not require a mediation participant who is represented by counsel to meet with the mediator without counsel present.

(iv) The mediator may set a deadline for the mediation participants to respond to a settlement proposal, including a settlement proposal by the mediator.

(v) Additional mediation procedures for the mediation may be agreed upon by the mediator and the mediation participants during the mediation process.

(d) Settlement Proposals by the Mediator. The mediator may, but shall not be required to, make a settlement proposal to the mediation participants. A settlement proposal by the mediator that is not accepted by the mediation participants shall not be disclosed to the Court.

(e) Failure to Comply With the Mediation Rule. If a mediation participant willfully fails to participate in good faith in the mediation process, then the mediator shall submit to the Clerk and serve on the mediation participants a report of the failure to participate. The report shall not be electronically filed, shall state on the first page at the top right corner that it is being submitted to the attention of the Clerk, and shall state that it is a report of a failure to mediate in good faith that should not be filed or given to the Judge. The report shall not be sent to the Judge presiding over the matter. The Clerk shall deliver the report to the Judge designated by the Chief Judge for mediation, who will take appropriate action, including holding a conference or hearing in person or telephone, and who may, in appropriate circumstances, impose sanctions.

(f) Post–Mediation Procedures.

(i) If the mediation participants reach an agreement, then the mediator shall serve upon the parties and file electronically with the Court a report stating that the matter has been settled.

(ii) If the mediation participants do not reach an agreement, and the mediator concludes that the mediation is at an impasse, then the mediator shall serve upon the parties and file with the Court a report stating that the mediation has reached an impasse and should be concluded.

(iii) Upon the filing of the mediator's report, the mediation will be placed in suspense and the mediator will be excused from undertaking any further actions, unless otherwise requested by the mediation participants or directed by the Court.

(g) Withdrawal from Mediation. At any time, the Court may withdraw a matter from mediation if the Court determines that the mediation referral is no longer appropriate. At any time, a party in interest, the United States trustee, or the mediator may request a conference with the Court or file a motion to withdraw a matter from mediation for cause.

(h) Mediator Compensation. The mediator shall be compensated on terms that are satisfactory to the mediator and the mediation participants. The mediator's compensation shall be subject to Court approval if the estate is to pay any part of the expense. The mediator and the mediation participants shall set forth the terms of the mediator's compensation in the Mediation Order. Absent agreement or order to the contrary, the mediation participants shall pay equal shares of the mediator's compensation. If the mediator and the mediation participants cannot agree on compensation terms, the Court shall fix terms that are reasonable and just. The Court may also request the mediator serve pro bono or on a reduced fee basis.

(i) Qualifications of the Mediator. The Clerk shall maintain a Mediation Register. Appointments to the Mediation Register shall be for 5–year terms. To qualify for appointment to the Mediation Register, a person must:

(i) file an application in the form established by the Clerk;

(ii) not have been suspended from a professional organization or have had a professional license revoked, not have pending any proceeding to suspend or revoke such license, not have resigned from any applicable professional organization while an investigation into allegations of misconduct which would warrant suspension, disbarment, or professional license revocation was pending; and not been convicted of a felony;

(iii) not have been employed by the Court during the 36–month period preceding the date of such person's appointment to the Mediation Register; and

(iv) meet the following minimum qualifications:

(A) For Lawyers Applying to be a Mediator: A lawyer must:

(1) be, or have been, a member in good standing of the New York State bar for at least 5 years;

(2) be admitted to practice in one of the district courts in the Second Circuit;

(3) have completed at least 12 hours of mediation training;

(4) be willing to undertake a minimum of 5 pro bono mediation assignments during the course of the 5–year term;

(5) file with the application original and current certificates of good standing from the department of the Supreme Court of New York Appellate Division in which he or she is admitted and from one of the district courts within the Second Circuit, or if retired, have been a member in good standing in such courts; and

(6) be certified by the Chief Judge.

(B) For Other Professionals Applying to be a Mediator: A person must:

(1) be, or have been, authorized to practice for at least 5 years under the laws of the State of New York as a professional, including but not limited to, an accountant, real estate broker, appraiser, engineer, or other professional occupation;

(2) be an active member in good standing and submit to the Clerk proof of his or her professional status, or if retired, have been a member in good standing, of any applicable professional organization;

(3) have completed a mediation course or courses consisting of at least 12 hours of training;

(4) be willing to undertake a minimum of five pro bono mediation assignments during the course of the 5–year term; and

(5) be certified by the Chief Judge.

The Chief Judge may waive any of the requirements of this subdivision for good cause set forth in the application. Each person certified as a mediator shall take an oath or affirmation before his or her appointment to the Mediation Register.

(j) Removal from the Mediation Register. A person may be removed from the Mediation Register at the person's request or by the Chief Judge.

(k) The Mediation Register. The Clerk shall maintain the Mediation Register at the Court's Website and in the Clerk's office. The Mediation Register shall list the persons appointed to the Mediation Register, together with a brief biography and fee information supplied by the mediator to the Clerk. The Clerk shall also maintain for public inspection the applications filed by persons appointed to the Mediation Register.

(*l*) Confidentiality. Any oral or written statements made by the mediator, the mediation participants, or others during the mediation process shall not be disclosed by any of the mediation participants, their agents, or the mediator, except that such statements may be disclosed to a Judge designated to hear a matter under subdivision (e) of this rule. Matters not to be disclosed include, without limitation:

(i) views expressed or suggestions made by a participant with respect to a possible settlement of the dispute;

(ii) whether a participant indicated a willingness to accept a proposal for settlement made by the mediator;

(iii) proposals made or views expressed by the mediator;

(iv) statements or admissions made by a participant; and

(v) documents prepared for use in the mediation.

Records, reports, or other documents received by a mediator shall be confidential and shall not be provided to the Court except as required by subdivision (e) of this rule. The mediator shall not be compelled to testify or disclose any information concerning the mediation in any forum or proceeding, except as required by subdivision (e) of this rule. Unless the mediation participants and the mediator agree or the Court orders otherwise, 60 days after the mediator files a report under subdivision (f) of this rule, the mediator may discard the submissions made by the mediation participants and any other documents or information relating to the mediation.

Rule 408 of the Federal Rules of Evidence and any applicable federal or state statute, rule, common law, or judicial precedent relating to the privileged nature of settlement discussions, mediation, or other alternative dispute resolution procedure shall apply to statements and information that may not be disclosed pursuant to this rule. Information otherwise discoverable or admissible in evidence shall not be immunized from discovery or inadmissible in evidence because it was disclosed in the mediation.

(m) Immunity. The mediator shall be immune from claims arising out of acts or omissions arising from or relating to his or her service as a Court appointee, to the maximum extent allowed by law.

[Effective May 28, 2008. Amended effective December 1, 2009.]

Reference: Federal Rule of Evidence 408.

RULE 9021–1. ENTRY OF ORDERS, JUDGMENTS AND DECREES

(a) Entry. The Clerk shall enter all orders, decrees, and judgments of the Court in the Electronic Case Filing system which shall constitute docketing of the order, decree, or judgment for all purposes. The Clerk's notation in the appropriate docket of an order, judgment, or decree shall constitute the entry of the order, judgment, or decree.

(b) Official Location. Each Court maintains a separate index of judgments signed by the Judges located at that site.

[Effective July 1, 1997. Amended effective July 1, 1999; May 28, 2008.]

RULE 9023–1. COSTS; NEW TRIALS; MOTIONS FOR RECONSIDERATION

(a) Costs. The expense of any party in obtaining all or any part of a transcript for purposes of a new trial or amended findings may be a cost taxable against the losing party.

(b) Motions for Reconsideration. A motion for reconsideration of an order may be made pursuant to Bankruptcy Rule 9023.

[Effective July 1, 1997. Amended effective May 28, 2008.]

RULE 9025–1. SURETIES

(a) Execution by Surety Only. If a bond, undertaking, or stipulation is required, an instrument executed only by the surety shall be sufficient.

(b) Security for Bond. Except as otherwise provided by law, every bond, undertaking, or stipulation referring to a bond shall be secured by:

(i) the deposit of cash or government bonds in the amount of the bond, undertaking, or stipulation;

(ii) the undertaking or guaranty of a corporate surety holding a certificate of authority from the Secretary of the Treasury; or

(iii) the undertaking or guaranty of two individual residents of the Eastern District or Southern District of New York, each of whom owns real or personal property within such district with an unencumbered value of twice the amount of the bond in excess of the surety's debts, liabilities, legal exemptions, and obligations on other bonds, guaranties, undertakings, or stipulations.

(c) Affidavit by Individual Surety. In the case of a bond, undertaking, or stipulation executed by individual sureties, each surety shall attach an affidavit of justification, giving the surety's full name, occupation, and residence and business addresses, and showing that the surety is not disqualified from acting as an individual surety under subdivision (d) of this rule.

(d) Persons Who May Not Act as Sureties. Members of the bar, administrative officers and employees of the Court, the marshal, and the marshal's deputies and assistants may not act as sureties in any pending case, adversary proceeding, or contested matter.

(e) Approval of Bonds of Corporate Sureties. Except as otherwise provided by Bankruptcy Code §§ 303 and 322(b) and Bankruptcy Rule 2010, all bonds, undertakings, and stipulations of corporate sureties holding certificates of authority from the Secretary of the Treasury, may be approved by the Clerk when the amount of such bonds or undertakings has been fixed by Court order or statute.

[Effective July 1, 1997. Amended effective July 1, 1999; May 28, 2008.]

Cross–Reference: E.D.N.Y. LBR 6005–1.

References: Bankruptcy Code §§ 303, 322(b); Bankruptcy Rule 2010.

RULE 9028–1. UNAVAILABILITY OF A JUDGE

In the event of the unavailability of a Judge, any other Judge may act. To obtain the assistance of an available Judge, the parties shall communicate first with the chambers staff of the assigned Judge or, if chambers staff is unavailable, then with the Clerk.

[Effective July 1, 1997. Amended effective July 1, 1999.]

RULE 9036–1. CONSENT TO NOTICE BY ELECTRONIC TRANSMISSION

The receipt of an Electronic Case Filing password from the Court shall constitute consent to electronic notice by the attorney receiving the password pursuant to Bankruptcy Rule 9036, and shall constitute a waiver by such attorney of the right to receive notice by other, non-electronic means.

[Effective May 28, 2008.]

RULE 9036–2. CONSENT TO SERVICE BY ELECTRONIC TRANSMISSION

(a) Consent to Electronic Service. The receipt of an Electronic Case Filing password from the Court shall constitute consent to electronic service by the attorney receiving the password pursuant to Bankruptcy Rule 9036, and except as otherwise provided in subdivision (c) of this rule, constitutes a waiver by such attorney of the right to receive service by other, non-electronic means.

(b) Service by Electronic Transmission. Whenever service is required to be made on a person who has consented to, or is deemed to have consented to, electronic service in accordance with Bankruptcy Rule 9036 or subdivision (a) of this rule, service shall be made by serving the "Notice of Electronic Filing" generated by the ECF system either by hand, facsimile, or e-mail, or by overnight mail if service by hand, facsimile, or e-mail is impracticable.

(c) Exceptions to Electronic Service. Notwithstanding E.D.N.Y. LBR 9036–1 and subdivisions (a) and (b) of this rule, paper copies of documents or notices shall be served in the following circumstances:

(i) Service made in accordance with Bankruptcy Rules 7004 and 9016; and

(ii) Upon commencement of a case, service by counsel for the debtor of the petition, schedules, and statement of affairs on the United States trustee, all applicable governmental agencies, and the trustee assigned to the case, when applicable.

(d) Proof of Service. Proof of service under this rule as required by E.D.N.Y. LBR 9013–1(f), shall include a list of parties electronically served and the e-mail address where service was transmitted.

[Effective May 28, 2008.]

Cross–Reference: E.D.N.Y. LBR 2002–2, 9013–1.

Reference: General Order on Electronic Filing Procedures, Bankruptcy Rules 2002, 7004, 9016; Federal Rules of Civil Procedure 4, 45.

RULE 9070–1. CUSTODY OF EXHIBITS

(a) Retention by Attorney. In any trial or contested hearing in which exhibits are introduced, exhibits shall not be filed with the Clerk unless the Court orders such filing, but shall be retained by the attorney or party who offered them in Court. That attorney or party shall permit their inspection by any party for the purpose of preparing the record on appeal and shall be charged with the responsibility for their safekeeping and transportation to the appellate court.

(b) Removal of Exhibits from Court. Exhibits that have been filed with the Clerk shall be removed by the party responsible for the exhibits:

(i) if no appeal has been taken, at the expiration of the time for taking an appeal; or

(ii) if an appeal has been taken, within 30 days after the record on appeal has been returned to the Clerk.

Parties failing to comply with this rule shall be notified by the Clerk to remove their exhibits, and, upon their failure to do so within 30 days of such notification, the Clerk may dispose of the exhibits at the expense of the party responsible.

[Effective July 1, 1997. Amended effective May 28, 2008.]

Cross–Reference: E.D.N.Y. LBR 8007–1.

RULE 9072–1. SETTLEMENT OR SUBMISSION OF ORDER, JUDGMENT OR DECREE

(a) Settlement of Order, Judgment or Decree. If, following a trial, hearing, or decision in an adversary proceeding or contested matter, the Court directs a party to settle an order, judgment, or decree, the party shall, within 14 days of the Court's direction, or such other time period as the Court may direct, file its proposed order, judgment, or decree upon at least 7 days' notice to all parties to the adversary proceeding

or contested matter, except that such notice period shall not apply if all parties to the adversary proceeding or contested matter have consented in writing to the proposed order, judgment, or decree. Counter-proposals of the proposed order, judgment, or decree shall be filed and served on at least 3 days' notice. If the proposed or counter-proposed order, judgment, or decree is served by first-class mail, an additional 3 days shall be added to the minimum service requirement. If the proposed or counter-proposed order, judgment, or decree is served by overnight mail or courier, an additional day shall be added to the minimum service requirement.

(b) Submission of Order, Judgment or Decree. If, following a trial, hearing or decision in an adversary proceeding or contested matter, the Court directs a party to submit an order, judgment, or decree, the party shall, within 14 days of the Court's direction, file its proposed order, judgment, or decree.

(c) Reference to Hearing Date. The proposed order, judgment, or decree and any counter-proposal shall refer to the hearing date to which the order applies.

(d) Abandonment of Matter. If the order is not timely submitted or settled, the matter may be deemed abandoned.

[Effective July 1, 1997. Amended effective May 28, 2008; December 1, 2009.]

RULE 9077–1. ORDERS TO SHOW CAUSE; EX PARTE ORDERS; ORDERS SHORTENING TIME

(a) Orders to Show Cause. An order to show cause shall be based on an affidavit or an affirmation showing reasons why proceeding other than by notice of motion is necessary. The affidavit or affirmation also shall state whether a previous application for similar relief has been made.

(b) Ex Parte Orders. An ex parte request for an order shall be based on an affidavit or an affirmation showing cause for ex parte relief, and stating whether a previous application for similar relief has been made.

(c) Orders Shortening Time. When expedited relief is thought necessary and the requirements for an order to show cause are not present and ex parte relief is not appropriate, the moving party may proceed by submitting a proposed order shortening time. A request for an order shortening time may be made ex parte and shall be supported by an affidavit or an affirmation showing cause for such expedited relief and stating whether a previous application for similar relief has been made.

[Effective July 1, 1997. Amended effective May 28, 2008; December 1, 2009.]

Reference: Bankruptcy Rule 9006.

SELECTED ORDERS

ADMINISTRATIVE ORDER 476. MANDATORY FILING OF DOCUMENTS BY ELECTRONIC MEANS

Whereas, the court having established, by General Order dated December 26, 2002, electronic filing procedures applicable to all bankruptcy cases and adversary proceedings filed on or after January 1, 2003, and

Whereas, it being in the court's interest to ensure compliance with such procedures by the practicing bar without any undue delay, it is

ORDERED, that effective October 1, 2003, any document (other than a proof of claim) filed by an attorney in a case which has been assigned to the court's Electronic Case Filing System shall be filed electronically, either over the Internet or on diskette in PDF format, and it is further,

ORDERED, that the Clerk is hereby authorized to reject for filing any document not submitted in accordance with the foregoing specification. Mandatory filing of all documents over the Internet will become effective as of a date to be determined by the court.

[Dated: June 4, 2003.]

ADMINISTRATIVE ORDER 487. TRANSFER OF CASES IN WHICH PETITION WAS INADVERTENTLY FILED IN THIS DISTRICT

Whereas, Pay.gov financial services are to be implemented in this Court effective May 1, 2005, and

Whereas, the implementation of Pay.gov requires that certain Court procedures be modified, it is

ORDERED, that effective May 1, 2005, in connection with any bankruptcy petition filed over the Internet, the Clerk is authorized and directed, upon being informed by the debtor's counsel that a bankruptcy petition was inadvertently filed in this district, to transfer the bankruptcy case to the appropriate district.

[Dated: March 31, 2005.]

ADMINISTRATIVE ORDER 488. DISMISSAL OF DUPLICATE PETITION FILED IN ERROR

Whereas, Pay.gov financial services are to be implemented in this Court effective May 1, 2005, and

Whereas, the implementation of Pay.gov requires that certain Court Procedures be modified, it is

ORDERED, that effective May 1, 2005, in connection with any bankruptcy petition filed over the Internet, the Clerk is authorized and directed, upon being informed by the debtor's counsel that a duplicate bankruptcy petition was inadvertently filed, to dismiss the duplicate bankruptcy case; and it is further

ORDERED, that the Clerk is authorized and directed to refund any filing fee which may have been paid in connection with such duplicate filing; and it is further

ORDERED, that the entry on the case docket of the order of dismissal shall be deemed sufficient notice of the dismissal of the case.

[Dated: March 31, 2005.]

ADMINISTRATIVE ORDER 491. DISMISSAL OF DUPLICATE ADVERSARY PROCEEDING FILED IN ERROR

Whereas, Pay.gov financial services are to be implemented in this Court effective May 1, 2005, and Whereas, the implementation of Pay.gov requires that certain Court procedures be modified, it is Ordered, that effective May 1, 2005, in connection with any adversary proceeding filed over the Internet, the Clerk is authorized and directed, upon being informed by counsel for the plaintiff that a duplicate adversary proceeding was inadvertently filed, to dismiss the duplicate adversary proceeding; and it is further

Ordered, that the Clerk is authorized and directed to refund any filing fee which may have been paid in connection with such duplicate filing; and it is further

Ordered, that the entry on the case docket of the order of dismissal shall be deemed sufficient notice of the dismissal of the adversary proceeding.

[Dated: April 14, 2005.]

ADMINISTRATIVE ORDER 512.   LIMITED ACCESS FILING OF DOCUMENTS BY ELECTRONIC MEANS

Whereas, the court having established, by General Order dated December 26, 2002, electronic filing procedures applicable to all bankruptcy cases and adversary proceedings filed on or after January 1, 2003, and

Whereas, it being in the court's interest to enable creditors (limited users) to utilize the court's Electronic Case Filing System to electronically file claims, transfers of claim and notices of appearance, and

Whereas, a creditor (limited user) will utilize the Limited Access Password Application to request access to the Electronic Case Filing system and will follow the rules of the ECF General Order and the Limited Access Password Application, it is

ORDERED, that effective January 3, 2007, all proofs of claim, transfers of claim and notices of appearance may be filed electronically in a case which has been designated as an electronic case in the court's Electronic Case Filing System (Chapter 11 cases filed on or after April 1, 2002 and all cases filed on or after January 1, 2003).

[Dated: December 11, 2006.]

GENERAL ORDER NO. 533.   IN RE: ADOPTION OF FORM FOR MOTIONS FOR RELIEF FROM STAY TO FORECLOSE A MORTGAGE ON REAL PROPERTY OR A SECURITY INTEREST IN A COOPERATIVE APARTMENT

BY resolution of the Board of Judges of the Bankruptcy Court for the Eastern District of New York, it is hereby

ORDERED, that all motions filed on or after September 1, 2008, in the United States Bankruptcy Court for the Eastern District of New York, in cases filed by individuals, seeking relief from the automatic stay pursuant to 11 U.S.C. § 362 to foreclose a mortgage on real property or a security interest in a cooperative apartment, shall include, as an exhibit to the motion, a completed copy of the annexed **Form for Motions for Relief from Stay to Foreclose a Mortgage on Real Property or a Security Interest in a Cooperative Apartment** (the "Form"); and it is further

ORDERED, that unexcused failure to comply with this order may constitute grounds for adjournment or denial of the motion.

[Dated: July 18, 2008.]

UNITED STATES BANKRUPTCY COURT
EASTERN DISTRICT OF NEW YORK
-- X

                          CASE NO. ___—____ (____)

                          CHAPTER ___

-- x

RELIEF FROM STAY—REAL ESTATE AND
COOPERATIVE APARTMENTS
BACKGROUND INFORMATION

1. ADDRESS OF REAL PROPERTY OR COOPERATIVE APARTMENT: _____
_____
_____

2. LENDER NAME: _____
_____

3. MORTGAGE DATE: _____

4. POST-PETITION PAYMENT ADDRESS: _____
_____
_____

DEBT AND VALUE REPRESENTATIONS

5. TOTAL PRE-PETITION AND POST-PETITION INDEBTEDNESS OF DEBTOR(S) TO MOVANT AS OF THE MOTION FILING DATE: $_____

(THIS MAY NOT BE RELIED UPON AS A "PAYOFF" QUOTATION.)

6. MOVANT'S ESTIMATED MARKET VALUE OF THE REAL PROPERTY OR COOPERATIVE APARTMENT AS OF THE MOTION FILING DATE: $_____

7. SOURCE OF ESTIMATED MARKET VALUE: _____

STATUS OF THE DEBT AS OF THE PETITION DATE

8. DEBTOR(S)'S INDEBTEDNESS TO MOVANT AS OF THE PETITION DATE:

    A. TOTAL: $_____

    B. PRINCIPAL: $_____

    C. INTEREST: $_____

    D. ESCROW (TAXES AND INSURANCE): $_____

    E. FORCED PLACED INSURANCE EXPENDED BY MOVANT: $_____

    F. PRE-PETITION ATTORNEYS' FEES CHARGED TO DEBTOR(S): $_____

    G. PRE-PETITION LATE FEES CHARGED TO DEBTOR(S): $_____

9. CONTRACT INTEREST RATE: _____

(IF THE INTEREST RATE HAS CHANGED, LIST THE RATE(S) AND DATE(S) THAT EACH RATE WAS IN EFFECT ON A SEPARATE SHEET AND ATTACH THE SHEET AS AN EXHIBIT TO THIS FORM. STATE THE EXHIBIT NUMBER HERE: ___.)

10. OTHER PRE-PETITION FEES, CHARGES OR AMOUNTS CHARGED TO DEBTOR(S)'S ACCOUNT AND NOT LISTED ABOVE: _____
_____
_____

(IF ADDITIONAL SPACE IS REQUIRED, LIST THE AMOUNT(S) ON A SEPARATE SHEET AND ATTACH THE SHEET AS AN EXHIBIT TO THIS FORM. STATE THE EXHIBIT NUMBER HERE: ___.)

AMOUNT OF POST–PETITION DEFAULT AS OF THE MOTION FILING DATE

11. DATE OF RECEIPT OF LAST PAYMENT: _____

12. NUMBER OF PAYMENTS DUE FROM PETITION DATE TO MOTION FILING DATE: ____ PAYMENTS.

13. POST–PETITION PAYMENTS IN DEFAULT:

PAYMENT DUE DATE	AMOUNT DUE	AMOUNT RECEIVED	AMOUNT APPLIED TO PRINCIPAL	AMOUNT APPLIED TO INTEREST	AMOUNT APPLIED TO ESCROW	LATE FEE CHARGED
TOTAL:	$	$	$	$	$	$

14. OTHER POST-PETITION FEES CHARGED TO DEBTOR(S):

     A. TOTAL: $_____

     B. ATTORNEYS' FEES IN CONNECTION WITH THIS MOTION: $_____

     C. FILING FEE IN CONNECTION WITH THIS MOTION: $_____

     D. OTHER POST-PETITION ATTORNEYS' FEES: $_____

     E. POST-PETITION INSPECTION FEES: $_____

     F. POST-PETITION APPRAISAL/BROKER'S PRICE OPINION FEES: $_____

     G. FORCED PLACED INSURANCE EXPENDED BY MOVANT: $_____

     15. AMOUNT HELD IN SUSPENSE BY MOVANT: $_____

16. OTHER POST-PETITION FEES, CHARGES OR AMOUNTS CHARGED TO DEBTOR(S)'S ACCOUNT AND NOT LISTED ABOVE: _____

_____

_____

(IF ADDITIONAL SPACE IS REQUIRED, LIST THE AMOUNT(S) ON A SEPARATE SHEET AND ATTACH THE SHEET AS AN EXHIBIT TO THIS FORM. STATE THE EXHIBIT NUMBER HERE: ____.)

REQUIRED ATTACHMENTS TO MOTION

PLEASE ATTACH THE FOLLOWING DOCUMENTS TO THIS MOTION AND INDICATE THE EXHIBIT NUMBER ASSOCIATED WITH EACH DOCUMENT.

(1) COPIES OF DOCUMENTS THAT ESTABLISH MOVANT'S INTEREST IN THE SUBJECT PROPERTY. FOR PURPOSES OF EXAMPLE ONLY, THIS MAY BE A COMPLETE AND LEGIBLE COPY OF THE PROMISSORY NOTE OR OTHER DEBT INSTRUMENT TOGETHER WITH A COMPLETE AND LEGIBLE COPY OF THE MORTGAGE AND ANY ASSIGNMENTS IN THE CHAIN FROM THE ORIGINAL MORTGAGEE TO THE CURRENT MOVING PARTY. (EXHIBIT ____.)

(2) COPIES OF DOCUMENTS THAT ESTABLISH MOVANT'S STANDING TO BRING THIS MOTION. (EXHIBIT ____.)

(3) COPIES OF DOCUMENTS THAT ESTABLISH THAT MOVANT'S INTEREST IN THE REAL PROPERTY OR COOPERATIVE APARTMENT WAS PERFECTED. FOR THE PURPOSES OF EXAMPLE ONLY, THIS MAY BE A COMPLETE AND LEGIBLE COPY OF THE FINANCING STATEMENT (UCC–1) FILED WITH THE CLERK'S OFFICE OR THE

REGISTER OF THE COUNTY IN WHICH THE PROPERTY OR COOPERATIVE APARTMENT IS LOCATED. (EXHIBIT ___.)

DECLARATION AS TO BUSINESS RECORDS *

I, _____, THE _____ OF _____, THE MOVANT HEREIN, DECLARE PURSUANT TO 28 U.S.C. SECTION 1746 UNDER PENALTY OF PERJURY THAT THE INFORMATION PROVIDED IN THIS FORM AND ANY EXHIBITS ATTACHED HERETO (OTHER THAN THE TRANSACTIONAL DOCUMENTS ATTACHED AS REQUIRED BY PARAGRAPHS 1, 2, AND 3, ABOVE) IS DERIVED FROM RECORDS THAT WERE MADE AT OR NEAR THE TIME OF THE OCCURRENCE OF THE MATTERS SET FORTH BY, OR FROM INFORMATION TRANSMITTED BY, A PERSON WITH KNOWLEDGE OF THOSE MATTERS; THAT THE RECORDS WERE KEPT IN THE COURSE OF THE REGULARLY CONDUCTED ACTIVITY; AND THAT THE RECORDS WERE MADE IN THE COURSE OF THE REGULARLY CONDUCTED ACTIVITY AS A REGULAR PRACTICE.

I FURTHER DECLARE THAT COPIES OF ANY TRANSACTIONAL DOCUMENTS ATTACHED TO THIS FORM AS REQUIRED BY PARAGRAPHS 1, 2, AND 3, ABOVE, ARE TRUE AND CORRECT COPIES OF THE ORIGINAL DOCUMENTS.

EXECUTED AT _____

on this ___ day of _____, 20___

<NAME>
<TITLE>
<MOVANT>
<STREET ADDRESS>
<CITY, STATE AND ZIP CODE>

DECLARATION

I, _____, THE _____ OF _____, THE MOVANT HEREIN, DECLARE PURSUANT TO 28 U.S.C. SECTION 1746 UNDER PENALTY OF PERJURY THAT THE FOREGOING IS TRUE AND CORRECT BASED ON PERSONAL KNOWLEDGE OF THE MOVANT'S BOOKS AND BUSINESS RECORDS.

EXECUTED AT _____

on this ___ day of _____, 20___

<NAME>
<TITLE>
<MOVANT>
<STREET ADDRESS>
<CITY, STATE AND ZIP CODE>

* [**Publisher's Note:** On February 11, 2009, the Court issued the following notice: "The two Declarations on the last page of the Form are both required to be executed by a qualified witness with personal knowledge of the facts being attested to, which will ordinarily be an employee of the movant, not an attorney. Where a judge of this Court requires an attorney's affidavit in support of a motion for relief from the automatic stay, this must be provided in addition to the Declarations required by General Order No. 533."]

GENERAL ORDER NO. 536. IN RE: ELECTRONIC CASE FILING OF DOCUMENTS IN NON–ELECTRONIC CASES

WHEREAS, the Court having established, by General Order No. 473, dated December 26, 2002, electronic filing procedures applicable to all bankruptcy cases and adversary proceedings filed on or after January 1, 2003, and

WHEREAS, E.D.N.Y. Local Bankruptcy Rule 5005–1, *Filing and Transmittal of Papers in Non–Electronic Cases*, requires the filing of all papers in any non-electronic case to be filed in the office of the Clerk located where the Judge who is assigned to the matter regularly sits, and

WHEREAS, it is in the Court's best interest to reduce the volume of paper filings submitted to the Court, and to allow practitioners the ability to file electronically in these cases, it is

ORDERED, that effective, January 1, 2009, all pending cases in the Eastern District of New York will be deemed electronic cases, and any document filed by an attorney on or after January 1, 2009, may be filed via the Internet, and it is further

ORDERED, that this Order supercedes Section II, A, 7, *Administrative Procedures on Electronic Filing and Service of Documents*, approved by this Court's General Order No. 473, and E.D.N.Y. Local Bankruptcy Rule 5005–1.

[Dated: December 18, 2008.]

ADMINISTRATIVE ORDER NO. 538.   IN THE MATTER OF ORDER ESTABLISHING PROCEDURES FOR MONTHLY COMPENSATION AND REIMBURSEMENT OF EXPENSES OF PROFESSIONALS

BY the Board of Judges of the Bankruptcy Court for the Eastern District of New York, it is resolved that in order to provide professionals with clear and concise procedures for seeking monthly compensation and reimbursement of expenses in chapter 11 cases (the "Monthly Fee Order"), all Monthly Fee Orders requested in the Bankruptcy Court for the Eastern District of New York shall be requested by motion on notice to the parties described in the Monthly Fee Order, and shall conform substantially to the form of Monthly Fee Order annexed hereto.

NOW, THEREFORE, it is

ORDERED, that the annexed form of Monthly Fee Order be, and the same is hereby adopted, effective immediately; and it is further

ORDERED, that nothing in this General Order shall be interpreted as creating any entitlement to monthly compensation; and it is further

ORDERED, that whether or not a motion for a Monthly Fee Order will be granted will be determined on a case-by-case basis by the Judge to whom the case is assigned.

[Dated: April 10, 2009.]

UNITED STATES BANKRUPTCY COURT
EASTERN DISTRICT OF NEW YORK
---x
     In re:

                                             Chapter 11

                                             Case No.

                     Debtor.
---x

ORDER PURSUANT TO 11 U.S.C. §§ 105(a) AND 331 ESTABLISHING PROCEDURES FOR MONTHLY COMPENSATION AND REIMBURSEMENT OF EXPENSES OF PROFESSIONALS

[NAMES OF DEBTOR], debtor and debtor-in-possession (the "Debtor"), moves, by a motion dated _____ ___, 200 ___ (the "Motion"), for an order, pursuant to §§ 105(a) and 331 of the United States Bankruptcy Code (the "Code"), establishing procedures for monthly compensation and reimbursement of expenses of professionals retained by order of this Court, and this Court having determined that the relief requested in the Motion is in the best interests of the Debtors, their estates, and creditors; and it appearing that proper and adequate notice has been given by service of the Motion on the Office of the United States Trustee, counsel to each official committee (if no committee is appointed, the 20 largest unsecured creditors), counsel to all post-petition lenders (or counsel to their agent(s)), and all parties who filed a notice of appearance; and that no other or further notice is necessary; and upon the record of the hearing herein; and upon the representation of the Debtors that this estate is administratively solvent; and after due deliberation thereon; and good and sufficient cause appearing therefor, it is hereby

ORDERED, that except as may otherwise be provided in Court orders authorizing the retention of specific professionals, all professionals in this case may seek monthly compensation in accordance with the following procedure:

(a) On or before the twentieth (20th) day of each month following the month for which compensation is sought, each professional seeking compensation under this Order will serve a monthly statement, by hand or overnight delivery on (i) _____, the officer designated by the Debtors to be responsible for such matters; (ii) counsel to the Debtors; (iii) counsel to all official committees; (iv) counsel for the Office of the United States Trustee, 271 Cadman Plaza East, Suite 4529, Brooklyn, New York 11201 (Attn: _____, Esq.); (vi) counsel to all postpetition lenders or their agent(s); and (v) _____ (anyone else the Court may designate);

(b) The monthly statement need not be filed with the Court and a courtesy copy need not be delivered to the presiding judge's chambers, because this Order is not intended to alter the fee application requirements outlined in §§ 330 and 331 of the Code and because professionals are still required to serve and file interim and final applications for approval of fees and expenses in accordance with the relevant provisions of the Code, the Federal Rules of Bankruptcy Procedure and the Local Rules for the United States Bankruptcy Court, Eastern District of New York;

(c) Each monthly fee statement must contain a list of the individuals and their respective titles (e.g. attorney, accountant, or paralegal) who provided services during the statement period, their respective billing rates, the aggregate hours spent by each individual, a reasonably detailed breakdown of the disbursements incurred (no professional should seek reimbursement of an expense which would otherwise not be allowed pursuant to the United States Trustee Guidelines for Reviewing Applications for Compensation and Reimbursement of Expenses Filed under 11 U.S.C. § 330 issued May 17, 1996 as amended from time to time), and contemporaneously maintained time entries for each individual in increments of tenths (1/10) of an hour;

(d) Each person receiving a statement will have at least fifteen (15) days after its receipt to review it and, in the event that he or she has an objection to the compensation or reimbursement sought in a particular statement, he or she shall, by no later than the thirty-fifth (35th) day following the month for which compensation is sought, serve upon the professional whose statement is objected to, and the other persons designated to receive statements in paragraph (a), a written "Notice Of Objection To Fee Statement," setting forth the nature of the objection and the amount of fees or expenses at issue;

(e) At the expiration of the thirty-five (35) day period, the Debtors shall promptly pay eighty percent (80%) of the fees and one hundred percent (100%) of the expenses identified in each monthly statement to which no objection has been served in accordance with paragraph (d);

(f) If the Debtors receive an objection to a particular fee statement, they shall withhold payment of that portion of the fee statement to which the objection is directed and promptly pay the remainder of the fees and disbursements in the percentages set forth in paragraph (e);

(g) If the parties to an objection are able to resolve their dispute following the service of a Notice Of Objection To Fee Statement and if the party whose statement was objected to serves on all of the parties listed in paragraph (a) a statement indicating that the objection is withdrawn and describing in detail the terms of the resolution, then the debtor shall promptly pay, in accordance with paragraph (e), that portion of the fee statement which is no longer subject to an objection;

(h) All objections that are not resolved by the parties, shall be preserved and presented to the Court at the next interim or final fee application hearing to be heard by the Court. See paragraph (j), below;

(i) The service of an objection in accordance with paragraph (d) shall not prejudice the objecting party's right to object to any fee application made to the Court in accordance with the Code on any ground, whether raised in the objection or not. Furthermore, the decision by any party not to object to a fee statement shall not be a waiver of any kind or prejudice that party's right to object to any fee application subsequently made to the Court in accordance with the Code;

(j) Approximately every 120 days, but no less frequently than every 150 days, each of the professionals shall serve and file with the Court an application for interim or final Court approval and allowance, pursuant to sections 330 and 331 of the Bankruptcy Code (as the case may be), of the compensation and reimbursement of expenses previously paid;

(k) Any professional who fails to file an application seeking approval of compensation and expenses previously paid under this Order within the time frame set forth in subparagraph (j) above shall (1) be ineligible to receive further monthly payments of fees or expenses as provided herein until further order of the Court and (2) may be required to disgorge any fees paid since the last fee application (or, if no fee application has been filed by such professional, since retention);

(*l*) The pendency of an objection or the entry of a Court order that payment of compensation or reimbursement of expenses was improper as to a particular statement shall not disqualify a professional from the future payment of compensation or reimbursement of expenses as set forth above, unless otherwise ordered by the Court;

(m) Neither the payment of, nor the failure to pay, in whole or in part, monthly compensation and reimbursement as provided herein shall have any effect on this Court's interim or final allowance of compensation and reimbursement of expenses of any professionals;

(n) Counsel for each official committee may, in accordance with the foregoing procedure for monthly compensation and reimbursement of professionals, collect and submit statements of expenses, with supporting vouchers, from members of the committee he or she represents; and it is further

ORDERED, that each professional may seek, in its first request for compensation and reimbursement of expenses pursuant to this Order, compensation for work performed and reimbursement for expenses incurred during the period beginning on the date of the professional's retention and ending on _____ ___, 200 ___; and it is further

ORDERED, that the amount of fees and disbursements sought be set out in U.S. dollars; [if the fees and disbursements are to be paid in foreign currency, the amount shall be set out in U.S. dollars and the conversion amount in the foreign currency, calculated at the time of the submission of the application;] and it is further

ORDERED, that the Debtors shall include all payments to professionals on their monthly operating reports, detailed so as to state the amount paid to each of the professionals; and it is further

ORDERED, that any party in interest may file a motion seeking modification or suspension of monthly payments to professionals pursuant to this order on any applicable grounds, including that the Debtors have not timely filed monthly operating reports, or remained current with their administrative expenses and 28 U.S.C. § 1930 fees, and in such event no further payments shall be made pursuant to this order until such motion is resolved; and it is further

ORDERED, that monthly payments to professionals pursuant to this Order may be suspended by the Court *sua sponte*; and it is further

ORDERED, that all time periods set forth in this Order shall be calculated in accordance with Federal Rule of Bankruptcy Procedure 9006(a); and it is further

ORDERED, that the Debtors shall serve a copy of this Order on all entities specified in paragraph (a) hereof.

Dated: Brooklyn, New York
_____ ___, 200___

_____
UNITED STATES BANKRUPTCY
JUDGE

ADMINISTRATIVE ORDER NO. 539. IN THE MATTER OF DISMISSAL OF CASES FOR WHICH FILING FEE HAS NOT BEEN PAID

Whereas, Pay.gov financial services were implemented in this Court effective May 1, 2005, and

Whereas, the implementation of Pay.gov requires that certain Court procedures be modified, it is

ORDERED, that effective December 1, 2009, where a bankruptcy petition is filed electronically over the Internet and the filing fee has not been paid in full, the Clerk is authorized and directed to send a notice to the debtor and the debtor's counsel informing them that the filing fee must be paid in full within five (5) days of the date of the Notice (the "Cure Period"), failing which the bankruptcy case may be dismissed.

[Dated: November 25, 2009.]

ADMINISTRATIVE ORDER NO. 540. IN THE MATTER OF: DISMISSAL OF ADVERSARY PROCEEDING FOR WHICH FILING FEE HAS NOT BEEN PAID

Whereas, Pay.gov financial services were implemented in this Court effective May 1, 2005, and

Whereas, the implementation of Pay.gov requires that certain Court procedures be modified, it is

ORDERED, that effective December 1, 2009, where an adversary proceeding is filed electronically over the Internet and the filing fee has not been paid in full, the Clerk is authorized and directed to send a notice to the debtor and the debtor's counsel informing them that the filing fee must be paid in full within five (5) days of the date of the Notice (the "Cure Period"), failing which the adversary proceeding may be dismissed.

[Dated: November 25, 2009.]

ADMINISTRATIVE ORDER NO. 541. IN RE: PROCEDURES FOR PAYMENT AND CURE OF PRE–PETITION JUDGMENT OF POSSESSION INVOLVING RESIDENTIAL PROPERTY [SUPERCEDED BY ADMINISTRATIVE ORDER 644, EFFECTIVE DECEMBER 10, 2015]

ADMINISTRATIVE ORDER NO. 542. IN THE MATTER OF DISMISSAL OF CASES EXHIBITING CERTAIN DEFECTS

Whereas, Pay.gov financial services were implemented in this Court effective May 1, 2005, and

Whereas, the implementation of Pay.gov requires that certain Court procedures be modified, it is

ORDERED, that effective December 1, 2009, in connection with any bankruptcy petition filed over the Internet, the Clerk is authorized and directed to send an electronic notice to the debtor's counsel (substantially in the form annexed hereto) that identifies one or more deficiency(ies) that, if not cured within five (5) days of transmission of such notice (the "Cure Period"), may result in dismissal of the bankruptcy case.

[Dated: November 30, 2009.]

NOTICE TO CURE DEFICIENCIES IN CONNECTION WITH ELECTRONICALLY FILED BANKRUPTCY PETITION

Bankruptcy Case No.: _____

Date of Filing: _____

Name(s) of Debtor(s): _____

Date of Notice: _____

The above-referenced bankruptcy filing has the following deficiency(ies) (indicated by an "X"):

____ 1. the bankruptcy petition was not attached at the time of filing;

____ 2. the bankruptcy petition for a different debtor was attached at the time of filing;

____ 3. the bankruptcy petition was not signed by the debtor; and/or

____ 4. the bankruptcy petition was not signed by the debtor's attorney;

The deficiencies identified in this Notice must be cured within five (5) days of the transmission of this Notice. If the deficiencies are not cured within this time period, the above-referenced bankruptcy filing may be dismissed.

[Dated: November 30, 2009.]

ADMINISTRATIVE ORDER NO. 556. IN RE: ADOPTION OF BAR DATE ORDER GUIDELINES

UPON the resolution of the Board of Judges for the United States Bankruptcy Court for the Eastern District of New York, it is hereby

ORDERED, that the annexed Bar Date Order Guidelines are adopted.

[Dated: March 29, 2010.]

BAR DATE ORDER GUIDELINES

The purpose of these guidelines is to provide a form order ("**Bar Date Order**") to establish deadlines for the filing of proofs of claim (the "**Bar Date**") in chapter 11 cases and thereby expedite court review and entry of such orders.

All proposed Bar Date Orders should conform to these guidelines and use the form of Bar Date Order and notice of Bar Date, with only such changes as are necessary under the circumstances of the individual case. **If a proposed Bar Date Order and accompanying notice of Bar Date do not comply with these guidelines, counsel should identify and explain, in the application for approval of the Bar Date Order, the reason for each change.** These forms and the guidelines apply only in chapter 11 cases and do not apply to deadlines for filing administrative claims.

GUIDELINES

1. An application for entry of a Bar Date Order should ordinarily be filed within 30 days after the earlier of (i) the initial case conference and (ii) the date which the Debtor's Schedules of Assets and Liabilities and Schedules of Executory Contracts and Unexpired Leases are due to be filed. If counsel believes that entry of a Bar Date Order should be delayed for any reason, counsel is urged to take up the matter at the initial case conference.

2. The application and accompanying papers may be submitted to the court without notice if these guidelines are followed and the application represents that the proposed Bar Date Order has been approved in form and substance by any official creditors' committee, any Debtor in Possession lender (or administrative agent thereof, if any) and any secured creditor (or administrative agent thereof, if any) with a lien on a significant percentage of the Debtor's assets. Otherwise, the proposed Bar Date Order should be submitted by notice of presentment or by notice of motion on notice to any official committee, Debtor in Possession lender, party requesting notice, and the United States trustee.

3. The application may contain suggested dates for the Bar Date, for mailing the notice of the Bar Date to creditors and, where appropriate, for publication. In most cases the suggested Bar Date should be at least 35 days after the mailing date and at least 28 days after the publication date. If possible, the proposed dates should provide the court with at least seven days after the application is submitted to enter the order. If applicable, the application should take into account the procedural provisions pertaining to creditors with foreign addresses. *See* Federal Rule of Bankruptcy Procedure ("**Bankruptcy Rules**") 2002(p). For cause shown, the court may reduce the notice period to 21 days after mailing in accordance with Bankruptcy Rules 2002(a)(7) and 9006(c)(2).

4. The form of Bar Date Order and the accompanying form of notice of the Bar Date to creditors assumes that the case is a single-debtor case. If more than one Debtor is present in jointly administered cases, the notice should list each of the Debtors and their related case numbers as part of, or as an addendum to, the notice of the Bar Date to creditors.

5. The form of Bar Date Order contains a paragraph in brackets providing for publication of notice of the Bar Date. These guidelines do not take any position as to whether publication notice of the Bar Date is required in a particular case. Counsel should state in the application for a Bar Date whether they believe publication is required and, if so, the proposed time, place and method of publication, and in appropriate cases should raise the issue at the initial case conference. The published notice should be substantially similar to the written notice to creditors.

6.   The form of Bar Date Order and notice of Bar Date contain instructions for proofs of claim to be filed electronically with the court, mailed to the court, or delivered by hand directly to the court site where the case is pending. Where it is anticipated that more than 1,000 proofs of claim will be filed, the Debtor should retain a claims/noticing agent ("**Claims Agent**") to receive mailed proofs of claim. In such cases, counsel should contact the Clerk's Office for procedures involving Claims Agents. In cases *without* Claims Agents, attorneys (with full access accounts) and employees of institutional creditors (with limited access accounts) may file proofs of claim electronically on the Court's Case Management/Electronic Case File ("**CM/ECF**") system.

7.   The form of Bar Date Order is intended for use only in connection with fixing a bar date for the filing of proofs of claim. If a Bar Date for the filing of proofs of equity interest is required, counsel may file a substantially similar motion or counsel may submit a proposed order and accompanying notice that sets a Bar Date for the filing of proofs of claim and proofs of interest. Notice of a deadline for the filing of administrative claims should **not** ordinarily be combined with notice of any other Bar Date.

8.   The forms of Bar Date Order and notice of Bar Date list persons and entities that are not required to file a proof of claim. While the list is not exhaustive, it is anticipated that these persons and entities will not be required to file proofs of claim in most chapter 11 cases. Some of the subparagraphs are bracketed, reflecting that the exemption may have no application or the Debtor may elect not to exempt the particular category from the requirement to file.

9.   The notice of Bar Date to creditors should contain the name and telephone number of an individual at the Debtor's counsel, or the bankruptcy services firm to whom questions may be addressed. The notice should not indicate that it has been signed by the bankruptcy judge but may provide that the notice is "By Order of the Court."

10.   The electronic copy of the proposed Bar Date Order submitted to the court should include both the form of the proposed Bar Date Order and the text of the notice of Bar Date to creditors.

[FORM OF BAR DATE ORDER]

UNITED STATES BANKRUPTCY COURT
EASTERN DISTRICT OF NEW YORK

---x

In re: Chapter 11

                                          Case No.: ___—_____(_____)

         Debtor.

---x

ORDER ESTABLISHING DEADLINE FOR FILING PROOFS OF CLAIM
AND APPROVING THE FORM AND MANNER OF NOTICE THEREOF

Upon the application of the Debtor and Debtor in Possession for an order, pursuant to Federal Rule of Bankruptcy Procedure ("**Bankruptcy Rule**") 3003(c)(3), fixing a deadline and establishing procedures for filing proofs of claim and approving the form and manner of service thereof, and it appearing that the relief requested is in the best interests of the Debtor, its estate, and creditors and that adequate notice has been given and that no further notice is necessary; and after due deliberation and good and sufficient cause appearing therefor, it is hereby

ORDERED, that except as otherwise provided herein, all persons and entities, (including, without limitation, individuals, partnerships, corporations, joint ventures, trusts and governmental units) that assert a claim, as defined in section 101(5) of 11 U.S.C. §§ 101 *et seq.* (the "**Bankruptcy Code**"), against the Debtor which arose prior to the filing of the Chapter 11 petition on _____, shall file a proof of such claim in writing so that it is received on or before _____, 20___ (the "**Bar Date**"); and it is further

[**ORDERED**, that notwithstanding any other provision hereof, proofs of claim filed by governmental units must be filed on or before _____, 20___ (the date that is 180 days after the date of the order for relief); and it is further][1]

ORDERED, that the following procedures for the filing of proofs of claim shall apply:

(a) Proofs of claim shall conform substantially to Official Bankruptcy Form No. 10;

(b) *[(1) Cases without Claims Agents—Insert this Subparagraph:]*[2] Attorneys (with full access accounts) and employees of institutional creditors (with limited access accounts) shall file proofs of claim electronically on the Court's Case Management/Electronic Case File ("**CM/ECF**") system. Those without accounts to the CM/ECF system shall file their proofs of claim by mailing or delivering the original proof of claim to the United States Bankruptcy Court, Eastern District of New York, [Conrad B. Duberstein U.S. Bankruptcy Courthouse, 271 Cadman Plaza East, Suite 1595, Brooklyn, NY 11201–1800] [Alfonse M. D'Amato U.S. Courthouse, 290 Federal Plaza, Central Islip, NY 11722];

[(2) Cases with Claims Agents—Insert this Subparagraph:] Proofs of claim shall be filed either by U.S. Postal Service mail or overnight delivery of the original proof of claim to the United States Bankruptcy Court, Eastern District of New York, c/o [address provided by Claims Agent] or by mailing or delivering the original proof of claim by hand to the United States Bankruptcy Court, Eastern District of New York, [Conrad B. Duberstein U.S. Bankruptcy Courthouse, 271 Cadman Plaza East, Suite 1595, Brooklyn, NY 11201–1800] [Alfonse M. D'Amato U.S. Courthouse, 290 Federal Plaza, Central Islip, NY 11722];

(c) Proofs of claim shall be deemed timely filed only when <u>received</u> by the Clerk of the Court on or before the Bar Date;

(d) Proofs of claim shall (i) be signed; (ii) include supporting documentation (if voluminous, attach a summary); (iii) be in the English language; and (iv) be denominated in United States currency;

(e) [In multiple debtor cases] Proofs of claim shall specify by name and case number the Debtor against which the claim is filed; if the holder asserts a claim against more than one Debtor or has claims against different Debtors, the holder shall file a separate proof of claim form for each Debtor; and it is further

ORDERED, that the following persons or entities need not file a proof of claim on or prior to the Bar Date:

(a) Any person or entity that has already filed a proof of claim against the Debtor in this case with the Clerk of the Bankruptcy Court for the Eastern District of New York in a form substantially similar to Official Bankruptcy Form No. 10;

(b) Any person or entity whose claim is listed on the Schedules of Assets and Liabilities filed by the Debtor (collectively, the "**Schedules**") [Docket Entry No. _____], if (i) the claim is <u>not</u> scheduled as "disputed," "contingent" or "unliquidated"; <u>and</u> (ii) the claimant agrees with <u>the</u> amount, nature and priority of the claim as set forth in the Schedules; [<u>and</u> (iii) the claimant does not dispute that the claim is an obligation of the specific Debtor against which the claim is listed in the Schedules];

(c) Any holder of a claim that has already been allowed in this case by order of the Court;

(d) Any holder of a claim for which a different deadline for filing a proof of claim in this case has already been fixed by this Court; or

(e) Any holder of a claim allowable under sections 503(b) and 507(a)(2) of the Bankruptcy Code as an expense of administration of the Debtor's estate; and it is further

ORDERED, that any person or entity that holds a claim that arises from the rejection of an executory contract or unexpired lease, as to which the order authorizing such rejection is dated on or before the date of entry of this Order, must file a proof of claim based on such rejection on or before the later of the Bar Date or the date that is 30 days after the date of the order authorizing such rejection, and any person or entity that holds a claim that arises from the rejection of an executory contract or unexpired lease, as to which an order authorizing such rejection is dated after the date of entry of this Order, must file a proof of claim on or before such date as the Court may fix in the applicable order authorizing such rejection; and it is further

ORDERED, that holders of equity security interests in the Debtor need not file proofs of interest with respect to the ownership of such interests, but if any such holder has a claim against the Debtor (including a claim relating to an equity interest or the purchase or sale of the equity interest), a proof of claim shall be filed on or prior to the Bar Date; and it is further

ORDERED, that if the Debtor amends or supplements the Schedules after the date of this Order, the Debtor shall give notice of any amendment or supplement to the holders of claims amended thereby, and holders of such claims shall have 30 days from the date of service of the notice to file proofs of claim and shall be given notice of that deadline; and it is further

ORDERED, that nothing in this Order shall prejudice the right of the Debtor or any other party in interest to dispute or assert offsets or defenses to any claim listed in the Schedules; and it is further

ORDERED, that pursuant to Bankruptcy Rule 3003(c)(2), a holder of a claim that fails to comply with this Order by timely filing a proof of claim in appropriate form shall not be treated as a creditor with respect to that claim for purposes of voting and distribution; and it is further

ORDERED, that notice of the Bar Date substantially in the form annexed hereto is approved and shall be deemed adequate and sufficient if served by first-class mail at least 35 days prior to the Bar Date on:

(a) the United States trustee;

(b) counsel to each official committee;

(c) all persons or entities that have requested notice of the proceedings in this case;

(d) all persons or entities that have filed claims in this case;

(e) all creditors and other known holders of claims as of the date of this Order, including all persons or entities listed in the Schedules as holding claims;

(f) all parties to executory contracts and unexpired leases of the Debtor;

(g) all parties to litigation with the Debtor;

(h) the Internal Revenue Service for the district in which the case is pending and, if required by Bankruptcy Rule 2002(j), the Securities and Exchange Commission and any other required governmental units;

and it is further

[**ORDERED**, that pursuant to Bankruptcy Rule 2002(*l*), the Debtor shall publish notice of the Bar Date in substantially the form annexed hereto as Exhibit ____ once, in the _____ [and the _____] at least 28 days prior to the Bar Date, which publication is hereby approved and shall be deemed good, adequate and sufficient publication notice of the Bar Date;[3] and it is further]

ORDERED, that the Debtor is authorized and empowered to take such steps and perform such acts as may be necessary to implement and effectuate the terms of this Order; and it is further

ORDERED, that entry of this Order is without prejudice to the right of the Debtor to seek a further order of this Court fixing a date by which holders of claims or interests not subject to the Bar Date established herein must file such proofs of claim or interest or be barred from doing so.

Dated: _____, New York

_____, 20___

UNITED STATES BANKRUPTCY
JUDGE

[FORM OF NOTICE OF BAR DATE]

UNITED STATES BANKRUPTCY COURT
EASTERN DISTRICT OF NEW YORK

---x

In re:

Debtor.

---x

Chapter 11

Case No.: ___—_____(_____)

NOTICE OF DEADLINE REQUIRING FILING OF PROOFS OF
CLAIM ON OR BEFORE _____

TO ALL PERSONS AND ENTITIES WITH CLAIMS AGAINST [NAME OF DEBTOR]

The United States Bankruptcy Court for the Eastern District of New York has entered an Order establishing [**set forth date in bold**] (the "**Bar Date**") as the last date for each person or entity (including individuals, partnerships, corporations, joint ventures, trusts and governmental units) to file a proof of claim against [Name of Debtor] (the "**Debtor**").

The Bar Date and the procedures set forth below for filing proofs of claim apply to all claims against the Debtor that arose prior to _____ (the "**Filing Date**"), the date on which the Debtor commenced a case under chapter 11 of 11 U.S.C. §§ 101 *et seq.* (the "**Bankruptcy Code**"), except for those holders of the claims listed in Section 4 below that are specifically excluded from the Bar Date filing requirement.

1. WHO MUST FILE A PROOF OF CLAIM

You MUST file a proof of claim to vote on a Chapter 11 plan filed by the Debtor or to share in distributions from the Debtor's bankruptcy estate if you have a claim that arose prior to the Filing Date, and it is not one of the types of claim described in Section 4 below. Claims based on acts or omissions of the Debtor that occurred before the Filing Date must be filed on or prior to the Bar Date, even if such claims are not now fixed, liquidated or certain or did not mature or become fixed, liquidated or certain before the Filing Date.

Under section 101(5) of the Bankruptcy Code and as used in this Notice, the word "claim" means: (a) a right to payment, whether or not such right is reduced to judgment, liquidated, unliquidated, fixed, contingent, matured, unmatured, disputed, undisputed, legal, equitable, secured, or unsecured; or (b) a right to an equitable remedy for breach of performance if such breach gives rise to a right to payment, whether or not such right to an equitable remedy is reduced to judgment, fixed, contingent, matured, unmatured, disputed, undisputed, secured or unsecured.

2. WHAT TO FILE

Your filed proof of claim must conform substantially to Official Form No. 10, a copy of which is annexed to this Notice. Additional proof of claim forms may be obtained at www.uscourts.gov/bkforms.

The proof of claim form must be **signed** by the claimant or, if the claimant is not an individual, by an authorized agent of the claimant. It must be written in English and be denominated in United States currency. You must attach to your completed proof of claim any documents on which the claim is based (if voluminous, attach a summary).

[Any holder of a claim against more than one Debtor must file a separate proof of claim with respect to each Debtor, and all holders of claims must identify on their proof of claim the specific Debtor against which their claim is asserted and the case number of that Debtor's bankruptcy case. A list of the names of the Debtors and their case numbers is [set forth in the case caption above] [attached to this Notice].]

Your proof of claim form shall not contain complete social security numbers or taxpayer identification numbers (only the last four digits), a complete birth date (only the year), the name of a minor (only the minor's initials) or a financial account number (only the last four digits of such financial account).

3. WHEN AND WHERE TO FILE

[(A) *Cases Without Claims Agents—Insert the following as Paragraph 3*:][4]

Except as provided for herein, all proofs of claim must be filed so as to be received **on or before** _____.

Attorneys (with full access accounts) and employees of institutional creditors (with limited access accounts) shall file proofs of claim electronically on the Court's Case Management/Electronic Case File ("**CM/ECF**") system. Those without accounts to the CM/ECF system shall file their proofs of claim by mailing or delivering the original proof of claim to the Court at the address provided below:

[United States Bankruptcy Court Eastern District of New York

Conrad B. Duberstein U.S. Bankruptcy Courthouse

271 Cadman Plaza East, Suite 1595

Brooklyn, NY 11201–1800]

[United States Bankruptcy Court Eastern District of New York

Alfonse M. D'Amato U.S. Courthouse

290 Federal Plaza

Central Islip, NY 11722]

A proof of claim will be deemed timely filed only when <u>received</u> by the Bankruptcy Court on or before the Bar Date. A proof of claim may not be delivered by facsimile, telecopy or electronic mail transmission.

[Governmental units may have until _____, the date that is 180 days after the order for relief, to file proofs of claim.][5]

[(B) *Cases with Claims Agents—Insert the following as Paragraph 3*:]

Except as provided for herein, all proofs of claim must be filed so as to be received **on or before** _____ at the following address:

[Insert address provided by claims agent]	**IF DELIVERED BY HAND:**
	United States Bankruptcy Court
	Eastern District of New York
	Conrad B. Duberstein U.S.
	Bankruptcy Courthouse
	271 Cadman Plaza East, Suite 1595
	Brooklyn, NY 11201–1800
	or
	United States Bankruptcy Court
	Eastern District of New York
	Alfonse M. D'Amato U.S. Courthouse
	290 Federal Plaza
	Central Islip, NY 11722

Proofs of claim will be deemed filed only when <u>received</u> at the address listed herein on or before the Bar Date. Proofs of claim may not be delivered by facsimile, telecopy or electronic mail transmission.

[Governmental units may have until _____, the date that is 180 days after the order for relief, to file proofs of claim.][6]

4. WHO NEED NOT FILE A PROOF OF CLAIM

You do **not** need to file a proof of claim on or before the Bar Date if you are:

(a) A person or entity that has already filed a proof of claim against the Debtor in this case with the Clerk of the Bankruptcy Court for the Eastern District of New York in a form substantially similar to Official Bankruptcy Form No. 10;

(b) A person or entity whose claim is listed on the Schedules of Assets and Liabilities filed by the Debtor (collectively, the "**Schedules**") [Docket Entry No. _____] if (i) the claim is not scheduled as "disputed," "contingent," or "unliquidated" and (ii) you agree with the amount, nature and priority of the claim as set forth in the Schedules [and (iii) you do not dispute that your claim is an obligation only of the specific Debtor against which the claim is listed in the Schedules];

(c) A holder of a claim that has already been allowed in this case by order of the Court;

(d) A holder of a claim for which a different deadline for filing a proof of claim in this case has already been fixed by this Court; or

(e) A holder of a claim allowable under sections 503(b) and 507(a)(2) of the Bankruptcy Code as an expense of administration of the Debtor's estate.

If you are a holder of an equity interest in the Debtor, you need not file a proof of interest with respect to the ownership of such equity interest at this time. But, if you assert a claim against the Debtor, including a claim relating to your equity interest or the purchase or sale of that interest you must file a proof of claim on or prior to the Bar Date in accordance with the procedures set forth in this Notice.

This Notice is being sent to many persons and entities that have had some relationship with or have done business with the Debtor but may not have an unpaid claim against the Debtor. The fact that you have received this Notice does not mean that you have a claim, or that the Debtor or the Court believes that you have a claim against the Debtor.

5. EXECUTORY CONTRACTS AND UNEXPIRED LEASES

If you have a claim arising out of the rejection of an executory contract or unexpired lease as to which the order authorizing such rejection is dated on or before _____, the date of entry of the Bar Order, you must file a proof of claim based on such rejection on or before the later of the Bar Date or the date that is 30 days after the date of the order authorizing such rejection. Any person or entity that has a claim arising from the rejection of an executory contract or unexpired lease, as to which the order is dated after the date of entry of the Bar Order, you must file a proof of claim with respect to such claim by the date fixed by the Court in the applicable order authorizing rejection of such contract or lease.

6. CONSEQUENCES OF FAILURE TO FILE A PROOF OF CLAIM BY THE BAR DATE

ANY HOLDER OF A CLAIM THAT IS NOT EXCEPTED FROM THE REQUIREMENTS OF THIS ORDER, AS SET FORTH IN SECTION 4 ABOVE, AND THAT FAILS TO TIMELY FILE A PROOF OF CLAIM IN THE APPROPRIATE FORM, WILL BE BARRED FROM ASSERTING ITS CLAIM AGAINST THE DEBTOR AND ITS CHAPTER 11 ESTATE, VOTING ON ANY PLAN OF REORGANIZATION FILED IN THIS CASE, AND PARTICIPATING IN ANY DISTRIBUTION IN THE DEBTOR'S CHAPTER 11 CASE ON ACCOUNT OF THAT CLAIM.

7. THE DEBTOR'S SCHEDULES AND ACCESS THERETO

You may be listed as the holder of a claim against the Debtor in the Debtor's Schedules. If you agree with the nature, amount and status of your claim as listed in the Debtor's Schedules, [and if you do not dispute that your claim is only against the Debtor specified by the Debtors,] and if your claim is not described as "disputed," "contingent," or "unliquidated," you do not need to file a proof of claim. Otherwise, you must file a proof of claim before the Bar Date in accordance with the procedures set forth in this Notice.

Copies of the Debtor's Schedules are available for inspection on the Court's Internet Website at http://www.nyeb.uscourts.gov. A login and password to the Court's Public Access to Electronic Court Records ("**PACER**") are required to access this information and can be obtained through the PACER Service Center at http://www.pacer.psc.uscourts.gov. Copies of the Debtor's Schedules may also be examined between the hours of 9:00 a.m. and 4:30 p.m., Monday through Friday at the Office of the Clerk of the Bankruptcy Court, [Conrad B. Duberstein U.S. Bankruptcy Courthouse, 271 Cadman Plaza East, Brooklyn, NY 11201–1800] [Alfonse M. D'Amato U.S. Courthouse, 290 Federal Plaza, Central Islip, NY 11722]. Copies of the Debtor's Schedules may also be obtained by written request to the Debtor's counsel at the address and telephone number set forth below:

[address and telephone number]

If you are unsure about any of these matters, including whether you should file a proof of claim, you may wish to consult an attorney.

Dated:_____, New York   **BY ORDER OF THE COURT**
        _____ ___, 20 __

_____
COUNSEL FOR THE DEBTOR AND
DEBTOR IN POSSESSION
FIRM NAME
ADDRESS
PHONE NUMBER

¹ For use only when the general Bar Date is less than 180 days after the Filing Date. Section 502(b)(9) of the Bankruptcy Code requires that governmental units have at least 180 days after the order for relief to file a proof of claim (however, a different deadline may apply for certain tax-related claims in a chapter 13 case).

² Choose either subparagraph 1 *or* subparagraph 2. If you have questions regarding the applicability of a claims agent to your case, please contact the Clerk's Office.

³ For Debtors that propose to publish notice of the Bar Date. *See* Guideline 5.

⁴ Choose either subparagraph A *or* subparagraph B. If you have questions regarding the applicability of a claims agent to your case, please contact the Clerk's Office.

⁵ *See* footnote 1, above.

⁶ *See* footnote 1, above.

ADMINISTRATIVE ORDER NO. 557. IN RE: ADOPTION OF SALE GUIDELINES

UPON the resolution of the Board of Judges for the United States Bankruptcy Court for the Eastern District of New York, it is hereby

ORDERED, that the annexed Sale Guidelines are adopted.

[Dated: March 29, 2010.]

_____

SALE GUIDELINES

The United States Bankruptcy Court for the Eastern District of New York (the "**Court**") has adopted the following guidelines (the "**Sale Guidelines**") for the conduct of asset sales under section 363(b) of 11 U.S.C. §§ 101, *et seq.* (the "**Bankruptcy Code**"). The Sale Guidelines are designed to: (a) help practitioners identify issues that typically are of concern to parties and the Court, so that, among other things, determinations can be made, if necessary, on an expedited basis, (b) highlight certain Extraordinary Provisions, defined below, which ordinarily will not be approved without good cause shown and (c) set forth best practices with respect to notice.

The Sale Guidelines do not: (a) address the circumstances under which an asset sale is appropriate (b) address other substantive legal issues or (c) constitute rules of the Court.

The Sale Guidelines supplement but do not replace, sections 363(b) and 365 of the Bankruptcy Code, Rules 2002 and 6004 of the Federal Rules of Bankruptcy Procedure (the "**Bankruptcy Rules**") and Rules 6004–1 and 6005–1 of the Local Bankruptcy Rules for the Eastern District of New York (the "**Local Rules**").

1. **Motions.**

(a) *Motion Content.* When an auction is contemplated in cases filed under chapter 11 and where appropriate under other chapters, the Debtor¹ should ordinarily file a single motion seeking the entry of two orders to be considered at two separate hearings. The first order (the "**Sale Procedures Order**") will approve procedures for the sale process, including any protections for an initial, or stalking horse bidder ("**stalking horse**"), and the second order (the "**Sale Order**") will approve the sale to the successful bidder at the auction. If no auction is contemplated or the Debtor has not actively solicited or will not actively solicit higher and better offers, the motion seeking approval of the sale should explain why the Debtor proposes to structure the sale in such manner.

(i) The proposed purchase agreement, or a form of proposed agreement acceptable to the Debtor if the Debtor has not yet entered into an agreement with a proposed buyer, should be attached to the motion.

(ii) The motion also should include a copy of the proposed order(s), particularly if the order(s) include any Extraordinary Provisions, defined below.

(iii) The motion must comply in form with the Local Rules.

(iv) If a hearing is required under section 363(b) of the Bankruptcy Code in connection with the sale of personally identifiable information subject to a privacy policy of the Debtor, the motion should request appointment of a consumer privacy ombudsman under section 332 of the Bankruptcy Code if the proposed sale does not fall under section 363(b)(1)(A) of the Bankruptcy Code.

(b) *Bidding Procedures.* Generally, a Sale Procedures Order should include a motion for proposed bidding procedures which are in the Debtor's reasonable business judgment, likely to maximize the sale price. Such procedures must not chill the receipt of higher and better offers and must be consistent with the Debtor's fiduciary duties. It is recommended that such procedures include the following:[2]

(i) Qualification of Bidders. An entity that is seeking to become a qualified bidder will deliver financial information by a stated deadline to the Debtor and other key parties (ordinarily excluding other bidders)[3] reasonably demonstrating such bidder's ability to consummate a sale on the terms proposed. Such financial information, which may be provided confidentially, if appropriate, may include current audited or verified financial statements of, or verified financial commitments obtained by, the potential bidder (or, if the potential bidder is an entity formed for the purpose of acquiring the property to be sold, the party that will bear liability for a breach). To be qualified, a prospective bidder also may be required by a stated deadline to make a non-binding expression of interest and execute a reasonable form of non-disclosure agreement before being provided due diligence access to non-public information.

(ii) Qualification of Bids Prior to Auction.

(1) The bidding procedures should state the criteria for a qualifying bid and any deadlines for (i) submitting such a bid and (ii) notification whether the bid constitutes a qualifying bid.

(2) The bidding procedures may require each qualified bid to be marked against the form of a stalking horse agreement or a form of proposed agreement, showing amendments and other modifications (including price and other terms) proposed by the qualified bidder. The bidding procedures may limit bidding to the terms of a stalking horse agreement or proposed form of agreement; provided, however, that, bidding on less than all of the assets proposed to be acquired by a stalking horse normally should be permitted, unless such bidding is inconsistent with the purpose of the sale.

(3) A qualified bid should clearly identify all conditions to the qualified bidder's obligation to consummate the purchase.

(4) A qualified bid should include a good faith deposit, which will be non-refundable if the bidder is selected as the successful bidder and fails to consummate the purchase (other than as a result of a breach by the seller) and refundable if it is not selected as the successful bidder (other than as a result of its own breach). The amount of, and rules governing, the good faith deposit will be determined on a case-by-case basis, but generally each qualified bidder, including any stalking horse should be required to make the same form of deposit.

(iii) Backup Buyer. The Sale Procedures Order may provide that the Debtor in the reasonable exercise of its judgment may accept and close on the second highest qualified bid received if the winning bidder fails to close the transaction within a specified period. In such case, the Debtor would retain the second highest bidder's good faith deposit until such bidder was relieved of its obligation to be a backup buyer.

(iv) Stalking Horse Protections/Bidding Increments.

(1) Break–Up/Topping Fees and Expense Reimbursement. The propriety of any break-up or topping fees and other bidding protections (such as the estate's proposed payment of out-of-pocket expenses incurred by a bidder in connection with the proposed transaction or the compensation of a bidder for lost opportunity costs) will be determined on a case-by-case basis. Generally such fees should be payable only from the proceeds of a higher or better transaction entered into with a third party within a reasonable time of the closing of the sale. Such provisions must be prominently disclosed and described with particularity in the motion.

(2) Bidding Increments. If a proposed sale contemplates the granting of a break-up or topping fee or expense reimbursement, the initial bidding increment must be more than sufficient to pay the maximum amount payable thereunder. Additional bidding increments should be appropriate in light of the value of the asset being sold and should not be so high as to chill further bids.

(3) Rebidding. If a break-up or topping fee is requested, the Sale Procedures Order should state whether the stalking horse will be deemed to waive the break-up or topping fee by rebidding. In the absence of a waiver, the Sales Procedure Order should state whether the stalking horse will receive a "credit" equal to the break-up or topping fee if the stalking horse is the successful bidder at a higher price than the stalking horse's initial bid.

(4) No–Shop or No–Solicitation Provisions. Limited no-shop or no-solicitation provisions may be permissible if they are necessary to obtain a sale, they are consistent with the Debtor's fiduciary duties, they do not chill the receipt of higher or better offers and they are appropriate under the circumstances of the case. Such provisions must be prominently disclosed in the motion and described with particularity.

(v) Auction Procedures.

(1) If an auction is proposed, the Sale Procedures Order generally should provide that the auction will be conducted in the presence of all qualified bidders and other interested parties, and that each bidder will be informed of the terms of the previous bid. The motion should explain the rationale for proposing a different auction format in the Sale Procedures Order.

(2) If a professional auctioneer will conduct the auction, the parties should refer to the statutory provisions and rules governing the conduct of professional auctioneers. *See* Bankruptcy Rule 6004 and Local Rules 6004–1 and 6005–1.

(3) If the auction is sufficiently complex or disputes can reasonably be expected to arise, it is advisable at the sale procedures hearing to ask the Court whether it will consider conducting the auction in open court, or otherwise be available to resolve disputes. If the Debtor proposes to conduct the auction outside the presence of the judge, the auction proceedings should be audiotaped, videotaped or otherwise recorded, or the motion should explain why this is not appropriate.

(4) Each bidder is expected to confirm at the auction that it has not engaged in any collusion with respect to the bidding or the sale.

(5) The Sale Procedures Order should provide that the Court will not consider bids made after the auction has been closed, unless a motion to reopen the auction is made and granted.

(c) *Sale Hearing*. The evidence presented or proffered at any sale hearing should be sufficient to enable the Court to make the following findings: (1) a sound business reason exists for the transaction; (2) the property has been adequately marketed, and the purchase price constitutes the highest or otherwise best offer and provides fair and reasonable consideration; (3) the proposed transaction is in the best interests of the Debtor's estate, its creditors, and where relevant, its interest holders; (4) the purchaser has acted in good faith, within the meaning of section 363(m) of the Bankruptcy Code; (5) adequate and reasonable notice has been provided; (6) the "free and clear" requirements of section 363(f) of the Bankruptcy Code, if applicable, have been met; (7) if applicable, the sale is consistent with the Debtor's privacy policy concerning personally identifiable information, or, after appointment of a consumer ombudsman in accordance with section 332 of the Bankruptcy Code and notice and a hearing, no showing was made that such sale would violate applicable nonbankruptcy law; (8) the requirements of section 365 of the Bankruptcy Code have been met in respect of the proposed assumption and assignment or rejection of any executory contracts and unexpired leases; (9) where necessary, the Debtor's board of directors or other governing body has authorized the proposed transaction; and (10) the Debtor and the purchaser have entered into the transaction without collusion, in good faith, and from arm's-length bargaining positions, and neither party has engaged in any conduct that would cause or permit the agreement to be avoided under section 363(n) of the Bankruptcy Code.

(i) Sound Business Purpose. The Debtor must demonstrate the facts that support a finding that a sound business reason exists for the sale.

(ii) Marketing Efforts. The Debtor must demonstrate the facts that support a finding that the property to be sold has been marketed adequately under the circumstances.

(iii) Purchase Price. The Debtor must demonstrate that fair and reasonable value will be received and that the proffered purchase price is the highest or best under the circumstances. If a bid includes deferred payments or any equity component, the Debtor should present evidence concerning, as applicable, its assessment of the proposed buyer's creditworthiness or ability to realize the projected earnings upon which future payments or other forms of consideration to the estate are based. Any material purchase price adjustment provisions should be identified.

(iv) Assumption and Assignment of Contracts and Leases. The Debtor must demonstrate at a minimum: (a) that it or the assignee has cured or will promptly cure all existing defaults under the agreement(s), and (b) that the assignee can provide adequate assurance that it will perform under the terms of the agreement(s) to be assumed and assigned under section 365 of the Bankruptcy Code. Additional notice and opportunity for a hearing for the non-debtor party to the lease or executory contract may be required if the offer to purchase a lease or executory contract sought to be approved at the sale hearing is submitted by a different entity than the stalking horse or the winning bid identifies different contracts or leases for assumption and assignment, or rejection, than the initial bid that was noticed for approval. If this possibility exists, the sale motion should acknowledge the Debtor will provide additional notice and opportunity to object under such circumstances.

(d) *Extraordinary Provisions.* The following provisions ("**Extraordinary Provisions**") must be disclosed conspicuously in a separate section of the sale motion and, where applicable, in the related proposed Sale Procedures Order or Sale Order, and the motion must provide substantial justification therefor:[4]

(i) Sale to Insider. If the motion proposes a sale to an insider, as defined in the Bankruptcy Code, the motion must disclose what measures have been taken to ensure the fairness of the sale process and the proposed transaction.

(ii) Agreements with Management. If the proposed buyer has discussed or entered into any agreements with management or key employees regarding compensation or future employment, the motion must disclose the material terms of any such agreements, and what measures have been taken to ensure the fairness of the sale and the proposed transaction in the light of any such agreements.

(iii) Private Sale/No Competitive Bidding. If no auction is contemplated, the Debtor has agreed to a limited no-shop or no-solicitation provision, or the Debtor has otherwise not sought or is not actively seeking higher or better offers, the sale motion must so state and explain why such sale is likely to maximize the sale price.

(iv) Deadlines that Effectively Limit Notice. If the proposed transaction includes deadlines for the closing or Court approval of the Sale Procedures Order or the Sale Order that have the effect of limiting notice to less than outlined in 2, below, the sale motion must provide an explanation.

(v) No Good Faith Deposit. If any qualified bidder, including a stalking horse, is excused from submitting a good faith deposit, the sale motion must provide an explanation.

(vi) Interim Arrangements with Proposed Buyer. If the Debtor is entering into any interim agreements or arrangements with the proposed purchaser, such as interim management arrangements (for which, approval, must also be sought after notice and a hearing under section 363(b) of the Bankruptcy Code), the sale motion must disclose the terms of such agreements.

(vii) Use of Proceeds. If the Debtor proposes to release sale proceeds on or after the closing without further Court order, or to provide for an allocation of sale proceeds between or among various sellers or secured creditors, the sale motion must describe the intended disposition of such amounts and the rationale therefor.

(viii) Tax Exemption. If the Debtor is seeking to have the sale declared exempt from taxes under section 1146(a) of the Bankruptcy Code, the sale motion must prominently disclose the type of tax (e.g., recording tax, stamp tax, use tax, capital gains tax) for which the exemption is sought. It is not sufficient to refer simply to "transfer" taxes. In addition, the Debtor must identify the state or states in which the affected property is located.

(ix) Record Retention. If the Debtor proposes to sell substantially all of its assets, the sale motion must confirm that the Debtor will retain, or have reasonable access to, its books and records to enable it to administer its bankruptcy case.

(x) Sale of Avoidance Actions. If the Debtor seeks to sell its rights to pursue avoidance claims under chapter 5 of the Bankruptcy Code, the sale motion must so state and provide an explanation of the basis therefor.

(xi) Requested Findings as to Successor Liability. If the Debtor seeks findings limiting the purchaser's successor liability, the sale motion must disclose the adequacy of the Debtor's proposed notice of such requested relief and the basis for such relief. Generally, the proposed Sale Order should not contain voluminous findings with respect to successor liability, or injunctive provisions, except as provided in 3, below.

(xii) Future Conduct. If the Debtor seeks a determination regarding the effect of conduct or actions that may or will be taken after the date of the Sale Order, the sale motion must set forth the legal authority for such a determination.

(xiii) Requested Findings as to Fraudulent Conveyance. If the Debtor seeks a finding to the effect that the sale does not constitute a fraudulent conveyance, it must explain why a finding that the purchase price is fair and reasonable is not sufficient.

(xiv) Sale Free and Clear of Unexpired Leases. If the Debtor seeks to sell property free and clear of a possessory leasehold interest, license or other right, the Debtor must identify the non-debtor parties whose interests will be affected, and explain what adequate protection will be provided for those interests.

(xv) Relief from Bankruptcy Rule 6004(h). If the Debtor seeks relief from the stay imposed by Bankruptcy Rule 6004(h), the sale motion must disclose the business or other basis for such request.

2. Notice.

(a) *General.* Notice is always required under section 363(b) of the Bankruptcy Code; however, a hearing is required only if there are timely objections or the Court otherwise schedules a hearing.

(b) *Notice of Proposed Sale Procedures*

(i) Notice Parties. Notice may be limited to those parties-in-interest best situated to articulate an objection to the limited relief sought at this stage, including:

(1) any official or unofficial creditors' committee or other committee, or if no creditors' committee exists, the 20 largest unsecured creditors;

(2) office of the United States Trustee;

(3) postpetition lenders (or administrative agent thereof, if any);

(4) indenture trustees;

(5) prepetition lenders (or administrative agent thereof, if any);

(6) all entities who have requested notice under Bankruptcy Rule 2002;

(7) entities known or reasonably believed to have asserted a lien, encumbrance, claim or other interest in any of the assets offered for sale; and

(8) parties to executory contracts and unexpired leases proposed to be assumed and assigned, or rejected as part of the proposed transaction.

To provide additional marketing of the assets, the Debtor also should send a copy of the motion to entities known or reasonably believed to have expressed an interest in acquiring any of the assets offered for sale. Nothing herein is meant to imply that prospective bidders have standing to be heard with respect to the sale procedures.

(c) *Notice Period.* As a general matter, the minimum 21–day notice period set forth in Bankruptcy Rule 2002(a) may be shortened with respect to the request for approval of a proposed Sale Procedures Order, that does not involve Extraordinary Provisions, and complies with these Sale Guidelines. The 14–day notice period provided for in EDNY LBR 9006–1(a) should provide sufficient time, under most circumstances, to enable any parties-in-interest to file an objection to proposed sale procedures.

(d) *Contents of Notice.* Notice should comport with Bankruptcy Rules 2002 and 6004.

3. Notice of Sale.

(a) *Notice Parties.* Generally the sale and hearing to approve the sale requires more notice than the hearing on approval of sale procedures. Notice of the sale and of the hearing to approve the sale should ordinarily be given to:[5]

(i) official and unofficial creditors' committee and other committees;

(ii) office of the United States Trustee;

(iii) entities who have requested notice under Bankruptcy Rule 2002[6] (and, if the proposed sale is of a significant portion of the Debtor's assets, all creditors of the Debtor);

(iv) postpetition lenders (or administrative agent thereof, if any);

(v) indenture trustees;

(vi) prepetition lenders (or administrative agent thereof, if any);

(vii) entities known or reasonably believed to have asserted a lien, encumbrance, claim or other interest in any of the assets offered for sale;

(viii) parties to executory contracts or unexpired leases to be assumed and assigned, or rejected as part of the transaction;

(ix) affected federal, state and local regulatory (including, for example, environmental agencies) and taxing authorities,[7] including the Internal Revenue Service;

(x) if applicable, a consumer privacy ombudsman appointed under section 332 of the Bankruptcy Code; and

(xi) the Securities and Exchange Commission (if appropriate).

If the contemplated sale implicates the antitrust laws of the United States, or a debt (other than for taxes) is owed by the Debtor to the United States government, notice also should be given to:

(xii) the Federal Trade Commission;

(xiii) the Assistant Attorney General in charge of the Antitrust Division of the Department of Justice; and

(xiv) the United States Attorney's Office.

To provide additional marketing of the assets, notice also should be sent to any entities known or reasonably believed to have expressed an interest in acquiring any of the assets.

See 1(c)(4), above, for circumstances in which it may be required, based on changes in the proposed transaction that had originally been noticed, to give additional notice to parties to executory contracts and unexpired leases proposed to be assumed and assigned or rejected under section 365 of the Bankruptcy Code.

(b) *Notice Period.* The statutory 21–day notice period should not be shortened for notice of the actual sale without a showing of good cause. The service of a prior notice or order, that discloses an intention to conduct a sale but does not state a specific sale date, does not affect the 21–day notice period.

(c) *Contents of Notice.* Proper notice should comport with Bankruptcy Rules 2002 and 6004 and should include:

(i) the Sale Procedures Order (including the date, time and place of any auction, the bidding procedures related thereto, the objection deadline for the sale motion and the date and time of the sale hearing);

(ii) reasonably specific identification of the assets to be sold, and instructions for promptly obtaining a bid package or any other detailed information being made available to prospective bidders;

(iii) the proposed form of asset purchase agreement, or instructions for promptly obtaining a copy;

(iv) if appropriate, representations describing the sale as being free and clear of liens, claims, interests and other encumbrances (other than any claims and defenses of a consumer under any consumer credit transaction that is subject to the Truth in Lending Act or a consumer credit contract (as defined in 16 C.F.R. § 433.1, as amended), with all such liens, claims, interests and other encumbrances attaching with the same validity and priority to the sale proceeds;

(v) any commitment by the buyer to assume liabilities of the Debtor; and

(vi) notice of proposed cure amounts and the right and deadline to object thereto and otherwise to object to the proposed assumption and assignment, or rejection of executory contracts and unexpired leases (*see* 1(c)(4), above, for additional notice that the Debtor may need to acknowledge may be required).[8]

4. Sale Order. In the typical case, the findings in a proposed Sale Order should be limited to those set out in 1(c), above, tailored to the particular case. The decretal paragraphs should also be limited, and if more than one decretal paragraph deals with the same subject matter or form of relief, the proponent of the Sale Order should explain the reason. Finally, if the order contains a decretal paragraph that approves the purchase agreement or authorizes the Debtor to execute the purchase agreement, it should not also contain separate decretal paragraphs that approve specific provisions of the purchase agreement or declare their legal effect.

With these admonitions, the Court may enter a Sale Order containing the following, if substantiated through evidence presented or proffered at the sale hearing:

(a) *Approval of Sale and Purchase Agreement.* The order should authorize the Debtor to (1) execute the purchase agreement, along with any additional instruments or documents that may be necessary to implement the purchase agreement, provided that such additional documents do not materially change its terms; (2) consummate the sale in accordance with the terms and conditions of the purchase agreement and the instruments and agreements contemplated thereby; and (3) take all further actions as may reasonably be requested by the purchaser for the purpose of transferring the assets.[9]

(b) *Transfer of Assets.* The order may provide that the assets will be transferred free and clear of all liens, claims, encumbrances and interests, other than any claims and defenses of a consumer under any consumer credit transaction subject to the Truth in Lending Act or a consumer credit contract, as defined in 16 C.F.R. § 433.1 (and as may be amended), with all such interests attaching to the sale proceeds with the same validity and priority, and the same defenses, as existed immediately prior to the sale,[10] and persons and entities holding any such interests will be enjoined from asserting such interests against the purchaser, its successors or assigns, or the purchased assets, unless the purchaser has otherwise agreed.

(c) *Assumption and Assignment of Executory Contracts and Leases to Purchaser.* The Debtor will be authorized and directed to assume and assign to the purchaser executory contracts and leases free and clear of all liens, claims, encumbrances and interests, with all such interests attaching to the sale proceeds with the same validity and priority as they had in the assets being sold (provided, however, that in certain circumstances additional notice may be required before assumption and assignment or rejection of executory contracts and leases can be granted. *See* 1(c)(4), above).

(d) *Statutory Provisions.* The proposed order should specify those sections of the Bankruptcy Code and Bankruptcy Rules that are being relied on, and identify those sections, such as Bankruptcy Rule 6004(h), that are, to the extent permitted by law, proposed to be limited or abridged.

(e) *Good Faith/No Collusion.* The transaction has been proposed and entered into by the Debtor and the purchaser without collusion, from arm's-length bargaining positions, and in good faith within the meaning of section 363(m) of the Bankruptcy Code. The proposed Sale Order should also specify that neither the Debtor nor the purchaser has engaged in any conduct that would cause or permit the transaction to be avoided under section 363(n) of the Bankruptcy Code.

[Dated: March 29, 2010.]

[1] The term "Debtor" includes "debtor in possession" and "trustee," as appropriate under the particular circumstances.

[2] When multiple asset sales over time are expected, the Debtor may consider seeking Court approval of global bidding procedures to avoid the need to obtain Court approval of procedures for each such sale. Similarly, the Debtor may consider seeking Court approval of global notice and other appropriate procedures to facilitate sales of assets of limited value or *de minimis* sales that do not warrant an auction or a separate motion for each sale. What constitutes a *de minimis* sale will depend on the facts of each case.

[3] It is expected that the Debtor will also share its evaluation of bids with key parties-in-interest, such as representatives of official committees, and that it will in its reasonable judgment identify the winning bidder only after consultation with such parties.

[4] The fact that a similar provision was included in an order entered in a different case does not constitute a justification.

[5] In larger cases, a sale of significant assets may also require notice of the proposed sale in publications of national circulation or other appropriate publications.

[6] In the case of publicly traded debt securities, notice to indenture trustees and record holders may be sufficient to the extent that the identity of beneficial holders is not known.

[7] Notice must be given to applicable taxing authorities, including the state attorney general or other appropriate legal officer, affected by the relief requested under section 1146(a) of the Bankruptcy Code.

8 This notice may be provided in a separate schedule sent only to the parties to such agreements.

9 Each and every federal, state and local government agency or department may be directed to accept any and all documents and instruments necessary and appropriate to consummate the transactions contemplated by the purchase agreement.

10 If any person or entity that has filed financing statements, mortgages, mechanic's liens, *lis pendens*, or other documents evidencing interests in the assets has not delivered to the Debtor prior to the closing date termination statements, instruments of satisfaction, and/or releases of all such interests, the Debtor may be authorized and directed to execute and file such statements, instruments, releases and other documents on behalf of such person or entity.

The Debtor should try to anticipate whether there are any allocation issues presented by the proposed "free and clear" relief.

ADMINISTRATIVE ORDER NO. 558. IN RE: ADOPTION OF GUIDELINES FOR FINANCING MOTIONS [SUPERCEDED BY ADMINISTRATIVE ORDER 655, EFFECTIVE JANUARY 13, 2017]

GENERAL ORDER NO. 559. IN RE: ELECTRONIC MEANS FOR FILING, SIGNING AND VERIFICATION OF DOCUMENTS

Electronic Filing Procedures

Applicable to All Bankruptcy Cases and Adversary Proceedings

WHEREAS, Federal Rule of Civil Procedure ("FRCP") 83 and Federal Rules of Bankruptcy Procedure ("FRBP") 5005(a)(2) and 9029 authorize this Court to establish practices and procedures for the filing, signing and verification of documents by electronic means; and

WHEREAS, by General Order No. 462, dated August 24, 2001, the Court established such practices and procedures; and

WHEREAS, by General Order No. 473, dated December 26, 2002, the Court revised such practices and procedures; and

WHEREAS, by General Order No. 559, dated April 23, 2010, the Court further revised such practices and procedures; and

WHEREAS, a proposal as to the adoption of Revised Administrative Procedures for Filing, Signing and Verifying Documents by Electronic Means ("Electronic Filing Procedures") has been reviewed by the Court; and

WHEREAS, the Electronic Filing Procedures are consistent with and enhance the responsibility of the Clerk of Court in the control of the Court's docket under FRBP 5003 and 5005, including safeguarding the integrity of the Court's docket; and

WHEREAS, the Electronic Filing Procedures do not impose fees inconsistent with the present fee structure adopted by the Judicial Conference of the United States pursuant to 28 U.S.C. §§ 1913, 1914, 1926 and 1930; and

WHEREAS, the Electronic Filing Procedures allow for the obtaining of a password by attorneys and limited users, which password identifies the party filing electronically; and

WHEREAS, the Electronic Filing Procedures provide for the signing of electronically filed documents in a manner consistent with terms set forth in E.D.N.Y. LBR 9011–1(b); and

WHEREAS, the Electronic Filing Procedures make adequate provision for the filing, review and retrieval of documents by parties who are not able to access the Electronic Filing System (the "System") from a remote location; and

WHEREAS, the Electronic Filing Procedures do not impair the ability of the Clerk of Court to discharge statistical reporting responsibilities both to the Court and the Administrative Office of the United States Courts; and

WHEREAS, the Electronic Filing Procedures are consistent with the notice requirements of FRBP 2002;

NOW, THEREFORE, IT IS ORDERED that:

The Electronic Filing Procedures, attached as Exhibit 1 to this Order, are approved by the Court.

1. Electronic files, consisting of the images of documents filed in cases or proceedings and documents filed by electronic means, are designated as and shall constitute the official record of the Court together with the other records kept by the Court.

2. No attorney or other person shall knowingly permit or cause to permit the attorney's password to be utilized by anyone other than an authorized member or employee of the attorney's law firm.

3. The signing of documents filed electronically shall conform to E.D.N.Y. LBR 9011–1(b).

4. The electronic filing of a document in accordance with the Electronic Filing Procedures together with the transmission of a Notice of Electronic Filing (NEF) from the Court shall constitute entry of that document on the docket kept by the Clerk under FRBP 5003, and shall be deemed accepted for filing by the Clerk's office.

5. The Office of the Clerk shall enter all applicable orders, decrees, judgments and proceedings of the Court in accordance with the Electronic Filing Procedures, which shall constitute entry of the order, decree, judgment or proceeding on the docket kept by the Clerk under FRBP 5003 and for purposes of FRBP 9021.

6. The request for and receipt of a System password from the Court shall constitute a request for electronic service by the attorney receiving the password pursuant to FRBP 9036, and except as otherwise provided in the Electronic Filing Procedures, a waiver by such attorney of the right to receive notice and service conventionally.

7. The original of this order shall be filed in accordance with the Electronic Filing Procedures.

8. Amendments to this order or the Electronic Filing Procedures may be entered from time to time in keeping with the needs of the Court.

9. This order shall become effective immediately, shall apply to all bankruptcy cases and adversary proceedings pending on or after the effective date, and shall supersede Revised General Order No. 559 dated April 23, 2010.

[Dated: March 18, 2016.]

EXHIBIT 1

Amended March 18, 2016

ADMINISTRATIVE PROCEDURES
FOR ELECTRONICALLY FILED CASES

UNITED STATES BANKRUPTCY COURT
EASTERN DISTRICT OF NEW YORK

Exhibit to General Order

REVISED ADMINISTRATIVE PROCEDURES

I. REGISTRATION FOR THE ELECTRONIC FILING SYSTEM

A. Designation of Cases. All bankruptcy cases and adversary proceedings shall be assigned to the Electronic Case Filing System (the "System").

B. Passwords. Each attorney and limited creditor ("Applicants") shall be entitled to one System password to permit them to participate in the electronic filing of documents in accordance with the System. Application for a password is governed by paragraphs I.C.1 and 2.

C. Registration.

1. To register to use the System, Applicants must submit a password application, using the forms provided on the Court's website at www.nyeb.uscourts.gov. Please note that there are separate applications for attorneys and limited creditors.

2. Completed applications are to be mailed or delivered to the Office of the Clerk, United States Bankruptcy Court, Eastern District of New York, Alphonse M. D'Amato U.S. Courthouse, 290 Federal Plaza, Central Islip, New York 11722, Attn: Electronic Case Filing System Registration.

3. Upon approval, Applicants will receive an e-mail from the Office of the Clerk containing their assigned System password.

4. System account holders are advised to change their Court assigned password periodically by using the ECF Password Reset Program available on the Court's website at https://ecf.nyeb.uscourts. gov/cgi-bin/lostPassword.pl. In the event a System account holder believes that the security of an

existing password has been compromised and a threat to the System exists, they shall give immediate telephonic notice to the Clerk of Court, Chief Deputy Clerk, Systems Manager or Assistant Systems Manager, confirmed by facsimile, to prevent access to the System through use of that password. Contact information for these individuals is available on the Court's website at www.nyeb.uscourts. gov.

II. ELECTRONIC FILING AND SERVICE OF DOCUMENTS

A. Filing.

1. All motions, pleadings, memoranda of law, or other documents required to be filed with the Court in connection with a case, with certain exceptions specified in paragraph III, below, shall be electronically filed on the System. For information regarding the filing of hard copies with chambers, please refer to the Judges' Procedures set forth on the Court's website. The date and time of the electronic filing shall be the official date and time of filing of the document.

2. Attorneys and Limited Creditors may file claims electronically on paper or PDF on diskette, CD, DVD or USB Flash Drive.

3. Creditors may also file claims without the requirement of a logon and password by using the Electronic Proof of Claim (ePOC) module located on the Court's website.

4. Attorneys who do not file electronically will be required to submit all filings to the Court in PDF on diskette, CD, DVD or USB Flash Drive in accordance with the Court's Administrative Order No. 476 dated June 4, 2003.

5. All documents that form part of a motion or pleading, and which are being filed at the same time and by the same party, may be electronically filed together under one document number, i.e., the motion and a supporting affidavit or application, with the exception of a memorandum of law. A memorandum of law must be filed separately and specified as related to the motion or pleading.

6. Persons filing documents that reference exhibits, which are not in electronic form shall scan and electronically file excerpts of the exhibits that are directly germane to the matter under consideration by the Court. Such filings must be clearly and prominently identified as excerpts, must not exceed twenty (20) pages, and state that the entire document is in the possession of the filing party and is available upon request. The entire exhibit must be made available forthwith to counsel and the Court on request, and must be available in the courtroom at any hearing pertaining to the matter. Persons filing excerpts of exhibits pursuant to these Procedures do so without prejudice to their right to file additional excerpts or the entire exhibit with the Court consistent with the Court's Local Bankruptcy Rules and the Judges' Procedures. *See, E.D.N.Y. LBR 5005–1(b)(iv).*

7. *Title of Docket Entries.* The person electronically filing a document is responsible for designating a title for the document using one of the main categories provided in the System, i.e., motion, application, etc.

8. *Payment of Filing Fees.* As part of the registration process, the attorneys affirm that they have a valid credit card or ACH debit card. All fee-related Internet filings will be paid through the Court's Internet credit card processing system known as Pay.gov, or by ACH debit card. These fees must be paid by midnight of the day of filing. Any failure to pay the fees due may result in revocation or suspension of the attorney's password.

B. Service.

1. *General Rule.* Except as otherwise provided in paragraph 2, below, all documents required to be served shall be served in paper (i.e., "hard copy") form in the manner mandated by the applicable law and rules.

2. *Consent to Electronic Service.* Whenever service is required to be made on a person who has requested, or is deemed to have requested, electronic notice in accordance with FRBP 9036 or paragraph 6 of the Court's Revised General Order on Electronic Filing Procedures, service may be made by serving the "Notice of Electronic Filing" generated by the System by hand, facsimile or e-mail in the first instance, or by overnight mail if service by hand, facsimile or e-mail is impracticable.

3. Notwithstanding the foregoing, hard copies of documents or notices shall be served in the following circumstances:

(a) A summons and complaint under FRBP 7004; a subpoena under FRBP 9016; and, a motion initiating a contested matter under FRBP 9014.

(b) Service shall be made upon an agency of the United States, including the United States Attorney, or chambers, in accordance with the FRBP, E.D.N.Y. Local Bankruptcy Rules, an order of the Court, or the Judges' Procedures.

(c) Notice served pursuant to FRBP 2002(a)(1).

(d) Upon the commencement of a case, service by counsel for the debtor, or by the debtor *pro se*, of the petition, schedules and statement of affairs on all applicable governmental agencies and the trustee assigned to the case, where applicable.

4. *Orders.* Attorney guidelines for submitting orders to the Court are posted on the Court's website.

5. *Notice of Electronic Filing Procedure, Adversary Proceedings.* Upon issuance by the Office of the Clerk of the Summons and Notice of Pretrial Conference, where applicable, the attorney for the plaintiff or the *pro se* party shall serve same along with a Notice of Electronic Filing upon all parties to the proceeding.

C. Signatures; Affidavits of Service.

1. Every petition, pleading, motion and other paper served or filed in accordance with these Procedures shall contain signatures that conform to E.D.N.Y. LBR 9011–1(b).

2. Petitions, lists, schedules, statements, amendments, pleadings, affidavits, stipulations and other documents which must contain original signatures, documents requiring verification under FRBP 1008, and unsworn declarations under 28 U.S.C.§ 1746, shall be filed electronically and bear "electronic signatures" that conform to E.D.N.Y. LBR 9011–1(b). The hard copy of the originally executed document, and/or original exhibits, shall be maintained by the filer for two years after the entry of a final order terminating the case or proceeding to which the document relates. On request of the Court, the filer must provide original documents for review.

3. Every order and judgment signed by the judge shall be filed electronically by the Clerk's Office at the direction of the Court and bear an "electronic signature."

D. Privacy Guidelines. Anyone filing documents with the Court shall comply with all guidelines pertaining to the privacy of individuals, including the provisions of Federal Rule of Bankruptcy Procedure 9037 and any guidelines implementing the E–Government Act of 2002. Among the privacy guidelines is the mandate to redact the first five digits of individuals' Social Security Numbers in any document intended for filing with the Court.

III. DOCUMENTS FILED UNDER SEAL

Documents filed under seal shall conform to E.D.N.Y. LBR 9018–1.

IV. PUBLIC ACCESS TO THE SYSTEM DOCKET

A. Pacer. Public Access to Court Electronic Records (PACER) is an electronic public access service that allows users to obtain case information via the Internet. All registered users will be charged a user fee. To register for the PACER System, or for more information, please visit the PACER Service Center at www.pacer.gov.

B. Access at the Court. Documents filed on the System and case dockets are available for viewing in the Office of the Clerk, United States Bankruptcy Court, Eastern District of New York, Alphonse M. D'Amato U.S. Courthouse, 290 Federal Plaza, Central Islip, New York, 11722 or the Conrad B. Duberstein United States Bankruptcy Courthouse, 271–C Cadman Plaza East, Brooklyn, New York 11201–1800 during regular business hours. No password is required to access documents at either of the Court's locations.

C. Conventional Copies and Certified Copies. Conventional copies and certified copies of electronically filed documents may be purchased at the Office of the Clerk, at Brooklyn or Long Island at the addresses noted above during regular business hours. Fees for copying and certification shall be in accordance with 28 U.S.C. § 1930.

D. Access Charges. At such time as the Court implements charges required by the Judicial Conference of the United States, as set out in 28 U.S.C. § 1930, for the usage of electronic access to the Court's records, users of the System will be charged in accordance with the fees and procedures established by the Administrative Office of the United States Courts.

ADMINISTRATIVE ORDER NO. 565. IN RE: ADOPTION OF GUIDELINES FOR FIRST DAY MOTIONS

UPON the resolution of the Board of Judges for the United States Bankruptcy Court for the Eastern District of New York, it is hereby

ORDERED, that the annexed Guidelines for First Day Motions are adopted.

[Dated: July 6, 2010.]

GUIDELINES FOR FIRST DAY MOTIONS

1. Statement of Purpose.

(a) The purpose of this document is to establish guidelines (the "**Guidelines**") for "first day" motions in business chapter 11 cases in the United States Bankruptcy Court for the Eastern District of New York (the "**Court**").

(b) The Guidelines are designed to help practitioners identify issues that typically are of concern to the Court where motions are brought before the Court shortly after the filing of a petition and to highlight such matters so that, among other things, determinations can be made, if necessary, on an expedited basis.

2. First Day Motions and Orders.

(a) "*First Day Orders*" are orders a Debtor seeks to have entered by the Court shortly after the filing of a petition. Generally, the purpose of First Day Orders is to address administrative matters, to facilitate the transition to debtor in possession status and to ensure that a Debtor's business and operations are stabilized. The request for a First Day Order should be made by motion (a "**First Day Motion**"), and a copy of the proposed First Day Order should be filed as an exhibit to the First Day Motion. The relief that may be granted by First Day Orders will depend upon the facts and circumstances of the case, the notice given and other related factors, and will take into account the needs of the Debtor and the rights of other parties in interest.

(b) While the Court recognizes the necessity and appropriateness of entertaining First Day Motions, only those motions seeking and appropriately requiring emergency relief will be heard on an expedited basis. Other motions may still be filed shortly after the filing of a petition, but they should seek relief at a future hearing in accordance with 11 U.S.C. §§ 101, *et seq.* (the "**Bankruptcy Code**"), the Federal Rules of Bankruptcy Procedure (the "**Bankruptcy Rules**") and the Local Bankruptcy Rules for the Eastern District of New York. The early filing of these motions will serve as useful guidance to the Court as to how the case may proceed.

3. Select First Day Motions and Orders.[1]

(a) *Joint Administration.*

(b) *Ministerial Matters.*

(i) This First Day Motion might request Court authorization to, among other things:

(A) extend the time to file schedules of assets and liabilities and the statement of financial affairs (which ordinarily should not exceed sixty (60) days from the date of the filing of the petition);

(B) establish procedures for mailing matrix/mailing issues;

(C) waive the requirement to file a list of creditors in cases where a motion to retain a claims/noticing agent has been filed; and

(D) use prepetition business forms, including letterhead, checks, etc.

(ii) The relief listed above should, where sought, ordinarily be sought in a single omnibus motion.

(iii) This First Day Motion should not include requests to use prepetition bank accounts or waive the investment requirements of section 345 of the Bankruptcy Code, which are discussed below.

(c) *Cash Collateral and Financing.* This First Day Motion should be brought in accordance with this Court's "Guidelines for Financing Motions" adopted pursuant to Administrative Order 558 dated April 15, 2010.

(d) *Cash Management Arrangements.*

(i) This First Day Motion should describe the proposed cash management system, including the rights and any procedures for the repayment of obligations incurred thereunder, and, in cases where money will be transferred between Debtors or from a Debtor to a non-debtor affiliate, give a business purpose for such transfers.

(ii) This First Day Motion should seek authorization (but not direction) for banks to follow the Debtor's instructions with respect to clearing checks, etc. The proposed First Day Order for this First Day Motion should also state that the banks are entitled to rely on the Debtor's representations as to which checks to clear.

(iii) This First Day Motion should not request relief that is inconsistent with the relief requested in connection with any debtor in possession financing and cash collateral motions.

(e) *Prepetition Employee Compensation, Benefits and Business Expenses.*

(i) This First Day Motion should disclose the gross amounts to be paid per employee or for lower level employees, by employee group (*i.e.,* general job categories) and in the aggregate.

(ii) This First Day Motion should estimate by category (salaries, commissions, reimbursable business expenses, etc.) the aggregate amounts proposed to be paid.

(iii) This First Day Motion should state whether, and the extent to which, the claims proposed to be paid constitute priority claims under section 507 of the Bankruptcy Code (**"Priority Claims"**) and, if such claims are not Priority Claims, this First Day Motion should explain why those claims should be afforded the treatment requested.

(iv) To the extent this First Day Motion requests Court authority to pay amounts in excess of the priority amount to any individual employees, a list of the names and position/job titles of all employees as to whom those excess payments will be made should be attached. The propriety of those requests will be considered on a case by case basis. There may be a need to present individual information confidentially in certain circumstances; however, the Court and the United States Trustee should receive this information (on a confidential basis where necessary).

(v) This First Day Motion should describe any relief that will be sought at a later hearing with respect to prepetition employee retention plans.

(f) *Critical Vendors.*

(i) This First Day Motion should ordinarily be brought as a single omnibus First Day Motion.

(ii) This First Day Motion and proposed First Day Order should identify, by category, the types of claims that the Debtor proposes to pay and should authorize specific non-cumulative capped amounts and describe the basis for the estimate of the expenditure. There may be a need to present vendor information confidentially in certain circumstances; however, the Court and the United States Trustee should receive this information (on a confidential basis where necessary).

(iii) This First Day Motion should state whether, and the extent to which, the prepetition claims proposed to be paid constitute (or are believed to constitute) claims under section 503(b)(9) of the Bankruptcy Code and, if such claims are not administrative expense claims, this First Day Motion should explain why those claims should be afforded the treatment requested.

(g) *Customer Claims.*

(i) This First Day Motion might request Court authorization to, among other things, satisfy or honor prepetition obligations with respect to refunds of deposits, lay-away plans, rebates, customer programs, warranty claims, etc.

(ii) This First Day Motion and the related proposed First Day Order should (other than for claims such as warranties or rebates) specify a cap on the amount to be paid or honored per claimant and in the aggregate, and the basis for such cap. There may be a need to present customer information confidentially in certain circumstances; however, the Court and the United States Trustee should receive this information (on a confidential basis where necessary).

(iii) This First Day Motion should state whether, and the extent to which, the claims proposed to be paid constitute (or are believed to constitute) Priority Claims and, if such claims are not Priority Claims, this First Day Motion should explain why those claims should be afforded the treatment requested.

(h) *Prepetition Taxes.* This First Day Motion should state whether, and the extent to which, the claims proposed to be paid constitute (or are believed to constitute) trust fund taxes, ad valorem taxes that result in liens and other taxes whose nonpayment gives rise to personal liability for officers, directors or employees, or other Priority Claims. If such claims are not Priority Claims, this First Day Motion should explain why those claims should be afforded the treatment requested.

(i) *Investment Guidelines.*

(i) This First Day Motion should disclose:

(A) the approximate amount of funds that the Debtor proposes to invest outside the enumerated investments permitted under section 345(b) of the Bankruptcy Code;

(B) the proposed types of investment to be made; and

(C) whether the United States Trustee has approved the Debtor's proposed arrangements.

(ii) If the Debtor proposes to invest or deposit money in or with an entity that has not satisfied the requirements of section 345(b) of the Bankruptcy Code (a "**Non–Qualified Entity**"), this First Day Motion should explain why such an investment or deposit is preferred and, to the extent known, why the Non–Qualified Entity cannot or has not satisfied the requirements of section 345(b) of the Bankruptcy Code. A list of United States Trustee-approved depositaries for the Eastern District of New York can be found at www.usdoj.gov/ust/r02.

(j) *Administrative Procedures.* This First Day Motion might request Court authorization to, among other things, establish a core service list and set omnibus hearing dates.

(k) *Retention of Claims/Noticing Agent.* Where it is anticipated that more than 1,000 proofs of claim will be filed, the Debtor should retain a claims/noticing agent to receive mailed proofs of claim. In such cases, counsel should contact the Clerk's Office for procedures involving claims/noticing agents.

(*l*) *Restrictions on Certain Transfers.* This First Day Motion might request Court authorization to, among other things, restrict certain transfers of claims against, and equity interests in, the Debtor and establish procedures for notice of certain transfers of claims against, and equity interests in, the Debtor.

4. Extraordinary Relief.

(a) Any First Day Motion requesting the relief identified in Bankruptcy Rule 6003 prior to the expiry of the twenty-one (21) day period provided by Bankruptcy Rule 6003 will be considered a request for "**Extraordinary Relief.**"

(b) If the Debtor requests any Extraordinary Relief, the First Day Motion, together with the omnibus affidavit or declaration, as applicable, should specifically state that Extraordinary Relief is sought and provide appropriate justification therefor, in accordance with E.D.N.Y. Local Bankruptcy Rule 9077–1.

(c) In connection with a request for Extraordinary Relief, the Court will consider, among other factors:

(i) the extent and adequacy of the notice provided;

(ii) whether only the minimal relief necessary is requested on an interim basis, with a broader final order to be submitted on notice;

(iii) whether an Official Committee of Unsecured Creditors appointed under section 1102 of the Bankruptcy Code (the "**Creditors' Committee**") or other parties in interest will have the ability to conduct an investigation and bring any appropriate proceedings related to the Extraordinary Relief (including, if relief is granted prior to any Creditors' Committee appointment, a motion to modify or prospectively vacate the relief granted, if appropriate); and

(iv) the urgency of the relief requested.

5. Participation of the Creditors' Committee.

(a) Absent good cause shown, the Court will not grant an order approving final substantive relief with respect to any matter that is granted on an interim basis pursuant to a First Day Motion unless the Creditors' Committee is in place for at least seven (7) days before the motion is heard.

(b) Absent good cause shown, the Creditors' Committee should be in place for at least seven (7) days before the following motions are heard:

(i) Rejection of leases and executory contracts. Affected landlords and other direct counterparties should receive appropriate notice of any motion.

(ii) Procedures establishing payment of interim compensation for retained professionals.

(iii) Approval of severance and employee retention programs.

(iv) Approval of the assumption of existing employment agreements.

6. Background and Factual Support. A single omnibus affidavit or declaration (or, if necessary, a small number of affidavits or declarations) should include the necessary general background as well as specific factual support for each First Day Motion, as necessary. The relevant affidavit or declaration may expressly be incorporated by reference into each motion in place of a lengthy background section of First Day Motions and other motions filed in the case.

7. Notice of First Day Motions.

(a) An index (the "**Index**") of First Day Motions and proposed First Day Orders that includes a brief summary of the relief sought in each (which summary may be in chart form and should not generally exceed one (1) paragraph per Motion) should be prepared by the Debtor. The Index also should note which First Day Motions, if any, include a request for Extraordinary Relief. The Index should inform parties that the First Day Motions and proposed First Day Orders may be viewed on the Court's website (http://www.nyeb.uscourts.gov/) with a login and password to the Court's Public Access to Court Electronic Records and that copies can be obtained from the Debtor's counsel and/or the Debtor's noticing agent. The Index will make the hearing on the First Day Motions more efficient as well as provide additional notice to parties in interest.

(b) The Index and a binder of all First Day Motions and proposed First Day Orders should ordinarily be provided to the United States Trustee, any party with a security interest in substantially all of the Debtor's assets and, if appropriate, any unofficial committee at least one (1) business day prior to the filing of the petition.

(c) Once the petition is filed and the Debtor is notified of the scheduling of the hearing on the First Day Motions, the Index should immediately be sent to the United States Trustee, counsel to any party with a security interest in substantially all of the Debtor's assets, counsel to any other party adversely affected by the relief requested, and the holders of the twenty (20) largest unsecured claims against each Debtor, if not onerous in view of the number of Debtor entities, or if a consolidated list is filed, to the holders of the thirty (30) largest unsecured claims, by hand delivery, facsimile or email, along with a notice of the time and place of the hearing on the First Day Motions, in the manner best designed to give adequate notice under the circumstances. It is understood that email addresses and/or facsimile numbers for some creditors may not be known by the Debtor at that time, and that such parties may not receive actual notice of the hearing.

(d) Whenever practicable, a list of email addresses for the Debtor, counsel to the Debtor, counsel to any party with a security interest in substantially all of the Debtor's assets, counsel to any other party adversely affected by the relief requested, and the holders of the twenty (20) largest unsecured claims against each Debtor, or if a consolidated list is filed, the holders of the thirty (30) largest unsecured claims should be provided to the United States Trustee before the First Day Motions are filed, and in any case, before the final hearing with respect to any matter that is granted on an interim basis pursuant to a First Day Motion.

8. List of Unsecured Creditors. Whenever practicable, a separate list of creditors holding the twenty (20) largest unsecured claims against each Debtor should be filed as required by Bankruptcy Rule 1007 before the hearing on the First Day Motions is held. In cases involving multiple Debtors, if it would be impracticable for each Debtor to file a separate list, an explanation should be set forth in the Bankruptcy Rule 1007 affidavit and a consolidated list of the holders of the thirty (30) largest unsecured claims should be filed.[2]

---

[1] This list does not preclude other relief from being sought on an expedited basis where necessary, and a Debtor is not required to seek all or any of the relief discussed herein. The inclusion of any item in this list should not be viewed or cited as justification for, or approval of, the legality or appropriateness of any such relief and does not guarantee that any or all of such relief will be granted.

2 The United States Trustee may require an expanded list of creditors depending on the circumstances of the case.

ADMINISTRATIVE ORDER NO. 568. IN RE: ADOPTION OF NEW YORK STATE STANDARDS OF CIVILITY

UPON the resolution of the Board of Judges for the United States Bankruptcy Court for the Eastern District of New York, it is

ORDERED, that the New York State Standards of Civility for the legal profession, New York Rules of Court, Part 1200, Appendix A, a copy of which is annexed hereto, are hereby adopted as guidelines for practice in all cases and proceedings in this Court.

[Dated: October 28, 2010.]

STANDARDS OF CIVILITY

1. Preamble. The New York State Standards of Civility for the legal profession set forth principles of behavior to which the bar, the bench and court employees should aspire. They are not intended as rules to be enforced by sanction or disciplinary action, nor are they intended to supplement or modify the Rules Governing Judicial Conduct, the Code of Professional Responsibility and its Disciplinary Rules, or any other applicable rule or requirement governing conduct. Instead they are a set of guidelines intended to encourage lawyers, judges and court personnel to observe principles of civility and decorum, and to confirm the legal profession's rightful status as an honorable and respected profession where courtesy and civility are observed as a matter of course. The Standards are divided into four parts: lawyers' duties to other lawyers, litigants and witnesses; lawyers' duties to the court and court personnel; court's duties to lawyers, parties and witnesses; and court personnel's duties to lawyers and litigants.

As lawyers, judges and court employees, we are all essential participants in the judicial process. That process cannot work effectively to serve the public unless we first treat each other with courtesy, respect and civility.

LAWYERS' DUTIES TO OTHER LAWYERS, LITIGANTS AND WITNESSES

I. Lawyers should be courteous and civil in all professional dealings with other persons.

A. Lawyers should act in a civil manner regardless of the ill feelings that their clients may have toward others.

B. Lawyers can disagree without being disagreeable. Effective representation does not require antagonistic or acrimonious behavior. Whether orally or in writing, lawyers should avoid vulgar language, disparaging personal remarks or acrimony toward other counsel, parties or witnesses.

C. Lawyers should require that persons under their supervision conduct themselves with courtesy and civility.

II. When consistent with their clients' interests, lawyers should cooperate with opposing counsel in an effort to avoid litigation and to resolve litigation that has already commenced.

A. Lawyers should avoid unnecessary motion practice or other judicial intervention by negotiating and agreeing with other counsel whenever it is practicable to do so.

B. Lawyers should allow themselves sufficient time to resolve any dispute or disagreement by communicating with one another and imposing reasonable and meaningful deadlines in light of the nature and status of the case.

III. A lawyer should respect the schedule and commitments of opposing counsel, consistent with protection of the client's interests.

A. In the absence of a court order, a lawyer should agree to reasonable requests for extensions of time or for waiver of procedural formalities when the legitimate interests of the client will not be adversely affected.

B.   Upon request coupled with the simple representation by counsel that more time is required, the first request for an extension to respond to pleadings ordinarily should be granted as a matter of courtesy.

C.   A lawyer should not attach unfair or extraneous conditions to extensions of time. A lawyer is entitled to impose conditions appropriate to preserve rights that an extension might otherwise jeopardize, and may request, but should not unreasonably insist on, reciprocal scheduling concessions.

D.   A lawyer should endeavor to consult with other counsel regarding scheduling matters in a good faith effort to avoid scheduling conflicts. A lawyer should likewise cooperate with opposing counsel when scheduling changes are requested, provided the interests of his or her client will not be jeopardized.

E.   A lawyer should notify other counsel and, if appropriate, the court or other persons at the earliest possible time when hearings, depositions, meetings or conferences are to be canceled or postponed.

IV.   A lawyer should promptly return telephone calls and answer correspondence reasonably requiring a response.

V.   The timing and manner of service of papers should not be designed to cause disadvantage to the party receiving the papers.

A.   Papers should not be served in a manner designed to take advantage of an opponent's known absence from the office.

B.   Papers should not be served at a time or in a manner designed to inconvenience an adversary.

C.   Unless specifically authorized by law or rule, a lawyer should not submit papers to the court without serving copies of all such papers upon opposing counsel in such a manner that opposing counsel will receive them before or contemporaneously with the submission to the court.

VI.   A lawyer should not use any aspect of the litigation process, including discovery and motion practice, as a means of harassment or for the purpose of unnecessarily prolonging litigation or increasing litigation expenses.

A.   A lawyer should avoid discovery that is not necessary to obtain facts or perpetuate testimony or that is designed to place an undue burden or expense on a party.

B.   A lawyer should respond to discovery requests reasonably and not strain to interpret the request so as to avoid disclosure of relevant and non-privileged information.

VII.   In depositions and other proceedings, and in negotiations, lawyers should conduct themselves with dignity and refrain from engaging in acts of rudeness and disrespect.

A.   Lawyers should not engage in any conduct during a deposition that would not be appropriate in the presence of a judge.

B.   Lawyers should advise their clients and witnesses of the proper conduct expected of them in court, at depositions and at conferences, and, to the best of their ability, prevent clients and witnesses from causing disorder or disruption.

C.   A lawyer should not obstruct questioning during a deposition or object to deposition questions unless necessary.

D.   Lawyers should ask only those questions they reasonably believe are necessary for the prosecution or defense of an action. Lawyers should refrain from asking repetitive or argumentative questions and from making self-serving statements.

VIII.   A lawyer should adhere to all express promises and agreements with other counsel, whether oral or in writing, and to agreements implied by the circumstances or by local customs.

IX.   Lawyers should not mislead other persons involved in the litigation process.

A.   A lawyer should not falsely hold out the possibility of settlement as a means for adjourning discovery or delaying trial.

B.   A lawyer should not ascribe a position to another counsel that counsel has not taken or otherwise seek to create an unjustified inference based on counsel's statements or conduct.

C.   In preparing written versions of agreements and court orders, a lawyer should attempt to correctly reflect the agreement of the parties or the direction of the court.

X. Lawyers should be mindful of the need to protect the standing of the legal profession in the eyes of the public. Accordingly, lawyers should bring the New York State Standards of Civility to the attention of other lawyers when appropriate.

LAWYERS' DUTIES TO THE COURT AND COURT PERSONNEL

I. A lawyer is both an officer of the court and an advocate. As such, the lawyer should always strive to uphold the honor and dignity of the profession, avoid disorder and disruption in the courtroom, and maintain a respectful attitude toward the court.

A. Lawyers should speak and write civilly and respectfully in all communications with the court and court personnel.

B. Lawyers should use their best efforts to dissuade clients and witnesses from causing disorder or disruption in the courtroom.

C. Lawyers should not engage in conduct intended primarily to harass or humiliate witnesses.

D. Lawyers should be punctual and prepared for all court appearances; if delayed, the lawyer should notify the court and counsel whenever possible.

II. Court personnel are an integral part of the justice system and should be treated with courtesy and respect at all times.

JUDGES' DUTIES TO LAWYERS, PARTIES AND WITNESSES

I. A Judge should be patient, courteous and civil to lawyers, parties and witnesses.

A. A Judge should maintain control over the proceedings and insure that they are conducted in a civil manner.

B. Judges should not employ hostile, demeaning or humiliating words in opinions or in written or oral communications with lawyers, parties or witnesses

C. Judges should, to the extent consistent with the efficient conduct of litigation and other demands on the court, be considerate of the schedules of lawyers, parties and witnesses when scheduling hearings, meetings or conferences.

D. Judges should be punctual in convening all trials, hearings, meetings and conferences; if delayed, they should notify counsel when possible.

E. Judges should make all reasonable efforts to decide promptly all matters presented to them for decision.

F. Judges should use their best efforts to insure that court personnel under their direction act civilly toward lawyers, parties and witnesses.

DUTIES OF COURT PERSONNEL TO THE COURT, LAWYERS AND LITIGANTS

I. Court personnel should be courteous, patient and respectful while providing prompt, efficient and helpful service to all persons having business with the courts.

A. Court employees should respond promptly and helpfully to requests for assistance or information.

B. Court employees should respect the judge's directions concerning the procedures and atmosphere that the judge wishes to maintain in his or her courtroom.

STATEMENT OF CLIENT'S RIGHTS

1. You are entitled to be treated with courtesy and consideration at all times by your lawyer and the other lawyers and personnel in your lawyer's office.

2. You are entitled to an attorney capable of handling your legal matter competently and diligently, in accordance with the highest standards of the profession. If you are not satisfied with

how your matter is being handled, you have the right to withdraw from the attorney-client relationship at any time (court approval may be required in some matters and your attorney may have a claim against you for the value of services rendered to you up to the point of discharge).

3. You are entitled to your lawyer's independent professional judgment and undivided loyalty uncompromised by conflicts of interest.

4. You are entitled to be charged a reasonable fee and to have your lawyer explain at the outset how the fee will be computed and the manner and frequency of billing. You are entitled to request and receive a written itemized bill from your attorney at reasonable intervals. You may refuse to enter into any fee arrangement that you find unsatisfactory.

5. You are entitled to have your questions and concerns addressed in a prompt manner and to have your telephone calls returned promptly.

6. You are entitled to be kept informed as to the status of your matter and to request and receive copies of papers. You are entitled to sufficient information to allow you to participate meaningfully in the development of your matter.

7. You are entitled to have your legitimate objectives respected by your attorney, including whether or not to settle your matter (court approval of a settlement is required in some matters).

8. You have the right to privacy in your dealings with your lawyer and to have your secrets and confidences preserved to the extent permitted by law.

9. You are entitled to have your attorney conduct himself or herself ethically in accordance with the Code of Professional Responsibility.

10. You may not be refused representation on the basis of race, creed, color, religion, sex, sexual orientation, age, national origin or disability.

ADMINISTRATIVE ORDER NO. 578. IN THE MATTER OF: TRANSITION OF AC-COUNTABILITY AND ADMINISTRATION OF THE COURT REGISTRY INVEST-MENT SYSTEM (CRIS) [SUPERSEDED BY ADMINISTRATIVE ORDER 655, EF-FECTIVE JANUARY 13, 2017]

GENERAL ORDER NO. 582. IN RE: ADOPTION OF MODIFIED LOSS MITIGATION PROGRAM PROCEDURES

Amending General Order #543

WHEREAS, by resolution of the Board of Judges of the United States Bankruptcy Court for the Eastern District of New York, General Order #543, dated December 8, 2009, instituted a uniform, comprehensive, court-supervised loss mitigation program in order to facilitate consensual resolutions for individual debtors whose residential real property is at risk of loss to foreclosure; and

WHEREAS, the loss mitigation program has helped avoid the need for various types of bankruptcy litigation, reduced costs to debtors and secured creditors, and enabled debtors to reorganize or otherwise address their most significant debts and assets under the United States Bankruptcy Code; and

WHEREAS, the Loss Mitigation Program Procedures were adopted, pursuant to 11 U.S.C. § 105(a), and shall apply in all individual cases assigned under Chapter 7, 11, 12 or 13 of the Bankruptcy Code, to Chief Judge Carla E. Craig, Judge Dorothy T. Eisenberg, Judge Elizabeth S. Stong and Judge Joel B. Rosenthal, and any other Judge of this Court who may elect to participate in the Loss Mitigation Program; and

WHEREAS, General Order #543 also provided that the Court may modify the Loss Mitigation Program Procedures from time to time by duly adopted General Order; and

WHEREAS, after further review of the Loss Mitigation Program, the Board of Judges has agreed to certain modifications to the procedures and forms; now therefor,

IT IS HEREBY ORDERED that the revised Loss Mitigation Program Procedures and forms are adopted effective immediately and shall be available in the Clerk's office and on the Court's web site.

[Dated: September 9, 2011.]

LOSS MITIGATION PROGRAM PROCEDURES

I. PURPOSE

The Loss Mitigation Program is designed to function as a forum in individual bankruptcy cases for debtors and lenders to reach consensual resolution whenever a debtor's residential property is at risk of foreclosure. The Loss Mitigation Program aims to facilitate resolution by opening the lines of communication between the debtors' and lenders' decision-makers. While the Loss Mitigation Program stays certain bankruptcy deadlines that might interfere with the negotiations or increase costs to the loss mitigation parties, the Loss Mitigation Program also encourages the parties to finalize any Settlement (as defined below) under bankruptcy court protection, instead of seeking dismissal of the bankruptcy case.

II. LOSS MITIGATION DEFINED

The term "loss mitigation" is intended to describe the full range of solutions that may avert the loss of a debtor's property to foreclosure, increased costs to the lender, or both. Loss mitigation commonly consists of the following general types of agreements, or a combination of them: loan modification, loan refinance, forbearance, short sale, or surrender of the property in full satisfaction. The terms of a loss mitigation solution will vary in each case according to the particular needs, interests, and goals of the parties.

III. ELIGIBILITY

The following definitions are used to describe the types of parties, properties, and loans that are eligible for participation in the Loss Mitigation Program:

A. Debtor. The term "Debtor" means any individual debtor in a case filed under Chapter 7, 11, 12, or 13 of the Bankruptcy Code, including joint debtors, whose case is assigned to Chief Judge Carla E. Craig, Judge Dorothy T. Eisenberg, Judge Elizabeth S. Stong, or Judge Joel B. Rosenthal, or any other judge who elects to participate in the Loss Mitigation Program.

B. Property. The term "Property" means any real property, including condominiums or cooperative apartments, used as the Debtor's principal residence, in which the Debtor holds an interest.

C. Loan. The term "Loan" means any mortgage, lien, or extension of money or credit secured by eligible Property or stock shares in a residential cooperative, regardless of whether the Loan (1) is considered to be "subprime" or "non-traditional;" (2) was in foreclosure prior to the bankruptcy filing; (3) is the first or junior mortgage or lien on the Property; or (4) has been "pooled," "securitized," or assigned to a servicer or to a trustee.

D. Creditor. The term "Creditor" means any holder, mortgage servicer, or trustee of an eligible Loan.

IV. ADDITIONAL PARTIES

A. Other Creditors. Any party may request, or the bankruptcy court may direct, more than one Creditor to participate in the Loss Mitigation Program, where it may be of assistance to obtain a global resolution.

B. Co–Debtors and Third Parties. Any party may request, or the bankruptcy court may direct, a co-debtor or other third party to participate in the Loss Mitigation Program, where the participation of such party may be of assistance, to the extent that the bankruptcy court has jurisdiction over the party or the party consents.

C. Chapter 13 Trustee. Any party may request, or the bankruptcy court may direct, the Chapter 13 Trustee to participate in the Loss Mitigation Program to the extent that such participation is consistent with the Chapter 13 Trustee's duty under Bankruptcy Code Section

1302(b)(4) to "advise, other than on legal matters, and assist the debtor in performance under the Chapter 13 plan."

D. Mediator. Any party may request, or the bankruptcy court may direct, a mediator from the Mediation Register maintained by the United States Bankruptcy Court for the Eastern District of New York to participate in the Loss Mitigation Program.

V. COMMENCEMENT OF LOSS MITIGATION

Parties are encouraged to request to enter into the Loss Mitigation Program as early in the case as possible, but a request may be made at any time as follows.

A. By the Debtor.

1. In a case under Chapter 13, the Debtor may request to enter into the Loss Mitigation Program with a particular Creditor in the Chapter 13 plan, and shall note the making of the request in the docket entry for the plan. The Creditor shall have 21 days to object. If no objection is filed, the bankruptcy court may enter an order referring the parties to the Loss Mitigation Program (a "Loss Mitigation Order").

2. A Debtor may serve and file a request to enter into the Loss Mitigation Program with a particular Creditor. The Creditor shall have 14 days to object. If no objection is filed, the bankruptcy court may enter a Loss Mitigation Order.

3. If a Creditor has filed a motion for relief from the automatic stay pursuant to Bankruptcy Code Section 362 (a "Lift–Stay Motion"), the Debtor may serve and file a request to enter into the Loss Mitigation Program at any time before the conclusion of the hearing on the Lift–Stay Motion. The bankruptcy court will consider the Debtor's request and any opposition by the Creditor at the hearing on the Lift–Stay Motion.

B. By a Creditor. A Creditor may serve and file a request to enter into the Loss Mitigation Program. The Debtor shall have 14 days to object. If no objection is filed, the bankruptcy court may enter a Loss Mitigation Order.

C. By the Bankruptcy Court. The bankruptcy court may enter a Loss Mitigation Order at any time after notice to the parties to be bound (the "Loss Mitigation Parties") and an opportunity to object.

D. Hearing on Objection. If any party files an objection, the bankruptcy court shall hold a hearing on the request to enter the Loss Mitigation Program and the objection, and shall not enter a Loss Mitigation Order until the objection has been heard.

VI. LOSS MITIGATION ORDER

A. Deadlines. A Loss Mitigation Order shall contain:

1. The date by which contact persons and telephone contact information shall be provided by the Loss Mitigation Parties

2. The date by which each Creditor shall initially contact the Debtor.

3. The date by which each Creditor shall transmit any request for information or documents to the Debtor.

4. The date by which the Debtor shall transmit any request for information or documents to each Creditor.

5. The date by which a written status report shall be filed, or the date and time for a status conference and oral status report (whether written or oral, a "Status Report"). In a Chapter 13 case, the status conference shall coincide, if possible, with a hearing on confirmation of the Chapter 13 plan. A date to file a written report shall be, if possible, not later than 7 days after the initial loss mitigation session.

6. The date when the loss mitigation process (the "Loss Mitigation Period") shall terminate, unless extended.

B. Effect. During the Loss Mitigation Period:

1.   A Creditor may contact the Debtor directly, and it shall be presumed that such contact does not violate the automatic stay.

2.   A Creditor may not file a Lift–Stay Motion, except where necessary to prevent irreparable injury. A Lift–Stay Motion filed by the Creditor before the entry of the Loss Mitigation Order shall be adjourned to a date following the Loss Mitigation Period, and the stay shall be extended pursuant to Bankruptcy Code Section 362(e).

3.   In a Chapter 13 case, the date by which a Creditor must object to confirmation of the Chapter 13 plan shall be extended to a date that is at least 14 days following the Loss Mitigation Period.

4.   Federal Rule of Evidence 408 shall apply to communications, information and documents exchanged by the Loss Mitigation Parties in connection with the Loss Mitigation Program.

VII. Duties Upon Commencement of Loss Mitigation

A.   Good Faith. The Loss Mitigation Parties shall negotiate in good faith. A party that does not participate in the Loss Mitigation Program in good faith may be subject to sanctions.

B.   Contact Information.

1.   *The Debtor*: The Debtor shall provide written notice to each Loss Mitigation Party of the manner in which the Creditor shall contact the Debtor or the Debtor's attorney. This may be done in the request to enter the Loss Mitigation Program.

2.   *The Creditor*: Each Creditor shall provide written notice to the Debtor of the name, address and direct telephone number of the contact person with authority to act on the Creditor's behalf. This may be done in the request to enter the Loss Mitigation Program.

C.   Status Report. The Loss Mitigation Parties shall provide a written or oral Status Report to the bankruptcy court within the period set in the Loss Mitigation Order. The Status Report shall indicate how many loss mitigation sessions have occurred, whether a resolution has been reached, and whether a Loss Mitigation Party believes that additional sessions may result in partial or complete resolution. A Status Report may include a request for an extension of the Loss Mitigation Period.

D.   Bankruptcy Court Approval. The Loss Mitigation Parties shall seek bankruptcy court approval of any Settlement reached during loss mitigation.

VIII. LOSS MITIGATION PROCESS

A.   Initial Contact. Following entry of a Loss Mitigation Order, the contact person designated by each Creditor shall contact the Debtor and any other Loss Mitigation Party within the time set by the bankruptcy court. The Debtor may contact any Loss Mitigation Party at any time. The purpose of the initial contact is to create a framework for the loss mitigation session and to ensure that the Loss Mitigation Parties are prepared. The initial contact is not intended to limit the issues or proposals that may arise during the loss mitigation session.

During the initial contact, the Loss Mitigation Parties shall discuss:

1.   The time and method for conducting the loss mitigation sessions.

2.   The loss mitigation alternatives that each party is considering.

3.   The exchange of information and documents before the loss mitigation session, including the date by when the Creditor shall request information and documents from the Debtor and the date by when the Debtor shall respond. All information and documents shall be provided at least seven days before the first loss mitigation session.

B.   Loss Mitigation Sessions. Loss mitigation sessions may be conducted in person, by telephone, or by video conference. At the conclusion of each loss mitigation session, the Loss Mitigation Parties shall discuss whether and when to hold a further session, and whether any additional information or documents should be exchanged.

C.   Bankruptcy Court Assistance. At any time during the Loss Mitigation Period, a Loss Mitigation Party may request a settlement conference or status conference with the bankruptcy judge.

D. Settlement Authority. At a loss mitigation session, each Loss Mitigation Party shall have a person with full settlement authority present. At a status conference or settlement conference with the bankruptcy court, each Loss Mitigation Party shall have a person with full settlement authority present. If a Loss Mitigation Party is appearing by telephone or video conference, that party shall be available beginning thirty minutes before the conference.

IX. DURATION, EXTENSION AND EARLY TERMINATION

A. Initial Period. The initial Loss Mitigation Period shall be set by the bankruptcy court in the Loss Mitigation Order.

B. Extension.

1. *By Agreement*: The Loss Mitigation Parties may agree to extend the Loss Mitigation Period by stipulation to be filed not less than one business day before the Loss Mitigation Period ends.

2. *In the Absence of Agreement*: A Loss Mitigation Party may request to extend the Loss Mitigation Period in the absence of agreement by filing and serving a request to extend the Loss Mitigation Period on the other Loss Mitigation Parties, who shall have seven days to object. If the request to extend the Loss Mitigation Period is opposed, then the bankruptcy court shall schedule a hearing on the request. The bankruptcy court may consider whether (1) an extension of the Loss Mitigation Period may result in a complete or partial resolution that provides a substantial benefit to a Loss Mitigation Party; (2) the party opposing the extension has participated in good faith and complied with these Loss Mitigation Procedures; and (3) the party opposing the extension will be prejudiced.

C. Early Termination.

1. *Upon Request of a Loss Mitigation Party*: A Loss Mitigation Party may request to terminate the Loss Mitigation Period by filing and serving a request to terminate the Loss Mitigation Period on the other Loss Mitigation Parties, who shall have seven days to object. If the request to terminate the Loss Mitigation Period is opposed, then the bankruptcy court shall schedule a hearing on the request. Notice may be modified for cause if necessary to prevent irreparable injury.

2. *Dismissal of the Bankruptcy Case*: A Chapter 13 bankruptcy case shall not be dismissed during the pendency of a Loss Mitigation Period, except (1) upon motion of the Chapter 13 Trustee or the United States Trustee for failure to comply with the requirements of the Bankruptcy Code; or (2) upon the voluntary request of the Chapter 13 Debtor. **A Chapter 13 Debtor may not be required to request dismissal of the bankruptcy case as part of a Settlement during the Loss Mitigation Period.** If a Chapter 13 Debtor requests voluntary dismissal during the Loss Mitigation Period, the Debtor shall indicate whether the Debtor agreed or intends to enter into a Settlement with a Loss Mitigation Party.

D. Discharge. The Clerk of the Court shall not enter a discharge during the pendency of a Loss Mitigation Period.

X. SETTLEMENT

The bankruptcy court shall consider any agreement or resolution (a "Settlement") reached during loss mitigation and may approve the Settlement, subject to the following provisions:

1. **Implementation:** A Settlement may be noticed and implemented in any manner permitted by the Bankruptcy Code and Federal Rules of Bankruptcy Procedure (the "Bankruptcy Rules"), including but not limited to a stipulation, sale, Chapter 11 plan of reorganization, or Chapter 13 plan.

2. **Fees, Costs, or Charges:** If a Settlement provides for a Creditor to receive payment or reimbursement of any expense arising from the Creditor's participation in the Loss Mitigation Program, that expense shall be disclosed to the Debtor and the bankruptcy court before the Settlement is approved.

3. **Signatures:** Consent to the Settlement shall be acknowledged in writing by the Creditor representative who participated in the loss mitigation session, the Debtor, and the Debtor's attorney, if applicable.

4. **Hearing:** Where a Debtor is represented by an attorney, a Settlement may be approved by the bankruptcy court without further notice, or upon such notice as the bankruptcy court directs,

unless additional notice or a hearing is required by the Bankruptcy Code or Bankruptcy Rules. Where a Debtor is not represented by counsel, a Settlement shall not be approved until the bankruptcy court conducts a hearing at which the Debtor shall appear in person.

5. Dismissal Not Required: A Debtor shall not be required to request dismissal of the bankruptcy case in order to effectuate a Settlement. In order to ensure that the Settlement is enforceable, the Loss Mitigation Parties shall seek bankruptcy court approval of the Settlement. Where the Debtor requests or consents to dismissal of the bankruptcy case as part of the Settlement, the bankruptcy court may approve the Settlement as a "structured dismissal," if such relief complies with the Bankruptcy Code and Bankruptcy Rules.

XI. LOSS MITIGATION FINAL REPORT

Debtor's counsel (or the Debtor, if the Debtor is proceeding without attorney representation) shall file with the Court a Loss Mitigation Final Report. The form of Loss Mitigation Final Report is on the Court's website. The Loss Mitigation Final Report shall be filed no later than 14 days after termination of the Loss Mitigation Period. Termination occurs:

1. when the Court enters an order terminating the Loss Mitigation Period;

2. when the Court approves a stipulated agreement that has been presented to the Court, which provides for settlement or resolution of the Loss Mitigation; or

3. upon expiration of the Loss Mitigation Period.

Where two or more requests for Loss Mitigation have been made in a case, for different properties or different mortgages on a property, a separate Loss Mitigation Final Report must be filed with respect to each request.

XII. COORDINATION WITH OTHER PROGRAMS

[Provision may be added in the future to provide for coordination with other loss mitigation programs, including programs in the New York State Unified Court System.]

UNITED STATES BANKRUPTCY COURT
EASTERN DISTRICT OF NEW YORK
-- X
In Re: Chapter

                                             Case No.

                   Debtor(s)
-- X

LOSS MITIGATION REQUEST—BY DEBTOR

I am a Debtor in this case. I hereby request to enter into the Loss Mitigation Program with respect to *[Identify the property, loan and creditor(s) for which you are requesting loss mitigation]*:

_____
[Identify the Property]

_____
[Loan Number]

_____
[Creditor's Name and Address]

SIGNATURE

I understand that if the Court orders loss mitigation in this case, I will be expected to comply with the Loss Mitigation Procedures. I agree to comply with the Loss Mitigation Procedures, and I will participate in the Loss Mitigation Program in good faith. I understand that loss mitigation is voluntary for all parties, and that I am not required to enter into any agreement or settlement with any other party as part of entry into the Loss Mitigation Program. I also understand that no other party is required to enter into any agreement or settlement with me. I understand that **I am not required to request dismissal of this case** as part of any resolution or settlement that is offered or agreed to during the Loss Mitigation Period.

Sign: _____ Date: _____, 20 ____

Print Name: _____
[First and Last Name]

Telephone Number: _____
[i.e. 999–999–9999]

E-mail Address [if any]: _____

UNITED STATES BANKRUPTCY COURT
EASTERN DISTRICT OF NEW YORK
--- X
In Re: Chapter

                                                Case No.

Debtor(s)
--- X

LOSS MITIGATION REQUEST—BY A CREDITOR

I am a Creditor (including a holder, servicer or trustee of a mortgage or lien secured by property used by the Debtor as a principal residence) of the Debtor in this case. I hereby request to enter into the Loss Mitigation Program with respect to *[Identify the property, loan and creditor(s) for which you are requesting loss mitigation]*:

_____
[Identify the Property]

_____
[Loan Number]

_____
[Creditor's Name and Address]

SIGNATURE

I understand that if the Court orders loss mitigation in this case, I will be expected to comply with the Loss Mitigation Procedures. I agree to comply with the Loss Mitigation Procedures, and I will participate in the Loss Mitigation Program in good faith. I understand that loss mitigation is voluntary for all parties, and that I am not required to enter into any agreement or settlement with any other party as part of entry into the Loss Mitigation Program. I also understand that no other party is required to enter into any agreement or settlement with me. I understand that **I am not required to request dismissal of this case** as part of any resolution or settlement that is offered or agreed to during the Loss Mitigation Period.

Sign: _____ Date: _____, 20 _____

Print Name: _____

[First and Last Name]

Telephone Number: _____

[i.e. 999–999–9999]

E-mail Address [if any]: _____

_____

UNITED STATES BANKRUPTCY COURT
EASTERN DISTRICT OF NEW YORK
--- x
In Re: Chapter

                                          Case No.

Debtor(s)   /
--- x

LOSS–MITIGATION ORDER

☐ A Loss Mitigation Request was filed by the debtor on *[Date]* _____, 20 ___.

☐ A Loss Mitigation Request was filed by a creditor on *[Date]* _____, 20 ___.

☐ The Court raised the possibility of loss mitigation, and the parties have had notice and an opportunity to object.

Upon the foregoing, it is hereby

ORDERED, that the following parties (the "Loss Mitigation Parties") are directed to participate in the Loss Mitigation Program:

1. The Debtor

2. _____, the Creditor with respect to _____ *[describe Loan and/or Property]*.

3. *[Additional parties, if any]* _____

It is further **ORDERED,** that the Loss Mitigation Parties shall comply with the Loss Mitigation Procedures annexed to this Order; and it is further

ORDERED, that the Loss Mitigation Parties shall observe the following deadlines:

1. Each Loss Mitigation Party shall designate contact persons and disclose contact information by *[suggested time is 7 days]*, unless this information has been previously provided. As part of this obligation, **a Creditor shall furnish each Loss Mitigation Party with written notice of the name, address and direct telephone number of the person who has full settlement authority.**

2. Each Creditor that is a Loss Mitigation Party shall contact the Debtor within **14 days of the date of this Order.**

3. Each Loss Mitigation Party shall make its request for information and documents, if any, within **14 days of the date of this Order.**

4. Each Loss Mitigation Party shall respond to a request for information and documents within **14 days after a request is made, or 7 days prior to the Loss Mitigation Session, whichever is earlier.**

5. The Loss Mitigation Session shall be scheduled not later than _____ *[suggested time is within 35 days of the date of the order]*.

6. The Loss Mitigation Period shall terminate on _____ [suggested time is within 42 days of the date of the date of the order], unless extended as provided in the Loss Mitigation Procedures.

320

It is further **ORDERED**, that a status conference will be held in this case on _____ *[suggested time is within 42 days of the date of the order]* (the "Status Conference"). The Loss Mitigation Parties shall appear at the Status Conference and provide the Court with an oral Status Report unless a written Status Report that is satisfactory to the Court has been filed not later than 7 days prior to the date of the Status Conference and requests that the Status Conference be adjourned or cancelled; and it is further

ORDERED, that at the Status Conference, the Court may consider a Settlement reached by the Loss Mitigation Parties, or may adjourn the Status Conference if necessary to allow for adequate notice of a request for approval of a Settlement; and it is further

ORDERED, that any matters that are currently pending between the Loss Mitigation Parties (such as motions or applications, and any objection, opposition or response thereto) are hereby adjourned to the date of the Status Conference to the extent those matters concern (1) relief from the automatic stay, (2) objection to the allowance of a proof of claim, (3) reduction, reclassification or avoidance of a lien, (4) valuation of a Loan or Property, or (5) objection to confirmation of a plan of reorganization; and it is further

ORDERED, that the time for each Creditor that is a Loss Mitigation Party in this case to file an objection to a plan of reorganization in this case shall be extended until 14 days after the termination of the Loss Mitigation Period, including any extension of the Loss Mitigation Period.

Dated:

BY THE COURT

_____
United States Bankruptcy Judge

UNITED STATES BANKRUPTCY COURT
EASTERN DISTRICT OF NEW YORK

--- x

In Re: Case No.
                                                    Chapter

Debtor(s)
--- x

LOSS MITIGATION FINAL REPORT

Name of Lender: _____

Property Address: _____

Last Four Digits of Account Number of Loan: _____

File Date of Request for Loss Mitigation: ___ / ___ / ___

Date of Entry of Order Granting Loss Mitigation: _____

Date of Entry of Order Approving Settlement *(if any):* _____

Other Requests for Loss Mitigation in this Case: ___ Yes   ___ No

The use of the Court's Loss Mitigation Procedures has resulted in the following (please check the appropriate box below):

☐ Loan modification.

  ☐   Loan refinance.

  ☐   Forbearance.

  ☐   Short sale.

  ☐   Surrender of property.

  ☐   No agreement has been reached.

  ☐   Other: _____

                   _____

                   _____

                   _____

Dated: _____   Signature: _____

1.   All capitalized terms have the meaning defined in the Loss Mitigation Procedures

GENERAL ORDER NO. 586. EXTENSION OF APPLICABILITY OF INTERIM RULE 1007–I

WHEREAS, this Court, by means of **General Order No. 535** (signed December 18, 2008), adopted Interim Rule 1007–I, which implements the 2008 amendments to 11 U.S.C. § 707(b) providing a temporary exclusion from the application of the means test for certain members of the National Guard and Reserves;

WHEREAS, the President of the United States, on December 13, 2011, signed into law the National Guard and Debt Relief Extension Act of 2011, which extended, until December 18, 2015, the temporary exclusion from the application of the means test for certain members of the National Guard and Reserves; it is, therefore,

ORDERED, that the applicability of Interim Rule 1007–I to cases filed in this district is extended for so long as such exclusion from the means test remains operative under federal law.

[Dated: December 20, 2011.]

Interim Rule 1007–I. Lists, Schedules, Statements, and Other Documents; Time Limits; Expiration of Temporary Means Testing Exclusion

* * * * *

(b) Schedules, Statements, and Other Documents Required.

* * * * *

(4) Unless either: (A) § 707(b)(2)(D)(i) applies, or (B) § 707(b)(2)(D)(ii) applies and the exclusion from means testing granted therein extends beyond the period specified by Rule 1017(e), an individual debtor in a chapter 7 case shall file a statement of current monthly income prepared as prescribed by the appropriate Official Form, and, if the current monthly income exceeds the median family income for the applicable state and household size, the information, including calculations, required by § 707(b), prepared as prescribed by the appropriate Official Form.

* * * * *

(c) Time Limits. In a voluntary case, the schedules, statements, and other documents required by subdivision (b)(1), (4), (5), and (6) shall be filed with the petition or within 15 days thereafter, except as otherwise provided in subdivisions (d), (e), (f), ~~and~~ (h), and (n) of this rule. In an involuntary case, the list in subdivision (a)(2), and the schedules, statements, and other documents required by subdivision (b)(1) shall be filed by the debtor within 15 days of the entry of the order for relief. In a voluntary case, the documents required by paragraphs (A), (C), and (D) of subdivision (b)(3) shall be filed with the petition. Unless the court orders otherwise, a debtor who has filed a statement under subdivision (b)(3)(B), shall file the documents required by subdivision (b)(3)(A) within 15 days of the order for relief. In a chapter 7 case, the debtor shall file the statement required by subdivision (b)(7) within 45 days after the first date set for the meeting of creditors under § 341 of the Code, and in a chapter 11 or 13 case no later than the date when the last payment was made by the debtor as required by the plan or the filing of a motion for a discharge under § 1141(d)(5)(B) or § 1328(b) of the Code. The court may, at any time and in its discretion, enlarge the time to file the statement required by subdivision (b)(7). The debtor shall file the statement required by subdivision (b)(8) no earlier than the date of the last payment made under the plan or the date of the filing of a motion for a discharge under §§ 1141(d)(5)(B), 1228(b), or 1328(b) of the Code. Lists, schedules, statements, and other documents filed prior to the conversion of a case to another chapter shall be deemed filed in the converted case unless the court directs otherwise. Except as provided in § 1116(3), any extension of time to file schedules, statements, and other documents 43 required under this rule may be granted only on motion for cause shown and on notice to the United States trustee, any committee elected under § 705 or appointed under § 1102 of the Code, trustee, examiner, or other party as the court may direct. Notice of an extension shall be given to the United States trustee and to any committee, trustee, or other party as the court may direct.

* * * * *

(n) Time Limits for, and Notice to, Debtors Temporarily Excluded From Means Testing.

(1) An individual debtor who is temporarily excluded from means testing pursuant to § 707(b)(2)(D)(ii) of the Code shall file any statement and calculations required by subdivision (b)(4) no later than 14 days after the expiration of the temporary exclusion if the expiration occurs within the time specified by Rule 1017(e) for filing a motion pursuant to § 707(b)(2).

(2) If the temporary exclusion from means testing under § 707(b)(2)(D)(ii) terminates due to the circumstances specified in subdivision (n)(1), and if the debtor has not previously filed a statement and calculations required by subdivision (b)(4), the clerk shall promptly notify the debtor that the required statement and calculations must be filed within the time specified in subdivision (n)(1).

Committee Note

This rule is amended to take account of the enactment of the National Guard and Reservists Debt Relief Act of 2008, which amended § 707(b)(2)(D) of the Code to provide a temporary exclusion from the application of the means test for certain members of the National Guard and reserve components of the Armed Forces. This exclusion applies to qualifying debtors while they remain on active duty or are performing a homeland defense activity, and for a period of 540 days thereafter. For some debtors initially covered by the exclusion, the protection from means testing will expire while their chapter 7 cases are pending, and at a point when a timely motion to dismiss under § 707(b)(2) can still be filed. Under the amended rule, these debtors are required to file the statement and calculations required by subdivision (b)(4) no later than 14 days after the expiration of their exclusion.

Subdivisions (b)(4) and (c) are amended to relieve debtors qualifying for an exclusion under § 707(b)(2)(D)(ii) from the obligation to file a statement of current monthly income and required calculations within the time period specified in subdivision (c).

Subdivision (n)(1) is added to specify the time for filing of the information required by subdivision (b)(4) by a debtor who initially qualifies for the means test exclusion under § 707(b)(2)(D)(ii), but whose exclusion expires during the time that a motion to dismiss under § 707(b)(2) may still be made under Rule 1017(e). If, upon the expiration of the temporary exclusion, a debtor has not already filed the required statement and calculations, subdivision (n)(2) directs the clerk to provide prompt notice to the debtor of the time for filing as set forth in subdivision (n)(1).

ADMINISTRATIVE ORDER 601. IN THE MATTER OF THE REFERRAL OF MATTERS TO THE BANKRUPTCY JUDGES [DISTRICT COURT ORDER]

UNITED STATES DISTRICT COURT
EASTERN DISTRICT OF NEW YORK

WHEREAS 28 U.S.C. § 157(a) provides that each district court may refer any or all cases under Title 11 and any or all proceedings arising under Title 11, or arising in or related to a case under Title 11, and

WHEREAS, by Order of this Court on August 28, 1986, all such cases and proceedings are referred to the Bankruptcy Judges for this District,

It is hereby

ORDERED that if a bankruptcy judge or district judge determines that a bankruptcy judge cannot enter a final order or judgment consistent with Article III of the United States Constitution in a particular proceeding referred under this order and designated as core under section 157(b) of title 28, unless the district court orders otherwise, the bankruptcy judge shall hear the proceeding and submit proposed findings of fact and conclusions of law to the district court, and it is further

ORDERED that the district court may treat any order or judgment of the bankruptcy court as proposed findings of fact and conclusions of law in the event that the district court concludes that a bankruptcy judge could not enter that order or judgment consistent with Article III of the United States Constitution, and it is further

ORDERED that this Order shall be given effect nunc pro tunc as of June 23, 2011.

[Dated: December 5, 2012.]

ADMINISTRATIVE ORDER NO. 609. IN THE MATTER OF: DUTY OF ATTORNEY TO REPORT DISCIPLINE

BY resolution of the Board of Judges of the Bankruptcy Court for the Eastern District of New York, it is

ORDERED, that if any federal, state or territorial court, agency or tribunal has entered an order disbarring or censuring an attorney who has appeared in a case or proceeding that is pending in this Court, or suspending the attorney from practice, whether or not on consent, the attorney shall deliver a copy of said order to the Clerk of this Court within fourteen days after the entry of the order; and it is further

ORDERED, that if any attorney who has appeared in a case or proceeding that is pending in this Court has resigned from the bar of any federal, state or territorial court, agency or tribunal while an investigation into allegations of misconduct against the attorney was pending, the attorney shall report such resignation to the Clerk of this Court within fourteen days after the submission of the resignation; and it is further

ORDERED, that if this Court has entered an order suspending an attorney from practice pursuant to E.D.N.Y. Local Bankruptcy Rule 2090–1(e), whether or not on consent, the attorney shall deliver a copy of said order within fourteen days after the entry of the order to the clerk of each federal, state or territorial court, agency and tribunal in which such attorney has been admitted to practice; and it is further

ORDERED, that any failure of an attorney to comply with the requirements of this order shall constitute a basis for referral to any federal, state or territorial court, agency or tribunal in which the attorney is or was admitted for discipline of said attorney.

[Dated: March 8, 2013.]

GENERAL ORDER 613.   RE: GUIDELINES FOR FEES AND DISBURSEMENTS FOR PROFESSIONALS IN EASTERN DISTRICT OF NEW YORK BANKRUPTCY CASES

By resolution of the Board of Judges for the United States Bankruptcy Court for the Eastern District of New York, it is resolved that in order to further provide professionals with clear and concise procedures for compensation and reimbursement of expenses and to combine into one order the requirements heretofore promulgated by this Court and the United States Trustee, applications for compensation and reimbursement of expenses filed in the Bankruptcy Court for the Eastern District of New York shall conform substantially to the annexed guidelines.

This order shall become effective on June 10, 2013, and apply to all fee applications filed on or after that date.

[Dated: June 4, 2013.]

GUIDELINES FOR FEES AND DISBURSEMENTS FOR PROFESSIONALS IN EASTERN DISTRICT OF NEW YORK BANKRUPTCY CASES

A.   Contents of Applications for Compensation and Reimbursement of Expenses.   All applications should include sufficient detail to demonstrate compliance with the standards set forth in 11 U.S.C. § 330.   The fee application should also contain sufficient information about the case and the applicant to facilitate a review without searching for relevant information in other documents.   The following will facilitate review of the application.

(1) *Information About the Applicant and the Application.*   The following information should be provided in every fee application:

(i) Date the bankruptcy petition was filed, date of the order approving employment, identity of the party represented, date services commenced, and whether the applicant is seeking compensation under a provision of the Bankruptcy Code other than section 330.

(ii) Terms and conditions of employment and compensation, source of compensation, existence and terms controlling use of a retainer, and any budgetary or other limitations on fees.

(iii) Names and hourly rates of all applicant's professionals and paraprofessionals who billed time, explanation of any changes in hourly rates from those previously charged, and statement of whether the compensation is based on the customary compensation charged by comparably skilled practitioners in cases other than cases under title 11.

(iv) Whether the application is interim or final, and the dates of previous orders on interim compensation or reimbursement of expenses along with the amounts requested and the amounts allowed or disallowed, amounts of all previous payments, and amount of any allowed fees and expenses remaining unpaid.

(v) Whether the person on whose behalf the applicant is employed has been given the opportunity to review the application and whether that person has approved the requested amount.

(vi) When an application is filed more than once every 120 days after the order for relief or after a prior application to the Court, the date and terms of the order allowing leave to file at shortened intervals.

(vii) Time period of the services or expenses covered by the application.

(2) *Case Status.*   The following information should be provided to the extent that it is known to or can be reasonably ascertained by the applicant:

(i) In a chapter 7 case, a summary of the administration of the case including all moneys received and disbursed in the case, when the case is expected to close, and, if applicant is seeking an interim award, whether it is feasible to make an interim distribution to creditors without prejudicing the rights of any creditor holding a claim of equal or higher priority.

325

(ii) In a chapter 11 case, whether a plan and disclosure statement have been filed and, if not yet filed, when the plan and disclosure statement are expected to be filed; whether all quarterly fees have been paid to the United States Trustee; and whether all monthly operating reports have been filed.

(iii) In a chapter 12 or 13 case, where the debtor's attorney is the applicant, whether the application is in accordance with the 2016(b) statement that was filed at the beginning of the case, and whether approval of the application would have an effect on the debtor's plan.

(iv) In every case, the amount of cash on hand or on deposit, the amount and nature of accrued unpaid administrative expenses, and the amount of unencumbered funds in the estate.

(v) In every case, any material changes in the status of the case that occur after the filing of the fee application should be raised, orally or in writing, at the hearing on the application or, if a hearing is not required, prior to the expiration of the time period for objection.

(3) *Summary Sheet.* All applications should contain a summary or cover sheet that provides a synopsis of the following information:

(i) Total compensation and expenses requested and any amount(s) previously requested;

(ii) Total compensation and expenses previously awarded by the court;

(iii) Name and applicable billing rate for each person who billed time during the period, and date of bar admission for each attorney;

(iv) Total hours billed and total amount of billing for each person who billed time during billing period; and

(v) Computation of blended hourly rate for persons who billed time during period, excluding paralegal or other paraprofessional time.

(4) *Project Billing Format.*

(i) To facilitate effective review of the application, all time and service entries should be arranged by project categories. The project categories set forth in Exhibit A should be used to the extent applicable. A separate project category should be used for administrative matters and, if payment is requested, for fee application preparation.

(ii) The Court has discretion to determine that the project billing format is not necessary in a particular case or in a particular class of cases.

(iii) Each project category should contain a narrative summary of the following information:

a. a description of the project, its necessity and benefit to the estate, and the status of the project including all pending litigation for which compensation and reimbursement are requested;

b. identification of each person providing services on the project; and

c. a statement of the number of hours spent and the amount of compensation requested for each professional and paraprofessional on the project.

(vi)* Time and service entries are to be reported in chronological order under the appropriate project category.

(vii) Time entries should be kept contemporaneously with the services rendered in time periods of tenths of an hour. Services should be noted in detail, with each service showing a separate time entry and not combined or "lumped" together; however, tasks performed on a project which total a de minimis amount of time can be combined or lumped together if they do not exceed 0.5 hours on a daily aggregate. Time entries for telephone calls, letters, and other communications should give sufficient detail to identify the parties to and the nature of the communication. Time entries for court hearings and conferences should identify the subject of the hearing or conference. If more than one professional from the applicant firm attends a hearing or conference, the applicant should explain the need for multiple attendees.

(5) *Reimbursement for Actual, Necessary Expenses.* Except to the extent that paragraph F, infra, is to the contrary, the following factors are relevant to a determination that an expense is proper:

(i) Whether the expense is reasonable and economical.

(ii) Whether the requested expenses are customarily charged to non-bankruptcy clients of the applicant.

(iii) Whether applicant has provided a detailed itemization of all expenses including the date incurred, description of expense (e.g., type of travel, type of fare, rate, destination), method of computation, and, where relevant, name of the person incurring the expense and purpose of the expense. Itemized expenses should be identified by their nature (e.g., long distance telephone, copy costs, messengers, computer research, airline travel, etc.) and by the month incurred. Unusual items require more detailed explanations and should be allocated, where practicable, to specific projects.

(iv) Whether applicant has prorated expenses where appropriate between the estate and other cases (e.g., travel expenses applicable to more than one case) and has adequately explained the basis for any such proration.

(v) Whether expenses incurred by the applicant to third parties are limited to the actual amounts billed to, or paid by, the applicant on behalf of the estate.

(vi) Whether applicant can demonstrate that the amount requested for expenses incurred in-house reflect the actual cost of such expenses to the applicant, or the actual cost cannot easily be determined.

(vii) Whether the expenses appear to be in the nature nonreimbursable overhead. Overhead consists of all continuous administrative or general costs incident to the operation of the applicant's office and not particularly attributable to an individual client or case. Overhead includes, but is not limited to: word processing, proofreading, administrative and other clerical services; rent, utilities, office equipment and furnishings; insurance, taxes, local telephones, and monthly car phone and cellular phone charges; lighting, heating and cooling; and library and publication charges.

(viii) Whether applicant has adhered to allowable rates for expenses as fixed by local rule or order of the Court.

B. Certification.

(1) Each application for fees and disbursements must contain a certification by the professional designated by the applicant with the responsibility in the particular case for compliance with these Amended Guidelines (the "Certifying Professional"), that (a) the Certifying Professional has read the application; (b) to the best of the Certifying Professional's knowledge, information and belief formed after reasonable inquiry, the fees and disbursements sought fall within these Amended Guidelines, except as specifically noted in the certification and described in the fee application; (c) except to the extent that fees or disbursements are prohibited by these Amended Guidelines, the fees and disbursements sought are billed at rates and in accordance with practices customarily employed by the applicant and generally accepted by the applicant's clients; and (d) in providing a reimbursable service, the applicant does not make a profit on the service, whether the service is performed by the applicant in-house or through a third party.

(2) Each application for fees and disbursements must contain a certification by the Certifying Professional that the United States Trustee, trustee, debtor, and, where applicable, the chair of each official committee, have been provided, not later than 21 days after the end of each month, with a statement of the fees and disbursements accrued during such month. The statement must contain a list of professionals and paraprofessionals providing services, their respective billing rates, the aggregate hours spent by each professional and paraprofessional, a general description of services rendered, a reasonably detailed breakdown of the disbursements incurred and an explanation of billing practices.

(3) Each application for fees and disbursements must contain a certification by the Certifying Professional that the United States Trustee, trustee, and, in a chapter 11 case, the chair of each official committee and the debtor have all been provided with a copy of the relevant fee application at least 21 days before the date set by the court or any applicable rules for filing fee applications.

C. Confidentiality Requests.
If an applicant believes that there is a need to omit any information or description of services as privileged or confidential, the applicant must first get the approval of the court; provided, however, that if such a request is granted, the court may require that any application also contain a set of unredacted time records for in camera inspection.

D. Fee Enhancement.

(1) Any request for an enhancement of fees over the fee which would be derived from the applicable hourly rates multiplied by the hours expended or from the court order authorizing

retention must be specifically identified in the application, including the amount being requested, and the justification for the requested enhancement must be set forth in detail.

(2) Any request for such an enhancement of fees must be set forth in the summary sheet required by these Amended Guidelines.

E. Voluntary Reduction of Fees or Disbursements. If an applicant is not requesting all of the fees or disbursements to which it might be entitled based on the applicable hourly rates multiplied by the hours expended or based on the court order authorizing retention, the voluntary reduction must be identified in the application, including the amount of the reduction taken. If the voluntary reduction pertains to services which that continue to appear in the detailed description of services rendered or to disbursements that continue to be listed, the entries for which no compensation or reimbursement is sought must be identified.

F. Provisions Regarding Disbursements.

(1) *No Enhanced Charges for Disbursements.* Except to the extent that disbursements are prohibited by these Amended Guidelines, the disbursements sought must be billed at rates, and in accordance with, practices customarily employed by the applicant and generally accepted by the applicant's clients.

(2) *Photocopies.* Photocopies shall be reimbursable at the lesser of $0.10 per page or cost.

(3) *Overtime Expense.* No overtime expense for non-professional and paraprofessional staff shall be reimbursable unless fully explained and justified. Any such justification must indicate, at a minimum, that:

(i) Services after normal closing hours are absolutely necessary for the case; and

(ii) That charges are for overtime expenses paid. The reasonable expenses of a professional required to work on the case after 8:00 p.m. are reimbursable provided that, if the professional dines before 8:00 p.m., the expense is reimbursable only if the professional returns to the office to work for at least one and one half hours. In any event, the expense for an individual's meal may not exceed $20.00.

The foregoing Guidelines have been approved by the Board of Judges and shall be subject to annual review as to adjustments to disbursement/reimbursement amounts set forth hereinabove in Provision F.

EXHIBIT A. PROJECT CATEGORIES

The following is a list of suggested project categories for use in most bankruptcy cases. Only one category should be used for a given activity. Professionals should make their best effort to be consistent in their use of categories, whether within a particular firm or by different firms working on the same case. It would be appropriate for all professionals to discuss the categories in advance and agree generally on how activities will be categorized. This list is not exclusive. The application may contain additional categories as the case requires. They are generally more applicable to attorneys in chapter 7 and chapter 11 cases, but may be used by all professionals as appropriate.

Asset Analysis and Recovery. Identification and review of potential assets including causes of action and non-litigation recoveries.

Asset Disposition. Sales, leases (§ 365 matters), abandonment and related transaction work.

Business Operations. Issues related to debtor-in-possession operating in chapter 11 such as employee, vendor, tenant issues and other similar problems.

Case Administration. Coordination and compliance activities, including preparation of statement of financial affairs; schedules; list of contracts; United States Trustee interim statements and operating reports; contacts with the United States Trustee; general creditor inquiries.

Claims Administration and Objections. Specific claim inquiries; bar date motions; analyses, objections and allowances of claims.

Employee Benefits/Pensions. Review issues such as severance, retention, 401K coverage and continuance of pension plan.

Fee/Employment Applications. Preparations of employment and fee applications for self or others; motions to establish interim procedures.

Fee/Employment Objections. Review of and objections to the employment and fee applications of others.

Financing. Matters under §§ 361, 363 and 364 including cash collateral and secured claims; loan document analysis.

Litigation. There should be a separate category established for each matter (e.g. XYZ Litigation).

Meetings of Creditors. Preparing for and attending the conference of creditors, the § 341(a) meeting and other creditors' committee meetings.

Plan and Disclosure Statement. Formulation, presentation and confirmation; compliance with the plan confirmation order, related orders and rules; disbursement and case closing activities, except those related to the allowance and objections to allowance of claims.

Relief From Stay Proceedings. Matters relating to termination or continuation of automatic stay under § 362.

The following categories are generally more applicable to accountants and financial advisors, but may be used by all professionals as appropriate.

Accounting/Auditing. Activities related to maintaining and auditing books of account, preparation of financial statements and account analysis.

Business Analysis. Preparation and review of company business plan; development and review of strategies; preparation and review of cash flow forecasts and feasibility studies.

Corporate Finance. Review financial aspects of potential mergers, acquisitions and disposition of company or subsidiaries.

Data Analysis. Management information systems review, installation and analysis, construction, maintenance and reporting of significant case financial data, lease rejection, claims, etc.

Litigation Consulting. Providing consulting and expert witness services relating to various bankruptcy matters such as insolvency, feasibility, avoiding actions; forensic accounting, etc.

Reconstruction Accounting. Reconstructing books and records from past transactions and bringing accounting current.

Tax Issues. Analysis of tax issues and preparation of state and federal tax returns.

Valuation. Appraise or review appraisals of assets.

* [**Publisher's Note:** So in original.]

ADMINISTRATIVE ORDER NO. 644. IN RE: PROCEDURES FOR PAYMENT AND CURE OF PRE–PETITION JUDGMENT OF POSSESSION INVOLVING RESIDENTIAL PROPERTY

```
------------------------------------------------------------x
In re:
```

PROCEDURES FOR PAYMENT AND CURE OF PRE–PETITION JUDGMENT OF POSSESSION INVOLVING RESIDENTIAL PROPERTY	**Administrative Order No. 644 Amending Administrative Order No. 541**

```
------------------------------------------------------------x
```

WHEREAS, the Bankruptcy Abuse Prevention and Consumer Protection Act of 2005, as codified in 11 U.S.C. § 362(b)(22) and 362(*l*), creates certain rights and obligations with respect to the cure of a monetary default giving rise to a pre-petition judgment for possession regarding residential property in which the debtor resides as a tenant under a lease or rental agreement, it is hereby

ORDERED, that a debtor shall be deemed to have complied with 11 U.S.C. § 362(*l*)(1) by:

1. Making the required certification by selecting the "Yes" box, listed in the voluntary petition under section 11 entitled, "Do you rent your residence?" and completing the *Initial Statement About an Eviction Judgment Against You* (Form 101A) and filing it with the bankruptcy petition, and

2. Delivering to the Clerk of Court ("Clerk"), together with the petition (or within one day of the filing, if the petition is filed electronically), a certified or cashier's check or money order, made payable to the lessor, in the amount of any rent that would become due during the 30-day period after the filing of the petition ("Rent Check"); and it is further

ORDERED, that if a debtor complies with the preceding paragraph, the Clerk shall, within two days, send notice of the debtor's compliance ("Notice of Compliance") to the lessor which notice shall also request that the lessor inform the Clerk whether it consents or declines to receive the Rent Check. If a lessor consents to receive the Rent Check, the notice will further request that the lessor provide the Clerk with an address to which the Rent Check should be sent; and it is further

ORDERED, that if a lessor fails, within 14 days of the date of the Notice of Compliance, to notify the Clerk whether it consents to or declines receipt of the Rent Check the lessor shall be deemed to have consented to receive the Rent Check and the Clerk shall send the Rent Check to the lessor at the address set forth in the debtor's certification; and it is further

ORDERED, that a lessor's consent to receive the Rent Check shall not preclude the lessor from objecting to a debtor's certification pursuant to 11 U.S.C. §§ 362(l)(1) and/or (2).

[Dated: December 10, 2015.]

ADMINISTRATIVE ORDER NO. 645. IN RE: ADOPTION OF PROCEDURAL GUIDELINES FOR PREPACKAGED AND PRENEGOTIATED CHAPTER 11 CASES

UPON the resolution of the Board of Judges for the United States Bankruptcy court for the Eastern District of New York, it is hereby

ORDERED, that the annexed Procedural Guidelines for Prepackaged and Prenegotiated Chapter 11 Cases are adopted.

UNITED STATES BANKRUPTCY COURT
EASTERN DISTRICT OF NEW YORK

PROCEDURAL GUIDELINES FOR PREPACKAGED AND PRENEGOTIATED CHAPTER 11 CASES IN THE UNITED STATES BANKRUPTCY COURT FOR THE EASTERN DISTRICT OF NEW YORK

I. **Statement of Purpose.** The purpose of this document is to establish guidelines (the "Guidelines") for commencing and administering Prepackaged Chapter 11 Cases, Partial Prepackaged Chapter 11 Cases, and Prenegotiated Chapter 11 Cases (as each such term is defined below), in the United States Bankruptcy Court for the Eastern District of New York (the "Court").

These Guidelines, which were developed by the Court in conjunction with the Chapter 11 Lawyers' Advisory Committee for the Eastern District of New York, are designed to help bankruptcy practitioners deal with practical matters which either are not addressed directly by statutes or rules or are addressed indirectly in a piecemeal fashion by statutes, general rules, and/or local rules that were not enacted specifically with Prepackaged Chapter 11 Cases and Prenegotiated Chapter 11 Cases in mind. Although each chapter 11 case is different, many issues are common to all Prepackaged Chapter 11 Cases and Prenegotiated Chapter 11 Cases, respectively. Judicial economy, as well as procedural predictability for debtors, creditors and other parties in interest, will be enhanced by the promulgation of these Guidelines in this Court.

These Guidelines are advisory only and the Court retains the authority to depart from these Guidelines. In the event there is a conflict between these Guidelines and any other Administrative Orders and General Orders of the Court concerning the subject matter of these Guidelines, such Administrative Orders or General Order of the Court shall govern and control.

II. **Definitions of Prepackaged Chapter 11 Case, Partial Prepackaged Chapter 11 Case, and Prenegotiated Chapter 11 Case.** For purposes of these Guidelines:

A. A "Prepackaged Chapter 11 Case" is one in which a debtor or potential debtor in a Chapter 11 Case ("Debtor") substantially contemporaneously with the filing of its chapter 11 petition, files a (i)

Prepack Scheduling Motion (as defined below), (ii) plan, (iii) disclosure statement (or other solicitation document), and (iv) voting certification, in accordance with the requirements set forth in Part III below.

B. A "Partial Prepackaged Chapter 11 Case" is one in which acceptances of the Debtor's plan were solicited prior to the commencement of the chapter 11 case from some, but not all, classes of claims or interests whose solicitation is required to confirm the Debtor's plan; and

C. A "Prenegotiated Chapter 11 Case" is one in which the Debtor has not solicited any acceptances of the Debtor's plan prior to the commencement of the chapter 11 case from any classes of claims or interests whose solicitation is required to confirm the Debtor's plan, but rather the Debtor and all, or a portion, of the Debtor's key creditors or stakeholders ("Supporting Creditors") have entered into a Plan Support Agreement (as defined below).

III. Criteria for Prepackaged Chapter 11 Case; Contents of Prepack Scheduling Motion.

A. *Requirements of Prepackaged Chapter 11 Case.* A Prepackaged Chapter 11 Case is one in which a Debtor, substantially contemporaneously with the filing of its chapter 11 petition, files a (i) **"Scheduling Motion For Prepackaged Chapter 11 Case"** in substantially the form attached to these Guidelines as Exhibit A which satisfies the criteria set forth in Part III(B) below (the "Prepack Scheduling Motion"), (ii) plan, (iii) disclosure statement (or other solicitation document), and (iv) voting certification.

B. *Content of Prepack Scheduling Motion.* A Prepack Scheduling Motion is a Motion filed with the Court that should:

1. Represent that (a) the solicitation of all votes to accept or reject the Debtor's plan required for confirmation of that plan was completed prior to the filing of the Debtor's chapter 11 petition or in accordance with 11 U.S.C. § 1125(g), and that no additional solicitation of votes on that plan is contemplated by the Debtor, or (b) the solicitation of all votes to accept or reject the Debtor's plan required for confirmation of that plan should be deemed adequate by the Court pursuant to Part III(D)(2) below such that no additional solicitation will be required;

2. Represent that the requisite acceptances of such plan have been obtained from each class of claims or interests as to which solicitation is required, except as provided in Part III(B)(3) below; and

3. With respect to any class of interests that has not accepted the plan, whether or not such class is deemed not to have accepted the plan under 11 U.S.C. § 1126(g), represent that the Debtor is requesting confirmation under 11 U.S.C. § 1129(b); and

4. Request entry of an order scheduling the hearing (a) on confirmation of the plan and (b) to determine whether the Debtor has satisfied the requirements of either 11 U.S.C. § 1126(b)(1) or 11 U.S.C. § 1126(b)(2), of the Bankruptcy Code, for a date that is not more than ninety (90) days following the petition date.

C. *Confirmation Pursuant to 11 U.S.C. § 1129(b)(2)(C).* A chapter 11 case may constitute a Prepackaged Chapter 11 Case for purposes of these Guidelines notwithstanding the fact that the Debtor proposes to confirm the plan pursuant to 11 U.S.C. § 1129(b)(2)(C) as to a class of interests.

D. *Filing of Petition after Solicitation Has Commenced but before Expiration of Voting Deadline.* Unless the Court orders otherwise, if a chapter 11 case is commenced by or against the Debtor, or if a chapter 7 case is commenced against the Debtor and converted to a chapter 11 case by the Debtor pursuant to 11 U.S.C. § 706(a), after the Debtor has transmitted all solicitation materials to holders of claims and interests whose vote is sought but before the deadline for casting acceptances or rejections of the Debtor's plan (the "Voting Deadline"):

1. The Debtor and parties in interest in its chapter 11 case should be permitted to accept but not solicit ballots until the Voting Deadline; and

2. After notice and a hearing, the Court may determine the effect of any and all such votes.

E. *Applicability of Guidelines to Cases Involving Cramdown of Classes of Claims and Partial Prepackaged Chapter 11 Cases.* The Court may, upon request of the Debtor or a party in interest in an appropriate chapter 11 case, apply some or all of these Guidelines to:

1. Cases in which the Debtor has satisfied the requirements of Part III(B)(1) above but intends to seek confirmation of the plan pursuant to 11 U.S.C. § 1129(b) as to a class of claims (a) which is deemed not to have accepted the plan under 11 U.S.C. § 1126(g), (b) which is receiving or retaining property under or pursuant to the plan but whose members' votes were not solicited prepetition

and whose rejection of the plan has been assumed by the Debtor for purposes of confirming the plan, or (c) which is receiving or retaining property under or pursuant to the plan and which voted prepetition to reject the plan, as long as no class junior to such rejecting class is receiving or retaining any property under or pursuant to the plan;

2.   Partial Prepackaged Chapter 11 Cases; and

3.   Prenegotiated Chapter 11 Cases, to the extent set forth in these Guidelines or as otherwise deemed appropriate by the Court; otherwise a Prenegotiated Chapter 11 Case should be subject to the Local Rules and all Administrative Orders and General Orders of the Court to the same extent a non–Prenegotiated Chapter 11 case is subject thereto.

IV.   Prefiling Notification to United States Trustee and Clerk of the Court of Prepackaged Chapter 11 Case.

A.   *Notice of Proposed Filing to United States Trustee.*   At least three (3) days prior to the anticipated filing date of the Prepackaged Chapter 11 Case, the Debtor should (i) notify the United States Trustee for the Eastern District of New York (the "United States Trustee") of the Debtor's intention to file a Prepackaged Chapter 11 Case, and (ii) supply the United States Trustee with two (2) copies of the Debtor's plan and disclosure statement (or other solicitation document).

B.   *Notice of Proposed "First Day Orders" to United States Trustee.*   At least three (3) days prior to the anticipated filing of the Prepackaged Chapter 11 Case the Debtor, if possible, should furnish to the United States Trustee drafts of all First Day Motions (as defined below), together with the proposed orders attached as exhibits.

C.   *Notice of Proposed Filing to Clerk of Court.*   At least three (3) days prior to the anticipated filing date of the Prepackaged Chapter 11 Case, counsel for the Debtor, without disclosing the name of the Debtor, should contact the Clerk of the Court to discuss the anticipated filing, the amount of the Debtor's assets, number and type of creditors, procedures for handling public inquiries (i.e., the names, addresses and telephone numbers of the persons to whom such inquiries should be directed), procedures for handling claims and proofs of claim or interest, whether the Debtor will request the Court to set a last date to file proofs of claim or interest, the need for appointment of a claims' agent for the Court (at the Debtor's expense), and related matters.

V.   Filing of Prepackaged Chapter 11 Case or Prenegotiated Chapter 11 Case.

A.   *Electronic Case Filing.*   Prepackaged Chapter 11 Cases and Prenegotiated Chapter 11 Cases, as with all cases filed with the Court, should be filed electronically in accordance with Administrative Order No. 476, "Mandatory Filing of Documents by Electronic Means", dated June 4, 2003, and General Order No. 559, "Electronic Means for Filing, Signing and Verification of Documents", dated April 23, 2010 (collectively, the "Electronic Filing Procedures"). In electronically filing a Prepackaged Chapter 11 Case or Prenegotiated Chapter 11 Case, the Debtor should file the petition(s) first, followed by the affidavit, motions and proposed orders. In order to expedite the filing process, the Debtor should file lengthy documents, such as the disclosure statement (or other solicitation materials) and plan, last.

B.   *Paper Copies Furnished to Assigned Judge.*   As soon as practicable following the filing of a Prepackaged Chapter 11 Case or Prenegotiated Chapter 11 Case, the Debtor should furnish to the judge assigned to the chapter 11 case, two (2) paper copies of the plan, the disclosure statement (or other solicitation document), First Day Motions (as defined below) (with proposed orders attached as exhibits), any other filed motion and any order to show cause on which the Court's signature is requested. Proposed orders should be presented in electronic format in Word or WordPerfect or other Windows-based format. (See the Electronic Filing Procedures.) To the extent that documents filed by the Debtor at or following the commencement of the Debtor's Prepackaged Chapter 11 Case or Prenegotiated Chapter 11 Case differ in substance from the versions supplied to the United States Trustee under Part IV(A) and/or Part IV(B) above, the Debtor should furnish to the judge assigned to the chapter 11 case and the United States Trustee two (2) paper copies of any such documents that have been modified, blacklined to show all changes.

VI.   First Day Orders.

A.   *Motions for Request for Entry of Immediate Orders.*   "First Day Orders" are orders which the Debtor seeks to have entered by the Court in a Prepackaged Chapter 11 Case, Prenegotiated Chapter 11 Case, or any other chapter 11 case filed in this Court, on or shortly after the filing of the petition.

The request for a First Day Order should be made by motion (a "First Day Motion") and, except as otherwise set forth in these Guidelines, should be in accordance with Administrative Order No. 565, "Adoption of Guidelines for First Day Motions", dated July 6, 2010 (the "Guidelines for First Day Motions"). A copy of the proposed First Day Order should be filed with and attached as an exhibit to the First Day Motion, in accordance with the Guidelines for First Day Motions.

Motions for related relief under First Day Orders need not be filed as separate motions. Refer to the Guidelines for First Day Motions for further information concerning the filing of separate and omnibus First Day Motions.

B. *Purpose of First Day Orders.* Generally, the purpose of First Day Orders in a Prepackaged Chapter 11 Case or Prenegotiated Chapter 11 Case is to address administrative matters and facilitate the transition of the Debtor to debtor in possession status, and to ensure that the Debtor's business and operations are stabilized and conducted in a manner consistent with past practice and the proposed plan, pending consideration of confirmation of that plan. While the Court recognizes the necessity and appropriateness of entertaining appropriate First Day Motions, only those motions seeking and appropriately requiring emergency relief will be heard on an expedited basis. The terms and conditions of First Day Orders necessarily will depend upon the facts and circumstances of the chapter 11 case, the terms of the plan, the notice given and other related factors, and will take into account the needs of the Debtor and the rights of other parties in interest.

C. *Certain Requirements Concerning First Day Motions and Orders.* In addition to the requirements set forth in the Guidelines for First Day Motions and elsewhere herein, a Debtor should comply with the following:

1. Application for an Order Setting the Last Date for Filing Proofs of Claim or Interest. All such applications should be filed in accordance with Administrative Order No. 556, "Adoption of Bar Date Order Guidelines", dated March 29, 2010 (the "Bar Date Order Guidelines"); provided, however, that the Debtor in a Prepackaged Chapter 11 Case may disregard the suggested timing in Paragraph 1 thereof concerning when the application should be filed.

2. Motion Under 11 U.S.C. § 363 for Interim Order Authorizing Debtor's Use of Cash Collateral on an Emergency Basis. All such motions should be brought in accordance Administrative Order No. 558, "Adoption of Guidelines for Financing Motions", dated April 15, 2010 (the "Guidelines for Financing Motions").

3. Motion Under 11 U.S.C. § 364 for Interim Order Authorizing Debtor to Obtain Post–Petition Financing on an Emergency Basis. All such motions should be brought in accordance with the Guidelines for Financing Motions.

4. Motion for Order Authorizing and Scheduling Auction and Approving Bidding and Auction Procedures. All such motions should be filed in accordance with Administrative Order No. 557, "Adoption of Sale Guidelines", dated March 29, 2010, subject to the Debtor seeking "Extraordinary Relief" in accordance with the Guidelines for First Day Motions.

VII. Voting Period; Ballot; Multiple Votes; Notice Presumptions for Prepackaged Chapter 11 Cases.

A. *Voting Period Guidelines.* Fed.R.Bankr.P. 3018(b) requires the Court to consider whether "an unreasonably short" time was prescribed for creditors and equity security holders to accept or reject the plan. Under ordinary circumstances, in determining whether the time allowed for casting acceptances and rejections on the Debtor's plan satisfied Fed.R. Bankr.P. 3018(b), the Court will generally approve as reasonable:

1. For securities listed or admitted to trading on the New York Stock Exchange or American Stock Exchange or any international exchanges quoted on NASDAQ, and for securities publicly traded on any other national securities exchange ("Publicly Traded Securities"), a twenty-one (21) day voting period, measured from the date of commencement of mailing.

2. For securities which are not Publicly Traded Securities and for debt for borrowed money which is not evidenced by a Publicly Traded Security, a fourteen (14) day voting period, measured from the date of commencement of mailing.

3. For all other claims and interests, a twenty-one (21) day voting period, measured from the date of commencement of mailing.

B. *Shorter or Longer Voting Period.* Nothing herein is intended to preclude (i) a shorter or longer voting period if it is justified in a particular case, or (ii) any party in interest from demonstrating that the presumptions set forth above were not reasonable in a particular case.

C. *Ballot.*

1.   The Debtor may use a ballot substantially in the form of the "**Ballot for Accepting or Rejecting Prepackaged Plan of Reorganization of Debtor Under Chapter 11 of the Bankruptcy Code**" attached to these Guidelines as <u>Exhibit B</u> in connection with a prepackaged plan solicitation.

2.   The "**Master Ballot for Accepting or Rejecting Prepackaged Plan of Reorganization of Debtor to be Filed Under Chapter 11 of the Bankruptcy Code**", attached to these Guidelines as <u>Exhibit C</u>, may be used to report voting by beneficial owners of claims and interests.

3.   The ballot may include information in addition to that set forth in the various Official Ballot Forms attached to these Guidelines, and may request and provide space for the holder of a claim or interest to vote on matters in addition to the plan.   By way of example, the ballot may seek and record (a) votes relating to an exchange offer, (b) consents to or votes with respect to benefits plans, and (c) elections provided for in the plan (or exchange offer).

D.   *Multiple Votes.*   If the holder of a claim or interest changes its vote during the pre-petition voting period, only the last timely ballot cast by such holder should be counted in determining whether the plan has been accepted or rejected unless the disclosure statement (or other solicitation document) provides for some other procedure for determining votes on the plan.   If a holder of a claim or interest wants to change a vote post-petition, Fed.R.Bankr.P. 3018(a) requires a showing of cause by the Debtor and Court approval.

E.   *Notice Guidelines.*   Fed.R.Bankr.P. 3018(b) requires the Court to consider whether the plan was transmitted to substantially all creditors and equity security holders of the same class.   In making that determination, the Court may take into account (i) whether the Debtor transmitted the plan and disclosure statement (or other solicitation document) in substantial compliance with applicable non-bankruptcy law, rules, or regulations and, (ii) the fact that creditors and equity security holders who are not record holders of the securities upon which their claims or interests are based generally assume the risk associated with their decision to hold their securities in "street name."

VIII.   Plan Support Agreements.

1.   Subject to the discretion and approval of the Court, a Debtor may enter into a Plan Support Agreement (as defined below) with Supporting Creditors.

2.   A "Plan Support Agreement" with respect to a Prepackaged Chapter 11 Case or Prenegotiated Chapter 11 Case is either a lock-up agreement, plan support agreement, restructuring support agreement, or similar type agreement, entered into prior to the commencement of the chapter 11 case, which may require:[1]

(i) the Debtor to (a) file the chapter 11 case and use commercially reasonable efforts to propose and seek confirmation of a plan containing agreed terms, usually according to an agreed timeline, as contemplated under the Plan Support Agreement, (b) take no action that is inconsistent with the Plan Support Agreement or plan, once filed, (c) take no action that would cause unreasonable delays or violate the agreed timeline, (d) not support any other plan or transaction, unless covered by the Debtor's Fiduciary Out, (e) pay the reasonable fees and expenses of certain advisors to the Supporting Creditors, (f) in certain circumstances, pay a termination fee (to be treated as an administrative expense) to the Supporting Creditors in the event the Debtor exercises its Fiduciary Out or breaches the Plan Support Agreement, (g) take no action that would be reasonably expected to breach the Plan Support Agreement or interfere with the Debtor's restructuring, and (h) assume the Plan Support Agreement after the Debtor has filed its chapter 11 petition; and

(ii) the Supporting Creditors to (a) support approval of the plan, disclosure statement, and the restructuring, (b) timely vote to accept the plan and not later withdraw or change their vote, (c) take no action in opposition to the plan or the solicitation of the plan, (d) waive and release any rights to exercise remedies against any collateral of the Debtor in connection with the applicable debt instruments or under any applicable non-bankruptcy law as of the effective date of the plan, and (e) take no action against the Debtor or any collateral that constitutes an enforcement action or remedy, as long as the Plan Support Agreement remains effective or after the effective date of the plan.

3.   A Plan Support Agreement entered into by the Debtor and Supporting Creditors after the Debtor has filed its chapter 11 petition may be approved by the Court in certain circumstances and in the Court's discretion.   However, to avoid violating 11 U.S.C. § 1125(b), such Plan Support

Agreement, should, at a minimum, require voting on a plan only after the Court's approval of the disclosure statement and only if the plan proposed by the Debtor substantially conforms to the terms of the Plan Support Agreement.

4. A Plan Support Agreement Should Include a Reasonable Form of Fiduciary Out. A "Fiduciary Out" permits a Debtor who is a party to a Plan Support Agreement to receive, but not solicit, proposals or offers for alternative transactions to the one set forth in the Plan Support Agreement from other parties and to negotiate, provide due diligence, discuss, and/or analyze such alternative transactions received without breaching or terminating the Plan Support Agreement.

IX. Organizational Meeting; Creditors' Committee.

1. Unless the Court finds that a meeting of creditors need not be convened pursuant to 11 U.S.C. § 341(e), after the filing of the chapter 11 petition, the Debtor should notify creditors of the date, time and place of the meeting of creditors pursuant to 11 U.S.C. § 341(a) ("Section 341 Meeting"), as well as the other information set forth in Part X(B)(2) below. The date set for the Section 341 Meeting should be no more than forty (40) days after the filing of the petition.

2. If a Section 341 Meeting has not yet been convened prior to the date upon which the plan is confirmed, no such meeting will be convened if the order confirming the plan (or an order entered substantially contemporaneously therewith) contains a provision waiving the convening of such a meeting.

3. Typically, no creditors' committee will be appointed in a Prepackaged Chapter 11 Case, particularly where the unsecured creditors are unimpaired. However, where members of a pre-petition committee seek to serve as a member of an official creditors' committee, they should demonstrate to the United States Trustee their compliance with Fed.R.Bankr.P. 2007(b).

X. Notice.

A. *In General.* Notice of the filing of the plan and disclosure statement (or other solicitation document) in a Prepackaged Chapter 11 Case or Prenegotiated Chapter 11 Case and of the hearing to consider compliance with disclosure requirements and confirmation of the plan, should be given to all parties in interest in the chapter 11 case. Paper copy of a notice should be mailed; service of a notice of electronic filing will generally not suffice. With respect to a Prepackaged Chapter 11 Case, no further distribution of the plan and disclosure statement (or other solicitation document) beyond that which occurred pre-petition is required unless requested by a party in interest.

B. *Hearing Notice.*

1. Where the disclosure statement has not been approved by the Court prior to plan confirmation in a Prepackaged Chapter 11 Case or Prenegotiated Chapter 11 Case, the Debtor should prepare and mail paper copies to all parties in interest in its chapter 11 case of a "**Summary of Plan of Reorganization and Notice of Hearing to Consider (i) Debtor's Compliance with Disclosure Requirements and (ii) Confirmation of Plan of Reorganization**" (or other solicitation documents) in substantially the form annexed hereto as Exhibit D (the "Hearing Notice"). The Hearing Notice should set forth:

- (i) the date, time and place of the hearing to consider compliance with disclosure requirements and confirmation of the plan, and (ii) the date and time by which objections to the foregoing must be filed and served;

- include a chart summarizing plan distributions;

- set forth the name, address and telephone number of the person from whom copies of the plan and disclosure statement (or other solicitation document) can be obtained (at the Debtor's expense); and

- state that the plan and disclosure statement (or other solicitation document) can be viewed electronically and explain briefly how electronic access to these documents may be obtained.

2. Either the Hearing Notice or a separate notice should set forth the date, time and place of the Section 341 Meeting and state that such meeting will not be convened if (a) the plan is confirmed prior to the date set for the Section 341 Meeting, and (b) the order confirming the plan (or an order entered substantially contemporaneously therewith) contains a provision waiving the convening of such a meeting.

C. *Service.*

1. The Hearing Notice should be served upon (a) record (registered) holders of debt and equity securities (determined as of the record date established in the disclosure statement or other

solicitation document) that were entitled to vote on the plan, (b) record (registered) holders of all other claims and interests of any class (determined as of a record date that is not more than fourteen (14) days prior to the date of the filing of the petition), (c) all other creditors of the Debtor, (d) the United States Trustee, (e) all indenture trustees, (f) any committee(s) that may have been appointed in the chapter 11 case, and (g) the United States in accordance with Fed.R.Bankr.P. 2002(j).

2. The Debtor should inform the Court of the proposed procedures for transmitting the Hearing Notice to beneficial holders of stock, bonds, debentures, notes, and other securities, and the Court may determine the adequacy of those procedures and enter such orders as it deems appropriate.

D. *Time Period.* The Hearing Notice should be mailed at least twenty-eight (28) days prior to the scheduled hearing date on confirmation of the plan and adequacy of disclosure, unless the Court shortens such notice period for cause.

XI. Combined Hearings. The hearings on the Debtor's compliance with either 11 U.S.C. § 1126(b)(1) or 11 U.S.C. § 1126(b)(2), as applicable, and on confirmation of the plan in a Prepackaged Chapter 11 Case should be combined whenever practicable.

[Dated: January 11, 2016.]

1 A form of Hearing Notice, which includes a summary of the Plan, also is appended to the Guidelines.

EXHIBIT "A"

UNITED STATES BANKRUPTCY COURT
EASTERN DISTRICT OF NEW YORK

In re [NAME], 　　　　Debtor.	Chapter 11 Case No. ＿＿＿＿＿＿ (＿＿＿) Tax ID No. ＿＿＿＿＿

SCHEDULING MOTION FOR
PREPACKAGED CHAPTER 11 CASE

TO THE HONORABLE UNITED STATES BANKRUPTCY JUDGE:

The **[NAME OF DEBTOR]**, as debtor and debtor in possession (the "Debtor"), respectfully represents:

Background

1. **[Brief background of the Debtor].**

Jurisdiction and Venue

2. This Court has jurisdiction to consider this application pursuant to 28 U.S.C. §§ 157 and 1334. Consideration of this application is a core proceeding pursuant to 28 U.S.C. § 157(b). Venue of this proceeding is proper in this district pursuant to 28 U.S.C. §§ 1408 and 1409.

The Debtor's Business

3. **[Brief Description of the Debtor's business].**

The Proposed Plan of Reorganization

4. **[Brief description of the proposed plan of reorganization].**

Key Dates

5. **[Chart of all key dates or milestones Debtor is seeking Court to approve in Chapter 11 case, including dates related to plan, DIP financing, asset sales, etc.]**

This Court Should Schedule a Hearing To Consider Confirmation of the Proposed Plan

6. Pursuant to section 1128(a) of the Bankruptcy Code, the Debtor requests that the Court set a hearing to consider confirmation of the Plan.

7. **[Summarize results of pre-petition solicitation].**

8. **[Indicate whether Debtor requests that confirmation hearing and disclosure hearing be combined].** **[Indicate proposed date and time for confirmation/disclosure hearings].**

9. The Debtor proposes to publish notice of the Confirmation and Disclosure Compliance Hearing (the "Hearing Notice") **[insert where notice will be published].** **[Indicate whether the proposed notice schedule complies with the minimum twenty-eight (28) days notice required under Rules 2002(b) and 3017(a) of the Federal Rules of Bankruptcy Procedure (the "Bankruptcy Rules".]**[1]

10. In addition to the Hearing Notice, the Debtor will transmit, in accordance with Bankruptcy Rule 3017(d), via first class mail, postage prepaid, a copy of the Disclosure Statement and the Plan to all holders of claims against, or equity interests in, the Debtor other than **[insert parties who received such materials pursuant to the prepetition solicitation],** which are the parties to whom the Disclosure Statement and Plan have already been transmitted pursuant to the prepetition solicitation.

Notice

11. Notice of this application has been given to **[insert names of persons to whom notice has been given, which should include the U.S. Trustee].**

12. No previous application for the relief sought herein has been made to this or any other court.

WHEREFORE, the Debtor respectfully requests entry of an order granting the relief requested herein and granting the Debtor such other and further relief as is just.

Dated: _____, _____

[1] A form of Hearing Notice, which includes a summary of the Plan, also is appended to the Guidelines.

EXHIBIT "B"

NO PERSON HAS BEEN AUTHORIZED TO GIVE ANY INFORMATION OR ADVICE, OR TO MAKE ANY REPRESENTATION, OTHER THAN WHAT IS INCLUDED IN THE MATERIALS MAILED WITH THIS BALLOT.

_____

[NAME OF DEBTOR],

        Debtor.

[DEBTOR'S ADDRESS]

Tax ID No. _____

**BALLOT FOR ACCEPTING OR REJECTING PREPACKAGED
PLAN OF REORGANIZATION OF [NAME OF DEBTOR]
UNDER CHAPTER 11 OF THE BANKRUPTCY CODE BALLOT
FOR VOTING___ % NOTES**

(Class: ___: ___ % Note Claims)

[Insert Exact Name of Notes/Bonds, If Applicable]*

[Insert CUSIP #, If Applicable]

If you are a beneficial owner of [NAME OF SECURITIES] (the ___ % Notes") issued by [NAME OF DEBTOR], please use this Ballot to cast your vote to accept or reject the chapter 11 plan of reorganization (the "Plan") which is being proposed by [DEBTOR]. The Plan is Exhibit [ ] to the Disclosure Statement, dated _____, _____, (the "Disclosure Statement"), which accompanies this Ballot. The Plan can be confirmed by the Bankruptcy Court and thereby made binding upon you if it is accepted by the holders of two-thirds in amount and more than one-half in number of claims in each class that vote on the Plan, and by the holders of two-thirds in amount of equity security interests in each class that vote on the Plan, and if it otherwise satisfies the requirements of section 1129(a) of the Bankruptcy Code. [If the requisite acceptances are not obtained, the Bankruptcy Court may nonetheless confirm the Plan if it finds that the Plan provides fair and equitable treatment to, and does not discriminate unfairly against, the class or classes rejecting it, and otherwise satisfies the requirements of section 1129(b) of the Bankruptcy Code.]

Important

VOTING DEADLINE: _____: _____.M., EASTERN TIME ON _____: _____.

REVIEW THE ACCOMPANYING DISCLOSURE STATEMENT FOR THE PLAN.

[BALLOTS WILL NOT BE ACCEPTED BY FACSIMILE TRANSMISSION.]

DO NOT RETURN ANY SECURITIES WITH THIS BALLOT. This Ballot is not a letter of transmittal and may not be used for any purpose other than to cast votes to accept or reject the Plan.

[Ballot Code]

HOW TO VOTE

1. COMPLETE ITEM 1 (if not already filled out by your nominee) AND ITEM 2 AND COMPLETE ITEM 3 (if applicable).

2. REVIEW THE CERTIFICATIONS CONTAINED IN ITEM 4.

3. **SIGN THE BALLOT** (unless your Ballot has already been signed or "prevalidated" by your nominee).

4. RETURN THE BALLOT IN THE PRE–ADDRESSED POSTAGE–PAID ENVELOPE (if the enclosed envelope is addressed to your nominee, make sure your nominee receives your Ballot in time to submit it before the Voting Deadline).

5. YOU WILL RECEIVE A SEPARATE BALLOT FOR EACH ISSUE OF SECURITIES YOU OWN WHICH IS ENTITLED TO BE VOTED UNDER THE PLAN.

6. YOU MUST VOTE *ALL YOUR* ___ % NOTES *EITHER* TO ACCEPT *OR* TO REJECT THE PLAN AND MAY NOT SPLIT YOUR VOTE.

Item 1. Principal Amount of % Notes Voted. The undersigned certifies that as of [the record date] the undersigned was either the beneficial owner, or the nominee of a beneficial owner, of % Notes in the following aggregate unpaid principal amount (insert amount in the box below). If your % Notes are held by a nominee on your behalf and you do not know the amount, please contact your nominee immediately.

$ _____

Item 2. Vote. The beneficial owner of the % Notes identified in Item 1 votes as follows (check one box only—if you do not check a box your vote will not be counted):

0 to **Accept** the Plan. 0 to **Reject** the Plan.

Item 3. Identify All Other % Notes Voted. By returning this Ballot, the beneficial owner of the % Notes identified in Item 1 certifies that (a) this Ballot is the only Ballot submitted for the % Notes owned by such beneficial owner, except for the % Notes identified in the following table, and (b) *all* Ballots for % Notes submitted by the beneficial owner indicate the same vote to accept or reject the Plan that the beneficial owner has indicated in Item 2 of this Ballot (please use additional sheets of paper if necessary):

ONLY COMPLETE ITEM 3 IF YOU HAVE SUBMITTED OTHER BALLOTS

Account Number	Name of Holder*	Principal Amount of Other ___ % Notes Voted
		$
		$

*Insert your name if the notes are held by you in record name or, if held in street name, insert the name of your broker or bank.

Item 4. Authorization. By returning this Ballot, the beneficial owner of the ___ % Notes identified in Item 1 certifies that it (a) has full power and authority to vote to accept or reject the Plan with respect to the ___ % Notes listed in Item 1, (b) was the beneficial owner of the ___ % Notes described in Item 1 on _____, _____, and (c) has received a copy of the Disclosure Statement (including the exhibits thereto) and understands that the solicitation of votes for the Plan is subject to all the terms and conditions set forth in the Disclosure Statement.

Name: _____
(Print or Type)
Social Security or Federal Tax I.D. No.: _____
(Optional)
Signature: _____
By: _____
(If Appropriate)
Title: _____
(If Appropriate)
Street Address: _____
City, State, Zip Code:
Telephone Number: (___)_____
Date Completed: _____

No fees, commissions, or other remuneration will be payable to any broker, dealer, or other person for soliciting votes on the Plan. This Ballot shall not constitute or be deemed a proof of claim or equity interest or an assertion of a claim or equity interest.

YOUR VOTE MUST BE FORWARDED IN AMPLE TIME FOR YOUR VOTE TO BE RECEIVED BY [DEBTOR or DEBTOR'S AGENT], BY: _____.M., EASTERN TIME, ON _____, _____, OR YOUR VOTE WILL NOT BE COUNTED. IF THE ENCLOSED ENVELOPE IS ADDRESSED TO YOUR NOMINEE, MAKE SURE YOUR NOMINEE RECEIVES YOUR BALLOT IN TIME TO SUBMIT IT BEFORE THE VOTING DEADLINE.

IF YOU HAVE ANY QUESTIONS REGARDING THIS BALLOT OR THE VOTING PROCEDURES, OR IF YOU NEED A BALLOT OR ADDITIONAL COPIES OF THE DISCLOSURE STATEMENT OR OTHER ENCLOSED MATERIALS, PLEASE CALL [DEBTOR or DEBTOR'S AGENT], AT _____.

* This form ballot does not contemplate multiple securities within the same class.

EXHIBIT "C"

NO PERSON HAS BEEN AUTHORIZED TO GIVE ANY INFORMATION OR ADVICE, OR TO MAKE ANY REPRESENTATION, OTHER THAN WHAT IS INCLUDED IN THE MATERIALS MAILED WITH THIS BALLOT.

_____

[NAME OF DEBTOR],

           Debtor.

[DEBTOR'S ADDRESS]

Tax ID No. _____

MASTER BALLOT FOR ACCEPTING OR REJECTING PREPACKAGED PLAN OF REORGANIZATION OF [NAME OF DEBTOR] TO BE FILED UNDER CHAPTER 11 OF THE BANKRUPTCY CODE MASTER BALLOT FOR VOTING % NOTES

(Class: % Note Claims)

[Insert exact name of Notes/Bonds]*

[Insert CUSIP # If Applicable]

THE **VOTING DEADLINE** BY WHICH YOUR MASTER BALLOT MUST BE *RECEIVED* BY [DEBTOR or DEBTOR'S AGENT] IS _____: _____.M., EASTERN TIME ON _____, _____. IF YOUR MASTER BALLOT IS NOT RECEIVED ON OR BEFORE THE VOTING DEADLINE, THE VOTES REPRESENTED BY YOUR MASTER BALLOT WILL <u>NOT</u> BE COUNTED.

This Master Ballot is to be used by you, as a broker, bank, or other nominee (or as their proxy holder or agent) (each of the foregoing, a "Nominee"), for beneficial owners of **[NAME OF SECURITIES]** (the ___ % Notes") issued by **[NAME OF DEBTOR]**, to transmit the votes of such holders in respect of their % Notes to accept or reject the chapter 11 plan of reorganization (the "Plan") described in, and attached as Exhibit "___" to the Disclosure Statement, dated _____, _____ (the "Disclosure Statement") provided to you. Before you transmit such votes, please review the Disclosure Statement carefully, including the voting procedures explained in Section _____.

The Plan can be confirmed by the Bankruptcy Court and thereby made binding upon you and the beneficial owners of % Notes for which you are the Nominee if it is accepted by the holders of two-thirds in amount and more than one-half in number of claims in each class that vote on the Plan, and by the holders of two-thirds in amount of equity security interests in each class that vote on the Plan, and if it otherwise satisfies the requirements of section 1129(a) of the Bankruptcy Code. [If the requisite acceptances are not obtained, the Bankruptcy Court may nonetheless confirm the Plan if it finds that the Plan provides fair and equitable treatment to, and does not discriminate unfairly against, the class or classes rejecting it, and otherwise satisfies the requirements of section 1129(b) of the Bankruptcy Code.]

PLEASE READ AND FOLLOW THE ATTACHED INSTRUCTIONS CAREFULLY. COMPLETE, SIGN, AND DATE THIS MASTER BALLOT, AND RETURN IT SO THAT IT IS RECEIVED BY [DEBTOR or DEBTOR'S AGENT] ON OR BEFORE THE VOTING DEADLINE OF _____: _____.M., EASTERN TIME, ON _____, _____. IF THIS MASTER BALLOT IS NOT COMPLETED, SIGNED, AND TIMELY RECEIVED, THE VOTES TRANSMITTED BY THIS MASTER BALLOT WILL NOT BE COUNTED.

                         [Master Ballot Code]

Item 1. Certification of Authority to Vote. The undersigned certifies that as of the _____, _____, record date, the undersigned (please check the applicable box):

[ ] Is a broker, bank, or other nominee for the beneficial owners of the aggregate principal amount of ___ % Notes listed in Item 2 below, and is the registered holder of such securities, or

[ ] Is acting under a power of attorney and/or agency (a copy of which will be provided upon request) granted by a broker, bank, or other nominee that is the registered holder of the aggregate principal amount of % Notes listed in Item 2 below, or

[ ] Has been granted a proxy (an original of which is attached hereto) from a broker, bank, or other nominee, or a beneficial owner, that is the registered holder of the aggregate principal amount of % Notes listed in Item 2 below, and,

accordingly, has full power and authority to vote to accept or reject the Plan on behalf of the beneficial owners of the % Notes described in Item 2 below.

Item 2. Class ___ (___ % Note Claims) Vote. The undersigned transmits the following votes of beneficial owners in respect of their ___ % Notes, and certifies that the following beneficial owners of ___ % Notes, as identified by their respective customer account numbers set forth below, are beneficial owners of such securities as of the _____, _____ record date and have delivered to the undersigned, as Nominee, Ballots casting such votes (Indicate in the appropriate column the aggregate principal amount voted for each account, or attach such information to this Master Ballot in the form of the following table. Please note: Each beneficial owner must vote *all* his, her, or its Class ___ claims (___ % Notes) *either* to accept or reject the Plan, and may *not* split such vote.):

Your Customer Account Number for Each Beneficial Owner of ___ % Notes	Principal Amount of ___ % Notes Voted to ACCEPT the Plan		Principal Amount of _____ % Notes Voted to REJECT the Plan
1.	$	OR	$
2.	$	OR	$
3.	$	OR	$
4.	$	OR	$
5.	$	OR	$
6.	$	OR	$
7.	$	OR	$
8.	$	OR	$
9.	$	OR	$
10.	$	OR	$
TOTALS	$		$

Item 3. Certification As to Transcription of Information From Item 3 As to Other ___ % Notes Voted by Beneficial Owners. The undersigned certifies that the undersigned has transcribed in the following table the information, if any, provided by beneficial owners in Item 3 of the ___ % Note Ballots, identifying any other ___ % Notes for which such beneficial owners have submitted other Ballots:

YOUR customer account number for each beneficial owner who completed Item 3 of the _____ % Note Ballot	TRANSCRIBE FROM ITEM 3 OF [ ]% NOTES BALLOT:		
	Account Number	Name Holder	Principal Amount of Other _____ % Notes Voted
	(Transcribe from Item 3 _____ of % Note Ballot)	*(Transcribe from Item 3 _____ of % Note Ballot)*	*(Transcribe from Item 3 ___ % of Note Ballot)*
1.			$
2.			$
3.			$
4.			$
5.			$
6.			$
7.			$

8. _____	$ _____
9. _____	$ _____
10. _____	$ _____

Item 4. Certification. By signing this Master Ballot, the undersigned certifies that each beneficial owner of ___ % Notes listed in Item 2, above, has been provided with a copy of the Disclosure Statement, including the exhibits thereto, and acknowledges that the solicitation of votes is subject to all the terms and conditions set forth in the Disclosure Statement.

Name of Broker, Bank, or Other Nominee:
_____
(Print or Type)
Name of Proxy Holder or Agent for Broker,
Bank, or Other Nominee (if applicable):
_____
(Print or Type)
Social Security or Federal Tax I.D. No.: _____
(If Applicable)
Signature: _____

By: _____
(If Appropriate)
Title: _____
(If Appropriate)
Street Address: _____
City, State, Zip Code: _____
Telephone Number:(   ) _____
Date Completed: _____

THIS MASTER BALLOT MUST BE RECEIVED BY [DEBTOR or DEBTOR'S AGENT], BEFORE _____: _____.M., EASTERN TIME, ON _____, _____ OR THE VOTES TRANSMITTED HEREBY WILL NOT BE COUNTED.

[PLEASE NOTE: BALLOTS AND MASTER BALLOTS WILL NOT BE ACCEPTED BY FACSIMILE TRANSMISSION.]

IF YOU HAVE ANY QUESTIONS REGARDING THIS MASTER BALLOT OR THE VOTING PROCEDURES, OR IF YOU NEED ADDITIONAL COPIES OF THE MASTER BALLOT, BALLOTS, DISCLOSURE STATEMENT, OR OTHER RELATED MATERIALS, PLEASE CALL [DEBTOR or DEBTOR'S AGENT], AT _____.

INSTRUCTIONS FOR COMPLETING THE MASTER BALLOT

VOTING DEADLINE:

The Voting Deadline is _____: _____.m., Eastern Time, on _____, _____, unless extended by the Debtor. To have the vote of your customers count, you must complete, sign, and return this Master Ballot so that it is received by **[DEBTOR or DEBTOR'S AGENT]**, **[ADDRESS]**, *on or before* the Voting Deadline.

HOW TO VOTE:

If you are both the registered owner *and* beneficial owner of any principal amount of _____ % Notes and you wish to vote such % Notes, you may complete, execute, and return to [DEBTOR or DEBTOR'S AGENT] *either* a ___ % Note Ballot or a ___ % Note Master Ballot.

If you are transmitting the votes of any beneficial owners of ___ % Notes other than yourself, you may *either*:

1.   Complete and execute the ___ % Note Ballot (other than Items 2 and 3) and deliver to the beneficial owner such "prevalidated" ___ % Note Ballot, along with the Disclosure Statement and other materials requested to be forwarded. The beneficial owner should complete Items 2 and 3 of that Ballot and return the completed Ballot to [DEBTOR or DEBTOR'S AGENT] so as to be received before the Voting Deadline;

OR

2. For any ___ % Note Ballots you do not "prevalidate":

Deliver the ___ % Note Ballot to the beneficial owner, along with the Disclosure Statement and other materials requested to be forwarded, and take the necessary actions to enable such beneficial owner to (i) complete and execute such Ballot voting to accept or reject the Plan, and (ii) return the complete, executed Ballot to you in sufficient time to enable you to complete the Master Ballot and deliver it to [**DEBTOR or DEBTOR'S AGENT**] before the Voting Deadline; and

With respect to all ___ % Note Ballots returned to you, you must properly complete the Master Ballot, as follows:

a. Check the appropriate box in Item 1 on the Master Ballot;

b. Indicate the votes to accept or reject the Plan in Item 2 of this Master Ballot, as transmitted to you by the beneficial owners of ___ % Notes. To identify such beneficial owners without disclosing their names, please use the customer account number assigned by you to each such beneficial owner, or if no such customer account number exists, please assign a number to each account (making sure to retain a separate list of each beneficial owner and the assigned number). **IMPORTANT: BENEFICIAL OWNERS MAY *NOT* SPLIT THEIR VOTES. EACH BENEFICIAL OWNER MUST VOTE *ALL* HIS, HER, OR ITS % NOTES *EITHER* TO ACCEPT OR REJECT THE PLAN. IF ANY BENEFICIAL OWNER HAS ATTEMPTED TO SPLIT SUCH VOTE, PLEASE CONTACT [DEBTOR or DEBTOR'S AGENT] IMMEDIATELY.** Any Ballot or Master Ballot which is validly executed but which does not indicate acceptance or rejection of the Plan by the indicated beneficial owner or which impermissibly attempts to split a vote will not be counted;

c. Please note that Item 3 of this Master Ballot requests that you transcribe the information provided by each beneficial owner from Item 3 of each completed ___ % Note Ballot relating to other ___ % Notes voted;

d. Review the certification in Item 4 of the Master Ballot;

e. Sign and date the Master Ballot, and provide the remaining information requested;

f. If additional space is required to respond to any item on the Master Ballot, please use additional sheets of paper clearly marked to indicate the applicable Item of the Master Ballot to which you are responding;

g. Contact [**DEBTOR or DEBTOR'S AGENT**] to arrange for delivery of the completed Master Ballot to its offices; and

h. Deliver the completed, executed Master Ballot so that it is actually *received* by [**DEBTOR or DEBTOR'S AGENT**] on or before the Voting Deadline. For each completed, executed ___ % Note Ballot returned to you by a beneficial owner, either forward such Ballot (along with your Master Ballot) to [**DEBTOR or DEBTOR'S AGENT**] or retain ___ % Note Ballot in your files for one such year from the Voting Deadline.

PLEASE NOTE:

This Master Ballot is *not* a letter of transmittal and may *not* be used for any purpose other than to cast votes to accept or reject the Plan. Holders should not surrender, at this time, certificates representing their securities. [**DEBTOR or DEBTOR'S AGENT**] will not accept delivery of any such certificates surrendered together with this Master Ballot. Surrender of securities for exchange may only be made by you, and will only be accepted pursuant to a letter of transmittal which will be furnished to you by the Debtor following confirmation of the Plan by the United States Bankruptcy Court.

No Ballot or Master Ballot shall constitute or be deemed a proof of claim or equity interest or an assertion of a claim or equity interest.

No fees or commissions or other remuneration will be payable to any broker, dealer, or other person for soliciting votes on the Plan. [We will, however, upon request, reimburse you for customary mailing and handling expenses incurred by you in forwarding the Ballots and other enclosed materials to the beneficial owners of _____ % Notes held by you as a nominee or in a fiduciary capacity. We will also pay all transfer taxes, if any, applicable to the transfer and exchange of your securities pursuant to and following confirmation of the Plan.]

NOTHING CONTAINED HEREIN OR IN THE ENCLOSED DOCUMENTS SHALL REN-
DER YOU OR ANY OTHER PERSON THE AGENT OF THE DEBTOR [OR THE DEBTOR'S
AGENT], OR AUTHORIZE YOU OR ANY OTHER PERSON TO USE ANY DOCUMENT OR
MAKE ANY STATEMENTS ON BEHALF OF ANY OF THEM WITH RESPECT TO THE
PLAN, EXCEPT FOR THE STATEMENTS CONTAINED IN THE ENCLOSED DOCUMENTS.

IF YOU HAVE ANY QUESTIONS REGARDING THIS MASTER BALLOT OR THE VOT-
ING PROCEDURES, OR IF YOU NEED ADDITIONAL COPIES OF THE MASTER BALLOT,
BALLOTS, DISCLOSURE STATEMENT, OR OTHER RELATED MATERIALS, PLEASE
CALL [DEBTOR or DEBTOR'S AGENT], AT _____.

* This form ballot does not contemplate multiple securities within the same class.

EXHIBIT "D"

UNITED STATES BANKRUPTCY COURT
EASTERN DISTRICT OF NEW YORK
_____X
In re   :
                                         :   Chapter 11 Case No.
[Name]   :   _____-_____ (_____)
                    Debtor.   :
                                         :   Tax Id No.
[DEBTOR'S ADDRESS]   :   _____
                                         :
_____X

SUMMARY OF PLAN OF REORGANIZATION AND NOTICE OF HEARING TO CONSIDER (i) DEBTOR'S COMPLIANCE WITH DISCLOSURE REQUIREMENTS AND (ii) CONFIRMATION OF PLAN OF REORGANIZATION

NOTICE IS HEREBY GIVEN as follows:

1. On _____, _____ (the "Petition Date"), **[NAME OF DEBTOR]**, the above-captioned
debtor (the "Debtor"), filed with the United States Bankruptcy Court for the Eastern District of New
York (the "Bankruptcy Court") a proposed plan of reorganization (the "Plan") and a proposed
disclosure statement (the "Disclosure Statement") pursuant to §§ 1125 and 1126(b) of title 11 of the
United States Code (the "Bankruptcy Code"). Copies of the Plan and the Disclosure Statement may
be obtained upon request of Debtor's counsel at the address specified below and are on file with the
Clerk of the Bankruptcy Court, **[ADDRESS]**, where they are available for review between the hours
of 9:00 a.m.—4:30 p.m. The Plan and Disclosure Statement also are available for inspection on the
Bankruptcy Court's internet site at www.nyeb.uscourts.gov.

Summary of Plan of Reorganization

2. [Provide one paragraph general description of salient Plan provisions, including whether
proponent requests confirmation pursuant to 11 U.S.C. § 1129(b).] Votes on the Plan were solicited
prior to the Petition Date. The following chart summarizes the treatment provided by the Plan to
each class of claims and interests and indicates the acceptance or rejection of the Plan by each class
entitled to vote.

CLASS	CLASS DESCRIPTION	IMPAIRMENT/ TREATMENT	ACCEPT/REJECT

Hearing to Consider Compliance with Disclosure Requirements

3.   A hearing to consider compliance with the disclosure requirements, any objections to the Disclosure Statement, and any other matter that may properly come before the Bankruptcy Court will be held before the Honorable _____, United States Bankruptcy Judge, in Room ___ of the United States Bankruptcy Court, [**ADDRESS**], on _____ at ___: ___.m. or as soon thereafter as counsel may be heard (the "Disclosure Compliance Hearing").   The Disclosure Compliance Hearing may be adjourned from time to time without further notice other than an announcement of the adjourned date or dates at the Disclosure Compliance Hearing or at an adjourned Disclosure Compliance Hearing and will be available on the electronic case filing docket.

4.   Any objections to the Disclosure Statement shall be in writing, shall conform to the Federal Rules of Bankruptcy Procedure and the Local Rules of the Bankruptcy Court, shall set forth the name of the objector, the nature and amount of any claims or interests held or asserted by the objector against the estate or property of the Debtor, the basis for the objection, and the specific grounds therefor, and shall be filed with the Bankruptcy Court at the address specified in the previous paragraph, with a copy delivered directly to Chambers, together with proof of service thereof, and served upon the following persons so as to be received on or before _____, _____ at 5:00 p.m. (Eastern Time):

(i)	[**NAME AND ADDRESS OF DEBTOR'S COUNSEL**]	(ii)	[**NAME AND ADDRESS OF COMMITTEE COUNSEL**]
(iii)	[**NAME AND ADDRESS OF BANK COUNSEL**]	(iv)	[**NAME AND ADDRESS OF INDENTURE TRUSTEE**]

(v)   OFFICE OF THE UNITED STATES TRUSTEE
U.S. Federal Office Building
201 Varick Street, Suite 1006
New York, NY 10014
Attn: Carolyn S. Schwartz, Esq.

[AND IF APPLICABLE:]

(vi)	OFFICE OF THE UNITED STATES ATTORNEY FOR THE EASTERN DISTRICT OF NEW YORK 271 Cadman Plaza East Brooklyn, NY 11201	(vii)	SECURITIES AND EXCHANGE COMMISSION 200 Vesey Street, Suite 400 New York, NY 10281

UNLESS AN OBJECTION IS TIMELY SERVED AND FILED IN ACCORDANCE WITH THIS NOTICE, IT MAY NOT BE CONSIDERED BY THE BANKRUPTCY COURT.

Hearing on Confirmation of the Plan

5.   A hearing to consider confirmation of the Plan, any objections thereto, and any other matter that may properly come before the Bankruptcy Court shall be held before the Honorable _____, United States Bankruptcy Judge, in Room _____ of the United States Bankruptcy Court, [**ADDRESS**], immediately following the Disclosure Compliance Hearing referred to above or at such later time as determined by the Bankruptcy Court at the conclusion of the Disclosure Compliance Hearing (the "Confirmation Hearing").   The Confirmation Hearing may be adjourned from time to time without further notice other than an announcement of the adjourned date or dates at the Confirmation Hearing or at an adjourned Confirmation Hearing.

6.   Objections to the Plan, if any, shall be in writing, shall conform to the Federal Rules of Bankruptcy Procedure and the Local Rules of the Bankruptcy Court, shall set forth the name of the objector, the nature and amount of any claims or interests held or asserted by the objector against the estate or property of the Debtor, the basis for the objection, and the specific grounds therefor, and shall be filed with the Bankruptcy Court at the address specified in the previous paragraph, with a copy delivered directly to Chambers, together with proof of service thereof, and served upon the

persons set forth in paragraph 4 above so as to be received on or before _____, _____, at 5:00 p.m. (Eastern Time). **UNLESS AN OBJECTION IS TIMELY SERVED AND FILED IN ACCORDANCE WITH THIS NOTICE, IT MAY NOT BE CONSIDERED BY THE BANKRUPTCY COURT.**

7. The times fixed for the Confirmation Hearing and objections to confirmation of the Plan may be rescheduled by the Bankruptcy Court in the event that the Bankruptcy Court does not find compliance with the disclosure requirements on, _____, _____. Notice of the rescheduled date or dates, if any, will be provided by an announcement at the Disclosure Compliance Hearing or at an adjourned Disclosure Compliance Hearing and will be available on the electronic case filing docket.

Section 341(a) Meeting

8. A meeting pursuant to section 341(a) of the Bankruptcy Code (the "Section 341(a) Meeting") will be held at the United States Bankruptcy Court, in room _____, **[ADDRESS]**, on _____, _____ at: _.m. Such meeting will not be convened if (i) the Plan is confirmed prior to the date set forth above for the Section 341(a) Meeting and (ii) the order confirming the Plan (or order entered substantially contemporaneously therewith) contains a provision waiving the convening of a Section 341(a) Meeting.

Dated: _____, New York

_____, _____

                                         BY ORDER OF THE COURT

                                         _____

                                         United States Bankruptcy Judge

**[NAME, ADDRESS, AND
TELEPHONE NUMBER OF
DEBTOR'S COUNSEL]**

ADMINISTRATIVE ORDER NO. 646. IN THE MATTER OF: ADOPTION OF PROCEDURES FOR THE ELECTRONIC FILING OF PROOFS OF CLAIM AND RELATED DOCUMENTS

WHEREAS, Local Bankruptcy Rule 5001–1 permits the electronic filing of Proofs of Claim, and

WHEREAS, the Court is implementing an Electronic Proof of Claim system ("ePOC") that permits the electronic filing of proofs of claim, amended proofs of claim, withdrawal of proofs of claim, and claim supplements (FRBP 3002.1 mortgage payment documents: Notice of Mortgage Payment Change; Notice of Postpetition Mortgage Fees, Expenses, and Charges; and Response to Notice of Final Cure Payment), it is hereby

ORDERED, that proofs of claim may be filed, amended, withdrawn and supplemented through ePOC without the need to obtain a CM/ECF login and password except in cases where the Court has appointed a Claims and Noticing Agent, and it is further

ORDERED, that any claim filed, amended, withdrawn or supplemented through ePOC shall constitute the filer's approved signature and have the same force and effect as if the individual signed a paper copy of such document, and it is further

ORDERED, that a claim filed through ePOC is considered the original proof of claim.

[Dated: March 18, 2016.]

ADMINISTRATIVE ORDER NO. 655. IN THE MATTER OF: DEPOSIT AND INVESTMENT OF REGISTRY FUNDS

The Court, having determined that it is necessary to adopt local procedures to ensure uniformity in the deposit, investment, and tax administration of funds in the Court's Registry,

IT IS ORDERED that the following shall govern the receipt, deposit, and investment of registry funds:

I.   Receipt of Funds.

A.   No money shall be sent to the Court or its officers for deposit in the Court's Registry without a court order signed by the presiding judge in the case or proceeding.

B.   The party making the deposit or transferring funds to the Court's registry shall serve the order permitting the deposit or transfer on the Clerk of Court.

C.   Unless provided for elsewhere in this Order, all monies ordered to be paid to the Court or received by its officers in any case pending or adjudicated shall be deposited with the Treasurer of the United States in the name and to the credit of this Court pursuant to 28 U.S.C. § 2041 through depositories designated by the Treasury to accept such deposit on its behalf.

II.   Investment of Registry Funds.

A.   Where, by order of the Court, funds on deposit with the Court are to be placed in some form of interest-bearing account or invested in a court-approved, interest-bearing instrument in accordance with Rule 67 of the Federal Rules of Civil Procedure, the Court Registry Investment System ("CRIS"), administered by the Administrative Office of the United States Courts under 28 U.S.C. § 2045, shall be the only investment mechanism authorized.

B.   Interpleader funds deposited under 28 U.S.C. § 1335 meet the IRS definition of a "Disputed Ownership Fund" (DOF), a taxable entity that requires tax administration. Unless otherwise ordered by the court, interpleader funds shall be deposited in the DOF established within the CRIS and administered by the Administrative Office of the United States Courts, which shall be responsible for meeting all DOF tax administration requirements.

C.   The Director of Administrative Office of the United States Courts is designated as custodian for all CRIS funds. The Director or the Director's designee shall perform the duties of custodian. Funds held in the CRIS remain subject to the control and jurisdiction of the Court.

D.   Money from each case deposited in the CRIS shall be "pooled" together with those on deposit with Treasury to the credit of other courts in the CRIS and used to purchase Government Account Series securities through the Bureau of Public Debt, which will be held at Treasury, in an account in the name and to the credit of the Director of Administrative Office of the United States Courts. The pooled funds will be invested in accordance with the principles of the CRIS Investment Policy as approved by the Registry Monitoring Group.

E.   An account will be established in the CRIS Liquidity Fund titled in the name of the case giving rise to the deposit invested in the fund. Income generated from fund investments will be distributed to each case based on the ratio each account's principal and earnings has to the aggregate principal and income total in the fund after the CRIS fee has been applied. Reports showing the interest earned and the principal amounts contributed in each case will be prepared and distributed to each court participating in the CRIS and made available to litigants and/or their counsel.

F.   For each interpleader case, an account shall be established in the CRIS Disputed Ownership Fund, titled in the name of the case giving rise to the deposit invested in the fund. Income generated from fund investments will be distributed to each case after the DOF fee has been applied and tax withholdings have been deducted from the fund. Reports showing the interest earned and the principal amounts contributed in each case will be available through the FedInvest/CMS application for each court participating in the CRIS and made available to litigants and/or their counsel. On appointment of an administrator authorized to incur expenses on behalf of the DOF in a case, the case DOF funds should be transferred to another investment account as directed by court order.

III.   Fees and Taxes.

A.   The custodian is authorized and directed by this Order to deduct the CRIS fee of an annualized 10 basis points on assets on deposit for all CRIS funds, excluding the case funds held in the DOF, for the management of investments in the CRIS. According to the Court's Miscellaneous Fee Schedule, the CRIS fee is assessed from interest earnings to the pool before a pro rata distribution of earnings is made to court cases.

B.   The custodian is authorized and directed by this Order to deduct the DOF fee of an annualized 20 basis points on assets on deposit in the DOF for management of investments and tax administration. According to the Court's Miscellaneous Fee Schedule, the DOF fee is assessed from interest earnings to the pool before a pro rata distribution of earnings is made to court cases. The custodian is further authorized and directed by this Order to withhold and pay federal taxes due on behalf of the DOF.

IV. Transition From Former Investment Procedure.

A. The Clerk of Court is further directed to develop a systematic method of redemption of all existing investments and their transfer to the CRIS.

B. Deposits to the CRIS DOF will not be transferred from any existing CRIS Funds. Only new deposits pursuant to 28 U.S.C. § 1335 from the effective date of this order will be placed in the CRIS DOF.

C. Parties not wishing to transfer certain existing registry deposits into the CRIS may seek leave to transfer them to the litigants or their designees on proper motion and approval of the judge assigned to the specific case.

D. This Order supersedes and abrogates all prior orders of this Court regarding the deposit and investment of registry funds.

E. The effective date of this order is the date the CRIS DOF begins accepting deposits.

[Dated: January 13, 2017.]

INDEX TO UNITED STATES BANKRUPTCY COURT
FOR THE EASTERN DISTRICT OF NEW YORK

UNITED STATES BANKRUPTCY COURT FOR THE NORTHERN DISTRICT OF NEW YORK

Including Amendments Received Through
September 1, 2017

———

RULE 1001–1. SHORT TITLE—APPLICABILITY

(a) **Short Title.** These local rules shall be known as the Local Bankruptcy Rules for the Northern District of New York and may be referred to and cited in papers filed in this Court as "Local Bankruptcy Rule ___–___" or "LBR ___–___."

(b) **Applicability.** The Local Bankruptcy Rules supplement the Federal Rules of Bankruptcy Procedure. These Local Bankruptcy Rules shall govern all proceedings in bankruptcy cases filed in the Northern District of New York.

(c) **Sectional References.** Unless otherwise indicated, all sectional references herein are to Title 11 of the United States Code.

(d) **Hyperlinks.** Unless otherwise indicated, hyperlinks are to Official Forms, Local Forms and Administrative Procedures for Filing, Signing, and Verifying Pleadings and Papers by Electronic Means ("Administrative Procedures") available on the Court's website located at www.nynb.uscourts.gov.

(e) **Defined Terms.** See LBR 9001–1.

[Effective January 1, 2012.]

Comment

Under the authority of Fed. R. Bankr. P. 9029, the District Court may make and amend rules of practice and procedure not inconsistent with the Federal Rules of Bankruptcy Procedure and that do not prohibit or limit the use of the official forms.

These Local Bankruptcy Rules, effective January 1, 2012, supersede and rescind the Local Bankruptcy Rules adopted October 27, 1994, January 1, 1998, and October 24, 2005. The numbering system used correlates each Local Bankruptcy Rule to the most closely associated Federal Rule of Bankruptcy Procedure, in conformity with the Uniform Numbering System prescribed by the Judicial Conference of the United States.

These Local Bankruptcy Rules incorporate certain Administrative Orders entered prior to October 1, 2011. Incorporated orders have been abrogated as indicated in Appendix III and are also noted on the court's website: www.nynb.uscourts.gov.

A Court may issue an Administrative Order that modifies or abrogates one or more of these Local Bankruptcy Rules. A list of Administrative Orders is available on the Court's website: www.nynb.uscourts.gov.

RULE 1002–1. COMMENCEMENT OF THE CASE

(a) **Electronic Case Filing and Signature.** Under the CM/ECF system, the Clerk no longer accepts original paper documents for filing. The petition must be signed and dated by the debtor contemporaneously with the filing. An electronic signature satisfies the requirement that petitions, verifications, resolutions, declarations, etc. be signed. An electronic signature is considered an original signature upon the filed documents for all purposes under the Bankruptcy Code, relevant federal and state statutes, and applicable federal rules. A pro se party may file a petition and other documents in paper format.

(b) **Filing Fees.** The Clerk shall not accept a petition to commence a case unless accompanied by: (1) the applicable filing fee; (2) an application pursuant to Fed. R. Bankr. P. 1006(b)(1) to pay the filing fee in installments (Official Form 103A); or (3) an application pursuant to Fed. R. Bankr. P. 1006(c) requesting a waiver of filing fee (Official Form 103B).

(c) **Where to File.**

(1) Except as set forth below, a petition, motion, pleading, memorandum of law, or other document required to be in writing must be filed electronically or in the Clerk's office where the assigned judge sits. The Clerk or the Court may make arrangements to permit the filing of a pleading or other paper at a location other than an official courthouse within the district after regular business hours on weekdays and on Saturdays, Sundays, and legal holidays for good cause shown.

(2) An attorney may use public scanners and computers located at the Public Intake Counter. A pro se party may file all papers and pleadings in paper format in any Clerk's office.

(d) **Corporate Resolution.** A voluntary petition filed by a corporation shall be accompanied by a copy of the corporate resolution or other appropriate authorization, duly attested to, authorizing such filing.

(e) **LLC Authority.** A voluntary petition filed by a limited liability company shall be accompanied by a copy of the appropriate authorization, duly attested to, authorizing such filing.

(f) **Partnership Declaration.** A voluntary petition filed by a partnership shall be accompanied by a copy of the appropriate authorization, duly attested to, authorizing such filing.

(g) **LLP Authority.** A voluntary petition filed by a limited liability partnership shall be accompanied by a copy of the appropriate authorization, duly attested to, authorizing such filing.

(h) **Deficient Petitions and Papers.** The Clerk may issue a notice specifying filing deficiencies to the filer of the document.

(i) **Noncompliance.** The failure to comply with the requirements of this Rule and the Federal Rules of Bankruptcy Procedure may subject the case to dismissal.

[Effective January 1, 2012. Amended effective December 1, 2015.]

Comment

Fed. R. Bankr. P. 5005(a)(2) permits a court by local rule to require documents to be filed, signed, or verified by electronic means. Although Fed. R. Bankr. P. 5005(a)(1) requires the Clerk to accept papers for filing that are not in proper form, paragraph (i) of this Rule makes clear that the Court may take appropriate action to enforce this Rule.

Once an initial waiver of the filing fee is granted under Fed. R. Bankr. P. 1006(c), that waiver shall apply to the debtor for all future fees assessed by the Clerk in that case, unless otherwise ordered by the Court.

Filing fees for the commencement of a case under the respective chapters of the Bankruptcy Code are set forth in 28 U.S.C. § 1930(a). Filing fees for the commencement of an adversary proceeding are authorized by 28 U.S.C. § 1930(b) and set forth in the Judicial Conference Schedule of Fees.

RULE 1003–1. INVOLUNTARY PETITION— FILING REQUIREMENTS

(a) Electronic Filing. An involuntary petition (Official Form 105 or 205) shall be filed using the CM/ECF system.

(b) Matrix. An involuntary petition shall be accompanied by a matrix, in proper form as set forth in LBR 1007–2(c), containing the name and address, including zip code and any post office address of all petitioning creditors, any attorneys for petitioning creditors, and any other parties in interest known to the petitioning creditors or their attorney.

(c) Certification of Matrix. The matrix required by paragraph (b) shall be certified in the manner directed in LBR 1007–2(f).

(d) Noncompliance. The failure to comply with the requirements of this Rule and the Federal Rules of Bankruptcy Procedure may subject the case to dismissal.

[Effective January 1, 2012. Amended effective January 1, 2014; December 1, 2015.]

RULE 1005–1. PETITION—CAPTION

(a) Individual Petition. The title of a case for an individual debtor shall include all names used by the debtor during the preceding eight years. This includes trade names, aliases, maiden names, and former married names. An individual debtor may not include as a d/b/a on the second line of the voluntary petition, which forms the basis for the caption of the case, the name of a corporation, partnership, limited liability company, limited liability partnership or any other separate and distinct legal entity when prompted to supply "All Other Names used by the Debtor in the last 8 years."

(b) Corporate, Partnership, LLC or LLP Petition. A corporate, partnership, limited liability corporation or limited liability partnership petition may not be combined with the petition of an individual or other separate legal entity. The caption of the petition must state the full and correct title of the entity and the entity's federal identification number.

[Effective January 1, 2012.]

Comment

Consult LBR 9004–1 for the format of a caption on a document for filing.

RULE 1007–1. STATEMENT OF SOCIAL SECURITY NUMBER, PAYMENT ADVICES AND FINANCIAL MANAGEMENT CERTIFICATE

(a) Verified Statement of Full Social Security Number. Fed. R. Bankr. P. 1007(f) requires the debtor to submit a verified statement (Official Form 121) of his or her full social security number. The verified statement is not filed in the case and does not become a part of the Court record or the public record. The completed and verified statement shall be retained by the debtor's attorney for two (2) years in accordance with LBR 9011–3(e) or, if the debtor is pro se, by the debtor for two (2) years.

(b) Submission With Petition Filed in Paper Format. When a petition is filed in paper format, the debtor is required to submit the original signed statement contemporaneously with the filing of the petition.

(c) Submission With Electronically Filed Petition. When a petition is electronically filed, the debtor is required to sign the statement of full social security number. The debtor's attorney is required to retain the original with his or her records. The form shall not be filed electronically with the petition and shall not be submitted to the Clerk.

(d) Amendment of Social Security Number. If a petition is filed with an incorrect social security number, debtor's counsel shall immediately:

(1) Submit, in paper format, to the Clerk an amended verified statement indicating both the incorrect social security number and the debtor's full and correct social security number;

(2) Serve the amended verified statement referenced in paragraph (d)(1) of this Rule upon all creditors, the trustee, and the United States trustee;

(3) File a certificate of service; and

(4) If the error affects the last four (4) digits of the debtor's social security number, in addition to submitting an amended - verified statement, also file an amended petition showing the corrected last four (4) digits of the debtor's social security number.

(e) Payment Advices. If a debtor cannot comply with § 521(a)(1)(B)(iv), the debtor shall complete and file a Payment Advice Form.

(f) Personal Financial Management Certificate. Every individual debtor in a case filed under chapter 7, chapter 11, or chapter 13 must complete a post-petition instructional course concerning personal financial management as required by Fed. R. Bankr. P. 1007(b)(7).

(1) *Failure to Timely File Evidence of Completion of Course.* If a debtor under chapter 7 or 13 fails to file a statement (Official Form 423) or a certificate from an approved provider evidencing completion of a course in financial management as required under Fed. R. Bankr. P. 1007(b)(7) within the time limits prescribed by Fed. R. Bankr. P. 1007(c), the Clerk may close the case without discharge and shall notify creditors. A motion to reopen the case to obtain a discharge will be subject to the applicable fee.

(2) *Deceased Debtor Excused From Compliance.* If a debtor dies after the filing of the petition and prior to completing the course in financial management, the debtor's attorney may file an ex parte application requesting a waiver of the completion of the course. A redacted version of the death certificate shall be attached as an exhibit to the application with service on the United States trustee and the case trustee.

(g) Noncompliance. The failure to comply with the requirements of this Rule and the Federal Rules of Bankruptcy Procedure may subject the case to dismissal.

[Effective January 1, 2012. Amended effective January 2, 2013; December 1, 2015.]

RULE 1007–2. MAILING MATRIX

(a) Matrix. When a list of creditors or list of equity security holders is required to be filed pursuant to Fed. R. Bankr. P. 1007, it shall be accompanied by a matrix containing the name and address of all creditors and other parties in interest. In addition, the list of the twenty (20) largest unsecured creditors filed pursuant to Fed. R. Bankr. P. 1007(d) shall be accompanied by a separate matrix. Each matrix shall be submitted in proper form, as described in paragraph (c) and (d) of this Rule.

(b) Reliance Upon the Matrix. The Clerk may rely upon the matrix as filed and any amendments thereto, for purposes of providing notice as required by these Local Bankruptcy Rules and the Federal Rules of Bankruptcy Procedure.

(c) Matrix Format. The mailing matrix must be formatted as follows:

(1) The matrix must be compatible with CM/ECF and must be formatted as a text file (*.txt) in ASCII format;

(2) The matrix must be typed in at least a 12–point font;

(3) The entries must appear in a column (left, center or right justified) with a one (1) inch margin;

(4) Entries should be in both uppercase and lowercase letters;

(5) Each creditor entry must consist of no more than five (5) single-spaced lines;

(6) Each line must contain no more than forty (40) characters, including spaces and punctuation;

(7) Each creditor's city, state, and zip code must all appear together on the final line;

(8) The two (2) letter state identifier as prescribed by the United States Post Office shall be used in an address with no periods included;

(9) If required under the Bankruptcy Code or Federal Rules of Bankruptcy Procedure, any attention lines or account numbers should be typed on the second line of the creditor's entry, and not on the last line. Account numbers should be in redacted format, identifying the last four (4) digits only; and

(10) There must be a double space between each creditor entry.

(d) Additional Copy of Mailing Matrix Required. In addition to the matrix filed in accordance with paragraph (c) above, a .pdf version of the matrix must be filed as either an attachment to the petition or as a stand-alone document.

(e) Matrix Certification. Whenever a matrix is required to be submitted pursuant to paragraph (a) of this Rule, paragraph (b) of LBR 1003–1, paragraph (d) of LBR 1009–1, paragraph (c) of LBR 1015–1, paragraph (c) of LBR 1019–1, or as otherwise required by the Court, the proponent or proponent's attorney must certify that the matrix contains the name, address, and zip code of all creditors and entities that appear in the list of creditors, list of equity security holders, list of twenty (20) largest unsecured creditors, or amendments thereto. The certification shall conform substantially to the following:

CERTIFICATION OF MAILING MATRIX

I (we), _____, the attorney for the debtor/petitioner (or, if appropriate, the debtor(s) or petitioners(s)) hereby certify under the penalties of perjury that the above/attached mailing matrix has been compared to and contains the names, addresses, zip codes and, if required, account numbers, in redacted form, of all persons and entities, as they appear on the list of creditors/list of equity security holders, or any amendment thereto filed herewith.

Dated:

_____
Attorney for Debtor/Petitioner
(Debtor(s)/Petitioner(s))

(f) Matrix Certification in an Involuntary Case. Whenever a matrix is required to be submitted in an involuntary case the proponent or proponent's attorney must certify that the matrix contains the name and address, of all petitioning creditors, their attorneys and any other parties in interest known to the petitioning creditors or their attorneys. The certification shall conform substantially to the following:

CERTIFICATION OF MAILING MATRIX IN AN INVOLUNTARY CASE

I (we), _____, the attorney for the petitioning creditors hereby certify under the penalties of perjury that the above/attached mailing matrix has been compared to and contains the names and addresses, zip codes and, if required, account numbers, in redacted form, of all persons and entities, as they appear on the list of creditors/list of equity security holders, or any amendment thereto filed herewith of the petitioning creditors, any attorneys for petitioning creditors and any other parties in interest known to the petitioning creditors or their attorney.

Dated:

_____
Attorney for Petitioning Creditors

(g) Noncompliance. The failure to comply with the requirements of this Rule and the Federal Rules of Bankruptcy Procedure may subject the case to dismissal.

[Effective January 1, 2012. Amended effective January 1, 2014.]

Comment

An example of an entry that complies with this Rule appears below.

XYZ, Inc.
Acct. No. XXX–XXX–1234
ATTN:
567 Avenue A
Albany, NY 12207

RULE 1007-3. NOTICE TO CREDITORS OMITTED FROM OR INCORRECTLY LISTED ON MAILING MATRIX

(a) Notice of Amendment to Add Creditor or Correct Creditor Information. If a debtor adds a creditor to the case or corrects the name or address of a creditor by amending either the schedules, the list of creditors, or matrix previously filed, the debtor must serve upon that creditor copies of the following:

(1) The amendment with the debtor's signed declaration (Official Form 106 Dec or 202 — Declaration);

(2) Notice of Meeting of Creditors;

(3) Verified Statement of Social Security Number (Official Form 121);

(4) Any matters previously noticed by the Clerk;

(5) Any other document filed in the case that affects the creditor's rights; and

(6) Any order that establishes or extends a bar date for claims or sets a deadline for creditors to file complaints to determine the dischargeability of certain debts or to object to the discharge of the debtor.

(b) Certificate of Compliance. The debtor must file a certificate of compliance with this Rule, together with a dated and clearly titled amended mailing matrix that lists only the name and correct mailing address of each newly scheduled or corrected creditor. The certification shall conform substantially to the following:

CERTIFICATION OF COMPLIANCE WITH LBR 1007-3

I (we)_____, the attorney for the debtor(s)/petitioner(s) (or if appropriate, the debtor(s) or petitioners(s)) hereby certify under the penalties of perjury that on date _____, schedules or an amended mailing matrix were filed.

The amended mailing matrix, which is clearly titled **AMENDED** matrix lists only the name and correct mailing address of each newly scheduled creditor or the corrected name and corrected mailing address of each creditor who was listed incorrectly on the mailing matrix filed with the petition.

I (we) further certify that any newly listed creditor and/or corrected creditor has been noticed as required by LBR 1007-3(a).

Dated:

Attorney for Debtor/Petitioner/Pro Se Debtor

[Effective January 1, 2012. Amended effective January 2, 2013; December 1, 2015.]

RULE 1009-1. AMENDMENT TO A PETITION, LIST, SCHEDULE, STATEMENT, SUMMARY OR MAILING MATRIX

(a) Caption. Each amendment to a petition, list, schedule, statement, summary, and mailing matrix shall contain a caption complying with Fed. R. Bankr. P. 1005 and 9004(b) and include the word "AMENDED" in the document's caption.

(b) Interlineation. No amendment by interlineations shall be permitted. The entire page or pages that the amendment affects shall be redrafted with the amendment "boxed in," and in such a manner that the amended page(s) will be complete without referring to the page or pages that have been amended.

(c) Schedules of Property—("A/B"), and Creditors ("D" and "E/F"). Each amendment to the schedules that affects the amount claimed shall be totaled on: (1) the amended schedule; and (2) the amended summary of schedules (Official Form 106Sum or 206Sum) and statistical summary of certain liabilities and related data (Official Form 106Sum or 206Sum).

(d) Mailing Matrix. Each amendment to the schedules that adds a party to the case or corrects the name or address of a party shall include an amended certified mailing matrix, listing only the new or corrected party and/or information.

(e) Amended List of Creditors. If the debtor files a list of creditors and their addresses in lieu of completed schedules as permitted by Fed. R. Bankr. P. 1007(c), and thereafter includes a creditor in the schedules not included in the original list of creditors, the schedules shall be treated as an amendment and the debtor shall file an amended list of creditors.

(f) Amendment to Claim of Exemption. An amendment to a claim of exemption pursuant to Fed. R. Bankr. P. 4003(a) shall be filed and served by the debtor or dependent of the debtor on the trustee, the United States trustee, and all creditors.

(g) Notice of Amendment. If the debtor amends a petition, list, schedule, statement, summary, or mailing matrix pursuant to Fed. R. Bankr. P. 1009, the debtor shall immediately serve notice of such amendment upon the United States trustee, trustee. and any entity affected thereby.

(h) Notice of Amendment to Add a Creditor. If a debtor adds a creditor to the case, the debtor must comply with the notice procedure as described in LBR 1007-3(a).

(i) Certificate of Service. Upon filing an amendment, the debtor shall file a certificate reflecting service of the notice of the amendment upon all parties entitled to notice under paragraph (g) of this Rule or paragraph (a) of LBR 1007-3.

(j) Filing Fee. Any fee required by 28 U.S.C. § 1930(b) and the appendix, must be paid at the time of the filing of the amendment.

[Effective January 1, 2012. Amended effective January 2, 2013; November 21, 2012; December 1, 2015.]

Comment

Amendments shall be filed in the form prescribed in LBR 9004-1 and in accordance with rules 1007-1 and 1007-3. A tutorial on how to comply with this rule is available on the court's website.

An example of an amendment that complies with this Rule appears below:

B6C (Official Form 6C) (04/10)

In re __James Greenstreet_____,   Case No. __11-98765_____
        Debtor   (If known)

Amended SCHEDULE C - PROPERTY CLAIMED AS EXEMPT

Debtor claims the exemptions to which debtor is entitled under: ☐ Check if debtor claims a homestead exemption that exceeds
(Check one box) $146,450.*
☒ 11 U.S.C. § 522(b)(2)
☐ 11 U.S.C. § 522(b)(3)

DESCRIPTION OF PROPERTY	SPECIFY LAW PROVIDING EACH EXEMPTION	VALUE OF CLAIMED EXEMPTION	CURRENT VALUE OF PROPERTY WITHOUT DEDUCTING EXEMPTION
Debtor's Homestead	CPLR § 5206	50,000	10,000
Primary Vehicle	Debtor Creditor Law § 282(1)	500.00	500.00

Amount subject to adjustment on 4/1/13 and every three years thereafter with respect to cases commenced on or after the date of adjustment.

RULE 1011-1. CONSENT TO INVOLUNTARY PETITION

(a) Corporation, LLC or LLP. A consent to an involuntary petition filed against a corporation, limited liability company, or limited liability partnership shall be accompanied by a copy of the corporate resolution or other appropriate authorization, duly attested to, authorizing such consent.

(b) Partnership. A consent to an involuntary petition filed against a partnership shall be accompanied by appropriate authorization, duly attested to by all general partners, authorizing such consent.

[Effective January 1, 2012.]

RULE 1014-1. INTERDISTRICT TRANSFER OF CASES OR PROCEEDINGS

After the expiration of fourteen (14) days from the date of entry of an order transferring a case or proceeding from this district to another district, the Clerk shall mail to the court to which the case is transferred: (1) an order of transfer; and (2) the original documents on file in the case or proceeding. If the documents in a transferred case or proceeding are only available in electronic format in the CM/ECF system, the Clerk shall mail to the court to which the case is transferred a notice to obtain the required documents from PACER.

[Effective January 1, 2012.]

Comment

Intradistrict transfer of cases is governed by LBR 1073–1.

RULE 1015–1. CONSOLIDATION OR JOINT ADMINISTRATION

(a) Joint Case.

(1) *Husband and Wife Joint Case.* A case filed by a husband and wife under § 302 shall be presumptively consolidated. In a chapter 7 asset case, the assets and liabilities shall be combined into a single pool to pay creditors, unless the court, upon motion made returnable prior to the final hearing on the trustee's final report and accounting, terminates the consolidation.

(2) *Motion to Sever.* At the request of one (1) or both of the joint debtors, and upon payment of the required fee, the joint bankruptcy case may be severed into two (2) separate cases, after which either debtor may convert his or her individual case. A motion to sever is not required for dismissal of a case with respect to one (1) of the joint debtors.

(b) Motion. A motion for joint administration or consolidation shall: (1) be filed in each of the affected cases; (2) be served on all creditors and parties in interest; and (3) designate one (1) of the cases as the main case.

(c) Matrix. Prior to the entry of an order of joint administration or consolidation, movant shall request copies from the Clerk or through PACER of the matrices for each of the cases affected by the order. Movant shall submit a supplemental certified matrix containing only those parties not already included on the matrix from the main case, without duplications or omissions. The matrix must comply with the filing requirements as set forth in LBR 1007–2 and shall be filed within seven (7) days of the entry of the order of consolidation or joint administration. This requirement shall not apply to the consolidation of a joint case under paragraph (a) of this Rule.

(d) Order. The proposed order of joint administration or consolidation must identify the main case and be uploaded in only the main case. The order shall be entered by the Clerk in each of the affected cases. In addition, the proposed order shall contain the following recitation:

Within seven (7) days of entry of this order, movant shall submit a supplemental certified mailing matrix, in conformance with LBR 1007–2, containing only those parties not previously included on the mailing matrix filed in the main case.

(e) Caption, Docket Entries and Filing. Prior to the entry of an order of consolidation or joint administration, all documents shall be captioned by their individual titles.

(1) *Consolidation.* Once separate cases have been ordered consolidated, they will be treated as one (1) case for all purposes, with a single case number, caption, claims register and docket.

(2) *Joint Administration.* Subsequent to the entry of an order of joint administration, all documents shall be captioned in the case or cases to which they pertain and shall be entered and filed in the main case. The Clerk may rely upon the document's caption in determining the case or cases to which a particular document applies.

(3) *Proofs of Claim.* A proof of claim should be filed in the case for the specific debtor against which the creditor holds the claim. It is the responsibility of the filing party to correctly identify the case in which to file the claim. A claim filed after cases have been ordered jointly administered is docketed per the case number identified on the claim.

(f) Noncompliance. Failure to comply with paragraph (c) of this Rule is cause for the Court to vacate its order of joint administration or consolidation and deny the relief requested.

[Effective January 1, 2012.]

Comment

Consolidation includes substantive consolidation.

An example of a caption for a jointly administered case is:

UNITED STATES BANKRUPTCY COURT
NORTHERN DISTRICT OF NEW YORK

In re:
     ABC COMPANY, LP, <u>et al.</u>,   Case No. 10–XXXXX
                                       Chapter 11(Main Case)
           Debtors.   Case No. 10–XXXXX
                                       Case No. 10–XXXXX

--- Jointly Administered

RULE 1017–1. DISMISSED CASE—MOTION TO VACATE ORDER OF DISMISSAL AND TO REINSTATE CASE

(a) Time to File a Motion. A motion to vacate or reconsider an order of dismissal shall be filed in accordance with the requirements of Fed. R. Bankr. P. 9023 and/or 9024, as applicable. The motion shall be served upon all creditors and parties in interest, at the address listed on the certificate of service of the notice of dismissal.

(b) Case Dismissed for Non–Payment. A motion filed in a case dismissed for failure of the debtor to make plan payments shall state with particularity:

(1) The circumstances that caused the debtor's non-payment;

(2) The circumstances that have changed so as to permit the debtor to make future payments;

(3) The date and manner of the proposed future payments by the debtor to the trustee; and

(4) Any new debt incurred by the debtor since the date of dismissal.

(c) Submission of Proposed Order. A proposed order granting a motion under this Rule shall be titled "Order Vacating Order of Dismissal and Reinstating Case."

(d) Service of Order. The debtor shall serve the order vacating the order of dismissal and reinstating the case upon all creditors and parties in interest at the address listed on the certificate of service of the notice of dismissal. The debtor shall file a certificate of service.

[Effective January 1, 2012.]

Comment

This motion may be pursued on a default basis under LBR 9013–3.

This Rule does not apply to a closed case. If the case is closed, parties must proceed under § 350 and Fed. R. Bankr. P. 5010, which require payment of a fee for reopening the case pursuant to 28 U.S.C. § 1930(b). The fee to be charged for reopening shall be the same as the filing fee in effect for commencing a new case as of the date of reopening.

RULE 1017–2. CONVERSION FROM CHAPTER 7 TO CHAPTER 13

A debtor who seeks to convert a chapter 7 case to a chapter 13 case must do so by motion. The debtor must assert facts that demonstrate eligibility for chapter 13 relief and that the conversion is sought in good faith. The motion must be served upon all creditors and parties in interest, the chapter 7 trustee, and the United States trustee. The debtor shall file a certificate of service.

[Effective January 1, 2012.]

Comment

This motion may be pursued on a default basis under LBR 9013–3.

RULE 1017–3. CONVERSION FROM CHAPTER 12 OR CHAPTER 13 TO CHAPTER 7

A debtor who seeks to convert a chapter 12 or 13 case to a chapter 7 need only file a notice of conversion, signed by the debtor. No order of conversion is required. The filing date of the notice of conversion becomes the date of the conversion order for purposes of applying § 348(c) and Fed. R. Bankr. P. 1019.

[Effective January 1, 2012.]

RULE 1019–1. CONVERSION—PROCEDURE FOLLOWING

(a) Filing of Additional Lists, Schedules, and Statements. In accordance with Fed. R. Bankr. P. 1019, the previously filed petition, lists, schedules, statements, and claims actually filed shall be deemed filed in the converted case. Only the lists, schedules, and any other statements necessary to complete the filing requirements in the newly converted case shall be filed upon conversion.

(b) Timeliness of Filing Schedule of Unpaid Debts. When the schedule of unpaid debts is filed in a case converted to chapter 7 within the period prescribed by Fed. R. Bankr. P. 1019(5), the Clerk shall notice each creditor listed on the schedule regarding the filing of post-petition claims pursuant to Fed. R. Bankr. P. 1019(6). When the schedule is untimely filed, the filer shall provide the notice required by this paragraph, and file a certificate of service.

(c) Supplemental Matrix. Any list, schedule, or statement filed as a result of a conversion that includes a creditor not previously listed on the case matrix, shall be accompanied by a supplemental certified matrix prepared as directed by LBR 1007–2, which lists, without duplication, only the additional creditor.

(d) Duties of Trustee or Debtor in Small Business Case Upon Conversion to Chapter 11. Within seven (7) days of the conversion of a chapter 7, 12, or 13 case to chapter 11, the trustee or the debtor in possession shall file the additional items required pursuant to § 1116(1)(A) or a statement pursuant to § 1116(1)(B).

(e) Debtor's Affidavit Upon Conversion to Chapter 11. In addition to the information required by LBR 2015–2, the debtor's affidavit shall set forth:

(1) If the case was originally commenced under chapter 7, 12, or 13, the name and address of any trustee appointed in the case and the name and address of each member elected to the creditors' committee in the chapter 7 case; and

(2) The name and address of each committee member and any attorney for such committee, organized prior to the order for relief in a chapter 11 case, and a brief description of the circumstances surrounding the formation of the committee, including the date of formation.

[Effective January 1, 2012.]

Comment

This Rule should be read in conjunction with LBRs 1002–1, 1007–2, 1007–3 and 2015–2.

RULE 1073–1. CASE ASSIGNMENT AND INTRADISTRICT TRANSFER

(a) Assignment of a Case and Adversary Proceeding to Albany. A case in which the domicile, residence, principal place of business, or principal asset(s) of the debtor is within Albany, Clinton, Essex, Rensselaer, Saratoga, Schenectady, Schoharie, Warren, or Washington county will be assigned to the Albany Court. A case filed by a resident of Columbia, Greene, or Ulster county will be treated as a Northern District case and assigned to the Albany Court when filed in the Northern District of New York.

(b) Assignment of a Case and Adversary Proceeding to Utica. A case in which the domicile, residence, principal place of business, or principal asset(s) of the debtor is within Broome, Chenango, Delaware, Franklin, Fulton, Hamilton, Herkimer, Lewis, Madison, Montgomery, Oneida, Otsego, or St. Lawrence county will be assigned to the Utica Court.

(c) Assignment of a Case and Adversary Proceeding to Syracuse. A case in which the domicile, residence, principal place of business, or principal asset(s) of the debtor is within Cayuga, Cortland, Jefferson, Onondaga, Oswego, Tioga, or Tompkins county will be assigned to the Syracuse Court.

(d) Assignment Generally. Except as otherwise provided in the Bankruptcy Code and Federal Rules of Bankruptcy Procedure, the assignment of a case to a Court includes the assignment of all proceedings arising under Title 11 or arising in or related to a case under Title 11.

(e) Intradistrict Transfer. Irrespective of the case assignment, a Court may transfer to another Judge within the district any case, contested matter, or adversary proceeding.

(f) Objections to Assignment. Objections to assignment of cases, adversary proceedings, or contested matters shall be filed with the Court assigned to the case.

[Effective January 1, 2012.]

Comment

Erroneous information on a petition may result in the incorrect assignment of a case. The Clerk may advise the Court if it appears that the case has been improperly assigned. Appropriate adjustment may be made pursuant to paragraph (e) of this Rule. The intentional furnishing of incorrect information may subject the person who provided such information to sanctions.

Interdistrict transfer of cases is governed by LBR 1014–1.

RULE 2002–1. NOTICE TO CREDITORS AND OTHER INTERESTED PARTIES

(a) Notice to All Creditors. Notice of the following actions shall be given by the proponent thereof, other than the United States trustee, to all creditors and parties in interest:

(1) A proposed use, sale, or lease of property other than in the ordinary course of business;

(2) The hearing on approval of a compromise or settlement of a controversy;

(3) In chapter 7, 11, and 12 cases, the hearing on the dismissal or conversion of the case to another chapter;

(4) The time fixed to accept or reject a proposed modification of a plan;

(5) Except as limited by paragraph (b), a hearing on all applications for compensation or reimbursement of expenses from the estate totaling in excess of $1,000.00;

(6) The time fixed for filing objections and the hearing to consider approval of a disclosure statement or, under § 1125(f), to make a final determination whether the plan provides adequate information so that a separate disclosure statement is not necessary;

(7) The time fixed for filing objections and the hearing to consider confirmation of a plan under chapter 9, 11 or 12;

(8) The notice of entry of an order confirming a plan under chapter 9, 11 or 12; and

(9) In a chapter 7 case, the notice of the trustee's final report.

(b) Limited Notice. Where an official creditors' committee has been appointed and as permitted by Fed. R. Bankr. P. 2002(i), required notice of hearings on the actions described below may be limited to such a committee or its authorized agent, the United States trustee, and to any creditor and equity security holder who files with the Court a request that all notices be mailed to them:

(1) Approval of a compromise or settlement; and

(2) Application for compensation or reimbursement of expenses from the estate totaling less than $25,000.00.

(c) Certificate of Service. A certificate of service conforming to LBR 9013–1(c) shall be filed within seven (7) days of effecting service and not later than seven (7) days prior to the return date of the hearing. For the purpose of preparing address labels, a copy of the updated matrix can be obtained from PACER or upon request from the Clerk.

(d) Notice to Committees. Except as the Court may otherwise designate, pursuant to Fed. R. Bankr. P. 9007, service of notice upon a committee may be made by serving the committee chairperson, the appointed attorney for the committee, if any and other authorized agent. Upon application by a party in interest, the Court may designate additional entities to which notice shall be given.

(e) Return Address on Court Generated Notices. The Clerk shall place the name and address of the debtor's attorney of record, or that of the pro se debtor, as the case may be, as the return address on all notices sent out by the Court to all creditors and other parties in interest.

(f) Returned Mail, Duty to Re–Notice, and File Certificate of Service. If a notice referred to in paragraph (e) is returned as undeliverable, debtor's counsel or the pro se debtor shall promptly send out the notice to any corrected address noted thereon. A certificate of service conforming to LBR 9013–1(c) shall be filed within seven (7) days of effecting service and not later than seven (7) days prior to the return date of a hearing.

[Effective January 1, 2012.]

Comment

This Rule is intended to facilitate the service of papers. The proponent of a notice under subparagraphs (a)(1), (2), (3), or (5) should consult LBR 9013–1(d) for the content of the notice.

RULE 2014–1. APPLICATION FOR EMPLOYMENT OF PROFESSIONAL PERSONS

(a) Requirements of the Application and Affidavit. Except as set forth in paragraph (e), an order approving the employment of a professional, shall be sought by application and supporting affidavit.

(1) *Application.* A copy of any written retainer agreement, and of any written guaranty agreement, shall be submitted with and appended to the application. An order approving the employment of a professional person pursuant to § 327 shall be granted only on application by the trustee, debtor in possession or committee. The application shall fully disclose:

(A) The reason the professional should be hired;

(B) The professional terms and conditions of employment, including any arrangement for retainer;

(C) The professional services to be rendered;

(D) The source of any retainer;

(E) The hourly rates for professional and paraprofessionals;

(F) Any contingency fee arrangement; and

(G) All of the professional's connections with the debtor or any party in interest, including disclosure of the terms of any guaranty agreement with respect to payment of the professional's fee by a third party.

(2) *Affidavit.* The application shall be accompanied by an affidavit of the professional, setting forth any facts which might reasonably lead to the conclusion the professional may not be disinterested or may hold or represent an interest adverse to the debtor as defined in § 101(14).

(3) *Order.* A proposed order approving the employment shall be submitted with and appended to the application required by paragraph (a) as an exhibit.

(b) Notice to the United States Trustee. The application for employment shall be electronically filed with the Court. The United States trustee shall file a response, if any, within twenty-one days from the date application is filed. The application will be deemed ripe for the Court's consideration upon the earlier of (1) the filing of a response by the United States trustee, or (2) the expiration of the twenty-one day period. If an objection to the application or the proposed order approving the employment is filed, a hearing on the application will be set by the Clerk. If no action is taken by the United States trustee within the twenty-one day period, the Court, in its discretion, may schedule a hearing on the application or enter an order approving the employment.

(c) Order Approving Employment. An order approving the application shall be submitted to the Court upon the earlier of (1) the United States trustee's consent to the application, (2) the expiration of the twenty-one day period referenced in paragraph (b), if no objection is filed, or (3) the conclusion of a hearing on the application. The order shall clearly state, inter alia, that no fees will be paid to the professional, including the use of any retainer received for post-petition services, without prior approval of the Court.

(d) Auctioneers Pursuant to § 327(a). In addition to the requirements of subparagraph (a)(2), the auctioneer's affidavit shall:

(1) Attest that the auctioneer is duly licensed, and include the auctioneer's license number and business address;

(2) Attach a copy of the surety bond referred to in LBR 6005–1(b) intended to cover the assets of the estate; and

(3) Where a blanket bond has been approved by the United States trustee and is on file with the Court, attest whether the affiant has been appointed as auctioneer in any other case, including the case name and case number, and state whether the affiant has or will, within a reasonable period of time, come into possession of property of any other estate in which the affiant has been appointed auctioneer, together with a reasonable estimation of the value of all such property.

(e) Employment of an Attorney Pursuant to § 327(e). If the chapter 7 trustee seeks to employ an attorney to pursue the estate's interest in a claim previously held by the debtor, approval of the retention shall be sought by motion on notice pursuant to LBR 9013–3. In addition to service on the United States trustee, the motion shall be served upon the debtor and attorney for the debtor.

[Effective January 1, 2012.]

Comment

The information required by this Rule shall be submitted at the same time as the information required by Fed. R. Bankr. P. 2014(a).

This Rule supplements Fed. R. Bankr. P. 6003.

RULE 2014–2. ADMISSION TO PRACTICE/DESIGNATION FOR SERVICE

(a) Attorney Admission. An attorney who is admitted to practice before the District Court of the Northern District of New York, unless otherwise restricted, is also admitted to practice before this Court.

(b) Pro Hac Vice Admission.

(1) *Application.* A member in good standing of the bar of any state or of any United States District Court not otherwise admitted to practice before the Court, may be permitted to practice on motion in this Court for a limited purpose only in a particular case, adversary proceeding, contested matter, or action. An attorney seeking admission pro hac vice shall provide an original certificate of good standing, as evidence of admission to the bar of the highest court of any state or of any United States District Court, and shall pay the required administrative fee. The application, original certificate of good standing, proposed order and a check made payable to the District Court Clerk shall be delivered in paper format to the Bankruptcy Court Clerk

(c) Limited Admission as Student Practitioner. A law student approved as a "Student Practitioner" may, under the supervision of an attorney and with prior Court approval, appear on behalf of a debtor who has completed and signed the Student Practice Authorization Form. The completed Student Practice Authorization Form shall be filed in the case pending before the Court.

(1) *Attorney Supervision.* The attorney who supervises a student shall:

(A) Be a member in good standing of the bar of the United States District Court for the Northern District of New York;

(B) Assume personal professional responsibility for the student's work;

(C) Assist the student to the extent necessary;

(D) Appear with the student in all proceedings before the Court unless his or her presence is waived by the Court; and

(E) Indicate in writing his consent to supervise the student on the prescribed application form for appearance as a Student Practitioner.

(2) *Student Eligibility.* In order to appear, the student shall:

(A) Be enrolled in a law school approved by the American Bar Association;

(B) Have completed legal studies amounting to at least three (3) semesters, or the equivalent;

(C) Be recommended by either the dean or a faculty member of his or her law school as a Student Practitioner, which recommendation may be withdrawn by the recommender at any time by mailing a notice to the Clerk;

(D) Neither ask for, nor receive any compensation or remuneration of any kind for the services performed from the person on whose behalf they are rendered, but this shall not prevent an attorney, legal aid bureau, law school, public defender agency, a State, or the United States from paying compensation to the eligible law student, nor shall it prevent any agency from making proper charges for its services. Neither the student, nor anyone on the student's behalf, shall seek recovery of attorneys' fees from an adverse party for the services rendered by the student as a student practitioner, except for the successful prosecution of a willful violation of the automatic stay or of the discharge injunction pursuant to §§ 362 and 524 and for the defense of an § 523(a)(2) nondischargeability action;

(E) Certify in writing that the student is familiar with the federal procedural and evidentiary rules as well as these rules; and

(F) Complete and file a Student Practice Authorization Form with the Court together with a proposed order for appearance as a Student Practitioner in the bankruptcy case and/or adversary proceeding in which the client consent has been obtained.

(3) *Permitted Student Services.* The Student Practitioner may:

(A) Appear as counsel in Court or at other proceedings when consent of the client and the supervising attorney has been filed and when the Court has approved the student's request to appear in the particular case;

(B) Prepare and sign affidavits, motions, petition, answers, objections, replies, memoranda and legal briefs, and other documents (collectively, "Documents") in connection with any matter in which the student has met the conditions of subparagraph (A) above. The Documents must also be signed by the supervising attorney with the original maintained in the case file.

(4) *Term of Student Admission.* A Student Practitioner whose application has been approved may continue to appear in a particular case as a Student Practitioner until the student has graduated from law school and is formally admitted to the bar or until termination by the Court. The Court sua sponte may terminate a Student Practitioner's right to appear at any time without notice of hearing and without showing of cause.

(d) **Designation for Service.** A Court may require an attorney who does not have an office in the Northern District of New York to designate a resident member of the bar of the Northern District of New York for service of process or papers.

[Effective January 1, 2012.]

RULE 2015–1. DEBTOR IN POSSESSION DUTIES

(a) **Monthly Statement of Operation Required in a Chapter 7 (Operating), Chapter 11 and Chapter 12 Case.** The operating report mandated by §§ 704(a)(8), 1106 and Fed. R. Bankr. P. 2015(b) must be filed monthly and, in addition, must be served upon the United States trustee, any governmental unit charged with responsibility for collection or determination of any tax arising out of the operations, and shall be served upon any official committee or its attorney.

(1) *Signature.* An operating report filed in accordance with paragraph (a) of this Rule must be signed by the debtor in possession, or if applicable, the chapter 7 trustee or § 1104 trustee. By signing the operating report, the debtor in possession or trustee verifies the accuracy of the information contained therein.

(b) **Monthly Statement of Operation Required in a Chapter 13 Business Case.** The operating report mandated by Fed.R.Bankr.P 2015(c)(1) must be filed monthly and, in addition, must be served upon the United States trustee, and any governmental unit charged with responsibility for collection or determination of any tax arising out of the operations.

(1) *Signature.* An operating report filed in accordance with paragraph (b) of this Rule must be signed by the debtor. By signing the operating report, the debtor verifies the accuracy of the information contained therein.

(c) **Requirements for a Chapter 12 or Chapter 13 Debtor Engaged in Business.** If a chapter 12 or 13 debtor is engaged in the operation of a business enterprise, including a family farm pursuant to § 1201, and is required to collect tax or for which the debtor incurs tax liability in the ordinary course of the debtor's business, the debtor shall:

(1) Provide the trustee a summary of business operations on such form as promulgated by the trustee or a copy of the debtor's most recent federal tax return when requested by the trustee and in such intervals as required by the trustee;

(2) Maintain a bank account that serves solely as a separate tax account ("Tax Account") for the deposit of all tax funds (including, but not limited to, funds held in trust for an employee's withholding tax, sales tax, and employer business tax, with the exception of income taxes) that may be collected by the debtor and for which the debtor may become liable during the pendency of this case. Such tax funds are to be withdrawn from the Tax Account only for the remittance to the appropriate taxing authority or to a federal tax depository;

(3) Contemporaneous with the payment of any salary paid to an employee of the debtor, deposit that portion of such salary as is required to be withheld for social security tax and the employer's portion of social security tax and disability and unemployment insurance taxes to the Tax Account;

(4) If the debtor is required to collect sales tax, deposit the sales tax in the Tax Account not later than the Monday following each week for that week's sales tax liability;

(5) Deposit any other tax that the debtor is required to collect, or for which the debtor incurs liability in the ordinary course of the debtor's business (such as federal excise taxes)

into the Tax Account not later than Wednesday of the week following the week in which such tax were collected or in which the liability was incurred;

(6) During the pendency of the case, timely file all required federal and state tax returns;

(7) During the pendency of the case, make required periodic deposits of federal and state taxes to a tax depository and provide the appropriate taxing authority with verification that such deposits were made within three (3) days from the date of any such deposit; and

(8) The debtor shall provide proof of compliance with paragraph (b) of this Rule upon request of the trustee.

[Effective January 1, 2012.]

Comment

This Rule addresses the requirement of filing monthly operating reports in a chapter 7 case when a business is authorized to be operated, in a chapter 11 and 12 case, and in a chapter 13 business case. Monthly Operating Report forms are located at: http://www.justice.gov/ust/r02/index.htm.

Pursuant to Fed. R. Bankr. P. 5003(e), counsel is referred to the Clerk's registry for the addresses for the filing of tax returns and remittance of payments.

RULE 2015–2. DEBTOR IN POSSESSION DUTIES—CHAPTER 11 AFFIDAVIT

(a) **Chapter 11 Debtor's Affidavit.** A debtor's affidavit shall be filed in each chapter 11 case and in any case converted to chapter 11 from chapter 7, 12, or 13.

(b) **Contents of Affidavit.** A debtor in possession shall file an original affidavit attesting:

(1) To the nature of the debtor's business and a concise statement of the circumstances leading to its chapter 11 filing;

(2) If the debtor failed to file its summary of schedules (Official Form 206Sum) with the initial filing, a summary of the debtor's assets and liabilities;

(3) A list of all property of the debtor in the possession or custody of any custodian, public officer, mortgagee, pledgee, assignee of rents, or secured creditor or agent for any such person, giving the name, address and telephone number of such person and the court, if any, in which a proceeding relating thereto is pending;

(4) If the debtor failed to file its Schedule "A/B" (Assets— Real and Personal Property) or Schedule "G" (Executory Contracts and Unexpired Leases) with the initial filing, a list of real and personal property owned, under lease or, held under other arrangement, including, but not limited to the property from which the debtor operates its business; and

(5) If the debtor failed to file its statement of financial affairs with the initial filing, the location of its substantial assets, the location of its books and records, and the nature, location and value of assets, if any, held by the debtor outside the territorial limits of the United States.

(c) **Additional Information Required if Business Continues.** If the debtor intends to continue the operation of its business, the affidavit shall so state and set forth the information described in subparagraphs (1)—(3) below:

(1) The estimated amount of the weekly payroll payable to employees (exclusive of any officer, partner, stockholder, and director) for the thirty (30) day period following the filing of the chapter 11 petition;

(2) The amount paid and proposed to be paid for services for the thirty (30) day period following the filing of the chapter 11 petition:

(A) If a corporation, to any officer, stockholder, and director;

(B) If an individual, partnership, limited liability company, or limited liability partnership, to the individual or any member of the partnership or limited liability entity; and

(C) If a consultant has been retained, to such consultant; and

(3) A schedule setting forth for the thirty (30) day period following the filing of the petition: estimated cash receipts and disbursements, net cash gain or loss, accrued but unpaid obligations, other than professional fees, and any other information relevant to an understanding of the foregoing.

(d) **When to File the Affidavit.** In a voluntary chapter 11 case, the affidavit pursuant to this Rule shall be filed within seven (7) days of the filing of the petition. In an involuntary chapter 11 case, the affidavit shall be filed within seven (7) days after entry of the order for relief or after the filing of debtor's consent to the petition, whichever is earlier.

(e) **Waiver of Requirements.** The Court may waive the requirements of this Rule, except for subparagraphs (1) and (2) of paragraph (b), upon application of the debtor and notice to the United States trustee, if it determines that compliance with this Rule is impracticable.

[Effective January 1, 2012. Amended effective December 1, 2015.]

Comment

This Rule supplements Fed. R. Bankr. P. 1007 and should be read in conjunction with LBR 1019–1(e) when a case converts to chapter 11.

RULE 2016–1. COMPENSATION OF PROFESSIONALS IN A CHAPTER 11 CASE

(a) **Applications for Compensation.** Applications for compensation shall comply with all requirements, including those related to format, outlined in Fed. R. Bankr. P. 2016(a) and the United States Trustee Fee Guidelines, which are available at www.justice.gov/ust/r02.

(b) **Filing and Paper Copy Requirements.** Applications for compensation are to be filed electronically. A paper copy marked "CM/ECF Case—Chambers Copy" is to be provided to the Court. In addition, the United States trustee is to be served with a paper copy of the application. Each application shall include:

(1) The date the applicant was appointed by the Court and, if applicable, the method of compensation, the maximum compensation, and any rate of compensation fixed in the order appointing applicant;

(2) A statement as to whether all services for which compensation is requested were performed for, or on behalf of, the party retaining applicant or on behalf of any other person or paraprofessional;

(3) A concise summary of the professional and paraprofessional services rendered, including:

(A) A factual explanation of the nature and extent of services performed, the results obtained, and the size of the estate; and

(B) For an interim fee request, an explanation of the status of the case, a projection as to the percentage of work that the current application covers in relation to the overall case, and any other matters that will enable the Court to determine the reasonable value of such services;

(4) An exhibit consisting of contemporaneous daily time records for all professionals and paraprofessionals, arranged in a project billing format as suggested by the United States Trustee Fee Guidelines. Applications seeking compensation less than $10,000.00, exclusive of expenses, are exempt from the project billing requirement. Entries in the time records must:

(A) Be legible and applicant shall define any codes, symbols, abbreviations, or non-legal technical terms used in the time records; and

(B) Be sufficiently specific to permit the Court to evaluate the reasonableness of the time allocated for the particular service. Failure to separately identify the time expended on each service with a single time entry may provide a basis for the Court to deny compensation for that service.

(5) A statement specifying the amounts, if any, within the total request that were previously received from any source, including guarantors, with or without Court authorization;

(6) A statement as to whether applicant has entered into any agreement to fix fees or to share compensation as prohibited by 18 U.S.C. § 155 and 11 U.S.C. § 504;

(7) A statement describing the estate's ability to pay the fees requested and the status of fees owed to other administrative claimants of equal priority to the extent the professional is employed pursuant to §§ 327 or 1103 and compensation is sought from the estate and not a third party;

(8) A specific description of the basis and justification for the request in terms related to the benefit of the services to the estate to the extent an enhancement of fees beyond those supported by the time records is sought; and

(9) An itemization of expenses incurred, conforming to paragraph (c) of this Rule.

(c) **Reimbursement of Expenses.** All requests for reimbursement of expenses shall be separately supported in the application by a detailed, itemized listing. Each category of expenses shall be separately totaled. A summary of all expense categories shall be included, which total should equal the aggregate request.

(1) The following expenses may be reimbursable if adequately supported in the application:

(A) Duplication of documents at actual cost at a rate not to exceed $0.20 per page or, if the photocopies were made by an entity unrelated to the applicant, at the rate charged by the entity as supported by a photocopy of the invoice appended to the application;

(B) Computer legal research at a rate not to exceed the cost of said service incurred by the applicant;

(C) Long distance travel expenses, if adequately described, including the mode of transportation, the date, destination, and purpose of the trip, and, if by automobile, the number of miles traveled, the rate used, and substantiation of incidental expenses, including lodging, tolls, and parking; and

(D) Facsimile transmission charges for outgoing transmissions to long distance numbers, reimbursable at either the actual toll charge or $1.00 per page.

(2) The applicant shall certify that all expenses for which reimbursement is sought were incurred on behalf of the client and no other person and that the reimbursement, if allowed in full, will not exceed the amount that applicant paid for the items.

(3) The following expenses may be considered unreasonable unless separately justified through a detailed itemization and explanation by the applicant as to why they were necessary and verification that the hourly rates charged by the professionals do not support said expenses as an overhead item within the applicant's office:

(A) Travel to and from the courthouse within a twenty-five (25)-mile radius;

(B) Any charges for typing, word processing and clerical assistance;

(C) A travel mileage rate in excess of that which the Administrator of General Services has prescribed for official travel of employees of the Federal Government, as amended from time to time, and set forth in http://www.gsa.gov/portal/content/100715; and

(D) Any meal expenses incurred while on long-distance travel.

(d) **Certification.** Each application for compensation shall be accompanied by a separate certification of the person or entity on whose behalf the applicant is employed, including the debtor, creditors' committee, or trustee. This certification must reflect both alternative options in substantially the form set forth below:

I, [person or representative of entity], certify that I have reviewed the [title of fee application] filed by [applicant], and

Check one:

☐   I do not object to allowance of the application and payment of fees and expenses in full as the services rendered and fees charged appear reasonable;

or

☐   I object to the application and to payment of the fees and expenses in full in the amounts and for the reasons set forth below:

Dated: _____

            [Person or Representative of Entity, with Title]

(g)* **Applications for Final Compensation in Chapter 11 Cases.** At the time of the hearing on the approval of the disclosure statement or at some later time, the Court may fix the time by which all applications for final compensation must be filed. Absent such directive, all applications for allowance of fees and expenses must be filed prior to or with the report of substantial consummation.

(1) *Estimate of Future Services.* An application for final compensation may include a reasonable estimate of the hours it is anticipated will be expended and the expenses incurred through the closing of the case. The estimate shall identify the specific tasks to be performed with an allocation of hours for each task.

(2) *Supplementary Exhibit.* Any estimate of future services and expenses shall be subject to later substantiation in the form of a supplementary exhibit, to be filed both on the return date of the hearing on the application for final compensation and with the application for final decree. The exhibit shall be filed in conformity with subparagraph (b)(4) governing professional compensation and Fed. R. Bankr. P. 2016(a). The supplementary exhibit must account for the actual services, hours and expenses which were estimated in the previously submitted application.

[Effective January 1, 2012.]

* [**Publisher's Note:** So in original.]

Comment

This Rule provides a procedure for the Court to fix final compensation of professionals in order to determine the total administrative expenses chargeable to the estate while at the same time compensate and monitor services required after confirmation through the closing of the case. Paragraph (e) is intended to clarify that professionals who are required to be appointed by the Court in order to be paid must receive Court approval of fees and expenses for services rendered during the case, before the case is closed. Failure to file the supplementary exhibit required by subparagraph (e)(2) in a timely manner may result in an order of the Court directing a party to disgorge compensation allowed on the basis of previously submitted estimates.

Compensation of auctioneers is addressed by LBR 6005–1.

The travel mileage rate changes referred to in subparagraph (c)(3)(C) of this Rule are available on the Court's website: www.nynb. uscourts.gov. Expenses specifically addressed in this Rule are not intended to be either an exclusive or exhaustive list of potentially reimbursable expenses.

RULE 2016–2. COMPENSATION OF PROFESSIONALS IN CHAPTER 13 CASE

(a) **Compensation.** In a chapter 13 case, the plan shall set forth the entire attorney's fee to be paid by or on behalf of the debtor in connection with the case including any amount paid pre-petition as a retainer and the amount to be paid through the plan. The trustee shall review the attorney's fee charged in each case and object to confirmation if the fee sought is unreasonable. Confirmation of the chapter 13 plan shall constitute Court approval of the attorney's fee. The Court may set a hearing sua sponte to review the attorney's fee requested, which may be scheduled at the same time as the confirmation hearing. By Administrative Order, the Court in each division may set a standard fee chargeable for standard legal services rendered in a chapter 13 case.

(b) **Notice to All Parties in Interest.** Notwithstanding any other provision of this Rule, if the compensation for debtor's counsel is an amount greater than one-half of the amount to be funded through the chapter 13 plan, the compensation is subject to further review and approval after notice and a hearing as provided for under Fed. R. Bankr. P. 2002(a)(6).

(c) **Fed. R. Bankr. P. 2016(b) Statement.** In addition to the disclosure requirements of Fed. R. Bankr. P. 2016(b), if counsel has represented the debtor in a prior bankruptcy case commenced within eight (8) years of the current case, any application submitted pursuant to paragraph (d) of this Rule, as well as the original 2016(b) statement, shall disclose the date of the prior filing(s) and the attorney's fees paid in connection with such prior filing(s). Unless otherwise ordered, when additional compensation for post-petition services is approved by the Court, said compensation shall be paid through the plan.

(d) **Application for Fees in Excess of Those Approved Under the Plan.** Any additional attorney's fees and expenses sought to be charged beyond those disclosed in the initial statement filed pursuant to Fed. R. Bankr. P. 2016(b) and/or approved by the confirmation order may be charged to the debtor only upon Court order, based upon prior application after notice and a hearing. The application shall disclose the fee allowed in the case to date, including amounts allowed to any prior counsel representing the debtor, the amount of allowed fees actually paid through the date of the application, and detail the specific services for which additional compensation is sought.

[Effective January 1, 2012.]

RULE 2016–3. REQUIRED SERVICES TO BE RENDERED BY DEBTOR'S ATTORNEY

(a) **Debtor Representation.** Unless otherwise ordered by the Court, an attorney representing a debtor shall be the attorney of record and represent the debtor until the case is administratively closed.

(b) **Required Attorney Duties in a Chapter 7, Chapter 12 and Chapter 13 Case.**

(1) *Retainer Agreement.* Absent special circumstances approved by the Court, an attorney representing the debtor in chapter 7, chapter 12 or chapter 13 proceeding in this district shall have a written retainer agreement that sets forth the fee arrangement and comprehensive services to be performed for the debtor in which the attorney agrees to:

(A) Analyze the client's financial situation, and advise and assist the client in determining whether to file a petition under the Bankruptcy Code;

(B) Prepare and file the petition, all required lists, schedules and statements, as well as any amendments that may be necessary or appropriate;

(C) File the certificate required from the individual debtor from an approved nonprofit budget and credit counseling agency for pre-petition credit counseling;

(D) File the debtor's payment advices together with the "Payment Advice Form" (Payment Advice Form);

(E) Appear personally and represent the debtor at any scheduled meeting of creditors under § 341, unless otherwise ordered by the Court;

(F) Amend any list, schedule, statement, and/or other document required to be filed with the petition as may be necessary or appropriate;

(G) Advise the debtor with respect to any reaffirmation agreement; negotiate, prepare and file reaffirmation agreements if in the best interest of the debtor; and attend all hearings scheduled on any reaffirmation agreement signed by the debtor;

(H) Prepare and file any motion as may be necessary or appropriate including but not limited to a motion to avoid a lien on exempt property, to obtain credit, to sell or abandon property, and to assume or reject a lease;

(I) Remove involuntary wage garnishments and/or voluntary wage assignments, as appropriate;

(J) Compile and forward to the trustee and the United States trustee any documents and information requested;

(K) Consult with the debtor and if there is a valid defense or explanation, respond to a motion for relief from the automatic stay;

(L) File the debtor's certification of completion of instructional course concerning financial management (Official Form 423);

(M) Represent the debtor in any adversary proceeding filed in the case; and

(N) Disclose any agreement and fee arrangement regarding the potential retention of co-counsel.

(2) *Chapter 7 Case.* In addition to the services identified in subparagraph (b)(1) above, and as may be needed or warranted by the facts of the case, the attorney retained in a chapter 7 case shall prepare and file a motion under § 722 to redeem exempt or abandoned personal property.

(3) *Chapter 12 and Chapter 13 Cases.* In addition to the duties identified in subparagraph (b)(1) above, and as may be needed or warranted by the facts of the case, the attorney retained in a chapter 12 or chapter 13 case shall:

(A) Attend the original and any adjourned confirmation hearing and address all objections to confirmation;

(B) Negotiate the value of secured claims or, as necessary, represent the debtor at valuation hearings in connection with the confirmation hearing;

(C) Prepare and file the necessary pleadings to partially or wholly avoid mortgage liens against the debtor's real property;

(D) Prepare necessary pre-confirmation amendments and post-confirmation modifications to the plan;

(E) Timely review all filed proofs of claim, and object to and file proofs of claim as appropriate;

(F) Oversee the filing of all operating reports in chapter 13 and any required in chapter 13;

(G) Represent the debtor in connection with motions for dismissal or conversion;

(H) File the appropriate affirmation required under Rule 4004–1(b) to permit the inference that the debtor is entitled to a discharge; and

(I) Attend any discharge hearing scheduled and address all objections to discharge.

[Effective January 1, 2012. Amended effective January 2, 2013; December 1, 2015.]

Comment

With reference to subparagraph (b)(3)(E) and the timely review of claims, practitioners are referred to LBR 3007–1(b) for the time by which claim objections are to be filed in chapter 13 cases.

RULE 2091–1. ATTORNEYS—WITHDRAWAL OTHER THAN BY SUBSTITUTION

(a) **Debtor's Attorney—Withdrawal Other Than by Substitution.** Withdrawal of an attorney who has appeared as the attorney of record for a debtor must comply with applicable rules of professional conduct. An attorney who has appeared as the attorney of record for a debtor may be relieved of representation only by order of the Court after notice and a hearing. Withdrawal may be permitted upon submission of an affidavit stating satisfactory reasons for withdrawal and a statement of the status of the case. Notice of the requested withdrawal in every instance shall be given to the debtor, the United States trustee, the trustee, any § 1104 trustee, any appointed committee, and any party having filed a notice of appearance.

(b) **Other Attorneys of Record.** Withdrawal of an attorney of record other than debtor's counsel must comply with applicable rules of professional conduct.

(1) An attorney who has appeared in a case or adversary proceeding, other than for the limited purpose of receiving notices, may be relieved of representation only by order of the Court after notice and a hearing, unless substitute counsel has made an appearance for that party. Counsel will not ordinarily be allowed to withdraw if withdrawal would delay the progress of an adversary proceeding or contested matter.

(2) An attorney who has appeared for the limited purpose of receiving notices, may be relieved of representation upon the filing of a written notice. Notice of the withdrawal shall be given to debtor's counsel or the debtor if pro se, the United States trustee, the case trustee, any § 1104 trustee, any appointed committee, and any party having filed a notice of appearance. Withdrawing counsel shall file a certificate of service in accordance with this Rule.

[Effective January 1, 2012.]

Comment

Attorneys shall be governed by applicable rules governing their practice, which for New York counsel are the New York Rules of Professional Conduct (22 NYCRR Part 1200).

RULE 2092–1. ATTORNEYS—SUBSTITUTION

(a) **Substitution.** A debtor's attorney may be substituted by order of the Court after such notice and hearing as the Court may direct. Substitution may be allowed upon submission of an affidavit stating satisfactory reasons for substitution and a statement of the status of the case, or, upon the submission of a stipulation signed by debtor(s), the attorney to be relieved, and the substituted attorney.

(b) Other Attorneys of Record. Substitution of an attorney of record other than debtor's counsel may be accomplished by providing written notice to the Court, all interested parties and any party having filed a notice of appearance. Substituted counsel shall file a certificate of service in accordance with this Rule.

[Effective January 1, 2012.]

RULE 3001-1. CLAIMS AND EQUITY SECURITY INTERESTS—ASSET CASE

In a chapter 11, 12 and 13 case, and in a chapter 7 case noticed as an asset case, an entity filing a proof of claim shall properly identify the case to which such claim relates by stating the applicable case name and number.

An amended or additional proof of claim filed after the bar date shall be served upon the trustee and upon the debtor's attorney.

[Effective January 1, 2012.]

Comment

Proper identification of the debtor estate by name and case number is essential for the Clerk to properly process a claim.

A filed claim and any documents attached thereto must not contain any personal identifiers and must comply with Fed. R. Bankr. P. 9037 and LBR 9037-1.

RULE 3001-2. CLAIMS AND EQUITY SECURITY INTERESTS—NO ASSET CASE

If a chapter 7 case is filed as a "no asset" case, pursuant to the Notice of Chapter 7 Bankruptcy Case — No Proof of Claim Deadline, no proof of claim shall be filed, unless the sole purpose for filing such proof of claim is to satisfy the requirements of § 521(a)(6). If the chapter 7 trustee determines that there are assets from which a dividend might be paid, the Clerk shall set a deadline for filing proofs of claim and issue a notice of the time to file claims, as required under Fed. R. Bankr. P.2002(f).

[Effective January 1, 2012. Amended effective December 1, 2015.]

RULE 3001-3. ELECTRONIC SUBMISSION OF PROOF OF CLAIM

Without the necessity of becoming a registered user, any claimant or the claimant's agent may utilize the feature available on the court's website for electronic submission of a proof of claim form. Any proof of claim filed electronically, using this court's website, shall have the same force and effect as if the individual signed a paper copy of the document.

[Effective January 2, 2013.]

RULE 3002-1. THIRD PARTY PROCESSING OF CLAIMS (CLAIMS AGENT)

(a) Request for Claims Agent. Upon motion, the Court may permit a third party to perform the docketing and processing of claims at the estate's expense.

(b) Docketing of Claims Via the CM/ECF System. A claims agent shall stamp the front of each claim with the date received, scan the claim and supporting documentation to PDF format, and docket the claim using the CM/ECF system. Claims shall be docketed by the claims agent within twenty-four (24) hours of receipt.

(c) Transfer of Claims. A claims agent shall process all transfer of claims forms and provide notice of the transfer as required by Fed. R. Bankr. P. 3001(e). A claims agent shall give notice of the filing of a claim in the name of a creditor by a debtor or trustee as required by Fed. R. Bankr. P. 3004.

(d) Retention of Original Claims. The claims agent shall retain all original claims until the case is closed unless the Court orders otherwise. Upon the closing of a case, the Court may direct the claims agent to transmit claims to the Federal Records Center for archiving.

[Effective January 1, 2012.]

RULE 3007-1. CLAIMS AND OBJECTIONS TO CLAIMS

(a) Time for Service of Objections to Claims. Objections to all claims must be served upon the claimant not later than 30 days prior to the hearing.

(b) Service of Objections to Claims. In addition to the service required by Fed. R. Bankr. P. 7004 and 9014, a claim objection must be served upon the claimant at the address (and in care of the individual) designated in Box 3 on the proof of claim (Official Form 410) and a certificate of service must be filed.

(c) Claim Objections in Chapter 11 Cases. Unless the Court orders otherwise, objections to claims in a chapter 11 case must be filed and served not later than fourteen (14) days after the entry of an order of confirmation.

(d) Claim Objections in Chapter 12 and 13 Cases. Unless the Court orders otherwise, objections to claims in a chapter 12 and 13 case must be filed and served within forty-five (45) days of the trustee's service of the "Notice of Claims Filed and of Trustee's Intent to Pay Claims as Listed." The trustee shall file the Notice of Claims Filed and of Trustee's Intent to Pay Claims as Listed.

(e) Objection to Additional or Amended Claim. Unless the Court orders otherwise, if an amended claim is filed or a claim is filed pursuant to LBR 3001-1, objections must be filed and served within forty-five (45) days of service by the trustee of the Notice of Additional or Amended Claim.

(f) Secured Claims. An entity holding an allowed secured claim that obtains relief from the automatic stay in a chapter 13 case shall not continue to receive the payments provided for in the confirmed plan once the trustee receives the order granting the relief. Funds to be distributed by the trustee on the allowed claim may recommence only upon the consent of the parties or upon application and order of the Court.

(g) Amended Secured Claims. The affected creditor referred to in paragraph (f) of this Rule shall retain the right to file an amended claim. The amended claim shall state:

(1) The date and terms of the disposition of the collateral;

(2) The name of the transferee of the collateral;

(3) The consideration received; and

(4) A detail of all charges claimed in retaking, holding, and disposing of the property.

[Effective January 1, 2012. Amended effective December 1, 2015.]

Comment

Paragraph (c) of this Rule sets a date by which objections to claims must be filed in chapter 11 cases in order to expedite the resolution of administrative matters remaining after confirmation. In many chapter 11 cases, a plan proponent should and will file objections to claims earlier and well in advance of confirmation in order to have objections resolved prior to confirmation.

RULE 3012–1. VALUATION OF COLLATERAL

Unless the Court orders otherwise, within fourteen (14) days of a written request by a party in interest, the debtor must make available any item of personalty for appraisal. The appraisal shall be conducted at the debtor's residence or place of business absent agreement of the parties. It shall be the affirmative duty of the debtor to contact the party in interest requesting the appraisal to arrange for the appraisal or to seek a protective order.

[Effective January 1, 2012. Amended effective January 2, 2013.]

RULE 3015–1. CHAPTER 13—PLAN

(a) Format of Plan. A debtor shall file a chapter 13 plan using the Model Plan.*

(b) Notice of Plan and the Time Fixed for Filing Objections to and the Hearing to Consider Confirmation of Chapter 13 Plan.

(1) *Plan Filed With Petition.* If the plan is filed with the petition, the Bankruptcy Noticing Center shall furnish copies of the plan to all parties in interest and notice the time fixed for filing objections to and the hearing to consider confirmation of the plan.

(2) *Plan Filed After Petition.* If the plan is filed after the petition, the debtor shall serve a copy of the plan and Notice of Time Fixed for Filing Objections To and the Hearing to Consider Confirmation of Chapter 13 Plan upon all parties in interest not later than 28 days prior to the confirmation hearing and, if necessary, adjourn the hearing date to provide the requisite 28 days' notice. Not later than seven (7) days prior to the confirmation hearing, the debtor shall file a certificate of service evidencing compliance with this Rule.

(c) Inclusion in Plan of Relief Governed by Fed. R. Bankr. P. 7001 (Adversary Proceeding) or Fed. R. Bankr. P. 9014 (Contested Matter).

(1) *Allowed Contested Matters.* If a plan includes a provision for relief that is governed by Fed. R. Bankr. P. 7001 or Fed. R. Bankr. P. 9014, such relief shall be obtained by separate adversary proceeding or motion except to the extent the plan proposes to do any of the following:

(A) Value collateral to establish the amount of a secured claim;

(B) Set the interest rate for a secured claim; or

(C) Assume and/or reject an unexpired lease or executory contract, each of which shall be deemed an "Allowed Contested Matter".

(2) *Notice Required If Plan Includes Allowed Contested Matter.* If the plan includes an Allowed Contested Matter as set forth in subparagraph (c)(1), a copy of the plan and Notice of Time Fixed for Filing Objections To and the Hearing to Consider Confirmation of Chapter 13 Plan must be served on all affected creditors by the debtor pursuant to Fed. R. Bankr. P. 7004. The Debtor shall promptly file a certificate of service evidencing compliance with the Rule but in no event later than seven (7) days prior to the confirmation hearing.

(d) Certification of Compliance With This Rule. The debtor shall certify in all cases proper notice and service in compliance with this Rule by filing, not later than fourteen (14) days prior to the confirmation hearing, a Certification Pursuant to Local Bankruptcy Rule 3015–1.

(e) Disbursement of § 1326 Payments.

(1) The debtor shall commence making plan payments to the trustee within thirty (30) days after the order for relief or the order converting the case to chapter 13. Said payment shall include the amounts necessary to pay pre-confirmation adequate protection payments plus the statutory trustee's fees. The debtor shall not reduce plan payments to the trustee under § 1326(a)(1)(C) as a result of these adequate protection payments, without an order of the Court.

(2) A creditor may file a motion requesting a change in the amount of § 1326(a)(1) pre-confirmation payments pursuant to § 1326(a)(3). Until the creditor's motion is resolved, the trustee shall continue to make pre-confirmation adequate protection payments to such creditor as set forth herein.

(3) The trustee is authorized to pay adequate protection to a secured creditor whose claim is secured by personal property pursuant to § 1326(a)(1) in an amount as set forth in the proposed plan. If the plan does not propose any such payment, then the trustee shall remit on a monthly basis to such creditor an amount equal to 1.5% of the value of the claim proposed to be paid by the debtor through the plan up until confirmation. However, no such payments shall be made to a creditor until a proof of claim is filed. Pre-confirmation adequate protection payments shall be made to the creditors with the trustee's first monthly disbursement within thirty (30) days of the filing of the proof of claim. At the time of such payments, the trustee is authorized to retain an administrative fee for effecting the payments described herein and shall collect such fee at the time of making the payment from the funds on hand with the trustee. The allowed fee shall be equal to the percentage fee established by the Attorney General pursuant to 28 U.S.C. § 586(e)(1)(B) in effect at the time

of disbursement. The trustee shall apply each § 1326(a)(1) pre-confirmation payment to the principal outstanding on the creditor's claim.

(4) If the case is dismissed prior to confirmation, the creditor shall receive from the trustee any § 1326 pre-confirmation adequate protection payment due and owing from funds collected by the trustee under § 1326(a)(1)(A), less statutory trustee fees and specifically allowed § 503(b) claims, including debtor's attorney fees.

[Effective January 1, 2012. Amended effective January 2, 2013.]

* [**Publisher's Note:** For a copy of the Chapter 13 Model Plan, *see* Selected Local Forms, *post.*]

Comment

The debtor is responsible for ensuring that notice of the plan, the time fixed for filing objections, and the hearing to consider confirmation of the plan be given in accordance with § 342(c)(2), as applicable, regardless of whether the plan is filed with or after the petition.

Paragraph (c) recognizes that it is inappropriate and may be considered bad faith to include as a plan provision relief that should be the subject of a separate adversary proceeding or motion. *See United Student Aid Funds, Inc. v. Espinosa*, 130 S. Ct. 1367, 1382 (2010) (referring to a plan provision that discharged a student loan).

RULE 3015–2. CHAPTERS 12 AND 13—OBJECTIONS TO CONFIRMATION

(a) Service of Objection. An objection to confirmation must be filed and served on the debtor, debtor's attorney, and the trustee not later than seven (7) days before the scheduled hearing on confirmation.

(b) Appearance Required Upon Objection. If an objection is filed, all parties or their counsel shall be present at the confirmation hearing. If the objecting creditor or creditor's counsel fails to appear at the confirmation hearing, the Court may treat the objecting party's absence as a waiver of the objection. If debtor's counsel fails to appear, the Court may deny confirmation.

(c) Required Contents. An objection to confirmation shall:

(1) Specify the number and letter section(s) of the Bankruptcy Code upon which the objection is grounded;

(2) Allege the specific facts that support the objections;

(3) Summarize the creditor's claim(s) against the debtor, including the alleged classification(s) (secured, unsecured, priority or administrative) and the amount of the claim(s); and

(4) Include within the case caption a reference to the document number of the plan or amended plan that is the subject of the objection.

(d) Separate Pleading Required. Objections to confirmation may not be combined with any motion seeking affirmative relief. Nothing within this Rule shall be deemed to limit or constrain the Court's authority to issue orders it deems appropriate at the time of a confirmation hearing.

[Effective January 1, 2012.]

RULE 3015–3. CHAPTERS 12 AND 13—SUBMISSION AND SERVICE OF CONFIRMATION ORDER

(a) Preparation of Confirmation Order. The Order of Confirmation shall be prepared and submitted by the trustee within sixty (60) days of the final hearing on confirmation, unless otherwise ordered by the Court.

(b) Service of Confirmation Order. The trustee shall serve the Order of Confirmation by regular first-class mail upon the debtor and any other interested party who makes a written request for service.

[Effective January 1, 2012. Amended effective January 1, 2014.]

RULE 3015–4. CHAPTERS 12 AND 13—MODIFICATION TO PLAN PRIOR TO AND AFTER CONFIRMATION

(a) Modification of Plan Prior to Confirmation.

(1) *Format.* A debtor seeking to modify a pan prior to confirmation shall use the Model Plan and check the box in the caption to indicate the Chapter 13 Plan is "Amended" (the "Amended Plan") and provide the date thereof.

(2) *Procedure.* The Amended Plan shall be filed and served on the trustee, the United States trustee, and all creditors that are being detrimentally affected by the proposed modification. The Amended Plan shall be served with Notice of Time Fixed for Filing Objections To and the Hearing to Consider Confirmation of Chapter 13 Plan not later than 28 days prior to the hearing. Not later than seven (7) days prior to the hearing, the debtor shall file a certificate of service evidencing compliance with this Rule.

(3) *Objections to an Amended Plan.* An objection to confirmation of an Amended plan must be filed and served on the debtor, debtor's attorney, and the trustee not later than seven (7) days prior to the confirmation hearing.

(b) Modification of Plan After Confirmation.

(1) *Format.* A debtor seeking to modify a plan after confirmation (the "Modified Plan") does not need to use the Model Plan. The Modified Plan shall set forth only those terms of the confirmed Chapter 13 plan that the proponent seeks to modify.

(2) *Procedure.* A Court order is required to modify a confirmed plan. A debtor, trustee, or holder of an allowed unsecured claim seeking to modify a confirmed plan shall:

(a) File the Modified Plan;

(b) File a notice of motion and a motion to modify confirmed plan;

(c) Serve the notice of motion on all creditors, and serve the notice of motion and motion to modify plan on the trustee, the debtor, and, if the debtor is not the movant, the debtor's attorney; and

(d) File a certificate of service not later than seven (7) days prior to the return date of the motion.

(3) *Notice of Motion.* The notice of motion to modify confirmed plan shall include the following disclosures:

(a) A clear statement of the proposed modification, with specific reference to the provisions of the previously filed plan that are being modified;

(b) Any change in the dividend to be paid to unsecured creditors, indicating the specific percentage change in the dividend;

(c) Any change in the time for the final payment under the plan;

(d) Any change in the plan payment;

(e) Any effect on the specific treatment of secured creditors under the plan; and

(f) The exact reasons for the modification, including specific and detailed changes in the budget of the debtor, or other circumstances of the debtor that would justify the modification.

(4) *Proposed Order Modifying Confirmed Plan.* Any proposed order that modifies a confirmed plan shall be captioned Order Modifying Confirmed Plan and must include the modified terms of the plan as requested in the motion to modify confirmed plan as approved by the Court.

[Effective January 1, 2012. Amended effective January 2, 2013; January 1, 2014.]

RULE 3015–5. CHAPTER 13—ADMINISTRATION OF PAYROLL DEDUCTION ORDER

(a) **Implementation of Payroll Deduction Order.** A proposed payroll deduction order shall be prepared and uploaded by the debtor's attorney or the trustee. A payroll deduction order shall contain the debtor's name, case number, redacted social security number (last four digits), employer's name, employer's address, the amount of the deduction, and the address where plan payments should be sent.

(b) **Termination of Payroll Deduction Order.** Upon completion of a plan, the debtor's attorney or the trustee shall prepare and upload a "cease deduction order."

(c) **New or Amended Payroll Deduction Order.** If the debtor changes employment, the debtor's attorney or the trustee shall prepare and upload a "cease deduction order" and then a new payroll deduction order. If there is an approved modification to the plan that changes the amount of the current payroll deduction, the debtor's attorney or trustee shall prepare and upload an amended payroll deduction order, which shall be clearly marked "amended" and that references, by document number within the order title, the original payroll deduction order being amended.

[Effective January 1, 2012.]

RULE 3016–1. CHAPTER 11—PLAN

Except in a case where the debtor is an individual, the jurisdictional statement in a chapter 11 plan shall provide that the Court will retain jurisdiction until there is substantial consummation of the plan. The Court may find a plan to be substantially consummated at the time the first payment is made pursuant to the plan if the other conditions of § 1101(2) are satisfied.

[Effective January 1, 2012.]

RULE 3016–2. DISCLOSURE STATEMENT

The first page of a proposed disclosure statement submitted for Court approval shall contain the following language, or words of similar import, in boldface type:

THIS IS NOT A SOLICITATION OF ACCEPTANCE OR REJECTION OF THE PLAN. ACCEPTANCE OR REJECTION MAY NOT BE SOLICITED UNTIL A DISCLOSURE STATEMENT HAS BEEN APPROVED BY THE BANKRUPTCY COURT AS CONTAINING ADEQUATE INFORMATION. THIS DISCLOSURE STATEMENT IS BEING SUBMITTED FOR APPROVAL BUT HAS NOT BEEN APPROVED BY THE COURT.

[Effective January 1, 2012.]

RULE 3017–1. AMENDED DISCLOSURE STATEMENT—CONDITION OF APPROVAL

(a) **Amended Disclosure Statement.** The amended disclosure statement, along with a redlined version showing changes to the last filed disclosure statement, shall be filed and served on the United States trustee and other parties in interest, with copies provided to chambers.

(b) **Condition of Approval.** Except for good cause shown, no order shall be entered approving the disclosure statement unless all operating statements have been filed and served pursuant to Fed. R. Bankr. P. 2015(a)(3) and LBR 2015–2.

(c) **Plan in Small Business Case Intended to Operate as Disclosure Statement.** If the proponent of a plan in a small business case (see § 101(51C)) intends the plan to jointly serve as the disclosure statement, paragraphs (a) and (b) of this Rule shall apply to any amendments of the plan.

[Effective January 1, 2012.]

RULE 3018–1. BALLOTS—VOTING ON CHAPTER 11 PLAN

(a) **Filing and Review.** Creditors and equity security holders shall return a Ballot for Accepting or Rejecting Plan (Official Form 314) to the plan proponent who shall retain the ballots and make them available for review, upon request, by any party in interest.

(b) **Certification.** At least seven (7) days prior to the hearing on confirmation, the plan proponent shall file a written certification of the amount and number of allowed claims or allowed interests of each class accepting or rejecting the plan, in accordance with § 1126. The ballots must be filed as an exhibit to the certification. The certification shall be served by the plan proponent upon the debtor, § 1104 trustee, if any, the United States trustee, and any committee. If an issue is raised as to the proponent's compliance with § 1126, the Court may hold an evidentiary hearing prior to any confirmation hearing.

(c) Failure to File Certification and Ballots. Failure to timely comply with paragraph (b) of this Rule is cause for the Court to adjourn the hearing on confirmation.

[Effective January 1, 2012. Amended effective December 1, 2015.]

RULE 3020–1. CHAPTER 11—CONFIRMATION OF A PLAN

(a) Objection to Confirmation. An objection to confirmation of a chapter 11 plan shall be served and filed not later than seven (7) days prior to the first date set for the confirmation hearing, unless otherwise ordered by the Court.

(b) Withdrawal of Objection. If an objection to confirmation of a chapter 11 plan is withdrawn or abandoned, the Court may deny confirmation of the plan unless the plan's proponent, or its counsel, states on the record or by affidavit the consideration promised or given, if any, directly or indirectly, for the withdrawal or abandonment of the objection.

(c) Motion to Confirm by "Cram–Down." If the plan proponent intends to seek confirmation of the plan as to one (1) or more classes pursuant to § 1129(b), the proponent shall file and serve upon the member or members of such class or classes, not less than seven (7) days prior to the confirmation hearing, notice of its intent to seek confirmation of the plan as to such class or classes pursuant to § 1129(b). Such notice shall be accompanied by an affidavit setting forth the facts and circumstances necessary to establish that the plan's treatment of such class or classes complies with the applicable provisions of § 1129(b).

[Effective January 1, 2012.]

RULE 3021–1. CHAPTER 11—AFFIDAVIT OF POST–CONFIRMATION DISBURSEMENTS

(a) Filing Requirements. The plan proponent or the disbursing agent defined by the plan or designated by the Court shall file and serve upon the United States trustee an affidavit reporting all cash disbursements for each month after confirmation of the plan, until such time provided in paragraph (b) of this Rule, unless the Court orders otherwise.

(b) Time for Filing. The affidavit shall be filed on the 20th of the month following the reported month. Unless the Court orders otherwise, the duty to file the monthly affidavit shall cease upon entry of the final decree pursuant to Fed R. Bankr. P. 3022, the conversion of the case to another chapter, or the dismissal of the case.

(c) Contents. The monthly affidavit shall disclose all disbursements, including but not limited to:

(1) The total amount of payments made for the reported month pursuant to the plan, with a subtotal of payments for each class defined within the plan, and a statement explaining whether the total amount paid to the class complies with the terms of the plan, whether the amount paid was in a lesser amount, or whether there is a good faith dispute about the amount owed;

(2) The administrative expenses paid; and

(3) The total of cash disbursements made.

[Effective January 1, 2012.]

Comment

The filing requirements of paragraph (a) of this Rule should be satisfied through the filing of Debtor's Post–Confirmation Quarterly Report, as provided by the United States trustee and made available at www.justice.gov/ust/r02.

RULE 3022–1. CHAPTER 11—FINAL REPORT AND MOTION FOR A FINAL DECREE

(a) Report of Substantial Consummation in Chapter 11 Case. The plan proponent shall file a report of substantial consummation that provides a basis for the Court to find that the plan proponent has satisfied the criteria of § 1101(2).

(1) *Motion for Final Decree.* The report of substantial consummation shall be accompanied by a motion for a final decree on notice to all creditors and parties in interest. Unless the Court orders otherwise, the final report, a proposed final decree, the cancelled checks, (or other evidence of payment in a form ordinarily provided by the payor's bank) representing the distributions made pursuant to the confirmed plan, and the supplementary exhibit to the application for final compensation required by LBR 2016–1 are not required to be served with the motion, but must be filed. In an individual chapter 11 case, the motion shall include the certification referenced in paragraph (c) of this Rule.

(2) *Final Decree.* Based on the information received, the Court may, in its discretion, ascertain whether the case has been fully administered and entertain the entry of the proposed final decree closing the case.

(b) Time for Filing Report of Substantial Consummation in Chapter 11 Case.

(1) *Non–Individual Chapter 11 Case.* The Court may require the report of substantial consummation to be filed as early as the time that all checks have cleared as to the first payments made under the plan. In no event shall the report be filed later than 180 days after the entry of a final order confirming a plan unless the Court, for cause shown, extends the time upon motion filed and served within the 180 day period.

(2) *Individual Chapter 11 Case.* The report of substantial consummation shall be filed not later than thirty (30) days after completion of all payments under the confirmed plan.

(3) *Form of Report of Substantial Consummation in Chapter 11 Case.* Unless otherwise ordered by the Court, the final report shall be signed and sworn to or affirmed under penalties of perjury, include the proper caption, and include, without limitation, at least the following information:

1. Administrative Expenses:

Trustee Compensation (if applicable)	$ __
Attorney for Trustee Compensation (if applicable)	$ __
Attorney for the Debtor Compensation	$ __
Other Professional Compensation	$ __
All Expenses	$ __
Total Administrative Expenses	$ __

2. Percentage of claims paid: ——%
    Percentage of claims paid to general unse-   ——%
    cured creditors

(c) Required Certification in Individual Chapter 11 Case. In an individual chapter 11 case, the motion for final decree shall include a Chapter 11 Debtor's Certification that the debtor is entitled to a discharge. Any party wishing to contest the entry of a discharge must file a written objection to the entry of a discharge not later than seven (7) days prior to the return date of the motion for final decree and serve the objection on the debtor, debtor's attorney, United States trustee, and any party having filed a notice of appearance in the case. If no objection to discharge is filed, the Clerk may issue a discharge in the case.

[Effective January 1, 2012.]

RULE 4001-1. RELIEF FROM THE AUTOMATIC STAY

(a) Motion Contents Generally. A motion for relief from the automatic stay shall include the following information to the extent applicable:

(1) The factual grounds that establish standing to bring the motion;

(2) The specific statutory basis and factual grounds for relief sought, including with specificity the contractual default of the debtor;

(3) The specific description of the collateral, including, where appropriate, the vehicle identification number (VIN), make, model, serial number, street address, and recording information (including the Clerk's office volume/page number);

(4) The names and purported interests of all parties known or, discovered after reasonable investigation, who claim to have an interest in the property;

(5) The amount of the outstanding indebtedness on each lien, admissible evidence as to value of the collateral, and the basis for the valuation;

(6) Legible and complete copies of movant's note, recorded mortgage, security agreement, modification(s), and assignment(s), if any; and

(7) Evidence of perfection of the movant's lien or interest.

(b) Motions Involving Real Property in Cases Where the Debtor Is an Individual. If the movant seeks stay relief with respect to a mortgage on real property and the basis for the motion is a payment default, and the debtor has not indicated in the petition and schedules or in a plan of reorganization that the debtor intends to surrender the real property, the movant shall file, as an exhibit to the motion, a completed copy of Certification of Payment History on the Note and Mortgage Dated and Related Information. If the Certification is not required, the movant shall indicate the reason why in its motion.

(c) Objections. A debtor objecting to the secured creditor's motion shall, to the extent applicable:

(1) State with specificity those allegations of the secured creditor that the debtor disputes;

(2) Articulate the debtor's legal and factual basis for asserting that the secured creditor is not entitled to relief from stay; and

(3) Include copies of records showing proof of any payments that the secured creditor has not acknowledged as having been received on the obligation or include an explanation as to why those records are not appended and the date they will be filed. If the motion is based upon a lack of equity in the property, then the debtor shall be required to include admissible evidence of value in the response.

(d) Grounds for Denial. Upon the request of a party in interest, the Court may deny without prejudice a motion for relief from stay involving encumbered real or personal property that fails to include the items recited in paragraph (a) of this Rule and/or that fails to include a completed copy of the form required under paragraph (b) of this Rule.

(e) Failure to Support Opposition. The debtor's failure to meet the requirements set forth in paragraph (c) of this Rule constitutes cause for the Court to deny the debtor's request for additional time to produce records and grant the motion as unopposed.

(f) Surplus Proceeds. Movant shall include in the proposed order granting a motion for relief from the stay a directive that (i) the case trustee be added as a necessary party to receive notice of the report of sale and surplus money proceedings; and (ii) closure of the case shall not constitute an abandonment of the trustee's interest, if any, in any surplus proceeds.

[Effective January 1, 2012. Amended effective January 1, 2014; July 15, 2016.]

RULE 4001-2. OBTAINING CREDIT

If authority for obtaining credit or incurring debt is sought pursuant to § 364(c) or (d), notice of the motion shall expressly state whether priority over any or all administrative expenses specified in §§ 503(b) or 507(b) is sought and, to the extent readily ascertainable, those creditors specifically affected thereby.

[Effective January 1, 2012.]

RULE 4001-3. CHAPTERS 12 AND 13—OBTAINING CREDIT

(a) Application. The debtor shall make written application to the trustee for approval to incur any non-emergency consumer debt in excess of $1,500.00 that does not involve a material modification of the debtor's budget. The debtor shall not file the application.

(1) *Trustee Approval.* If approved by the trustee, the trustee shall file the approval and the application.

(2) *Trustee Denial.* If denied by the trustee, the debtor may file a motion to incur non-emergency consumer debt. The motion shall contain as an attachment the trustee's denial. If a motion is required, the motion shall be on notice to the trustee, the United States trustee, and all creditors.

[Effective January 1, 2012.]

RULE 4002–1. CHANGE OF ADDRESS OF DEBTOR AND DEBTOR'S COUNSEL

(a) If the address of the debtor changes at any time prior to closure of the case, the debtor shall immediately file with the court a Change of Address Form.

(b) If the address of debtor's counsel changes at any time prior to closure of the case, debtor's counsel shall immediately send a letter to the Court's CM/ECF Administrator that advises of the address change to the below address:

CM/ECF Administrator
United States Bankruptcy Court
James T. Foley Courthouse
445 Broadway
Suite 330
Albany, NY 12207

[Effective January 1, 2012. Amended effective February 1, 2017.]

RULE 4002–2. CHANGE OF ADDRESS OF PARTY IN INTEREST

If the address of a party in interest changes at any time prior to closure of the case, the party in interest may file a Change of Address Form with the Clerk. The notice shall contain the debtor's name, case number, the party's name, the original address given to the Clerk, and the party's complete new address.

[Effective January 1, 2012. Amended effective February 1, 2017.]

RULE 4002–3. DUTY TO MAINTAIN A VALID E–MAIL ADDRESS

(a) Valid E–Mail Address. A registered user of the CM/ECF system must maintain a valid e-mail address and promptly resolve any technical issue with the user's e-mail account.

(b) Change of E–Mail Address. A registered user must immediately update their CM/ECF user account if there is any change to their e-mail address. This may be accomplished by using the feature "Maintain Your ECF Account" found under the "Utilities Menu."

(c) Undeliverable E–Mails. The Clerk may disable a registered user's account if an e-mail is returned to the Clerk as undeliverable. Common reasons why e-mails are undeliverable include a full mailbox or a filter issue. The holder of a disabled account cannot file electronically and may be brought before the Court on an order to show cause for failing to comply with the Court's electronic filing requirements.

[Effective January 1, 2012.]

RULE 4004–1. COMPLETION OF PLAN AND ENTRY OF A CHAPTER 12 OR CHAPTER 13 DISCHARGE

(a) Trustee's Final Report. Upon completion of payments under a Chapter 12 or 13 plan, the trustee shall file a report that all payments required under the plan have been made.

(b) Debtor's Certifications.

1. *Requirement Prior to Issuance of Discharge.* In a case filed on or after October 17, 2005, within thirty (30) days of the filing of Trustee's Final Report, the debtor shall file a Chapter 12 Debtor(s) Certifications Regarding Domestic Support Obligations and §§ 522(q) and 1228 or Chapter 13 Debtor(s) Certifications Regarding Domestic Support Obligations and §§ 522(q) and 1328 under penalties of perjury as part of the necessary basis for the issuance of a discharge. If the certifications are filed prior to the Trustee's Final Report, the filing party will be notified that the filing is premature, and current certifications will need to be refiled after the Trustee's Final Report is filed.

2. *Request for Waiver of Certifications for Deceased Debtor.* Upon *ex parte* application and submission of a proposed order, the court may consider the waiver of certifications required under LBR 4004–1(b) for a deceased debtor. The *ex parte* application must be supported by a properly redacted death certificate.

(c) Discharge Hearing.

(1) *Chapter 13 Case.* Upon the timely filing of the certifications regarding domestic support obligations and §§ 522(q) and 1328 and Official Form 423—Debtor's Certification of Completion of Instructional Course Concerning Financial Management, the Clerk shall issue a Notice of Default Hearing on Request for Discharge Pursuant to § 1328. If the certifications and Official Form 423 or a motion to extend time to file are not timely filed, the Clerk may close the case without discharge and notify creditors of the same.

(2) *Chapter 12 Case.* Upon the timely filing of the certifications regarding domestic support obligations and §§ 522(q) and 1228, the Clerk shall issue a Notice of Default Hearing on Request for Discharge Pursuant to § 1228. If the certifications or a motion to extend time to file are not timely filed, the Clerk may close the case without discharge and notify creditors of the same.

(d) Objection to Entry of Discharge. Any party wishing to contest the entry of a discharge must file a written objection to the entry of a discharge not later than seven (7) days prior to the date set by the Clerk for the hearing on the Request for Discharge and serve such objection on the debtor, debtor's attorney, the trustee, the United States trustee, and any party having filed a notice of appearance. In the event no objections to discharge are filed, and the debtor is otherwise eligible to receive a discharge, the Clerk may issue a discharge in the case.

(e) Case Closed Without Discharge. If a case is closed without a discharge under paragraph (c) of this Rule, the debtor shall file a motion to reopen the case and pay a fee equal to the filing fee for a chapter 12 or 13 petition, as applicable, in order to obtain a discharge. The fee to reopen a case to obtain a discharge cannot be waived.

[Effective January 1, 2012. Amended effective January 2, 2013.]

RULE 4004–2. MOTION FOR HARDSHIP DISCHARGE

(a) Content of Motion. Motions for discharge under 11 U.S.C. § 1328(b) shall be filed with the court and served on the trustee, United States trustee, any party having filed a notice of appearance and all creditors, at least 21 days preceding the date fixed for hearing. The motion shall set forth the basis for the discharge and provide evidence in support of the motion. A copy of a proposed order shall be attached to the motion as an exhibit to the motion.

(b) Requirements Prior to Issuance of Hardship Discharge. Prior to a discharge being entered by the Court, debtor or debtors are required to file with the court the Chapter 13 Debtor(s) Certifications Regarding Domestic Support Obligations and Section 522(q) and 1328 [local form O1328C] and the Debtor's Certification of Completion of Instructional Course Concerning Financial Management [Official Form 423]. Both certifications are required for any case filed AFTER October 16, 2005, unless waived by application and an order of the court.

(c) Objections to Entry of Discharge. Any party wishing to contest the entry of a discharge must file a written objection to the entry of a discharge not later than (7) days prior to the date set by the Clerk for the hearing on the Request for Discharge and serve such objection on the debtor, debtor's attorney, the trustee, the United States trustee, and any party having filed a notice of appearance. In the event no objections to discharge are filed, and the debtor is otherwise eligible to receive a discharge, the Clerk may issue a discharge in the case.

[Effective January 1, 2014. Amended effective December 1, 2015.]

RULE 4080–1. CHAPTERS 12 AND 13—EMERGENCY REFUND OR CREDIT

(a) Written Request to Trustee. The trustee is authorized to issue an emergency refund or allow an emergency credit in a chapter 12 or 13 case from property of the estate in an amount not to exceed one monthly payment or credit per case, per year, provided that:

(1) The request for such refund or credit is in writing;

(2) The request is signed by the debtor (both debtors in a joint case) or by the debtor's counsel;

(3) Exigent circumstances support such emergency refund or credit; and

(4) The issuance of the refund or allowance of the credit will not substantially affect distributions to creditors.

(b) Form of Emergency Refund or Credit. The trustee has discretion to issue an emergency refund check or allow the debtor to forego the next monthly payment.

[Effective January 1, 1998. Amended effective January 1, 2012.]

RULE 5005–1. ELECTRONIC FILING

(a) Filing. A list, schedule, statement, proof of claim, complaint, motion, application, objection and other papers (each a "document") must be filed electronically in accordance with the Administrative Procedures, unless otherwise ordered by the court.

(b) Deficient Documents. The Clerk may issue to the filer of a document a notice of deficiency that specifies the error and contains instructions on how to correct a filing that does not conform to the Administrative Procedures.

(c) Signature. The electronic filing of a document bearing an electronic signature (example: /s/ Jane Smith) constitutes the signature of the filer under Fed. R. Bankr. P. 9011.

(d) Use of Court's Website to File an Electronic Proof of Claim (EPOC).* Any proof of claim filed electronically, using this court's website, shall have the same force and effect as if the individual signed a paper copy of the proof of claim.

(e) Use of Court's Website to Submit an Electronic Registration for CM/ECF Password. Any CM/ECF registration form submitted electronically, using this court's website, shall have the same force and effect as if the individual signed a paper copy of the registration form.

(f) Filing Fees. A filing fee is to be paid via the on-line payment program on the same day it is incurred. Failure to pay a filing fee will result in the suspension of the filer's ECF ability to electronically file documents. Said suspension will be lifted once the fee is paid.

(g) Filing in a Dismissed Case. Until an order revoking a dismissal order is entered, the only permissible filings in a dismissed case are a required filing by a trustee, an administrative filing by the Clerk and the Bankruptcy Noticing Center, and a motion to vacate or reconsider a dismissal order.

(h) Filing in a Closed Case. The only permissible filing in a closed case is a motion to reopen, unless otherwise ordered by the court.

(i) Violation. Any filings made in contravention of paragraphs (g) or (h) may be stricken sua sponte by the Court.

[Effective January 1, 2012.]

* [Publisher's Note: *See also* LBR 3001–3, *ante*.]

RULE 5005–2. ELECTRONIC CASE FILING PASSWORDS

(a) Password for Electronic Filing. A Court-issued CM/ECF password is required to file electronically. Attorneys and certain non-attorney participants are eligible to receive CM/ECF passwords. CM/ECF Training for attorneys and staff members is available upon request to CMECFTraining@nynb.uscourts.gov.

Attorney—Admitted Within District. An attorney admitted to practice in the Northern District of New York will be issued a password after submitting a completed Attorney Registration Form to the Court.

(1) *Attorney—Not Admitted in the District.* An attorney not admitted to practice in the Northern District of New York who is a registered CM/ECF user in another federal court will be issued a limited-use password after submitting a completed Attorney Registration Form to the Court.

(2) *Filing Agent.* An attorney or trustee may request multiple logins and passwords for legal staff who file as agents on their behalf. When an agent files on behalf of the attorney, the docket text displays the name of the attorney as the filer.

A filing agent may obtain a login and password by submitting a completed Filing Agent Registration Form.

(3) *Non–Attorney (Limited Use).* A creditor who is not represented by an attorney or a claims agent may obtain a limited-use password. The limited-use password may only be used to file a proof of claim, objection to claim, transfer of claim, objection to transfer of claim, request to reclassify a claim, withdrawal of a claim, notice of appearance and request for notices, reaffirmation agreement, and certificate of service. A participant will be issued a limited-use password upon submitting to the Court the appropriate Limited Use Registration Form.

(b) Submission of a Registration Form for Obtaining a Password. Registration for a CM/ECF password shall be completed electronically by submitting the appropriate registration form.

(c) Misuse of CM/ECF Account Holder. No account holder may permit his/her password to be used other than by an authorized employee of his/her firm. A CM/ECF account holder's misuse of a password will result in the suspension of CM/ECF account privileges.

(d) Misuse of Password by Non–Account Holder. A non-account holder's misuse of a password is punishable by contempt and the imposition of sanctions.

[Effective January 1, 2012. Amended effective January 2, 2013; February 1, 2017.]

Comment

Issuance of a limited-use password under subparagraph (a)(2) of this Rule is not a substitute for admission pro hac vice.

RULE 5007–1. PHOTOGRAPHY, RECORDING DEVICES AND BROADCASTING

(a) Prohibition. All photographing, oral or video tape recording, and radio or television broadcasting is prohibited in the courtroom during the progress of or in connection with judicial proceedings, whether or not Court is actually in session. None of the foregoing activities are allowed in a jury room, the office of a judge, or in any room, hallway, or corridor of the floor of the building in which a courtroom is located.

(b) Court Exception. Notwithstanding paragraph (a), the Court may permit recording of ceremonial, investiture, and educational proceedings, and the actions of its personnel while acting in an official capacity.

(c) Court Personnel Exception. Court personnel are not prohibited by this Rule from making a recording for the sole purpose of discharging their official duties. Any recording made in furtherance of those duties shall not be used for any other purposes by any other person.

[Effective January 1, 2012.]

RULE 5007–2. RECORD OF PROCEEDINGS

(a) Audio Record of Court Hearings. Digital audio recordings will be available on PACER for select hearings and trials conducted on or after March 16, 2015. The audio recording will appear on the docket as a PDF with an embedded MP3 file. It generally will be available within 48 hours after the conclusion of the subject hearing.

(b) Transcripts. The official record of any Court hearing remains the written transcript.

[Effective March 16, 2015.]

Comment

This is a pilot program; currently, the audio record of a proceeding is only available in the Syracuse Division. This technology is provided as a courtesy to document the record of the hearing and should not be treated as a substitute for a required appearance.

RULE 5010–1. REOPENING A CASE

(a) Closed Cases. The only permissible filing in a closed case is a motion to reopen.

(b) Filing Fee. A motion to reopen a case pursuant to Fed. R. Bankr. P. 5010 shall be in writing and shall be accompanied by the appropriate filing fee.

(1) *Waiver.* The Court may waive payment of the filing fee when a case is reopened to correct an administrative error or on account of actions relating to the debtor's discharge.

(2) *Deferral.* The Court may defer payment of the filing fee when a case is reopened by a trustee and there is no asset available from which to pay the filing fee. The filing fee shall be paid promptly upon the trustee's ability to do so. The trustee shall notify the Court if no assets are discovered and payment of the filing fee will be waived.

(c) Retrieval Fee. A separate retrieval fee must accompany the motion if the case has been transmitted to the Federal Records Center for storage. The retrieval fee may not be waived by the Court.

(d) Notice of Motion to Reopen. Unless the Court orders otherwise, notice of a motion to reopen shall be given to the former trustee, the United States trustee and, when the moving party is not the debtor, to the debtor and debtor's counsel. Except as provided in paragraph (e) of this Rule, a motion to reopen a case must be noticed for a hearing pursuant to LBR 9013–3.

(e) Ex Parte Relief. A motion to reopen a case may be considered ex parte if the purpose of the motion is (1) to file a debtor's certificate of completion of financial management course, (2) to correct an administrative error, (3) on account of actions relating to the debtor's discharge, or (4) to avoid a judicial lien pursuant to § 522(f).

(f) Request for Other Relief. No other relief may be requested in a closed case until the order reopening the case is entered. A motion filed in a closed case will not be acted upon and will result in a deficiency notice being issued by the Clerk.

[Effective January 1, 2012. Amended effective January 1, 2014.]

RULE 5011–1. WITHDRAWAL OF A CASE OR PROCEEDING (WITHDRAWAL OF REFERENCE)

(a) Form of Request and Place for Filing. A request for withdrawal of a case, in whole or in part, or proceeding, other than a sua sponte request by the Court, shall be by motion in accordance with LBR 9013–1. The Court may not conduct a hearing on a motion for withdrawal, but the motion should be filed with the Clerk with the appropriate fee. The fee is equal to the civil action filing fee under 28 U.S.C. § 1914(a). All such motions shall clearly and conspicuously state that: RELIEF IS SOUGHT FROM A UNITED STATES DISTRICT JUDGE under Fed. R. Bankr. P. 5011(a).

(b) Stay of Proceedings. The filing of a motion for withdrawal does not automatically stay proceedings in the Court. Any motion for a stay shall be filed in accordance with the requirements of Fed. R. Bankr. P. 5011(c).

(c) Responses to a Motions for Withdrawal. A response to a motion for withdrawal shall be filed with the Clerk and served on all interested parties within fourteen (14) days of service of the motion.

(d) Designation of Record.

(1) *Withdrawal of Bankruptcy Case.* Upon the Clerk's entry of a District Court order withdrawing a bankruptcy case, in whole or in part, the moving party shall file a list designating those portions of the record of the proceedings in the Court that the moving party believes will be reasonably necessary or pertinent. If the record designated includes a transcript of any proceeding or a part thereof, the designating party shall immediately deliver to the ECRO a written request for the transcript and make satisfactory arrangements for payment of its cost.

(2) *Withdrawal of Adversary Proceeding.* Where the District Court orders the withdrawal of an adversary proceeding, the Court shall designate the entire record of the adversary proceeding.

(e) Proceedings in District Court. After the record is transmitted to the District Clerk, documents pertaining to the matter under review by the District Court shall be filed with the District Clerk, but all documents relating to other matters in the bankruptcy case or adversary proceeding shall continue to be filed with the Clerk.

[Effective January 1, 2012.]

RULE 6004–1. SALE OF ESTATE PROPERTY

(a) Appraisal Filed With the Court Prior to Sale. The appraisal prepared by a court-appointed appraiser shall be filed not later than seven (7) days prior to the return date of the motion to approve the sale of the appraised property, unless the Court orders otherwise. Property subject to an appraisal shall not be sold until the appraisal has been filed with the Clerk and served upon the United States trustee.

(b) Access and Confidentiality of Filed Appraisal. A confidential appraisal may be submitted in paper format to the Clerk in a sealed envelope marked "CONFIDENTIAL APPRAISAL." The envelope shall also include the complete caption of the case/proceeding and identification of the property appraised. The Clerk, the United States trustee and the appraiser shall maintain the confidentiality of the appraisal, unless the Court directs otherwise.

(c) Contents of Sale Motion. In addition to the requirements set forth in LBR 6004–2(b) and LBR 6004–3(a), if applicable, a motion to sell estate property shall contain the following, unless the Court orders otherwise:

(1) A description of the property;

(2) The name and address of the buyer;

(3) The sale price, and whether the sale is an arm's-length transaction;

(4) Marketing efforts;

(5) The name of each lien holder and amount of each lien;

(6) Whether the sale is free and clear of liens and encumbrances, or is subject to liens and encumbrances;

(7) Whether the proceeds will be subject to any exemption by the debtor, and if so, the amount and nature of the exemption;

(8) The estimated benefit to be realized by the estate from the sale;

(9) That the sale is subject to higher or better offers at the hearing; and

(10) The proposed attorney's fee payable upon sale, a list and explanation of other proposed deductions from the sale proceeds, and the approximate amount of closing costs.

(d) Sale of Firearms. A motion or application to sell a firearm requiring a license shall state that the proposed purchaser holds a valid license. A sale will not be approved unless proof that the purchaser has the required license is filed with the Court.

[Effective January 1, 2012.]

RULE 6004–2. CHAPTER 11—SALE OF ESTATE PROPERTY OTHER THAN IN THE ORDINARY COURSE OF BUSINESS

(a) Sale Prior to Confirmation. In a chapter 11 case, if the debtor or trustee seeks authority to sell property of the estate under § 363(b) prior to the entry of an order of confirmation, the notice of motion shall contain a clear and conspicuous statement to that effect.

(b) Content of Notice. In addition to the information required under Fed. R. Bankr. P. 2002(c), the notice of motion to sell property of the estate under § 363(b) shall specify:

(1) The benefit to be realized by each class of creditors from the proceeds of sale;

(2) The extent of the debtor's liabilities;

(3) The estimated net value of any of the remaining assets not subject to the proposed sale; and

(4) The business justification for disposing of estate assets outside the ordinary course of business before a disclosure statement has been approved or a plan confirmed.

[Effective January 1, 2012.]

RULE 6004–3. CHAPTERS 12 AND 13—SALE OR OTHER DISPOSITION OF ESTATE PROPERTY

(a) Disposition of Real Property. The debtor shall file a motion for approval of the sale of real property after a contract of sale is procured. The motion shall be on notice to all parties in interest, all potential bidders, and the trustee. In addition to the requirements of LBR 6004–1(c), the motion shall state the following:

(1) Whether the debtor's plan has been confirmed;

(2) Whether the property is the debtor's residence;

(3) Notwithstanding LBR 6004–1, the motion shall provide an itemized valuation of all property to be sold together with the basis for each valuation and whether the property has been appraised and, if so, when, and by whom;

(4) The approximate amount of unpaid real estate taxes;

(5) The name of any realtors and the proposed real estate commission;

(6) The approximate amount of the sale proceeds to be paid into the plan; and

(7) Whether the plan provides for a sale.

(b) Exhibits. A copy of the contract shall be provided as an exhibit.

(c) Statement of Sale. The debtor shall provide the trustee with a copy of the statement of sale not later than seven (7) days after the closing of the sale. In the event the sale does not close, the debtor shall notify the trustee promptly.

(d) Fees. Fees to be paid to any professional attendant to the sale of real property including, without limitation, a real estate agent, a broker, and the debtor's real estate attorney must be approved by the Court prior to payment.

(e) Disposition of Real or Personal Property Valued at Less Than $2,500. To sell or otherwise dispose of real or personal property with a value of $2,500 or less, the debtor shall make written application to the trustee and any other creditor with a lien on the property. The debtor shall not file the application. If approved by the trustee, the debtor may dispose of or sell the property in accordance with the terms and conditions approved by the trustee. The trustee shall file the approval and application. If not approved by the trustee, the debtor may file a motion to dispose of or sell property of the estate and the motion shall contain as an attachment a copy of the trustee's denial. The motion shall be on notice to all parties in interest.

[Effective January 1, 2012.]

RULE 6005–1. APPRAISERS AND AUCTIONEERS

(a) Compensation of Auctioneers. An auctioneer shall be allowed compensation and reimbursement of expenses as follows, unless the Court orders otherwise:

(1) *Maximum Commissions.* The maximum allowable commissions are as follows:

(A) 12% of any gross proceeds of sale on the first $100,000. or less;

(B) 5.5% of any gross proceeds of sale between $100,001 and $200,000; and

(C) 2.5% of any gross proceeds of sale in excess of $200,000.

(2) *Expenses.*

(A) The auctioneer shall be reimbursed for the reasonable and necessary expenses directly related to the sale, including bond or blanket bond premium costs attributable to said sale, labor, printing, advertising and insurance, but excluding worker's compensation, social security, unemployment insurance or other payroll taxes. An auctioneer shall be reimbursed for a blanket bond at the rate of $100 per case or 10% of the gross proceeds from an auction, whichever is less, less any amounts previously reimbursed for said bond, unless the Court orders otherwise.

(B) If directed by the trustee to transport goods, the associated costs shall be reimbursable.

(b) Bond. An auctioneer employed with Court approval shall not act until a surety bond in favor of the United States of America is provided in each estate, at the auctioneer's expense. The bond shall be approved by the Court and shall be in an amount sufficient to cover the aggregate appraised value of all property to be sold, or in such sum as may be fixed by the Court, conditioned upon:

(1) The faithful and prompt accounting for all monies and property which may come into the possession of the auctioneer;

(2) Compliance with all rules, orders, and decrees of the Court; and

(3) The faithful performance of duties in all respects in all cases in which the auctioneer may act.

(c) Report of Sale. The auctioneer shall file a report with the Clerk and serve the United States trustee within thirty (30) days after conclusion of the sale. The report of sale shall set forth:

(1) The time, date and place of sale;

(2) The gross amount realized by the sale;

(3) An itemized statement of commissions sought under this Rule and disbursements made, including the name of the payee and the original receipts or cancelled checks, or copies thereof, substantiating the disbursements. Where labor charges are included, the report shall specify the name(s) of the person(s) employed, the hourly wage, and the number of hours worked by each person. If the cancelled checks are not available at the time the report is filed, then the report shall so state, and the cancelled checks shall be filed as soon as they become available;

(4) Where the auctioneer has a blanket insurance policy covering all sales conducted for which original receipts and cancelled checks are not available, an explanation of how the insurance expense charged to the estate was allocated;

(5) The names of all purchasers at the sale;

(6) The sign-in sheet, indicating the number of people attending the sale;

(7) The disposition of any items for which there were no bid;

(8) The terms and conditions of sale read to the audience immediately prior to the commencement of the sale;

(9) A statement of the manner and extent of advertising the sale and the availability of the items for inspection prior to the sale;

(10) The amount of sales tax collected; and

(11) Such other information as the Court may require.

(d) Proceeds of Sale. Unless the Court orders otherwise, the proceeds of sale less the auctioneer's reimbursable expenses, shall be turned over to the trustee as soon as practicable and not later than twenty-one (21) days from the date of sale or shall be deposited in a separate interest-bearing account. The Court retains the jurisdiction to review the auctioneer's reimbursable expenses for reasonableness. In the event the Court determines that a portion of the expenses deducted from the proceeds of the sale are unreasonable, the auctioneer shall be required to return those funds to the trustee.

(e) Application for Commissions and Expenses. An auctioneer shall apply to the Court for approval of commissions and expenses on not less than twenty-one (21) days' notice as required by Fed. R. Bankr. P. 2002 and in conformance with LBR 2002–1. No such application shall be granted unless the report referred to in paragraph (c) has been filed.

(f) Purchase Prohibited by Auctioneer, Appraiser, and/or Agent. An auctioneer or officer, director, stockholder, agent, or employee of an auctioneer shall not purchase directly or indirectly, or have a financial interest in, the purchase of any property of the estate which the auctioneer has been employed to sell. Likewise, an appraiser or officer, director, stockholder, agent, or employee of an appraiser shall not purchase directly or indirectly, or have a financial interest in, the purchase of any property of the estate that the appraiser has been employed to appraise.

[Effective January 1, 2012.]

RULE 6007–1. ABANDONMENT OR DISPOSITION OF DEBTOR'S BOOKS, RECORDS AND PAPERS

(a) Available Options. Unless the Court orders otherwise, the trustee, subject to applicable non-bankruptcy law, may

(1) Place in storage, at the expense of the estate, the debtor's books, records, and papers;

(2) Return the debtor's books, records, and papers to the debtor or its principal(s) after issuance of the final decree; or

(3) Dispose of all the debtor's books, records, and papers in the trustee's possession, after issuance of the final decree, provided that the debtor's books, records, and papers are first offered to the debtor.

(b) Privacy Protection. Any trustee disposing of a debtor's books, records, and papers shall redact and/or shred any confidential and/or personal information including, but not limited to billing records, medical records, social security numbers, tax identification numbers, and financial account numbers.

[Effective January 1, 2012.]

RULE 7003–1. ADVERSARY PROCEEDING COVER SHEET

A complaint filed to commence an adversary proceeding shall be accompanied by an Adversary Proceeding Cover Sheet (Official Form 1040).

[Effective January 1, 1998. Amended effective January 1, 2012; December 1, 2015.]

RULE 7004–1. SUMMONS

(a) Issuance of Summons. Upon the filing of an adversary complaint or a third party complaint, the summons will be automatically generated and docketed through the CM/ECF system. The plaintiff shall be responsible for printing the summons and serving it pursuant to Fed. R. Bankr. P. 7004. In the case of multiple defendants the plaintiff shall be responsible for making such duplicate copies of the summons as are necessary to effect service.

(b) Reissuance of Summons. If a party fails to effect service of the summons within seven (7) days of its issuance as required by Fed. R. Bankr. P. 7004, the Clerk shall reissue a summons upon written request.

[Effective January 1, 2012. Amended effective May 12, 2017.]

Comment

A complaint should be filed electronically. The CM/ECF system will electronically transmit the summons to the filer. If a complaint is filed in paper format by a pro se filer, an unregistered user of the CM/ECF system, or a registered user who is unable to utilize the CM/ECF system, the Clerk will generate the summons and provide it to the filer electronically, by mail, or by personal delivery if the filer is present in the Clerk's office at the time of issuance.

RULE 7016–1. PRE–TRIAL PROCEDURES

Insofar as Fed. R. Civ. P. 16(b), made applicable in adversary proceedings by Fed. R. Bankr. P. 7016, mandates a scheduling order and describes its contents, it shall not be applicable to adversary proceedings or contested matters in this district.

[Effective January 1, 2012.]

Comment

The Court will issue pretrial orders, as appropriate. This Rule should be read in conjunction with LBR 7026–1.

RULE 7026–1. DISCOVERY—GENERAL

(a) Required Disclosure. The initial disclosures required under Fed. R. Civ. P. 26(a)(1), (2), and (3), made applicable in adversary proceedings by Fed. R. Bankr. P. 7026, shall be operative unless the Court orders otherwise.

(b) Meeting of Parties. The provisions of Fed. R. Civ. P. 26(d) and (f), made applicable in adversary proceedings by Fed. R. Bankr. P. 7026, insofar as they mandate an actual meeting of the parties twenty-one (21) days before a scheduling conference, require the submission of a written report, and prohibit a party from seeking discovery from any source prior to any such meeting, shall not apply to a contested matter or adversary proceeding, unless the Court orders otherwise.

[Effective January 1, 2012.]

Comment

This provision permits the Court to limit the provisions of Fed. R. Civ. P. 26, as made applicable in adversary proceedings by Fed. R. Bankr. P. 7026, on a case by case basis.

This Rule should be read in conjunction with LBR 7016–1.

RULE 7026–2. DISCOVERY MOTIONS

(a) Required Affidavit. No discovery motion shall be heard by the Court unless counsel for the movant files a supporting affidavit certifying that counsel for the movant has conferred with counsel for the opposing party in a good faith effort to resolve by agreement the issues raised by the motion and that counsel have been unable to reach such an agreement.

(b) Partial Resolution. If one or more of the issues have been resolved by agreement prior to the return date of the motion, movant's counsel shall file a supplemental affidavit that identifies the issues so resolved and the issues that remain unresolved.

[Effective January 1, 2012.]

RULE 7040–1. TRIAL EXHIBITS

(a) Exhibits to Be Offered. Except as otherwise ordered by the Court or as directed by the Court's scheduling order, three (3) sets of all exhibits (original and two (2) copies) to be offered into evidence must be submitted to the Court in hard copy.

(b) Retention and Return. Unless otherwise ordered by the Court, the original exhibits from a trial or evidentiary hearing shall be retained by the Clerk until such time as a decision or verdict has been rendered and expiration of the time allowed for an appeal or, if an appeal is filed, after the appeal is adjudicated. Exhibits shall thereafter be available for return, pick up or destruction. The Court will contact the party who introduced the exhibits for their instruction.

[Effective January 1, 2012.]

RULE 7040–2. ADJOURNMENT OF TRIAL AND EVIDENTIARY HEARING

An adjournment of a trial or evidentiary hearing shall not be granted, except upon a showing to the Court of exceptional circumstances. Any such request shall be filed electronically and indicate whether all parties have consented. For cases assigned to the Albany division, the request shall also be faxed to Chambers.

[Effective January 1, 2012.]

RULE 7041–1. DISMISSAL OF ADVERSARY PROCEEDING BROUGHT PURSUANT TO 11 U.S.C. § 727

(a) Voluntary Dismissal. An adversary proceeding commenced pursuant to § 727 shall be dismissed only upon Court approval.

(b) Obtaining Court Approval. Court approval of the voluntary dismissal is conditioned upon full disclosure as to the circumstances of the dismissal, including the terms of any agreement entered into between the parties. If the action is not dismissed in the presence of the Court on the record, then plaintiff shall file a proposed order of dismissal accompanied by a stipulation fully disclosing the circumstances of the dismissal and any consideration promised to be given, directly or indirectly, for the dismissal of the action. The Court may, alternatively, direct the defendant to prepare and file the stipulation required by this Rule.

(c) Notice. Notice of the proposed voluntary dismissal shall be given to the trustee, the United States trustee, and such other persons as the Court may direct.

[Effective January 1, 2012.]

Comment

This Rule shall apply without regard to whether a dispute is settled through mediation.

RULE 7055–1. DEFAULT JUDGMENT

(a) Default Judgment Application Deadline. A plaintiff entitled to a default judgment due to defendant's failure to answer, appear, or otherwise defend the action, must file the appropriate application for default judgment within forty-five days after the first day plaintiff is entitled to entry of default. Failure to seek a default judgment within forty-five (45) days after default occurs may result in the Court dismissing the adversary proceeding pursuant to Fed. R. Bankr. P. 7041.

(b) Clerk's Entry of Default. Prior to filing an application for default judgment, the party seeking default judgment shall obtain the Clerk's Entry of Default by filing an affidavit containing sufficient factual allegations to determine the following:

(1) The summons and complaint have been timely and properly served on the defaulting party as required by Fed. R. Bankr. P. 7004;

(2) An accurate and complete certificate of service has been filed and a copy included as an exhibit to the affidavit;

(3) The defaulting party is not an infant, an incompetent person, nor in the military service (see comment); and

(4) The defaulting party has failed to plead or otherwise defend the action.

(c) Obtaining a Default Judgment From the Clerk. The Clerk may enter a default judgment if the defaulting party is not the debtor, the underlying action is a core proceeding and the default judgment is for a sum certain and does not include a request for attorney's fees or other substantive relief. A party seeking entry of a default judgment by the Clerk must file the following:

(1) An affidavit of the amount due and the basis for the same;

(2) A copy of the Clerk's Entry of Default; and

(3) A proposed judgment for signature by the Clerk.

(d) Obtaining a Default Judgment From the Court.

(1) *Core Proceeding.* Where the adversary proceeding is a core proceeding, a party seeking entry of default judgment by the Court shall file:

(A) A motion for default judgment;

(B) An affidavit under Fed. R. Civ. P. 55(b)(2), made applicable by Fed. R. Bankr. P. 7055;

(C) A copy of the Clerk's Entry of Default;

(D) An affidavit of amount due including a statement of the damages being requested and the basis for them;

(E) A proposed order granting the motion for judgment by default;

(F) A proposed judgment, if applicable, for signature by the Court; and

(G) If the party against whom a default judgment is sought has appeared in the proceeding or is the debtor, an affidavit of service indicating notice of the motion was provided to the defaulting party as required by Fed. R. Bankr. P. 9014.

(2) *Non–Core Proceeding.* Where the adversary proceeding is a non-core proceeding, plaintiff may seek a Recommendation from the Court to the District Court that a default judgment be entered by filing the following:

(A) An affidavit under Fed. R. Civ. P. 55(b)(2), made applicable by Fed. R. Bankr. P. 7055;

(B) A copy of the Clerk's Entry of Default;

(C) An affidavit of amount due including a statement of the damages being requested and the basis for them;

(D) A proposed order transmitting record to District Court, combined with the finding that the complaint has been properly served and the time within which to answer or other respond has passed and no pleading has been filed and that it is recommended that the Default Judgment enter default judgment;

(E) A proposed order granting the motion for judgment by default for signature by the District Court; and

(F) A proposed judgment, if applicable, for signature by the District Court.

[Effective January 1, 2012.]

Comment

Securing a default judgment is a two-step process. A party seeking a default judgment must follow (1) the procedure outlined in paragraph (b) of this Rule, and then (2) either the procedure outlined in paragraphs (c) or (d) of this Rule.

In his discretion or where entry of default judgment by the Clerk is not permissible, the Clerk may present any application for default judgment to the Court for its consideration.

Through use of the following website, the U.S. Department of Defense will advise either that it does possess information regarding whether an individual is on active duty, or it does not possess information indicating that the individual is or was on active duty:

http://www.dmdc.osd.mil/appj/scra/scraHome.do

RULE 7056-1.   SUMMARY JUDGMENT

(a) Motion for Summary Judgment. A summary judgment motion under Fed. R. Bankr. P. 7056 shall include a separate, concise statement, in numbered paragraphs, of the material facts as to which the moving party contends there is no genuine issue, supported by specific citations to the record.

(b) Memorandum in Support. The moving party shall file with the motion a memorandum of law that cites all authorities upon which the party relies. The memorandum must disclose all controlling authorities, including those contrary to movant's position.

(c) Response. The papers opposing the motion shall include a separate, concise statement, in numbered paragraphs, of each material fact as to which the opposing party contends there is a genuine issue, supported by specific citations to the record. The Court may deem admitted each material fact set forth in the statement served by the moving party if not controverted by the statement served by the opposing party.

(d) Memorandum in Opposition. The respondent shall file with its opposition to the motion a memorandum of law that cites all authorities upon which the respondent relies. The memorandum must disclose all controlling authorities, including those contrary to respondent's position.

(e) Grounds for Denial of Motion. The Court may deny the motion for summary judgment if the moving party fails to comply with the requirements of this Rule.

[Effective January 1, 2012.]

Comment

Syracuse division only: All motions for summary judgment shall be set by the Court. CM/ECF will prompt a filer of a motion for summary judgment to contact the Court's courtroom deputy for a hearing date.

RULE 7067-1.   REGISTRY FUND

a. Deposits in Court. No money shall be sent to the Court or to the Clerk of the Court for deposit into the Court's registry without a court order signed by the presiding judge. Unless provided for elsewhere in this Rule, all money ordered to be paid into the Court or received by the Clerk of the Court in any case pending or adjudicated shall be deposited with the Treasury of the United States in the name and to the credit of this Court pursuant to 28 U.S.C. § 2041 through institutions that the Treasury has designated to accept such deposit on its behalf. The party making the deposit or transferring funds to the Court's registry shall serve the Clerk of the Court with the Order permitting the deposit or transfer.

b. Order Directing the Investment of Funds. The Clerk of the Court or his designee shall place the funds on deposit with the Court in some form of interest bearing account using the Court Registry Investment System ("CRIS") administered by the Administrative Office of the United States Courts. Any order directing the Clerk of the Court to invest funds deposited with the Court's CRIS pursuant to 28 U.S.C. § 2041 shall specify the amount to be invested. The Clerk of the Court shall take all reasonable steps to invest the funds within fourteen (14) days of the filing date of the order.

c. Investment of Registry Funds.

1) When the Court orders funds on deposit with the Court be placed in some form of interest-bearing account, CRIS shall be the only investment mechanism authorized.

2) Money from each case deposited into CRIS shall be "pooled" together with those on deposit with Treasury to the credit of other courts in CRIS and used to purchase Government Account Series securities through the Bureau of Public Debt, which will be held at Treasury, in an account in the name and to the credit of the Director of the Administrative Office of the United States Courts as custodian for CRIS.

3) An account for each case will be established in CRIS titled in the name of the case giving rise to the investment in the fund. Income generated from fund investments will be distributed to each case based on the ratio each account's principal and earnings has to the aggregate principal and income total in the fund. Reports showing the interest earned and the principal amounts contributed in each case will be prepared and distributed to each court participating in CRIS and made available to the litigants and/or their counsel.

d. Deductions of Fees.

1) The custodian is authorized to deduct the investment services fee for the management of investments in the CRIS and the registry fee for maintaining accounts deposited with the Court.

2) The investment services fee is assessed from interest earnings to the pool according to the Court's Miscellaneous Fee Schedule and is to be assessed before a pro rata distribution of earnings to court cases.

3) The registry fee is assessed by the custodian from each case's pro rata distribution of the earnings and is to be determined on the basis of the rates published by the Director of the Administrative Office of the United States Courts as approved by the Judicial Conference of the United States.

e. Withdrawal of a Deposit. Any person seeking withdrawal of money deposited in the Court, pursuant to Fed. R. Civ. P. 67 and this local rule, shall provide a completed Internal Revenue Service Form W–9 with the motion papers seeking withdrawal of the funds. See 28 U.S.C. § 2042.

[Effective January 1, 2012. Amended effective March 16, 2015.]

RULE 8007–1. STAY PENDING APPEAL (SUPERSEDEAS BOND)

(a) Amount of Bond When Money Judgment Only. A supersedeas bond, where the judgment is for a sum of money only, shall be in the amount of the judgment, plus 11% to cover interest and such damages for delay as may be awarded, plus an amount to be determined by the Court, to cover costs.

(b) Amount of Bond When Judgment Not Solely for a Sum of Money. When the stay may not be effected solely by the giving of the supersedeas bond, because the judgment or order is not solely for a sum of money, the Court, on notice, shall fix the amount of the bond and grant a stay on such terms as to security and otherwise as it may deem proper.

(c) Objections. Upon approval, a supersedeas bond shall be filed with the Clerk, and a copy thereof, with notice of filing, promptly served on all parties affected thereby. If the appellee raises objections to the form of the bond, or to the sufficiency of the surety, the Court shall hold a hearing on expedited notice to all parties.

[Former Rule 8005–1 effective January 1, 2012. Renumbered and amended effective December 1, 2015.]

RULE 8009–1. DESIGNATION OF RECORD ON APPEAL

(a) Contents. Each party preparing and filing a designation of the items to be included in the record on appeal shall set forth the document number from the Court's docket, filing date and the title or a description of each item designated.

(b) PDF Format. Immediately after filing a designation of the items to be included in the record on appeal, the filing party shall provide to the Clerk a copy of the items designated in PDF format on a CD, unless otherwise directed by the Court.

(c) Noncompliance. If a party fails to deliver the CD to the Clerk pursuant to paragraph (b) of this Rule, the Court shall prepare the CD at the party's expense. The expense shall be calculated in accordance with the Appendix entitled Bankruptcy Court Miscellaneous Fee Schedule issued pursuant to 28 U.S.C. § 1930.

[Former Rule 8006–1 effective January 1, 2012. Renumbered and amended effective December 1, 2015.]

Comment

The current fee charged for reproducing designated items to a c.d. is $30.

RULE 8024–1. REMAND BY APPELLATE COURT

If the order or judgment of the appellate court remands for further proceedings, the Court will notice a hearing or enter any further order as directed.

[Former Rule 8016–1 effective January 1, 2012. Renumbered and amended effective December 1, 2015.]

RULE 8024–2. ENTRY OF APPELLATE COURT'S ORDER OR JUDGMENT

When an order or judgment of an appellate court is filed with the Clerk, it shall be entered on the docket of the main bankruptcy case or adversary proceeding, as appropriate, without further order.

[Former Rule 8016–2 effective January 1, 2012. Renumbered and amended effective December 1, 2015.]

RULE 9001–1. DEFINITIONS

In these Local Bankruptcy Rules:

1) "Administrative Order" means any order signed by a bankruptcy judge that amends, modifies, or supplements procedures of the United States Bankruptcy Court for the Northern District of New York;

2) "Administrative Procedure" means any procedure published by the United States Bankruptcy Court for the Northern District of New York which may amend, modify, or supplement these Local Bankruptcy Rules and orders of the Court;

3) "Allowed Contested Matters" refer in chapter 13 cases to those provision which value collateral to establish the amount of a secured claim; set the interest rate for a secured claim; and assume and/or reject an unexpired lease and/or executory contract.

4) "Appellate Court" means the district court where the appeal was taken;

5) "Bankruptcy Code" and "Code" refers to the Bankruptcy Reform Act of 1978, as amended and set forth in Title 11 of the United States Code;

6) "Clerk" means the "clerk or deputy clerk" of the Court;

7) "Court" means the United States Bankruptcy Court for the Northern District of New York established by 28 U.S.C. §§ 151 and 152 or, with respect to a case which has not been referred, means the District Court;

8) "District Clerk" means the clerk or deputy clerk of the District Court;

9) "District Court" means the United States District Court for the Northern District of New York;

10) "District Judge" means any United States District Judge appointed to or sitting by designation in the Northern District of New York;

11) "CM/ECF" means case-management/electronic case filing;

12) "ECRO" means Electronic Court Recording Operator;

13) "E–Orders" means electronically submitted orders;

14) "Fed. R. Bankr. P." means the Federal Rules of Bankruptcy Procedure and Official Bankruptcy Forms promulgated pursuant to 28 U.S.C. § 2075 in effect on the effective date of these Local Bankruptcy Rules, and as thereafter amended or enacted;

15) "Judge" means any United States Bankruptcy Judge appointed to or sitting by designation in the Northern District of New York, or with respect to a case which has not been referred, it means the District Judge;

16) "Model Plan" means the court-approved standard chapter 13 plan that is to be exclusively used by chapter 13 debtors in the Northern District of New York;

17) "PACER" means public access to court electronic records http://www.pacer.gov/psco/cgi-bin/links.pl;

18) "Public Intake Counter" means the counter located within the Clerk's office where the public may interact with the Clerk's staff;

19) "Red-lined" means a revised version of a document showing additions in bold or colored type and deletions crossed out;

20) "Student Practitioner" means a law student admitted to practice before the court pursuant to LBR 2014–2;

21) "United States trustee" means the United States trustee, acting United States trustee, assistant United States trustee, or attorney therefore, for the Northern District of New York, Region 2; and

22) "United States Trustee Fee Guidelines" means the United States Trustee Fee Guidelines for Reviewing Applications for Compensation and Reimbursement of Expenses filed under 11 U.S.C. § 330 adopted by the Executive Office for United States Trustees on January 30, 1996, as subsequently revised.

The meanings of other words and phrases used in these Rules shall, unless inconsistent with the context, be construed in accordance with the Bankruptcy Code and Federal Rules of Bankruptcy Procedure.

[Effective January 1, 2012.]

Comment

These definitions apply only to the interpretation of these Local Bankruptcy Rules.

RULE 9004–1. DOCUMENTS—REQUIREMENTS OF FORM AND CAPTION

(a) **Form Generally.** Any pleading, motion, and other document presented for filing shall be formatted as follows:

(1) Text, whether in the body of a document or in a footnote, must be:

(A) A minimum of 12–point font;

(B) Double-spaced, except that text in a block quotation or footnote may be single-spaced;

(C) Plainly and legibly written, typewritten, printed or reproduced without defacing erasures or interlineations;

(D) Printed on only a single-side of a page; and

(E) Printed in black ink.

(2) A page must be:

(A) Formatted with a one-inch margin on all four sides;

(B) Consecutively numbered; and

(C) Letter-size, 8½ × 11 inch layout.

(b) **Footnotes.** Extensive footnotes must not be used to circumvent page limitations.

(c) **Caption.** The caption on a document presented for filing shall contain the name of the Court, the title of the case, case number and chapter number assigned thereto, only the last four digits of the debtor's social security number and/or taxpayer identification number and, if pertinent to an adversary proceeding, the adversary proceeding name and assigned number. The caption shall also contain a short title that identifies the document and the name of the party on whose behalf it is filed.

Sample Caption:

UNITED STATES BANKRUPTCY
COURT
NORTHERN DISTRICT OF NEW
YORK

In re:

	Hearing Date:	April 1, 2011
Alex B. Casper and Alice B. Casper,	Hearing Time:	10:00 a.m.
(SSN: H: xxx-xx-1234; W: xxx-xx-4321)	Hearing Location:	Syracuse
Debtors.		
	Case No. XX–XXXXX	
	Chapter 13	

Objection by the Chapter 13 Trustee to Debtors'
Motion to Modify Chapter 13 Plan

(d) Noncompliance. The Court reserves the right to not consider a document that fails to comply with this Rule.

[Effective January 1, 2012.]

Comment

Paragraph (c) of this Rule should be read in conjunction with LBR 9022–1. The caption for a proposed judgment affecting the title or lien on real property or for the recovery of money or property has additional requirements.

RULE 9010–1. ATTORNEYS—NOTICE OF APPEARANCE

The filing and service of a notice of appearance in a case (as distinguished from the filing of a notice of appearance in an adversary proceeding) containing a request for service of papers filed in the case will be deemed to be a request for only such papers and notices which these rules or the Federal Rules of Bankruptcy Procedure require to be served on such party.

[Effective January 1, 1998. Amended effective January 1, 2012.]

Comment

This Rule allows a party to avoid the unnecessary expense of service upon a party not otherwise entitled to service. Service of papers on an attorney is governed by Fed. R. Bankr. P. 7005. See also Fed. R. Bankr. P. 7004(g) and 9014(b).

RULE 9010–2. REQUIREMENT OF COUNSEL FOR NON–INDIVIDUALS

(a) Non–Individual Debtor. A non-individual debtor shall not be permitted to proceed under chapters 7, 9, 11, 12, or 15 without representation by an attorney duly admitted to the Northern District of New York.

(b) Withdrawal of Counsel. In the event that counsel for a non-individual debtor is permitted to withdraw, the case is subject to dismissal unless new counsel is substituted.

(c) Non–Individual Entity. A non-individual entity shall not be permitted to appear in any case without representation

by an attorney duly admitted to the Northern District of New York.

[Effective January 1, 2012.]

RULE 9011–1. ATTORNEYS—DUTIES [DELETED EFFECTIVE JANUARY 1, 2012]

Comment

See LBR 2016–3 for specific required duties of debtor's counsel.

RULE 9011–2. DUTIES OF AN UNREPRESENTED DEBTOR OR PARTY

(a) Contact Information. An unrepresented debtor shall file with the Clerk a designation of the debtor's residential and mailing address, if different, and telephone number where the debtor can be reached during daytime hours. This designation shall be filed along with the debtor's initial filing in the case.

(b) Notification of Change of Address. An unrepresented debtor is required to file with the Clerk a notification of any change of address. The notice of an address change must contain the debtor's name, the case number, the responsible party's name (if different from debtor) and original address given to the Court, together with the debtor's complete new mailing address.

(c) Local Address Requirement. An unrepresented individual who is not a resident of the Northern District of New York may be required by the Court to designate a mailing address within the Northern District of New York. This requirement shall not apply to a party who has appeared without representation solely for the purpose of filing a proof of claim or interest.

[Effective January 1, 1998. Amended effective January 1, 2012.]

Comment

A Pro Se Petitioner's Packet containing information for an unrepresented (pro se) debtor and information regarding pro bono resources is available on the Court's website: www.nynb.uscourts.gov.

RULE 9011–3. SIGNATURE AND ELECTRONIC FILING

(a) Original Signature and Electronic Filing. Any petition, list, schedule, statement, amendment, pleading, affidavit, or other document that requires an original signature or verification under Fed. R. Bankr. P. 1008 or an unsworn declaration, as provided in 28 U.S.C. § 1746, may be filed electronically by a registered user.

(b) Signature Block. In addition to the requirement under Fed. R. Bankr. P. 9011(a) that each paper states the signer's address and telephone number, the attorney's signature block shall include the signer's e-mail address and Northern District of New York attorney bar roll identification number.

(c) Format of Electronic Signature. A pleading or other document electronically filed shall indicate a signature, in the format "/s/name" unless the document has been scanned and shows the actual signature.

(d) Unregistered Attorney's Use of a Registered Attorney's Login and Password Is Not Permitted. The attorney login name must match the attorney name signed on an electronically-filed document. Attorneys who are not registered with the Bankruptcy Court for the Northern District of New York, and therefore, have not been issued a login and password are not permitted to electronically file documents using the login and password of a registered attorney, unless the registered attorney is a co-filer of the document and that status is clearly apparent from the document.

(e) Retention of Original Signature. The document bearing the original signature must be retained by the filer for a minimum of two (2) years after the closing of the case and all time periods for appeals have expired unless the Court orders a different period. In an adversary proceeding, the parties shall maintain the original documents for a minimum of two (2) years after the proceeding is closed and all time periods for appeals have expired unless the Court orders a different period. These retention periods do not affect or replace any other periods required by other applicable laws or rules. Upon request of the Court, the filer must provide the document bearing the original signature for review.

(f) Presentation of Original Petition at § 341 Meeting. Counsel for the debtor shall bring to the § 341 meeting of creditors the original petition bearing the original signature of the debtor.

(g) Electronic Signature on Stipulations or Other Documents Requiring Multiple Signatures. The following procedure applies when a stipulation or other document requires two or more signatures:

(1) The filer shall obtain the physical signatures of all parties required to sign the document. For purposes of this Rule a facsimile signature is permitted.

(2) Depending on the preference within each division of this district, the filer shall either (i) scan the document reflecting the actual script signatures and upload the same, or (ii) indicate each signature using the format "/s/name."

(3) The filing party originating the document shall maintain the document bearing original signatures as provided for in paragraph (e) above.

(h) Proposed Order Submitted for Signature. Unless otherwise directed by the Court, all proposed orders shall be submitted electronically in accordance with the requirements of the E–Orders program and shall be submitted after the scheduled time of the hearing or trial:

(1) A proposed order shall conform to the following:

(A) There must be a four (4) inch margin (i.e., four inches of white space) at the top of the first page of the proposed order;

(B) The character sequence ### must appear on the last page of the proposed order, centered, and at the end of the text; and

(C) The proposed order shall not contain a signature line, block or date.

(2) DO NOT ELECTRONICALLY FILE A PLEADING THAT CONTAINS A PROPOSED ORDER IN THE BODY OF THE PLEADING.

[Effective January 1, 2012.]

Comment

With reference to the electronic filing of signed stipulations, the Syracuse division requires a scanned document that reflects actual script signatures. The Albany and Utica divisions accept either: (i) a scan of the actual script signatures on the document; or (ii) a typed representation of each signature in the format "/s/ name" as set forth in subparagraph (f)(2) of this Rule.

RULE 9013–1. MOTION PRACTICE

(a) Notice. Unless otherwise ordered by the Court, notice of a motion shall be provided in the time and manner prescribed by the Federal Rules of Bankruptcy Procedure, Local Bankruptcy Rules, and the Administrative Procedures.

(1) *Identification of Hearing Date, Time, and Location.* The date, time, and location of the hearing shall be included in the body of the notice of motion and above the case number in the caption.

(2) *Identification of Relief Sought and Statutory Basis.* The notice of motion shall set forth, in concise, plain terms, the specific relief sought, the party or parties against whom such relief is sought, and the rule or statute upon which the motion or application is predicated. Failure to provide the basis for relief sought is cause for the Court to deny the relief requested.

(b) Notice of Electronic Filing. When a pleading or other document is electronically filed, the CM/ECF system generates a "Notice of Electronic Filing" that is transmitted to the filing party and all registered users of the CM/ECF system having appeared in the case in which the filing is made.

(1) *Service Upon a Registered User Who Has Appeared in the Case.* Transmission of the Notice of Electronic Filing to a registered user via the CM/ECF system, constitutes service of the pleading or other document.

(2) *Service Upon a Non–Registered User or a Registered User Who Has Not Appeared in the Case.* A party who is not a registered user of the CM/ECF system must be served with the filed pleading or other document in compliance with the Federal Rules of Bankruptcy Procedure and these rules.

(c) Certificate of Service. A certificate of service upon both registered and non-registered users of the CM/ECF system is required. The certificate must state the manner in which service or notice was accomplished on each party. The moving party shall file a certificate of service, not later than seven (7) days prior to the return date of the motion. Failure to file a certificate of service may result in the motion not appearing on the Court's calendar. Sample language for a certificate of service can be found in the Administrative Procedures.

(d) Supporting Affidavit, Application, and Exhibits.

(1) *Service Not Required.* Except as provided in the subparagraphs below, where a motion is made for the relief set forth in subparagraphs (a)(1), (2), (3), and (5) of LBR 2002–1 and the relief sought and the affected parties are clearly and unambiguously stated in the notice of motion, a supporting affidavit, application, or exhibits need not be served on all parties in interest. In such case, the notice of motion must clearly indicate that a copy of the supporting affidavit, application, or exhibit is available, without charge, from the movant upon request. The movant must provide a contact name and telephone number and/or email address to which such a request may be made.

(2) *Service Required.* A complete copy of a motion with any supporting affidavit, application, and exhibits shall be served upon the United States trustee, the trustee, any official committee, opposing counsel, and any party that may be directly adversely affected by the granting of the requested relief.

(3) *Filing Requirements.* Any motion, supporting affidavit, and application must be filed with the Court. For filing requirements related to exhibits, see LBR 9013–2.

(e) Timeliness of Filing and Service of a Motion. Unless otherwise specified in the Federal Rules of Bankruptcy Procedure (particularly Rules 2002, 3007, and 4007), these rules, the Administrative Procedures, or as ordered by the Court, any motion shall be filed and served at least twenty-one (21) days before the return date of the motion.

(f) Filing Deadlines. An electronic filing is considered timely if received by the Court before midnight on the date set as a deadline, unless the Court or these rules specifically require an earlier filing.

(g) Answering Papers.

(1) *Timeliness of Filing and Service.* Answering papers shall be served and filed so as to be received not later than seven (7) days prior to the return date of the motion. The date, time, and location of the hearing shall be included above the case number in the caption.

(2) *Form.* Answering papers shall identify the date, time and location of the hearing above the case number in the caption.

(3) *Oral Opposition.* If the Court permits oral opposition to a motion without an answer or response being filed and adjourns the hearing, the answer or response substantiating the oral opposition shall be filed and served within seven (7) days of the original hearing date.

(h) Chambers Copy. A paper chambers copy is required for the matters listed below. The chambers copy is to be submitted to the Clerk contemporaneously with the electronic filing of the pleading or other document. The copy must be clearly marked as "ECF CASE—CHAMBERS COPY." The chambers copy need not contain a copy of the original signature. Unless otherwise directed by the Court, copies should be sent via regular mail or hand delivery, not by facsimile. Parties who fail to provide a chambers copy may be billed for copies.

(1) *Albany Chambers:*

(A) Notice of motion, motion, application, and certificate of service, except for chapter 13 trustee's motion to dismiss and to determine/expunge claim;

(B) Opposition, response, or any pleading relating to a hearing;

(C) Opposition to disclosure statement in a chapter 11 case;

(D) Objection to confirmation of a chapter 11 plan;

(E) Pretrial statement;

(F) Memoranda of law and any pleading and other document filed in regard to a submitted matter; and

(G) All pleadings related to loss mitigation.

(2) *Syracuse and Utica Chambers:*

(A) Notice of motion, motion, application and certificate of service;

(B) Any pleading filed in an adversary proceeding;

(C) Pretrial statement;

(D) Memoranda of law and any pleading or other document filed in regard to a submitted matter;

(E) Any document regarding an appeal;

(F) Withdrawal of reference;

(G) Any objection pursuant to Fed. R. Bankr. P. 9033; and

(H) All pleadings related to loss mitigation.

(i) Adjournment Generally. The Court requires a written request for an adjournment that affirmatively indicates the consent of opposing counsel, states the reasons for the request, and states whether any previous request for an adjournment has been made. Chambers will notify the requesting party only if the request is denied.

(j) Procedure for Requesting Adjournment. An adjournment request shall be made by electronically filing not later than 2:00 p.m. the day prior to the hearing an Adjournment Request/Withdrawal/Settlement Notification for Motion Related Matters form or an Adjournment Request/Withdrawal/Settlement Notification for Confirmation Hearings form.

(1) *Inability to Obtain Opposing Counsel's Consent.* The inability to affirmatively indicate opposing counsel's consent to an adjournment will require an appearance for the purpose of requesting the adjournment, unless the Court directs otherwise.

(k) Withdrawal of Pleading or Other Document Generally. Any party who seeks to withdraw a motion, pleading or other document shall provide written notification to the Court and all parties who have filed and served related papers.

(*l*) Procedure for Notification of Withdrawal. Notice of the withdrawal of a motion shall be provided not later than 2:00 p.m. the day prior to the hearing by electronically filing an Adjournment Request/Withdrawal/Settlement Notification for Motion Related Matters form.

(m) Notification of Settlement—Generally. Where movant and opposing counsel have agreed to the terms of an order, movant shall provide written notification to the Court and all parties who have filed and served responding papers.

(n) Procedure for Notification of Settlement. Notice of the settlement of a motion shall be provided not later than 2:00 p.m. the day prior to the hearing by electronically filing an Adjournment Request/Withdrawal/Settlement Notification for Motion Related Matters form.

(*o*) Motion to Avoid Judicial Lien Pursuant to § 522(f). A motion to avoid a judicial lien pursuant to § 522(f) shall be served upon the judgment creditor pursuant to Fed. R. Bankr. P. 7004 and upon the attorney who obtained the judgment on behalf of the creditor.

[Effective January 1, 2012. Amended effective January 2, 2013; January 1, 2014; February 1, 2017.]

Comment

The service fee for copies made by Clerk's Office staff is governed by the Bankruptcy Court Miscellaneous Fee Schedule.

RULE 9013–2. MOTION EXHIBITS

An exhibit and other attachment to a motion that is capable of being electronically imaged (scanned) should be electronically filed. An exhibit and attachment may be summarized and only the relevant excerpts electronically filed. The size of an electronic file should be no larger than 5 Megabytes (MB). An attachment larger than 5 Megabytes (MB) must be split into separate PDF files, all of which shall be attached to the pleading. Any proposed order submitted as an exhibit shall prominently bear on its face the word "EXHIBIT".

[Effective January 1, 1998. Amended effective October 24, 2005; January 1, 2012; January 2, 2013.]

RULE 9013–3. DEFAULT MOTION PRACTICE

(a) Default Notice. Any motion listed in paragraph (c) of this Rule, if pursued on a default basis, shall clearly and conspicuously contain the following paragraph (which may be single-spaced):

IF YOU INTEND TO OPPOSE THIS MOTION, WRITTEN OPPOSITION MUST BE FILED WITH THE CLERK OF THE COURT AND SERVED ON MOVANT'S COUNSEL AT LEAST SEVEN (7) DAYS PRIOR TO THE RETURN DATE. IF YOU DO NOT FILE AND SERVE WRITTEN OPPOSITION, NO HEARING WILL BE HELD ON THE RETURN DATE AND THE COURT MAY GRANT THE MOTION AS UNOPPOSED.

(b) Timely Opposition Not Filed. If no opposition is timely filed and served upon movant's counsel as outlined in the above notice, the motion will not appear on the Court's motion calendar on the return date, and the motion will be considered by the Court without the necessity of any appearance by movant's counsel.

(1) *Timely Opposition Filed.* If written opposition to the motion is timely filed and served upon movant's counsel, the motion will appear on the Court's motion calendar on the return date and the parties are required to appear.

(2) *Proposed Order.* A proposed order should not be submitted for signature until after the return date of the motion.

(c) Default Motions. The default motion practice outlined in this Rule applies to the following types of motions:

(1) Abandon Property (§ 554(b));

(2) Allow Administrative Expenses Other Than Professional Fees (§ 503(b));

(3) Allow Administrative Expenses for Professional Fees: (A) in a chapter 13 case which are not in excess of $1,000.00 provided, however, that said fees are requested for services rendered in connection with a motion brought by default under this Rule and (B) which are in excess of $1.000.00 provided, however, that said fees are requested solely for services rendered in connection with a loss mitigation;

(4) Approve Settlement of Adversary Proceeding or Contested Matter (Fed. R. Bankr. P. 9019);

(5) Assume or Reject Executory Contract or Unexpired Lease (§ 365);

(6) Change Venue (28 U.S.C. § 1412);

(7) Compel Turnover of Property from the Debtor by the Trustee or Pursuant to § 542(e);

(8) Convert (§§ 706, 1112(a)) or Dismiss Case (§§ 707, 1112(b), 1208, and 1307);

(9) Disallow or Modify Claim (§ 502);

(10) Dismiss for Failure to Pay Filing Fee (Fed. R. Bankr. P. 1006(a));

(11) Extend Time to Assume or Reject an Unexpired Nonresidential Lease (§ 365(d)(4));

(12) Extend Time to File Complaint (Fed. R. Bankr. P. 4004(b), 4007(c));

(13) Extend Time to File Plan and Disclosure Statement—Chapter 11 (§ 1121(d));

(14) Extend Time to File Plan—Chapter 12 and 13 (§§ 1221 and 1321);

(15) Extend Time to Pay Filing Fee (Fed. R. Bankr. P. 1006(b));

(16) Conduct Fed. R. Bankr. P. 2004 Exam;

(17) Object to Claimed Exemption (Fed. R. Bankr. P. 4003(b));

(18) Obtain Credit (§ 364(b), (c), and (d));

(19) Modify Chapter 12 or 13 Plan Post–Confirmation (§§ 1229 and 1329);

(20) Reopen Case (Fed. R. Bankr. P. 5010 and Local Bankruptcy Rule 5010);

(21) Terminate or Modify the Automatic Stay and/or Co-Debtor Stay, provided, however, that movant shall include in the proposed order granting a motion for relief from the stay a directive that (i) the case trustee be added as a necessary party to receive notice of the report of sale and surplus money proceedings; and (ii) closure of the case shall not constitute an abandonment of the trustee's interest, if any, in any surplus proceeds. (§ 362(d));

(22) Use Cash Collateral (§ 363(e));

(23) Revoke/Reconsider Order of Dismissal (Fed. R. Bankr. P. 9024);

(24) Waive Debtor's Appearance at Section 341 Meeting of Creditors;

(25) Application to Employ a Professional under § 327(e) in a Chapter 7 Case When the Trustee Seeks to Employ an Attorney to Pursue a Claim of the Estate Previously Held by the Debtor (§ 327(e));

(26) Confirm Automatic Stay Has Been Terminated (§ 362(j));

(27) Extend the Automatic Stay (§ 362(c)(3)(B));

(28) Seal a Document (Fed. R. Bankr. P. 9018); and

(29) Avoid Judicial Lien and Non–Possessory, Non–Purchase Money Security Interest (§ 522(f)).

(d) Rules 9013–1 and 9013–2 also apply to default motion practice.

(e) The default motion practice only applies to motions listed in paragraph (c) of this Rule. Any other motion shall require the appearance of movant's counsel, regardless of whether written opposition is filed.

[Effective January 1, 2012. Amended effective January 1, 2014; July 1, 2014; July 18, 2016; February 1, 2017.]

Comment

Essential to the Court granting a default motion is proper service of the default motion evidenced by a timely filed certificate of service. In this regard, particular reference is made to Fed. R. Bankr. P. 3007 and 6007 and to the provisions of Fed. R. Bankr. P. 7004(b)(1)–(10), which are applicable to contested matters pursuant to Fed. R. Bankr. P. 9014.

Certain applications to employ a professional in a chapter 7 case are required to be on notice so that the debtor and debtor's counsel are cognizant that any professional retained by the chapter 7 trustee is retained to represent the bankruptcy estate's interest and not the debtor's interest, despite the fact the professional may have represented the debtor prior to the bankruptcy filing. See LBR 2014–1(e).

See also LBR 4001–1 with respect to a motion to lift the automatic stay.

RULE 9013–4. ORDERS AND JUDGMENTS

(a) Orders. Unless otherwise ordered by the Court, all oral orders of the Court, including any order resulting from a default motion under LBR 9013–3, shall be reduced to writing and submitted electronically as an e-order by the prevailing party not later than 30 days from the date of ruling, except for confirmation orders in chapter 12 and 13 cases. See LBR 3015–3.

(b) Noncompliance. Failure to comply with paragraph (a) of this Rule is cause for the Court to vacate its oral order and deny the relief requested.

(c) Settlement of Order or Judgment. Unless otherwise ordered by the Court, to settle an order or to settle a judgment shall mean the following:

(1) *Service.* The prevailing party or other party as directed by the Court shall serve a proposed order or judgment upon any opposing party who has appeared or has requested service thereof within 14 days of the hearing. Any counter proposal must be served not later than 7 days from the date of service.

Counsel who served the proposed order or judgment shall submit it to the Court, together with any counter proposal.

(2) *Required Notice.* All proposed orders or judgments shall be served together with a separate notice which shall clearly and conspicuously contain the following paragraph (which may be single-spaced):

THE ATTACHED PROPOSED ORDER IS BEING SERVED UPON YOU ON [INSERT DATE]. PURSUANT TO LOCAL BANKRUPTCY RULE 9013–4, IF YOU INTEND TO SUBMIT ANY COUNTER PROPOSAL, YOU MUST SERVE UPON THE UNDERSIGNED A WRITTEN COUNTER PROPOSAL TO THE ORDER OR JUDGMENT ATTACHED HERETO NOT LATER THAN SEVEN DAYS FROM SERVICE HEREOF. IN THE EVENT THAT NO WRITTEN COUNTER PROPOSAL IS RECEIVED, THE ORDER OR JUDGMENT ATTACHED HERETO SHALL BE SUBMITTED TO THE COURT. IF A COUNTER PROPOSAL IS TIMELY RECEIVED, IT SHALL BE SUBMITTED, TOGETHER WITH THE PROPOSED ORDER, TO THE COURT.

(3) *Submission.* If counsel, having served the proposed order or judgment, does not receive any written counter proposal, then the proposed order or judgment shall be uploaded electronically as an e-order after counsel has electronically filed the original notice and certificate of service. If a written counter proposal is timely received, it shall be submitted in paper format, together with the proposed order in paper format, with a letter to the Court advising the Court of the parties' inability to settle the order or judgment. The letter shall also be electronically filed.

(d) Order With Attachment. If an order has an attachment, the character sequence ### must appear on the last page of the attachment, centered and at the end of the text.

[Effective January 1, 2012.]

Comment

Electronic orders shall be filed in the format prescribed in LBR 9011–3(h).

RULE 9013–5. EX PARTE ORDER— ORDER SHORTENING TIME— ORDER TO SHOW CAUSE

(a) Ex Parte Order.

(1) *Application.* A request for ex parte relief shall be made by affidavit or motion containing a clear and specific showing of cause for both ex parte action as well as the relief requested and whether previous application for similar relief has been made.

(2) *Submission.* The underlying affidavit or motion shall be filed electronically and the proposed ex parte order shall be uploaded immediately following the filing of the underlying application via the E–Orders menu. The application shall not be uploaded as one PDF document via E–Orders. If the relief requested would be defeated by prior notice, the application may be filed in paper format pursuant to paragraph (d) of this Rule.

(b) Order Shortening Time.

(1) *Application.* A request for an order shortening any specified notice period shall be made by application for an expedited hearing on the motion pursuant to Fed. R. Bankr. P. 9006(d). Such application shall contain a clear and specific showing by affidavit of good and sufficient reasons for shortening the notice period and whether previous application for similar relief has been made. Law office failure does not provide good and sufficient cause.

(2) *Submission.* The underlying motion shall be filed electronically, and then the application for an expedited hearing shall be filed electronically and linked to the underlying motion. A proposed order shortening time shall be emailed to Chambers in Word format and not filed on the docket. The proposed order shortening time should specify the proposed manner of service and provide for the proposed motion hearing date and time. Chambers must be notified before filing an application for an order shortening time.

(c) Order to Show Cause.

(1) *Application.* No order to show cause to bring on a motion will be entered except upon a clear and specific showing by affidavit of good and sufficient reasons why proceeding other than by notice of motion is necessary. Law office failure does not provide good and sufficient cause relief has been made. The papers shall also state whether a previous application for similar relief has been made.

(2) *Submission.* The underlying affidavit shall be filed electronically. A proposed order to show cause shall be emailed to Chambers in Word format and not filed on the docket. Chambers must be notified before filing an order to show cause.

(d) Prior Notice of Temporary Restraining Order. Unless the purpose of an order to show cause would be defeated by prior notice, any party seeking an order to show cause which contains temporary restraining relief shall give an opposing party or, if known, counsel for an opposing party, at least 24 hours prior notice, if possible, of the presentation of the order to show cause and the underlying papers, including the date and time of the proposed presentment of said order to show cause to the Court. Proof of notice of presentment shall be filed with the Court.

[Effective January 1, 2012. Amended effective February 1, 2017.]

RULE 9013–6. MOTION TO AVOID JUDICIAL LIEN—11 U.S.C. § 522(f)(1)(A)

(a) Contents. A motion to avoid a judicial lien shall include:

(1) The date the bankruptcy was filed ("petition date");

(2) A description of the real property owned by the debtor on the petition date to which the lien has attached;

(3) A statement that the debtor has claimed the property as exempt on Schedule C, the amount of the claimed exemption and the statutory basis for the exemption (i.e., 11 U.S.C. § 522(b)(3) and N.Y. CPLR 5206(a), or, 11 U.S.C. § 522(b)(2) and (d)(1) and/or (d)(5));

(4) Whether the debtor owns the property solely or jointly and, if owned jointly, the nature of the debtor's ownership interest in the property (*e.g.*, joint tenant, tenant by the entirety or tenant in common);

(5) Proof as to the value of the real property as of the petition date;

(6) The name(s) of the judicial lien creditor(s), <u>listed in order of their priority</u>, the amount(s) of the lien(s) sought to be avoided, and the recording information for each judgment;

(7) For each lien sought to be avoided, a statement that the lien does not secure a debt arising out of a domestic support obligation of the kind described in § 523(a)(5);

(8) A copy of the recorded judgment or transcript of the judgment that reflects recording information and the name and address of the attorney who obtained the judgment on behalf of the creditor;

(9) The name(s) of the holder(s) of each additional lien against the property, the nature of such lien(s) (*e.g.*, mortgage, tax, or statutory) and proof of the amount of each lien as of the petition date;

(10) The address of all other real property owned by the debtor (i.e., rental property, commercial property);

(11) The date on which the debtor acquired an interest in the real property; and

(12) A showing that the lien impairs the claimed exemption in that the sum of the amounts described in subparagraphs (3), (6) and (9) above exceeds the value that the debtor's interest in the property would have in the absence of any liens.

(b) Service. A motion to avoid a judicial lien pursuant to § 522(f) shall be served upon the judgment creditor pursuant to Fed. R. Bankr. P. 7004 and upon the attorney who obtained the judgment on behalf of the creditor.

[Effective July 1, 2014. Amended effective March 16, 2015.]

Comment

With reference to establishing the fair market value of the property or the balances owed on outstanding liens as of the petition date, values contained in debtors' schedules shall <u>not</u> constitute adequate proof thereof. Among other things, the court may consider a broker's price opinion or appraisal as evidence of value of real property and a proof of claim, payoff letter or account statement as evidence of a lien amount.

Code § 522(f) operates solely with respect to judicial liens. See § 101(36) for the definition of "judicial lien." A statutory lien, as *e.g.* a mechanic's lien, cannot be avoided under this section. See § 101(53) for the definition of "statutory lien." Papers submitted in support of the motion should allow the court to readily ascertain the nature of the lien. See *In re Schick*, 418 F.3d 321 (3d Cir. 2005) (discussing the distinction between judicial liens, which are avoidable under § 522(f), and statutory liens, which are not.)

RULE 9015–1. JURY TRIAL

If the right to a jury trial applies and a timely demand has been filed pursuant to Fed. R. Civ. P. 38(b), the parties may consent to have a jury trial conducted by a bankruptcy judge under 28 U.S.C. § 157(e) by jointly or separately filing a statement of consent within twenty-one (21) days after the last date to file a pleading.

[Effective January 1, 1998. Amended effective December 1, 2009; January 1, 2012.]

Comment

The Court is specifically designated to conduct jury trials in all proceedings commenced in cases filed under Title 11 of the United States Code where the right to a jury trial applies and where all the parties have expressly consented thereto, pursuant to Rule 76.1 of the Local Rules of Practice for the United States District Court for the Northern District of New York.

RULE 9018–1. FILING UNDER SEAL

(a) Request to Seal a Document. A party requesting the sealing of a document must file a motion with the Court with notice to parties in interest, unless the Court orders otherwise. The motion may be filed electronically or in paper format. The motion shall include the reason for the request to seal the document and, the parties, if any, who may have access to the document to be sealed. Care should be given to not disclose in the motion information sought to be sealed.

(b) Order to Seal Document. A document will not be sealed without a Court order. The proposed order submitted to the Court shall direct the Clerk to place the document under seal and it shall identify the parties, if any, who may have access to the document that is under seal. In addition, the proposed order shall contain the following recitation:

The original sealed document filed with the Clerk may be destroyed sixty (60) days following disposition of the case/adversary proceeding, unless the original filer requests its return in writing.

(c) Access to Document. If the Court orders access to the document by other parties under paragraph (b) of this Rule, it shall be provided by the filer of the sealed document.

(d) Filing Sealed Document With the Clerk. The party requesting the sealing of a document must contact the Clerk's office to arrange for the filing of the document. The original document must be in a sealed envelope with the caption (case name, case number, adversary proceeding number, if applicable, and title of document) on the front of the envelope. A paper copy of the signed order granting the motion to seal must accompany the document to be sealed.

(e) Disposition of Sealed Documents. The original document filed with the Clerk under paragraph (d) of this Rule will be destroyed sixty (60) days after the closing of the case or adversary proceeding, unless the original filer requests its return in writing from the Clerk.

[Effective January 1, 2012.]

Comment

This motion may be pursued on a default basis under LBR 9013–3.

RULE 9019–1. ALTERNATIVE DISPUTE RESOLUTION

The mediation program developed by the Court, as set forth in the Appendix to these Rules and incorporated by reference, is adopted.

[Effective January 1, 2012.]

RULE 9022–1. NOTICE OF ENTRY OF JUDGMENT AND ORDER

(a) Notice of Entry. Whenever notice of entry of a contested order or judgment is required by Fed. R. Bankr. P. 9022, the party submitting said order or judgment shall provide the Clerk with a list of names and addresses of the parties contesting entry, including the name and address of the submitting party and the name and address of their respective attorneys.

(b) Delivery of Notice of Entry. The Clerk must mail or deliver by electronic means to the contesting parties a copy of a judgment or order showing the date the judgment or order was entered. Immediately upon entry of an order or judgment in a case or proceeding, the Clerk will electronically transmit to the registered users in the case or proceeding, a "Notice of Electronic Filing." Electronic transmission of the Notice of Electronic Filing constitutes the notice required by Fed. R. Bankr. P. 9022. The Clerk must give notice in paper form to persons who have not consented to electronic service in accordance with the Federal Rules of Bankruptcy Procedure and these Rules.

(c) Proposed Judgments and Orders. Unless otherwise directed by the Court, all proposed judgments and orders must be uploaded electronically as an e-order. To facilitate the Clerk's compliance with Fed R. Bankr. P. 5003(c), any judgment or order that affects the title to or lien on real property or involves the recovery of money or property shall contain the word "Index" in the caption under the case number and/or adversary proceeding number.

[Effective January 1, 2012.]

Comment

An example of a caption that complies with paragraph (c) of this Rule appears below.

UNITED STATES BANKRUPTCY COURT
NORTHERN DISTRICT OF NEW YORK

In re:

    JOHN DOE,   Case No. XX–XXXXX
          Debtor.   Chapter 7

    JOHN DOE,

          Plaintiff,   Adv. Proc. No. XX–XXXXX

    v.

    JOE SMITH,   **INDEX**
          Defendant.

[INSERT TITLE OF DOCUMENT]

RULE 9025–1. SURETIES

(a) Execution by Surety Only. Whenever a bond, undertaking or stipulation is required, it shall be sufficient if the instrument is executed by the surety or sureties only.

(b) Security for Bond. Except as otherwise provided by law, every bond, undertaking or stipulation must be secured by:

(1) The deposit of cash or government bonds in the amount of the bond, undertaking or stipulation, or

(2) The undertaking of a corporate surety holding a certificate of authority from the United States Secretary of the Treasury.

(c) Affidavit by Individual Surety. In the case of a bond, undertaking or stipulation executed by an individual surety, each surety shall attach an affidavit of justifications, giving the full name, occupation, residence and business address, and showing that the individual is qualified as an individual surety under paragraph (b) of this Rule.

(d) Persons Who May Not Act as Surety. Unless otherwise ordered by the Court, a member of the bar, administrative officer, Court employee, the marshal, deputy or assistant, may not act as surety in any case, adversary proceeding, contested matter or action pending in this Court.

[Effective January 1, 2012.]

RULE 9027–1. REMOVAL AND REMAND

(a) Removal—List of Parties. In addition to compliance with the requirements in Fed. R. Bankr. P. 9027, a party removing a civil action to this Court shall file a list containing the name of each party to the removed case, and the names, addresses and telephone numbers of their counsel, or the party, if pro se.

(b) Procedure After Remand. If the Court remands the case, a certified copy of the order of remand shall be mailed by the Clerk to the clerk of the court from which the civil action or proceeding was removed, and that court may thereupon proceed with the case.

(c) Service. Service of the notice of removal or remand shall be served on all parties to the removed or remanded case, in the manner provided for in Fed. R. Bankr. P. 7004.

[Effective January 1, 2012.]

RULE 9034–1. NOTICE TO AND SERVICE UPON THE UNITED STATES TRUSTEE

(a) Notice. In addition to the notice required to be given to the United States trustee pursuant to Fed. R. Bankr. P. 2002(k) and 9034, the United States trustee has requested that any entity filing the following documents shall also transmit an electronic and paper copy to the United States trustee.

(1) Any pleading and other document related to the appointment of any Chapter 11 trustee or examiner pursuant to § 1104;

(2) Any pleading and other document related to a motion filed under § 363(b) in a Chapter 11 case;

(3) Any fee application and objection filed in connection with §§ 330 and 331 in a Chapter 11 case;

(4) Any disclosure statement, plan and amendment filed thereto, pursuant §§ 1121 and 1125; and

(5) All operating reports required under LBR 2015–2.

(b) Service. The time and manner of service shall conform to these Local Bankruptcy Rules, the Court's Administrative Procedures and the Federal Rules of Bankruptcy Procedure and shall be effected contemporaneously with service upon all other parties in interest.

[Effective January 1, 2012.]

Comment

The address for notice to or service upon the United States trustee is available at the United States trustee's website: www.justice.gov/ust/r02

This Rule is intended to supplement the requirements of notice to the United States trustee pursuant to Fed. R. Bankr. P. 2002(k), 5005(b), and 9034.

Motions filed in a chapter 7 or chapter 13 case shall not be served in paper form upon the United States trustee.

RULE 9037–1. PRIVACY PROTECTION— REDACTION OF A PERSONAL IDENTIFIER

(a) Personal Identifier. Unless otherwise ordered by the Court, in an electronic or paper filing made with the Court that contains an individual's social security number, taxpayer identification number, or birth date, the name of an individual, other than the debtor known to be and identified as a minor, or a financial-account number (individually and collectively referred to as "Personal Identifier"), a party or nonparty making the filing may include only:

(1) The last four (4) digits of the social security number and taxpayer identification number;

(2) The year of the individual's birth;

(3) The minor's initials; and

(4) The last four digits of the financial account number.

(b) Responsibility for Redaction. As noted in Fed. R. Bankr. P. 9037, responsibility for redacting a Personal Identifier in a pleading or other document filed with the Court rests solely with counsel and unrepresented parties filing such pleadings or other documents. The Clerk will not review each pleading or other document for compliance with Fed. R. Bankr. P. 9037 and this Rule and absent a request, as provided in paragraph (c), will not redact a Personal Identifier, erroneously including in a filing.

(c) Request for Redaction of Personal Identifier. A request for the redaction of a Personal Identifier should be made by electronically filing an ex parte application for an Order Directing Clerk to (i) Restrict Document(s) from Public Access and (ii) Substitute Redacted Document(s). The redacted document(s) should be filed as an exhibit to the application. The applicant should then upload as an E–Order the proposed order that grants the application.

(d) Sanctions. The Court may impose sanctions on counsel or any party who files a pleading or other document containing a Personal Identifier in violation of Fed. R. Bankr. P. 9037.

[Effective January 1, 2012. Amended effective January 1, 2014; February 1, 2017.]

Comment

On occasion counsel or parties may have the need to file multiple requests for redaction of personal identifiers. Counsel or parties should contact the Clerk's office prior to filing the requests for redaction.

RULE 9037–2. TRANSCRIPT REDACTION

(a) Notice of Intent to Request Redaction. Within seven (7) days of the filing of the transcript, any person who wishes to redact from a transcript a Personal Identifier defined in Rule 9037–1 and as set forth in Fed. R. Bankr. P. 9037(a) must file a Notice of Intent to Request Redaction with the Clerk and serve a copy of the notice on the transcriber.

(b) Request for Redaction Under Fed. R. Bankr. P. 9037(a). A Request for Redaction must be filed within twenty-one (21) days of the filing of the transcript and served upon the transcriber. The Request for Redaction must include the location of the Personal Identifier by page and line number, as well as the type of Personal Identifier (e.g., social security number, taxpayer identification number, date of birth, minor's name or financial account number) to be redacted.

[Effective January 1, 2012.]

Comment

Redaction of information not covered in Fed. R. Bankr. P. 9037(a) must be done by a motion for a protective order pursuant to Fed. R. Bankr. P. 9037(d).

APPENDICES

APPENDIX I. COUNTY ASSIGNMENT AND HEARING LOCATIONS

COUNTY	DIVISIONAL ASSIGNMENT	USUAL HEARING LOCATION*
Albany	Albany	Albany
Broome	Utica	Binghamton
Cayuga	Syracuse	Syracuse
Chenango	Utica	Binghamton
Clinton	Albany	Albany
Columbia	Albany	Albany
Cortland	Syracuse	Syracuse
Delaware	Utica	Binghamton
Essex	Albany	Albany
Franklin	Utica	Utica "Court Call"
Fulton	Utica	Utica "Court Call"
Greene	Albany	Albany
Hamilton	Utica	Utica
Herkimer	Utica	Utica
Jefferson	Syracuse	Syracuse
Lewis	Utica	Utica
Madison	Utica	Utica
Montgomery	Utica	Utica "Court Call"
Oneida	Utica	Utica
Onondaga	Syracuse	Syracuse
Oswego	Syracuse	Syracuse
Otsego	Utica	Binghamton
Rensselaer	Albany	Albany
St. Lawrence	Utica	Utica "Court Call"
Saratoga	Albany	Albany
Schenectady	Albany	Albany
Schoharie	Albany	Albany
Tioga	Syracuse	Syracuse
Tompkins	Syracuse	Syracuse
Ulster	Albany	Albany
Warren	Albany	Albany
Washington	Albany	Albany

* For cases assigned to the Utica division, all Chapter 11 matters are held on a Utica Chapter 11 motion calendar.

NOTE: Assignment location and hearing location are subject to change without notice on a case by case basis if the Court deems it necessary for ease of administration.

[Effective January 1, 2012.]

APPENDIX II. LOCAL FORMS

Adjournment Request/Withdrawal/Settlement Notification for Motion Calendar Related Matters—Utica

Adjournment Request/Withdrawal/Settlement Notification for Trials/Evidentiary Hearings—Utica

Adjournment Request/Withdrawal/Settlement Notification for Motion Calendar Related Matters—Syracuse

Adjournment Request/Withdrawal/Settlement Notification for Confirmation Hearings—Syracuse

Attorney Registration Form

Chapter 13 Debtor's Certifications Regarding Domestic Support Obligations and Sections 522(q) and 1328

Chapter 12 Debtor's Certifications Regarding Domestic Support Obligations and Sections 522(q) and 1228

Chapter 11 Debtor's Certification Regarding Domestic Support Obligations and Sections 522(q)

Certification of Payment History on the Note and Mortgage Dated and Related Information

Certification Pursuant to Local Bankruptcy Rule 3015–1(b) and (c)

Filing Agent Form

Model Plan

Notice of Time Fixed for Filing Objections To and Hearing to Consider Confirmation of a Chapter 13 Plan

Order of Confirmation

Participant Registration Form

Payment Advice Form

Student Practice Authorization Form

[Effective January 1, 2012.]

APPENDIX III. ADMINISTRATIVE ORDERS

Administrative Order 17–01	Adoption of Revised Local Bankruptcy Rules Effective February 1, 2017
Administrative Order 16–09	Order Establishing Claims Bar Dates for Cases Converted from Chapter 11 to Chapter 7
Administrative Order 16–07	Order Regarding Deposit and Investment of Registry Funds
Administrative Order 16–03	Debtor's Attorney Fee in Chapter 13 Cases Filed in the Albany Division
Administrative Order 16–02	Debtor's Attorney Fee in Chapter 13 Cases filed in the Utica Division
Administrative Order 16–01	Adoption of Modified Loss Mitigation Program Procedures Effective March 15, 2016
Administrative Order 15–04	Adoption of Revised Local Bankruptcy Rules Effective December 1, 2015
Administrative Order 14–06	In the Matter of the Appointment of Chief Bankruptcy Judge for the Northern District of New York
Administrative Order 14–05	Order Regarding Deposit and Investment of Registered Funds **ABROGATED by Administrative Order 16–07**
Administrative Order 13–05	Adoption of Loss Mitigation Program Procedures
Administrative Order 13–03	Debtor's Attorney Fee in Chapter 13 Cases Filed in the Albany Division **ABROGATED by Administrative Order 16–03**
Amended Administrative Order 13–02A	Debtor's Attorney Fee in Chapter 13 Cases Filed in the Utica Division **ABROGATED by Administrative Order 16–02**
Administrative Order13–02	Debtor's Attorney Fee in Chapter 13 Cases Filed in the Utica Division
Administrative Order 12–03	Debtor Counsel Fees in Chapter 13 Cases Filed in the Albany Division
Administrative Order 11–03	Abrogated Administrative Orders
Administrative Order 11–02	Procedural Rules for Electronic Case Filing
Administrative Order 09–09	Revised Local Procedure Governing Time Computation **ABROGATED January 1, 2012**—The language, policy and/or procedure set forth within this Order was incorporated into the Local Bankruptcy Rules for the Northern District of New York effective January 1, 2012 and are in compliance with the amendments to the Federal Rules of Bankruptcy, Civil, Appellate and Criminal Procedure effective December 1, 2009. Accordingly, this Order was abrogated effective January 1, 2012.
Administrative Order 09–08	Rights and Responsibilities of Chapter 13 Debtors and Their Attorneys for the Albany and Utica divisions
Administrative Order 09–07	Debtor Counsel Fees in Chapter 13 Cases Filed in the Utica Division
Administrative Order 09–04	Employee Disclosure
Administrative Order 09–03	Appearance by Student Practitioners
Administrative Order 08–11	Appointment of Judge Robert E. Littlefield, Jr., as Chief Bankruptcy Judge
Administrative Order 08–02	Repeal of Order Adopting Interim Bankruptcy Rules

	ABROGATED January 1, 2012 – Interim Rule 5012 has been replaced by a permanent national rule. Accordingly, this Order was abrogated effective January 1, 2012.
Administrative Order 08–01	Debtor Counsel Fees in Chapter 13 Cases Filed in the Albany Division
Administrative Order 07–05	Issuance of Chapter 13 Discharges
	ABROGATED January 1, 2012 – The language, policy and/or procedure set forth within this Order was incorporated into the Local Bankruptcy Rules for the Northern District of New York effective January 1, 2012. Accordingly, this Order was abrogated effective January 1, 2012. (LBR 4004–1)
Administrative Order 07–04	Increase to Transcript Fee Rates
Administrative Order 05–03	Disbursement of Sec. 1326 Pre–Confirmation Adequate Protection Payments in Chapter 13 Cases Filed on or after 10/17/05
	ABROGATED January 1, 2012 – The language, policy and/o procedure set forth within this Order was incorporated into the Local Bankruptcy Rules effective January 1, 2012. Accordingly, this Order was abrogated effective January 1, 2012. (LBR 3015–1)
Administrative Order 05–02	Adoption of Interim Bankruptcy Rules
	ABROGATED January 1, 2012 – Interim Rules have been replaced by a permanent national rule. Accordingly, this Order was abrogated effective January 1, 2012.
Administrative Order 04–05	Designation of Property Disposal Officer
	ABROGATED December 1, 2010 – Chief Judge Robert E. Littlefield Jr. signed new designation. Accordingly, this Order was abrogated effective December 1, 2010.
Administrative Order 04–04	Designation of Property Custodial Officer
	ABROGATED December 1, 2010 – Chief Judge Robert E. Littlefield, Jr. signed new designation. Accordingly, this Order was abrogated effective February 1, 2010.
Administrative Order 04–03	Delegation of Property Disposal Officer
	ABROGATED December 1, 2010 – Chief Judge Robert E. Littlefield Jr. signed a new designation. Accordingly, this Order was abrogated effective December 1, 2010.
Administrative Order 04–02	Designation of Automation Property Custodial Officer
	ABROGATED December 1, 2010 – Chief Judge Robert E. Littlefield, Jr. signed new designation. Accordingly, this Order was abrogated effective December 1, 2010.
Administrative Order 04–01	Delegation of Authority to Designate Property Custodial and Disposal Officers
	ABROGATED February 1, 2010 – Chief Judge Robert E. Littlefield Jr. signed new appointment. Accordingly, this Order was abrogated effective February 1, 2010.
Administrative Order 03–01	Electronic Case Filing

	ABROGATED January 1, 2012 – The language, policy and/or procedure set forth within this Order was incorporated into the Local Bankruptcy Rules for the Northern District of New York effective January 1, 2012. Accordingly, this Order was abrogated effective January 1, 2012.
Administrative Order 02–03	Administrative Procedures for Filing, Signing, and Verifying Pleadings and Papers by Electronic Means
	ABROGATED January 1, 2012 – The language, policy and/o procedure set forth within this Order was incorporated into the Local Bankruptcy Rules effective January 1, 2012. Accordingly, this Order was abrogated effective January 1, 2012.
Administrative Order 02–02	Order Authorizing Clerk to Sign Ministerial Orders for Cases Assigned to Robert E. Littlefield, Jr., U.S. Bankruptcy Judge
	ABROGATED January 1, 2012 – All the orders referenced within this order are executed by Chief Judge Robert E. Littlefield, Jr. Accordingly, this Order was abrogated effective January 1, 2012.
Administrative Order 02–01A	Order Authorizing Clerk to Sign Ministerial Orders
	ABROGATED January 1, 2012 – All of the orders referenced within this order are executed by Chief Judge Robert E. Littlefield, Jr Accordingly, this Order was abrogated effective January 1, 2012.
Administrative Order 02–01	Delegation of Duties to Clerk of the Court
	ABROGATED January 1, 2012 – All of the orders referenced within this order are executed by Chief Judge Robert E. Littlefield, Jr. Accordingly, this Order was abrogated effective January 1, 2012.
Administrative Order 01–01	Requirements for filing an Assignment of Claim
	ABROGATED January 1, 2012.
Administrative Order 00–02	Matter of the Termination of the Bankruptcy Appellate Panel Service of the Second Judicial Circuit, Effective 06/30/00.
Administrative Order 00–01	Designating Judge Robert E. Littlefield, Jr., of the NDNY to sit in the Bankruptcy Court—District of Vermont on an intermittent basis
	ABROGATED January 1, 2012 – Bankruptcy Judge Colleen Brown was appointed in 2000. Accordingly, this Order was abrogated effective January 1, 2012.
Administrative Order 99–06	Designation of Bankruptcy Judge John J. Connelly
	ABROGATED January 1, 2012 – All pending matters are completed. Accordingly, this Order was abrogated effective January 1, 2012.
Administrative Order 99–05	Designation of Bankruptcy Judge Robert E. Littlefield, Jr.
	ABROGATED January 1, 2012 – All pending matters are completed. Accordingly, this Order was abrogated effective January 1, 2012.
Administrative Order 99–04	Designation of Bankruptcy Judge

	ABROGATED January 1, 2012 – All pending matters are completed. Accordingly, this Order was abrogated effective January 1, 2012.
Administrative Order 99–03	Designation of Bankruptcy Judge
	ABROGATED January 1, 2012 – All pending matters are completed. Accordingly, this Order was abrogated effective January 1, 2012.
Administrative Order 99–02	Designation of Chief Bankruptcy Judge Michael Kaplan
	ABROGATED January 1, 2012 – All pending matters are completed. Accordingly, this Order was abrogated effective January 1, 2012.
Administrative Order 99–01	Application of Fleet Bank to Withdraw and be Discharged from its Bond
Administrative Order Effective 01/02/97	Re: Default Motions (LBR 913.1k)
	ABROGATED January 1, 2012 – The language, policy and/or procedure set forth within this Order was incorporated into the Local Bankruptcy Rules effective January 1, 2012. Accordingly, this Order was abrogated effective January 1, 2012.

[Effective January 1, 2012. Amended effective January 23, 2017.]

APPENDIX IV. MEDIATION PROGRAM FOR THE U.S. BANKRUPTCY COURT, NORTHERN DISTRICT OF NEW YORK

1.0 PRELIMINARY STATEMENT

Litigation in bankruptcy cases frequently imposes significant economic and other burdens on parties and often delays resolution of disputes. Alternate dispute resolution procedures have the potential to reduce delay, cost, stress and other burdens often associated with litigation. Mediation, in particular, allows parties more active involvement in determining the resolution of their disputes without sacrificing the quality of justice to be rendered or the right of the litigants to a full trial on all issues not resolved through mediation.

Mediation is a process in which an impartial person, the mediator, facilitates communication between disputing parties and counsel to promote understanding, reconciliation and settlement. Mediation enables litigants to take control of their dispute and encourages amicable resolutions.

The mediator may, among other things, suggest alternatives, analyze issues, question perceptions, use logic, conduct private caucuses and stimulate negotiations between opposing sides. The mediator is an advocate for settlement and uses the mediation process to ensure that the parties fully explore all areas of agreement. The mediator does not serve as a judge or arbitrator and has no authority to render decisions on questions of fact or law or to force settlements.

2.0 ASSIGNMENT OF MATTERS TO MEDIATION

A matter may be assigned to mediation only by order of the Court ("Order of Assignment"). Upon motion of a party to the matter or the United States trustee, written stipulation, or by sua sponte order the court may assign to mediation any dispute arising in an adversary proceeding, contested matter or otherwise in a bankruptcy case. Federal Rules of Bankruptcy Procedure 7016 hereby is made applicable to all matters in which mediation is requested.

3.0 EFFECT OF MEDIATION ON PENDING MATTERS

The assignment of a matter to mediation does not relieve the parties to that matter from complying with any other court orders or applicable provisions of the United States Code, the Federal Rules of Bankruptcy Procedure, or the local rules of this court. Unless otherwise ordered by the court, the assignment to mediation does not delay or stay discovery, pretrial, hearing dates, or trial schedules.

4.0 THE MEDIATOR

4.1 Registration of Mediators/Mediation Administrator

The clerk of the court shall establish and maintain a register of persons (the "Panel") qualified under this section and designated by the court to serve as mediators in the Mediation Program.

4.2 Application and Certification of Mediators

4.2.1 Application and Qualification Requirements

Each applicant shall submit to the Mediation Administrator a statement of professional qualifications, experience, training, and other information demonstrating, in the applicant's opinion, why the applicant should be designated to the Panel. The applicant shall have completed eight hours of formal mediation training. The applicant shall submit the statement in the form attached hereto as Form A. The statement also shall set forth whether the applicant has been removed from any professional organization, or has resigned from any professional organization while an investigation into allegations of professional misconduct was pending, and the circumstances of such removal or resignation. This statement shall constitute an application for designation to the Mediation Program.

4.2.2 Court Certification

The court in its sole discretion shall grant or deny an application submitted pursuant to subsection 4.2.1 of this rule. If the court grants the application, the applicant's name shall be added to the Panel, subject to removal pursuant to section 4.4 of this rule.

4.2.3 Reaffirmation of Qualifications

Each applicant accepted for designation to the Panel shall reaffirm annually the continued existence and accuracy of the qualifications, statements and representations made in the application. Failure to comply with this section shall be grounds for removal under section 4.4.

4.3 Mediator's Oath or Affirmation

Upon appointment to the Panel or selection as a mediator, every mediator must sign a written oath or affirmation (see 28 U.S.C. § 453), as if the person were a judge, and file the oath or affirmation with the Mediation Administrator.

4.4 Ethical Standards for Mediators

All mediators shall adhere to the Standards of Conduct for Mediators as promulgated by the American Arbitration Association ("AAA standards"). A failure to adhere to the AAA standards may constitute sufficient cause for the removal from the Panel. Such failure will not void any consensual agreement between the parties unless both parties consent to the rescission of the agreement or, on motion of any party to the mediation or, sua sponte, the court finds that the mediator's conflict of interest or failure to abide by the AAA standards caused actual prejudice to a party.

4.5 Removal from Panel

A person shall be removed from the Panel either at the person's written request to the Mediation Administrator or by court order for cause. If removed by court order, the personal shall not be returned to the Panel absent a court order obtained on motion to the Mediation Administrator supported by an affidavit sufficiently explaining the circumstances of such removal and the reasons justifying the return of the person to the Panel.

5.0 APPOINTMENT OF MEDIATOR

5.1.1 Selection by Parties

Within 15 calendar days of the date of service of the Order of Assignment of a matter to mediation, the parties to the matter to be mediated shall select a mediator, and an alternate mediator, and shall present the court with a proposed order of appointment. If such selection is not from the Panel, the parties shall submit with the proposed order of appointment a stipulation by the parties that the person is not on the Panel but is qualified to mediate the matter. If the court approves the parties' selection, immediately after entry of the order of appointment, the court shall notify the parties, the mediator and the alternate mediator of the appointment.

5.1.2 Selection/Appointment by Court

If the parties cannot agree upon a mediator within 15 calendar days of the date of service of the Order of Assignment, the court shall appoint a mediator and an alternate mediator from the Panel and shall notify the parties, the mediator, and the alternate mediator of such appointment.

5.2.1 Inability of Mediator to Serve

If the mediator is unable to serve due to a conflict or other reason precluding acceptance of the appointment, the mediator shall file and serve on all parties to the mediation and on the alternate mediator, within five calendar days after receipt of the notice of appointment, a notice of inability to accept the appointment. The alternate mediator then shall become the mediator if the alternate does not file and serve on all parties to the mediation a notice of inability to accept the appointment within five calendar days after receipt of the original mediator's notice of inability to accept the appointment. If neither the mediator nor the alternate mediator can serve, the court shall appoint another mediator and alternate mediator.

5.2.2 Mediator's Prior Service

A mediator has the option of declining to accept the mediation based on having served as a mediator on four previous occasions within a period of one year.

5.3 Disqualification of Mediator

5.3.1 Disqualifying Events

Any person selected as a mediator may be disqualified for bias or prejudice in the same manner that a judge may be disqualified under 28 U.S.C. § 144. Any person selected as a mediator shall be disqualified in any matter where 28 U.S.C. § 455 would require disqualification if that person were a judge. Any member of the bar who is certified and designated as a mediator pursuant to this rule shall not solely for that reason be disqualified from appearing or acting as counsel in any other matter or case pending before this court.

5.3.2 Inquiry by Mediator; Disclosure

Promptly after receiving notice of appointment, the mediator shall make inquiry sufficient to determine whether there is a basis for disqualification under subsection 5.3.1 of this rule. The inquiry shall include, but shall not be limited to, a search for conflicts of interest in the manner prescribed by the applicable rules of professional conduct for attorney mediators, and by the applicable rules pertaining to the mediator's profession for non-attorney mediators. Within seven calendar days after receiving notice of appointment, the mediator shall file with the court and serve on the parties to the mediation either (a) a statement that there is no basis for disqualification under subsection 5.3.1 and that the mediator has no actual or potential conflict of interest or (b) a notice of withdrawal.

5.3.3 Objection Based on Conflict of Interest

A party to the mediation who believes that the assigned mediator and/or the alternate mediator has a conflict of interest promptly shall bring the issue to the attention of the mediator and/or the alternate mediator, as applicable, and to other parties to the mediation. If the mediator does not withdraw, the issue shall be brought to the court's attention by the mediator or any of the parties to the mediation. The court shall take such action as the court deems necessary or appropriate to resolve the alleged conflict of interest.

5.4 Mediator's Liability

There shall be no liability on the part of, and no cause of action shall arise against, any person who is appointed as a mediator pursuant to this rule on account of any act or omission in the course and scope of such person's duties as a mediator. *See e.g., Wagshal v. Foster*, 28 F.3d 1249 (D.C. Cir. 1994).

6.0 COMPENSATION

6.1 Compensation of Mediator

The mediator shall serve on a pro bono basis and shall not require compensation or reimbursement of expenses. It is anticipated that the mediation shall not exceed six hours in length. If, at the conclusion of the six hours of mediation, it is determined by the mediator and the parties to the mediation that additional time will be necessary and productive in order to complete the mediation, then:

(1) If the mediator consents to continue to serve on a pro bono basis, the parties to the mediation may agree to continue the mediation conference; or

(2) If the mediator does not consent to continue to serve on a pro bono basis, the mediator's fees and expenses shall be on such terms as are satisfactory to the mediator and the parties to the mediation, subject to prior court approval if the estate is to be charged. The parties to the mediation shall share equally all mediation fees and expenses unless the parties to the mediation agree otherwise. The court may, in the interest of justice, determine a different allocation. In no case will compensation exceed an hourly rate of $150 per hour.

7.0 THE MEDIATION

7.1 Time and Place of Mediation Conference

After consulting with all counsel and pro se parties, the mediator shall schedule a convenient time and place for the mediation conference, and promptly give all counsel and pro se parties at least 14 calendar days' written notice of the time and place of the mediation conference. The mediator shall schedule the mediation to begin as soon as practicable.

7.2 Submission Materials

Not less than seven calendar days before the mediation conference, each party shall submit directly to the mediator, and serve on all counsel and pro se parties, any materials (the "Submission") the mediator directs to be prepared and assembled. The mediator shall so direct not less than 14 calendar days before the mediation conference. Prior to the mediation conference, the mediator may talk with the participants to determine what materials would be helpful. The Submissions shall not be filed with the court and the court shall not have access to them.

7.3 Attendance at Mediation Conference

7.3.1 Persons Required to Attend

The following persons personally must attend the mediation conference:

(1) Each party that is a natural person;

(2) If the party is not a natural person, a representative who is not the party's attorney of record and who has full authority to negotiate and settle the matter on behalf of the party;

(3) If the party is a governmental entity that requires settlement approval by an elected official or legislative body, a representative who has authority to recommend a settlement to the elected official or legislative body;

(4) The attorney who has primary responsibility for each party's case; and

(5) Other interested parties such as insurers or indemnitors, or one or more of their representatives, whose presence is necessary for a full resolution of the matter assigned to mediation.

7.3.2 Excuse

A person required to attend the mediation is excused from appearing if all parties and the mediator agree that the person need not attend. The court for cause may excuse a person's attendance.

7.3.3 Failure to Attend

Willful failure to attend any mediation conference, and any other material violation of this rule, shall be reported to the court by the mediator and may result in the imposition of sanctions by the court. Any such report of the mediator shall comply with the confidentiality requirements of section 8.1 of this rule.

7.4 Mediation Conference Procedures

The mediator may establish procedures for the mediation conference.

8.0 CONFIDENTIALITY OF MEDIATION PROCEEDINGS

8.1 Protection of Information Disclosed at Mediation

The mediator and the participants in mediation are prohibited from divulging, outside of the mediation, any oral or written information disclosed by the parties or by witnesses in the course of the mediation. No person may rely on or introduce as evidence in any arbitral, judicial, or other proceedings, evidence pertaining to any aspect of the mediation effort, including but not limited to: (a) views expressed or suggestions made by a party with respect to a possible settlement of the dispute; (b) the fact that another party had or had not indicated willingness to accept a proposal for settlement made by the mediator; (c) proposals made or views expressed by the mediator; (d) statements or admissions made by a party in the course of the mediation; and (e) documents prepared for the purpose of, in the course of, or pursuant to the mediation. In addition, without limiting the foregoing, Rule 408 of the Federal Rules of Evidence and any applicable federal or state statute, rule, common law or judicial precedent relating to the privileged nature of settlement discussions, mediation or other alternative dispute resolution procedure shall apply. Information otherwise discoverable or admissible in evidence, however, does not become exempt from discovery, or inadmissible in evidence, merely by being used by a party in a mediation.

8.2 Discovery from Mediator

The mediator shall not be compelled to disclose to the court or to any person outside the mediation conference any of the records, reports, summaries, notes, communications, or other documents received or made by a mediator while serving in such capacity. The mediator shall not testify or be compelled to testify in regard to the mediation in connection with any arbitral, judicial or other proceeding. The mediator shall not be a necessary party in any proceedings relating to the mediation. Nothing contained in this section shall prevent the mediator from reporting the status, but not the substance, of the mediation effort to the court in writing, from filing a report as required by section 9.1, or from complying with the obligations set forth in section 10.

8.3 Protection of Proprietary Information

The parties, the mediator, and all mediation participants shall protect proprietary information during and after the mediation conference.

8.4 Preservation of Privileges

The disclosure by a party of privileged information to the mediator does not waive or otherwise adversely affect the privileged nature of the information.

9.0 RECOMMENDATIONS BY MEDIATOR

The mediator is not required to prepare written comments or recommendations to the parties. Mediators may present a written settlement recommendation memorandum to attorneys or pro se litigants, but not to the court.

10.0   POST MEDIATION PROCEDURES

10.1   Preparation of Orders

If a settlement is reached at a mediation, a party designated by the mediator shall submit a fully executed stipulation and proposed order to the court within twenty calendar days after the end of the mediation. If the party fails to prepare the stipulation and order, the court may impose appropriate sanctions.

10.2   Mediator's Certificate of Completion

Promptly after the mediation conference, the mediator shall file with the court, and serve on the parties and the Mediation Administrator, a certificate in the form provided by the court showing compliance or noncompliance with the mediation conference requirements of this rule and whether or not a settlement has been reached. Regardless of the outcome of the mediation conference, the mediator shall not provide the court with any details of the substance of the conference.

10.3   Mediator's Report

In order to assist the Mediation Administrator in compiling useful data to evaluate the Mediation Program, and to aid the court in assessing the efforts of the members of the Panel, the mediator shall provide the Mediation Administrator with an estimate of the number of hours spent in the mediation conference and other statistical and evaluative information on a form provided by the court. The mediator shall provide this report whether or not the mediation conference results in settlement.

11.0   WITHDRAWAL FROM MEDIATION

Any matter assigned to mediation pursuant to this rule may be withdrawn from mediation by the court at any time upon determination that the matter is not suitable for mediation. In addition, where mediation is brought about either by sua sponte order or motion, a party may withdraw from the mediation at any time after attending the first scheduled mediation conference only upon notice and motion. In order to withdraw, the withdrawing party shall, no later than five business days prior to any subsequently scheduled mediation activity, file with the court a motion seeking to withdraw from the mediation, briefly stating the reasons for the request and serve on the Mediator, Administrator, mediator and other parties (or their counsel). The method of service of the motion for withdrawal shall provide for actual receipt by the parties and the mediator no later than three business days prior to the next scheduled mediation activity. The court shall rule upon the motion without argument. All mediation activity shall be stayed pending an order from the court.

12.0   TERMINATION OF MEDIATION

Upon the filing of a mediator's certificate pursuant to section 10.2 or the entry of an order withdrawing a matter from mediation pursuant to section 11.0, the mediation will be deemed terminated, and the mediator excused and relieved from further responsibilities in the matter without further court order. If the mediation conference does not result in a resolution of all of the disputes in the assigned matter, the matter shall proceed to trial or hearing pursuant to the court's scheduling order.

13.0   REEVALUATION/REVISION PROCEDURE

The purpose and administration of this rule shall be reviewed and reevaluated at such time and in such manner as the court deems appropriate.

[Effective January 1, 2012. Amended effective May 21, 2012.]

APPENDIX V. BANKRUPTCY COURT MISCELLANEOUS FEE SCHEDULE

Fee Schedule for the United States Bankruptcy Court (EFFECTIVE 12/01/2016)

Chapter	Filing Fee	Split/Sever	Reopen	Conv to Ch 7	Conv to Ch 11
7	$ 335.00	$ 335.00	$ 260.00	—	$ 922.00
12	$ 275.00	$ 275.00	$ 200.00	$ 60.00	NO FEE
13	$ 310.00	$ 310.00	$ 235.00	$ 25.00	$ 932.00
11	$1717.00	$1717.00	$1167.00	$ 15.00	—
9 or 15	$1717.00	$1213.00	$1167.00	$ 15.00*	n/a
				*Ch 9 Only	

Other Filing Fees

Amend Schedules D, E, F, Matrix, List of Creditors	$ 31.00 new
Motion to Lift Stay (362) or Abandonment	$ 181.00 new
Adversary Filing Fee (no fee to reopen)	$ 350.00
Notice of Appeal	$ 5.00
Appeal/Cross Appeal	$ 293.00
Direct Appeal/Direct Cross Appeal (in addition to $298.00 for Notice and Appeal)	$ 207.00
File a Misc. Document or Register a Foreign Judgment	$ 47.00 new
Withdrawal of the Reference	$ 181.00 new
Transfer of Claim Filing Fee	$ 25.00
Sale Motion Free & Clear 11 USC § 363(f)	$ 181.00 new
Motion to Redact (Fed. R. of Bankr. P. 9037)	$ 25.00 *

*NO fee to reopen case if motion for redaction only.

Service Fees

NSF Charge for ANY form of Pmt Returned or Denied	$ 53.00		
Record Retrieval from Federal Records Center	$ 64.00		(1st box) $39.00 ea. Add'l box
SmartScan Electronic Record Retrieval- 100 page limit	$19.90		Plus $.65 per page
Search of Records (per name or item searched)	$ 31.00	new	
Microfilm or Microfiche Duplication	$ 5.00		
Reproduction of Audio Recording (tape or CD)	$ 31.00	new	
Photocopies produced via public terminal (per page)	$ 00.10		
Photocopy requests by mail or phone (per page)	$ 00.50		
Document Certification (plus copy charge)	$ 11.00		
Document Exemplification (plus copy charge)	$ 22.00	new	
Pro Hac Vice Registration (payable to Dsct Court Clerk)	$100.00		

Transcript of Hearing (typed)				
Turnaround Time (in days)	30	14	7	Daily
Cost per Page	$ 3.65	$ 4.25	$ 4.85	$ 6.05

[Effective January 1, 2012. Amended effective November 21, 2012; December 1, 2013; December 1, 2016.]

SELECTED LOCAL FORMS

CHAPTER 13 MODEL PLAN

UNITED STATES BANKRUPTCY COURT
NORTHERN DISTRICT OF NEW YORK

In re:

Case No.
Chapter 13

Debtor(s).

CHAPTER 13 PLAN
(□ Amended as of _____)

The chapter 13 plan ("Plan") does one or more of the following (if the box is checked):

☐ Values Collateral to Establish Amount of Secured Claims (Section II(B)(ii))

☐ Sets Interest Rates for Secured Claims (Section II(B)(ii) and (iii))

☐ Assumes and/or Rejects Unexpired Leases and Executory Contracts (Section II(I))

Hereinafter the matters checked are referred to as "Allowed Contested Matters."

☐ **IF THIS BOX IS CHECKED, THE PLAN CONTAINS NON-STANDARD PROVISIONS AT SECTION V THAT ARE CONTROLLING AND THAT SHALL SUPERSEDE ANY OTHER PROVISIONS OF THE PLAN.**

☐ **IF THIS IS AN AMENDED PLAN,** the reason for filing the Amended Plan is: _____
_____ .

NOTICE TO ALL CREDITORS:

YOUR RIGHTS WILL BE AFFECTED.   You should read these papers carefully and consult an attorney as to their legal effect. Anyone who wishes to oppose any provision of this Plan or the included Allowed Contested Matters **MUST** file with the United States Bankruptcy Court a timely written objection, so as to be received not later than seven (7) days prior to the hearing on Confirmation of the Plan and approval of the Allowed Contested Matters, and appear at the hearing. Unless a written objection is timely filed, this Plan may be confirmed and become binding, and the included Allowed Contested Matters may be granted, without further notice or hearing.

UNLESS A WRITTEN OBJECTION IS TIMELY FILED, the Court will find at confirmation that the chapter 13 Debtor has complied with the filing requirements of 11 U.S.C. § 521(a)(1) (mandatory documents) and 11 U.S.C. § 521(b) (credit counseling certificate).

EVEN IF A DEBT IS SPECIFICALLY LISTED IN THIS PLAN, A CREDITOR SHOULD TIMELY FILE A PROOF OF CLAIM.

I.   **PAYMENT AND LENGTH OF PLAN.**

A.   **STANDARD PLAN TERMS.**

Required Monthly Payments: _____

Lump-sum payment(s) in the amount(s) of _____ from the following source(s):
_____ lawsuit proceeds

STANDARD PLAN TERMS cont. ...

_____ sale proceeds (include description of property to be sold, location, method of sale and anticipated date of sale) _____

_____

_____ other _____

The Debtor shall immediately turn over to the Trustee any tax refund in excess of $1,500.00 during the life of the Plan.

Term of Plan: _____

Minimum Amount to be paid into the Plan: _____

Minimum amount to be paid to General Unsecured Creditors under the Plan shall be the greater of:

Liquidation: $_____
Disposable Income (B 122C-2 - Line 45): $_____
Percentage Repayment: _____%

B.   SPECIAL NOTICES.

SPECIAL NOTICE TO CREDITORS HOLDING UNSECURED CLAIMS:

UNSECURED CREDITORS ARE DIRECTED TO CAREFULLY REVIEW THE ORDER OF DISTRIBUTION OF PLAN PAYMENTS BY THE TRUSTEE AT PARAGRAPH I(C) OF THIS PLAN AND CONSULT AN ATTORNEY REGARDING THE PROPOSED TREATMENT OF THEIR CLAIM(S) UNDER THIS PLAN.

Under 11 U.S.C. § 1325(b)(1)(B), if an unsecured creditor objects to this Plan, the Court may not approve this Plan unless the Plan provides that all of the Debtor's projected disposable income will be applied to make payments to unsecured creditors under the Plan. Absent an objection, distribution of payments under this Plan will be made pursuant to the order of distribution set forth at paragraph I(C) below. This distribution scheme may result in the secured and priority claims being paid *prior to your unsecured claim*. To avoid this result, you must file an objection.

SPECIAL NOTICE TO DOMESTIC SUPPORT OBLIGATION CLAIMANTS:

THE DEBTOR IS REQUIRED TO MAKE PAYMENTS FOR POST-PETITION DOMESTIC SUPPORT OBLIGATIONS AS THAT TERM IS DEFINED UNDER 11 U.S.C. § 101(14A), COMMENCING ON THE DATE OF FILING AND CONTINUING DURING THE TERM OF THE PLAN. PRE-PETITON DOMESTIC SUPPORT OBLIGATION ARREARS, IF ANY, ARE ADDRESSED AT SECTION II(F).

THE FOLLOWING IS THE NAME AND ADDRESS OF EACH INDIVIDUAL ENTITLED TO RECEIVE DOMESTIC SUPPORT OBLIGATION PAYMENTS, AND THE AMOUNT(S) OF SUCH PAYMENTS:

☐ **Not Applicable**

2

(Rev. 11/30/2015)

DOMESTIC SUPPORT OBLIGATION CLAIMANTS AND AMOUNTS CONT. ...

Payee Name and Address   **Ongoing Payment Obligation**

_____ $_____

_____

_____

_____

_____

C.   ORDER OF DISTRIBUTION OF PLAN PAYMENTS BY THE TRUSTEE. Subject to any alternate provision in Section V, funds received by the Trustee for distribution to creditors under the Plan, absent objection, shall be applied, after payment of applicable Trustee's fees, in the following order of distribution:

First:	To pay any and all equal monthly payments required on allowed secured claims under Section II(B)(ii) and (iii).
Second:	To pay allowed administrative expenses, including attorney's fees, *pro rata*, until paid in full under Section II(A)(i) and (ii).
Third:	To pay allowed secured claims *pro rata* until paid in full under Section II(B)(i)(a), (iv) and (v).
Fourth:	To pay allowed priority claims *pro rata* until paid in full under Section II(F).
Fifth:	To pay allowed unsecured claims *pro rata*.

However, in the event the Debtor pays ongoing mortgage payments through the Plan under Section II(B)(i)(c), those payments shall be made prior to payment to any other creditor and after payment of applicable Trustee fees.

D.   REQUIREMENTS FOR COMPLETION. The Plan will be considered complete when:

(i)   all allowed secured and priority unsecured claims have been paid in full except those specified in Section II(B)(i)(b);

(ii)   all payments as set forth in Section I have been received by the Trustee for payment to creditors; and

(iii)   allowed unsecured claims not separately classified and provided for in Section II(H) have received at least _____% or $_____ . (either liquidation or disposable income), whichever provides a greater distribution.

II.   TREATMENT OF CREDITORS.

A.   ADMINISTRATIVE EXPENSE CLAIMS. All allowed administrative claims shall be paid in full. The amount to be paid shall be the amount listed below unless the creditor holding the claim timely files a proof of claim with the Court setting forth a different amount, which claim amount shall control.

(i)   **Debtor's attorney's fees:** Debtor's attorney shall be paid $_____, of which $_____ was paid pre-petition and $_____ shall be paid as an allowed administrative claim as part of the Plan.

3

(Rev. 11/30/2015)

TREATMENT OF CREDITORS Cont. ...

     (ii)   **Other Administrative Claims:**

Creditor	Estimated Claim

☐ **None**

B.   **SECURED CLAIMS.**

<u>NOTICES TO ALL CREDITORS HOLDING SECURED CLAIMS:</u>

LIEN RETENTION: With the exception of those creditors whose liens are subject to avoidance under 11 U.S.C. § 522(f) and whose liens are subsequently avoided by court order as impairing the Debtor's exemption, all secured creditors shall retain the lien(s) securing their claim(s) until the earlier of payment in full of the underlying debt determined in accordance with nonbankruptcy law or discharge of such claim under 11 U.S.C. § 1328. If paid by the Trustee, the claim shall be paid *pro rata* in accordance with the Plan terms providing for the order of distribution or in monthly payments, as indicated below.

CLAIM ALLOWANCE AND AMOUNT: The allowance and amount of the secured claim shall be determined in accordance with the creditor's timely filed proof of claim.

ONGOING NOTICES: Creditors being paid directly by the Debtor under the Plan shall continue to send customary payment coupons, statements, and notices to the parties making ongoing payments. Debtor agrees that such actions shall not constitute or form the basis for finding a violation of the automatic stay.

POST-PETITION FEES AND COSTS FOR CLAIMS SECURED BY REAL PROPERTY: No creditors holding claims secured with real property shall ever assess, charge or collect, from either the Debtor or the real estate collateral, any assessments, fees, costs, expenses or any other monetary amounts, exclusive of principal, interest, taxes, late fees and insurance, that arose from the date of filing of the bankruptcy petition to the entry of the order of discharge except as may be allowed as part of an allowed secured claim pursuant to Federal Rule of Bankruptcy Procedure 3002.1 or a court order.

    (i)   Real Property Mortgage Claims:

        a.   Mortgage Arrears: Mortgage arrears owed to the creditors listed below shall be paid through the Plan by the Trustee in accordance with the secured creditor's timely filed proof of claim.

Creditor	Collateral Address	Amount of Arrears

☐ **None**

4

(Rev. 11/30/2015)

SECURED CLAIMS Cont. ...

      b.   Ongoing Post-Petition Mortgage Payments to be Paid by the Debtor Directly to the Creditor:

Creditor	Collateral Address

☐ **None**

      c.   Post-Petition Mortgage Payments to be Paid by the Trustee to the Creditor Through the Plan:

Creditor	Payment Amount	Interest Rate

☐ **None**

    (ii)   Payment of Bifurcated Claim with Secured Portion Based on Collateral Value:

The creditors listed below will be paid a secured claim through the Plan based upon the value of their collateral pursuant to 11 U.S.C. § 506 ("Collateral Value") with present value interest pursuant to 11 U.S.C. § 1325(a)(5) in the amount set forth below. Any filed claim requesting payment of a higher secured claim amount shall be deemed to be an unsecured claim to the extent that the amount of the filed claim exceeds the Collateral Value stated below. Further, any request for interest at a rate which is higher than the rate listed below shall be disallowed. Finally, a filed proof of claim seeking a lower secured claim amount or lower rate of interest on its secured claim shall be deemed to be the creditor's consent to accept payment of said lower amount(s) notwithstanding this Court's determination of the secured claim amount or interest rate as set forth below. Monthly payments received prior to the date of confirmation of the Plan shall constitute adequate protection pursuant to 11 U.S.C. § 1326 and shall be applied to reduce the principal balance of the claim. After confirmation, the balance of the claim shall be paid with interest at the rate set forth below through equal monthly payments as required under 11 U.S.C. § 1325(a)(5). The remaining balance of the creditor's claim (above the Collateral Value) shall be treated as an unsecured claim.

Creditor	Collateral Value	Interest Rate	Equal Monthly Payment	Pre-confirmation Adequate Protection Payment

☐ **None**

Collateral Description: _____

Collateral Description: _____

Collateral Description: _____

5

(Rev. 11/30/2015)

SECURED CLAIMS Cont. ...

(iii)   Payment in Full of Secured Claim With Present Value Interest:

The creditors listed below will be paid principal owed in full, with present value interest pursuant to 11 U.S.C. § 1325(a)(5). The amounts set forth in the timely filed proof of claim shall control the amount paid, however, any filed proof of claim will be disallowed to the extent that the interest rate sought exceeds the rate listed below. Further, a filed claim seeking a lower secured claim amount or lower interest rate on its secured claim shall be deemed to be the creditor's consent to accept payment at the lower amount and/or rate notwithstanding this Court's determination of the secured claim amount or interest rate as set forth below. Monthly payments prior to the date of confirmation of the Plan shall constitute adequate protection pursuant to 11 U.S.C. § 1326 and shall be applied to reduce the principal balance of the claim. After confirmation, the balance of the claim shall be paid with interest at the rate set forth below through equal monthly payment as required pursuant to 11 U.S.C. § 1325(a)(5).

Creditor	Full Claim Amount	Interest Rate	Equal Monthly Payment	Pre-confirmation Adequate Protection Payment
☐ **None**				

Collateral Description:_____

Collateral Description:_____

Collateral Description:_____

(iv) Payment of Arrearage Only on Claims Secured By Personalty:

Arrears owed to the creditors listed below shall be paid through the Plan by the Trustee in accordance with the secured creditor's timely filed proof of claim.

Creditor	Collateral	Amount of Arrears Claim	Interest Rate
☐ **None**			

(v) Payment in Full of All Other Secured Claims:

These claims may include, but are not limited to, claims secured by unavoidable judgments and real property tax liens. The creditors listed below will receive payment in full in accordance with the secured creditor's timely filed proof of claim.

Creditor	Lien Amount	Interest Rate
☐ **None**		

6

(Rev. 11/30/2015)

SECURED CLAIMS Cont. ...

Collateral Description: _____

Collateral Description: _____

Collateral Description: _____

     (vi) Other Ongoing Direct Payments on Secured Claims:

     The creditors listed below will not receive payments through the Plan:

Creditor	Collateral

☐ **None**

Collateral Description: _____

Collateral Description: _____

C.   **MORTGAGE CLAIMS MODIFIED PURSUANT TO 11 U.S.C. § 506.** The following claims shall be treated as unsecured claims and an appropriate motion will be filed and heard on or before confirmation of the Plan:

Creditor	Amount of Claim

☐ **None**

D.   **COLLATERAL SUBJECT TO SURRENDER.** Debtor surrenders his or her interest in the following collateral in satisfaction of the secured portion of such creditor's allowed claim. If the creditor has timely filed a secured claim, the creditor may file an amended claim, which claim shall be treated as a non-priority unsecured claim for any remaining deficiency balance after liquidation by the creditor of their secured collateral in accordance with applicable state law. Upon confirmation, creditor may submit for entry an ex parte order lifting the automatic stay as to the surrendered collateral.

Creditor	Collateral	Amount of Claim (if known)

☐ **None**

E.   **CLAIMS SUBJECT TO SALE OF COLLATERAL.** The collateral securing the claims held by the following secured creditors will be sold during the Plan and the claim shall be paid from sale proceeds at the time of sale. **No disbursements shall be made to the creditor from the regular monthly Plan payments.**

Creditor	Collateral	Amount of Claim

☐ **None**

7

(Rev. 11/30/2015)

F.   PRIORITY CLAIMS. All allowed claims entitled to priority under 11 U.S.C. § 507 shall be paid in full. The amount of the claim shall be determined in accordance with the creditor's timely filed proof of claim.

Creditor	Estimated Claim	Basis for priority treatment

☐ **None**

G.   CO-SIGNED AND OTHER SEPARATELY CLASSIFIED UNSECURED CLAIMS. The claims listed below have been separately classified pursuant to 11 U.S.C. § 1322(b)(1) and will be paid in full. The amount of the claim shall be determined in accordance with the creditor's timely filed proof of claim.

Creditor	Amount of Claim

☐ **None**

H.   UNSECURED NON-PRIORITY CLAIMS. Allowed unsecured non-priority claims will be paid *pro rata* in accordance with the minimum distribution set forth in Section I(A).

I.   UNEXPIRED LEASES AND EXECUTORY CONTRACTS. Creditors holding an arrearage claim on any assumed lease or executory contract shall be paid through the Plan. The amount to be paid shall be in accordance with the creditor's timely filed proof of claim.

The following unexpired leases and executory contracts are **ASSUMED:**

Creditor	Property Subject to the Lease or Contract	Amount of Claim

☐ **None**

The following unexpired leases and executory contracts are **REJECTED:**

Creditor	Property Subject to the Lease or Contract	Amount of Claim

☐ **None**

Any unexpired leases and executory contracts not listed above are deemed **REJECTED**.

III.   CONFIRMATION ORDER CONTROLS. The provisions of this Plan are subject to modification as provided in the Order of Confirmation. In the event of an inconsistent provision contained in this Plan and the Order of Confirmation, the Order of Confirmation shall control.

IV.   VESTING OF PROPERTY OF THE ESTATE. All property of the Debtor's chapter 13 estate shall remain property of the estate and under this Court's jurisdiction until the Plan is completed.

8

(Rev. 11/30/2015)

V.   NON-STANDARD PLAN PROVISIONS.

☐ NONE

☐ PAY WITHOUT CREDITOR'S PROOF OF CLAIM (Albany Division Only)
BE ADVISED, that if this box is checked:

The Debtor requests that the specific claims set forth herein held by the creditors listed below be allowed and paid through the Plan with the claims deemed filed by the Debtor, subject to being amended by the creditor's timely filed proof of claim:

Creditor   Collateral Description

_____   _____

_____   _____

_____   _____

If no proof of claim is filed by a creditor listed above, Debtor requests that the Court find that the Plan conforms substantially to the Federal Rules of Bankruptcy Procedure and the Official Proof of Claim form so as to support allowance and payment of the claim for that creditor in the amount set forth herein.

☐ OTHER

_____

_____

_____

_____

Dated:_____   _____
                                          Debtor Signature

Dated:_____   _____
                                          Joint Debtor Signature

Dated:_____   _____
                                          Attorney Signature
                                          Attorney Name and Address

9

(Rev. 11/30/2015)

[Effective January 17, 2012.   Revised September 1, 2012;   December 1, 2014;   November 30, 2015.]

FORM LM1. LOSS MITIGATION REQUEST BY DEBTOR(S) AND CERTIFICATE OF SERVICE

UNITED STATES BANKRUPTCY COURT
NORTHERN DISTRICT OF NEW YORK

In re: _____   Case No.
                                             Chapter
                    _____
                    Debtor(s).

LOSS MITIGATION REQUEST BY DEBTOR(S) AND CERTIFICATE OF SERVICE

PURSUANT TO SECTION V OF THE COURT'S LOSS MITIGATION PROGRAM PROCEDURES, THE CREDITOR NAMED HEREIN HAS 14 DAYS FROM SERVICE OF THIS REQUEST TO FILE AND SERVE AN OBJECTION TO LOSS MITIGATION REQUEST AND A NOTICE OF HEARING ON OBJECTION TO LOSS MITIGATION REQUEST ON THE DEBTOR(S), DEBTOR(S)' ATTORNEY, AND THE CASE TRUSTEE. IF AN OBJECTION TO LOSS MITIGATION REQUEST AND A NOTICE OF HEARING ON OBJECTION TO LOSS MITIGATION REQUEST ARE NOT FILED, THE COURT MAY ENTER A LOSS MITIGATION ORDER.

I. IDENTIFICATION OF THE PROPERY AND THE PARTIES:

I am/We are the Debtor(s) in this case and hereby request to enter into the Loss Mitigation Program with respect to my/our Property located at:

Address: _____

          _____ ;

With the following Creditor:

Creditor's Name and Address: With respect to the Property, Creditor
                                            is the holder of a:

_____   ☐ First Mortgage

_____   ☐ Second Mortgage

                                            ☐ Other (please specify): _____

_____   _____.

II. SIGNATURE:

I understand that if the court orders Loss Mitigation in this case, I am required to comply with the Loss Mitigation Program Procedures and will participate in good faith. **I understand that Loss Mitigation is voluntary for all parties and that I am not required to enter into any agreement or settlement with any other party as part of entry into the Loss Mitigation Program. I also understand that no other party is required to enter into any agreement or settlement with me.** I understand that I am not required to request dismissal of my case as part of any resolution or settlement that is offered or agreed to during Loss Mitigation. I also understand that if a Loss Mitigation Order is entered, I am responsible pursuant to section VII(B) of the Loss Mitigation Program Procedures for adjourning any matters pending between the Loss Mitigation Parties for which I am the movant. I certify that the Property in question consists only of real property used as my principal residence in which I hold an interest.

Dated: _____

                     Debtor

Dated: _____

                     Joint Debtor

III. LOSS MITIGATION CONTACT INFORMATION FOR ATTORNEY FOR DEBTOR(S):

Name: _____

Title: _____

Firm: _____

Address: _____

Address 2: _____

City: _____ State: _____ Zip Code: _____

Phone No.: _____ Facsimile No.: _____

Email Address: _____.

2

(LM:01 Request by Debtor(s) rev. 03-15-2016)

IV. CERTIFICATE OF SERVICE:

I, _____, state under penalty of perjury that the following is true and accurate.

(1) That I am not a party to this action, am over 18 years of age, and reside in _____, New York.

(2) That on _____, 20____, I served a true and accurate copy of the above Loss Mitigation Request by Debtor(s)—

—by notice of electronic filing (NEF) via the CM/ECF system upon the following parties at the email addresses listed below:

—by first class mail upon the following parties at the addresses listed below:

—by certified mail upon the following parties at the addresses listed below:

Dated: _____, 20____
_____, New York
                                                   _____
                                                   Name

Sworn to before me this

_____ day of _____, 20_____
_____
Notary Public, State of New York

3

(LM:01 Request by Debtor(s) rev. 03-15-2016)

[Effective June 21, 2013.   Revised March 15, 2016.]

FORM LM2. LOSS MITIGATION REQUEST BY CREDITOR AND CERTIFICATE OF SERVICE

UNITED STATES BANKRUPTCY COURT
NORTHERN DISTRICT OF NEW YORK

In re: Case No.
                                                Chapter

_____ Debtor(s).

LOSS MITIGATION REQUEST BY CREDITOR AND CERTIFICATE OF SERVICE

PURSUANT TO SECTION V OF THE COURT'S LOSS MITIGATION PROGRAM PROCEDURES, THE ABOVE-CAPTIONED DEBTOR(S) HAS/HAVE 14 DAYS FROM SERVICE OF THIS REQUEST TO FILE AND SERVE AN OBJECTION TO LOSS MITIGATION REQUEST AND A NOTICE OF HEARING ON OBJECTION TO LOSS MITIGATION REQUEST ON THE CREDITOR AND THE CASE TRUSTEE. IF AN OBJECTION TO LOSS MITIGATION REQUEST AND A NOTICE OF HEARING ON OBJECTION TO LOSS MITIGATION REQUEST ARE NOT FILED, THE COURT MAY ENTER A LOSS MITIGATION ORDER.

I am/represent a Creditor (including a holder, servicer or trustee of a mortgage or lien secured by Property used by the Debtor(s) as a principal residence) of the Debtor(s). I/Creditor hereby requests to enter into the Loss Mitigation Program with respect to:

Property Address: _____

_____

With respect to the Property, I am/Creditor is the holder of a:

☐ First Mortgage
☐ Second Mortgage
☐ Other (please specify): _____

Signature:

I understand that if the court orders Loss Mitigation in this case, I am required to comply with the Loss Mitigation Program Procedures and will participate in good faith. **I agree that I will not require the Debtor(s) to request or cause dismissal of this case as part of any**

1

(LM:02 Request by Creditor rev. 03-15-2016)

resolution or settlement that is offered or agreed to during the Loss Mitigation Period. I also understand that if a Loss Mitigation Order is entered, I am responsible pursuant to section VII(B) of the Loss Mitigation Program Procedures for adjourning any matters pending between the Loss Mitigation Parties for which I am the movant.

Dated:

_____
Creditor Name

By: _____

_____
Printed Name

_____
Title

Loss Mitigation Contact Information for Attorney for Creditor:

Name: _____

Title: _____

Firm: _____

Address: _____

Address 2: _____

City: _____ State: _____ Zip Code: _____

Phone No.: _____ Facsimile No.: _____

Email Address: _____.

Name of the Creditor representative in-house who has full settlement authority to act on the Creditor's behalf with respect to the Loan:

Name: _____

Title: _____

Phone No.: _____

2

(LM:02 Request by Creditor rev. 03-15-2016)

CERTIFICATE OF SERVICE

I, _____, state under penalty of perjury that the following is true and accurate.

(1) That I am not a party to this action, am over 18 years of age, and reside in _____, New York.

(2) That on _____, 20____, I served a true and accurate copy of the above Loss Mitigation Request by Creditor—

—by notice of electronic filing (NEF) via the CM/ECF system upon the following parties at the email addresses listed below:

—by first class mail upon the following parties at the addresses listed below:

—by certified mail upon the following parties at the addresses listed below:

Dated: _____, 20____

_____, New York

_____
Name

Sworn to before me this

_____ day of _____, 20_____

_____
Notary Public, State of New York

(LM:02 Request by Creditor rev. 03-15-2016)

3

[Effective June 21, 2013.   Revised March 15, 2016.]

FORM LM3.   OBJECTION TO LOSS MITIGATION REQUEST

UNITED STATES BANKRUPTCY COURT
NORTHERN DISTRICT OF NEW YORK
_____

In re: Case No.
                                                   Chapter
                            Debtor(s).
_____

OBJECTION TO LOSS MITIGATION REQUEST

_____, attorney(s) for
_____, affirms under penalty of perjury as follows:

1. This Objection is submitted in response to the Loss Mitigation Request by
   _____ and Certificate of Service filed on _____, 20____.

2. _____
   _____
   _____
   _____.

3. _____
   _____
   _____
   _____.

4. _____
   _____
   _____
   _____.

5. _____
   _____
   _____
   _____.

1

6. _____

_____

_____

_____ .

7. _____

_____

_____

_____ .

8. _____

_____

_____

_____ .

9. _____

_____

_____

_____ .

10. _____

_____

_____

_____ .

Dated: _____   _____

Name

Firm

Attorney(s) for ☐ Debtor(s) ☐ Creditor

Address

Telephone Number

Email Address

N.D.N.Y. Bar Roll Identification No.

2

[Effective June 12, 2013.]

FORM LM4. NOTICE OF HEARING ON OBJECTION TO LOSS MITIGATION REQUEST AND CERTIFICATE OF SERVICE

UNITED STATES BANKRUPTCY COURT
NORTHERN DISTRICT OF NEW YORK

In re:

Case No.
Chapter

_____ Debtor(s).

NOTICE OF HEARING ON OBJECTION TO LOSS MITIGATION REQUEST
AND CERTIFICATE OF SERVICE

   PLEASE TAKE NOTICE that _____ objects to the

Loss Mitigation Request by _____ filed on _____, 20____, as more

fully set forth in the Objection filed herewith.

   PLEASE TAKE FURTHER NOTICE that a hearing to consider the Loss Mitigation

Request and the Objection filed herewith shall be held at _____

_____,

on _____, 20____ at _____ , or as soon thereafter as counsel may be heard.

   PLEASE TAKE FURTHER NOTICE that if you wish to be heard on the Request or

the Objection, you must appear at the hearing. Any written response to the Objection must be

served and filed with the court no later than seven (7) days prior to the hearing.

Dated: _____
                                               Name
                                               Firm
                                               Attorney(s) for ☐ Debtor(s) ☐ Creditor
                                               Address
                                               Telephone Number
                                               Email Address
                                               N.D.N.Y. Bar Roll Identification No.

CERTIFICATE OF SERVICE

I, _____, state under penalty of perjury that the following is true and accurate.

(1) That I am not a party to this action, am over 18 years of age, and reside in _____, New York.

(2) That on _____, 20____, I served a true and accurate copy of the above Notice of Hearing on Objection to Loss Mitigation Request and the Objection to Loss Mitigation Request referenced therein—

—by notice of electronic filing (NEF) via the CM/ECF system upon the following parties at the email addresses listed below:

—by first class mail upon the following parties at the addresses listed below:

—by certified mail upon the following parties at the addresses listed below:

Dated: _____, 20____
_____, New York

_____
Name

Sworn to before me this

_____ day of _____, 20_____

_____
Notary Public, State of New York

[Effective June 12, 2013.]

FORM LM5. LOSS MITIGATION ORDER

UNITED STATES BANKRUPTCY COURT
NORTHERN DISTRICT OF NEW YORK

In re: Case No.
                                                                Chapter
                            Debtor(s).
_____

LOSS MITIGATION ORDER

☐   A Loss Mitigation Request[1] was filed by the Debtor(s) on _____, 20_____,

☐   A Loss Mitigation Request was filed by a Creditor on _____, 20_____,

☐   The court raised the possibility of Loss Mitigation,

and the parties have had notice and an opportunity to object, and the court has reviewed any objections filed thereto.

NOW, it is hereby

ORDERED that

(1)   The following parties (the "Loss Mitigation Parties") are directed to participate in Loss Mitigation and are bound by the court's Loss Mitigation Program Procedures:

Debtor(s): _____,

Creditor: _____,

_____

[1] All capitalized terms have the meanings defined in the Loss Mitigation Program Procedures.

(2)   **Within seven (7) days** after the entry of this Order,

- Each Loss Mitigation Party shall designate contact persons and disclose contact information, unless this information has been previously provided in the Loss Mitigation Request,

- The Creditor shall contact the Debtor(s)' attorney or the Debtor(s), if *pro se*, and

- Requests for information and documents, if any, must be served upon the opposing party and counsel, and the requesting party shall file a Loss Mitigation Affidavit on the form prescribed by the court identifying the information and/or documents requested.

(3)   **Within thirty-five (35) days** after the entry of this Order and at least seven (7) days prior to the initial Loss Mitigation Session, each Loss Mitigation Party shall respond to a request for information and documents, and the party responding shall file a Loss Mitigation Affidavit on the form prescribed by the court identifying the information and/or documents provided.

(4)   **Within forty-five (45) days** after the entry of this Order but in any event prior to the initial Status Conference, the Loss Mitigation Parties shall conduct the initial Loss Mitigation session.

(5)   A status conference will be held in this case at the <u>United States Bankruptcy Court,_____</u> on _____, 20___ at _____ (the "Status Conference"). The Loss Mitigation Parties shall appear at the Status Conference. Seven (7) days prior to the date of the initial Status Conference or any adjournments thereof by the court, the party that requested Loss Mitigation shall file and serve upon all Loss Mitigation Parties a Loss Mitigation Status Report on the form prescribed by the court.

(6)   At the Status Conference, the court may consider a Settlement reached by the Loss Mitigation Parties, or may adjourn the Status Conference, as necessary.

(7)   Any proceedings (*e.g.* motions or applications) that are currently pending between the Loss Mitigation Parties shall be adjourned by the party who commenced such proceeding pursuant to L.B.R. 9013-1(i) and (j) to the date of the Status Conference indicated above to the extent those proceedings concern (1) objection to the allowance of a proof of claim, (2) reduction, reclassification or avoidance of a lien, or (3) valuation of a lien or the Property. A pending Motion for Relief from Stay by the Creditor shall be adjourned pursuant to section VI(B)(2) of the Loss Mitigation Procedures.

(8)   If the underlying bankruptcy case is one filed under chapter 12 or 13, the standing trustee may participate in the Loss Mitigation ordered herein, including—but not necessarily limited to—appearing at the Status Conference and filing a response, if any, to Creditor's motion to terminate Loss Mitigation made pursuant to section IX(B)(4) of the Loss Mitigation Program Procedures. The standing trustee shall not need to make a specific request in order to participate in Loss Mitigation. The standing trustee may participate to the extent that such participation is consistent with the trustee's duties under, respectively, 11 U.S.C. §§ 1202(b) or 1302(b)(4).

(9)   If the underlying bankruptcy case is one filed under chapter 13 and Debtor(s)' counsel seeks to receive a portion of fees for the case through the plan, then, in the month following entry of this Order or the first month after the initial 11 U.S.C. § 341 Meeting of Creditors, whichever is later, the standing trustee shall disburse payment to Debtor(s)' counsel of the requested attorney fee, up to a maximum of $1,500.00, with said amount to be paid in the manner prescribed in Debtor(s)' proposed plan. The amount disbursed shall be deemed allowed immediately. This amount shall be exclusive of any amounts received by counsel prior to the filing of the petition. The balance of the attorney fee shall only be allowed and paid pursuant to the Order of Confirmation or further order of this court.

(10)   If the underlying bankruptcy case is one filed under chapter 7, the entry of this Order automatically defers the entry of an order granting the Debtor(s)' discharge until one day after an Order Terminating Loss Mitigation and Final Report is filed pursuant to Federal Rule of Bankruptcy Procedure 4004(c)(2). The deadline to object to the Debtor(s)' discharge or the dischargeability of a debt is NOT extended by this Order.

(11)   This Order shall remain in effect until an Order Terminating Loss Mitigation and Final Report is entered or the Debtor(s)' case is dismissed.

# # #

[Effective June 21, 2013.   Revised January 1, 2014;   March 15, 2016;   November 1, 2016.]

FORM LM6.   LOSS MITIGATION AFFIDAVIT OF DEBTOR(S) AND CERTIFICATE OF SERVICE

UNITED STATES BANKRUPTCY COURT
NORTHERN DISTRICT OF NEW YORK

In re: Case No.
                                                    Chapter

                        Debtor(s).
_____

**LOSS MITIGATION AFFIDAVIT OF DEBTOR(S)
AND CERTIFICATE OF SERVICE**

STATE OF   ) ss.:
COUNTY OF   )

        I, _____, being sworn, say: I am not a party to this

action, am over 18 years of age, and reside in _____, _____.

Instructions:

    (1)   Complete, as is appropriate, either Part A: Request for Documents/Information by
          Debtor(s) <u>or</u> Part B: Debtor(s)' Response to Request for Documents/Information.

    (2)   Complete Part C: Loss Mitigation Contact Information, unless the information was
          provided in the Loss Mitigation Request by Debtor(s) and Certificate of Service.

    (3)   Complete Part D: Certificate of Service.

On behalf of Debtor(s):

Part A: Request for Documents/Information by Debtor(s)

        On _____, 20___, I served a true and accurate copy of the
Debtor(s)' Request for the following documents/information:

    ☐   A copy of Debtor(s)' payment history;

    ☐   Other (please specify): _____

                 _____

                 _____

                 _____.

1

Part B: Debtor(s)' Response to Request for Documents/Information

On _____, 20____, I served a true and accurate copy of the Debtor(s)' Response to Creditor's Request for documents/information, including the following:

☐   A copy of the Debtor(s)' two (2) most recent federal income tax returns;

☐   A copy of the Debtor(s)' last two (2) paycheck stubs, proof of social security income, pensions, or any other income received by the Debtor(s);

Or, if the Debtor(s) is/are self-employed:

A copy of the Debtor(s)' Profit and Loss Statements, setting forth a breakdown of the monthly income and expenses for the Debtor(s)' business (es), for the two (2) most recent months of _____ and _____;

☐   A completed copy of the Creditor's Financial Worksheet;

☐   Proof of second/third party income by affidavit of the party, including the party's last two (2) paycheck stubs;

☐   Other (please specify): _____

_____

_____

_____.

2

Part C: Loss Mitigation Contact Information

The Loss Mitigation contact information for the Attorney for the Debtor(s) is as follows:

Name: _____

Title: _____

Firm: _____

Address: _____

Address 2: _____

City: _____ State: _____ Zip Code: _____

Phone No.: _____ Facsimile No.: _____

Email Address: _____.

Part D: Certificate of Service

On _____, 20____, I served a true and accurate copy of the above Loss Mitigation Affidavit by Debtor(s)—

—by notice of electronic filing (NEF) via the CM/ECF system upon the following parties at the email addresses listed below:

—by first class mail upon the following parties at the addresses listed below:

3

—by certified mail upon the following parties at the addresses listed below:

Dated: _____, 20_____

_____, New York

                                      _____

                                      Name

Sworn to before me this

_____ day of _____, 20_____

_____

Notary Public, State of New York

4

[Effective June 12, 2013.]

FORM LM7.   LOSS MITIGATION AFFIDAVIT OF CREDITOR AND CERTIFICATE OF SERVICE

UNITED STATES BANKRUPTCY COURT
NORTHERN DISTRICT OF NEW YORK

In re: Case No.
                                        Chapter

                     Debtor(s).

LOSS MITIGATION AFFIDAVIT OF CREDITOR
AND CERTIFICATE OF SERVICE

STATE OF   ) ss.:
COUNTY OF   )

     I, _____, being sworn, say: I am not a party to this action, am over 18 years of age, and reside in _____, _____.

Instructions:

     (1)   Complete, as is appropriate, either Part A: Request for Documents/Information by Creditor or Part B: Creditor's Response to Request for Documents/Information.

     (2)   Complete Part C: Loss Mitigation Contact Information, unless the information was provided in the Loss Mitigation Request by Creditor and Certificate of Service.

     (3)   Complete Part D: Certificate of Service.

On behalf of Creditor _____ *[insert Creditor's Name]*:

☐ **If this box is checked, THERE ARE NO PROGRAMS UNDER WHICH THIS LOAN MAY BE MODIFIED.**

Part A: Request for Documents/Information by Creditor

     On _____, 20____, I served a true and accurate copy of the Creditor's Financial Packet and a Request for the following documents/information:

     ☐   A copy of the Debtor(s)' two (2) most recent federal income tax returns;

     ☐   A copy of the Debtor(s)' last two (2) paycheck stubs, proof of social security income, pensions, or any other income received by the Debtor(s);

     Or, if the Debtor(s) is/are self-employed:

(LM:07 Affid. of Creditor rev. 03-15-2016)

1

A copy of the Debtor(s)' Profit and Loss Statements, setting forth a breakdown of the monthly income and expenses for the Debtor(s)' business(es), for the two (2) most recent months of _____ and _____;

☐ A completed copy of the Creditor's Financial Worksheet;

☐ Proof of second/third party income by affidavit of the party, including the party's last two (2) paycheck stubs;

☐ Other (please specify): _____

_____

_____

_____

Part B: Creditor's Response to Request for Documents/Information

On _____, 20____, I served a true and accurate copy of the Creditor's Response to the Debtor(s)' Request for documents/information, including the following:

☐ A copy of Debtor(s)' payment history;

☐ Other (please specify): _____

_____

_____

_____

_____

2

(LM:07 Affid. of Creditor rev. 03-15-2016)

Part C: Loss Mitigation Contact Information

The Loss Mitigation contact information for the Attorney for the Creditor is as follows:

    Name: _____

    Title: _____

    Firm: _____

    Address: _____

    Address 2: _____

    City: _____ State: _____ Zip Code: _____

    Phone No.: _____ Facsimile No.: _____

    Email Address: _____.

Name of the Creditor representative in-house who has full settlement authority to act on the Creditor's behalf with respect to the Loan:

    Name: _____

    Title: _____

    Phone No.: _____

Part D: Certificate of Service

    On _____, 20____, I served a true and accurate copy of the above Loss Mitigation Affidavit by Creditor—

    ☐ by notice of electronic filing (NEF) via the CM/ECF system upon the following parties at the email addresses listed below:

3

(LM:07 Affid. of Creditor rev. 03-15-2016)

☐ by first class mail upon the following parties at the addresses listed below:

☐ by certified mail upon the following parties at the addresses listed below:

Dated: _____, 20____

_____, New York   _____
                                                                    Name

Sworn to before me this

_____ day of _____, 20_____

_____
Notary Public, State of New York

4

(LM:07 Affid. of Creditor rev. 03-15-2016)

[Effective June 21, 2013.   Revised March 15, 2016.]

FORM LM8. LOSS MITIGATION STATUS REPORT

UNITED STATES BANKRUPTCY COURT
NORTHERN DISTRICT OF NEW YORK

In re: Case No.
                                                    Chapter

                        Debtor(s).

LOSS MITIGATION STATUS REPORT

This Loss Mitigation Status Report is submitted pursuant to the court's Loss Mitigation Program Procedures.

PART I — GENERAL INFORMATION

a. Full description of the Property:

b. Name and address of Creditor:	Name, address, and telephone number of Creditor's attorney:
Has Creditor filed a proof of claim? ☐ Yes ☐ No	

(LM:08 Loss Mitigation Status Report rev. 03-15-2016)

PART II — LOSS MITIGATION PROGRAM

a. On _____ , a Loss Mitigation Request was filed by:

☐ Debtor(s).   ☐ Other party: _____.

☐ Creditor.   ☐ The court raised the possibility of Loss Mitigation.

b. Loss Mitigation Order:

☐ A Loss Mitigation Order was entered on _____.

☐ The Loss Mitigation Order was served on _____.

c. At this time, the Debtor(s) is/are:

☐ making on-going post-petition monthly mortgage payments in the amount of $_____

  ☐ directly to the Creditor.

  ☐ to the standing trustee.

  ☐ not making on-going post-petition monthly mortgage payments.

d. If the underlying bankruptcy case is one filed under chapter 12 or 13, has a plan been confirmed?

☐ Yes   ☐ No

e. Creditor served a Request for Information and Documents on _____.

Debtor(s) served a Response to the Creditor's Request on _____.

☐ All Information and Documents have been produced.

☐ The following Information and Documents are still outstanding:

_____

_____

f. Debtor(s) served a Request for Information and Documents on _____.

Creditor served a Response to the Debtor(s)' Request on _____.

☐ All Information and Documents have been produced.

☐ The following Information and Documents are still outstanding:

_____

_____

(LM:08 Loss Mitigation Status Report rev. 03-15-2016)

g. The Loss Mitigation Parties have participated in _____ Loss Mitigation Session(s) and:

☐ A resolution has been reached.

☐ A resolution has not been reached because:

_____

_____

h. Prior Loss Mitigation Status Report (if applicable):

A Prior Loss Mitigation Status Report was submitted on _____.

A Prior Loss Mitigation Status Report was submitted on _____.

A Prior Loss Mitigation Status Report was submitted on _____.

i. Additional information relevant to the Loss Mitigation Parties reaching a final resolution:

_____

_____

_____

_____

PART III — OTHER MORTGAGES/LIENS AGAINST THE PROPERTY

_____

_____

_____

Dated: _____

_____
Name
Firm
Attorney(s) for Debtor(s)/Creditor
Address
Telephone Number
Email Address
N.D.N.Y. Bar Roll Identification No.

(LM:08 Loss Mitigation Status Report rev. 03-15-2016)

[Effective June 21, 2013.   Revised February 7, 2014;   March 15, 2016.]

FORM LM9. REQUEST FOR ADDITIONAL LOSS MITIGATION CONFERENCE AND CERTIFICATE OF SERVICE

UNITED STATES BANKRUPTCY COURT
NORTHERN DISTRICT OF NEW YORK

In re: Case No.
                                                    Chapter

                Debtor(s).

REQUEST FOR ADDITIONAL LOSS MITIGATION CONFERENCE
AND CERTIFICATE OF SERVICE

The Status Conference ordered in paragraph (5) of the Loss Mitigation Order—

□ is scheduled for   □ was held on   _____, 20____.

Pursuant to section VIII(C) of the court's Loss Mitigation Program Procedures,

_____ requests an additional conference to address

the following: _____

_____

_____.

A copy of this Request has been served upon all other Loss Mitigation Parties and the

case trustee as indicated on the attached certificate of service.

Dated: _____
                                          Name
                                          Firm
                                          Attorney(s) for □ Debtor(s) □ Creditor
                                          Address
                                          Telephone Number
                                          Email Address
                                          N.D.N.Y. Bar Roll Identification No.

CERTIFICATE OF SERVICE

I, _____, state under penalty of perjury that the following is true and accurate.

(1) That I am not a party to this action, am over 18 years of age, and reside in _____, New York.

(2) That on _____, 20____, I served a true and accurate copy of the above Request for Additional Loss Mitigation Conference—

—by notice of electronic filing (NEF) via the CM/ECF system upon the following parties at the email addresses listed below:

—by first class mail upon the following parties at the addresses listed below:

—by certified mail upon the following parties at the addresses listed below:

Dated: _____, 20____

_____, New York

_____
Name

Sworn to before me this

_____ day of _____, 20_____

_____
Notary Public, State of New York

[Effective June 12, 2013.]

FORM LM10. STIPULATION AND ORDER AUTHORIZING PARTIES TO ENTER INTO LOAN MODIFICATION AND DIRECTING TREATMENT OF MORTGAGE CLAIM

UNITED STATES BANKRUPTCY COURT
NORTHERN DISTRICT OF NEW YORK

In re:

                                                     Case No.
                                                     Chapter 13

                      Debtor(s).

STIPULATION AND ORDER AUTHORIZING PARTIES TO ENTER INTO LOAN MODIFICATION AND DIRECTING TREATMENT OF MORTGAGE CLAIM

WHEREAS, the Debtor(s) are owners of property located at _____ ("Property") and _____ ("Creditor") is the holder of a note in the original amount of $_____ ("Note") and mortgage ("Mortgage") against the Property securing the Note; and

WHEREAS, a Loss Mitigation Order granting Debtor(s)' Loss Mitigation Request was entered on _____; and

WHEREAS, the Loss Mitigation Parties and their respective attorneys have negotiated in good faith and reached an agreement to modify the terms of the Note and Mortgage ("Loan Modification Agreement") and require court approval to enter into such modification.

NOW, IT IS HEREBY STIPULATED AND AGREED as follows:

1.   The automatic stay imposed by 11 U.S.C. § 362(a) upon the filing of the Debtor(s)' petition is hereby modified solely for the purpose of allowing the Debtor(s) and Creditor to execute and record a Loan Modification Agreement; and

2.   Debtor(s) and Creditor are hereby authorized to execute and record the Loan Modification Agreement annexed hereto as **Exhibit A**; and

3.   Below is a comparison of the terms of the Note and Mortgage and Loan Modification Agreement:

Current Terms		Modified Terms	
Unpaid Principal Balance	$	Unpaid Principal Balance	$
		Principal Amount Forgiven	$
Maturity Date		Maturity Date	
		Term of modification	
Payment Due Date		Payment Due Date	
Monthly Payment	$	Monthly Payment	$
Principal and Interest	$	Principal and Interest	$
Escrow	$	Escrow	$
Interest Rate		Interest Rate	
Other Salient Terms (*e.g.*, balloon payment)		Other Salient Terms (*e.g.*, balloon payment)	
		Additional Amount Capitalized	$

4.   The secured claim for prepetition mortgage arrears filed by the Creditor as Claim No. -_____ on the PACER Claim Register ("Claim") is deemed modified to reflect the amount paid by the Trustee as of the date of entry of this Order, with any and all balance due on said Claim reduced to zero ($0.00); and

5.   The Trustee is hereby directed to *[please check appropriate box below]*:

      ☐ Cease all further payments to Creditor on the Claim and on any and all Notices of Postpetition Fees and Costs filed in connection with the Claim in this case.

      ☐ Make the ongoing post-petition mortgage payment to Creditor as set forth in Debtor(s)' chapter 13 plan.

Dated: _____   _____, Esq.

                                           (Print Name) Attorney for Debtor(s)

Dated: _____   _____

                                           Debtor

Dated: _____   _____

                                           Debtor

Dated: _____   _____, Esq.

                                           (Print Name) Attorney for Creditor

Dated: _____   _____

                                           Choose Trustee
                                           Standing Chapter 13 Trustee

###

[Effective June 12, 2013. Revised January 30, 2014; May 16, 2014; March 15, 2016; January 4, 2017.]

FORM LM11. STIPULATION TERMINATING LOSS MITIGATION

IUNITED STATES BANKRUPTCY COURT
NORTHERN DISTRICT OF NEW YORK

In re: Case No.
                                                  Chapter

_____ Debtor(s).

STIPULATION TERMINATING LOSS MITIGATION

Pursuant to the Loss Mitigation Program Procedures, the Loss Mitigation Parties agree and consent to the termination of Loss Mitigation prior to a Settlement. Concurrently with the filing of this Stipulation, the party that requested Loss Mitigation shall upload an Order Terminating Loss Mitigation and Final Report via the court's E-Order system.

Dated: _____   _____
                            Name
                            Firm
                            Attorney for Debtor(s)
                            Address
                            Telephone number
                            Email Address
                            N.D.N.Y. Bar Roll Identification No.

Dated: _____   _____
                            Name
                            Firm
                            Attorney(s) for Creditor
                            Address
                            Telephone number
                            Email Address
                            N.D.N.Y. Bar Roll Identification No.

1

(LM:11 Stip. Terminating 03-15-2016)

[Effective June 21, 2013. Revised January 30, 2014; May 16, 2014; March 15, 2016.]

FORM LM12. ORDER TERMINATING LOSS MITIGATION AND FINAL REPORT

UNITED STATES BANKRUPTCY COURT
NORTHERN DISTRICT OF NEW YORK
_____

In re:

                                        Case No.
                                        Chapter ___

                        Debtor(s).
_____

ORDER TERMINATING LOSS MITIGATION AND FINAL REPORT

Name of Creditor: _____

Property Address: _____

Last Four Digits of Account Number of Loan: _____

Filing Date of Loss Mitigation Request: __/__/__

Date of Entry of Loss Mitigation Order: __/__/__

Other Requests for Loss Mitigation in this Case: Yes ☐   No ☐

       The use of the Court's Loss Mitigation Program Procedures has resulted in the following

[please check appropriate box below]:

☐   Creditor granted a loan modification

☐   Debtor[1] rejected Creditor's offer of a loan modification

☐   Creditor and Debtor were unable to reach an agreement

----

[1] In joint cases, use of the term "Debtor" shall be read as referring to both Debtors.

(LM:12 Order Terminating & Final Rpt. 03-15-2016)

☐   Debtor surrendered the real property

☐   Creditor agreed to a short sale

☐   Loss Mitigation was terminated due to Debtor's voluntary dismissal of the case

☐   Loss Mitigation was terminated because the case was involuntarily dismissed

☐   Other - Loss Mitigation was terminated for the following

reason(s):_____

_____

_____

NOW, based upon the foregoing, it is hereby

ORDERED, that Loss Mitigation is terminated with respect to the Loan identified above by the last four digits of the account number.

###

(LM:12 Order Terminating & Final Rpt. 03-15-2016)

[Effective June 21, 2013. Revised March 15, 2016.]

FORM LM13. EX PARTE APPLICATION AND CERTIFICATION IN SUPPORT OF APPROVAL AND PAYMENT OF ATTORNEY FEES FOR LOSS MITIGATION

UNITED STATES BANKRUPTCY COURT
NORTHERN DISTRICT OF NEW YORK

In re: Case No.
                                                    Chapter
                          Debtor(s).

EX PARTE APPLICATION AND CERTIFICATION IN SUPPORT OF
APPROVAL AND PAYMENT OF ATTORNEY FEES FOR LOSS MITIGATION

Upon the request to enter Loss Mitigation filed by _____

and after the parties having had notice and an opportunity to be heard, the court entered a Loss

Mitigation Order on _____, 20____.

I certify that:

1. I am counsel for the above-captioned Debtor(s).

2. I completed all requirements of Debtor(s)' counsel pursuant to the Loss Mitigation

    Program Procedures.

3. A resolution has been reached as follows:

    ☐   Loan modification request granted.

    ☐   Loan modification request denied.

    ☐   Loss Mitigation was terminated due to Debtor(s)' voluntary dismissal of the case.

    ☐   Loss Mitigation was terminated because the case was involuntarily dismissed.

    ☐   Loss Mitigation was terminated for the following reason(s): _____

         _____.

    ☐   Other (please describe): _____

         _____.

4. A Loss Mitigation Program Final Report was filed on _____, 20____.

1

All requirements necessary to complete the Loss Mitigation Program having now been met, I hereby request, pursuant to section XI(B) of the Loss Mitigation Program Procedures, approval and payment of attorney fees for Loss Mitigation in the amount of $1,000.00, which, if a chapter 12 or 13 case, are to be paid as an administrative expense through Debtor(s)' plan.

Dated: _____

　　　　　　　　　　　　　　　　　　　　Name
　　　　　　　　　　　　　　　　　　　　Firm
　　　　　　　　　　　　　　　　　　　　Attorney for Debtor(s)
　　　　　　　　　　　　　　　　　　　　Address
　　　　　　　　　　　　　　　　　　　　Telephone Number
　　　　　　　　　　　　　　　　　　　　Email Address
　　　　　　　　　　　　　　　　　　　　N.D.N.Y. Bar Roll Identification No.

2

[Effective June 12, 2013.]

FORM LM14. ORDER APPROVING ATTORNEY FEES FOR LOSS MITIGATION AND AUTHORIZING PAYMENT

UNITED STATES BANKRUPTCY COURT
NORTHERN DISTRICT OF NEW YORK

In re: Case No.
                                                              Chapter
                              Debtor(s).

ORDER APPROVING ATTORNEY FEES FOR LOSS MITIGATION AND AUTHORIZING PAYMENT

An Ex Parte Application and Certification in Support of Approval and Payment of Attorney Fees for Loss Mitigation having been submitted by _____, Esq., counsel for the Debtor(s), and after due consideration, it is hereby

ORDERED that attorney fees in the sum of $1,000.00 are awarded to counsel for the Debtor(s) for services rendered in connection with representation of the Debtor(s) in the Loss Mitigation Program; and is it further

ORDERED that said attorney fees shall be paid to _____, Esq. by the Debtor(s) in conformance with the retainer agreement between Debtor(s) and counsel.

#

[Effective June 12, 2013.]

FORM LM15. ORDER APPROVING ATTORNEY FEES FOR LOSS MITIGATION AND AUTHORIZING PAYMENT

UNITED STATES BANKRUPTCY COURT
NORTHERN DISTRICT OF NEW YORK

In re: Case No.
                                                    Chapter
                        Debtor(s).

ORDER APPROVING ATTORNEY FEES FOR LOSS MITIGATION
AND AUTHORIZING PAYMENT

An Ex Parte Application and Certification in Support of Approval and Payment of

Attorney Fees for Loss Mitigation having been submitted by _____, Esq.,

counsel for the Debtor(s), and after due consideration, it is hereby

ORDERED that attorney fees in the sum of $1,000.00 are awarded to counsel for the

Debtor(s) for services rendered in connection with representation of the Debtor(s) in the Loss

Mitigation Program; and is it further

ORDERED that said attorney fees shall be paid to _____, Esq. as

an administrative claim through the Debtor(s)' plan.

#

[Effective June 12, 2013.]

FORM LM16A. ADJOURNMENT REQUEST/WITHDRAWAL/SETTLEMENT NOTIFI-CATION OF LOSS MITIGATION STATUS CONFERENCES; RELATED MOTIONS FOR RELIEF FROM STAY AND/OR CONFIRMATION HEARINGS ONLY

United States Bankruptcy Court
Northern District of New York (Albany & Syracuse Divisions)

Adjournment Request/Withdrawal/Settlement Notification of Loss Mitigation Status Conferences; Related Motions for Relief from Stay and/or Confirmation Hearings ONLY

Case Name:

Case No.:   Division:

☐   Adjournment Request: Loss Mitigation Request at Docket No.: _____
☐   Adjournment Request: Related Motion for Relief from Stay at Docket No.: _____
☐   Adjournment Request: Confirmation Hearing at Docket No.: _____

Reason for Adjournment Request:

☐ Parties are still exchanging documents and explanatory Status Report has been filed.
☐ Creditor has deemed package complete and is reviewing documents.
☐ Trial modification offered and waiting for debtor(s) approval.
☐ Parties have entered into a trial modification.
☐ Parties are finalizing documentation for final modification and order.
☐ A motion to approve a loan modification has been filed and is returnable on _____.
☐ Other: (Please Explain)_____

Date Loss Mitigation Order Filed: _____

☐ Notification of Withdrawal of Loss Mitigation Request at Docket No.: _____
☐ Notification of Settlement or Approval of Loan Modification at Docket No.: _____, mooting out the need for a status hearing.

Current Conference Date: _____ Requested Adjourned Date: _____

Requesting Attorney's Name, Office Address, Phone and Email Address:

Consent of Loss Mitigation Parties Obtained? ☐ Yes ☐ No
In a Chapter 13 case, Trustee notified of Adjournment Request? ☐ Yes ☐ No

Absent compelling reasons, adjournments will not be granted without the consent of all parties. If your request is denied, you will be notified by Chambers.

This Form Must Be E-Filed By **2 p.m. on the Day Prior to the Conference/Hearings** and **Be Linked** to the related Loss Mitigation Request, Motion for Relief from Stay/Confirmation (if applicable).

REMINDER: You Must File a Status Report (7) Seven Days Prior to Your Initial Conference Even if the First Scheduled Conference Was Adjourned.

[Effective March 15, 2016. Revised January 12, 2017.]

FORM LM16B. ADJOURNMENT REQUEST/WITHDRAWAL/SETTLEMENT NOTIFI-CATION OF LOSS MITIGATION STATUS CONFERENCES; RELATED MOTIONS FOR RELIEF FROM STAY, CONFIRMATION HEARINGS, AND/OR MOTIONS TO DISMISS ONLY

United States Bankruptcy Court
Northern District of New York (Utica Division)

Adjournment Request/Withdrawal/Settlement Notification of Loss Mitigation Status Conferences; Related
Motions for Relief from Stay, Confirmation Hearings, and/or Motions to Dismiss ONLY

Case Name: _____   Case No.: _____

☐   Adjournment Request: Loss Mitigation Request at Docket No.: _____
☐   Adjournment Request: Related Motion for Relief from Stay at Docket No.: _____
☐   Adjournment Request: Confirmation Hearing at Docket No.: _____
☐   Adjournment Request: Trustee's Motion to Dismiss at Docket No.: _____
    Reason for Adjournment Request:

    ☐ Parties are still exchanging documents and explanatory Status Report has been filed.
    ☐ Creditor has deemed package complete and is reviewing documents.
    ☐ Trial modification offered and waiting for debtor(s) approval.
    ☐ Parties have entered into a trial modification.
    ☐ Parties are finalizing documentation for final modification and order.
    ☐ A motion to approve a loan modification has been filed and is returnable on _____.
    ☐ Other: (Please Explain) _____.

    Date Loss Mitigation Order Filed: _____

☐   Notification of Withdrawal of Loss Mitigation Request at Docket No.: _____
☐   Notification of Settlement or Approval of Loan Modification at Docket No.: _____,   mooting out
    the need for a status hearing.

Current Conference Date: _____   Requested Adjourned Date: _____

REMINDER: Stand Alone Loss Mitigation matters must be adjourned to 11:30 a.m. Loss Mitigation matters that accompany confirmation or motion practice, however, must be adjourned to 10:30 a.m. or the proper motion time.

Requesting Attorney's Name, Office Address, Phone and Email Address:

Consent of Loss Mitigation Parties Obtained? ☐ Yes ☐ No
In a Chapter 13 case, Trustee notified of Adjournment Request? ☐ Yes ☐ No

Absent compelling reasons, adjournments will not be granted without the consent of all parties. If your request is denied, you will be notified by Chambers.

This Form Must Be E-Filed By **2 p.m. on the Day Prior to the Conference/Hearings** and **Be Linked** to the related Loss Mitigation Request, Motion for Relief from Stay, Confirmation, and/or Motion to Dismiss (if applicable).

REMINDER: You Must File a Status Report (7) Seven Days Prior to Your Initial Conference Even if the First Scheduled Conference Was Adjourned.

[Effective March 15, 2016. Revised January 12, 2017; February 1, 2017.]

FORM LM17. ADDENDUM TO CONFIRMATION ORDER WHEN LOSS MITIGATION IS PENDING

ADDENDUM TO CONFIRMATION ORDER

WHEN LOSS MITIGATION IS PENDING

Loss Mitigation is pending between Debtor and _____ (the "Mortgagee Creditor"). The following terms and conditions shall govern the rights of Debtor and Mortgagee Creditor under the confirmed Chapter 13 plan:

1.   The Court and the parties acknowledge that the plan is dependent upon the success of the pending loss mitigation and modification of the mortgage terms. Mortgagee Creditor's right to seek dismissal of the case based upon Debtor's inability to successfully complete the plan and Debtor's right to seek to modify the plan terms are preserved in all respects.

2.   While Loss Mitigation is pending, the Trustee shall reserve all funds which would otherwise be disbursed on any claim timely filed by the Mortgagee Creditor. Reserved funds may be disbursed by the Trustee only with the consent of the Mortgagee Creditor or upon entry of an Order after notice and a hearing.

3.   If the confirmed plan provides that Debtor will remit to the Trustee a sum certain every month as an ongoing post-petition mortgage payment for the Mortgagee Creditor, then the Trustee shall reserve and shall not disburse said funds while Loss Mitigation is pending absent consent of the Mortgagee Creditor or entry of an Order authorizing disbursement after notice and a hearing.

(LM:17 Addendum to Conf. Order 03-15-2016)

[Effective March 15, 2016.]

SELECTED ADMINISTRATIVE ORDERS
ADMINISTRATIVE ORDER NO. 07–04. INCREASE TO TRANSCRIPT FEE RATES

The Judicial Conference of the United States, at its September 2007 session, approved an increase of ten percent to the maximum original and copy transcript fee rates, to be effective in fiscal year 2008. The Judicial Conference also approved a new rate for the delivery of transcripts within 14 days and agreed that the rate be set at the mid-point between the rates authorized for expedited (7–day) and ordinary (30–day) delivery. It is hereby

ORDERED, that this Court adopts a revised schedule of Maximum Rates for all categories of transcript, as attached hereto. Transcripts ordered prior to the effective date of this Order shall be billed at the rates in effect at the time the transcript order was placed with the Electronic Court Recorder Operator. The rates reflected in the attachment shall remain in effect until further order of this Court.

[Dated: November 20th, 2007.]

Attachment

Maximum Transcript Fee Rates—All Parties Per Page

	Original	First Copy to Each Party	Each Add'l Copy to the Same Party
Ordinary Transcript (30 day) A transcript to be delivered within thirty (30) calendar days after receipt of an order.	$3.65	$.90	$.60
14–Day Transcript A transcript to be delivered within fourteen (14) calendar days after receipt of an order.	$4.25	$.90	$.60
Expedited Transcript (7 day) A transcript to be delivered within seven (7) calendar days after receipt of an order.	$4.85	$.90	$.60
Daily Transcript A transcript to be delivered following adjournment and prior to the normal opening hour of the court on the following morning whether or not it actually is a court day.	$6.05	$1.20	$.90
Hourly Transcript A transcript of proceedings ordered under unusual circumstances to be delivered within two (2) hours.	$7.25	$1.20	$.90
Realtime Transcript A draft unedited transcript produced by a certified realtime reporter as a byproduct of realtime to be delivered electronically during proceedings or immediately following adjournment.	$3.05	$1.20	

ADMINISTRATIVE ORDER NO. 09–03.   APPEARANCE
BY STUDENT PRACTITIONERS

The Court hereby approves the following regulations regarding appearance before the Court by Student Practitioners.

1.   A law student approved as a "Student Practitioner" may, under the supervision of an attorney and with prior court approval, appear on behalf of any person who has consented in writing on forms adopted pursuant to this Order and attached as Exhibit A, as may be amended from time to time, and filed in the case pending before the United States Bankruptcy Court.

2.   The attorney who supervises a student shall:

(a) be a member in good standing of the bar of the United States District Court for the Northern District of New York;

(b) assume personal professional responsibility for the student's work;

(c) assist the student to the extent necessary;

(d) appear with the student in all proceedings before the court unless his or her presence is waived by the court; and

(e) indicate in writing his consent to supervise the student on the prescribed forms.

3.   In order to appear, the student shall:

(a) be duly enrolled in a law school approved by the American Bar Association;

(b) have completed legal studies amounting to at least three semesters, or the equivalent;

(c) be recommended by either the dean or a faculty member of his or her law school as a Student Practitioner, which recommendation may be withdrawn by the recommender at any time by mailing a notice to the Clerk;

(d) neither ask for nor receive any compensation or remuneration of any kind for the services performed from the person on whose behalf they are rendered, but this shall not prevent an attorney, legal aid bureau, law school, public defender agency, a State, or the United States from paying compensation to the eligible law student, nor shall it prevent any agency from making proper charges for its services.   Neither the student, nor anyone on the student's behalf, shall seek recovery of attorneys' fees from an adverse party for the services rendered by the student as a student practitioner, except for the successful prosecution of a willful violation of the automatic stay or of the discharge injunction pursuant to §§ 362 and 524 of Title 11 of the United States Code and for the defense of a § 523(a)(2) nondischargeability action on a consumer debt;

(e) certify in writing that the student is familiar with the federal procedural and evidentiary rules as well as the Local Bankruptcy Rules for the Northern District of New York;

(f) complete and file an application with the United States Bankruptcy Court together with a proposed order for appearance as a Student Practitioner in the bankruptcy case and/or adversary proceeding in which client consent has been obtained on the form supplied by the Clerk.

4.   The bankruptcy judge for the division within which the completed application form is filed will consider the application and, if deemed appropriate, issue an order approving the applicant's appearance as a Student Practitioner in the bankruptcy case and/or adversary proceeding.

5.   The Student Practitioner may:

(a) appear as counsel in court or at other proceedings when consent of the client and the supervising attorney has been filed and when the court has approved the student's request to appear in the particular case;

(b) prepare and sign affidavits, motions, petitions, answers, objections, replies, memoranda and legal briefs and other documents (collectively, "Documents") in connection with any matter in which the student has met the conditions of (a) above, which Documents must also be signed by the supervising attorney with the original maintained in the case file.

6.   A Student Practitioner whose application has been approved may continue to appear in a particular case as a Student Practitioner until the student has graduated law school and is formally admitted to the bar or until termination by the court.   The court sua sponte may terminate a Student Practitioner's right to appear at any time without notice of hearing and without showing of cause.

7. The application form for appearance as a Student Practitioner and form of proposed order, as amended from time to time, is available on the court's website at www.nynb.uscourts.gov.

[Dated: March 17, 2009.]

EXHIBIT A TO ADMINISTRATIVE ORDER 09–03

UNITED STATES BANKRUPTCY COURT
FOR THE NORTHERN DISTRICT OF NEW YORK

In re:

                                                    Case No. _____
                              Debtor.   Chapter _____

_____

APPLICATION FOR ADMISSION AS A STUDENT PRACTITIONER
PURSUANT TO ADMINISTRATIVE ORDER 09–03

_____
(Name of Student)

_____   _____
(Telephone Number)   (Address of Student)*

_____   _____
(Email Address)   (City, State, Zip)

NAME OF LAW SCHOOL STUDENT IS ATTENDING: _____

SEMESTERS STUDENT HAS COMPLETED: _____

ANTICIPATED GRADUATION DATE: _____

* Please note that this address is the address to which all notices and correspondence are to be mailed by the court.

TO BE COMPLETED BY THE LAW STUDENT:

I certify that I have completed at least three (3) semesters of law school. I certify that I have read and am familiar with the provisions of the Judicial Code (Title 28 of the United States Code) that pertain to the jurisdiction of, and practice in, the United States District Courts, the Federal Rules of Civil Procedure; the Local Bankruptcy Rules, the District Court Rules and General Orders for the Northern District of New York and the Code of Professional Responsibility and that I will faithfully adhere thereto. I certify that I will receive no compensation from the person on whose behalf I am rendering services, except as provided in Part 3(d) of Administrative Order 09–03 pertaining to Student Practice in the Northern District of New York.

CERTIFICATION OF APPLICANT

_____   _____
(Date)   (Signature of Student)

The Student Practitioner's admission shall automatically expire upon graduation and admission to the bar unless an application for extension is granted.

STUDENT PRACTICE AUTHORIZATION FORM

AUTHORIZATION BY THE CLIENT FOR WHOM THE LAW STUDENT IS RENDERING SERVICES.

I authorize _____, a law student, to appear in court or at other proceedings on my behalf and to prepare documents on my behalf in connection with the case listed below.

_____   _____
(Date)   (Signature of Client)

                                                         _____
                                                              (Print Name)

(If more than one client is involved, approval from each client must be attached.)

Bankruptcy Case Name: _____

Bankruptcy Case No. _____   Chapter ____

Adversary Proceeding No. (if applicable) _____

Assigned to Judge: _____

TO BE COMPLETED BY THE LAW STUDENT'S SUPERVISING ATTORNEY:

I will carefully supervise all of this student's work. I authorize this student to appear in court or at other proceedings, and to prepare documents. I will accompany the student at such appearances, and I will sign all documents prepared by the student. I assume personal responsibility for the student's work. I will notify the Clerk in writing when this student is no longer under my direct supervision.

_____   _____
(Date)   (Signature of Attorney)

                                                         _____
                                                              (Address)

                                                         _____
                                                           (City, State, Zip Code)

TO BE COMPLETED BY THE DEAN OR A FACULTY MEMBER OF THE STUDENT'S LAW SCHOOL:

I certify that this law student has completed at least three (3) semesters of law school work, and I recommend that the student be admitted to the court as a student practitioner.

_____   _____
(Date)   (Signature of Dean)

                                                                  -or-

                                                         _____
                                                         (Signature of Faculty Member)

Procedural Note: The Application for Admission as a Student Practitioner pursuant to Administrative Order 09–03 of the U.S. Bankruptcy Court, N.D.N.Y. and Student Practice Authorization

Form should he electronically <u>filed</u> on the Court's docket via CM/ECF. The proposed order should be electronically <u>uploaded as an order</u> via CM/ECF. Do not electronically file the proposed order on the Court's docket. A sample proposed order follows.

UNITED STATES BANKRUPTCY COURT
<u>NORTHERN DISTRICT OF NEW YORK</u>

In re:

                                 Case No. _____
                                 Chapter _____

              Debtor.

ORDER APPROVING APPLICATION TO APPEAR AS STUDENT PRACTITIONER

Based upon this court's review of the completed Application to Appear as a Student Practitioner pursuant to Administrative Order 09–03 filed on behalf of (name of student) by supervising attorney, (name of supervising attorney, it is hereby

Ordered that (name of student) is authorized to appear as a Student Practitioner in reference to the pending case; and it is further

Ordered that (name of supervising attorney) shall exercise professional oversight and assume responsibility for the Student Practitioner's work.

ADMINISTRATIVE ORDER NO. 09–08. RIGHTS AND RESPONSIBILITIES OF CHAPTER 13 DEBTORS AND THEIR ATTORNEYS FOR THE ALBANY AND UTICA DIVISIONS

WHEREAS, administrative orders 08–01 and 09–07 refer to a form titled *Rights and Responsibilities of Chapter 13 Debtors and their Attorneys.*

NOW, after due deliberation, it is hereby,

ORDERED, as follows:

Chapter 13 debtor counsel shall file the form titled *Rights and Responsibilities of Chapter 13 Debtors and their Attorneys* with the court.

[Dated: October 8, 2009.]

**United States Bankruptcy Court
for the Northern District of New York**

Albany and Utica Division

RIGHTS AND RESPONSIBILITIES OF CHAPTER 13 DEBTORS AND THEIR ATTORNEYS

It is important for Chapter 13 debtors to understand their rights and responsibilities. It is also important that the debtors know that communicating with their attorney(s) is essential to successfully completing their plan. Debtors should also know that they may expect certain services to be performed by their attorney.

In order to assure that debtors and their attorney understand their rights and responsibilities in the bankruptcy process, the following guidelines approved by the Court are hereby agreed to by the debtors and their attorneys **unless the Court orders otherwise:**

(Nothing in this Agreement shall be construed to excuse an attorney for any ethical duties or responsibilities under FRBP 9011 or applicable non-bankruptcy law.)

Before the Case Is Filed

The debtor agrees to:

1. Provide the attorney with accurate financial information and timely provide all requested documentation.

2. Discuss with the attorney the debtor's objectives in filing the case.

The attorney agrees to:

1. Meet with the debtor to review the debtor's debts, assets, liabilities, income, and expenses.

2. Counsel the debtor regarding the advisability of filing either a Chapter 7 or Chapter 13 case, outlining the procedures with the debtor, and answering the debtor's questions.

3. Explain what payments will be made directly by the debtor and what payments will be made through the debtor's Chapter 13 plan, with particular attention to mortgage and vehicle loan payments, as well as any other claims which accrue interest.

4. Explain to the debtor how, when, and where to make the Chapter 13 plan payments.

5. Explain to the debtor how the attorney's fees are paid and provide an executed copy of this document to the debtor.

6. Explain to the debtor that the first plan payment must be made to the Trustee within 30 days of the date the plan is filed.

7. Advise the debtor of the requirement to attend the 341 Meeting of Creditors, and instruct the debtor as to the date, time, and place of the meeting.

8. Advise the debtor of the necessity of maintaining liability and hazard insurance on all real property as well as liability, collision, and comprehensive insurance on vehicles securing loans or leases.

9. Timely prepare and file the debtor's petition, plan, statements, and schedules.

AFTER THE CASE IS FILED

The debtor agrees to:

1. Keep the Trustee and attorney informed of the debtor's address and telephone number.

2. Inform the attorney of any wage garnishments or attachments of assets which occur or continue after the filing of the case.

3. Contact the attorney promptly if the debtor loses his/her job or has other financial problems.

4. Let the attorney know if the debtor is sued during the case.

5. Inform the attorney if any tax refunds the debtor is entitled to are seized or not returned to the debtor by the IRS or Franchise Tax Board.

6. Contact the attorney before buying, selling or refinancing any property and before entering into any loan agreements to find out what approvals are required.

The attorney agrees to:

1. Appear at the 341 Meeting of Creditors with the debtor.

2. Respond to objections to plan confirmation, and where necessary, prepare an amended plan

3. Prepare, file, and serve necessary modifications to the plan which may include suspending, lowering, or increasing plan payments.

4. Prepare, file, and serve necessary amended statements and schedules, in accordance with information provided by the debtor.

5. Prepare, file, and serve such motions as are needed during the case including, but not limited to, motions to avoid liens, sell property, approve settlements, approve new debt etc.

6. Timely review all proofs of claim.

7. Timely object to improper or invalid proofs of claims based upon information and documentation provided by the debtor if such objection is necessary and beneficial to the debtor or to the estate.

8. Represent the debtor in connection motions for relief from stay and for dismissal or conversion of the case.

9. Where appropriate, prepare, file, and serve necessary motions to partially or wholly avoid liens on real or personal property pursuant to sections 506 or 522.

10. Communicate with the debtor by telephone or by being available for office appointments to discuss pending issues or matters of concern.

11. Provide such other legal services as are necessary for the proper administration of the present case before the Bankruptcy Court.

Approval for legal fees in the total sum of $ _____ will be requested by the attorney. The attorney has received $ _____ prepetition (the initial retainer) and requests payment of the balance of $ _____ through the Chapter 13 plan.

Legal fees to be paid to the attorney shall be a "flat fee" for all services to be rendered in this case. Additional fees may be awarded and paid to the attorney if an extraordinary level of service is provided. If such occurs, the attorney shall apply to the Court for any additional fees and all such fees shall be paid through the plan unless otherwise ordered. The attorney may not receive fees directly from the debtor other than the initial retainer.

If the debtor disputes the legal services provided or charged by the attorney, the debtor must advise the Court or the Chapter 13 Trustee in writing and the matter set for hearing.

The attorney may move to withdraw pursuant to Local Bankruptcy Rule 2091–1, or the client may discharge the attorney at any time.

Dated: _____   _____

                            Debtor

Dated: _____   _____

                            Debtor

Dated: _____   _____

                            Attorney for Debtor(s)

ADMINISTRATIVE ORDER NO. 11–02.   IN RE: PROCEDURAL RULES FOR ELECTRONIC CASE FILING (ECF)

Federal Rule of Civil Procedure, hereafter FRCP, 83 and Federal Rules of Bankruptcy Procedure, hereafter FRBP, 5005(a)(2), 9011, and 9029 authorize this Court to establish practices and procedures for the filing, signing, and verification of pleadings and papers by electronic means; and

The *Administrative Procedures for Filing, Signing, and Verifying Pleadings and Papers by Electronic Means*, hereafter *Administrative Procedures*, have been reviewed by this Court; and

The *Administrative Procedures* are consistent with and further the responsibility of the Clerk of Court for the control of the Court's docket under FRBP 5003, including safeguarding the integrity of the Court's docket; and

The *Administrative Procedures* do not impose fees inconsistent with the present fee structure adopted by the Judicial Conference of the United States pursuant to 28 U.S.C. § 1930; and

The *Administrative Procedures* provide adequate procedures for filing pleadings and papers and provide access to review and retrieve records and dockets of this Court by parties who are not able to access the Electronic Case Filing System over the internet, thereby complying with the requirements contained in 11 U.S.C. § 107(a); and

The *Administrative Procedures* do not impair the ability of the Clerk of the Court to perform statistical reporting responsibilities for both the Court and the Administrative Office of the United States Courts; and

The *Administrative Procedures* are consistent with notice requirements of the FRBP and the Local Bankruptcy Rules for the Northern District of New York, hereafter LBR.

IT IS ORDERED that:

1. Introduction and Definitions.

a. The Clerk of the Bankruptcy Court for the Northern District of New York is authorized to implement, publish, and update the *Administrative Procedures* for the district, including but not limited to the procedures for registration for attorneys and other participants, and for the distribution of logins and passwords to permit electronic filing and notice of pleadings and other papers.

b.   In the event of a conflict between the *Northern District of New York Local Bankruptcy Rules* and the *Administrative Procedures*, the *Administrative Procedures*, as relating to the electronic filing of petitions, pleadings, orders and other papers shall govern.

c.   "Electronic Case Files", as referred to in the *Administrative Procedures*, are petitions, pleadings, and other papers that are stored in a fixed electronic format instead of on paper. This Court accepts documents only in the Portable Document Format (PDF or PDF/A) and creditor matrices in Text format (TXT).

NOTE: The newer PDF/A standard addresses concerns raised about the security and long term archival storage of documents. Standard word processing software is now capable of producing PDF/A documents. Although no target date has been set, in the future the court will require users to file documents in PDF/A format. Users of the NDNY *System* will be notified when the PDF/A format becomes mandatory.

d.   The Clerk's Office will not maintain a paper court file in any case except as otherwise provided by the Local Bankruptcy Rules and the Administrative Procedures. The official court record shall be an electronic file maintained on the court's file server. Any documents received in paper format in Chambers or the Clerk's Office may be shredded when it is determined that they are no longer needed.

e.   "Filer", as referred to in the *Administrative Procedures*, is defined as the attorney of record or the actual party in interest, if not represented by counsel, who transmits any pleading or document to the Court.

2. Electronic Filing of Documents.

a.   The electronic filing of a pleading or other paper in accordance with electronic filing procedures shall constitute entry of that pleading or other paper on the docket kept by the Clerk under FRBP 5003.

b.   The Office of the Clerk shall enter all orders, decrees, judgments and proceedings of the court in accordance with electronic filing procedures, which shall constitute entry of the order, decree, judgment or proceeding on the docket kept by the Clerk under FRBP 5003 and 9021.

c.   For filings that require a fee to be paid, the fees are to be paid through the on-line payment program (Pay.gov) in CM/ECF.

d.   A "Chambers Copy" in paper format for Chambers is required for the following matters. The copy must be clearly marked as "ECF CASE—CHAMBERS COPY" and must be submitted in compliance with the requirements of LBR 9013–1. The Chambers Copy need not contain a copy of the original signature. Unless directed by the Court, copies should not be faxed to Chambers or Courtroom Services. Copies should be sent via the mail or hand delivered.

Albany Chambers

- Notice of motion, motion, application, and certificate of service, except for chapter 13 trustee's motion to dismiss and to determine/expunge claim and chapter 7 trustee's final meeting notice;
- Opposition, response, or any pleading relating to a hearing;
- Opposition to disclosure statement in a chapter 11 case;
- Objection to confirmation of a chapter 11 plan;
- Pretrial statement; and
- Memoranda of law and any pleading and other document filed in regard to a submitted matter.

Syracuse Chambers

- Notice of motion, motion, application and certificate of service;
- Chapter 7 final meeting notice;
- Any pleading filed in an adversary proceeding; Pretrial statement;
- Memoranda of law and any pleading or other document filed in regard to a submitted matter;
- Any document regarding an appeal;
- Withdrawal of reference; and
- Any objection pursuant to *Fed. R. Bankr. P. 9033*.

Utica Chambers

- Notice of motion, motion, application and certificate of service;

- Chapter 7 final meeting notice;
- Any pleading filed in an adversary proceeding;
- Pretrial statement;
- Memoranda of law and any pleading or other document filed in regard to a submitted matter;
- Any document regarding an appeal;
- Withdrawal of reference; and
- Any objection pursuant to *Fed. R. Bankr. P. 9033*.

3. Logins and Passwords.

a.   Each attorney admitted to practice in the Northern District of New York and currently in good standing, and creditor participants filers shall be entitled to a single Electronic Case Filing System login and password to permit him/her to electronically file and electronically receive pleadings and other documents. The Bankruptcy Court reserves the right to deny a request for a login and password. Pro se debtors are not eligible for a login and password.

b.   An attorney or trustee may request multiple logins and passwords for legal staff who file as agents on their behalf. When an agent files on behalf of the attorney, the docket text displays the name of the attorney as the filer. A filing agent may obtain a login and password by submitting a completed Case Management/Electronic Case Files (CM/ECF) System Electronic Filing Agent Registration Form.

c.   Login and password registration forms are available in the Office of the Clerk and on the Court's Internet site which is www.nynb.uscourts.gov.

d.   A trustee or standing trustee who also serves as private counsel should submit two separate Case Management/Electronic Case Files (CM/ECF) System Attorney Registration Forms and will receive two separate logins and passwords; one in his/her role as trustee and one in his/her role as private counsel.

e.   No attorney shall knowingly permit or cause his/her password to be utilized by anyone other than an authorized employee of his/her law firm.

e.*   No person shall knowingly utilize or cause another person to utilize the password of a registered attorney unless such person is an authorized employee of the law firm.

f.   Misuse of the Electronic Case Filing System login and password may result in revocation of the login and password of the attorney or party and/or the imposition of sanctions.

4. Signatures.

a.   The electronic filing of a petition, motion, or other paper by an attorney or participant who is a registered user in the electronic case filing system shall constitute the signature of that filer under FRBP 9011.

b.   Any pleading, affidavit or other document filed electronically shall contain an electronic signature of the filer, e.g., *"/s/name."*

5. Notice of Electronic Filing and Service.

a.   Whenever a pleading or other paper if filed electronically, a *Notice of Electronic Filing* will be automatically generated by the Electronic Case Filing System at the time of the filing and sent electronically to the party filing the pleading or other paper, as well as to all parties in the case who are registered participants in the Electronic Case Filing System or have otherwise consented to electronic service.

b.   If the recipient of notice or service is a registered participant in the Electronic case Filing System and has consented to electronic service, service of the *Notice of Electronic Filing* shall be the equivalent of service of the pleading or other paper by first class mail, postage prepaid.

c.   Pleadings or other documents which are not filed electronically shall be served in accordance with the FRBP and LBR except as otherwise provided by order of the Court.

d.   **Participation in the Electronic Case Filing System by receipt of a login and password from the Court shall constitute a request for service and notice electronically pursuant to FRBP 9036. Participants in the Electronic Case Filing System, by receiving a login and password from the Court, agree that notice and service by electronic means constitutes proper service.**

e. It is not necessary to submit a paper summons to the Clerk's Office to have it signed, sealed and issued for service on the defendant(s). The *System* will electronically generate the initial summons in an adversary proceeding. The electronic summons will contain the Clerk's signature and court seal. Multiple copies can be printed for service upon the defendant(s). Proof of service will still be required. Service of a summons in an involuntary bankruptcy petition shall continue to be made pursuant to FRBP 1010 and 7004.

f. Service by electronic means is not effective if the party making service learns that the attempted service did not reach the person to be served.

6. The provisions of this Order shall apply to all cases and proceedings filed in the U.S. Bankruptcy Court for the Northern District of New York. Amendments to this Order may be entered from time to time in keeping with the needs of the Court.

7. The effective date of this Administrative Order is January 1, 2012.

[Dated: December 28, 2011.]

* [**Publisher's Note:** So in original.]

ADMINISTRATIVE ORDER NO. 11–03. IN RE: ABROGATED ADMINISTRATIVE ORDERS

Due to the implementation of the Local Bankruptcy Rules which become effective on January 1, 2012, amendments to the Federal Rules of Bankruptcy Procedure, and some matters now being moot, the following orders are abrogated:

Administrative Order 09–09, Revised Local Procedure Governing Time Computation

Administrative Order 08–02, Repeal of Order Adopting Interim Bankruptcy Rules

Administrative Order 07–05, Issuance of Chapter 13 Discharges

Administrative Order 05–03, Disbursement of Sec. 1326 Pre–Confirmation Adequate Protection Payments in Chapter 13 Cases Filed on or after 10/17/05

Administrative Order 05–02, Adoption of Interim Bankruptcy Rules

Administrative Order 04–05, Designation of Property Disposal Officer

Administrative Order 04–04, Designation of Property Custodial Officer

Administrative Order 04–03, Delegation of Property Disposal Officer

Administrative Order 04–02, Designation of Automation Property Custodial Officer

Administrative Order 04–01, Delegation of Authority to Designate Property Custodial and Disposal Officers

Administrative Order 02–03, Procedural Rules for Electronic Case Filing (ECF) [See Administrative Order 11–02]

Administrative Order 02–02, Order Authorizing Clerk to Sign Ministerial Orders for Cases Assigned to Robert E. Littlefield, Jr., U.S. Bankruptcy Judge

Administrative Order 02–01A, Order Authorizing Clerk to Sign Ministerial Orders

Administrative Order 02–01, Delegation of Duties to Clerk of the Court

Administrative Order 01–01, Requirements for filing an Assignment of Claim

Administrative Order 00–01, Designating Judge Robert E. Littlefield, Jr., of the NDNY to Sit in the Bankruptcy Court—District of Vermont on an Intermittent Basis

Administrative Order 99–06, Designating Judge Robert E. Littlefield, Jr., of the NDNY to Sit in the Bankruptcy Court—District of Vermont on an Intermittent Basis

Administrative Order 09–05, Designation of Bankruptcy Judge Robert E. Littlefield, Jr.

Administrative Order 09–04, Designation of Bankruptcy Judge

Administrative Order 09–03, Designation of Bankruptcy Judge

Administrative Order 09–02, Designation of Chief Bankruptcy Judge Michael Kaplan

Administrative Order Effective 01/02/97, Re: Default Motions (LBR 913.1K)

[Dated: December 28, 2011.]

AMENDED ADMINISTRATIVE ORDER 13–02. DEBTOR'S ATTORNEY FEE IN CHAPTER 13 CASES FILED IN THE UTICA DIVISION [SUPERSEDED BY ADMINISTRATIVE ORDER 16–02, EFFECTIVE APRIL 1, 2016]

ADMINISTRATIVE ORDER 13–03. DEBTOR'S ATTORNEY FEES IN CHAPTER 13 CASES FILED IN THE ALBANY DIVISION [SUPERSEDED BY ADMINISTRATIVE ORDER 16–03, EFFECTIVE APRIL 1, 2016]

ADMINISTRATIVE ORDER 13–05. IN RE: ADOPTION OF LOSS MITIGATION PROGRAM PROCEDURES*

WHEREAS a uniform, comprehensive, court-supervised loss mitigation program may facilitate consensual resolutions for individual debtors whose residential real property is at risk of loss to foreclosure (the "Loss Mitigation Program" or "Loss Mitigation"); and

WHEREAS the Loss Mitigation Program may avoid the need for various types of bankruptcy litigation, reduce costs to debtors and secured creditors, and enable debtors to reorganize or otherwise address their most significant debts and assets under the United States Bankruptcy Code;

Now, therefore, it is hereby

ORDERED that the "Loss Mitigation Program Procedures" annexed to this Administrative Order and the Loss Mitigation Program described therein are adopted, pursuant to 11 U.S.C. § 105(a); and it is further

ORDERED that effective July I, 2013, the Loss Mitigation Program Procedures shall apply in all individual cases filed under chapter 7, 11, 12, or 13 of the Bankruptcy Code, within the United States Bankruptcy Court for the Northern District of New York; and it is further

ORDERED that the Loss Mitigation Program Procedures and related forms, including the Loss Mitigation Request by Debtor(s) and Certificate of Service, shall be available on the court's website. The court may modify the Loss Mitigation Program Procedures from time to time by Administrative Order, and in that event shall make the revised Loss Mitigation Program Procedures available immediately on the court's website.

[Dated: June 21, 2013.]

LOSS MITIGATION PROGRAM PROCEDURES[1]

Current as of June 27, 2013

I. Purpose. The Loss Mitigation Program is designed to function as a forum in individual bankruptcy cases for debtors and lenders to reach consensual resolution whenever a debtor's principal residence is at risk of foreclosure. The Loss Mitigation Program aims to facilitate resolution by opening the lines of communication between debtors' and lenders' decision-makers. While the Loss Mitigation Program stays certain bankruptcy deadlines that might interfere with negotiations or increase costs to the parties, the Loss Mitigation Program also encourages the parties to finalize any Settlement (as defined below) under bankruptcy court protection, instead of seeking dismissal of the bankruptcy case.

II. Loss Mitigation Defined. The term "Loss Mitigation" is intended to describe the full range of solutions that may avert the loss of a debtor's property to foreclosure, increased costs to the lender, or both. Loss Mitigation commonly consists of the following general types of agreements, or a combination of them: loan modification, loan refinance, forbearance, short sale, or surrender of the property in full satisfaction. The terms of a Loss Mitigation resolution will vary in each case according to the particular needs, interests, and goals of the parties.

III. Other Definitions. The following definitions are used to describe the types of parties, properties, and loans that are eligible for participation in the Loss Mitigation Program.

A. *Debtor.* The term "Debtor" means any individual debtor in a case filed under chapter 7, 11, 12, or 13 of the Bankruptcy Code, including joint debtors, in the Northern District of New York.

B. *Property.* The term "Property" means any real property, including condominiums or cooperative apartments, used as the Debtor's principal residence, in which the Debtor holds an interest.

C. *Loan.* The term "Loan" means any mortgage, lien, or extension of money or credit secured by eligible Property or stock shares in a residential cooperative, regardless of whether the Loan (1) is considered to be "subprime" or "non-traditional;" (2) was in foreclosure prior to the bankruptcy filing; (3) is the first or junior mortgage or lien on the Property; or (4) has been "pooled," "securitized," or assigned to a servicer or trustee.

D. *Creditor.* The term "Creditor" means any holder, mortgage servicer, or trustee of an eligible Loan.

E. *Loss Mitigation Party.* The term "Loss Mitigation Party" means any party participating in the Loss Mitigation Program as identified in the Loss Mitigation Order.

IV. Additional Parties.

A. *Other Creditors.* Any Loss Mitigation Party may request or the court may direct, after notice and a hearing, more than one Creditor to participate in the Loss Mitigation Program if it may be of assistance to obtain a global resolution.

B. *Non–Filing Co–Debtors and Third Parties.* Any Loss Mitigation Party may request or the court may direct, after notice and a hearing, a non-filing co-debtor or other third party to participate in the Loss Mitigation Program if the participation of such party may be of assistance and if the court has jurisdiction over the party or the party consents.

C. *Chapter 13 / Chapter 12 Trustee.* In a chapter 13 case, the chapter 13 trustee may participate in the Loss Mitigation Program to the extent that such participation is consistent with the chapter 13 trustee's duty under 11 U.S.C. § 1302(b)(4) to "advise, other than on legal matters, and assist the debtor in performance under the [chapter 13] plan."

In a chapter 12 case, the chapter 12 trustee may participate in the Loss Mitigation Program to the extent that such participation is consistent with the chapter 12 trustee's duties under 11 U.S.C. § 1202(b).

V. Commencement of Loss Mitigation.
Parties are encouraged to request to enter into the Loss Mitigation Program as early in the case as possible, but a request may be made at any time as follows.

A. *By Written Request of the Debtor.*

1. At any time during the pendency of the case, a Debtor may file a completed Loss Mitigation Request by Debtor(s) and Certificate of Service to enter into the Loss Mitigation Program with one or more named Creditors. The Debtor shall serve the Loss Mitigation Request by Debtor(s) and Certificate of Service on the case trustee and the named Creditor(s) pursuant to Rule 7004 of the Federal Rules of Bankruptcy Procedure ("Bankruptcy Rules") and, if a proof of claim has been filed, on the individual who signed the proof of claim by first class mail. The Creditor(s) shall have 14 days to file and serve an Objection to Loss Mitigation Request and a Notice of Hearing on Objection to Loss Mitigation Request and Certificate of Service on the Debtor, Debtor's attorney, and the case trustee. If an Objection to Loss Mitigation Request and a Notice of Hearing on Objection to Loss Mitigation Request and Certificate of Service are not filed, the court may enter a Loss Mitigation Order.

2. The Debtor may file and serve a Loss Mitigation Request by Debtor(s) and Certificate of Service as part of a timely response to a motion pursuant to 11 U.S.C. § 362(d) for relief from the automatic stay ("Motion for Relief from Stay") as follows:

 a. The Debtor shall state in the response to the Motion for Relief from Stay that the Debtor wishes to enter Loss Mitigation with the Creditor and that a completed Loss Mitigation Request by Debtor(s) and Certificate of Service has been attached as an exhibit thereto for the court's consideration; and

 b. The Debtor shall allege in the response facts sufficient to support the conclusion that the Debtor can and will proceed in Loss Mitigation in good faith; and

 c. The Debtor shall attach a copy of the completed Loss Mitigation Request by Debtor(s) and Certificate of Service as an exhibit to Debtor's response.

A request for Loss Mitigation is not, in itself, a defense to a Motion for Relief from Stay. Therefore, the Debtor should still advance any other legal or factual defenses to the Motion for

Relief from Stay in Debtor's response. The court will treat the Debtor's request for Loss Mitigation as an application for permission to file the Loss Mitigation Request by Debtor(s) and Certificate of Service, and will consider the Debtor's request and any opposition by the Creditor at the hearing on the Motion for Relief from Stay.

In the event the court grants the Debtor leave to file a request for Loss Mitigation, the Debtor shall file the Loss Mitigation Request by Debtor(s) and Certificate of Service within three (3) days after the hearing on the Motion for Relief from Stay, and shall serve the Loss Mitigation Request by Debtor(s) and Certificate of Service in accordance with section V(A)(1). The court will treat the Debtor's request for Loss Mitigation as if it had been made pursuant to section V(A)(1), and will proceed on the request pursuant to these Procedures as if the request had been so made.

B. *By Written Request of a Creditor.*

1. At any time during the pendency of the case, a Creditor may file a completed Loss Mitigation Request by Creditor and Certificate of Service to enter into the Loss Mitigation Program with the Debtor. The Creditor shall serve the Loss Mitigation Request by Creditor and Certificate of Service on the case trustee and Debtor's counsel by a notice of electronic filing (NEF) via the CM/ECF system and on the Debtor by first class mail. The Debtor shall have 14 days to file and serve an Objection to Loss Mitigation Request and a Notice of Hearing on Objection to Loss Mitigation Request and Certificate of Service on the Creditor and case trustee. If an Objection to Loss Mitigation Request and a Notice of Hearing on Objection to Loss Mitigation Request and Certificate of Service are not filed, the court may enter a Loss Mitigation Order.

2. The Creditor may serve and file a Loss Mitigation Request by Creditor and Certificate of Service as a reply to any opposition received to a Motion for Relief from Stay that was filed by the Creditor as follows:

    a. The Loss Mitigation Request by Creditor and Certificate of Service shall be filed not later than three (3) days prior to the return date of the Motion for Relief from Stay, and shall be served in accordance with section V(B)(1); and

    b. The Creditor shall adjourn the hearing on its Motion for Relief from Stay pursuant to Local Bankruptcy Rule ("L.B.R.") 9013–1(i) and (j) to a date that is at least 20 days but no more than 60 days from the date of the hearing on its Motion for Relief from Stay.

The court will treat the Creditor's request for Loss Mitigation as if it had been made pursuant to section V(B)(1), and will proceed on the request pursuant to these Procedures as if the request had been so made.

C. *Hearing on Loss Mitigation Request.* If a party files either an Objection to Loss Mitigation Request and a Notice of Hearing on Objection to Loss Mitigation Request and Certificate of Service or a Loss Mitigation Request as provided in sections V(A)(2) or V(B)(2), the court shall hold a hearing on the request for Loss Mitigation, and shall not enter a Loss Mitigation Order until the parties have had an opportunity to be heard.

D. *Service of the Loss Mitigation Order.* Within three (3) days after entry of the Loss Mitigation Order, the party that requested Loss Mitigation shall serve the Loss Mitigation Order on all other Loss Mitigation Parties and the case trustee, and shall file a certificate of service.

VI. Loss Mitigation Order.

A. *Deadlines.* A Loss Mitigation Order shall contain:

1. The date by which contact persons and telephone, facsimile and email contact information shall be provided by the Loss Mitigation Parties.

2. The date by which the Debtor and each Creditor shall transmit any request for information or documents to other Loss Mitigation Parties, and shall file the appropriate Loss Mitigation Affidavit (Debtor(s) / Creditor) itemizing the information and/or documents requested.

3. The date by which the Debtor and each Creditor shall respond to any request for information or documents, and shall file the appropriate Loss Mitigation Affidavit (Debtor(s) / Creditor) itemizing the information and/or documents provided.

4. The date by which the initial Loss Mitigation Session shall be conducted.

5. The date and time of the Status Conference with the court and a requirement that the Loss Mitigation Party that requested Loss Mitigation file with the court a Loss Mitigation Status Report not later than seven (7) days prior to the Status Conference.

6. The date when the Loss Mitigation process shall terminate, unless extended (the "Loss Mitigation Period").

7. The date by which the Loss Mitigation Party that requested Loss Mitigation shall file a Loss Mitigation Program Final Report.

B. *Effect.* During the Loss Mitigation Period:

1. A Creditor that is a Loss Mitigation Party may not file a Motion for Relief from Stay regarding Property that is subject to Loss Mitigation. A pending Motion for Relief from Stay by a Creditor that is a Loss Mitigation Party filed before the entry of the Loss Mitigation Order shall be adjourned by the Creditor pursuant to L.B.R. 9013–1(i) and (j) to the date of the Status Conference, and the stay shall be extended pursuant to 11 U.S.C. § 362(e).

A Loss Mitigation Party that wishes to file a Motion for Relief from Stay or to restore a pending Motion for Relief from Stay to the court's calendar must first make a motion requesting early termination of the Loss Mitigation Period pursuant to section IX(C) of these procedures. A Loss Mitigation Party that wishes to restore a pending Motion for Relief from Stay to the court's calendar may request that relief as ancillary to its motion requesting early termination of the Loss Mitigation Period.

2. The time for each Creditor that is a Loss Mitigation Party to file an objection to an unconfirmed plan of reorganization in Debtor's case shall be extended until fourteen (14) days after the termination of the Loss Mitigation Period, including any extension thereof.

3. Federal Rule of Evidence 408 shall apply to communications, information and documents exchanged by the Loss Mitigation Parties in connection with the Loss Mitigation Program.

VII. Duties Upon Commencement of Loss Mitigation.

A. *Good Faith.* The Loss Mitigation Parties shall negotiate in good faith. A party that does not participate in the Loss Mitigation Program in good faith may be subject to sanctions.

B. *Adjourn Other Proceedings.* Other proceedings (*e.g.* motions or applications) that are currently pending between the Loss Mitigation Parties shall be adjourned by the party who commenced such proceeding pursuant to L.B.R. 9013–1(i) and (j) to the date of the Status Conference as indicated in the Loss Mitigation Order to the extent that those proceedings concern (1) relief from the automatic stay; (2) objection to the allowance of a proof of claim; (3) reduction, reclassification or avoidance of a lien; or (4) valuation of a lien or the Property.

C. *Contact Information.*

1. The Debtor. If the Debtor is represented by counsel in the underlying bankruptcy case, the Debtor shall be represented during all phases of the Loss Mitigation Program. Debtor's counsel shall provide the name, address, direct telephone number, facsimile number and email of the attorney(s) with authority to act on the Debtor's behalf to each Loss Mitigation Party. If the Debtor is pro se, the Debtor shall provide written notice to each Loss Mitigation Party of the manner in which the Creditor shall contact the Debtor. This information may be conveyed in the Loss Mitigation Request by Debtor(s) and Certificate of Service.

2. The Creditor. Each Creditor shall provide written notice to the Debtor's attorney or the Debtor, if pro se, of the name, address, direct telephone number, facsimile number and email of the contact person with authority to act on the Creditor's behalf. This may be done in the Loss Mitigation Request by Creditor and Certificate of Service.

D. *Status Report.* Unless the court orders otherwise in the Loss Mitigation Order, the party that requested Loss Mitigation shall file and serve upon all other Loss Mitigation Parties a Loss Mitigation Status Report as provided in section VIII(C) of these procedures. The date on which the Loss Mitigation Status Report is due shall be governed by the Loss Mitigation Order.

E. *Bankruptcy Court Approval.* The Loss Mitigation Parties shall seek court approval of any Settlement reached during the Loss Mitigation Period.

F. *File Final Report Upon Resolution of Loss Mitigation.* Upon expiration or termination of Loss Mitigation, whether by dismissal of the case or otherwise, a Loss Mitigation Program Final

Report shall be filed by the party that requested Loss Mitigation, unless the court directs otherwise in the Loss Mitigation Order.

VIII. Loss Mitigation Process After Loss Mitigation is Ordered.

A. *Initial Contact Period.* The purpose of the initial contact period is to create a framework for the Loss Mitigation Sessions and to ensure that the Loss Mitigation Parties are prepared. The initial contact period is not intended to limit the issues or proposals that may arise during the Loss Mitigation Sessions.

1. Within fourteen (14) days after the entry of the Loss Mitigation Order, the following shall occur:

a. Each Loss Mitigation Party shall designate contact persons and disclose contact information, unless this information was previously provided.

b. Each Creditor that is a Loss Mitigation Party shall contact the Debtor's attorney or the Debtor, if pro se.

c. Each Loss Mitigation Party shall make its request for information and documents, if any, and file the appropriate Loss Mitigation Affidavit (Debtor(s) / Creditor) itemizing the information and/or documents requested.

2. Within thirty-five (35) days after the entry of the Loss Mitigation Order and at least seven (7) days prior to the initial Loss Mitigation Session, each Loss Mitigation Party shall respond to any request for information and documents, and shall file the appropriate Loss Mitigation Affidavit (Debtor(s) / Creditor) identifying the information and/or documents provided.

3. Within forty-five (45) days after the entry of the Loss Mitigation Order, the Loss Mitigation Parties shall conduct the initial Loss Mitigation Session.

B. *Loss Mitigation Sessions.* Loss Mitigation Sessions may be conducted in person, by telephone, or by video conference. At the conclusion of each Loss Mitigation Session, the Loss Mitigation Parties shall discuss whether and when to hold a further session and whether any additional information or documents should be exchanged.

C. *Status Conference / Additional Conferences.* Pursuant to the Loss Mitigation Order, the court shall conduct a Status Conference at which the Loss Mitigation Parties shall appear. The Loss Mitigation Parties shall appear through counsel unless unrepresented, in which case, the party shall appear. In its discretion, the court may order that the Loss Mitigation Parties appear with their counsel. Seven (7) days prior to the Status Conference or any adjournments thereof by the court, the party that requested Loss Mitigation shall file and serve upon all Loss Mitigation Parties a Loss Mitigation Status Report.

At any time during the Loss Mitigation Period, a Loss Mitigation Party may request additional conferences with the court by filing on notice to the other Loss Mitigation Parties a Request for Additional Loss Mitigation Conference and Certificate of Service.

D. *Persons with Settlement Authority.* At both a Loss Mitigation Session and a Status Conference with the court, each Loss Mitigation Party shall have a person with full settlement authority present or immediately available by telephone. If a Loss Mitigation Party is appearing at a Status Conference by telephone or video conference, that party shall be available beginning thirty minutes before the conference.

IX. Duration, Extension, and Resolution.

A. *Initial Period.* The initial Loss Mitigation Period shall be set by the court in the Loss Mitigation Order.

B. *Extension.*

1. By Agreement. The Loss Mitigation Parties may agree to extend the Loss Mitigation Period for up to ninety (90) days beyond the initial Loss Mitigation Period by Stipulation and Order Extending Loss Mitigation Period signed by the Loss Mitigation Parties [2] and filed not later than three (3) business days before the termination of the initial Loss Mitigation Period, to be so ordered by the court. If the parties desire an extension of the Loss Mitigation Period for a period beyond ninety (90) days from the initial termination date provided in the Loss Mitigation Order, a joint motion shall be filed and heard prior to the termination of the Loss Mitigation Period. The motion shall set forth the original termination date of the Loss Mitigation Period, any previous extensions granted, the current extension desired, and the reason for the request.

2. In the Absence of Agreement. A Loss Mitigation Party may request to extend the Loss Mitigation Period in the absence of agreement by motion filed and heard prior to the termination of the initial Loss Mitigation Period. The motion shall set forth the original termination date of the Loss Mitigation Period, any previous extensions granted, the current extension desired, the reason for the request, and that no agreement can be reached. A certificate of service evidencing service of the motion on the other Loss Mitigation Parties shall be filed not later than seven (7) days prior to the return date of the motion.

In determining whether to grant an extension of the Loss Mitigation Period, the court shall consider whether: (1) an extension of the Loss Mitigation Period may result in a complete or partial resolution that provides a substantial benefit to a Loss Mitigation Party; (2) the Loss Mitigation Party opposed to the extension has participated in good faith and has complied with the Loss Mitigation Program Procedures; and (3) the Loss Mitigation Party opposed to the extension will be prejudiced.

C. *Early Termination.*

1. By Agreement. The Loss Mitigation Parties may agree to early termination of the Loss Mitigation Period by Stipulation and Order Terminating Loss Mitigation Period signed by the Loss Mitigation Parties[3] and filed at any time during the Loss Mitigation Period, to be so ordered by the court.

2. In the Absence of Agreement. A Loss Mitigation Party may request early termination of the Loss Mitigation Period in the absence of agreement by filing and serving on the other Loss Mitigation Parties a motion requesting early termination. The motion shall set forth the reason for the request and that no agreement can be reached. A certificate of service shall be filed not later than seven (7) days prior to the return date of the motion.

In determining whether to grant early termination of the Loss Mitigation Period, the court shall consider whether: (1) early termination of the Loss Mitigation Period is appropriate; (2) the Loss Mitigation Party seeking early termination has participated in good faith and has complied with the Loss Mitigation Program Procedures; and (3) the Loss Mitigation Party opposed to the early termination will be prejudiced.

3. Early Termination by Dismissal of the Bankruptcy Case. If the Debtor's case is dismissed during the Loss Mitigation Period, the Loss Mitigation shall terminate on the date the dismissal order is entered. If the dismissal is the result of a chapter 12 or chapter 13 debtor requesting voluntary dismissal of the bankruptcy case pursuant to 11 U.S.C. § 1208(b) or § 1307(a) respectively, the Debtor shall indicate in the request for dismissal whether the Debtor agreed to or intends to enter into a Settlement with a Loss Mitigation Party.

X. Settlement. The court shall consider any agreement or resolution (a "Settlement") reached during the Loss Mitigation Period and may approve the Settlement, subject to the following provisions.

A. *Implementation.* A Settlement may be noticed and implemented in any manner permitted by the Bankruptcy Code and Bankruptcy Rules, including, but not limited to, a stipulation, sale, or chapter 11, 12, or 13 plan of reorganization.

B. *Fees, Costs, or Charges.* If a Settlement provides for a Creditor to receive payment or reimbursement of any expense arising from the Creditor's participation in the Loss Mitigation Program, that expense shall be disclosed to the Debtor and the court before the Settlement is approved.

C. *Signatures.* Consent to the Settlement shall be acknowledged in writing by the Creditor's representative who participated in the Loss Mitigation Session(s), the Debtor, Debtor's counsel, if applicable, and, in a chapter 12 or 13 case, the chapter 12 or chapter 13 trustee.

D. *Hearing.* Where a Debtor is represented by an attorney, a Settlement may be approved by the court without further notice, or upon such notice as the court directs, unless additional notice or a hearing is required by the Bankruptcy Code or Bankruptcy Rules. Where a Debtor is not represented by counsel, the Creditor shall file a motion to approve the Settlement. The Settlement shall not be approved until the court conducts a hearing at which the pro se Debtor shall appear in person.

E. *Dismissal not Required.* A Debtor shall not be required to request dismissal of the bankruptcy case in order to effectuate a Settlement.

XI. Debtor's Counsel Fees When Utilizing Loss Mitigation Program.

A. *Allowance and Payment of Portion of Fee Before Confirmation of Chapter 13 Plan.* The Loss Mitigation Order shall provide that in a chapter 13 case where Debtor's counsel is to receive a portion of fees through the plan, in the month following entry of the Loss Mitigation Order or the first month after the initial 11 U.S.C. § 341 Meeting of Creditors, whichever is later, the chapter 13 trustee shall disburse payment to Debtor's counsel of the requested attorney fee—up to a maximum of $1,500.00—with said amount to be paid in the manner prescribed in the Debtor's proposed plan. The amount disbursed shall be deemed allowed immediately. This amount shall be exclusive of any amounts received by counsel prior to the filing of the petition. The balance of the attorney fee shall only be allowed and paid pursuant to a Confirmation Order or further order of the court.

B. *Allowance and Payment of Additional Fee for Loss Mitigation Upon Conclusion of Loss Mitigation Program.* Upon completion of the Loss Mitigation Program, Debtor's counsel may submit an Ex Parte Application and Certification in Support of Approval and Payment of Attorney Fees for Loss Mitigation. The court may thereafter enter an Order Approving Attorney Fees for Loss Mitigation and Authorizing Payment (chapter 7 or 11 / chapter 12 or 13). In a chapter 12 or 13 case, the court may direct the chapter 12 or chapter 13 trustee to pay said fees as an administrative expense through the Debtor's plan.

Except as otherwise ordered by the court, a fee in the sum of $1,000.00 shall be presumed reasonable for services rendered in connection with the Loss Mitigation Program without further documentation. The award of this fee is without prejudice to the rights of counsel to request approval of additional fees by filing and serving a Notice of Hearing and an Application for Compensation under 11 U.S.C. § 331. Any such Application for Compensation shall be accompanied by an appropriate narrative of services rendered and contemporaneous time records.

XII. Loss Mitigation Program Required Forms. The following forms are available on the court's website and shall be used, as indicated above, by the Loss Mitigation Parties:

- Loss Mitigation Request by Debtor(s) and Certificate of Service
- Loss Mitigation Request by Creditor and Certificate of Service
- Objection to Loss Mitigation Request
- Notice of Hearing on Objection to Loss Mitigation Request and Certificate of Service
- Loss Mitigation Order
- Loss Mitigation Affidavit of Debtor(s) and Certificate of Service
- Loss Mitigation Affidavit of Creditor and Certificate of Service
- Loss Mitigation Status Report
- Request for Additional Loss Mitigation Conference and Certificate of Service
- Stipulation and Order Extending Loss Mitigation Period
- Stipulation and Order Terminating Loss Mitigation Period
- Loss Mitigation Program Final Report
- Ex Parte Application and Certification in Support of Approval and Payment of Attorney Fees for Loss Mitigation
- Order Approving Attorney Fees for Loss Mitigation and Authorizing Payment—chapter 7 or 11
- Order Approving Attorney Fees for Loss Mitigation and Authorizing Payment—chapter 12 or 13

[Dated: June 21, 2013.]

1 Text appearing in Blue denotes a Loss Mitigation Program Form. The Loss Mitigation Program Forms, which are listed in section XII, are required under these Loss Mitigation Program Procedures and are available on the court's website at www.nynb. uscourts.gov. [**Publisher's Note:** Font style in the court record is not reproduced herein. The forms referenced in these procedures are set forth, *post.*]

2 The parties are reminded to comply with L.B.R. 9011–3(g).

3 The parties are reminded to comply with L.B.R. 9011–3(g).

* [**Publisher's Note:** This Administrative Order has been augmented by Administrative Order 16–01, dated March 14, 2016, *post.*]

ADMINISTRATIVE ORDER 16–01. ADOPTING MODIFIED LOSS MITIGATION PROGRAM PROCEDURES

WHEREAS, on June 21, 2013 the Loss Mitigation Program Procedures and the Loss Mitigation Program described therein were adopted by Administrative Order #13–05 to facilitate consensual resolutions for individual debtors whose residential real property is at risk of loss to foreclosure; and

WHEREAS, pursuant to Administrative Order #13–05, the Loss Mitigation Program Procedures may be modified by Administrative Order from time to time as deemed necessary by the Judges of the Northern District of New York Bankruptcy Court; and

WHEREAS, the Judges of the Northern District of New York Bankruptcy Court comprised a working group of creditor and debtor attorneys, standing trustees, law clerks and Clerk's office personnel to review and recommend changes to the Loss Mitigation Program Procedures and the related forms.

Now, therefore, it is hereby

ORDERED, that the revised "Loss Mitigation Program Procedures" annexed to this Administrative Order and the Loss Mitigation Program described therein are adopted, pursuant to 11 U.S.C. § 105(a); and it is further

ORDERED, that the revised Loss Mitigation Program Procedures shall take effect March 15, 2016. and apply to any pending and future request for Loss Mitigation; and it is further

ORDERED, that the revised Loss Mitigation Program Procedures and related forms shall be available on the court's website; and it is further

ORDERED, that this Administrative Order augments Administrative Order #13–05, which shall remain in full force and effect.

[Dated: March 14, 2016.]

LOSS MITIGATION PROGRAM PROCEDURES[1]

Current as of March 15, 2016

I. PURPOSE

The Loss Mitigation Program[2] is designed to function as a forum in individual bankruptcy cases for debtors and lenders to reach consensual resolution whenever a debtor's principal residence is at risk of foreclosure. The Loss Mitigation Program aims to facilitate resolution by opening the lines of communication between debtors and lenders' decision-makers. While the Loss Mitigation Program stays certain bankruptcy deadlines that might interfere with negotiations or increase costs to the parties, the Loss Mitigation Program also encourages the parties to finalize any Settlement (as defined below) under bankruptcy court protection, instead of seeking dismissal of the bankruptcy case.

II. LOSS MITIGATION DEFINED

The term "Loss Mitigation" is intended to describe the full range of solutions that may avert the loss of a debtor's property to foreclosure, increased costs to the lender, or both. Loss Mitigation commonly consists of the following general types of agreements, or a combination of them: loan modification, loan refinance, forbearance, short sale, or surrender of the property in full satisfaction. The terms of a Loss Mitigation resolution will vary in each case according to the particular needs, interests, and goals of the parties.

III. OTHER DEFINITIONS

The following definitions are used to describe the types of parties, properties, and loans that are eligible for participation in the Loss Mitigation Program.

A. **Debtor.** The term "Debtor" means any individual debtor in a case filed under chapter 7, 11, 12, or 13 of the Bankruptcy Code, including joint debtors, in the Northern District of New York.

B. Property. The term "Property" means any real property, including condominiums or cooperative apartments, used as the Debtor's principal residence, in which the Debtor holds an interest.

C. Loan. The term "Loan" means any mortgage, lien, or extension of money or credit secured by eligible Property or stock shares in a residential cooperative, regardless of whether the Loan (1) is considered to be "subprime" or "non-traditional;" (2) was in foreclosure prior to the bankruptcy filing; (3) is the first or junior mortgage lien on the Property; or (4) has been "pooled," "securitized," or assigned to a servicer or trustee.

D. Creditor. The term "Creditor" means any holder, mortgage servicer, or trustee of an eligible Loan.

E. Loss Mitigation Party. The term "Loss Mitigation Party" means any party participating in the Loss Mitigation Program as named in the Loss Mitigation Order. In a chapter 12 or 13 case, the standing trustee, although a participant in the Loss Mitigation Program, is not a Loss Mitigation Party.

F. Status Conference. The term "Status Conference" means the conference set by the court which requires appearances by the Loss Mitigation Parties.

IV. ADDITIONAL PARTIES

A. Other Creditors. Any Loss Mitigation Party may request or the court may direct, after notice and a hearing, more than one Creditor to participate in the Loss Mitigation Program if it may be of assistance to obtain a global resolution.

B. Non-Filing Co-Debtors and Third Parties. Any Loss Mitigation Party may request or the court may direct, after notice and a hearing, a non-filing co-debtor or other third party to participate in the Loss Mitigation Program if the participation of such party may be of assistance and if the court has jurisdiction over the party or the party consents.

C. Chapter 12 & Chapter 13 Trustees. In a chapter 12 or 13 case, the standing trustee may participate in the Loss Mitigation Program to the extent that such participation is consistent with the trustee's duties under, respectively, 11 U.S.C. §§ 1202(b) or 1302(b)(4).

A Loss Mitigation Order shall provide that, in a chapter 12 or 13 case, the standing trustee may participate in Loss Mitigation, including—but not necessarily limited to—appearing at the Status Conference and filing a response, if any, to the Creditor's motion to terminate Loss Mitigation made pursuant to section IX of these Procedures. The standing trustee need not make a specific request in order to participate in Loss Mitigation.

V. COMMENCEMENT OF LOSS MITIGATION

Generally, a request for Loss Mitigation may be made at any time during the pendency of the case. However, when there is a pending motion pursuant to 11 U.S.C. § 362(d) for relief from the automatic stay ("Motion for Relief from Stay") as to the Property, a request may be presented to the court only as provided in subsections (A)(2) and (B)(2). Parties are encouraged to request to enter into the Loss Mitigation Program as early in the case as possible.

A. By Written Request of the Debtor.

1. *Generally.* Except as provided in subsection (A)(2), a Debtor may file at any time during the pendency of the case a completed Loss Mitigation Request by Debtor(s) and Certificate of Service to enter into the Loss Mitigation Program with a Creditor. In a chapter 12 or 13 proceeding, the Debtor's plan payments or such modified payments as agreed to by the standing trustee must be current at the time Loss Mitigation is requested. A separate Loss Mitigation Request by Debtor(s) and Certificate of Service must be filed for each Loan subject to Loss Mitigation. The Debtor shall serve the Loss Mitigation Request by Debtor(s) and Certificate of Service on the case trustee and the named Creditor pursuant to Rule 7004 of the Federal Rules of Bankruptcy Procedure ("Bankruptcy Rules") and, if a proof of claim has been filed, on the individual who signed the proof of claim by first class mail.

The Creditor shall have 14 days to file and serve an Objection to Loss Mitigation Request and a Notice of Hearing on Objection to Loss Mitigation Request and Certificate of Service on 14 days' notice to the Debtor, Debtor's attorney, and the case trustee. If an Objection to Loss Mitigation Request and a Notice of Hearing on Objection to Loss Mitigation Request and Certificate of Service are not filed, the court may enter a Loss Mitigation Order.

2. *When a Motion for Relief from Stay is Pending as to the Property.* The Debtor may include a Loss Mitigation Request by Debtor(s) and Certificate of Service as part of a timely response to a Motion for Relief from Stay in the manner provided below:

a. The Debtor shall state in the response to the Motion for Relief from Stay that the Debtor wishes to enter Loss Mitigation with the Creditor and that a completed Loss Mitigation Request by Debtor(s) and Certificate of Service is attached as an exhibit thereto for the court's consideration; **and**

b. The Debtor shall allege in the response facts sufficient to support the conclusion that the Debtor can and will proceed in Loss Mitigation in good faith; **and**

c. The Debtor shall attach a copy of the completed Loss Mitigation Request by Debtor(s) and Certificate of Service as an exhibit to Debtor's response. The Loss Mitigation Request by Debtor(s) and Certificate of Service shall not be separately filed and served at this juncture because the court will treat the Debtor's request for Loss Mitigation as an application for permission to file the Loss Mitigation Request by Debtor(s) and Certificate of Service. The Debtor's request and any opposition by the Creditor will be considered by the court at the hearing on the Motion for Relief from Stay.

A request for Loss Mitigation is not, in itself, a defense to a Motion for Relief from Stay. Therefore, the Debtor must still advance any legal defenses to the Motion for Relief from Stay in Debtor's response.

In the event the court grants the Debtor leave to file a request for Loss Mitigation, the Debtor shall file the Loss Mitigation Request by Debtor(s) and Certificate of Service within three (3) business days after the hearing on the Motion for Relief from Stay, and shall serve the Loss Mitigation Request by Debtor(s) and Certificate of Service in accordance with subsection (A)(1). The court will treat the Debtor's request for Loss Mitigation as if it had been made pursuant to subsection (A)(1), and will proceed on the request pursuant to these Procedures as if the request had been so made.

B. By Written Request of a Creditor.

1. *Generally.* Except as provided in subsection (B)(2), a Creditor may file a completed Loss Mitigation Request by Creditor and Certificate of Service to enter into the Loss Mitigation Program with the Debtor at any time during the pendency of the case. The Creditor shall serve the Loss Mitigation Request by Creditor and Certificate of Service on the trustee and Debtor's counsel by notice of electronic filing (NEF) via the CM/ECF system and on the Debtor by first class mail.

The Debtor shall have 14 days to file and serve an Objection to Loss Mitigation Request and a Notice of Hearing on Objection to Loss Mitigation Request and Certificate of Service on 14 days' notice to the Creditor and case trustee. If an Objection to Loss Mitigation Request and a Notice of Hearing on Objection to Loss Mitigation Request and Certificate of Service are not filed, the court may enter a Loss Mitigation Order.

2. *When a Motion for Relief from the Stay is Pending as to the Property.* The Creditor may serve and file a Loss Mitigation Request by Creditor and Certificate of Service as a reply to any opposition received to a Motion for Relief from Stay that was filed by the Creditor in the manner provided below:

a. The Loss Mitigation Request by Creditor and Certificate of Service shall be filed not later than three (3) days prior to the return date of the Motion for Relief from Stay, and shall be served in accordance with subsection (B)(1); **and**

b. The Creditor shall adjourn the hearing on its Motion for Relief from Stay pursuant to Local Bankruptcy Rule ("L.B.R.") 9013–1(i) and (j) to a date that is at least 20 but no more than 60 days from the date of the hearing on its Motion for Relief from Stay.

The court will treat the Creditor's request for Loss Mitigation as if it had been made pursuant to subsection (B)(1), and will proceed on the request pursuant to these Procedures as if the request had been so made.

C. Hearing on an Opposed Request for Loss Mitigation. If a party files an Objection to Loss Mitigation Request and a Notice of Hearing on Objection to Loss Mitigation Request and Certificate of Service, the court shall hold a hearing on the request for Loss Mitigation, and shall not enter a Loss Mitigation Order until the parties have had an opportunity to be heard. In a chapter 12 or 13 case, the standing trustee may attend and participate in the hearing without making a request to appear.

D. Service of the Order on the Request for Loss Mitigation. Within three (3) business days after entry of a Loss Mitigation Order or an order denying a request for Loss Mitigation, the party that requested Loss Mitigation shall serve the order on (i) all parties named in the request for Loss Mitigation, (ii) the case trustee, and (iii) any party not named in the request for Loss Mitigation but designated a Loss Mitigation Party in the Loss Mitigation Order, and shall file a certificate of service.

VI. LOSS MITIGATION ORDER

A. Deadlines. A Loss Mitigation Order shall contain:

1. The date by which contact persons and telephone, facsimile and email contact information shall be provided by the Loss Mitigation Parties.

2. The date by which the Debtor and the Creditor shall transmit any request for information or documents to other Loss Mitigation Parties, and shall file the appropriate Loss Mitigation Affidavit (Debtor(s) / Creditor) itemizing the information and/or documents requested.

3. The date by which the Debtor and the Creditor shall respond to any request for information or documents, and shall file the appropriate Loss Mitigation Affidavit (Debtor(s) / Creditor) itemizing the information and/or documents provided.

4. The date by which the initial Loss Mitigation session shall be conducted.

5. The date and time of the initial Status Conference with the court and a requirement that the Loss Mitigation Party that requested Loss Mitigation file with the court a Loss Mitigation Status Report not later than seven (7) days prior to the initial Status Conference. Failure to file the initial Loss Mitigation Status Report may, at the discretion of the court, result in termination of Loss Mitigation.

B. Effect. During Loss Mitigation:

1. Absent consent of counsel or as otherwise ordered by the court, it is expected that communications between the Loss Mitigation Parties shall be made through the Loss Mitigation Parties' designated attorneys.

2. A Creditor may not file a Motion for Relief from Stay regarding Property that is subject to Loss Mitigation. A pending Motion for Relief from Stay by a Creditor that is a Loss Mitigation Party filed before the entry of the Loss Mitigation Order shall be adjourned by the Creditor to the date of the initial Status Conference by filing an Adjournment Request/Withdrawal/Settlement Notification of Loss Mitigation Status Conferences; Related Motions for Relief from Stay and/or Confirmation Hearings (Albany & Syracuse Divisions) form, or Adjournment Request/Withdrawal/Settlement Notification of Loss Mitigation Status Conferences; Related Motions for Relief from Stay, Confirmation Hearings, and/or Motions to Dismiss (Utica Division) form, and the stay shall be extended pursuant to 11 U.S.C. § 362(e).

A Loss Mitigation Party that wishes to file a Motion for Relief from Stay or to restore a pending Motion for Relief from Stay to the court's calendar must first make a motion requesting termination of Loss Mitigation pursuant to section IX(B)(4) of these Procedures. A Loss Mitigation Party that wishes to restore a pending Motion for Relief from Stay to the court's calendar may request that relief as ancillary to its motion requesting termination of Loss Mitigation.

3. In the Albany Division only, if a chapter 13 plan is confirmed while Loss Mitigation is pending, an Addendum to Confirmation Order When Loss Mitigation is Pending will be submitted to the court by the standing trustee as part of the proposed Order of Confirmation.

4. Federal Rule of Evidence 408 shall apply to communications, information, and documents exchanged by the Loss Mitigation Parties in connection with the Loss Mitigation Program.

5. Unless otherwise ordered by the court, in a chapter 7 case, entry of a Loss Mitigation Order defers entry of an order discharging the Debtor until one day after an Order Terminating Loss Mitigation and Final Report is entered, pursuant to Federal Rule of Bankruptcy Procedure

4004(c)(2). The deadline to object to the Debtor's discharge or the dischargeability of a debt is not extended by the entry of a Loss Mitigation Order.

VII. DUTIES UPON COMMENCEMENT OF LOSS MITIGATION

A. Good Faith.

1. *Participation.* The Loss Mitigation Parties shall negotiate in good faith. A party that does not participate in the Loss Mitigation Program in good faith may be subject to sanctions.

2. *Mortgage Payments.* During the pendency of Loss Mitigation, a Debtor in a chapter 13 proceeding shall make the contractually due post-petition monthly payment ("Payment") directly to the Creditor, or submit the Payment or such lesser amount as the Debtor can afford to the standing trustee for the benefit of the Creditor.

3. *Plan Payments.* In a chapter 12 or 13 proceeding, the Debtor's failure to remain current with plan payments may, at the discretion of the court, result in termination of Loss Mitigation.

B. Adjourn Other Proceedings.
Other proceedings (*e.g.* motions or applications) that are currently pending between the Loss Mitigation Parties shall be adjourned by the party who commenced such proceeding pursuant to L.B.R. 9013–1(i) and (j) to the date of the initial Status Conference as indicated in the Loss Mitigation Order to the extent that those proceedings concern (1) objection to the allowance of a proof of claim; (2) reduction, reclassification or avoidance of a lien; or (3) valuation of a lien or the Property. A pending Motion for Relief from Stay by a Creditor shall be adjourned as provide in section VI(B)(2) of these Procedures.

C. Contact Information.

1. *The Debtor.* If the Debtor is represented by counsel in the underlying bankruptcy case, the Debtor shall be represented during all phases of the Loss Mitigation Program. Debtor's counsel shall provide the name, address, direct telephone number, facsimile number and email of the attorney(s) with authority to act on the Debtor's behalf to each Loss Mitigation Party. If the Debtor is *pro se*, the Debtor shall provide written notice to each Loss Mitigation Party of the manner in which the Creditor shall contact the Debtor. This may be done in the Loss Mitigation Request by Debtor(s) and Certificate of Service.

2. *The Creditor.* The Creditor shall provide written notice to the Debtor's attorney or the Debtor, if *pro se*, of the names, addresses, direct telephone numbers, facsimile numbers and email addresses of the attorney(s) representing the Creditor in Loss Mitigation and the person in-house who has full settlement authority to act on the Creditor's behalf with respect to the Loan. This may be done in the Loss Mitigation Request by Creditor and Certificate of Service or Loss Mitigation Affidavit of Creditor and Certificate of Service.

D. Status Report.
Unless the court orders otherwise in the Loss Mitigation Order, the party that requested Loss Mitigation shall file and serve upon all other Loss Mitigation Parties and, in a chapter 12 or 13 case, the standing trustee, a Loss Mitigation Status Report as provided in section VIII(C)(2) of these Procedures. The date on which the Loss Mitigation Status Report is due shall be governed by the Loss Mitigation Order.

E. Submission of Order Terminating Loss Mitigation and Final Report Upon Resolution of Loss Mitigation.
Upon completion of Loss Mitigation, whether by agreement or resolution reached by the Loss Mitigation Parties ("Settlement"), dismissal of the case, or otherwise, an Order Terminating Loss Mitigation and Final Report shall be filed by the party that requested Loss Mitigation, unless the court directs otherwise.

VIII. LOSS MITIGATION PROCESS AFTER LOSS MITIGATION IS ORDERED

A. Initial Contact Period.
The purpose of the initial contact period is to create a framework for the Loss Mitigation sessions and to ensure that the Loss Mitigation Parties are prepared. The initial contact period is not intended to limit the issues or proposals that may arise during the Loss Mitigation sessions. During the initial contact phase, the Loss Mitigation Parties should hold a telephone conference to discuss (1) the types of Loss Mitigation solutions under consideration by each party; and (2) a plan for the exchange of required information prior to the Loss Mitigation session.

1. Within seven (7) days after the entry of the Loss Mitigation Order, the following shall occur:

    a.   Each Loss Mitigation Party shall designate contact persons and disclose contact information, unless this information was previously provided.

    b.   The Creditor shall contact the Debtor's attorney or the Debtor, if *pro se.*

    c.   Each Loss Mitigation Party shall make its request for information and documents, if any, and file the appropriate Loss Mitigation Affidavit (Debtor(s) / Creditor) itemizing the information and/or documents requested.

2.   Within thirty-five (35) days after entry of the Loss Mitigation Order and at least seven (7) days prior to the initial Loss Mitigation session, each Loss Mitigation Party shall respond to any request for information and documents, and shall file the appropriate Loss Mitigation Affidavit (Debtor(s) / Creditor) identifying the information and/or documents provided.

3.   Within forty-five (45) days after entry of the Loss Mitigation Order but in any event prior to the initial Status Conference, the Loss Mitigation Parties shall conduct the initial Loss Mitigation session. The initial Loss Mitigation session shall include a discussion of both the federally regulated and in-house loan modification programs for which the Loan of the Debtor may qualify.

B. Loss Mitigation Sessions. Loss Mitigation sessions may be conducted in person, by telephone, or by video conference. At the conclusion of each Loss Mitigation session, the Loss Mitigation Parties shall discuss whether and when to hold a further session and whether any additional information or documents should be exchanged.

C. Status Conference / Additional Conferences.

1.   *Status Conference.* Pursuant to the Loss Mitigation Order, the court shall conduct an initial Status Conference at which the Loss Mitigation Parties shall appear. The Loss Mitigation Parties shall appear through counsel unless unrepresented, in which case, the party shall appear. In its discretion, the court may order that the Loss Mitigation Parties appear with their counsel at such intervals as directed by the court. In a chapter 12 or 13 case, the standing trustee may attend and participate in the Status Conference without making a request to appear.

    a.   Procedure for Requesting Adjournment. An adjournment request shall be made by not later than 2:00 p.m. the day prior to the Status Conference by filing an Adjournment Request/Withdrawal/Settlement Notification of Loss Mitigation Status Conferences; Related Motions for Relief from Stay and/or Confirmation Hearings (Albany & Syracuse Divisions) form, or Adjournment Request/Withdrawal/Settlement Notification of Loss Mitigation Status Conferences; Related Motions for Relief from Stay, Confirmation Hearings, and/or Motions to Dismiss (Utica Division) form.

2.   *Loss Mitigation Status Report.* Seven (7) days prior to the initial Status Conference or any adjournments thereof by the court, the party that requested Loss Mitigation shall file and serve upon all Loss Mitigation Parties and, in a chapter 12 or 13 case, the standing trustee, a Loss Mitigation Status Report. After the filing of the initial Loss Mitigation Status Report, the format, responsible party, and due date of any subsequent status reports, shall be as directed by the court.

3.   *Additional Conferences.* At any time during Loss Mitigation, a Loss Mitigation Party may request additional conferences with the court by filing a Request for Additional Loss Mitigation Conference and Certificate of Service on notice to the other Loss Mitigation Parties and, in a chapter 12 or 13 case, the standing trustee.

D. Persons With Settlement Authority. At both a Loss Mitigation session and a Status Conference with the court, each Loss Mitigation Party shall have a person with full settlement authority present or immediately available by telephone. If a Loss Mitigation Party is appearing at a Status Conference by telephone or video conference, that party shall be available beginning thirty minutes before the conference.

IX. DURATION AND TERMINATION

A. Duration. Once a Loss Mitigation Order has been entered by the court, it shall remain in effect until an order is entered terminating Loss Mitigation or dismissing the Debtor's case.

B. Termination.

1.   *By the Court.* The court may *sua sponte* terminate Loss Mitigation at any time for failure to comply with these Procedures.

2. *By Debtor.* The Debtor may terminate Loss Mitigation prior to a Settlement by filing a letter with the court on notice to all Loss Mitigation Parties and, in a chapter 12 or 13 case, the standing trustee, stating the reason for the termination. Once the letter is filed, the Debtor shall present an Order Terminating Loss Mitigation and Final Report to the court by uploading the document via the court's E–Order system.

3. *By Agreement.* The Loss Mitigation Parties may agree to termination of Loss Mitigation prior to a Settlement by filing a Stipulation Terminating Loss Mitigation signed by the Loss Mitigation Parties.[3] Concurrently, the party that requested Loss Mitigation shall upload an Order Terminating Loss Mitigation and Final Report via the court's E–Order system.

4. *By Creditor in the Absence of Agreement.* The Creditor may request termination of Loss Mitigation in the absence of agreement by filing and serving a motion requesting termination on the other Loss Mitigation Parties and, in a chapter 12 or 13 case, the standing trustee. The motion shall set forth the reason for the request and that no agreement can be reached. A certificate of service shall be filed not later than seven (7) days prior to the return date of the motion.

In determining whether to grant termination of Loss Mitigation, the court shall consider whether: (1) termination of Loss Mitigation is appropriate; (2) the Loss Mitigation Party seeking termination has participated in good faith and has complied with these Procedures; and (3) the Loss Mitigation Party opposed to the termination will be prejudiced.

5. *By Dismissal of the Bankruptcy Case.* If the Debtor's case is dismissed during Loss Mitigation, Loss Mitigation shall terminate on the date the dismissal order is entered. If the dismissal is the result of a chapter 12 or chapter 13 debtor requesting voluntary dismissal of the bankruptcy case pursuant to 11 U.S.C. §§ 1208(b) or 1307(a), respectively, the Debtor shall indicate in the request for dismissal whether the Debtor agreed to or intends to enter into a Settlement with a Loss Mitigation Party.

X. SETTLEMENT

The court shall consider any Settlement reached during Loss Mitigation and may authorize the Settlement, subject to the following provisions.

A. Implementation. If the Settlement consists of a loan modification, a Stipulation and Order Authorizing Parties to Enter Into Loan Modification and Directing Treatment of Mortgage Claim[4] shall be executed and presented to the court by uploading the document via the court's E–Order system. Approval of all other Settlements shall be sought by motion on notice as required under the Bankruptcy Code and Bankruptcy Rules.

B. Fees, Costs, or Charges. If a Settlement provides for a Creditor to receive payment or reimbursement of any expense arising from the Creditor's participation in the Loss Mitigation Program, that expense shall be disclosed to the Debtor and the court before the Settlement is approved.

C. Signatures. Consent to the Settlement shall be acknowledged in writing by the Creditor's attorney who participated in the Loss Mitigation, the Debtor, Debtor's counsel, if applicable, and, in a chapter 12 or 13 case, the standing trustee.

D. Hearing. Where a Debtor is represented by an attorney, a Settlement may be authorized by the court without further notice, or upon such notice as the court directs, unless additional notice or a hearing is required by the Bankruptcy Code or Bankruptcy Rules. Where a Debtor is not represented by counsel, the Creditor shall file a motion to approve the Settlement. The Settlement shall not be authorized until the court conducts a hearing at which the *pro se* Debtor shall appear in person. In a chapter 12 or 13 case, the standing trustee may attend and participate in the hearing without making a request to appear.

E. Dismissal Not Required. A Debtor shall not be required to request dismissal of the bankruptcy case in order to effectuate a Settlement.

XI. DEBTOR'S COUNSEL FEES WHEN UTILIZING LOSS MITIGATION PROGRAM

A. Allowance and Payment of Portion of Fee Before Confirmation of Chapter 13 Plan. The Loss Mitigation Order shall provide that in a chapter 13 case where Debtor's counsel is to receive a portion of fees through the plan, in the month following entry of the Loss Mitigation Order or the first month after the initial 11 U.S.C. § 341 Meeting of Creditors, whichever is later, the chapter 13 trustee shall disburse payment to Debtor's counsel of the requested attorney fee—up to a maximum of $1,500.00—with said amount to be paid in the manner prescribed in the Debtor's proposed plan. The amount disbursed shall be deemed allowed immediately. This amount shall be exclusive of any amounts received by counsel prior to the filing of the petition. The balance of the attorney fee shall only be allowed and paid pursuant to a Confirmation Order or further order of the court.

B.   Allowance and Payment of Additional Fee for Loss Mitigation Upon Conclusion of Loss Mitigation Program.

If Debtor's counsel seeks fees in an amount of $1,000 or less, the fees sought may be presumed reasonable for services rendered in connection with the Loss Mitigation Program without further documentation. After submitting an Order Terminating Loss Mitigation and Final Report, Debtor's counsel may file an Ex Parte Application and Certification in Support of Approval and Payment of Attorney Fees for Loss Mitigation. Concurrently therewith, Debtor's counsel shall upload via the court's E–Order system a proposed Order Approving Attorney Fees for Loss Mitigation and Authorizing Payment (chapter 7 or 11 / chapter 12 or 13). The court may thereafter enter the proposed order and, in a chapter 12 or 13 case, may direct the standing trustee to pay approved fees as an administrative expense through the Debtor's plan.

Counsel seeking approval of fees in excess of $1,000.00 shall file and serve a Notice of Hearing and an Application for Compensation under 11 U.S.C. §§ 330 and 331. Any such Application for Compensation shall be accompanied by an appropriate narrative of services rendered and contemporaneous time records.

XII.   LOSS MITIGATION PROGRAM REQUIRED FORMS

The following forms are available on the court's website and shall be used, as indicated above, by the Loss Mitigation Parties:

- Loss Mitigation Request by Debtor(s) and Certificate of Service
- Loss Mitigation Request by Creditor and Certificate of Service
- Objection to Loss Mitigation Request
- Notice of Hearing on Objection to Loss Mitigation Request and Certificate of Service
- Loss Mitigation Order
- Loss Mitigation Affidavit of Debtor(s) and Certificate of Service
- Loss Mitigation Affidavit of Creditor and Certificate of Service
- Loss Mitigation Status Report
- Request for Additional Loss Mitigation Conference and Certificate of Service
- Stipulation and Order Authorizing Parties to Enter Into Loan Modification and Directing Treatment of Mortgage Claim
- Stipulation Terminating Loss Mitigation
- Order Terminating Loss Mitigation and Final Report
- Ex Parte Application and Certification in Support of Approval and Payment of Attorney Fees for Loss Mitigation
- Order Approving Attorney Fees for Loss Mitigation and Authorizing Payment—chapter 7 or 11
- Order Approving Attorney Fees for Loss Mitigation and Authorizing Payment—chapter 12 or 13
- Adjournment Request/Withdrawal/Settlement Notification of Loss Mitigation Status Conferences; Related Motions for Relief from Stay and/or Confirmation Hearings (Albany & Syracuse Divisions)
- Adjournment Request/Withdrawal/Settlement Notification of Loss Mitigation Status Conferences; Related Motions for Relief from Stay, Confirmation Hearings, and/or Motions to Dismiss (Utica Division)
- Addendum to Confirmation Order When Loss Mitigation is Pending

CM/ECF Filing Instructions for each prescribed form are available on the court's website. Please visit the link entitled "Loss Mitigation Filing Event Codes in CM/ECF."

[Dated: March 14, 2016.]

1 Text appearing in Blue denotes a Loss Mitigation Program Form. The Loss Mitigation Program Forms, which are listed in section XII, are required under these Loss Mitigation Program Procedures and are available on the court's website at www.nynb. uscourts.gov.

2 The Loss Mitigation Program Procedures were adopted by Administrative Order #13–05 and modified by Administrative Order #16–01.

3 The parties are reminded to comply with L.B.R. 9011–3(g).

4 *See supra* note 3.

ADMINISTRATIVE ORDER 16–02. DEBTOR'S ATTORNEY FEE IN CHAPTER 13 CASES FILED IN THE UTICA DIVISION

WHEREAS, a need exists to be certain that every Chapter 13 debtor understands (1) his or her rights and responsibilities to the Court, to the Chapter 13 trustee, and to the creditors of his or her bankruptcy estate, (2) the importance of honest and continuous communication with his or her attorney to make the Chapter 13 case successful, (3) the attorney fee and costs being charged for Chapter 13 representation, and (4) the services to be provided in connection with the attorney fee and costs; and

WHEREAS, a need exists to be certain that every Chapter 13 debtor's attorney understands what legal services he or she is expected to provide when a Chapter 13 case is filed in the Utica Division of the United States Bankruptcy Court for the Northern District of New York; and

WHEREAS, the purpose of this Administrative Order is to set forth the procedures that will generally be followed by this Court with respect to the attorney fee and costs that will be routinely allowed without a fee application and supporting time records for an attorney representing a Chapter 13 debtor in a case filed in the Utica Division.

NOW, after due deliberation, it is hereby,

ORDERED, as follows:

A Chapter 13 debtor's attorney shall set forth the amount of the attorney fee to be charged for services rendered to the debtor both in the Rule 2016(b) Statement required by Federal Rule of Bankruptcy Procedure 2016(b) (the "Rule 2016(b) Statement") and in the Chapter 13 plan filed with the Court. The attorney fee requested, when it falls within the range permitted by this Administrative Order, shall constitute the Flat Fee for all services rendered and to be rendered in connection with the case in accordance with this Court's *Rights and Responsibilities of Chapter 13 Debtors and Their Attorneys,* unless otherwise specified in the Rule 2016(b) Statement. Pursuant to Administrative Order 09–08 titled "Rights and Responsibilities of Chapter 13 Debtors and Their Attorneys for the Albany and Utica Divisions," entered on October 8, 2009, the attorney shall also file a copy of the executed *Rights and Responsibilities of Chapter 13 Debtors and Their Attorneys* in each case. Except as otherwise ordered by the Court, after a confirmation hearing held on notice to all parties in interest, the Flat Fee, whether paid through the Chapter 13 plan or directly by the debtor, shall neither be more than $4,325.00, nor more than 50% of the amount to be funded through the Chapter 13 plan.

The *Rights and Responsibilities of Chapter 13 Debtors and Their Attorneys* form shall apply regardless of whether the debtor and the debtor's attorney select the Flat Fee option or an hourly fee option in a given case. In a case where the attorney elects to represent the debtor on an hourly fee basis, the attorney shall request approval by filing and serving an appropriate application for compensation pursuant to 11 U.S.C. §§ 330 and/or 331. Such an application must be accompanied by a narrative of services rendered, accurate and contemporaneous time records, and a summary of any attorney fee previously paid to the attorney of record to date in the case.

The Flat Fee established by this Administrative Order shall be deemed allowed without application or further order of the Court, to be paid as an 11 U.S.C. § 503(b)(2) administrative expense under the terms of a confirmed plan.

Establishment of the Flat Fee does not inalterably determine the reasonableness of the attorney fee requested. Nothing herein is meant to limit the right of the Court, debtor, Chapter 13 Trustee, or any other party in interest to object to the reasonableness of the Flat Fee in a particular case. In such cases, the burden to support the challenged fee request still remains on the Chapter 13 debtor's attorney.

To obtain a partial Flat Fee award in an amount not to exceed $2,500.00 from the funds held by the Chapter 13 Trustee that are otherwise subject to return to the debtor pursuant to 11 U.S.C. § 1326(a)(2) because the case has been dismissed or converted prior to confirmation, the attorney must file an application on 21-day notice and serve the debtor, the Chapter 13 trustee, and any other party otherwise entitled to a share of those funds pursuant to an order of the Court. Such application must be heard and adjudicated prior to the dismissal or conversion of the case to avoid jurisdictional limitations.

The Flat Fee includes ordinary and reasonable costs incurred in connection with notice and service of routine matters for which representation is required during the case. The Flat Fee does not include costs for the statutory filing fee or any fee charged by a third-party provider for credit counseling and the education course required by the Bankruptcy Abuse Prevention and Consumer Protection Act of 2005.

This Administrative Order shall be effective with respect to all Chapter 13 cases filed in the Utica Division on or after April 1, 2016.

This Administrative Order supersedes Administrative Order 09-07 and Administrative Order 13-02.

[Dated: March 24, 2016.]

ADMINISTRATIVE ORDER 16-03. DEBTOR'S ATTORNEY FEE IN CHAPTER 13 CASES FILED IN THE ALBANY DIVISION

WHEREAS, a need exits to be certain that debtors understand (1) their rights and responsibilities to the court, to the Chapter 13 trustee, and to creditors of their estates, (2) the importance of honest and continual communication with their attorneys to make their cases successful, and (3) the attorney fees being charged for their cases by their attorneys; and

WHEREAS, a need exists to be certain that debtors' attorneys understand what legal services they are expected to provide when a Chapter 13 case is filed in the Albany Division of the United States Bankruptcy Court for the Northern District of New York.

NOW, therefore, it is hereby

ORDERED, as follows:

Chapter 13 debtors' attorneys shall set forth the amount of the legal fee to be charged for services rendered to the debtor in both the statement required by Federal Rule of Bankruptcy Procedure 2016(b) (the "2016(b) Statement") and the Chapter 13 plan filed with the court. The attorney fee requested shall constitute a flat fee for all services rendered and to be rendered in connection with the case in accordance with this court's *Rights and Responsibilities of Chapter 13 Debtors and Their Attorneys* (a copy is attached hereto) (the "Flat Fee"), unless otherwise specified in the 2016(b) Statement. Chapter 13 debtors' attorneys shall file the executed *Rights and Responsibilities of Chapter 13 Debtors and Their Attorneys* in each case.

Except as otherwise ordered by the court, after a hearing held on notice to all parties in interest, the Flat Fee, whether paid through the Chapter 13 plan or directly by the debtor, shall not he more than **$4,325**, nor more than 50% of the amount to be funded through the Chapter 13 plan. Commencing April 1, 2019, and at each 3-year interval ending on April 1 thereafter, the Flat Fee shall be reviewed and adjusted, if appropriate.

If the 2016(b) Statement provides that the attorney is representing the debtor on an hourly fee basis rather than the Flat Fee option, no fee shall be awarded absent entry of a separate order. In those instances, the debtor's attorney shall request approval by filing and serving an appropriate Application for Compensation pursuant to 11 U.S.C. §§ 330 and/or 331. Such an application shall be accompanied by a narrative of services rendered and contemporaneous time records. The *Rights and Responsibilities of Chapter 13 Debtors and Their Attorneys* shall apply regardless of whether the debtor and debtor's attorney select the Flat Fee or an hourly fee option is a case.

Nothing contained herein is meant to limit the rights of the Chapter 13 trustee or an interested party to object to the reasonableness of the fees or method of payment sought by debtor's attorney.

This Administrative Order shall be effective with respect to all Chapter 13 cases filed with the Albany Division on or after April 1, 2016.

This Administrative Order supersedes Administrative Order 13–03.

[Dated: March 29, 2016.]

United States Bankruptcy Court
for the Northern District of New York
Albany and Utica Division

RIGHTS AND RESPONSIBILITIES OF CHAPTER 13 DEBTORS AND THEIR ATTORNEYS

It is important for Chapter 13 debtors to understand their rights and responsibilities. It is also important that the debtors know that communicating with their attorney(s) is essential to successfully completing their plan. Debtors should also know that they may expect certain services to be performed by their attorney.

In order to assure that debtors and their attorney understand their rights and responsibilities in the bankruptcy process, the following guidelines approved by the Court are hereby agreed to by the debtors and their attorneys **unless the Court orders otherwise:**

(Nothing in this Agreement shall be construed to excuse an attorney for any ethical duties or responsibilities under FRBP 9011 or applicable non-bankruptcy law.)

BEFORE THE CASE IS FILED

The debtor agrees to:

1. Provide the attorney with accurate financial information and timely provide all requested documentation.

2. Discuss with the attorney the debtor's objectives in filing the case.

The attorney agrees to:

1. Meet with the debtor to review the debtor's debts, assets, liabilities, income, and expenses.

2. Counsel the debtor regarding the advisability of filing either a Chapter 7 or Chapter 13 case, outlining the procedures with the debtor, and answering the debtor's questions.

3. Explain what payments will be made directly by the debtor and what payments will be made through the debtor's Chapter 13 plan, with particular attention to mortgage and vehicle loan payments, as well as any other claims which accrue interest.

4. Explain to the debtor how, when, and where to make the Chapter 13 plan payments.

5. Explain to the debtor how the attorney's fees are paid and provide an executed copy of this document to the debtor.

6. Explain to the debtor that the first plan payment must be made to the Trustee within 30 days of the date the plan is filed.

7. Advise the debtor of the requirement to attend the 341 Meeting of Creditors, and instruct the debtor as to the date, time, and place of the meeting.

8. Advise the debtor of the necessity of maintaining liability and hazard insurance on all real property as well as liability, collision and comprehensive insurance on vehicles securing loans or leases.

9. Timely prepare and file the debtor's petition, plan, statements, and schedules.

AFTER THE CASE IS FILED

The debtor agrees to:

1. Keep the Trustee and attorney informed of the debtor's address and telephone number.

2. Inform the attorney of any wage garnishments or attachments of assets which occur or continue after the filing of the case.

3. Contact the attorney promptly if the debtor loses his/her job or has other financial problems.

4. Let the attorney know if the debtor is sued during the case.

5. Inform the attorney if any tax refunds the debtor is entitled to are seized or not returned to the debtor by the IRS or Franchise Tax Board.

6. Contact the attorney before buying, selling or refinancing any property and before entering into any loan agreements to find out what approvals are required.

The attorney agrees to:

1. Appear at the 341 Meeting of Creditors with the debtor.

2. Respond to objections to plan confirmation, and where necessary, prepare an amended plan

3. Prepare, file, and serve necessary modifications to the plan which may include suspending, lowering, or increasing plan payments.

4. Prepare, file, and serve necessary amended statements and schedules, in accordance with information provided by the debtor.

5. Prepare, file, and serve such motions as are needed during the case including, but not limited to, motions to avoid liens, sell property, approve settlements, approve new debt, etc.

6. Timely review all proofs of claim.

7. Timely object to improper or invalid proofs of claims based upon information and documentation provided by the debtor if such objection is necessary and beneficial to the debtor or to the estate.

8. Represent the debtor in connection motions for relief from stay and for dismissal or conversion of the case.

9. Where appropriate, prepare, file, and serve necessary motions to partially or wholly avoid liens on real or personal property pursuant to sections 506 or 522.

10. Communicate with the debtor by telephone or by being available for office appointments to discuss pending issues or matters of concern.

11. Provide such other legal services as are necessary for the proper administration of the present case before the Bankruptcy Court.

Approval for legal fees in the total sum of $ ＿＿＿ will be requested by the attorney. The attorney has received $ ＿＿＿ prepetition (the initial retainer) and requests payment of the balance of $ ＿＿＿ through the Chapter 13 plan.

Legal fees to be paid to the attorney shall be a "flat fee" for all services to be rendered in this case. Additional fees may be awarded and paid to the attorney if an extraordinary level of service is provided. If such occurs, the attorney shall apply to the Court for any additional fees and all such fees shall be paid through the plan unless otherwise ordered. The attorney may not receive fees directly from the debtor other than the initial retainer.

If the debtor disputes the legal services provided or charged by the attorney, the debtor must advise the Court or the Chapter 13 Trustee in writing and the matter set for hearing.

The attorney may move to withdraw pursuant to Local Bankruptcy Rule 2091–1, or the client may discharge the attorney at any time.

Dated: ＿＿＿＿＿＿＿＿＿＿＿＿＿＿
                                     Debtor

Dated: ＿＿＿＿＿＿＿＿＿＿＿＿＿＿
                                     Debtor

Dated: ＿＿＿＿＿＿＿＿＿＿＿＿＿＿
                                     Attorney for Debtor(s)

ELECTRONIC CASE FILING
ADMINISTRATIVE PROCEDURES FOR FILING, SIGNING AND VERIFYING PLEADINGS AND PAPERS BY ELECTRONIC MEANS

Revised January 1, 2012

I. REGISTRATION FOR THE ELECTRONIC FILING SYSTEM

A. Designation of Cases.

1. All documents submitted for filing in this district, shall be filed electronically using the Electronic Case Filing System (hereafter *System*) or shall be scanned and uploaded to the *System*.

2. Parties proceeding pro se shall not be required to file electronically. All filing requirements as provided in the *Fed. R. Bankr. P.* and the *Local Bankruptcy Rules* will apply.

B. Mandatory Electronic Case Filings. Petitions, pleadings, motions and all other documents filed in all cases after July 1, 2004 must be filed electronically pursuant to Administrative Order No. 03–01.*

C. Logins and Passwords. Each attorney admitted to practice in the Northern District of New York, an out of district attorney in good standing in his/her district, legal staff filing on behalf of an attorney or trustee or a creditor participant in any case or proceeding shall be eligible for a *System* login and password from the Bankruptcy Court. The login and password permit the attorney or party to participate in the electronic retrieval and filing of pleadings and other papers in accordance with the *System*. Registration for a login and password is governed by Section I.D. below and *Local Bankruptcy Rule* 5005–3. The Bankruptcy Court reserves the right to deny a request for a *System* login and password. Pro se debtors are not eligible for a *System* login and password.

D. Registration and Access to the System.

1. Each attorney admitted to practice in the Northern District of New York or a participant desiring to file pleadings or other papers electronically must:

- Complete and sign a Case Management/Electronic Case Files (CM/ECF) System Attorney Registration Form (attached as Form A to this procedure) and

- Complete the court's on-line test (CM/ECF Certification Exam) with a passing score of at least 80.

- **Note**: Registered Electronic Case Filing participants of the United States District Court for the Northern District of New York can also receive a login and password to the Bankruptcy Court ECF System by completing a Case Management/Electronic Case Files (CM/ECF) System Attorney Registration Form (attached to this procedure as Form A) **and** completing the court's on-line test with a passing score of at least 80. CM/ECF training classes will be held periodically throughout the year for interested attorneys and staff members.

2. An Out of District attorney desiring to file pleadings or other papers electronically must:

- Complete and sign a Case Management/Electronic Case Files (CM/ECF) System Attorney Registration Form (attached to this procedure as Form A);

- Be a registered Electronic Case Filing participant in a United States Bankruptcy Court in another state or district; and

- Complete the court's on-line test (CM/ECF Certification Exam) with a passing score of at least 80.

3. An attorney or trustee may request multiple logins and passwords for legal staff who file as agents on their behalf. When an agent files on behalf of the attorney, the docket text displays the name of the attorney as the filer. A filing agent may obtain a login and password by submitting a completed Case Management/Electronic Case Files (CM/ECF) System Electronic Filing Agent Registration Form (attached to this procedure as Form B).

4. A Creditor Participant is permitted to electronically file proofs of claim, reaffirmation agreements, notices of appearance and other documents. A creditor participant desiring to file electronically must:

- Complete, sign and submit a Case Management/Electronic Case files (CM/ECF) System Limited Filing Privileges Registration Form (attached as Form C to this procedure) and

- Correctly file test documents in the CM/ECF test database prior to receiving a login and password.

The above mentioned forms are available on the Court's web site at: www.nynb.uscourts.gov.

5.   All signed original Attorney Registration Forms and Limited Filing Privileges Registration Forms shall be mailed or delivered to:

> **Director of I.T.**
> **United States Bankruptcy Court**
> **James T. Foley U.S. Court House**
> **445 Broadway, Suite 330**
> **Albany, NY 12207**

6.   To ensure that the Clerk's Office has correctly entered a registering attorney's or participant's Internet e-mail address in the *System*, the Clerk's Office will send the attorney or participant an Internet e-mail message which will contain either the date and time of his/her training session at the Clerk's Office or instructions on completing the certification requirements remotely. The attorney or participant may indicate on his/her registration form the name(s) of his/her support staff that he/she would like included in the same training. The login and password will only be given to the registering attorney or participant.

7.   A registered participant should change the court assigned password. This change can be made by logging into the *System* and accessing the menu option "Maintain Your ECF Account" under Utilities. In the event a filer believes that the security of an existing password has been compromised and in order to prevent unauthorized access to the *System* by use of that password, the registered participant shall immediately change his/her password in the *System* and thereafter provide notice to the Albany NDNY Help Desk (518–257–1616) and confirm by facsimile to the I.T. Director. If a registered participant forgets his/her password, the I.T. Director will assign a new password.

8.   If any of the information on the Registration Form changes, e.g., mailing address, e-mailing address, etc., the registered participant must submit the appropriate amended form addressed to the I.T. Director as indicated in section I.D.5. above.

E.   Withdrawal From the System.   A registered attorney or participant may withdraw from using the *System* by providing the Clerk's Office with notice of withdrawal. Such notice must be in writing, and mailed or delivered to the Clerk of Court. Upon receipt, the Clerk's Office will immediately cancel the password and will delete the attorney or participant's name from any applicable electronic service list.

The mailing address is:

Clerk of Court
United States Bankruptcy Court
James T. Foley U.S. Court House
445 Broadway, Suite 330
Albany, NY 12207

II.   ELECTRONIC FILING, SERVICE OF DOCUMENTS, AND TIMELINESS

A.   Filing.

1.   *Administrative Procedures and Local Rules.*   The Administrative Procedures for Electronic Case Filing and the Administrative Order for Electronic Case Filing are to be read in conjunction with the *Local Bankruptcy Rules* for the Northern District of New York. In the event of a conflict between the Northern District of New York *Local Bankruptcy Rules* and the Administrative Procedures, the Administrative Procedures, as it relates to the electronic filing of petitions, pleadings, and other papers, shall govern.

2.   *Portable Document Format.*   Registered filers shall submit electronically all petitions, motions, pleadings, briefs, memoranda of law, proofs of claim, orders or other documents required to be filed with the court in connection with a case or proceeding, except as provided by this procedure or the *Local Bankruptcy Rules*, in Portable Document Format (PDF) or PDF/A.

NOTE: The newer PDF/A standard addresses concerns raised about the security and long term archival storage of documents. Standard word processing software is now capable of producing PDF/A documents. Although no target date has been set, in the future the court will require users to file documents in PDF/A format. Users of the NDNY *System* will be notified when the PDF/A format becomes mandatory.

3. *Creditor Matrix.* The creditor matrix is to be prepared with bankruptcy software or with word processing software and uploaded to the system as a Text (TXT) file. In addition a separate creditor mailing matrix is also to be prepared (in PDF format) and filed along with the Certification of Mailing Matrix in conformity with Local Bankruptcy Rule 1007-2 (c). Creditors are to be listed in a single column format (left, center or right justified) with a one inch left margin. Creditors are to be single spaced (each on no more than 5 lines with no more than 40 characters per line) with a double space separating one creditor from the next. Account information must be placed on line 2 or 3 only. The city, state and zip code must all be on the last line.

Examples of the proper format for the matrix are as follows:

```
MBNA
Attn: Payment Center
Acct.No. XXX—XXX—1234
P.O. Box 15019
Wilmington, DE 19886-5019

Wells Fargo Financial
Acct. No. XXX-XX-5678
Attn: The Collection Center
5 Gateway Drive, Suite 5000
Columbia, MD 21046
```

4. *Applications for Compensation.* Applications for compensation are to be filed electronically. A paper copy marked **ECF Case—Chambers Copy** is to be provided to the court. In addition, the U.S. Trustee is also to be provided with a paper copy of the application. The Chambers copy and the U.S. Trustee copy are to include all the items listed in subsections (b)(1) through (b)(9) of Local Bankruptcy Rule 2016-1.

5. *Chambers Copies.* A "Chambers Copy" in paper format for Chambers is required for the matters listed below. The copy must be clearly marked as **"ECF CASE—CHAMBERS COPY"** and must be submitted in compliance with the requirements of *Local Bankruptcy Rule 9013-1* and should be submitted immediately after papers are filed electronically. The "Chambers Copy" need not contain an original signature. Unless directed by the court, copies should not be faxed to Chambers or Courtroom Services. Copies should be sent via the mail or hand delivered. *Attorneys who fail to provide Chambers Copy will be billed by the Clerk's Office for copying services.*

Note: The "Chambers Copy" is to be submitted to the actual physical location of the judge assigned to the case. Chambers copies for Judge Davis are to be submitted to Utica; chambers copies for Judge Littlefield are to be submitted to Albany; chambers copies for Judge Cangilos-Ruiz are to be submitted to Syracuse.

Albany Chambers

A. Notice of motion, motion, application, and certificate of service, except for chapter 13 trustee's motion to dismiss and to determine/expunge claim and chapter 7 trustee's final meeting notice;

B. Opposition, response, or any pleading relating to a hearing;

C. Opposition to disclosure statement in a chapter 11 case;

D. Objection to confirmation of a chapter 11 plan;

E. Pretrial statement; and

F. Memoranda of law and any pleading and other document filed in regard to a submitted matter.

Syracuse Chambers

A. Notice of motion, motion, application and certificate of service;

B. Chapter 7 final meeting notice;

C. Any pleading filed in an adversary proceeding;

D. Pretrial statement;

    E. Memoranda of law and any pleading or other document filed in regard to a submitted matter;

    F. Any document regarding an appeal;

    G. Withdrawal of reference; and

    H. Any objection pursuant to *Fed. R. Bankr. P. 9033.*

Utica Chambers

    A. Notice of motion, motion, application and certificate of service;

    B. Chapter 7 final meeting notice;

    C. Any pleading filed in an adversary proceeding;

    D. Pretrial statement;

    E. Memoranda of law and any pleading or other document filed in regard to a submitted matter;

    F. Any document regarding an appeal;

    G. Withdrawal of reference; and

    H. Any objection pursuant to *Fed. R. Bankr. P. 9033.*

6. *Summons.* It is not necessary to submit a paper summons to the Clerk's Office to have it signed, sealed and issued for service on the defendant(s). The *System* will electronically generate the initial summons in an adversary proceeding. The electronic summons will contain the Clerk's signature and court seal. Multiple copies can be printed for service upon the defendant(s). Proof of service will still be required.

7. *Paper Documents.* The Clerk's Office will not maintain a paper court file in any case except as otherwise provided by this procedure. The official court record shall be an electronic file maintained on the court's file server. Any documents received in paper format in Chambers or the Clerk's Office may be shredded when it is determined that they are no longer needed.

8. *Adjournment Requests.* Adjournment letters and status conference requests are to be filed electronically. They shall also be faxed to Chambers in Albany.

9. *Expedited Matters.* In expedited matters, the movant shall contact Chambers staff by phone as soon as possible before filing the item needing expedited treatment.

B. Service.

1. Whenever a pleading or other paper is filed electronically, in accordance with these procedures and the *Local Bankruptcy Rules*, the *System* shall generate a "Notice of Electronic Filing," (attached to this procedure as Form H), to the filing party and any other party who has requested electronic notice in that case.

    a. If the recipient is a registered participant in the *System*, the Clerk's e-mailing of the "Notice of Electronic Filing" shall be the equivalent of service of the pleading or other paper by first class mail, postage prepaid.

    b. Service of the "Notice of Electronic Filing" on a party who is not a registered participant in the System may be accomplished by e-mail, subject to the additional service requirements of paragraph II.B.3. below.

    c. There is no opt out option to electronic service via the "Notice of Electronic filing".

2. A certificate of service on all parties entitled to service or notice is still required when a party files a document electronically. The certificate must state the manner in which service or notice was accomplished on each party so entitled. Sample language for a Certificate of Service is attached to these procedures as Form D.

3. A party who is not a registered participant of the *System* is entitled to a paper copy of any electronically filed pleading or paper. The filing party must therefore provide the non-registered party with the pleading or paper according to the *Fed. R. Bankr. P.* and *Local Bankruptcy Rules.*

C. Section 341(a) Meeting of Creditors. The attorney for the debtor or the pro se debtor shall bring to the section 341(a) meeting of creditors the electronically filed petition, schedule, lists and statement of affairs bearing the original signatures.

D. Timeliness.

1. Filing of documents electronically does not alter the filing deadline for that document.

2. Local Bankruptcy Rule 9013–1(f) requires that a pleading or other document electronically filed on the last day for filing must be filed by 4:00 PM Eastern Standard Time. Generally, electronic filings are considered timely if received by the court before midnight on the date set as a deadline, unless the judge or *Local Bankruptcy Rules* specifically require an earlier filing.

3. Any answering papers filed electronically on the last day for filing pursuant to Local Bankruptcy Rule 9013–1(g) must be filed by 4:00 PM Eastern Standard Time.

4. Any motions filed electronically on the last day for filing pursuant to Local Bankruptcy Rule 9013–1(e) must be filed by 4:00 PM Eastern Standard Time.

5. Due to variations in time zones, timeliness is established based on the Eastern time zone where the Northern District of New York is located.

6. A filer whose document is made untimely as the result of a technical failure of the court's CM/ECF site, as prescribed in Section X. of this procedure, may seek appropriate relief from the court.

III. SIGNATURES

A. Petitions, lists, schedules and statements, amendments, pleadings, affidavits, and other documents which must contain original signatures or which require verification under *Fed. R. Bankr.P.* 1008 or an unsworn declaration as provided in 28 U.S.C. § 1746, may be filed electronically by attorneys registered in the *System.*

B. Attorneys who are not registered with the Bankruptcy Court for the Northern District of New York and who do not have a login and password provided by the Court are not permitted to electronically file documents using the login and password of another registered attorney. The attorney login and name shown on a filed document must match.

C. A pleading or other document electronically filed shall indicate a signature in the format, "/s/ name," unless the document has been scanned and shows the original signature.

D. A copy containing an original signature must be retained by the filer for a minimum of two (2) years after the closing of the case and all time periods for appeals have expired unless the court orders a different period. In adversary proceedings, the parties shall maintain the original documents for a minimum of two (2) years after the proceeding ends and all time periods for appeals have expired unless the court orders a different period. These retention periods do not affect or replace any other periods required by other applicable laws or rules. Upon request of the court, the filer must provide original documents for review. Compliance with *Fed. R. Bankr. P.* 9011 is required.

E. The following procedure applies when a stipulation, which does not require an order, or another document requires two or more signatures:

1. The filer shall obtain the physical signature of all parties required to sign the document. For purposes of this procedure a facsimile signature is permitted.

2. Depending on the preference within each division of the district, the filer shall either (i) scan the document reflecting the actual script signatures and upload the same, or (ii) indicate each signature using the format "/s/name."

3. The filing party originating the document shall maintain the original signed document as provided for in Section III. D. above.

IV. FEES

A. Fee Payment Through pay.gov. Filing fees are to be paid through the on-line payment program (Pay.gov) in CM/ECF. The court will not manually charge an attorney's credit card for filing fees incurred through CM/ECF.

B. Accepted Credit Cards. Only VISA, MASTERCARD, AMERICAN EXPRESS, DISCOVER, and DINER'S CLUB credit cards are accepted.

C. Fees due same day Incurred. Filing fees are to be paid through the on-line payment program (Pay.gov) on the same day they are incurred. Failure to pay filing fees will result in your

ECF account being automatically locked. Participants will be unable to file on-line until fees are paid in full. PACER access to view dockets will be unaffected.

D. Fee Schedule. Except as otherwise provide, all registered participants in the System shall be subject to the fees set forth in the Fee Schedule for Electronic Public Access (EPA Fee schedule), adopted by the Judicial Conference of the United States.

E. Viewing Document Through PACER. Attorneys of record and parties in a case receive one free electronic viewing of all filed documents through PACER from which he or she can save or print the document. Additional PACER access to the pleading is subject to PACER fees.

F. Filing Fee Refunds. Filing fees will not be refunded unless so ordered by the court. Requests for refunds are to be made by motion or application and order.

V. ATTACHMENTS

A. Registered participants must submit all documents referenced as attachments including but not limited to leases, notes and the like in Portable Document Format (PDF) unless the court permits conventional paper filing. Attachments may be summarized (using attached Form E) and only the relevant excerpts electronically filed.

B. The size of the electronic file shall be no larger than 2 megabytes. Attachments larger than 2 megabytes must be split into separate PDF files and the multiple PDF files attached to the pleading.

C. If an attachment is not available in electronic form, it is preferred that such documents, or the relevant portions thereof, be electronically imaged, i.e., scanned, and filed using the Portable Document Format (PDF). Excerpted material must be clear and prominently identified as such. The file size limits as stated in section V.B. above are required.

D. The filing party of electronic excerpts of documents as attachments do so without prejudice to their right to timely file additional excerpts or complete attachments.

E. The filing party must promptly provide excerpted documents in full if the court or a responding party makes such a request.

VI. SEALED DOCUMENTS

A. A motion to file a document under seal may be filed electronically unless prohibited by law.

B. Documents ordered to be placed under seal must be filed conventionally in paper format and **NOT** electronically, unless specifically authorized by the court.

C. The filing party must submit to the clerk a paper copy of the signed order attached to the documents to be sealed by the clerk.

VII. ORDERS

- All proposed orders, must be submitted electronically using the E–Orders feature of CM/ECF and shall only be submitted *after the return date of the hearing or trial*, unless otherwise ordered by the court. Registered users will be notified when and how to file certain orders and applications electronically if not already allowed.

- A copy of a proposed order can be included as an attachment to an electronically filed pleading if the proposed order is clearly marked as an "EXHIBIT" only. This copy will not be considered by the court and will not be signed by the court.

- Any order filed electronically by the court without the original signature of a judge has the same force and effect as if the judge had affixed his/her signature to a paper copy of the order and it had been entered on the docket in paper format.

- Any ministerial order filed electronically by the Clerk without the original signature of the Clerk has the same force and effect as if the Clerk had affixed his/her signature to a paper copy of the order and it had been entered on the docket in paper format.

A. Ex Parte Orders.

Application. A request for ex parte relief shall be made by affidavit or motion containing a clear and specific showing of cause for both *ex parte* action as well as the relief requested and whether previous application for similar relief has been made.

Submission. The underlying affidavit or motion shall be filed electronically and the proposed ex parte order shall be uploaded immediately following the filing of the underlying application via the E–Orders menu. The application shall not be uploaded as one PDF document via E–Orders. If the relief requested would be defeated by prior notice, the application may be filed in paper format pursuant to paragraph (D) of this procedure.

B. Order Shortening Time.

Application. A request for an order shortening any specified notice period shall be made by application for an expedited hearing on the motion pursuant to Fed. R. Bankr. P. 9006(d). Such application shall contain a clear and specific showing by affidavit of good and sufficient reasons for shortening the notice period and whether previous application for similar relief has been made. Law office failure to act does not provide good and sufficient cause.

Submission. The underlying motion shall be filed electronically, and then the application for an expedited hearing shall be filed electronically and linked to the underlying motion. A proposed order shortening time shall be emailed to Chambers in either Word or WordPerfect format and not filed on the docket. The proposed order shortening time should specify the proposed manner of service and provide for the motion hearing date and time. Chambers must be notified before filing an application for an order shortening time.

C. Order to Show Cause.

Application. No order to show cause to bring on a motion will be entered except upon a clear and specific showing by affidavit of good and sufficient reasons why proceeding other than by notice of motion is necessary. Law office failure to act does not provide good and sufficient cause. The papers shall also state whether a previous application for similar relief has been made.

Submission. The underlying affidavit shall be filed electronically. A proposed order shortening time shall be emailed to Chambers in either Word or WordPerfect format and not filed on the docket. Chambers must be notified before filing an affidavit in support of an order to show cause.

D. Prior Notice of Temporary Restraining Order.
Unless the purpose of an order to show cause would be defeated by prior notice, any party seeking an order to show cause which contains temporary restraining relief shall give an opposing party or, if known, counsel for an opposing party, at least 24 hours prior notice, if possible, of the presentation of the order to show cause and the underlying papers, including the date and time of the proposed presentment of said order to show cause to the court. Proof of notice of presentment shall be filed with the court.

E. Retention/Employment Orders.

Application. The application for employment shall be electronically filed with the court on twenty-one (21) days notice to the United States trustee. The application will be deemed ripe for the court's consideration upon the earlier of (1) the filing of a response by the United States trustee, or (2) the expiration of the twenty-one (21) day period. If an objection to the application or the proposed order approving the employment is filed, a hearing on the application will be set by the clerk. If no action is taken by the United States trustee within the twenty-one (21) day period, the court, in its discretion, may schedule a hearing on the application or enter an order approving the employment.

Submission. An order approving the application shall be submitted to the court upon the earlier of (1) the United States trustee's consent to the application, (2) the expiration of the twenty-one (21) day period, if no objection is filed, or (3) the conclusion of a hearing on the application. The order shall clearly state, inter alia, that no fees will be paid to the professional, including the use of any retainer received for post-petition services, without prior approval of the court.

NOTE: Employment of an Attorney Pursuant to § 327(e). If the chapter 7 trustee seeks to employ an attorney to pursue the estate's interest in a claim previously held by the debtor, approval of the retention shall be sought by motion on notice pursuant to *Local Bankruptcy Rule* 9013–3. In addition to service on the United States trustee, the motion shall be served upon the debtor and attorney for the debtor.

VIII. DOCKET ENTRIES

A. A filer who electronically submits a pleading or other document shall be responsible for designating a docket entry for the document by using one of the docket event categories prescribed by the court. This action constitutes an entry on the official court docket as provided in *Fed. R. Bankr. P.* 5003.

B. The clerk shall enter all orders and judgments in the *System*, which constitute docketing of the order and judgment for all purposes. The clerk's notation in the appropriate docket of an order or judgment shall constitute the entry of the order or judgment as provided in *Fed. R. Bankr. P.* 5003.

IX. CORRECTING DOCUMENTS FILED IN ERROR

A. Once a document is submitted and becomes part of the case docket, corrections to the docket are made only by the Clerk's Office.

B. A document incorrectly filed in a case may be the result of posting the wrong PDF file to a docket entry, or selecting the wrong document type from the menu, or entering the wrong case number and not catching the error before the transaction is completed. **Do not attempt to re-file the document if an error in filing is discovered.**

C. As soon as possible after an error is discovered, the filer shall contact the Help Desk in the Clerk's Office which has jurisdiction over the case or proceeding. Be sure to have the case number and document number for which the correction is being requested. If appropriate, the clerk will make an entry indicating that the document was filed in error. You will be advised if you need to re-file the document. The *System* will not permit you to make changes to the document(s) or docket entry filed in error once the transaction has been accepted.

X. TECHNICAL FAILURES

A. The Clerk's Office shall deem this district's CM/ECF site to be subject to technical failure on any given day if the site is unable to accept filings continuously or intermittently over the course of any period of time greater than one hour after 12:00 PM (Noon) that day. Known systems outages will be posted on our web site, if possible.

B. Problems on the filer's end, such as with phone lines, filer's Internet Service Provider (ISP), or hardware or software, will not constitute a technical failure under these procedures nor excuse an untimely filing. A filer who cannot file a document electronically because of a problem on the filer's end must file the document conventionally.

XI. SECURITY OF THE SYSTEM

Each electronically filed paper shall be assigned a special identification number which can be traced, if necessary, to detect post filing alterations to a document.

XII. PRIVACY

A. To address the privacy concerns created by Internet access to court documents, filers may modify or partially redact certain personal data identifiers appearing in pleadings or other papers. This data and the suggested modifications are as follows:

1. *Minor's Name*: Use the minor's initials;

2. *Financial Account Numbers*: Identify the name or type of account and the financial institution where maintained, but use only the last four numbers of the account number;

3. *Social Security Numbers*: Documents filed with the court should only contain the last four digits of the Social Security number. Attorneys are required to obtain the debtor's full social security number and maintain the originally signed "Form 21, Statement of Social Security Number" in their files;

4. *Dates of Birth*: Use only the year; and

5. Other data as permitted by order of the court.

B. Information posted on the *System* must not be downloaded for uses inconsistent with the privacy rights of any person.

XIII. PUBLIC ACCESS TO THE SYSTEM DOCKET

A. Electronic access to the electronic docket and documents filed in the *System* is available for viewing to the public at no charge at each Clerk's Office public counter during regular business hours. A fee for a paper copy of an electronic document is required in accordance with 28 U.S.C. § 1930.

B. Although any person can retrieve and view the documents in the *System* and access information from it without charge access to the *System*, for viewing purposes is otherwise limited to subscribers to the Public Access to Court Electronic Records ("PACER") *System* and, in accordance with the ruling of the Judicial Conference of the United States, a user fee will be charged for accessing detailed case information, such as reviewing filed documents and docket sheets, but excluding review of calendars and similar general information.

C. Conventional copies and certified copies of the electronically filed documents may be purchased at the Clerk's Office. The fee for copying and certification will be in accordance with 28 U.S.C. § 1930.

* [**Publisher's Note:** So in original. *See* Administrative Order 11–02, *ante*.]

United States Bankruptcy Court
Northern District of New York

Case Management / Electronic Case Files (CM/ECF) System
Attorney Registration Form

(Form A)

This form is to be used by attorneys to register for filing privileges to electronically file documents using the CM/ECF System in the U.S. Bankruptcy Court for the Northern District of New York.

First/Middle/Last Name: _____

Bar ID No: _____

State of Admission: _____

Admitted to Practice in U.S. District Court NDNY   ☐ Yes
                                                      ☐ No

If No checked above, you must list what U.S. District you are admitted to practice:

_____

Firm Name: _____

Mailing Address: _____

_____

_____

Telephone Number: _____

Facsimile Number: _____

E-mail Address: _____

Other districts in which I am certified to file electronically using CM/ECF: _____

_____

_____

Send Electronic Notices to (check one)   ☐ Each Filing   ☐ End of Day Summary
Send Electronic Notices in the following format (check one)

☐   HTML for ISP mail service (i.e., AOL, Hotmail, Yahoo)
☐   Text for cc:mail, Groupwise, Outlook, Outlook Express
☐   Other (please list): _____

Who do you primarily represent   ☐ Debtors   ☐ Creditors   ☐ Both

I, the attorney filer, certify under penalty of perjury that I agree to adhere to all the rules and regulations in the NDNY Administrative Order for Filing, Signing, and Verifying Pleadings and Papers by Electronic Means currently in effect and any changes or additions that may be made to such Administrative Order and to the following:

1. I understand that use of my login and password constitutes my signature on an electronically filed document for all purposes, including those under Rule 9011 and 28 U.S.C. § 1746, and shall have the same force and effect as if I had affixed my signature on a paper document being filed. Signatures will be indicated by "/s/" and the typed name of the person signing in the following format: "/s/ Jane Smith" on the signature line.

2. Registration shall constitute a request and an agreement to receive service of pleadings and other papers electronically pursuant to Fed. Rules of Bankruptcy Procedure 9036, where service of pleadings and other papers electronically is otherwise permitted by first class mail, postage paid.

3. I shall protect and secure the login and password issued by the court, and I shall be solely responsible to the court regarding each record entered into the CM/ECF system using my login and password. The login and password will be used only by me. If there is any reason to suspect misuse of the password, it is my duty to change my password and immediately contact the court to report the suspected misuse.

4. I may notify the court to terminate my status at anytime. If I cease to be an employee or agent of the firm on whose behalf documents are being electronically filed with the court, or for any other reason cease to be authorized to file electronically, I will promptly notify the court.

5. I shall maintain the accuracy of my account (e.g., mailing address, telephone number, fax number, e-mail address).

6. I understand that electronically filed documents requiring original signatures from any person other than me, must be maintained by me in paper form, bearing the original signatures, for two years after closing of the case or proceeding in which the documents were filed. Upon the court's request, I must provide the original signed documents for review.

7. I agree to adhere to all rules and procedures of the U.S. Bankruptcy Court for the Northern District of New York concerning the use of CM/ECF.

8. This access is for use only in CM/ECF cases filed in the U.S. Bankruptcy Court for the Northern District of New York. It may be used to file and view electronic documents, docket sheets and reports. [Note: A PACER Account is necessary for this access. A PACER login and password may be obtained from the PACER Service Center. Registration for a PACER account is available online at http://pacer.psc.uscourts.gov. For assistance, call 1–800–676–6856.]

9. At any time without advance notice, the court may, sua sponte, terminate my account for any reason and future documents to be filed conventionally or in any other format specified by the court.

_____   _____

Date   Attorney Filers Signature

                                            _____

                                            Last Four Digits of Social Security
                                            Number

Return form to: U.S. Bankruptcy Court, NDNY
                     Attn: Director of IT
                     James T. Foley Courthouse
                     445 Broadway, Suite 330
                     Albany, N.Y. 12207

United States Bankruptcy Court
Northern District of New York

Case Management / Electronic Case Files (CM/ECF) System
Electronic Filing Agent Registration Form

(Form B)

A person desiring to register as a Filing Agent for filing documents through the Court's Case Management / Electronic Case Filing system on behalf of a Registered Filing User (an attorney or trustee registered with the Court as a CM/ECF user) must provide the information requested below.

This form must be signed by **_both_** the Filing Agent requesting a login and password and the Registered Filing User.

Filing Agent Name: _____

Attorney / Trustee Name: _____

Firm Name: _____

Mailing Address: _____

Telephone Number: _____ Facsimile Number: _____

E–Mail Address: _____

By signing and submitting this registration form, the Filing Agent agrees to abide by the following requirements:

1. The Filing Agent agrees to adhere to all orders, rules and procedures of the U.S. Bankruptcy Court for the Northern District of New York concerning the use of CM/ECF.

2. Pursuant to Rule 9011 and Local Bankruptcy Rule 5005–2, electronically filed documents shall be signed by an attorney of record and that signature shall be indicated by "/s/" and the typed name of the person signing in the following format: "/s/ Jane Smith" on the signature line. The unique user name and password issued to each Registered Filing User and to each Filing Agent identifies the user upon login and constitutes the signature of the Registered Filing User.

3. The Filing Agent must protect and secure the login and password issued by the Court. The login and password must be used exclusively by the Filing Agent on behalf of the Registered Filing User. The Filing Agent must not knowingly permit the login and password to be used by anyone who is not authorized. After the password has been issued by the Court, the Filling Agent is encouraged to change the password every 90 days. The Filing Agent must immediately notify the Court if misuse of a password is suspected.

4. The Registered Filing User must immediately notify the Court if a Filing Agent is no longer authorized to act as a Filing Agent.

5. The Filing Agent agrees to maintain the accuracy of his or her account (mailing address, telephone number, fax number, e-mail address) and to notify the Court whenever there is a change to the account information.

6. If the Filing Agent ceases to be an employee or agent of the firm on whose behalf documents are electronically filed, or for any other reason ceases to be authorized to file electronically, the Filing Agent will promptly notify the Court.

7. At any time without advance notice, the Court may revoke the login and password of a Filing Agent or a Registered Filing User.

_____   _____
Date   Filing Agent Applicant

I hereby acknowledge that the above applicant is authorized to act on my behalf as a Filing Agent for filing documents in the Court's Case Management/Electronic Case Filing system. I further acknowledge that any document filed by the above applicant as my Filing Agent is deemed to be signed and filed by me for purposes of Federal Rule of Bankruptcy Procedure 9011 and Local Bankruptcy Rule 5005.

_____

Date

_____

Registered Filing User

_____

Bar ID Number and State of Admission

Return form to: U.S. Bankruptcy Court, NDNY
                   Attn: Director of IT
                   James T. Foley Courthouse
                   445 Broadway, Suite 330
                   Albany, N.Y. 12207

_____

United States Bankruptcy Court
Northern District of New York

Case Management / Electronic Case Files (CM/ECF) System
Limited Filing Privileges Registration Form

(Form C)

This form is to be used by creditors to register for limited filing privileges to electronically file documents using the CM/ECF System in the U.S. Bankruptcy Court for the Northern District of New York. The limited filer may only perform specified transactions, as set forth in paragraph 7 of this form. NOTE: If you are an attorney, complete the attorney registration form.

First/Middle/Last Name: _____
Title: _____
Entity Name: _____
Mailing Address: _____
_____
_____

Telephone Number: _____
Facsimile Number: _____
E-mail Address: _____
Other districts in which I am certified to file electronically using CM/ECF: _____
_____
_____

Send Electronic Notices to (check one)   ☐ Each Filing   ☐ End of Day Summary
Send Electronic Notices in the following format (check one)
☐   HTML for ISP mail service (i.e., AOL, Hotmail, Yahoo)
☐   Text for cc:mail, Groupwise, Outlook, Outlook Express
☐   Other (please list): _____

I, the limited filer, certify under penalty of perjury that I am authorized by the above-named entity to submit this registration form, and I understand and agree to adhere to the following:

1. I understand that use of my login and password constitutes my signature on an electronically filed document for all purposes, including those under Rule 9011 and 28 U.S.C. § 1746, and shall have the same force and effect as if I had affixed my signature on a paper document being filed. Signatures will be indicated by "/s/" and the typed name of the person signing in the following format: "/s/ Jane Smith" on the signature line.

2. I shall protect and secure the login and password issued by the court, and I shall be solely responsible to the court regarding each record entered into the CM/ECF system using my login and password. The login and password will be used only by me. If there is any reason to suspect misuse

of the password, it is my duty to change my password and immediately contact the court to report the suspected misuse.

3. I may notify the court to terminate my status as a limited filer at anytime. If I cease to be an employee or agent of the entity on whose behalf documents are being electronically filed with the court, or for any other reason cease to be authorized to file electronically on behalf of the entity, I will promptly notify the court.

4. I shall maintain the accuracy of my account (e.g., mailing address, telephone number, fax number, e-mail address).

5. I understand that electronically filed documents requiring original signatures from any person other than me, must be maintained by me in paper form, bearing the original signatures, for two years after closing of the case or proceeding in which the documents were filed. Upon the court's request, I must provide the original signed documents for review.

6. I agree to adhere to all rules and procedures of the U.S. Bankruptcy Court for the Northern District of New York concerning the use of CM/ECF.

7. Limited filing privileges are narrow in scope. I will only use CM/ECF to electronically file the following:

> File a Claim, Transfer a claim, Withdraw a claim, Object to claim, Object to transfer of claim, File a Certification of Service, File a Creditor Request for Notices, File a Letter, File a Notice of Appearance and Request for Notice, File a Reaffirmation Agreement

The court reserves the right to modify these options or add additional options as deemed necessary.

8. I understand that using my limited filer account to monitor general activity in any case in which I have not filed a document is beyond the scope of my limited filing privileges. The limited filer account is intended for performing the specified transactions in Paragraph 7. In order to view and retrieve electronic docket sheets and documents available on CM/ECF, I will use PACER. [Note: A PACER login and password may be obtained from the PACER Service Center. Registration for a PACER account is available online at http://pacer.psc.uscourts.gov. For assistance, call 1–800–676–6856.]

9. If the court determines that limited filers may receive notices electronically, then I expressly consent to receive notice and service of pleadings and other papers by electronic means from the court and other filing users in all cases, except with regard to service of a summons and complaint under Bankruptcy Rule 7004, a motion initiating a contested matter under Bankruptcy Rule 9014, or a subpoena under Bankruptcy Rule 9016.

10. At any time without advance notice, the court may, sua sponte, terminate my account for any reason and require future documents to be filed conventionally or in any other format specified by the court.

Date   Limited Filer Signature

                                          Last Four Digits of Social Security Number

Return form to: U.S. Bankruptcy Court, NDNY
                      Attn: Director of IT
                      James T. Foley Courthouse
                      445 Broadway, Suite 330
                      Albany, N.Y. 12207

Form D

(SAMPLE FORMAT)

UNITED STATES BANKRUPTCY COURT
NORTHERN DISTRICT OF NEW YORK
_____

In Re:

                                      Case No.

                                      Chapter

                    Debtor(s).
_____

CERTIFICATE OF SERVICE

I hereby certify that on, _____ (Date), I electronically filed the foregoing with the Clerk of the Bankruptcy Court using the CM/ECF system which sent notification of such filing to the following:

And, I hereby certify that I have mailed by the United States Postal Service the document to the following non CM/ECF participants:

/s/ name

_____

Form E

(SAMPLE FORMAT)

UNITED STATES BANKRUPTCY COURT
FOR THE NORTHERN DISTRICT OF
NEW YORK
_____

In Re:

                                      Case No.

                                      Chapter

                    Debtor(s).
_____

SUMMARY OF ATTACHMENT(s) AND CERTIFICATE OF SERVICE

The following attachment(s) in reference to _____ are available upon request:

     1. ....
     2. ....
     3. ....

                                  Respectfully submitted

                                  /s/ name

                                  ATTORNEY FOR _____

Copy of the above served this

____ day of _____, ____ on:

[respondent parties if motion]
[debtor's (s') attorney and trustee if claim]

E–ORDER FORMAT (Unsigned)—Sample (Form F)

THIS AREA IS LEFT BLANK FOR THE SIGNATURE OF THE JUDGE.
ALLOW AT LEAST FOUR INCHES AT THE TOP FOR THE SIGNATURE.

UNITED STATES BANKRUPTCY COURT
NORTHERN DISTRICT OF NEW YORK

In re John Debtorman   )
)
            Debtor(s)   )   Case No. 06–10001
)
)
)   Chapter 7
)

ORDER VACATING FINAL DECREE

IT APPEARING that the Final Decree filed in the above-entitled case on May 31, 2005 was filed in error as there are still matters pending in the case, It is hereby ORDERED that said Final Decree is hereby vacated.

E–ORDER FORMAT (Signed)—Sample (Form G)

GRANTED. SO ORDERED
SIGNED this 2nd day of March, 2011.

                                    Robert E. Littlefield, Jr.
                                    Chief United States Bankruptcy Judge

UNITED STATES BANKRUPTCY COURT
NORTHERN DISTRICT OF NEW YORK

In re John Debtorman   )
)
            Debtor(s)   )   Case No. 06–10001
)
)
)   Chapter 7
)

ORDER VACATING FINAL DECREE

IT APPEARING that the Final Decree filed in the above-entitled case on May 31, 2005 was filed in error as there are still matters pending in the case, It is hereby ORDERED that said Final Decree is hereby vacated.

Sample Notice of Electronic Filing

499

Form H

NOTE TO PUBLIC ACCESS USERS Judicial Conference of the United States policy permits attorneys of record and parties in a case (including pro se litigants) to receive one free electronic copy of all documents filed electronically, if receipt is required by law or directed by the filer. PACER access fees apply to all other users. To avoid later charges, download a copy of each document during this first viewing. However, if the referenced document is a transcript, the free copy and 30–page limit do not apply.

U.S. Bankruptcy Court

Northern District of New York

Notice of Electronic Filing

The following transaction was received from Perry Mason entered on 12/20/2011 at 10:50 AM EST and filed on 12/20/2011

Case Name: Ferdie Mouse **Case Number:06–60125–6Document Number:187 Docket Text:** Ex Parte Motion for Relief from Stay. Receipt Number EXEMPT, Fee Amount of $0.00 is Exempt Filed by Ferdie Mouse. (Mason, Perry)

The following document(s) are associated with this transaction:

Document description: Main Document

Original filename: Motion.PDF

Electronic document Stamp: [STAMP bkecfStamp_ID=1007484561 [Date=12/20/2011] [FileNumber=120618   –0][830361e0f320ef4e054adce1f3d424b47fcb4c8dbdbbfdcef483a841ccc4ff2206d522 64993bef62abdf939a7b04ddd5baac3ddf3f05681dfed56c0ad6577c79]]

06–60125–6 Notice will be electronically mailed to:

Julian Mayfair

dina_ventura@nynb.uscourts.gov

06–60125–6 Notice will not be electronically mailed to:

American Trust,

Cornerstone on behalf of Debtor Danielle Richardson,

Perry Mason on behalf of Creditor Citibank

10 Raymond Burr Apartments

Ironsides, NY 12207

Out of Money, Inc.,

James F. Selbach on behalf of Attorney James Selbach

One Lincoln Center

108 W. Fayette Street

Suite 720

Syracuse, NY 13202–1191

James F. Selbach on behalf of Spec. Counsel James Selbach

One Lincoln Center

108 W. Fayette Street

Suite 720

Syracuse, NY 13202–1191

Guy Van Baalen

Office of the United States Trustee

105 U.S. Courthouse

10 Broad St.

Utica, NY 13501

[Effective January 1, 2012.]

INDEX TO UNITED STATES BANKRUPTCY COURT
FOR THE NORTHERN DISTRICT OF NEW YORK

TRANSCRIPTS
Redaction, **NDNY LBR 9037–2**

TRANSFERS
Cases, **NDNY LBR 1014–1, 1073–1**
Claims, **NDNY LBR 3002–1**

TRUSTS AND TRUSTEES
Consent, orders, **NDNY LBR 9013–1**
Credit, approval, **NDNY LBR 4001–3**
Motions, process, **NDNY LBR 9013–1**
Notice, **NDNY LBR 9034–1**
Process, **NDNY LBR 9034–1**

VACATION
Dismissal and nonsuit, **NDNY LBR 1017–1**

VALUATION
Collateral, chapter 13 proceedings, **NDNY LBR 3012–1**

VIDEO TAPES
Courthouses, **NDNY LBR 5007–1**

WAGES
Compensation and Salaries, generally, this index

WAIVER
Affidavits, business and commerce, debtors in possession,
    NDNY LBR 2015–6

WEAPONS
Sales, **NDNY LBR 6004–1**

WITHDRAWAL
Attorneys, **NDNY LBR 2091–1**
    Dismissal and nonsuit, **NDNY LBR 9010–2**
Motions, **NDNY LBR 9013–1**
Reference and referees, motions, **NDNY LBR 5011–1**

WORDS AND PHRASES
Generally, **NDNY LBR 9001–1**

UNITED STATES BANKRUPTCY COURT FOR THE WESTERN DISTRICT OF NEW YORK

Including Amendments Received Through
September 1, 2017

APPENDICES

ELECTRONIC CASE FILING

SELECTED ADMINISTRATIVE ORDERS

SELECTED STANDING ORDERS

RULE 1001. SCOPE OF LOCAL RULES OF BANKRUPTCY PROCEDURE

1001–1. Title and Numbering Sequence.

These local rules, to be known as the "Local Rules of Bankruptcy Procedure" for the Western District of New York, supplement the Federal Rules of Bankruptcy Procedure, and shall govern bankruptcy practice in the United States District Court and United States Bankruptcy Court for the Western District of New York, and supersede all previous Local Bankruptcy Rules.

[Former Rule 1]

[Effective May 13, 1997.]

RULE 1007. LISTS, SCHEDULES AND STATEMENTS

1007–1. Number of Copies.

A. For conventionally filed cases, an original and three (3) copies of a petition, lists, schedules and statements under chapter 7 or chapter 13 of the Bankruptcy Code and amendments thereto shall be filed. These documents shall be filed in the order prescribed by the Clerk of the U.S. Bankruptcy Court.

B. For conventionally filed cases, an original and six (6) copies of a petition, lists, schedules and statements under chapter 9, chapter 11, or chapter 12 of the Bankruptcy Code and amendments thereto shall be filed. An original and six (6) copies of chapter 11 disclosure statements and plans shall be filed.

C. "Courtesy copies" for the Court, in paper format, of Voluntary Chapter 7 Petitions, Schedules Lists and Statements are not required to be provided by Filing Users electronically filing Voluntary Chapter 7 Petitions.

D. For electronically-filed cases, the filer is directed to provide one paper copy each of the petition, statements, lists, schedules, etc., directly to each of the United States Trustee and the assigned case Trustee, immediately upon notification of the Trustee assignment.

[Former Rule 11A & B] [SO 8/14/85]

1007–2. Master Mailing Matrix. In addition to the list of creditors required by Rule 1007(a) Fed.R.Bankr.P., in all cases a list of creditors shall be filed by the debtor, or such party as may be ordered, in a form specified by the Bankruptcy Clerk which shall be known as the matrix. The matrix shall be supplemented or modified by the responsible party, to include all parties that are required to be given notice, so the Clerk can rely on the matrix in the performance of his or her duties.

[Former Rule 18B]

[Effective May 13, 1997. Amended effective June 16, 2003.]

RULE 1009. AMENDMENTS OF VOLUNTARY PETITIONS, LISTS, SCHEDULES AND STATEMENTS

1009–1. Amendments. Amendments to voluntary petitions, lists (including the mailing matrix), schedules and state-ments must have a completed "Amendment Cover Sheet" affixed to the front thereof in a form prescribed by the Clerk. (A paper cover sheet is required for conventional filings, a cover sheet in .pdf form is required to be attached for electronic filings.) No purported amendment of any type will be acknowledged, recognized or processed as such by the Office of the Clerk in the absence of an Amendment Cover Sheet. The term "amendment" includes the delayed initial filing of a schedule, statement, list or other document that discloses the existence of parties-in-interest who were not disclosed in the list of creditors that accompanied the petition. Guidelines regarding amendments are available in the Bankruptcy Court Clerk's Office.

The title of the cover sheet has been changed and its required use expanded to include additional categories of documents, in addition to amendments. A "Cover Sheet for Schedules, Statements, Lists and/or Amendments" must be completed and attached to the front of the following types of documents:

 a. Amendments to previously-filed document(s);

 b. Schedules, Statements, Lists, etc. not previously filed;

 c. Schedules, Statements, Lists, etc. filed pursuant to Fed.R.Bankr.P. Rule 1019 upon the conversion from one chapter to another.

An affidavit of service listing all parties served must be filed with the types of documents identified above. None of the document types identified above will be acknowledged, recognized or processed as such by the Office of the Clerk in the absence of a "Cover Sheet for Schedules, Lists, Statements, and/or Amendments." A paper cover sheet is required for conventional filings, a cover sheet in .pdf format is required to be attached for electronic filings.

[General Orders 3/21/88 & 1/18/92]

[Effective May 13, 1997. Amended effective June 16, 2003.]

RULE 1014. CHANGE OF VENUE

1014–1. Reassignment of Cases. If the convenience or best interests of creditors would be served by the scheduling of a case in a geographical area served by another Judge, the assigned Bankruptcy Judge may reassign the case, on application of a party in interest.

[Former Rule 10B]

[Effective May 13, 1997.]

RULE 1015. CONSOLIDATION OR JOINT ADMINISTRATION

1015–1.

A. Upon the entry of an Order of Joint Administration of two or more related cases, the Clerk shall:

 1. Designate any one of said cases to be the lead case for purposes of docketing and filing.

 2. Enter the Order of Joint Administration simulta-neously on the dockets of all cases covered by the Order and

file a copy of the Order of Joint Administration in the case file of all cases covered by the Order, except the lead case.

3. File the original of the Order of Joint Administration in the case file of the lead case.

4. Thereafter, maintain only the lead case file and docket for all activity affecting any of the jointly-administered cases.

B. The party which obtained the Order for Joint Administration shall, within ten (10) days of the entry of said Order, file with the Court a consolidated matrix comprising a total mailing list of all interested parties in all the jointly administered cases, without duplication.

C. Adequate safeguards shall be established by the Clerk to assure that parties interested in examining the docket or file of a case that is not the lead case will be directed thereby to the docket and file of the lead case for further matters affecting the case in question. Furthermore, to the extent that a docketable paper or event clearly pertains to less than all of the jointly-administered cases, the docket entry made on the lead docket shall so indicate this to enable parties to more readily examine the activities in any one of the jointly-administered cases.

D. Notwithstanding the above, the Clerk may require parties in interest, or request the Court to seek, obtain, or execute separate documents for each case where necessary for purposes of clarity, statistical reporting, case closing or other similar cause.

[Former Rule 17A thru D]

[Effective May 13, 1997. Amended effective December 1, 2009.]

RULE 1019.   CONVERSION—PROCEDURE FOLLOWING [RESERVED]

[Former Rule 20]

RULE 1020.   CHAPTER 11 SMALL BUSINESS CASES, GENERAL

[Former Rule 41]

1020–1.

A. *Election to Be Considered a Small Business in a Chapter 11 Reorganization Case:* In a chapter 11 reorganization case, a debtor that is a small business may elect to be considered a small business by filing a written statement of election no later than 60 days after the date of the order for relief or by a later date as the Court, for cause, may fix.

B. *Approval of Disclosure Statement:*

1. Conditional Approval: If the debtor is a small business and has made a timely election to be considered a small business in a chapter 11 case, the Court may, on application of the plan proponent, conditionally approve a disclosure statement filed in accordance with Rule 3016 Fed. R.Bankr.P. On or before conditional approval of the disclosure statement, the Court shall:

(a) fix a time within which the holders of claims and interests may accept or;

(b) fix a time for filing objections to the disclosure statement;

(c) fix a date for the hearing on final approval of the disclosure statement to be held if a timely objection is filed; and

(d) fix a date for the hearing on confirmation.

2. Application of Rule 3017 Fed.R.Bankr.P.: If the disclosure statement is conditionally approved, Rule 3017(a), (b), (c) and (e) Fed.R.Bankr.P. do not apply. Conditional approval of the disclosure statement is considered approval of the disclosure statement for the purpose of applying Rule 3017(d) Fed.R.Bankr.P.

3. Objections and Hearing on Final Approval: Notice of the time fixed for filing objections and the hearing to consider final approval of the disclosure statement shall be given in accordance with Rule 2002 Fed.R.Bankr.P. and may be combined with notice of the hearing on confirmation of the plan. Objections to the disclosure statement shall be filed, transmitted to the United States Trustee, and served on the debtor, the trustee, any committee appointed under the Bankruptcy Code and any other entity designated by the Court at any time before final approval of the disclosure statement or by an earlier date as the Court may fix. If a timely objection to the disclosure statement is filed, the Court shall hold a hearing to consider final approval before or combined with the hearing on confirmation of the plan.

[Former Rule 41]

[Effective May 13, 1997.]

RULE 1072.   PLACES OF HOLDING COURT

1072–1.   Sessions of Court. Regular and continuous sessions of the Bankruptcy Court shall be held at Buffalo and Rochester. Special sessions of the Court shall be held at Mayville, Olean, Niagara Falls, Batavia and Watkins Glen at such times as may be necessary.

[Former Rule 8]

1072–2.   Scheduling of Cases and Proceedings as Among Places of Holding Court. Giving due regard to the convenience of a debtor, creditors, and equity holders, as well as to the availability of Court support services, the Judge assigned to the case or, if delegated to the Clerk, the Clerk may schedule hearings and trials in a case at a place of holding Court other than that which is in closest proximity to the debtor's residence or of place of business.

[Former Rule 10E]

[Effective May 13, 1997.]

RULE 1073.   ASSIGNMENT OF CASES

1073–1.   Assignment of Bankruptcy Cases to Bankruptcy Judges.

A. Upon filing, the Clerk shall assign each bankruptcy case to a specific Bankruptcy Judge in accordance with the following directives:

1. As to cases arising in Erie County, assignment shall be made by random selection as between the two Bankrupt-

cy Judges stationed at Buffalo, utilizing a formula assuring an equitable distribution of those cases based upon their total case loads.

2. As to cases arising in Niagara, Orleans, Genesee, and Wyoming Counties, to a Bankruptcy Judge stationed at Buffalo as specified by the Chief Judge.

3. As to cases arising in Chautauqua, Cattaraugus, and Allegany Counties, to a Bankruptcy Judge stationed at Buffalo as specified by the Chief Judge.

4. As to cases arising in Monroe, Chemung, Livingston, Ontario, Schuyler, Seneca, Steuben, Wayne, and Yates Counties, to a Bankruptcy Judge stationed at Rochester.

5. General Provisions:

a. For the purposes of these subsections, a business debtor's case shall be deemed to have arisen in the county in which the principal place of business is located if there is a principal place of business within the district.

b. If these rules of assignment result in a disproportionate load of cases falling upon a Bankruptcy Judge, they may be changed upon a majority vote of the Judges.

c. Any case inadvertently assigned to a Judge in contravention of this rule shall be reassigned by the Chief Judge.

B. *Exigencies.* To expedite the flow of cases, proceedings or matters, the Judges may agree to the reassignment of cases, matters, or proceedings to meet exigencies arising in the conduct of a given Judge's calendar. In the absence of the Judge assigned to a case, adversary proceeding, or contested matter, any other Judge may act.

[Former Rule 10A(1) thru A(5) and Former Rule 10D]

[Effective May 13, 1997.]

RULE 2002. NOTICES TO CREDITORS, EQUITY SECURITY HOLDERS, UNITED STATES, AND UNITED STATES TRUSTEE

2002–1.

A. A party filing a motion which requires notice to creditors and/or a creditors' committee in addition to service upon adverse parties shall arrange with the Clerk for such noticing and schedule the hearing accordingly.

B.[1] Notices to creditors required by 2002(a) Fed. R.Bankr.P. in chapter 13 cases will be issued and served by the Standing Chapter 13 Trustee. The Chapter 13 Trustee will file an affidavit of service with the Court to evidence service of each notice. The cost of issuing such notices shall be considered an administrative expense of each Chapter 13 Office.

C. Debtors-in-Possession (or plan proponent if other than the debtor) are directed to serve the Notice of the Hearing on Confirmation of a Plan complete with a copy of the Disclosure Statement, Plan and Ballot and upon confirmation of a plan, the notice of entry of the Order Confirming the Plan pursuant to the requirements of Rule 2002(d)(6) Fed.R.Bankr.P.

[Former Rule 14G] [SO 4/22/86]

[Effective May 13, 1997.]

1 *See also* Notice to Creditors in Chapter 13 Cases under "Standing Orders," *post.*

RULE 2007. TRUSTEES AND EXAMINERS

Rule 2007-1. [Reserved]

[Former Rule 18]

2007–1.1. Election of Trustee in a Chapter 11 Reorganization Case.

A. *Request for an Election:* A request to convene a meeting of creditors for the purpose of electing a trustee in a chapter 11 reorganization shall be filed and transmitted to the United States Trustee in accordance with Rule 5005 Fed. R.Bankr.P. within the time prescribed by § 1104(b) of the Bankruptcy Code. Pending Court approval of the person elected, a person appointed trustee under § 1104(d) shall serve as trustee.

B. *Matter of Election and Notice:* An election of a trustee under § 1104(b) of the Code shall be conducted in the manner provided in Rules 2003(b)(3) and 2006 Fed.R.Bankr.P. Notice of the meeting of creditors convened under § 1104(b) shall be given in the manner and within the time provided for notices under 2002(a) Fed.R.Bankr.P. A proxy for the purpose of voting in the election may be solicited by a committee appointed under § 1102 of the Code and by any other party entitled to solicit a proxy under Rule 2006 Fed.R.Bankr.P.

C. *Application for Approval of Appointment and Resolution of Disputes:* If it is not necessary to resolve a dispute regarding the election of the trustee or if all disputes have been resolved by the Court, the United States Trustee shall promptly appoint the person elected to be trustee and file an application for approval of the appointment of the elected person under Rule 2001.1(b) Fed.R.Bankr.P., except that the application does not have to contain names of parties in interest with whom the United States Trustee has consulted.

If it is necessary to resolve a dispute regarding the election, the United States Trustee shall promptly file a report informing the Court of the dispute. If no motion for the resolution of the dispute is filed within 14 days after the date of the creditors' meeting called under § 1104(b), a person appointed by the United States Trustee in accordance with § 1104(d) of the Code and approved in accordance with Rule 2007(b) Fed. R.Bankr.P. shall serve as trustee.

[Rule 40]

[Effective May 13, 1997. Amended effective December 1, 2009.]

RULE 2008. NOTICE TO TRUSTEE OF SELECTION

2008–1. Filing of Blanket Trustee Designation in Chapter 13 Cases. The Court will accept a blanket designation for standing Chapter 13 Trustees in lieu of a separate designation for each chapter 13 case filed in the Western District of New York. A separate designation must be filed in the event of a substitution of trustee so designated under the blanket designation.

[SO 4/23/96]

[Effective May 13, 1997.]

RULE 2010. QUALIFICATION BY TRUSTEE; PROCEEDING ON BOND

2010–1. Trustee's Reimbursement of Blanket Bond Premiums.

A. The trustee shall issue one check or money order for the entire bond premium and provide a copy of that check to the Office of the United States Trustee.

B. The trustee may be reimbursed from that trustee's estates pending on the date of issuance of the premium check, at the bond premium rate, or,

C. In the alternative, the trustee may allocate the premium paid pro rata to those cases comprising the substantial majority (in dollar amount) of assets under the trustees administration on the date of issuance of the premium check. The trustee shall issue reimbursement checks from the individual estates according to their pro rata share.

D. In no event shall the aggregate amount of the reimbursement checks exceed the amount of the premium paid.

[SO 7/31/90]

[Effective May 13, 1997.]

RULE 2014. EMPLOYMENT OF PROFESSIONALS

2014–1. Definition. "Counsel for the estate." An attorney who has obtained an order of the Court approving his or her employment as attorney for a chapter 11 debtor-in-possession or for a chapter 7, 12, or 13 trustee is counsel for the estate of the debtor. Corporate debtors must be represented by an attorney of record. Papers, including petitions, filed by a corporate debtor which has no attorney of record, may be received but later dismissed, sua sponte, by the Judge to whom the case is assigned.

[Former Rule 5A]

2014–2. Duty of Counsel for the Estate With Regard to Estate's Employment of Other Professionals.

A. Appraisers, auctioneers, accountants, brokers, special counsels, consultants, independent managers, and other professional persons employed by the debtors' estates are often unfamiliar with the requirements of bankruptcy law regarding the need for prior Court approval of their employment; regarding the record keeping and reporting requirements applicable to sustain their claim to subsequent compensation from the estate; and regarding the risk that there may be insufficient assets in the estate to satisfy such claims. Whether or not a professional person is familiar with such considerations, it is necessary and desirable that the responsibility for obtaining Court approval of such employment and for advising professionals of the responsibilities and risks of such employment be placed on the attorney for the estate.

B. Whenever the estate employs any other professional whose employment requires Court approval under the Bankruptcy Code or Rules, it is the duty of counsel for the estate to ensure that such approval is properly sought, and to advise the professional of the requirements and risks, if any, pertaining to the professional's ability to subsequently obtain compensation and reimbursement of expenses from the estate.

C. Estate counsel who fails to satisfy such duties may be determined by the Court to be personally responsible for any compensation and reimbursement of expenses lost to any professional as a result thereof.

[Former Rule 5B]

2014–3. Duty of Attorney Commencing a Chapter 11 Case on Behalf of a Debtor Which Is a Corporation.

A. A corporation which is a debtor-in-possession must be represented by an attorney duly admitted to practice before this Court and duly approved to serve as counsel for the estate by order of the Court.

B. It is the duty of an attorney who commences a chapter 11 case (whether by original petition or by obtaining an order of conversion to such chapter) on behalf of a corporate debtor to ensure that the debtor properly seeks approval of estate counsel promptly upon such commencement, or, in the alternative, to file with the Court an affidavit reciting that he or she has advised the debtor that the case would be dismissed or converted for absence of a counsel for the estate, reciting the diligent efforts made by the attorney both before and after the commencement of the chapter 11 case in assisting the debtor in obtaining such counsel, and explaining why such counsel was not obtained.

C. An attorney who fails in such duties may be found personally liable to any party who is damaged by the failure of the estate to be suitable represented.

[Former Rule 5C]

[Effective May 13, 1997.]

RULE 2015. TRUSTEES, DEBTORS–IN–POSSESSION DUTIES [RESERVED]

[Former Rule 18]

RULE 2016. COMPENSATION OF PROFESSIONALS

2016–1. Professional Persons—Compensation and Reimbursement of Expenses. In all cases under Title 11, requests for interim or final compensation shall be in a form prescribed by the Bankruptcy Clerk, who shall, at a minimum, require the applicant to include a one page face sheet bearing the caption of the case, the name and address of the applicant or applicants, the dates upon which the case was filed and the applicant was appointed, the nature and the date or the period of services rendered, a typewritten time sheet with a description of services rendered, and the amount of compensation or expense reimbursement sought. (If both compensation and reimbursement are sought, the amounts shall be separately stated.) The application should also include a statement of prior applications and prior allowances.

A. All supporting documentation shall be attached to the application and, if it is an application for interim compensation, it shall also contain an affidavit or unsworn declaration reciting why the applicant should not be required to await the filing of a final report in the case. The Court may take judicial notice of any facts of record warranting denial of the application as having been prematurely made.

B. All applications must be filed at least twenty-five (25) days prior to a calendar at which the application is to be considered.

C. Non-appearance of an applicant at the scheduled hearing shall be deemed to be a consent to the disposition of the application on the filed papers and record, if any, of the hearing.

To aid the Court and any party in interest in reviewing compensation statements filed by attorneys:

(a) The "compensation" paid or to be paid to an attorney shall include all legal fees and all charges of whatever character paid or to be paid by the debtor or other entity. Charges shall be identified and, if not self explanatory, justified.

(b) Basic services to be performed are:

(1) Analysis of the financial situation and rendering advice and assistance to the client in determining whether to file a petition under Title 11, United States Code;

(2) Preparation and filing of the petition, lists, statements or schedules in a chapter 7 or 13 case;

(3) Representation of the debtor at the § 341 meeting;

(4) Amend lists, statements or schedules to comport with developments which may have occurred before or at the § 341 meeting;

(5) Motions under § 522(f) to avoid liens on exempt property;

(6) Motions, such as motions for abandonment, or proceedings to clear title to real property owned by the debtor;

(7) Removal of garnishments or wage assignments;

ADDITIONAL SERVICES REQUIRED IN CHAPTER 7 CASES

(8) Negotiate, prepare and file reaffirmation agreements;

(9) Motions under § 722 to redeem exempt personal property from liens;

ADDITIONAL SERVICES REQUIRED IN CHAPTER 13 CASES

(10) Attend confirmation hearings;

(11) Negotiate valuation of secured claims and/or present evidence thereon at confirmation hearing.

(c) If, in the attorneys judgment, the performance of the above basic services required or will require unusual expenditures of time he or she should so state and annex time sheets or projections of time supporting the claim.

[Former Rules 38 & 39] [SO 7/30/90]

2016–2. Applications for Fees by the Attorney for the Debtor in Chapter 7 Cases.

A. The expeditious administration of chapter 7 estates is hindered by the delays by debtors' attorneys in the filing of applications for allowances from the estate under 11 U.S.C. Sec. 330. Therefore, the failure to file any fee allowance application by such an attorney before fifteen (15) days after the mailing of the Rule 2002(f)(9) Fed.R.Bankr.P. notice of the trustee's final report in any case shall be deemed a waiver of the allowance.

B. All actual compensation and disbursements whether charged by attorneys to the debtor, debtor's estate or any entity paying on behalf of the debtor or debtor's estate prior to or during the pendency of a case must be fully disclosed in a supplemental statement filed in accordance with Rule 2016(b) Fed.R.Bankr.P. [A disclosed fee which is to be charged in the event of a contingent future service, and which is charged, shall be disclosed in a supplemental statement].

C. Supplemental statements by attorneys as to compensation sought from the estate shall be supported by time sheets and detail as to any disbursements charged and shall be accompanied by a motion [notice thereof to be given by the requesting party to parties in interest in accordance with Rule 2002(a)(7) Fed.R.Bankr.P.].

[Former Rule 39] [SO 6/12/84; SO 7/30/90]

[Effective May 13, 1997. Amended effective December 1, 2009.]

RULE 2020. SERVICE ON THE OFFICE OF THE UNITED STATES TRUSTEE

2020–1. Duties of Clerk of Court.

A. For conventionally filed cases, the Clerk of the Court shall ensure that the Office of the United States Trustee for the district is placed on the mailing matrix in each case filed with the Court and is sent notices (including notices of appeal) issued by the Clerk or such other person as the Court may direct.

B. For conventionally filed cases, the Clerk's office shall collect enough copies of petitions, statements, schedules, and amendments thereof to furnish the Office of the United States Trustee with two (2) copies of each.

C. For electronically-filed cases, the filer is directed to provide one paper copy each of the petition, statements, lists, schedules, etc., directly to each of the United States Trustee and the assigned case Trustee, immediately upon notification of the Trustee assignment.

[Former Rule 15A & B]

2020–2. Duties of Parties.

A. Parties shall serve a copy of all documents initiating a request for a Court order or judgment, except proofs of claim or interest, on the Office of the United States Trustee. This includes but is not limited to all pleadings in adversary proceedings and contested matters.

[Former Rule 15C]

[Effective May 13, 1997. Amended effective June 16, 2003.]

RULE 2081. CHAPTER 11

[Former Rule 19]

2081–1. Chapter 11 Reports. [Reserved]

RULE 2090. ATTORNEYS—ADMISSION TO PRACTICE

2090–1. Admission to Bankruptcy Practice and Attorneys of Record.

A. *Prior Admission.* A person admitted to practice in the United States District Court for the Western District of New York before October 1, 1979, is admitted for bankruptcy practice in the Western District of New York. A person subsequently admitted to bankruptcy practice under prior local bankruptcy rules is admitted for bankruptcy practice in the Western District of New York.

B. *Who May Apply.* A person admitted to practice before the United States District Court for the Western District of New York.

C. *Verified Petition.* Each applicant for admission shall file with the Clerk of the Bankruptcy Court a verified petition for admission stating:

(1) Applicant's residence and office address;

(2) That the applicant has been admitted to practice before the United States District Court for the Western District of New York and the date of said admission;

(3) That the applicant has read and is familiar with:

(a) The provisions of Judicial Code 28 U.S.C., section 1334, sections 151 through 158, and sections 1408 through 1412, and section 1452, which pertain to jurisdiction over and venue of bankruptcy cases, proceedings and matters.

(b) The Bankruptcy Code, Title 11 U.S.C.;

(c) The Federal Rules of Bankruptcy Procedure;

(d) The Local Rules of Bankruptcy Procedure for the Western District of New York.

D. *Other Admission Prerequisites.* Upon the filing of the aforesaid verified petition, taking of the oath, and signing of the attorneys' roll, a person shall be admitted for bankruptcy practice and the Clerk shall issue a certificate to that effect.

E. *Admission Pro Hac Vice.* An attorney duly admitted to practice in any state, territory, district, or foreign country may be admitted pro hac vice to participate in a bankruptcy case or proceeding before the District or Bankruptcy Court under such terms or conditions as may be appropriate.

F. *Government Attorneys.* An attorney duly appointed to represent the United States is permitted to appear on any matter within the scope of his or her employment.

G. Only members admitted under LBR 2090 may represent a debtor, be approved for employment as counsel in a bankruptcy case, or appear before the District or Bankruptcy Court in the litigation of adversary proceedings and contested matters.

H. An attorney who has not obtained District or Bankruptcy Court approval to represent a party when required by Bankruptcy Codes and Rules may not appear in representation of that party.

I. An attorney who accepts employment by a debtor in connection with the filing of a case under Title 11, United States Code, has the duty to render complete and competent service, to file with the Court a statement disclosing all payments rendered from a debtor or debtor-in-possession, and may not withdraw from that undertaking without the permission of the District or Bankruptcy Court.

J. Applications to approve employment as attorney of record (whenever Court approval of such employment is required by statute or rule) *must* include the following:

(1) an application, signed by the party seeking to retain counsel, which sets forth the reason this attorney should be hired, the services this attorney will provide, the arrangements reached with regard to when and how the attorney will be paid, the prior relationship between the applicant and the attorney, and the fact that no fees are to be paid unless and until there is specific Court approval;

(2) an affidavit from the attorney setting forth when he or she was admitted to practice in New York State and to bankruptcy practice in the Western District of New York, his or her qualifications; a statement of disinterestedness sufficient to persuade the Court that there is no conflict of interest; attorney's prior relationship with the debtor-client and the date upon which the petition was filed;

(3) an Order appointing counsel which clearly sets forth that no fees are to be paid without Court approval and the date from which the appointment is effective.

K. An attorney who seeks an order approving employment may do so ex parte unless the initial post-petition services date back more than thirty (30) days. The attorney otherwise shall file a motion and notice all parties in interest of the motion and hearing date. The attorney must submit the application and notice to the Clerk of the Bankruptcy Court and obtain approval that they are adequate as to form and content before mailing the notices. The attorney shall prepare and mail such applications, unless the Court orders otherwise.

[Former Rule 2A thru F; Former Rule 3A thru E]

2090–2. Attorneys—Discipline and Disbarment.

A. Any person admitted to bankruptcy practice in the Western District of New York may be disbarred from practice or otherwise disciplined after hearing, after such notice as the District or Bankruptcy Court may direct. Any member of the bar who has been disbarred in a state in which he or she was admitted to practice shall have his or her name stricken from the roll of attorneys or, if suspended from practice for a period at said bar, shall be suspended automatically for a like period from bankruptcy practice in the Western District of New York.

B. Discipline and/or suspension from practice specifically may be directed against any attorney who conducts himself or herself in a manner demonstrating inability to properly represent his or her clients' interests. [See "Malpractice in Bankruptcy—Observations from the Bench" in Commercial Law Journal (March 1985) pp. 95–100, Hon. Harold Lavien, U.S. Bankruptcy Judge for the District of Mass.]

[Former Rule 4A & B]

[Effective May 13, 1997.]

RULE 2091. ATTORNEYS—WITHDRAWAL

2091–1. Withdrawal.

A. Withdrawal shall be permitted only by order granted upon:

(1) motion to withdraw, served upon the withdrawing attorney's client and such other parties as the Court directs; or

(2) if satisfactory to the Court, stipulation of counsel and parties affected thereby.

B. An attorney who has appeared in a case under chapters 7 and 13 as the attorney of record for the debtor may be displaced without order of the Court by filing with the Court a Notice of Substitution of Attorney.* The successor attorney shall file with the Court a Statement of Compensation pursuant to Rule 2016 Fed.R.Bankr.P. within ten (10) days of the Notice of Substitution of Attorney.

C. An order granting permission to withdraw or to substitute shall become effective upon ten (10) days notice to all attorneys of record unless the Court specifically directs that the order shall become effective upon entry.

[Former Rule 3F & G]

* [**Publisher's Note:** On or about June 3, 2010, the Court made available certain procedures concerning substitution of counsel in bankruptcy matters that are set forth below.

Procedure for Substitution of Attorney or Law Firms:

This procedure is to be used if there is a change in attorney or law firms. This includes (1) substituting one attorney for another in the same law firm as the lead attorney, (2) a transfer to the same lead attorney at a new law firm, and (3) a transfer of one attorney to another attorney in different law firms.

1. A "Consent to Substitute Attorney" must be completed and signed by the withdrawing attorney (individually and on behalf of the law firm), the successor attorney (individually and on behalf of the law firm), and the affected client. Parties are encouraged to use the form available on the Court's website.

2. A fully executed Consent to Substitute Attorney must be prepared and docketed in each case for which the attorney is being substituted. To generate a complete list of cases in which you are involved, login to the ECF System (https://ecf.nywb.uscourts.gov), click on "Query", and enter your last and first name.

3. The Court's records will not be updated unless and until the Consent to Substitute Attorney is completed and docketed in each case. Consequently, the attorney who is withdrawing from the case will remain as the attorney of record, and will continue to receive notices, in electronic or other format, from the Court until the necessary form has been filed. Docket the Consent form under *Bankruptcy > Other > Attorney Substitution* for bankruptcy cases or *Adversary > Adversary Misc. > Attorney Substitution* for adversary proceedings.

4. Successor attorneys must also file with the Court a Statement of Compensation pursuant to Bankruptcy Rule 2016 and Local Rule 2091–1(B) within ten (10) days of the Consent to Substitute Attorney.

Procedure to Request a Change of Contact Information in the ECF System for Attorney:

This procedure is to be used only by attorneys requesting a change in their contact information, such as address, phone number, fax number, and/or e-mail address. If there will be a substitution of attorney or change in law firms, you must follow the "Procedures for Substitution of Attorney."

1. Complete the "Request for Change of Contact Information" available as a writeable form on the Court's website.

2. Submit the completed, signed form in paper to the Clerk's Office, at either of the following addresses:

Clerk of Court	Clerk of Court
United States Bankruptcy Court, WDNY	United States Bankruptcy Court, WDNY
Olympic Towers	1220 U.S. Courthouse
300 Pearl St., Suite 250	100 State Street
Buffalo, New York 14202	Rochester, New York 14614

3. Your CM/ECF account and the Court's records will not be updated unless and until the Request for Change of Contact Information form is completed and submitted to the Clerk's Office. Please note that only records for pending cases will be updated. Records for closed cases will not be updated.]

[Effective May 13, 1997. Amended effective December 1, 2009.]

RULE 3001. CLAIMS AND EQUITY SECURITY INTERESTS—GENERAL

3001–1. Transfer or Claim. The Clerk of Court is to accept for filing a waiver of notice of a claim other than for security after proof filed when said notice is signed by the transferring entity and further notice need not be made. When said waiver of notice is accompanied by a properly completed assignment of claim form, the Clerk of Court shall substitute the transferee for the transferor.

[SO 7/15/94]

[Effective May 13, 1997.]

RULE 3007. OBJECTIONS TO CLAIMS

3007–1. Rochester and Watkins Glen objections to claims may be granted without a hearing after the Court has considered the objection and determined the sufficiency of the claim and the objection, unless a request for a hearing is served and filed within the time permitted. Guidelines designed to comply with this procedure are available in the Bankruptcy Court Clerk's Office.

[SO 5/20/93]

[Effective May 13, 1997.]

RULE 4001. RELIEF FROM AUTOMATIC STAY; CASH COLLATERAL AND FINANCING ORDERS

4001–1.

A. *Applicability of Local Bankruptcy Rule 9013.* Except as otherwise provided herein, Local Bankruptcy Rule 9013 applies to motions for relief from stay, use of cash collateral, adequate protection, and financing orders.

B. *Motions for Relief From Stay.* The thirty (30) days within which the Court must preliminarily rule on such a motion under 11 U.S.C. § 362(e) shall be computed from the date on which a motion is served on opposing parties and filed with the Court. In addition to those parties listed in Rule 4001 Fed.R.Bankr.P., notice shall be given to the debtor, attorney for the debtor, trustee or examiner, the United States Trustee, to any persons requesting special notice under Rule

2002(i) Fed.R.Bankr.P., and any chapter 11 creditors' committee or other official committee duly appointed in a chapter 11 case.

[SO 8/4/83]

4001–2. [Reserved].

[Former Rules 18 & 24]

Cash Collateral or Adequate Protection Agreements. All requests for orders approving adequate protection or cash collateral agreements or stipulations shall be sought by written motion and notice of motion, and shall be the subject of a hearing. The party seeking the order shall prepare and serve the motion and notice of motion. Notice shall be given to the parties to the agreement, all parties having any other interest in the collateral, and the creditors' committee, if any, and the United States Trustee. If there is no creditors' committee, notice shall be given to the twenty largest creditors. At the hearing, after inquiry into the content and consequences of the agreement, the Court may direct a further hearing on notice to all creditors or all parties-in-interest. The Court will entertain without a hearing, requests for an order approving a cash collateral agreement or a stipulation which provides for nothing more than a replacement lien on post-petition assets, in an amount equal to the amount of cash collateral used.

[Effective May 13, 1997.]

RULE 4008. DISCHARGE AND REAFFIRMATION HEARING

4008–1. Reaffirmation agreements submitted must be accompanied by Form B240 (or a form which substantially conforms to Form B240) and must be completed and signed. Debtors will no longer be required to attend a discharge hearing, except as provided below. Discharge Hearing Calendars will be conducted on a regular basis throughout the district, at which debtors may present themselves for a full explanation of the meaning of discharge and of reaffirmation. Times and places of such calendars are available from the Clerk.

A. *Pro Se Debtors.* A discharge hearing must be attended by a pro se debtor filing a reaffirmation agreement. The Clerk will issue an informational letter to the debtor and a form to request a § 524(d) hearing.

B. *Reaffirmation Agreement Accompanied by Attorney's Declaration.* The debtor shall not be required to attend a discharge hearing if the debtor is represented by an attorney who attaches a declaration prepared pursuant to § 524(c)(3).

C. *Reaffirmation Agreement Not Accompanied by Attorney's Declaration.* A discharge hearing must be attended by the debtor if a reaffirmation agreement is not accompanied by a completed Attorney's Declaration. The Clerk will issue an information letter to the debtor and a form to request a § 524(d) hearing.

[GO 11/21/86]

[Effective May 13, 1997.]

RULE 5073. PHOTOGRAPHY, RECORDING DEVICES & BROADCASTING

5073–1. Cameras and Recording Devices.

A. The taking of photographs, or making of oral or video tape recordings, or radio or television broadcasting in a courtroom during the progress of or in connection with judicial proceedings, whether or not Court is actually in session, is prohibited. None of the foregoing activities is allowed in the jury rooms, the offices of the Judges or Court reporters, or in any room, hallway or corridor of the floor of the building in which the courtrooms are located, except with the express consent of the Court.

B. The Court may except ceremonial and investitive proceedings from this prohibition.

C. Court reporters are not prohibited by this rule from making sound recordings for the sole purpose of discharging their official duties. No recording made for that purpose shall be used for any other purpose by any person. Likewise, personnel of the Court are not prohibited by Section A of this rule from making sound recordings in the course of their work.

[Former Rule 9]

[Effective May 13, 1997.]

RULE 5080. FEES—GENERAL

5080–1. Payment of Fees. The Bankruptcy Clerk, unless otherwise ordered by the Court, shall not be required to render any service for which a fee is prescribed by statute or by the Judicial Conference of the United States unless the fee for such service is paid in advance and as specified in LBR Rule 5081.

[Former Rule 22]

[Effective May 13, 1997.]

RULE 5081. FEES—FORM OF PAYMENT

5081–1. Form of Payments. Fees must be tendered in cash or by certified check, bank draft, or money order. The Clerk may specify other forms of payment.

[Former Rule 22]

[Effective May 13, 1997.]

RULE 6004. USE, SALE OR LEASE OF PROPERTY

6004–1. Statement, Form, and Notice.

A. Except as to sales in the ordinary course of operating a business, the trustee or debtor in possession shall file with the Bankruptcy Court a statement identifying any estate property proposed to be sold and the date and manner of such sale. The statement shall contain sufficient detail to enable creditors to make an informed judgment as to the wisdom of the proposed disposition. At a minimum, the statement shall contain a description of the property. A statement of sale shall contain a description of the manner and terms of sale, the name of the buyer and purchase price, if known. If the case is a chapter 11 case, a statement as to whether the sale is all or substantially all of the debtor's assets, and the effect the sale will have upon the debtor's ability to reorganize.

B.   Except as provided in Rule 6004(c) Fed.R.Bankr.P., and subdivision C hereof, notice of the filing of the statement and a summary thereof shall be sent to all creditors. The notice also shall advise creditors that they may obtain a hearing on the proposed disposition by filing a written demand for a hearing with the Court within twenty (20) days of the notice date.

C.   Where the statement discloses a sale of all or substantially all of the assets, the Clerk shall set the matter for hearing and notice shall be sent to all creditors.

[Former Rule 25 and Rule 26 (RESERVED)] [SO 8/9/83]

[Effective May 13, 1997. Amended effective December 1, 2009.]

RULE 6007.   ABANDONMENT

6007–1.   Statement, Form and Notice.

A.   The trustee or debtor in possession shall file with the Bankruptcy Court a statement identifying any estate property proposed to be abandoned and the date and manner of such abandonment. That statement shall contain sufficient detail to enable creditors to make an informed judgment as to the wisdom of the proposed disposition. At a minimum, the statement shall contain a description of the property.

B.   Notice of the filing of the abandonment statement and a summary thereof shall be sent to all creditors. The notice also shall advise creditors that they may obtain a hearing on the proposed disposition by filing a written demand for a hearing with the Court within twenty (20) days of the notice date.

[Former Rule 25; parts of A & B]

[Effective May 13, 1997. Amended effective December 1, 2009.]

RULE 6070.   TAX RETURNS & TAX REFUNDS

6070–1.

A.   *In General.* The failure of a debtor in an asset case under any chapter of Title 11 of the United States Code to file any required tax return promptly after filing the petition or after conversion may constitute "cause" for dismissal or conversion of the case upon a request by a party in interest and after hearing on notice.

B.   *As to "Estimated" Tax Claims.* Concurrent with the debtor's duty to file tax returns is the duty to assure that improper distributions are not made upon "estimated" tax claims resulting from the Debtor's failure to file returns.

Overpayment of taxes by allowance of unduly-high "estimated" tax claims may occur to the prejudice of other unsecured creditors, whose percentage distribution may be reduced for the benefit of the excessive "priority" tax claim.

Underpayment of taxes by allowance of unduly-low "estimated" tax claims leaves the Debtor liable for the deficiency after he or she emerges from bankruptcy. And it may have resulted in a windfall for other creditors.

When the tax claim is an "estimated" claim only because no return was filed, the burden must be placed on the Debtor to take steps to avoid prejudice to other creditors (and the Debtor may wish to take steps to protect himself or herself as well.)

At the least, the Debtor shall within 30 days of service of a copy of an "estimated" tax claim that is "estimated" because of non-filing of returns, object to such claim under Rule 3007 Fed.R.Bankr.P. even if the Debtor does not disagree with the amount. A copy of the proposed return or other evidence of the amount of the liability shall accompany the objection. If the Debtor is not served with a copy of the "estimated claim", then the objection must be filed within 30 days after the closing of the 180 day opportunity for the filing of tax claims under § 502.

At the hearing on the objection the Debtor shall appear and shall be prepared to tender the tax return thereat or to provide evidence to the Court as to a proper "estimate" of the tax claim, whether higher, lower, or the same as that filed by the taxing entity.

The Court will thus "estimate" the claim for the purpose of allowance but will not at that hearing determine the Debtor's tax liability under § 505 or the applicable tax laws. The duty to file a return and the risk of additional liability remains at all times on the Debtor, and any discharge shall not discharge the unpaid balance of any actual tax liability, interest or penalties. Determination of tax liability under § 505 requires an Adversary Proceeding.

If the objection required by this rule is not made, the case may on motion on notice to the Debtor and counsel be converted or dismissed, as to the Court appears proper.

The taxing entities may assert other remedies, such as objections to confirmation of a plan. If a plan is confirmed "pending" the estimation of the tax claims as above, then confirmation shall be without prejudice to any objections properly arising out of the hearing on the claim, such as (but not limited to) objections based on feasibility, projected disposable income, or lack of good faith.

[Former Rule 42]

[Effective May 13, 1997.]

RULE 7004.   SERVICE OF PROCESS

7004–1.   Service Upon the United States in Contested Matters.

A.   Rule 9014 Fed.R.Bankr.P. requires that a motion be served "in the manner provided for service of a summons and complaint by Rule 7004 Fed.R.Bankr.P." of those Rules. Rule 7004(a) Fed.R.Bankr.P. [by incorporating Rule 4(d) of the Federal Rules of Civil Procedure and Rule 7004(b)(4), (5)] require:

1.   that the United States be served whenever an officer or agency of the United States is served; and

2.   that service upon the United States is obtained by serving the United States Attorney for the District in which the action is brought, together with mailing a copy of the process to the Attorney General of the United States at Washington, D.C.

[Former Rule 16]

[Effective May 13, 1997.]

RULE 7016. PRE–TRIAL PROCEDURES

7016–1. Pre–Trial Conferences in Adversary Proceedings.

A. At the pre-trial conference required by Rule 7016 Fed. R.Bankr.P., counsel shall be prepared to report on the following matters:

(1) status of the pleadings and joinder of other parties or actions;

(2) anticipated discovery proceedings and the time required for the completion thereof;

(3) unusual problems of law or fact which may arise;

(4) anticipated motions;

(5) narrowing of the issues and stipulation as to matters which avoid unnecessary proof;

(6) the time when the case will be ready for trial;

(7) such other matters as may aid in disposition of the case.

B. Upon the completion of the conference, an order will be entered by the Bankruptcy Court setting the time within which all pre-trial motions and discovery are to be completed and imposing such additional requirements as may be appropriate. Thereafter, further discovery shall not be permitted except by leave of the Court for good cause shown.

[Former Rule 27]

7016–2. Authority of Clerk.

The authority of this Court to set pre-trial conferences in adversary proceedings and other disputed matters is hereby delegated non-exclusively to the Clerk, who shall, in directing litigants to appear thereat, give them notice that such direction is by order of the Court and that the Court may impose sanctions, including a default judgment for failure to appear.

[Former Rule 28] [SO 5/7/84]

[Effective May 13, 1997.]

RULE 7024. UNCONSTITUTIONALITY, CLAIM OF

7024–2. Notice of Claim of Unconstitutionality.

If at any time prior to the trial of any adversary proceeding or contested matter, to which neither the United States, an individual state, nor any agency, officer or employee of either is a party, a party draws in question the constitutionality of an Act of Congress or a state statute affecting the public interest, the party shall, in writing, notify the Bankruptcy Court of the existence of such question and specifically identify the statute and the respects in which it is claimed to be unconstitutional. *See* 28 U.S.C. § 2403(a) and (b).

[Former Rule 23]

[Effective May 13, 1997.]

RULE 7026. DISCOVERY

7026–1. Cooperation of Counsel.

No motion for discovery and production of documents under Rules 7026 through 7037 Fed.R.Bankr.P. shall be heard unless and until moving counsel certify that they have attempted to resolve the discovery dispute on their own.

[Former Rule 29]

[Effective May 13, 1997.]

RULE 7040. ASSIGNMENT OF ADVERSARY PROCEEDINGS

7040–1.

The assignment of the bankruptcy case to a Judge includes, subject to LBR 1073–1(B) herein, the assignment of adversary proceedings and contested matters arising in the case.

[Former Rule 10C]

[Effective May 13, 1997.]

RULE 7054. COSTS—TAXATION/PAYMENT

7054–1. Costs in the Bankruptcy Case.

A. A party entitled to recover costs shall file with the Bankruptcy Clerk, upon forms provided by the Clerk, a verified bill of costs. The date on which the parties will appear before the Clerk for taxation of the costs and proof of service of a copy upon the party liable for the costs shall be endorsed thereon. The Clerk's action may be reviewed by the Court if a motion to retax the costs is filed within five (5) days after the costs are taxed.

B. *Standards for Taxing Costs.*

(1) The Clerk's filing fee is allowable if paid by the claimant.

(2) Fees of the marshal as set forth in 28 U.S.C. § 1921 are allowable to the extent actually incurred. Fees for service of process by someone other than the marshal are allowable to the extent that they do not exceed those permitted by 28 U.S.C. § 1921.

(3) Reporters' Transcripts.

(a) The cost of transcripts necessarily obtained for an appeal are allowable.

(b) The cost of a transcript of a statement by a Judge from the bench which is to be reduced to a formal order prepared by counsel is allowable.

(c) The cost of other transcripts is not normally allowable unless, before it is incurred, it is approved by a Judge or stipulated to be recoverable by counsel.

(4) Depositions.

(a) The cost of an original and one copy of any deposition used for any purpose in connection with the case is allowable.

(b) The expenses of counsel in attending depositions are not allowable.

(c) The cost of reproducing exhibits to depositions is allowable where the cost of the deposition is allowable.

(d) Notary fees incurred in connection with taking depositions are allowable.

(e) The attendance fee of a reporter when a witness fails to appear is allowable if the claimant made use of available process to compel the attendance of the witness.

(5) Reproduction and Exemplification.

(a) The cost of reproducing and certifying or exemplifying government records for use in the case is allowable.

(b) The cost of reproducing documents used for any purpose in connection with the trial is allowable.

(c) The cost of reproducing copies of motions, pleadings, notices and other routine case papers is not allowable.

(d) The cost of reproducing trial exhibits is allowable to the extent that a Judge requires copies to be provided.

(e) The cost of preparing charts, diagrams and other visual aids to be used as exhibits is allowable if such exhibits are reasonably necessary to assist the jury or the Court in understanding the issues at the trial.

(f) The cost of reproducing the required number of copies of the Clerk's record on appeal is allowable.

(6) Witness Expenses. Per diem, subsistence and mileage payments for witnesses are allowable to the extent reasonably necessary. No other witness expenses, including fees for expert witnesses, are allowable.

(7) Such other costs, not heretofore provided for, authorized under Rule 39, Federal Rules of Appellate Procedure, are allowable.

(8) Premiums on undertaking bonds and costs of providing security required by law, by order of a Judge, or otherwise necessarily incurred are allowable.

(9) The certificate of counsel required by 28 U.S.C. § 1924 shall be prima facie evidence of the facts recited therein. The burden is on the opposing party to establish that a claim is incorrectly stated, unnecessary or unreasonable.

[Former Rule 34]

[Effective May 13, 1997. Amended effective December 1, 2009.]

RULE 7055. DEFAULT—FAILURE TO PROSECUTE

7055–1. Procedure for Granting of Default Judgments.

Before seeking default judgment, plaintiff's attorney should make certain that he or she has (1) properly and timely served the defendant, and (2) filed an accurate certificate of service. Then, once the time to answer has expired, he or she may seek entry of default judgment, following the procedures described below.

When the underlying action is a core matter, the Clerk of the Bankruptcy Court may enter the default judgment if:

A. the underlying action is a core matter; and

B. the default judgment is for a sum certain.

In order to obtain a default judgment, in this circumstance, the attorney for the plaintiff is to file (1) an application for default judgment addressed to the Clerk of Court; (2) a certificate of default; (3) a request for judgment by default and affidavit of amount due; and (4) an affidavit of non-military service.

When the underlying action is a non-core matter

A. The Bankruptcy Judge to whom the matter has been assigned may execute a recommendation that default judgment be entered, without requiring a hearing, if the judgment is for a sum certain. When it is a non-core matter at issue, final judgment—even default judgment—must be entered in the District Court.

In order to obtain such a recommendation, the plaintiff's attorney is to file: (1) a recommendation for default judgment addressed to the Bankruptcy Judge; (2) an affidavit of non-military service; (3) an order to transmit record in a non-core proceeding to District Court, combined with findings of fact, conclusions of law and recommendation regarding plaintiff's request for entry of default judgment; (4) an affidavit of amount due; and (5) judgment (for execution by a U.S. District Judge).

B. When the Bankruptcy Judge, on the basis of the submitted recommendation for default judgment, determines that a hearing is necessary, the Clerk will inform the parties of the date of that hearing. (For example, if the defendant appeared, but did not answer, the defendant has a right to be heard on the question of the amount of damages.) After that hearing, the plaintiff's attorney is to submit a revised order to transmit, a revised affidavit of amount due, and a judgment (for execution by the U.S. District Judge).

Appropriate sample forms are available from the Bankruptcy Court Clerk.

The Clerk of Court shall enter the fact of default in an adversary proceeding only when requested to do so by the nondefaulting party. Upon entry of the fact of default under Fed.R.Civ.P. Rule 55(a), the nondefaulting party may seek judgment by default from the Clerk or the Court as appropriate under Fed.R.Civ.P. Rule 55(b), (d), and (e). Where relief has been sought against multiple parties not all of whom have failed to plead or defend, the fact of default may be entered as to any party who failed to plead or defend, but no judgment by default shall be entered against such party until the case shall have been decided with respect to the nondefaulting parties, unless the Court orders otherwise. A plaintiff entitled to a default for the failure to answer a complaint must request entry of the fact of default, and make suitable request for judgment, within 60 days after the last day to answer. Failure to make these requests will result in the entry of an order placing the proceeding on a calendar for a hearing on the question of why the complaint should not be dismissed for want of prosecution.

[Former Rule 33] [SO 12/5/83; SO 4/19/84]

[Effective May 13, 1997.]

RULE 7069. JUDGMENT, PAYMENT OF

7069–1. Interest on Judgments.

Interest on Judgments entered in the United States Bankruptcy Court for the Western District of New York shall be based on the rate applicable in the Federal District Court, pursuant to Title 28 U.S.C. § 1961.

Satisfaction of Judgments. [Reserved].

[Former Rules 35 & 36 (Reserved)] [GO 1/3/84]

[Effective May 13, 1997.]

RULE 8008. APPEALS

8008–1. Filing Papers—Appeal.

Upon filing a notice of appeal, the appellant shall furnish the Clerk with a sufficient number of copies thereof for mailing.

[Former Rule 14F]

[Effective May 13, 1997.]

RULE 9004. PAPERS

9004–1. Form of Papers.

All pleadings and other papers shall be plainly and legibly written, preferably typewritten, printed or reproduced; shall be without erasures or interlineations materially defacing them; shall be in ink or its equivalent on durable, white paper of good quality; and, except for exhibits, shall be on letter size paper.

To assist the Court in its efforts to scan all documents and make them electronically available, the requirement to securely fasten and two-hole punch all pleadings and other papers in durable covers is hereby discontinued for all filings, both electronic and conventional (paper). Documents should be fastened using a device which can be easily removed, such as a large paper clip or clamp. However, "Courtesy Copies" of electronically filed documents submitted to the Court should be bound with exhibits clearly marked.

[Former Rule 13A]

9004–2. Caption.

All pleadings and other papers shall be captioned with the name of the Court, the title of the case, the proper docket number or numbers, including the initial at the end of the number indicating the Judge to whom the matter has been assigned, and a description of their nature. All pleadings and other papers, unless excepted under Rule 9011 Fed.R.Bankr. P., shall be dated, signed and have thereon the name, address and telephone number of each attorney, or if no attorney, then the litigant appearing.

[Former Rule 13B]

9004–3.

Papers not conforming with this rule generally shall be received by the Bankruptcy Clerk, but the effectiveness of any such papers shall be subject to determination of the Court.

[Former Rule 13D]

[Effective May 13, 1997. Amended effective June 16, 2003.]

RULE 9006. TIME PERIODS

9006–1. Reduction.

If a party wishes to shorten the notice requirements prescribed by Rule 9013 Fed.R.Bankr.P., the party must make written application to the appropriate Judge for an expedited hearing.

[Former Rule 14D]

[Effective May 13, 1997.]

RULE 9010. ATTORNEYS—NOTICE OF APPEARANCE

9010–1. Student Law Clerks.

A. An eligible law student may, with the approval of his or her law school dean or a member of the law school faculty and of a Bankruptcy Judge of the Western District of New York, serve as a part-time student law clerk to that Bankruptcy Judge.

B. In order to so serve, the law student shall:

(1) be duly enrolled in a law school approved by the American Bar Association;

(2) have completed legal studies amounting to at least two semesters or the equivalent;

(3) be enrolled in a course or program at his or her law school offering academic credit for serving as a part-time law clerk to a Judge or be certified by the dean of his or her law school for non-credit clinical experience;

(4) be supervised by a member of a law school faculty. This faculty advisor shall, to the extent possible, review all aspects of the student's work before it is submitted to the Judge;

(5) be certified by the dean or a faculty member of his or her law school as being of good character and competent legal ability. This certification may be withdrawn by the certifier at any time by mailing a notice to the Judge supervising the student. Termination of certification by the certifier shall not reflect on a student's character or ability unless otherwise specified. A copy of such certification and decertification shall be filed with the Clerk of the Court;

(6) neither be entitled to ask for not receive compensation of any kind from the Court or anyone in connection with service as a part-time law clerk to a Judge;

(7) certify in writing, which certification shall be filed with the Clerk of the Bankruptcy Court, that he or she:

(a) has read and is familiar with and will comply with the Code of Professional Responsibility, and relevant provisions of the Code of Judicial Conduct for United States Judges, and

(b) will abstain from revealing any information and making any comment at any time, except to his or her faculty advisor or to the Court personnel as specifically permitted by the Judge to whom he or she is assigned, concerning any proceeding pending or impending in this Court while he or she is serving as a part-time clerk.

C. A Judge supervising a part-time clerk may terminate or limit the clerk's duties at any time without notice or hearing and without showing of cause. Such termination or limitation shall not be considered a reflection on the character or ability of the part-time clerk unless otherwise specified.

D.   An attorney in a pending proceeding may at any time request that a part-time clerk not be permitted to work on or have access to information concerning that proceeding and, on a showing that such restriction is necessary, a Judge shall take appropriate steps to restrict the clerk's contact with the proceeding.

E.   For the purpose of Canons 3–A(4) and 3–A(6) of the Code of Judicial Conduct for United States Judges, a part-time law clerk is deemed to be a member of the Court's personnel.

F.   Forms for designating compliance with the rule are available in the Clerk's office.

[Former Rule 6]

9010–2. Student Practice.

A.   An eligible law student, with the Court's approval, under supervision of an attorney, may appear on behalf of any person, including the United States Attorney, who has consented in writing.

B.   The attorney who supervises a student shall:

(1) be admitted to bankruptcy practice in the United States District and Bankruptcy Courts for the Western District of New York;

(2) assume personal professional responsibility for the student's work;

(3) assist the student to the extent necessary;

(4) appear with the student in all proceedings before the Court;

(5) indicate in writing his or her consent to supervise the student.

C.   In order to appear, the student shall:

(1) be duly enrolled in a law school approved by the American Bar Association;

(2) have completed legal studies amounting to at least two semesters or the equivalent;

(3) be certified by either the dean or a faculty member of his or her law school as qualified to provide the legal representation permitted by these rules. This certification may be withdrawn by the certifier at any time by mailing a notice to the Clerk or by termination by the Judge presiding in the case in which the student appears without notice or hearing and without showing of cause. The loss of certification by action of a Judge shall not be considered a reflection on the character or ability of the student;

(4) be introduced to the Court by an attorney admitted to bankruptcy practice before the Court;

(5) neither ask for nor receive any compensation or remuneration of any kind for his or her services from the person on whose behalf he or she renders services, but this shall not prevent an attorney, legal aid bureau, law school, a state or the United States from paying compensation to the eligible law student, nor shall it prevent any agency from making proper charges for its services;

(6) certify in writing that he or she is familiar with and will comply with the Code of Professional Responsibility of the American Bar Association;

(7) certify in writing that he or she is familiar with the procedural and evidentiary rules relevant to the action in which he or she is appearing.

D.   The law student, supervised in accordance with these rules, may:

(1) appear as counsel in Court or at other proceeding when written consent of the client (on the form available in the Clerk's Office) or of the United States Attorney, when the client is the United States, and the supervising attorney have been filed, and when the Court has approved the student's request to appear in the particular case to the extent that the Judge presiding at the hearing or trial permits;

(2) prepare and sign motions, petitions, answers, briefs, and other documents in connection with any matter in which he or she had met the conditions of "1" above; each such document also shall be signed by the supervising attorney.

E.   Forms for designating compliance with this rule shall be available in the Bankruptcy Court Clerk's Office. Completed forms shall be filed with the Bankruptcy Clerk.

F.   Participation by students under the rule shall not be deemed a violation in connection with the rules for admission to the bar of any jurisdiction concerning practice of law before admission to that bar.

[Former Rule 7]

[Effective May 13, 1997.]

RULE 9013.   MOTIONS: FORM AND SERVICE

9013–1.

A.   All pleadings, notices and other papers shall be served and filed in accordance with the Federal Rules of Bankruptcy Procedure and these Local Rules.

B.   Except as otherwise provided by rule or ordered by the Court, notices of motion along with supporting affidavits and memoranda shall be served on the parties and filed with the Bankruptcy Clerk at least five (5) days prior to the return date of the motion [eight (8) days if served by mail]. Motion dates may be obtained from the Clerk. Discretionary responses to motions (those not required by order) shall be filed and served upon the adverse party or parties as soon as practicable.

C.   Rochester and Watkins Glen motions filed pursuant to, including but not limited to § 362, § 554, § 522(f), § 722 and § 1229 and § 1339 Modification motions may be granted by the Court by default without a hearing. Sample forms and guidelines designed to comply with this procedure are available in the Bankruptcy Court Clerk's Office.

[Former Rule 14A & C] [SO 8/4/93; SO 8/5/92; SO 3/9/93, SO 4/13/93; SO 7/25/94; SO 7/26/95]

[Effective May 13, 1997. Amended effective December 1, 2009.]

RULE 9014. CONTESTED MATTERS

9014–1. Objections to Trustee's Final Report and Account in a Chapter 7 Case.

A. Parties to whom a summary of the trustee's final report and account have been sent in a chapter 7 case pursuant to Rule 2002(f)(9) Fed.R.Bankr.P. may object to the final report and account by written objection filed with the Bankruptcy Clerk and served on the Office of the United States Trustee within fifteen (15) days of the date of the summary so sent. Unless the Court orders otherwise, no trustee shall distribute dividends unless and until said fifteen (15) days have elapsed without the filing of an objection.

An objection to the trustee's final report and account is a contested matter governed by Rule 9014 Fed.R.Bankr.P.

If the summary of the final report and account is coupled with a notice of a hearing on allowances, an objection to the allowances sought may be made at or before the hearing. The party objecting shall serve a copy of the objection upon or give notice of an intention to object to the Office of the United States Trustee.

B. Responses to written questions or demands, including answers to interrogatories, depositions upon written questions, letters interrogatory or a notice demanding admissions, shall set forth each question or demand verbatim with the party's response set forth immediately thereafter. Objections to interrogatories should set forth the question, the answer and the objection thereto. Objections to responses to interrogatories should set forth the question, the answer, and the objection thereto.

C. An objection to a trustee's final report and account is a contested matter governed by Rule 9014 Fed.R.Bankr.P. Parties to whom a summary of the trustee's final report and account have been sent in a chapter 7 case pursuant to Rule 2002(f)(9) Fed.R.Bankr.P. may object to the final report and account by written objection filed with the Bankruptcy Clerk and served on the Office of the United States Trustee within fifteen (15) days of the date of the summary so sent. Unless the Court orders otherwise, no trustee shall distribute dividends unless and until said fifteen (15) days have elapsed without the filing of an objection.

If the summary of the final report and account is coupled with a notice of a hearing on allowances, an objection to the allowances sought may be made at or before the hearing. The party objecting shall serve a copy of the objection upon or give notice of an intention to object to the Office of the United States Trustee.

[Former Rule 37; Former Rule 13C]

[Effective May 13, 1997. Amended effective December 1, 2009.]

RULE 9015. JURY TRIALS

A. **Applicability of Certain Federal Rules of Civil Procedure.** Rules 38, 39 and 47–51 Fed.R.Civ.P. and Rule 81(c) Fed.R.Civ.P. insofar as it applies to jury trials, apply in cases and proceedings, except that a demand made under Rule 38(b) Fed.R.Civ.P. shall be filed in accordance with Rule 5005 Fed.R.Bankr.P.

B. **Consent to Have Trial Conducted by Bankruptcy Judge.** If the right to a jury trial applies, a timely demand has been filed under Rule 38(b) Fed.R.Civ.P., and the Bankruptcy Judge has been specially designated to conduct the jury trial, the parties may consent to have a jury trial conducted by a Bankruptcy Judge under 38 U.S.C. § 157(e) by jointly or separately filing a statement of consent.

[Former Rule 31]

[Effective May 13, 1997.]

RULE 9022. JUDGMENTS AND ORDERS, NOTICE OF

9022–1. Number of Copies.

All orders and judgments shall be filed in duplicate by the party who secures them if such party desires a conformed copy be returned to them. The copies will be placed at the intake counter for pickup unless accompanied by a postage-paid, self-addressed envelope. Such party also shall furnish the Clerk with a sufficient number of additional copies thereof for mailing with the notice of entry, whenever notice of entry is required. All orders, whether made on notice or ex parte, together with the papers on which they were granted, shall be filed forthwith or within the time otherwise permitted by law.

[Former Rule 14E]

[Effective May 13, 1997. Amended effective June 16, 2003.]

RULE 9024. RELIEF FROM JUDGMENT OR ORDER

General reference regarding proceedings to set aside judgments of the District Court in "Non–Core" Bankruptcy Proceedings under 28 U.S.C. § 157 is covered in the General Order regarding same entered in the U.S. District Court on September 14, 1988.

[GO 9/14/88]

[Effective May 13, 1997.]

RULE 9070. EXHIBITS

9070–1.

A. In an adversary proceeding or a contested matter, the exhibits shall be marked by counsel or the parties prior to trial or hearing.

B. Unless the Bankruptcy Court otherwise directs, exhibits (except those produced by non-parties) shall not be filed with the Bankruptcy Court Clerk but shall be retained in the custody of the respective attorneys or persons who produce them in Court. Upon submission to the trier of fact, all exhibits which were received into evidence shall be delivered to the Court. Following decision or verdict, exhibits will be returned to the parties. In the case of an appeal or other review by an appellate Court, all exhibits necessary to perfect the appeal shall be made available for inclusion in the record on appeal.

C. Exhibits produced by non-parties may be held by the Clerk or a party as the Court may direct. Whenever practicable, copies of such exhibits shall be substituted for originals.

Upon expiration of the time allowed for appeal, or following an appeal, any originals retained by the Court or a party shall be returned to non-parties.

[Former Rule 30A thru C]

[Effective May 13, 1997.]

RULE 9071. STIPULATIONS

9071-1.

A. *Stipulations.* All stipulations affecting an adversary proceeding before this Court, except stipulations which are made in open Court and recorded by the court reporter, shall be in writing and signed, and shall be filed. Except to prevent injustice, no stipulation which does not satisfy these requirements shall be given in effect.

B. *Settlements.* When an adversary proceeding is settled, the parties shall file within thirty (30) days a signed agreement for judgment or stipulation for dismissal as appropriate. If no such agreement is filed, the Court may enter an order dismissing the adversary proceeding as settled, with prejudice and without costs.

[Former Rule 32]

[Effective May 13, 1997.]

APPENDICES

APPENDIX 1. CONVERSION TABLE OF FORMER BANKRUPTCY RULES, STANDING ORDERS, AND GENERAL ORDERS TO CURRENT LOCAL RULES OF BANKRUPTCY PROCEDURE

Former Local Bankruptcy Rule, General and/or Standing Order	New Local Bankruptcy Rule
1. Rule 1	LBR 1001–1
2. Rule 2	LBR 2090–1
3. Rule 3	LBR 2090–1
4. Rule 4	LBR 2090–1
5. Rule 5	LBR 2014–1; 2014–2; 2014–3
6. Rule 6	LBR 9010–1
7. Rule 7	LBR 9010–2
8. Rule 8	LBR 1072–1
9. Rule 9	LBR 5073–1
10. Rule 10	LBR 1014–1; 1072–2; 1073–1; 1073–2; 7040–1
11. Rule 11	LBR 1007–1
12. Rule 12	ABROGATED
13. Rule 13	LBR 9004–1; 9004–2; 9004–3; 9014–1
14. Rule 14	LBR 2002; 8008–1; 9006; 9013–1; 9022–1
15. Rule 15	LBR 2020–1; 2020–2
16. Rule 16	LBR 7004–1
17. Rule 17	LBR 1015–1
18. Rule 18	LBR 1007–2; 2007–1; 2015–1; 2015–2; 2015–4; 2015–5; 4001–2
19. Rule 19	LBR 2081
20. Rule 20	LBR 1019
21. Rule 21	LBR 1019
22. Rule 22	LBR 5080–1; 5081–1
23. Rule 23	LBR 7024–2
24. Rule 24	LBR 4001–2
25. Rule 25	LBR 6004–1; 6007–1
26. Rule 26	LBR 6004–1
27. Rule 27	LBR 7016–1
28. Rule 28	LBR 7016–2
29. Rule 29	LBR 7026–1
30. Rule 30	LBR 9070–1
31. Rule 31	LBR 9015–1
32. Rule 32	LBR 9071
33. Rule 33	LBR 7055–1
34. Rule 34	LBR 7054–1
35. Rule 35	LBR 7069–1
36. Rule 36	LBR 7069–1
37. Rule 37	LBR 9014–1
38. Rule 38	LBR 2016–1
39. Rule 39	LBR 2016–2
40. Rule 40	LBR 2007–1
41. Rule 41	LBR 1020–1
42. Rule 42	LBR 6070
43. Standing Order 8/4/83; Motions Under 11 U.S.C. § 362(d) Seeking Relief from an Automatic Stay	LBR 4001; 9013

44. Standing Order 8/9/83; The Content of a Debt-   LBR 6004
    or-in-Possession's Statement of Intent to Sell
    Property Outside the Ordinary Course of Busi-
    ness
45. Standing Order 12/5/83; Defaults in Adversary   LBR 7055
    Proceedings
46. General Order 1/3/84; Interest on Judgments   LBR 7069
47. Standing Order 4/19/84; Defaults in Adversary   LBR 7055
    Proceedings
48. Standing Order 5/7/84; Directing Litigants to   LBR 7016-1
    Appear at Pre–Trial Conferences
49. Standing Order 6/12/84; Applications for Fees   LBR 2016-1
    by the Attorney for the Debtor in Chapter 7
    Cases
50. Standing Order 8/14/85; Number of Copies   LBR 1007
    Required in Chapter 11 Cases
51. Standing Order 10/30/85; Cash Collateral or   LBR 4001-2
    Adequate Protection Agreements
52. Standing Order 4/22/86; Issuing Notices by the   LBR 2002
    Standing Chapter 13 Trustee
53. General Order 11/21/86; Discharge Hearings   LBR 4008
    and Reaffirmation Agreements Under the 1986
    Amendments to 11 U.S.C. 524(c) and (d)
54. Standing Order 4/29/87; Petitions: Number of   LBR 1007-1
    copies to be filed in the Bankruptcy Court and
    Minimum Filing Requirements
55. General Order 3/21/88; Amendments to Peti-   LBR 1009
    tions, Lists, Schedules, and Statements
56. General Order 9/14/88; Proceedings to Set   LBR 9024
    Aside Judgments of the District Court in
    "Non–Core" Bankruptcy Proceedings Under 18
    U.S.C. § 157
57. Standing Order 7/30/90; Trustee's Reimburse-   LBR 2016-1; 2016-2
    ment of Blanket Bond Premiums
58. Standing Order 7/31/90; Compensation in   LBR 2010
    Chapter 7 & 13 Cases
59. General Order & Notice 1/8/92; Amendments   LBR 1009-1
    to Petitions, Lists, Schedules, and Statements
60. Standing Order 7/15/94; Waiver of Notice of   LBR 3001(e)(2)
    Claim
61. Standing Order 4/23/96; Blanket Trustee Des-   LBR 2008
    ignation in Chapter 13 Cases
62. Standing Order 8/5/92; Section 362 Motions in   LBR 9013
    Chapter 7 and Chapter 13 Cases in Rochester
    and Watkins Glen
63. Standing Order 3/9/93; Section 554 Motions in   LBR 9013
    Rochester and Watkins Glen
64. Standing Order 3/9/93; Section 522(f) Motions   LBR 9013
    in Rochester and Watkins Glen
65. Standing Order 4/13/93; Revised re: Section   LBR 9013
    522(f) Motions in Rochester and Watkins Glen
66. Standing Order 5/20/93; Rule 3007—Objec-   LBR 3007
    tions to Claims—Procedure in Rochester and
    Watkins Glen
67. Standing Order 7/25/94; Section 722 Motions in   LBR 9013
    Rochester and Watkins Glen
68. Standing Order 7/26/95; Section 1229 and 1329   LBR 9013
    Modification Motions in Rochester and Watkins
    Glen

[Effective May 13, 1997.]

APPENDIX 2.   IN RE: STANDING ORDER OF REFERENCE
RE: TITLE 11 [DISTRICT COURT ORDER]

Pursuant to 28 U.S.C. Section 157(a) any and all cases under title 11 and any and all proceedings arising under title 11 or arising in or related to a case under title 11 are referred to the bankruptcy judges for this district.

If a bankruptcy judge or district judge determines that entry of a final order or judgment by a bankruptcy judge would not be consistent with Article III of the United States Constitution in a particular proceeding referred under this order and determined to be a core matter, the bankruptcy judge shall, unless otherwise ordered by the district court, hear the proceeding and submit proposed findings of fact and conclusions of law to the district court. The district court may treat any order of the bankruptcy court as proposed findings of fact and conclusions of law in the event the district court concludes that the bankruptcy judge could not have entered a final order or judgment consistent with Article III of the United States Constitution.

[Dated: February 29, 2012.]

APPENDIX 3. IMPLEMENTATION OF THE ACT
OF JULY 10, 1984, PUBLIC LAW 98–353

UNITED STATES DISTRICT COURT
WESTERN DISTRICT OF NEW YORK

IMPLEMENTATION OF THE ACT
OF JULY 10, 1984, PUBLIC LAW 98–353

Supplementing this Court's Order dated July 13, 1984 which provided "Procedure for the Handling of Cases Under and Proceedings Arising Under, and Proceedings Arising in or Related to a Case Under Title 11 U.S.C." and by way of further implementation of the Act of July 10, 1984, Public Law 98–353, it is

ORDERED, pursuant to § 154(b), Title 28, United States Code, that Beryl E. McGuire is designated Chief Judge of the Bankruptcy Court for the Western District of New York, and it is

FURTHER ORDERED that the Bankruptcy Judges of this District are authorized to promulgate local rules consistent with and necessary to the implementation of Public Law 98–353; the provisions of Title 11, United States Code, as amended; and the provisions of the Rules of Bankruptcy Procedure, as amended; and it is

FURTHER ORDERED, pursuant to § 157(b)(5), Title 28, United States Code, that personal injury tort and wrongful death claims shall be tried in the district court in which the bankruptcy case is pending, or in the district court in the district in which the claim arose, as determined by the district court in which the bankruptcy case is pending.

[Dated: September 18, 1984.]

APPENDIX 4. REAFFIRMATION OF THE ORDERS IMPLEMENTING THE ACT OF JULY 10, 1984, PUBLIC LAW 98–353

UNITED STATES DISTRICT COURT
WESTERN DISTRICT OF NEW YORK

REAFFIRMATION OF THE ORDERS
THE ACT OF JULY 10, 1984, PUBLIC LAW 98–353

In reaffirmation of the Order of this Court dated July 13, 1984, which provided "Procedure for the Handling of Cases Under and Proceedings Arising Under, and Proceedings Arising in or Related to a Case Under Title 11 U.S.C." and the Order of this Court dated September 18, 1984, which further implemented the Act of July 10, 1984, Public Law 98–353, it is

ORDERED, pursuant to § 154(b), Title 28, United States Code, that Beryl E. McGuire is designated Chief Judge of the Bankruptcy Court for the Western District of New York, and it is

FURTHER ORDERED that the Bankruptcy Judges of this District are authorized to promulgate local rules consistent with and necessary to the implementation of Public Law 98–353; the provisions of Title 11, United States Code, as amended; and the provisions of the Rules of Bankruptcy Procedure, as amended; and it is

FURTHER ORDERED, pursuant to § 157(b)(5), Title 28, United States Code, that personal injury tort and wrongful death claims shall be tried in the district court in which the bankruptcy case is pending, or in the district court in the district in which the claim arose, as determined by the district court in which the bankruptcy case is pending.

[Dated: May 20, 1992.]

APPENDIX 5.   ORDER OF APPOINTMENT OF CHIEF BANKRUPTCY JUDGE

UNITED STATES DISTRICT COURT
WESTERN DISTRICT OF NEW YORK

IN THE MATTER OF THE APPOINTMENT OF CHIEF JUDGE, BANKRUPTCY
COURT, WESTERN DISTRICT OF NEW YORK

ORDER OF APPOINTMENT OF CHIEF BANKRUPTCY JUDGE

The Court having been advised by the Honorable Beryl E. McGuire that he intends to resign as Chief Judge of the Bankruptcy Court for the Western District of New York effective January 1, 1993, and the Court having selected the Honorable Michael J. Kaplan as his successor pursuant to 28 U.S.C. § 154(b), it is hereby

ORDERED, that the Honorable Michael J. Kaplan is appointed Chief Judge of the Bankruptcy Court for the Western District of New York commencing January 1, 1993, and expiring December 31, 1999.

SO ORDERED.

[Dated: December 21, 1992.]

ELECTRONIC CASE FILING

ADMINISTRATIVE ORDER NO. 7. IN THE MATTER OF: PROCEDURAL RULES FOR ELECTRONIC CASE FILING (ECF)

In and by "Administrative Order No. 1," dated May 28, 2003, and effective June 16, 2003, this Court adopted and approved "Administrative Procedures for Filing, Signing and Verifying Pleadings and Papers by Electronic Means," revised December 1, 2003 ("ECF Administrative Procedures"). The Court has identified the need to revise the ECF Administrative Procedures to clarify many of the procedures governing the Court's Case Management/Electronic Case Files ("ECF") System, it is hereby

ORDERED,that the ECF Administrative Procedures governing the Court's ECF System are hereby amended and the Clerk of Court is directed to publish on the Court's website the Amended ECF Administrative Procedures and to send a broadcast e-mail through the ECF System advising of the amendments to the ECF Administrative procedures, and it is further

ORDERED,that the Amended ECF Administrative Procedures dated October 1, 2010, are effective as of October 15, 2010, and supercede all prior versions thereof.

[Dated: October 13, 2010.]

AMENDED ADMINISTRATIVE PROCEDURES FOR FILING, SIGNING AND VERIFYING PLEADINGS AND PAPERS ELECTRONICALLY

Effective October 15, 2010

Section 1. THE CASE MANAGEMENT/ELECTRONIC CASE FILES SYSTEM.

A. Mandatory Electronic Filing and the Official Court Record

1. All documents submitted for filing in this District must be filed electronically using the Case Management/Electronic Case Files System ("ECF System") See also, Administrative Order No. 5 dated May 14, 2004.

2. All service requirements as provided in the Federal Rules of Bankruptcy Procedure ("Bankruptcy Rule(s)") and the Local Rules of Bankruptcy Procedure ("Local Rule(s)") are to be followed. Electronic filing is not a substitute for conventional service in paper, except as provided in Section 3(B) of these Administrative Procedures

3. Parties proceeding pro se, or parties granted an exemption ("Non–ECF Registered Participants"), will not be permitted to file electronically and must follow all filing requirements of the Bankruptcy Rules and Local Rules.

4. The Official Court record for all pleadings, papers, and documents filed on or after June 13, 2003 is the ECF System.

Section 2. REGISTRATION FOR THE ECF SYSTEM.

A. Logins and Passwords.

1. Attorneys admitted to practice in this Court, United States Trustees and their assistants, private Trustees, and others as the Court deems appropriate, may register with the Court's ECF System ("ECF Registered Participant"). Registration is in a form directed by the Clerk of Court and requires the ECF Registered Participant's name, address, telephone number, email address, and, in the case of an attorney, a declaration that the attorney is admitted to practice before this Court. The process of registering for a login and password is governed by Section 2(B) of these Administrative Procedures.

2. Issuance of a login and password to an ECF Registered Participant immediately activates access to the Court's ECF System, together with all procedures and responsibilities related thereto.

3. Registration as an ECF Registered Participant constitutes: (1) waiver of the receipt of <u>notice</u> from the Clerk of Court by first class mail and consent to receive <u>notice</u> from the Clerk of Court electronically pursuant to Bankruptcy Rule 9036; and (2) consent to <u>electronic service of responsive pleadings and papers</u> through the ECF System. Any pleading that is not an Initiating Paper (as defined below) is considered a Responsive Pleading for purposes of this Administrative Order.

4. Registration as an ECF Registered Participant does NOT constitute waiver of the right to service of any "Initiating Paper", which includes, but is not limited to: (1) pleading or other paper required to be served to initiate a request for an order or request for relief pursuant to Bankruptcy Rules 9013 and 9014, (2) an adversary proceeding commenced pursuant to Bankruptcy Rule 7003, or (3) responsive pleading or paper that asserts a counterclaim or cross-claim (individually or collectively, "Initiating Paper(s)"). Initiating Papers must be served in paper on all parties in interest in the manner required by Bankruptcy Rules 7004 and 7005. See also, Section 3(B) of these Administrative Procedures.

B. Registration.

1. Each attorney or authorized participant filing pleadings or other papers electronically with the Court must complete and sign an Attorney Registration Form (Form A) or a Pro Hac Vice Registration Form (Form B). These forms are available on the Court's website www.nywb.uscourts.gov.

2. The Court does allow non-attorney filers, such as creditors or governmental agencies, to become ECF Registered Participants, but non-attorneys may only be allowed to become Limited Access Filers ("Limited Access Filers") pursuant to Administrative Order No. 4, dated February 2, 2004. Limited Access Filers must complete and sign a Creditor/Limited Filing Registration Form (Form E). Attendance at the training is optional for Limited Access Filers.

3. All signed original Attorney, Pro Hac Vice, or Limited Access Filer Registration Forms are to be mailed or delivered to the Clerk of Court, United States Bankruptcy Court, Olympic Towers, 300 Pearl Street, Suite 250, Buffalo, New York 14202.

4. The Clerk's Office will send the ECF Registered Participant or Limited Access Filer an e-mail message assigning a login and password.

5. Each ECF Registered Participant is strongly encouraged to promptly change the Court-assigned password. This change can be made, once logged into the ECF System, by clicking on the "Utilities" tab and selecting "Maintain Your ECF Account" under "Your Account."

6. In the event that an ECF Registered Participant believes that the security of an existing password has been compromised and in order to prevent unauthorized access to the ECF System through the use of that password, the ECF Registered Participant should immediately change the password in the ECF System and provide notice to the Clerk of Court. If an ECF Registered Participant forgets the password, the Clerk of Court will assign a new password.

7. All signed original Credit Card Blanket Authorization Forms (Form C) are to be mailed or delivered to the Clerk's Office in an envelope marked "CONFIDENTIAL" and addressed to the Administrative Manager, United States Bankruptcy Court, Olympic Towers, 300 Pearl Street, Suite 250, Buffalo, New York 14202. Submission of a Credit Card Blanket Authorization Form by an ECF Registered Participant is optional.

8. An ECF Registered Participant may withdraw from using the ECF System by providing the Clerk's Office with notice of withdrawal. Such notice must be in writing, and mailed or delivered to the Clerk of Court, United States Bankruptcy Court, Olympic Towers, 300 Pearl Street, Suite 250, Buffalo, New York 14202. Upon receipt, the Clerk's Office will immediately cancel the ECF Registered Participant's password and will delete the participant's name from any applicable electronic service list. However, such a withdrawal will not operate to excuse the former ECF Registered Participant from the requirements of electronically filing all documents with the Court as mandated by Administrative Order No. 5 and Section 1(A)(1) of these Administrative Procedures. A request for withdrawal from use of the ECF System does not effect a substitution of attorney or withdrawal of representation.

9. If any of the information on the Attorney, Pro Hac Vice or Limited Access Filer Registration Forms, or the Credit Card Blanket Authorization Form changes, including but not limited to mailing address, e-mail address or credit card information, the ECF Registered Participant must submit the appropriate amended form addressed to the Clerk of Court and/or the Administrative Manager, pursuant to Section 2(B)(3) or (7) of these Administrative Procedures.

10. If any change in information is required because of a substitution of attorney, then the ECF Registered Participant must follow the process for Substitution of Attorney. The forms are available on the Court's website www.nywb.uscourts.gov at New York Western Procedural Forms.

Section 3. ELECTRONIC FILING OF PLEADINGS AND PAPERS, NOTICE AND SERVICE OF PLEADINGS AND PAPERS, AND TIMELINESS.

A. Filing of Pleadings and Papers.

1. Except as otherwise provided by these Administrative Procedures, ECF Registered Participants must electronically file all petitions, motions, pleadings, briefs, memoranda of law, proofs of claim or other documents required to be filed with the Court in connection with a case or proceeding. The filing must be done using the ECF System and electronically filed documents must be in Portable Document Format ("PDF").

2. ECF Registered Participants are required to ensure that information categorized as a "personal identifier" or protected under the privacy guidelines established by the Judicial Conference of the United States (see, http://www.privacy.uscourts.gov) and Bankruptcy Rule 9037 are to be redacted by the ECF Registered Participants before electronic filing. The Clerk of Court is not responsible for redaction of or monitoring of the content of documents filed in the ECF System. See also, Section 13 of these Administrative Procedures.

3. The Creditor Matrix is to be prepared in a single column format, one inch from the left edge of each page (not centered). The name and address of each creditor must not exceed 5 lines and each line may not contain more than 40 characters, including blank spaces. "Attention" lines should be placed on the second line of the name/address. Creditor names and addresses are to be single spaced, with a double space separating each creditor. The city, state, and zip code must all be on the last line. State names must be two-letter abbreviations. The Creditor Matrix must be saved as a **plain text (".TXT") file** and uploaded to the ECF System in the manner described in the CM/ECF Attorney Quick Reference Filing Guide available on the Court's website www.nywb.uscourts.gov.

4. The Clerk's Office will not maintain a paper Court file for any case filed after June 13, 2003, the date on which the ECF Administrative Procedures first became effective, unless otherwise provided by these Administrative Procedures. The official Court Record is the electronic case file maintained on the Court's ECF System.

5. Chambers courtesy copies of all documents filed electronically are required to be provided to the Court within two (2) business days of the electronic filing, EXCEPT voluntary Chapter 7 initiating petitions, schedules and statements, which do not require courtesy copies.[1] The courtesy copy must be submitted in paper and clearly marked as "**ELECTRONICALLY FILED DOCUMENT—CHAMBERS COPY.**" See also, Administrative Order No. 2 dated June 11, 2003.

6. Single-sided printing is required for documents received in paper format. Any documents received in paper format either in Chambers or in the Clerk's Office will be disposed of when it is determined that the paper copy is no longer needed.

7. In expedited matters, the movant will contact, by telephone, the Clerk's Office in Rochester or the presiding Judge's secretary in Buffalo, promptly after filing the pleading or paper for which expedited treatment is requested. Compliance with Bankruptcy Rule 9006 is required.

8. The United States Trustee requires that, immediately upon filing a **Chapter 11 case only**, the attorney for the debtor must provide the United States Trustee with a paper copy of the electronically filed petition, lists, schedules, statement of financial affairs, Rule 2016(b) Statement and any amended schedules, together with an attached copy of the Notice of Electronic Filing. The United States Trustee requires that, within two (2) business days of the notification of the trustee assignment, the attorney for the debtor or the pro se debtor must submit to the **Chapter 7 Case Trustee in Buffalo and Rochester** and the **Chapter 13 Case Trustee in Rochester only**, a paper copy of the electronically filed petition, lists, schedules, statement of affairs, Rule 2016(b) Statement, and any amended schedules, together with a copy of the Notice of Electronic Filing. See also, Notice of Amendment to Administrative Procedures for Filing, Signing and Verifying Pleadings and Papers by Electronic Means, Effective Immediately, dated October 18, 2004.

9. Upon conversion of a case, the attorney for the debtor must provide paper copies of the electronically filed documents listed above in Section 3(A)(8) of these Administrative Procedures, together with any documents filed pursuant to this Court's Local Rules, to the United States Trustee within two (2) business days of the conversion and to the newly appointed case trustee within two (2) business days of notification of the trustee assignment.

10. Papers, pleadings and other documents filed in the ECF System must not include advertisements by or on behalf of the ECF Registered Participant or any third-party.

B. Notice and Service of Pleadings and Papers.

1. When a pleading or other paper is filed electronically, notice of which is required to be given by the Clerk of Court pursuant to the Bankruptcy Rules, the ECF System will generate a Notice of

Electronic Filing and send it to the filing party and any other party who has requested electronic notice in that case, which electronic notice will substitute for paper notice by mail in accordance with Bankruptcy Rule 9036. Attached is a sample Notice of Electronic Filing (Form G).

2. Any Initiating Paper must be e-filed, but also must be served conventionally in paper in the manner required by Bankruptcy Rules 7004 and 7005. Initiating Papers include, but are not limited to: (1) pleading or other paper required to be <u>served</u> to initiate a request for an order or request for relief pursuant to Bankruptcy Rules 9013 or 9014, or (2) an adversary proceeding commenced pursuant to Bankruptcy Rule 7003, or (3) responsive pleading or paper that asserts a counterclaim or cross-claim.

3. A pleading or other paper required to be <u>served</u> in response to an Initiating Paper or in reply to a responsive paper (individually or collectively "Responsive Paper(s)"), may be served electronically using the ECF System upon any ECF Registered Participant required to be served with such responsive papers. Responsive Papers that assert a counterclaim or cross-claim are considered Initiating Papers and must be served in the manner set out in Section (3)(B)(2) of these Administrative Procedures.

4. A Certificate of Service must be filed with the electronic version of each pleading or paper required to be served and filed in the ECF System. The Certificate of Service must comply with the Bankruptcy Rules and state the manner in which service was made on each party served (Form D).

5. A party who is a Non–ECF Registered Participant is entitled to a paper copy of <u>any</u> electronically filed pleading or paper. The filing party must, therefore, serve any Non–ECF Registered Participant with any Initiating or Responsive pleading or paper conventionally in paper, in the manner specified by the Bankruptcy Rules or Local Rules.

C. Section 341(a) Meeting of Creditors.

1. The attorney for the debtor must bring to the Section 341(a) Meeting of Creditors a paper copy of the electronically filed petition, schedules, lists and statement of affairs bearing the original signatures of the debtor(s) and counsel and the date on which the signatures were made, as required by Section 4(B) of these Administrative Procedures. Debtors and their attorneys will execute a "Declaration Re: Electronic Filing" at the Meeting of Creditors (Form H).

2. The attorney for the debtor must also bring to the Section 341(a) Meeting of Creditors the Statement of Social Security Number(s) (Official Form B21) bearing the original signatures of the debtor(s).

D. Timeliness.

1. Filing a document electronically does not alter the filing deadline for that document.

2. Filings are considered timely if received by the Court before midnight on the date set as a deadline, unless the presiding Judge specifically requires an earlier filing, such as by the close of business.[2]

3. Due to variations in time zones, timeliness is established based on the Eastern Time Zone in which the Court is located.

4. An ECF Registered Participant whose filing is made untimely as the result of a technical failure of the Court's ECF System may seek appropriate relief from the Court, pursuant to Section 11 of these Administrative Procedures.

Section 4. SIGNATURES AND RETENTION OF DOCUMENTS BEARING INK SIGNATURES.

A. Petitions, lists, schedules and statements, amendments, pleadings, affidavits, and other documents that must contain original signatures or that require either verification pursuant to Bankruptcy Rule 1008 or an unsworn declaration pursuant to 28 U.S.C. § 1746, must be filed electronically. **THE ELECTRONIC FILING OF ANY DOCUMENT REQUIRING AN INK SIGNATURE CONSTITUTES A REPRESENTATION BY THE ECF REGISTERED PARTICIPANT THAT THE ORIGINAL SIGNATURE(S) WERE OBTAINED AND AFFIXED TO SUCH DOCUMENT(S) PRIOR TO THE ELECTRONIC FILING. VIOLATIONS OF THIS REQUIREMENT WILL BE SUBJECT TO DISCIPLINARY ACTION AGAINST THE ECF REGISTERED PARTICIPANT.** The Statement of Social Security Number (Official Form 21) must be verified and signed prior to the electronic filing of the petition. Official Form B21 must <u>not</u> be electronically filed with the Court.

B. For a period of not less than five (5) years after the closing of the bankruptcy case, the ECF Registered Participant that made the filing of each pleading, paper or other document must retain the original paper version of such pleading, paper or other document bearing original ink signatures pursuant to the verification requirements under Bankruptcy Rule 1008 or 28 U.S.C. § 1746, whether the signature is that of the ECF Registered Participant or made by someone other than the ECF Registered Participant. Upon request of the Court, the ECF Registered Participant must provide original documents for review in the manner directed by the Court.

C. Each pleading or other document electronically filed must indicate the presence of an original signature by using an "/s/" signature and the date on which the signature was made, unless the document is a scanned PDF document and shows each handwritten signature and date on which the signature was made.

D. The following procedure applies when a stipulation or other document requires two or more signatures:

1. The ECF Registered Participant must initially confirm that the content of the document is acceptable to all persons required to sign the document and must obtain the handwritten signatures of all necessary parties on the document.

2. The ECF Registered Participant must submit the document or stipulation containing the signatures of all signatory parties to the Clerk's Office. After the stipulation has been approved and signed by the presiding Judge, the stipulated order will be filed and entered by the Clerk's Office into the ECF System.

E. Statement of Social Security Number(s) (Official Form B21), must be signed by the debtor(s) before the petition is electronically filed with the Court and must be retained by the debtor(s)' attorney in paper with original ink signatures in accordance with the requirements of Section 4(A) and (B) of these Administrative Procedures. Official From B21 must <u>not</u> be filed with the Court.

Section 5. FEES.

A. Fees for electronic filing of any pleading or paper requiring a filing fee must be paid by the ECF Registered Participant by credit card over the internet, through the Pay.Gov application that is integrated with the ECF System.

B. The Court is authorized to accept only VISA, MASTERCARD, AMERICAN EXPRESS, DISCOVER, and DINER'S CLUB credit cards. Should other forms of electronic payment be authorized in the future, the Court will amend the Administrative Procedures accordingly.

C. The fee for any transaction declined by the credit card issuer for any reason must be paid to the Court by cash, attorney's check or money order by the close of business on the next business day following notification by Court staff of the deficiency. The failure to make payment of fees following such notification will result in the ECF Registered Participant's account being "locked-out" of the ECF System, preventing any further electronic filings, until payment is made. "Lock-out" occurs within 48 hours of the declined transaction. The ECF Registered Participant has the responsibility to furnish updated credit card information to the Court.

D. Except as otherwise provided, all ECF Registered Participants will be subject to the fees set forth in the Fee Schedule for Electronic Public Access ("EPA Fee Schedule"), adopted by the Judicial Conference of the United States.

E. ECF Registered Participants in a case receive one free electronic viewing of each filed document through Public Access to Court Electronic Records ("PACER"), for a limited time after the document is filed. Users are encouraged to print or save the document at that time to avoid additional PACER fees. Should the ECF Registered Participant not print or otherwise save the document, any subsequent PACER access to documents is subject to PACER fees, as set by the Judicial Conference of the United States.

Section 6. ATTACHMENTS.

A. ECF Registered Participants must file, in PDF format, documents referenced as Exhibits, or, if voluminous, only those relevant excerpts that are directly relevant to the matter under consideration by the Court, including, but not limited to, leases, notes and mortgages, unless the Court permits conventional filing. Exhibits may be summarized using Summary of Exhibits/Attachment(s) and Certificate of Service (Form F). Cover sheets are considered attachments.

B. The ECF System will not allow the filing of documents larger than four megabytes (4mb), so as not to degrade system performance. Attachments exceeding four megabytes (4mb) must be split into separate PDF files and the multiple PDF files attached to the document.

C. Documents not available in electronic form must be converted to PDF format by the ECF Registered Participant, using scanning technology. It is recommended that the scanner resolution be set to 300 pixels per inch (ppi) or higher, to support archival preservation of documents filed in the ECF System.

D. ECF Registered Participants filing excerpts of documents do so without prejudicing their opportunity to timely file additional excerpts or complete documents, on request of the Court or a party in interest. ECF Registered Participants may not file excerpts if the Bankruptcy Rules or Local Rules require the complete document be attached at the time of filing.

E. ECF Registered Participants must promptly provide complete versions of excerpted documents upon the request of the Court or a party in interest.

Section 7. SEALED DOCUMENTS.

A. A motion to file a document under seal may be filed electronically unless prohibited by law.

B. Documents ordered to be filed under seal must be filed in paper, and NOT electronically, unless specifically authorized by the Court.

C. The filing party must file with the Clerk of Court a paper copy of a proposed order, together with the documents to be sealed.

Section 8. ORDERS.

A. Proposed orders must be submitted in paper to the Court, with the following exception: proposed orders submitted as part of the Default Motion Procedures in effect for cases filed in Rochester and Watkins Glen may be submitted electronically as a separate attachment to the motion. All other proposed orders should be submitted to the Court by the party requesting the Order, in paper, no later than three (3) business days of the granting of said order. Document backers should not be affixed.

B. Proposed orders may not be combined with the application or motion as a single document, so that orders may be printed out for signature by the Judge. The application or motion must be entered on the docket prior to submitting the proposed order. **DO NOT ELECTRONICALLY FILE A PLEADING THAT CONTAINS A PROPOSED ORDER IN THE BODY OF THE PLEADING.** Pleadings that contain a proposed order within the body of the pleading or are not properly labeled as "proposed" will be disregarded.

C. Any order filed and entered on the docket by the Court without the original signature of the presiding Judge, but indicating the approval of the presiding Judge, has the same force and effect as if the Judge had affixed a signature to a paper copy of the Order and it had been entered on the docket in a conventional manner. Only the Court and authorized Clerk's Office Staff may file and enter Orders electronically. Orders purported to be filed electronically by filers other than the Court or authorized Clerk's Office Staff shall have no validity.

Section 9. DOCKET ENTRIES.

A. An ECF Registered Participant who electronically submits a pleading or other document is responsible for designating the appropriate docket entry for the document by using one of the docket event categories prescribed by the Court. This action constitutes an entry on the Official Court Docket as provided in Bankruptcy Rule 5003. ECF Registered Participants are responsible for accurately describing all documents, including attachments, filed on the docket.

B. The Clerk of Court will enter all orders and judgments in the ECF System, which constitutes the entry of an order or judgment on the Official Court Docket. The Clerk's notation in the appropriate docket of an order or judgment will constitute the entry of the order or judgment as provided in Bankruptcy Rule 5003.

Section 10. CORRECTING DOCUMENTS FILED IN ERROR.

A. When a document is electronically filed, it becomes part of the case docket. Corrections to the docket are only able to be made by the Clerk's Office Staff, at the direction of the Clerk of Court.

B. A document incorrectly filed in a case may be the result of posting the wrong PDF file to a docket entry, or selecting the wrong document type from the menu, or entering the wrong case number and not discovering the error before the transaction is completed. **ECF Registered Participants are cautioned not to attempt to re-file the document.**

C.   As soon as possible after an error is discovered, the ECF Registered Participant must contact the Clerk's Office in Buffalo or Rochester, whichever has jurisdiction over the case or proceeding. As appropriate, the Clerk of Court may either make an entry indicating that the ECF Registered Participant has represented that a document was filed in error or the error will be brought to the attention of the Court for proper resolution. The ECF Registered Participant will be advised as to how the error will be corrected and what additional actions will need to be taken by the ECF Registered Participant, such as re-filing the document. The ECF System will not permit ECF Registered Participants to make changes to any document or to any docket entry once an electronic filing has occurred.

Section 11.   TECHNICAL FAILURES.

A.   Technical failure of the Court's ECF System that prevents an ECF Registered Participant from being able to timely file documents may be resolved by the ECF Registered Participant seeking appropriate relief from the Court or by filing such documents with the Clerk of Court conventionally in paper. Known systems outages, for maintenance and system upgrades, will be posted to the Court's website and broadcast to all ECF Registered Participants by e-mail with as much advance notification as possible.

B.   Problems with an ECF Registered Participant's system(s), such as phone line problems, problems with an Internet Service Provider, or hardware or software problems, do not constitute a technical failure under these Administrative Procedures. An ECF Registered Participant who cannot file a document electronically because of a problem with the ECF Registered Participant's hardware, software, internet connection or other such problems, may file the document(s) at the Clerk's Office during regular business hours, in person, using the computer equipment available in the Clerk's Office lobby area and docketing such documents using the ECF Registered Participant's login and password. An ECF Registered Participant's technical failures do not excuse a late filing. An ECF Registered Participant may seek appropriate relief from the Court in the event that a technical failure of the ECF Registered Participant's system resulted in the inability to file documents timely.

Section 12.   SECURITY OF THE ECF SYSTEM.

Each electronically filed paper will be assigned a special identification number which can be traced, if necessary, to detect post filing alterations to a document. The security of the ECF System is provided by protocols established and enforced by the Administrative Office of the United States Courts.

Section 13.   PRIVACY.

A.   To address potential privacy concerns created by internet access to Court documents, the Judicial Conference of the United States has directed that filers of electronic or paper documents must limit certain personal identifiers appearing in pleadings or other papers. ECF Registered Participants and those filing documents in paper are cautioned of the requirement to ensure that information categorized as a "personal identifier" or protected under the privacy guidelines established by the Judicial Conference of the United States (see, http://www.privacy.uscourts.gov) and Bankruptcy Rule 9037 are to be redacted by the ECF Registered Participants and those filing conventionally in paper before electronic filing. ECF Registered Participants will be required to affirmatively acknowledge their obligation to comply with the redaction rules for each filing in the ECF System.

B.   Information posted on the ECF System must not be downloaded for uses inconsistent with the privacy rights of any person.

Section 14.   PUBLIC ACCESS TO THE ECF SYSTEM DOCKET.

A.   Electronic view-only access to the docket and documents filed in the ECF System is available free of charge to the public at each Clerk's Office public area during regular business hours. A fee for a paper copy of an electronic document is required in accordance with 28 U.S.C. § 1930.

B.   Although any person can retrieve and view the documents in the ECF System and access information without charge by using the public access terminals located within the Clerk's Office, electronic access to the ECF System for viewing purposes is otherwise limited to subscribers to the PACER System. In accordance with the policy of the Judicial Conference of the United States, a "per-page fee" will be charged for accessing detailed case information, such as reviewing filed documents and docket sheets.

C. Paper copies and certified copies of electronically filed documents may be obtained at the Clerk's Office. The fee for copying and certification will be in accordance with 28 U.S.C. § 1930.

1 Judge Kaplan does not require courtesy copies of petitions, schedules, and statements for Bankruptcy proceedings filed under any Chapter.

2 For matters returnable before Judge Ninfo please consult the Court's website www.nywb.uscourts.gov for additional procedural information.

FORM A

UNITED STATES BANKRUPTCY COURT
WESTERN DISTRICT OF NEW YORK

CASE MANAGEMENT/ELECTRONIC CASE FILES SYSTEM (ECF)
ATTORNEY REGISTRATION FORM

LIVE SYSTEM

This form will be used by a licensed attorney to register for the U.S. Bankruptcy Court for the Western District of New York Electronic Case Files System (ECF System). A registered attorney will be provided attorney access level privileges to file documents electronically, and to view and retrieve docket sheets and documents for all cases assigned to the Western District Bankruptcy Court's ECF System. (**NOTE: A PACER account is necessary for access to files and documents.** You may register for a PACER account either online at http://pacer.psc.uscourts.gov or by calling 1–800–676–6856).

First/Middle/Last Name: _____

NYS Bar "Attorney Registration Number":
[Listed on Biennial Registration Receipt]   _____

Dated Admitted to Practice in U.S. District Court for the WDNY: _____

Dated Admitted to Practice in U.S. Bankruptcy Court for the WDNY: _____

Firm Name, if applicable   _____

Mailing Address: _____

_____

Voice Phone Number: _____

Fax Phone Number: _____

Internet E–MAIL Address: _____

Send Notices to these additional E–MAIL Addresses: _____
_____

Send Electronic Notice (check one)   ☐ Each Filing   ☐ End of Day Summary

Send Electronic Notice in the following format (check one):

    ☐ HTML for Webmail providers, e.g., Google, Hotmail, Yahoo, AOL
    ☐ Text for Outlook, Outlook Express, Lotus Notes, other (please list): _____

I have a current Trading Partner agreement for Electronic Bankruptcy Noticing: ☐ Yes ☐ No
    If yes, I wish to continue to receive notices through EBN via: ☐ EDI ☐ Fax or, ☐ I
    wish to discontinue EDI or FAX service provided through EBN

In order to schedule you for the appropriate training class, please indicate your type of legal practice.

☐ Debtor   ☐ Creditor   ☐ Trustee   ☐ Other (please specify) _____.

By submitting this registration form the applicant agrees to adhere to the following:

1. This access is for use only in ECF cases filed in the U.S. Bankruptcy Court for the Western District of New York. It may be used to file and view electronic documents, docket sheets, and reports. **NOTE: A PACER account is necessary for this access and the registration information is referenced above.**

2. Rule 9011 of the Federal Rules of Bankruptcy Procedure ("Bankruptcy Rules") requires that every pleading, motion, and other paper (except lists, schedules, statements, or amendments thereto) filed with Court be signed by at least one attorney of record or, if the party is not represented by an attorney, by the party. The unique password issued to a participant identifies that participant to the Court each time he or she logs onto the ECF System. The use of a participant's password constitutes a signature for purposes of Bankruptcy Rule 9011 on any document or pleading filed electronically using that participant's password. Therefore, a participant must protect and secure the password issued by the Court. If there is any reason to suspect the password has been compromised, it is the duty of the participant to immediately change his or her password through the "Utilities" menu in the ECF System. After doing so, the participant must contact the Clerk's Office to report the suspected password compromise.

3. Registration will constitute a request and an agreement to receive notice of pleadings and other papers from the Clerk of Court electronically pursuant to Bankruptcy Rule 9036, where notice of pleadings and other papers is otherwise permitted by first class mail, postage prepaid.

4. I understand that by submitting an application for a password I agree to adhere to all of the rules and regulations in the WDNY Administrative Order for Filing, Signing, and Verifying Pleadings and Papers by Electronic Means currently in effect, and any changes or additions that may be made to such Administrative Orders. The Court may periodically post announcements and updates to the Court's website that are pertinent to CM/ECF practice and use.

5. I assume all responsibility and liability for the payment of all applicable filing fees due at the time the document is electronically filed.

6. I understand that prior to electronically filing any document with the Court, I must obtain the original signature of the party or parties I represent on a paper copy of the document and that I must retain the original of that signed document for the length of time set forth in the Administrative Procedures.

7. I understand that prior to the electronic filing of a petition, I must obtain the original signature(s) of the debtor(s) I represent on a paper copy of the Statement of Social Security Number(s), (Official Form B21), and that I must retain the original of that signed document for the length of time set forth in the Administrative Procedures. I also understand I must compare the Social Security number(s) provided by the debtor(s) on Official Form B21 to the numbers entered into the Court's ECF System to ensure they are the same.

8. I understand that should I enter into a Trading Partner Agreement to receive notices via Electronic Bankruptcy Noticing by EDI or fax in addition to e-mail service through the Court's ECF System, that I must notify the Court in writing. Failure to advise the Court will result in my receipt of notice through the Court's ECF System only.

9. My signature below constitutes my affirmation that I am an attorney holding a current and valid license to practice law.

_____
Applicant's Signature

_____
Last four Digits of Social Security Number (for security purposes)

Privacy Disclaimer: The information contained within this application will not be sold or otherwise distributed by this office to outside sources.

Please return this form to the New York Western Office at: **U.S. Bankruptcy Court, Attention: Clerk of Court, Olympic Towers, 300 Pearl Street, Suite 250, Buffalo, NY 14202.**

FORM B

UNITED STATES BANKRUPTCY COURT
WESTERN DISTRICT OF NEW YORK

CASE MANAGEMENT/ELECTRONIC CASE FILES SYSTEM (ECF)
PRO HAC VICE ATTORNEY REGISTRATION FORM

LIVE SYSTEM

This form will be used to register an out of district attorney on the U. S. Bankruptcy Court for the Western District of New York Electronic Case Files System (ECF System) by attorneys who (1) reside and **practice outside of this district** and (2) represent parties in New York State on **a pro hac vice basis.** A registered participant will have privileges to submit documents electronically, and to view and retrieve docket sheets and documents for all cases assigned to the Western District ECF System. (**NOTE: A PACER account is necessary for access to files and documents.** You may register for a PACER account either online at http://pacer.psc.uscourts.gov or by calling 1–800–676–6856).

First/Middle/Last Name: _____

Bar ID #: _____

State of Admission: _____

Admitted to Practice in the U.S. District Court for _____

Firm Name, if applicable: _____

Mailing Address: _____

_____

Voice Phone Number: _____

Fax Phone Number: _____

Internet E–MAIL Address: _____

Send Notices to these additional E–MAIL Addresses: _____

_____

Send Electronic Notice (check one)   ☐ Each Filing   ☐ End of Day Summary

Send Electronic Notice in the following format (check one):

       ☐ HTML for Webmail providers e.g., Google, Hotmail, Yahoo, AOL
       ☐ Text for Outlook, Outlook Express, Lotus Notes, other (please list): _____

In order to schedule you for the appropriate training class, please indicate your type of legal practice.
☐ Debtor ___ ☐ Creditor ___ ☐ Trustee ___ ☐ Other (please specify) _____.

In order to qualify for an account on the ECF System, the out-of- state attorney/participant must certify that he or she meets one of the following conditions. **Please check the applicable box(es):**

       ☐   I am registered as an ECF participant in the United States Bankruptcy Court in another state or district. Please indicate court or district(s): _____

☐   I have read the WDNY Administrative Orders and Procedures regarding ECF and have completed training as required by the WDNY Administrative Procedures.

By submitting this registration form the applicant agrees to adhere to the following:

1. This access is for use only in ECF cases filed in the U.S. Bankruptcy Court for the Western District of New York. It may be used to file and view electronic documents, docket sheets, and reports. **NOTE: A PACER account is necessary for this access and the registration information is referenced above.**

2. Rule 9011 of the Federal Rules of Bankruptcy Procedure ("Bankruptcy Rules") requires that every pleading, motion, and other paper (except lists, schedules, statements, or amendments thereto) filed with Court be signed by at least one attorney of record or, if the party is not represented by an attorney, by the party. The unique password issued to a participant identifies that participant to the Court each time he or she logs onto the ECF System. The use of a participant's password constitutes a signature for the purposes of Bankruptcy Rule 9011 on any document or pleading filed electronically using that participant's password. Therefore, a participant must protect and secure the password issued by the Court. If there is any reason to suspect the password has been compromised, it is the duty of the participant to immediately change his or her password through the "Utilities" menu in the ECF System. After doing so, the participant must contact the Clerk's Office to report the suspected password compromise.

3. Registration will constitute a request and an agreement to receive notice of pleadings and other papers from the Clerk of Court electronically pursuant to Bankruptcy Rule 9036, where notice of pleadings and other papers is otherwise permitted by first class mail, postage prepaid.

4. I understand that by submitting an application for a password I agree to adhere to all of the rules and regulations in the WDNY Administrative Order for Filing, Signing, and Verifying Pleadings and Papers by Electronic Means currently in effect, and any changes or additions that may be made to such Administrative Orders. The Court may periodically post announcements and updates to the Court's website that are pertinent to CM/ECF practice and use.

5. I assume all responsibility and liability for the payment of all applicable filing fees due at the time the document is electronically filed.

6. I understand that prior to electronically filing any document with the Court, I must obtain the original signature of the party or parties I represent on a paper copy of the document and that I must retain the original of that signed document for the length of time set forth in the "Administrative Procedures."

7. I understand that prior to the electronic filing of a petition, I must obtain the original signature(s) of the debtor(s) I represent on a paper copy of the Statement of Social Security Number(s), (Official Form B21), and that I must retain the original of that signed document for the length of time set forth in the Administrative Procedures. I also understand I must compare the Social Security number(s) provided by the debtor(s) on Official Form B21 to the numbers entered into the Court's ECF System to ensure they are the same.

8. I understand that should I enter into a Trading Partner Agreement to receive notices via Electronic Bankruptcy Noticing by EDI or fax in addition to e-mail service through the Court's ECF System, that I must notify the Court in writing. Failure to advise the Court will result in my receipt of notice through the Court's ECF System only.

9. My signature below constitutes my affirmation that I am an attorney holding a current and valid license to practice law.

_____
Applicant's Signature

_____
Last four Digits of Social Security Number (for security purposes)

Privacy Disclaimer: The information contained within this application will not be sold or otherwise distributed by this office to outside sources.

Please return this form to the New York Western Office at: **U.S. Bankruptcy Court, Attention: Clerk of Court, 300 Pearl Street, Suite 250, Buffalo, New York 14202.**

_____

FORM C

UNITED STATES BANKRUPTCY COURT
WESTERN DISTRICT OF NEW YORK

CREDIT CARD BLANKET AUTHORIZATION FORM

I hereby authorize the U.S. Bankruptcy Court for the Western District of New York to charge the bank card listed below for payment of fees, costs and expenses which are incurred by the authorized users listed below. I understand if a document requiring a fee is received without the fee, the court will automatically charge the account number listed on this form. **A copy of both sides of the credit card must accompany this form.** I certify that I am authorized to sign this form on behalf of my law firm.

THIS FORM MUST BE TYPED, FILLED OUT COMPLETELY WITH ORIGINAL SIGNATURES, AND DELIVERED TO THE U.S. BANKRUPTCY COURT FOR THE WESTERN DISTRICT OF NEW YORK. A new original form must be submitted to the Court upon <u>any</u> change of <u>any</u> of the information below. It is the responsibility of the cardholder to notify the Court if a card has been stolen or cancelled. If the information on the form is not current, the transaction will not be processed. This form will remain in effect until the expiration date of the credit card or the form is specifically revoked in writing. Photo identification will be requested from the authorized users listed on this form when appearing personally at the Court.

Name as it appears on card _____

Card Type: ☐ MasterCard ☐ Visa ☐ Discover ☐ American Express ☐ Diners Club

Account Number: _____ *AmEx ID#:* _____ *Expiration Date:* _____

Security Code: _____ *Signature:* _____ *Date:* _____

Names and signatures of individuals authorized to use account number listed above for payment of fees, costs, or expenses:

_____   _____
Name   Signature

_____   _____
Name   Signature

_____   _____
Name   Signature

Name of Firm: _____
(Sole practitioner, type or print your name)

Billing Address: _____

_____

Contact Person: _____ *Phone No:* _____

e-mail address: _____

Please send your form to:

U.S. Bankruptcy Court, WDNY
300 Pearl St., Suite 250
ATTN: Admin. Manager
Buffalo, NY 14202

Court Use Only:
Date Received: _____   CC copy attached: Y N   Info verified: Y N By: _____

_____

FORM D

(Sample Format)

UNITED STATES BANKRUPTCY COURT
WESTERN DISTRICT OF NEW YORK

In re:

                                                   Case No.
                                                   Chapter
          Debtor(s)
_____

CERTIFICATE OF SERVICE

I, _____ certify that on, _____, I served true and correct copies of _____
on the following parties in the manner specified for each party below:

Name and Address of Party*   Method of Service
                                        (If by mail, describe the mode of mailing)

Dated: _____

* If a corporation, note name of officer, director or managing agent. See Federal Rules of Bankruptcy Procedure 7003, 7004, 9013 and 9014 and additional rules, as applicable, for service requirements.

FORM E

UNITED STATES BANKRUPTCY COURT
WESTERN DISTRICT OF NEW YORK

CASE MANAGEMENT/ELECTRONIC CASE FILES SYSTEM (CM/ECF)
CREDITOR/LIMITED ACCESS FILER REGISTRATION FORM

LIVE SYSTEM

This form is to be used to register for **LIMITED ACCESS FILER PRIVILEGES** to file and view documents electronically using the Electronic Case Files System (ECF System) in the U.S. Bankruptcy Court for the Western District of New York. (**NOTE: A PACER account is necessary for access to files and documents.** You may register for a PACER account either online at http:// pacer.psc.uscourts.gov or by calling 1–800–676–6856).

545

First/Middle/Last Name: _____

Company/Firm Name: _____

Mailing Address: _____

_____

Voice Phone Number: _____

Fax Phone Number: _____

Internet E–Mail Address: _____

Send Notice to these additional E–Mail Addresses: _____

_____

By submitting this registration form the applicant certifies under penalty of perjury that he or she is authorized to submit this registration form on behalf of the Company/firm identified above and agrees to adhere to the following:

1. This access is for use only of cases filed in the U.S. Bankruptcy Court for the Western District of New York. It may be used to file and view electronic documents, docket sheets and reports. NOTE: A PACER account is necessary for this access and the registration information is referenced above.

2. Rule 9011 of the Federal Rules of Bankruptcy Procedure ("Bankruptcy Rules") require that every pleading, motion, and other paper (except lists, schedules, statements, or amendments thereto) filed with Court be signed by at least one attorney of record or, if the party is not represented by an attorney, by the party. The unique password issued by the Court to a participant identifies that participant to the Court each time he or she logs onto the ECF System. The use of a participant's password constitute a signature for the purposes of Bankruptcy Rule 9011, on any document or pleading filed electronically using that participant's password. Therefore, a participant must protect and secure the password issued by the Court. If there is any reason to suspect the password has been compromised, it is the duty of the participant to immediately change their password through the "Utilities" menu in the ECF System. After doing so, the participant must contact the Clerk's Office to report the suspected compromise of the password.

3. I understand that a signature will be indicated by "/s/" and the typed name of the person signing in the following format: "/s/ Jane Smith" on the signature line. The ECF password constitutes my signature. The login and password for filing with the Court over the internet will be used by me and by any of my employees to whom I give authorization. I will not knowingly permit my login and password to be used by anyone who is not so authorized.

4. Registration will constitute a request and an agreement to receive notice of pleadings and other papers from the Clerk of Court electronically pursuant to Bankruptcy Rule 9036, where notice of pleadings and other papers is otherwise permitted by first class mail, postage prepaid. I agree to maintain a current postal address to receive notification from the Bankruptcy Noticing Center.

4.* I understand that, by submitting an application for a password, I agree to adhere to all of the rules and procedures of the U.S. Bankruptcy Court for the Western District of New York concerning the use of the ECF System, set forth in the Administrative Procedures for Filing, Signing, and Verifying Pleadings and Papers Filed by Electronic Means. I also understand that the Court may periodically post announcements and updates to the Court's website that are pertinent to ECF practice and use.

5. I understand that the use of my login and password in filing a document containing the signature of another person is my representation to the Court that, to the best of my knowledge, the document is a true and correct copy of the original document bearing such other person's signature. I also understand that I must retain the original of the signed document for the length of time set forth in the Administrative Procedures.

6. As a participant with limited filing privileges, participant will only have access in ECF to perform limited transactions including transactions relating to Claims, Reaffirmation Agreements, and

Notice of Appearance. The Court reserves the right to add or remove options available to the participant, as deemed necessary.

7. The Company/Firm will be responsible for adding correct name and address information to the creditor mailing matrix for receipt of notices.

_____

Applicant's Signature

_____

Last four digits of Social Security Number (for security purposes)

Privacy Disclaimer: The information contained within this application will not be sold or otherwise distributed by this office to outside sources.

Return my login and password by: ☐ Email to the following address: _____

Please return the completed for to:

> U.S. Bankruptcy Court
> Olympic Towers
> 300 Pearl Street, Suite 250
> Attn: Clerk of Court
> Buffalo, New York 14202

_____

FORM F

(SAMPLE FORMAT)

UNITED STATES BANKRUPTCY COURT
WESTERN DISTRICT OF NEW YORK

_____

In Re:

                                                    Case No.

                                                    Chapter

                    Debtor(s).

_____

SUMMARY OF EXHIBITS/ATTACHMENT(S) AND CERTIFICATE OF SERVICE

Complete versions of the following exhibits or attachment(s) in reference to _____ are available upon request:

                                        Respectfully submitted

                                        /s/ name

                                        ATTORNEY FOR _____

Copy of the above served this _____ day of _____, _____ on:

_____

FORM G

SAMPLE NOTICE OF ELECTRONIC FILING GENERATED BY ECF SYSTEM WHEN A DOCUMENT IS FILED

00–00000–ABC Notice of Electronic Filing

The following transaction was received from Jim C. Doe on 01/01/2001 at 12:01 AM

Case Name: Debtor name

Case Number: 00–00000–ABC

Document Number: 14

Docket Text:

MOTION FOR RELIEF FROM STAY filed by Jim C. Doe of Creditor's law firm on behalf of Creditor. (Doe, Jim C.)

The following document(s) are associated with this transaction:

Document description: Main Document

Original filename: x:/XXX/12345.pdf

Electronic Document Stamp:

[STAMP NYWBStamp_ID=1111111111[Date=01/01/2001][File Number=11111–1][other codes]

00–00000–ABC Notice will be electronically mailed to:

John Doe

jdoe@hotmail.com

Jim Doe

James@hotmail.com

00–00000–ABC Notice will not be electronically mailed to:

Jane Doe

111 Main Street

Anywhere, USA 11111

FORM H

**UNITED STATES BANKRUPTCY COURT
WESTERN DISTRICT OF NEW YORK**

In Re:

                                        Case No.

        Debtor(s)

**DECLARATION RE: ELECTRONIC FILING OF
PETITION, SCHEDULES & STATEMENTS**

PART I—DECLARATION OF PETITIONER

I (WE) and, the undersigned debtor(s), *hereby declare under penalty of perjury* that the information provided in the electronically filed petition, statements, and schedules is true and correct and that I signed these documents prior to electronic filing. I consent to my attorney sending my petition, statements and schedules to the United States Bankruptcy Court. I understand that this DECLARATION RE: ELECTRONIC FILING is to be executed at the First Meeting of Creditors and filed with the Trustee. I understand that failure to file the signed and dated original of this

DECLARATION may cause my case to be dismissed pursuant to 11 U.S.C. § 707(a)(3) without further notice. I (we) further declare under penalty of perjury that I (we) signed the original Statement of Social Security Number(s), (Official Form B21), prior to the electronic filing of the petition and have verified the 9–digit social security number displayed on the Notice of Meeting of Creditors to be accurate.

☐ If petitioner is an individual whose debts are primarily consumer debts and who has chosen to file under a chapter: I am aware that I may proceed under chapter 7, 11, 12 or 13 of Title 11, United States Code, understand the relief available under each chapter, and choose to proceed under this chapter. I request relief in accordance with the chapter specified in this petition. I (WE) and, the undersigned debtor(s), *hereby declare under penalty of perjury* that the information provided in the electronically filed petition, statements, and schedules is true and correct.

☐ If petitioner is a corporation or partnership: I declare under a penalty of perjury that the information provided in the electronically filed petition is true and correct, and that I have been authorized to file this petition on behalf of the debtor. The debtor requests relief in accordance with the chapter specified in this petition.

☐ If petitioner files an application to pay filing fees in installments: I certify that I completed an application to pay the filing fee in installments. I am aware that if the fee is not paid within 120 days of the filing date of filing the petition, the bankruptcy case may be dismissed and, if dismissed, I may not receive a discharge of my debts.

Dated:

Signed:_____   _____
         (Applicant)   (Joint Applicant)

PART II—DECLARATION OF ATTORNEY

I *declare under penalty of perjury* that the debtor(s) signed the petition, schedules, statements, etc., including the Statement of Social Security Number(s) (Official Form B21) before I electronically transmitted the petition, schedules, and statements to the United States Bankruptcy Court, and have followed all other requirements in Administrative Orders and Administrative Procedures, including submission of the electronic entry of the debtor(s) Social Security number into the Court's electronic records. If an individual, I further declare that I have informed the petitioner (if an individual) that [he or she] may qualify to proceed under chapter 7, 11, 12 or 13 of Title 11, United States Code, and have explained the relief available under each chapter. This declaration is based on the information of which I have knowledge.

Dated:

Attorney for Debtor(s)
_____

Address of Attorney
_____
_____

[Effective December 30, 2004. Amended effective October 15, 2010.]

* [**Publisher's Note:** So in original.]

SELECTED ADMINISTRATIVE ORDERS

ADMINISTRATIVE ORDER NO. 3.   IMPLEMENTATION OF BANKRUPTCY RULE AMENDMENTS CONCERNING PRIVACY AND PUBLIC ACCESS TO ELECTRONIC CASE FILES

The Judicial Conference of the United States has proposed changes to the Federal Rules of Bankruptcy Procedure ["FRBP"] to protect the privacy of debtors, including limitations on inclusion of Social Security Numbers on court documents. These changes will take effect on December 1, 2003, unless Congress acts to overturn the Bankruptcy Rule Amendments before that date.

The proposed amendment of FRBP Rule 1005 requires, among other things, that the title of the bankruptcy case include only the last four digits of the debtor's Social Security Number. The proposed change to FRBP Rule 1007(f) requires the debtor to *submit* to the Clerk of Court a verified statement listing the debtor's full Social Security Number or that the debtor does not have a Social Security Number. However, the debtor(s)' Social Security Number will not become part of the Court's file. "Statement of Social Security Number(s)" (Official Form 21) has been proposed as the document on which the debtor will provide his or her full Social Security Number to the Clerk of Court, although that form will not be filed with the Court.

IT IS HEREBY ORDERED that:

1.   For bankruptcy petitions filed electronically, the completed and verified "Statement of Social Security Number(s)" (Official Form 21) as required by FRBP 1007(f), must be signed by the debtor(s) prior to the electronic filing of the petition and must be retained in paper form by the debtor(s)' attorney in accordance with this Court's Administrative Orders and Administrative Procedures for Filing, Signing and Verifying Pleadings and Papers by Electronic Means. The original Statement of Social Security Number will not be filed electronically and is to be brought to the "Meeting of Creditors."

2.   For bankruptcy petitions filed conventionally in paper format, the signed original "Statement of Debtor's Social Security Number(s) "(Official Form 21) as required by FRBP 1007(f), must be *submitted* with the filing of the petition. The term *"submitted"* as used in FRBP 1007(f) means that Official Form 21 will require special handling by the Clerk's Office to ensure that the document is not available to the public and will neither be filed in the bankruptcy case nor retained in electronic format attached to the case docket.

3.   The Clerk of Court will make necessary modifications to the Administrative Procedures for Electronic Case Filing and related forms to incorporate local procedures to ensure full compliance with privacy related rules.

4.   The Clerk of Court will make necessary modifications to the electronic case filing system (CM/ECF) to ensure that notices and information provided through electronic means are in full compliance with the privacy related rules.

The effective date of this Administrative Order is December 1, 2003 concurrent with the enactment of various proposed amendments to the Federal Rules of Bankruptcy Procedure.

[Dated: October 20, 2003.]

ADMINISTRATIVE ORDER NO. 4.   PROCEDURAL RULES CONCERNING ELECTRONIC FILING OF CLAIMS AND RELATED DOCUMENTS OF CREDITOR/LIMITED FILER ACTIVITIES
Supplement to CM/ECF Administrative Orders 1, 2, and 3

Federal Rule of Civil Procedure ("FRCP") 83 and Federal Rules of Bankruptcy Procedure ("FRBP") 5005(a)(2) and 9029 authorize this Court to establish practices and procedures for the filing, signing, and verification of documents by electronic means.

By Administrative Order No. 1, dated May 28, 2003, this Court established practices and procedures, as set forth in the "Administrative Procedures for Filing, Signing, and Verifying Pleadings and Papers by Electronic Means," as revised December 1, 2003, ("Revised Electronic Filing Procedures") pertaining to the Court's Case Management/Electronic Case Files ("CM/ECF") System.

The Practice under the Revised Electronic Filing Procedures limited to attorneys admitted to practice before this Court the ability to obtain a CM/ECF login and password. The use by such attorneys of that login and password constitutes the signature of the attorney for all purposes, including, but not limited to, Rule 11 of the FRBP and FRCP.

To enable creditors, particularly large-volume institutional creditors, to utilize CM/ECF to electronically file documents related to claims, the Court will now permit creditors and limited filer users to access CM/ECF for the limited purpose of electronically filing certain documents relating to claims, notices of appearance and reaffirmation agreements ("Limited Access Filers"). To obtain a limited-access login and password to the CM/ECF System, an individual must apply to the Court in writing and complete such training as the Court may require.

The Administrative Procedures for Filing, Signing and Verifying Pleadings and Papers by Electronic Means, together with the Administrative Orders entered in regard to Electronic Case Filing, apply in all respects to the Limited Access Filers. The user login and password required to file documents using the CM/ECF System serve as the Filing User's signature on all documents electronically filed with the Court. The user login and password also serve as a signature, with the same force and effect as a written signature, for purposes of the Federal Rules of Bankruptcy Procedure, including, but not limited to, Rules 9001 and 3001, the Local Rules of this Court, and any other purpose for which a signature is required in connection with proceedings before or filings with the Court. Limited Access Filers bear the responsibility of keeping the limited-access password secure and have the duty to immediately notify the Court in the event the Limited Access Filer obtains greater access to CM/ECF than the limited-access password is intended to permit or if the Limited Access Filer believes that the security of the password has been compromised.

The Clerk of the Court may cancel the password of any individual who does not comply in all respects with this Standing Order and/or the provisions contained in the Revised Electronic Filing Procedures or any other Order of this Court regarding electronic filing of documents using the CM/ECF System.

[Dated: February 2, 2004.]

ADMINISTRATIVE ORDER NO. 5.   MANDATORY ELECTRONIC FILING OF DOCUMENTS BY INTERNET TRANSMISSION

In and by "Administrative Order No. 1," dated May 28, 2003 and effective June 16, 2003, this Court adopted and approved "Administrative Procedures for Filing, Signing and Verifying Pleadings and Papers by Electronic Means," revised December 1, 2003 ("Administrative Procedures"). The Court having determined that it is necessary to substantially reduce the volume of paper filings made with the Court, given the increasing case load and the demonstrated reliability of electronic filing using the Case Management/Electronic Case Files (CM/ECF) System, it is hereby

ORDERED, that effective October 1, 2004, the Clerk of Court shall no longer be required to accept for filing any paper submission, except by contrary direction of a Judge of this Court or for papers submitted in connection with pro bono services rendered through VLP, NLPS, VLPS or the like.

[Dated: May 14, 2004.]

ADMINISTRATIVE ORDER NO. 6.   ELECTRONIC TRANSMISSION OF NOTICES BY THE CLERK AND ELIMINATION OF REDUNDANT PAPER NOTICES FOR REGISTERED CM/ECF E-FILERS

In and by "Administrative Order No. 1," dated May 28, 2003 and effective June 16, 2003, this Court adopted and approved "Administrative Procedures for Filing, Signing, and Verifying Pleadings and Papers by Electronic Means," revised December 1, 2003 ("Administrative Procedures"). Notices required to be provided by the Clerk of the Court are not sent to "Registered CM/ECF E-Filers" both electronically through the Case Management/Electronic Case Files (CM/ECF) System and in a redundant paper mode through Bankruptcy Noticing Center ("BNC"). The Court has observed that (1) many attorneys e-filing papers through CM/ECF have indicated that receipt of the redundant paper notices is burdensome, wasteful, and unnecessary, (2) the cost for producing and mailing redundant paper notices through the BNC is an unnecessary budgetary expenditure that should be avoided, and (3) the formal process of amending Bankruptcy Rule 9036 to eliminate the electronic return receipt requirement is underway. In order to accommodate the requests of counsel to eliminate redundant paper notice and in an effort to reduce mailing expenses to the Judiciary budget, it is hereby

ORDERED, that effective December 1, 2004, the Clerk of the Court will discontinue the practice of sending redundant paper notices to registered CM/ECF e-filers through the BNC, except for the "Notice of the Meeting of Creditors" which will continue to be sent in paper through the BNC, and the electronic transmission of notices by the Clerk will be deemed complete upon transmission, and it is further

ORDERED that the Clerk of Court will establish an opt-out procedure to ensure that redundant paper notices are sent through the BNC to any registered CM/ECF e-filer requesting such, in writing.

[Dated: October 18, 2004.]

SELECTED STANDING ORDERS
DEBTORS ASSERTING AN EXCEPTION TO THE LIMITATION OF THE AUTOMATIC STAY UNDER 11 U.S.C. § 362(l) AND PROCEDURE FOR RECEIVING RENT DEPOSITS

WHEREAS, the Bankruptcy Abuse Prevention and Consumer Protection Act of 2005 amended 11 U.S.C. § 101 et seq. ("Code") including the automatic stay provision of 11 U.S.C. § 362 in regards to actions to recover possession of residential property occupied by a Debtor by the enactment of 11 U.S.C. § 362(l), and

WHEREAS, the Court requires uniformity in the procedure for the deposit of rent by Debtors and transmittal of rent to Lessors under § 362(l)(1)(B) and § 362(l)(5)(D) of the Code, it is hereby

ORDERED, that any deposit of rent made by or on behalf of a Debtor, pursuant to § 362(l)(1)(B) of the Code, must be in the form of a **certified check or money order payable to the order of the Lessor,** and delivered to the Clerk of Court upon filing of the Petition and the Certification made under § 362(l)(1)(A) of the Code, and it is further

ORDERED, that the debtor must file a copy of the Judgment of Eviction together with the Petition, and it is further

ORDERED, that upon the Clerk's receipt of a **certified check or money order payable to the order of the Lessor,** with a copy of the Judgment of Eviction, tendered by a Debtor pursuant to § 362(l)(1) of the Code, the Clerk is directed to promptly transmit the certified check or money order to the Lessor, by certified mail/return receipt requested, to the address listed on the petition.

[Dated: October 17, 2005.]

NOTICE TO CREDITORS IN CHAPTER 13 CASES

The Court orders the following interim amendment to Local Rule 2002–1(B) with respect to certain Chapter 13 notices:

1. Effective for Chapter 13 cases filed on or after November 17, 2005, the Clerk will provide creditors with notice of the initial § 341 meeting and hearing on confirmation of the Chapter 13 Plan ("Plan"), together with a copy of the plan, if filed with the Petition.

2. Effective November 17, 2005, any Chapter 13 Plan and any Modified or Amended Chapter 13 Plan filed after the date that the petition was filed must be timely served on the Chapter 13 Trustee and all creditors in the case **by the debtor,** together with the notice of hearing on confirmation. The Chapter 13 Trustee will provide the debtor with the hearing date/time/location and a notice ready form. The debtor must file a certificate of service within 48 hours of completion of service required by this Rule.

3. Effective November 17, 2005, pursuant to Bankruptcy Rule 2002, the Clerk, unless otherwise directed by the Court, will give the debtor, the trustee, all creditors and indenture trustees notice by mail or electronic means in Chapter 13 cases, notwithstanding the provisions contained in this Standing Order.

IT IS FURTHER ORDERED, that pursuant to 11 U.S.C. § 1342(b), **for Chapter 13 cases filed in Erie, Niagara, Genesee, Orleans, Wyoming, Allegany, Chautauqua, or Cattaraugus only,** the confirmation hearing on the debtor's Plan will be scheduled for same date as the first meeting of creditors, unless an objection is filed by a party-in-interest.

[Dated: October 21, 2005.]

"REFUND" OF FILING FEES

All requests for the refund of the payment of fees collected without authority or due to administrative error on the part of the Clerk's Office must be submitted in the form of an application or motion and proposed order and filed in the appropriate case. If approved, refunds will be processed through the electronic credit card system. The motion must specify which of the two circumstances identified in the paragraph below of this Standing Order warrant consideration of the relief requested.

The Clerk of Court is hereby delegated the authority to (1) refund any duplicate filing fee collected as a result of a "pay.gov" error and (2) delete any fee due (prior to payment) of a duplicate fee or a fee not due. The Clerk's office will not notify parties of duplicate payments already received or if payment was made without a fee being due.

IT IS ORDERED that refunds will not be permitted on fees due upon filing, even if the party files the document in error and even if the court dismisses the case or pleading.

[Dated: April 14, 2006.]

IMPLEMENTATION OF INCREASE TO TRANSCRIPT FEE RATES AND NEW TRANSCRIPT DELIVERY CATEGORY

WHEREAS, the Judicial Conference, at its September 2007 session, approved an increase of ten percent to the maximum original and copy transcript fee rates to be effective in fiscal year 2008, and also approved a new rate for the delivery of transcripts within 14 days and agreed that the rate be set at the mid-point between the rates authorized for expedited (7–day) and ordinary (30–day) delivery, it is hereby

ORDERED, that this Court adopts a revised Schedule of Maximum Rates for all categories of transcript, as attached hereto. Transcripts ordered prior to the effective date of this Order shall be billed at the rates in effect at the time the transcript order was placed with the official court reporter.

[Dated: November 1, 2007.]

Attachment

Maximum Transcript Fee Rates—All Parties Per Page

	Original	First Copy to Each Party	Each Add'l Copy to the Same Party
Ordinary Transcript (30 day) A transcript to be delivered within thirty (30) calendar days after receipt of an order.	$3.65	$.90	$.60
14–Day Transcript A transcript to be delivered within fourteen (14) calendar days after receipt of an order.	$4.25	$.90	$.60
Expedited Transcript (7 day) A transcript to be delivered within seven (7) calendar days after receipt of an order.	$4.85	$.90	$.60
Daily Transcript A transcript to be delivered following adjournment and prior to the normal opening hour of the court on the following morning whether or not it actually is a court day.	$6.05	$1.20	$.90
Hourly Transcript A transcript of proceedings ordered under unusual circumstances to be delivered within two (2) hours.	$7.25	$1.20	$.90
Realtime Transcript A draft unedited transcript produced by a certified realtime reporter as a byproduct of realtime to be delivered electronically during proceedings or immediately following adjournment.	$3.05	$1.20	

IN THE MATTER OF ISSUANCE OF CHAPTER 13 DISCHARGES

WHEREAS, the Bankruptcy Abuse Prevention and Consumer Protection Act of 2005 (BAPCPA) requires the debtor to meet certain requirements before a discharge can be issued in a Chapter 13 case, including those set out at 11 USC §§ 1328(h) and 522(q) ("Bankruptcy Code"); and whereas, Procedural Form B283, entitled "Chapter 13 Debtor's Certifications regarding Domestic Support Obligations and Section 522(q)," has been approved for use by the Judicial Conference of the United States to satisfy these requirements, it is therefore

ORDERED, that Procedural Form B283, entitled "Chapter 13 Debtor's Certifications regarding Domestic Support Obligations and Section 522(q)," issued by the Director of the Administrative Office of the United States Courts is required for use in this District; and it is further

ORDERED, that the Chapter 13 debtor's failure to timely file Procedural Form B283 will result in the case being closed without a discharge; and it is further

ORDERED, that parties be provided notice of an opportunity to file objections and/or request a hearing regarding the applicability of § 522(q) of the Bankruptcy Code as it relates to the issuance of a discharge. Pursuant to Bankruptcy Rule 2002(f)(11), said notice will be included in the Summary of Trustee's Case Closing Report and Account, or by separate notice issued by the Court, beginning with notices issued on or after January 1, 2009; and it is further

ORDERED, that if no objections and/or requests for a hearing are filed with respect to the possible applicability of § 1328(h), and the debtor is otherwise eligible to receive a discharge, the Court may issue a discharge in the case; and it is further

ORDERED, that if the case is closed without a discharge, the debtor must file a motion to reopen the case and pay the requisite filing fee in order to obtain a discharge. The fee to reopen a case to obtain a discharge will not be waived; and it is further

ORDERED, that these procedures become effective for all Chapter 13 cases commenced under BAPCPA for which notice of an opportunity to request a hearing was provided, as indicated above.

[Dated: December 11, 2008.]

IN THE MATTER OF ADOPTION OF AMENDMENT
TO INTERIM BANKRUPTCY RULE 1007–I

WHEREAS, the National Guard and Reservists Debt Relief Act of 2008, Pub.L. 110–438, ("Act",) provides a temporary exclusion from the bankruptcy means test for Reservists and members of the National Guard called to active duty or homeland defense activity for at least 90 days after September 11, 2001; and

WHEREAS, by Standing Order dated December 11, 2008, this Court adopted Interim Rule 1007–I in its entirety to implement the Act; and

WHEREAS, the Judicial Conference has proposed amendments to Bankruptcy Procedure Rule 1007(c) which will become effective on December 1, 2012, and which Interim Rule 1007–I incorporates by reference, it is now hereby

ORDERED, that the attached Interim Rule 1007–I is adopted in its entirety, effective December 1, 2012, to conform to the amendments incorporated by reference. This Interim Rule shall remain in effect until further Order of this Court.

[Dated: November 8, 2012.]

Interim Rule 1007–I.[1] **Lists, Schedules, Statements, and Other Documents; Time Limits; Expiration of Temporary Means Testing Exclusion**[2]

* * * * *

(b) Schedules, Statements, and Other Documents Required.

* * * * *

(4) *Unless either*: (A) § 707(b)(2)(D)(I) applies, or (B) § 707(b)(2)(D)(ii) applies and the exclusion from means testing granted therein extends beyond the period specified by Rule 1017(e), an individual debtor in a chapter 7 case shall file a statement of current monthly income prepared as prescribed by the appropriate Official Form, and, if the current monthly income exceeds the median

family income for the applicable state and household size, the information, including calculations, required by § 707(b), prepared as prescribed by the appropriate Official Form.

* * * * *

(c) Time Limits. In a voluntary case, the schedules, statements, and other documents required by subdivision (b)(1), (4), (5), and (6) shall be filed with the petition or within 14 days thereafter, except as otherwise provided in subdivisions (d), (e), (f), (h), and (n) of this rule. In an involuntary case, ~~the list in subdivision (a)(2), and~~ the schedules, statements, and other documents required by subdivision (b)(1) shall be filed by the debtor within 14 days of the entry of the order for relief. In a voluntary case, the documents required by paragraphs (A), (C), and (D) of subdivision (b)(3) shall be filed with the petition. Unless the court orders otherwise, a debtor who has filed a statement under subdivision (b)(3)(B), shall file the documents required by subdivision (b)(3)(A) within 14 days of the order for relief. In a chapter 7 case, the debtor shall file the statement required by subdivision (b)(7) within 60 days after the first date set for the meeting of creditors under § 341 of the Code, and in a chapter 11 or 13 case no later than the date when the last payment was made by the debtor as required by the plan or the filing of a motion for a discharge under § 1141(d)(5)(B) or § 1328(b) of the Code. The court may, at any time and in its discretion, enlarge the time to file the statement required by subdivision (b)(7). The debtor shall file the statement required by subdivision (b)(8) no earlier than the date of the last payment made under the plan or the date of the filing of a motion for a discharge under §§ 1141(d)(5)(B), 1228(b), or 1328(b) of the Code. Lists, schedules, statements, and other documents filed prior to the conversion of a case to another chapter shall be deemed filed in the converted case unless the court directs otherwise. Except as provided in § 1116(3), any extension of time to file schedules, statements, and other documents required under this rule may be granted only on motion for cause shown and on notice to the United States trustee, any committee elected under § 705 or appointed under § 1102 of the Code, trustee, examiner, or other party as the court may direct. Notice of an extension shall be given to the United States trustee and to any committee, trustee, or other party as the court may direct.

* * * * *

(n) Time Limits for, and Notice to, Debtors Temporarily Excluded from Means Testing.

(1) An individual debtor who is temporarily excluded from means testing pursuant to § 707(b)(2)(D)(ii) of the Code shall file any statement and calculations required by subdivision (b)(4) no later than 14 days after the expiration of the temporary exclusion if the expiration occurs within the time specified by Rule 1017(e) for filing a motion pursuant to § 707(b)(2).

(2) If the temporary exclusion from means testing under § 707(b)(2)(D)(ii) terminates due to the circumstances specified in subdivision (n)(1), and if the debtor has not previously filed a statement and calculations required by subdivision (b)(4), the clerk shall promptly notify the debtor that the required statement and calculations must be filed within the time specified in subdivision (n)(1).

[1]Interim Rule 1007–I has been adopted by the bankruptcy courts to implement the National Guard and Reservists Debt Relief Act of 2008, Public Law No: 110–438, as amended by Public Law No. 112–64. The amended Act, which provides a temporary exclusion from the application of the means test for certain members of the National Guard and reserve components of the Armed Forces, applies to bankruptcy cases commenced in the seven-year period beginning December 19, 2008.

[2]Incorporates (1) time amendments to Rule 1007 which took effect on December 1, 2009, ~~and~~ (2) an amendment, effective December 1, 2010, which extended the time to file the statement of completion of a course in personal financial management in a chapter 7 case filed by an individual debtor, and (3) a conforming amendment effective December 1, 2012, which removed an inconsistency created by the 2010 amendment.

Committee Note

This rule is amended to take account of the enactment of the National Guard and Reservists Debt Relief Act of 2008, which amended § 707(b)(2)(D) of the Code to provide a temporary exclusion from the application of the means test for certain members of the National Guard and reserve components of the Armed Forces. This exclusion applies to qualifying debtors while they remain on active duty or are performing a homeland defense activity, and for a period of 540 days thereafter. For some debtors initially covered by the exclusion, the protection from means testing will expire while their chapter 7 cases are pending, and at a point when a timely motion to dismiss under § 707(b)(2) can still be filed. Under the amended rule, these debtors are required to file the statement and calculations required by subdivision (b)(4) no later than 14 days after the expiration of their exclusion.

Subdivisions (b)(4) and (c) are amended to relieve debtors qualifying for an exclusion under § 707(b)(2)(D)(ii) from the obligation to file a statement of current monthly income and required calculations within the time period specified in subdivision (c).

Subdivision (n)(1) is added to specify the time for filing of the information required by subdivision (b)(4) by a debtor who initially qualifies for the means test exclusion under § 707(b)(2)(D)(ii), but whose exclusion expires during the time that a motion to dismiss under § 707(b)(2) may still be made under Rule 1017(e). If, upon the expiration of the temporary exclusion, a debtor has not already filed the required statement and calculations, subdivision (n)(2) directs the clerk to provide prompt notice to the debtor of the time for filing as set forth in subdivision (n)(1).

IN THE MATTER OF HEARING LOCATION FOR MATTERS IN CHAPTER 11 CASES IN THE ROCHESTER DIVISION

WHEREAS, there is only one Watkins Glen Term each month during which the Court hears matters in Watkins Glen, New York, and

WHEREAS, the Court hears matters in Rochester, New York every week, and

WHEREAS, it would be more convenient for counsel and the parties in Chapter 11 cases in the Rochester Division to have matters heard in Rochester, where the Court is in session every week and where participation by telephone conference is available, and

WHEREAS, to allow the Court to more expeditiously and effectively handle Chapter 11 cases in the Rochester Division, it is hereby

ORDERED, that all matters in Chapter 11 cases in the Rochester Division will be heard in Rochester, New York; and it is further

ORDERED, that this procedure is effective immediately.

[Dated: August 26, 2013.]

INDEX TO UNITED STATES BANKRUPTCY COURT
FOR THE WESTERN DISTRICT OF NEW YORK

RITZ LIBRARY DUTCHESS COMM COLLEGE

7027964